Course   A200:
Foundations of Accounting
INDIANA UNIV BLOOMINGTON

http://create.mheducation.com

ISBN-10: 130812709X   ISBN-13: 9781308127095

Contents

Credits

CHAPTER 1

An Introduction to Accounting

LEARNING OBJECTIVES

After you have mastered the material in this chapter, you will be able to:

SECTION 1: COLLECTING AND ORGANIZING INFORMATION

LO 1-1   Explain the role of accounting in society.

LO 1-2   Construct an accounting equation and show how business events affect the equation.

LO 1-3   Interpret information shown in an accounting equation.

LO 1-4   Classify business events as asset source, use, or exchange transactions.

SECTION 2: REPORTING INFORMATION

LO 1-5   Use general ledger account information to prepare four financial statements.

LO 1-6   Explain the closing process.

LO 1-7   Record business events using a horizontal financial statements model.

 Video lectures and accompanying self-assessment quizzes are available for all learning objectives through McGraw-Hill Connect® Accounting.

The Curious Accountant

Who owns Google? Who owns the American Heart Association (AHA)? Many people and organizations other than owners are interested in the operations of Google and the AHA. These parties are called *stakeholders*. Among others, they include lenders, employees, suppliers, customers, benefactors, research institutions, local governments, heart patients, lawyers, bankers, financial analysts, and government agencies such as the Internal Revenue Service and the Securities and Exchange Commission. Organizations communicate information to stakeholders through *financial reports*.

How do you think the financial reports of Google differ from those of the AHA? (Answer on page 11.)

SECTION 1:

COLLECTING AND ORGANIZING INFORMATION

Why should you study accounting? You should study accounting because it can help you succeed in business. Businesses use accounting to keep score. Imagine trying to play football without knowing how many points a touchdown is worth. Like sports, business is competitive. If you do not know how to keep score, you are not likely to succeed.

Accounting is an information system that reports on the economic activities and financial condition of a business or other organization. Do not underestimate the importance of accounting information. If you had information that enabled you to predict business success, you could become a very wealthy Wall Street investor. Communicating economic information is so important that accounting is frequently called the *language of business*.

ROLE OF ACCOUNTING IN SOCIETY

LO 1-1

Explain the role of accounting in society.

How should society allocate its resources? Should we spend more to harvest food or cure disease? Should we build computers or cars? Should we invest money in IBM or General Motors? Accounting provides information that helps answer such questions.

Using Free Markets to Set Resource Priorities

Suppose you want to start a business. You may have heard "you have to have money to make money." In fact, you will need more than just money to start and operate a business. You will likely need such resources as equipment, land, materials, and employees. If you do not have these resources, how can you get them? In the United States, you compete for resources in open markets.

A **market** is a group of people or entities organized to exchange items of value. The market for business resources involves three distinct participants: consumers, conversion agents, and resource owners. *Consumers* use resources. Resources are frequently not in a form consumers want. For example, nature provides trees but consumers want furniture. *Conversion agents* (businesses) transform resources such as trees into desirable products such as furniture. *Resource owners* control the distribution of resources to conversion agents. Thus resource owners provide resources (inputs) to conversion agents who provide goods and services (outputs) to consumers.

For example, a home builder (conversion agent) transforms labor and materials (inputs) into houses (output) that consumers use. The transformation adds value to the inputs, creating outputs worth more than the sum of the inputs. A house that required

$220,000 of materials and labor to build could have a market value of $250,000.

Common terms for the added value created in the transformation process include **profit, income,** or **earnings.** Accountants measure the added value as the difference between the cost of a product or service and the selling price of that product or service. The profit on the house described above is $30,000, the difference between its $220,000 cost and $250,000 market value.

Conversion agents who successfully and efficiently (at low cost) satisfy consumer preferences are rewarded with high earnings. These earnings are shared with resource owners, so conversion agents who exhibit high earnings potential are more likely to compete successfully for resources.

Return to the original question. How can you get the resources you need to start a business? You must go to open markets and convince resource owners that you can produce profits. Exhibit 1.1 illustrates the market trilogy involved in resource allocation.

The specific resources businesses commonly use to satisfy consumer demand are financial resources, physical resources, and labor resources.

Financial Resources

Businesses (conversion agents) need **financial resources** (money) to get started and to operate. *Investors* and *creditors* provide financial resources.

- **Investors** provide financial resources in exchange for ownership interests in businesses. Owners expect businesses to return to them a share of the business including a portion of earned income.

- **Creditors** lend financial resources to businesses. Instead of a share of the business, creditors expect the businesses to repay borrowed resources plus a specified fee called **interest.**

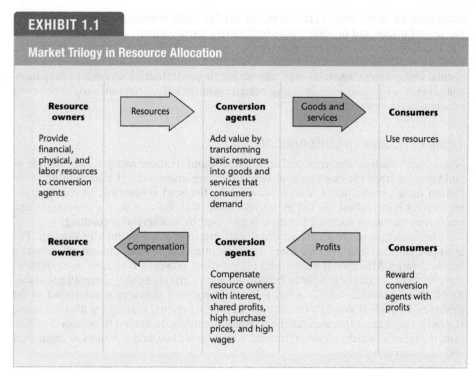

EXHIBIT 1.1

Market Trilogy in Resource Allocation

Investors and creditors prefer to provide financial resources to businesses with high earnings potential because such companies are better able to share profits and make interest payments. Profitable businesses are also less likely to experience bankruptcy.

Physical Resources

In their most primitive form, **physical resources** are natural resources. Physical resources often move through numerous stages of transformation. For example, standing timber may be successively transformed into harvested logs, raw lumber, and finished furniture. Owners of physical resources seek to sell those resources to businesses with high earnings potential because profitable businesses are able to pay higher prices and make repeat purchases.

Labor Resources

Labor resources include both intellectual and physical labor. Like other resource providers, workers prefer businesses that have high income potential because these businesses are able to pay higher wages and offer continued employment.

Accounting Provides Information

How do providers of financial, physical, and labor resources identify conversion agents (businesses) with high profit potential? Investors, creditors, and workers rely heavily on accounting information to evaluate which businesses are worthy of receiving resources. In addition, other people and organizations have an interest in accounting information about businesses. The many **users** of accounting information are commonly called **stakeholders.** Stakeholders include resource providers, financial analysts, brokers, attorneys, government regulators, and news reporters.

The link between conversion agents (businesses) and those stakeholders who provide resources is direct: businesses pay resource providers. Resource providers use accounting information to identify companies with high earnings potential because those companies are more likely to return higher profits, make interest payments, repay debt, pay higher prices, and provide stable, high paying employment.

The link between conversion agents and other stakeholders is indirect. Financial analysts, brokers, and attorneys may use accounting information when advising their clients. Government agencies may use accounting information to assess companies' compliance with income tax laws and other regulations. Reporters may use accounting information in news reports.

Types of Accounting Information

Stakeholders such as investors, creditors, lawyers, and financial analysts exist outside of and separate from the businesses in which they are interested. The accounting information these *external users* need is provided by **financial accounting.** In contrast, the accounting information needed by *internal users,* stakeholders such as managers and employees who work within a business, is provided by **managerial accounting.**

The information needs of external and internal users frequently overlap. For example, external and internal users are both interested in the amount of income a business earns. Managerial accounting information, however, is usually more detailed than financial accounting reports. Investors are concerned about the overall profitability of Wendy's versus Burger King; a Wendy's regional manager is interested in the profits of individual Wendy's restaurants. In fact, a regional manager is also interested in nonfinancial measures, such as the number of employees needed to operate a restaurant, the times at which customer demand is high versus low, and measures of cleanliness and customer satisfaction.

Nonbusiness Resource Usage

The U.S. economy is not *purely* market based. Factors other than profitability often influence resource allocation priorities. For example, governments allocate resources to national defense, to redistribute wealth, or to protect the environment. Foundations, religious groups, the Peace Corps, and other benevolent organizations prioritize resource usage based on humanitarian concerns.

Like profit-oriented businesses, civic or humanitarian organizations add value through resource transformation. For example, a soup kitchen adds value to uncooked meats and vegetables by converting them into prepared meals. The individuals who consume the meals, however, are unable to pay for the kitchen's operating costs, much less for the added value. The soup kitchen's motivation is to meet humanitarian needs, not to earn profits. Organizations that are not motivated by profit are called **not-for-profit entities** (also called *nonprofit* or *nonbusiness organizations*).

Stakeholders interested in nonprofit organizations also need accounting information. Accounting systems measure the cost of the goods and services not-for-profit organizations provide, the efficiency and effectiveness of the organizations' operations, and the ability of the organizations to continue to provide goods and services. This information serves a host of stakeholders, including taxpayers, contributors, lenders, suppliers, employees, managers, financial analysts, attorneys, and beneficiaries.

The focus of accounting, therefore, is to provide information that is useful to a variety of business and nonbusiness user groups for decision-making. The different types of accounting information and the stakeholders that commonly use the information are summarized in Exhibit 1.2.

Careers in Accounting

An accounting career can take you to the top of the business world. *Bloomberg Businessweek* studied the backgrounds of the chief executive officers (CEOs) of the 1,000 largest public corporations. More CEOs had backgrounds in finance and accounting than any other field. Exhibit 1.3 provides additional detail regarding the career paths followed by these executives.

EXHIBIT 1.2

Accounting as Information Provider

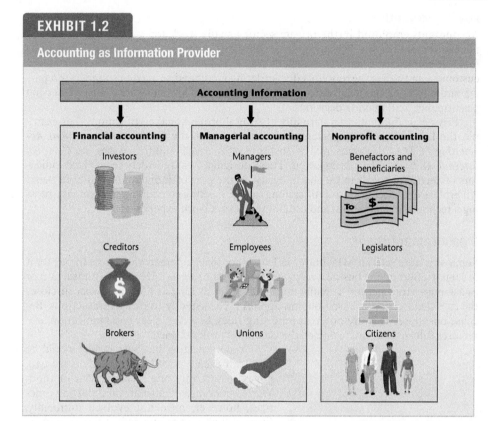

What do accountants do? Accountants identify, record, analyze, and communicate information about the economic events that affect organizations. They may work in either public accounting or private accounting.

Public Accounting

You are probably familiar with the acronym CPA. CPA stands for certified *public* accountant. Public accountants provide services to various clients. They are usually paid a fee that varies depending on the service provided. Services typically offered by public accountants include (1) audit services, (2) tax services, and (3) consulting services.

- *Audit services* involve examining a company's accounting records in order to issue an opinion about whether the company's financial statements conform to generally accepted accounting principles. The auditor's opinion adds credibility to the statements, which are prepared by the company's management.

- *Tax services* include both determining the amount of tax due and tax planning to help companies minimize tax expense.

- *Consulting services* cover a wide range of activities that includes everything from installing sophisticated computerized accounting systems to providing personal financial advice.

All public accountants are not certified. Each state government establishes certification requirements applicable in that state. Although the requirements vary from state to state, CPA candidates normally must have a college education, pass a demanding technical examination, and obtain work experience relevant to practicing public accounting.

EXHIBIT 1.3

Career Paths of Chief Executive Officers

Private Accounting

Accountants employed in the private sector usually work for a specific company or nonprofit organization. Private sector accountants perform a wide variety of functions for their employers. Their duties include classifying and recording transactions, billing customers and collecting amounts due, ordering merchandise, paying suppliers, preparing and analyzing financial statements, developing budgets, measuring costs, assessing performance, and making decisions.

Private accountants may earn any of several professional certifications. For example, the Institute of Management Accountants issues the *Certified Management Accounting (CMA)* designation. The Institute of Internal Auditors issues the *Certified Internal Auditor (CIA)* designation. These designations are widely recognized indicators of technical competence and integrity on the part of individuals who hold them. All professional accounting certifications call for meeting education requirements, passing a technical examination, and obtaining relevant work experience.

Measurement Rules

Suppose a store sells an MP3 player in December to a customer who agrees to pay for it in January. Should the business *recognize* (report) the sale as a December transaction or as a January transaction? It really does not matter as long as the storeowner discloses the rule the decision is based on and applies it consistently to other transactions. Because businesses may use different reporting rules, however, clear communication also requires full and fair disclosure of the accounting rules chosen.

Communicating business results would be simpler if each type of business activity were reported using only one measurement method. World economies and financial reporting practices, however, have not evolved uniformly. Even in highly sophisticated countries such as the United States, companies exhibit significant diversity in reporting methods. Providers of financial reports assume that users are educated about accounting practices.

The **Financial Accounting Standards Board (FASB)**[1] is a privately funded organization with the primary authority for establishing accounting standards in the United States. The measurement rules established by the FASB are called **generally accepted accounting principles (GAAP).** Financial reports issued to the public must follow GAAP. This textbook introduces these principles so you will be able to understand business activity reported by companies in the USA.

Companies are not required to follow GAAP when preparing *management accounting* reports. Although there is considerable overlap between financial and managerial accounting, managers are free to construct internal reports in whatever fashion best suits the effective operation of their companies.

Reporting Entities

Think of accountants as you would of news reporters. A news reporter gathers and discloses information about some person, place, or thing. Likewise, an accountant gathers and discloses financial information about specific people or businesses. The

---

[1] The FASB consists of seven full-time members appointed by the supporting organization, the Financial Accounting Foundation (FAF). The FAF membership is intended to represent the broad spectrum of individuals and institutions that have an interest in accounting and financial reporting. FAF members include representatives of the accounting profession, industry, financial institutions, the government, and the investing public.

FOCUS ON INTERNATIONAL ISSUES

IS THERE GLOBAL GAAP?

As explained in this chapter, accounting is a measurement and communication discipline based on rules referred to as *generally accepted accounting principles (GAAP)*. The rules described in this text are based on GAAP used in the United States, but what rules do the rest of the world use? Is there a global GAAP, or does each country establish its own unique GAAP?

Until recently, each country developed its own unique GAAP. Global companies were required to prepare multiple sets of financial statements to satisfy each country's GAAP. The use of multiple accounting standards across the globe made comparing company performance difficult and expensive. To address the need for a common set of financial standards, the International Accounting Standards Committee was formed in 1973. The committee was reorganized as the **International Accounting Standards Board (IASB)** in 2001. The IASB issues **International Financial Reporting Standards (IFRS),** which are rapidly gaining support worldwide. In 2005,

companies in the countries who were members of the European Union were required to use the IFRS as established by the IASB, which is headquartered in London. Today, over 100 countries require or permit companies to prepare their financial statements using IFRS.

As of 2013 most of the major economic countries had switched from their local GAAP to IFRS. One notable exception is the United States, but even here, the Securities and Exchange Commission announced in 2008 that it was seriously considering adopting rules that would allow our companies to use either GAAP or IFRS. Although not finalized when this book was being prepared, many accountants in the United States believe this will occur. Additionally, there is an active process in place to reduce the differences between IFRS and U.S. GAAP.

There are many similarities between the IASB and the FASB. Both the FASB and the IASB are required to include members with a variety of backgrounds, including auditors, users of financial information, academics, and so forth. Also, both groups primarily require that their members work full-time for their respective boards; they cannot serve on the board while being compensated by another organization. (The IASB does allow up to three of its members to be part-time.) Members of each board serve five-year terms, and can be reappointed once. The funds to support both boards, and the large organizations that support them are obtained from a variety of sources, including selling publications and private contributions. To help maintain independence of the board's members, fundraising is performed by separate sets of trustees.

There are significant differences between the IASB and the FASB, and one of these relates to size and geographic diversity. The FASB has only seven members, all from the United States. The IASB has sixteen members, and these must include at least four from Asia, four from Europe, four from North America, one from Africa, and one from South America.

Not only is the structure of the standards-setting boards different but the standards and principles they establish may also differ significantly. In this chapter, you will learn that GAAP employs the *historical cost concept*. This means that the assets of most U.S. companies are shown on the balance sheet at the amount for which they were purchased. For example, land that has a market value of millions of dollars may be shown on US Steel's financial statements with a value of only a few hundred thousand dollars. This occurs because GAAP requires US Steel to show the land at its cost rather than its market value. In contrast, IFRS permits companies to show market values on their financial statements. This means that the exact same assets may show radically different values if the statements are prepared under IFRS rather than GAAP.

Throughout this text, where appropriate, we will note the differences between U.S. GAAP and IFRS. However, by the time you graduate, it is likely that among the major industrialized nations, there will be a global GAAP.

---

people or businesses accountants report on are called **reporting entities.** When studying accounting you should think of yourself as the accountant. Your first step is to identify the person or business on which you are reporting. This is not always as easy as it may seem. To illustrate, consider the following scenario.

Jason Winston recently started a business. During the first few days of operation, Mr. Winston transferred cash from his personal account into a business account for a company he named Winston Enterprises. Mr. Winston's brother, George, invested cash in Winston Enterprises for which he received an ownership interest in the company. Winston Enterprises borrowed cash from First Federal Bank. Winston Enterprises paid cash to purchase a building from Commercial Properties, Inc. Winston Enterprises earned cash revenues from its customers and paid its employees cash for salaries expense.

How many reporting entities are described in this scenario? Assuming all of the customers are counted as a single entity and all of the employees are counted as a single entity, there are a total of seven entities named in the scenario. These entities include: (1) Jason Winston, (2) Winston Enterprises, (3) George Winston, (4) First Federal Bank, (5) Commercial Properties, Inc., (6) the customers, and (7) the employees. A separate set of accounting records would be maintained for each entity.

Your ability to learn accounting will be greatly influenced by how you approach the entity concept. Based on your everyday experiences you likely think from the perspective of a customer. In contrast, this text is written from the perspective of a business entity. These opposing perspectives dramatically affect how you view business events. For example, as a customer you consider a sales discount a great bargain. The view is different from the perspective of the business granting the discount. A sales discount means an item did not sell at the expected price. To move the item, the business had to accept less money than it originally planned to receive. From this perspective, a sales discount is not a good thing. To understand accounting, train yourself to interpret transactions from the perspective of a business rather than a consumer. Each time you encounter an accounting event ask yourself, how does this affect the business?

☑ CHECK YOURSELF 1.1

In a recent business transaction, land was exchanged for cash. Did the amount of cash increase or decrease?

Answer The answer depends on the reporting entity to which the question pertains. One entity sold land. The other entity bought land. For the entity that sold land, cash increased. For the entity that bought land, cash decreased.

ELEMENTS OF FINANCIAL STATEMENTS

LO 1-2

Construct an accounting equation and show how business events affect the equation.

The individuals and organizations that need information about a business are called *stakeholders.* Stakeholders include owners, lenders, government agencies, employees, news reporters, and others. Businesses communicate information to stakeholders through four financial statements:[2] (1) an income statement, (2) a statement of changes in equity, (3) a balance sheet, and (4) a statement of cash flows.

The information reported in **financial statements** is organized into ten categories known as **elements.** Eight financial statement elements are discussed in this chapter: assets, liabilities, equity, contributed capital, revenue, expenses, distributions, and net income. The other two elements, gains and losses, are discussed in a later chapter. In practice, the business world uses various titles to identify several of the financial statement elements. For example, business people use net income, net *earnings,* and net *profit* interchangeably to describe the same element. Contributed capital may be called *common stock* and equity may be called *stockholders' equity, owner's capital,* and *partners' equity.* Furthermore, the transfer of assets from a business to its owners may be called *distributions, withdrawals,* or *dividends.* Think of accounting as a language. Different terms can describe the same business event. Detailed definitions of the elements and their placement on financial statements will be discussed in the following sections of the chapter.

---

[2]In practice these statements have alternate names. For example, the income statement may be called *results of operations* or *statement of earnings.* The balance sheet is sometimes called the *statement of financial position.* The statement of changes in equity might be called *statement of capital* or *statement of stockholders' equity.* Since the Financial Accounting Standards Board (FASB) called for the title *statement of cash flows,* companies do not use alternate names for that statement.

Answers to The Curious Accountant

Anyone who owns stock in Google owns a part of the company. Google has many owners. In contrast, nobody actually owns the American Heart Association (AHA). The AHA has a board of directors that is responsible for overseeing its operations, but the board is not its owner.

Ultimately, the purpose of a business entity is to increase the wealth of its owners. To this end, it "spends money to make money." The expense that Google incurs for developing software is a cost incurred in the hope that it will generate revenues when it sells advertising. The financial statements of a business show, among other things, whether and how the company made a profit during the current year. For example, Google's income statements show how much expense was incurred from "research and development" operations versus from "sales and marketing."

The AHA is a not-for-profit entity. It operates to provide services to society at large, not to make a profit. It cannot increase the wealth of its owners, because it has no owners. When the AHA spends money to conduct CPR classes, it does not spend this money in the expectation that it will generate revenues. The revenues of the AHA come from contributors who wish to support efforts related to fighting heart disease. Because the AHA does not spend money to make money, it has no reason to prepare an *income statement* like that of Google. The AHA's statement of activities shows how much revenue was received from "contributions" versus from "special events."

Not-for-profit entities do prepare financial statements that are similar in appearance to those of commercial enterprises. The financial statements of not-for-profit entities are called the *statement of financial position*, the *statement of activities*, and the *cash flow statement*.

Using Accounts to Gather Information

Detailed information about the elements is maintained in records commonly called **accounts.** For example, information regarding the element *assets* may be organized in separate accounts for cash, equipment, buildings, land, and so forth. The types and number of accounts used by a business depends on the information needs of its stakeholders. Some businesses provide very detailed information; others report highly summarized information. The more detail desired, the greater number of accounts needed. Think of accounts like the notebooks students keep for their classes. Some students keep detailed notes about every class they take in a separate notebook. Other students keep only the key points for all of their classes in a single notebook. Similarly, some businesses use more accounts than other businesses.

Diversity also exists regarding the names used for various accounts. For example, employee pay may be called salaries, wages, commissions, and so forth. Do not become frustrated with the diversity of terms used in accounting. Remember, accounting is a language. The same word can have different meanings. Similarly, different words can be used to describe the same phenomenon. The more you study and use accounting, the more familiar it will become to you.

Accounting Equation

You have probably heard the adage "you have to have money to make money." Indeed, you usually need a lot more than just money. For example, Carmike Cinemas, Inc., uses buildings, seating, screens, projection equipment, vending machines, cash registers, and so on in order to make money from ticket sales. The resources a business uses to make money are called **assets.** So, where do businesses get assets? There are three distinct sources.

First, a business can borrow assets from creditors. Usually a business acquires cash from creditors and then uses the cash to purchase the assets it needs to conduct its operations. When a business receives cash from creditors it accepts an obligation to return the cash to the creditors at some future date. In accounting terms, the obligations a business has to its creditors are called **liabilities.**

The second source of assets is investors. When a business acquires assets from investors it commits to keep the assets safe and to use the assets in a manner that benefits the investors. The business also grants the investor an ownership interest in the business thereby allowing the investor (owner) to share in the profits generated by the business. The specific commitments made to the investors are described in certificates called **common stock.** In accounting terms investors are called **stockholders.** Further, the business's commitment to the stockholders is called **stockholders' equity.**

The third source of assets is operations. Businesses use assets in order to produce higher amounts of other assets. For example, Best Buy may sell a TV that cost the company $500 for $600. The $100 difference between the sales price and the cost of the TV results in an increase in Best Buy's total assets. This explains how operations can be a source of assets. Of course operations may also result in a decrease in assets. If Best Buy has to discount the sales price of the TV to $450 in order to sell it, the company's total assets decrease by $50.

Net increases in assets generated from operations are commonly called *earnings* or *income.* Net decreases in assets caused by operations are called *losses.* As a result of their ownership status, the stockholders reap the benefits and suffer the sacrifices that a business experiences from its operations. A business may distribute all or part of the assets generated through operations to the shareholders. The distribution of assets generated through earnings is called a *dividend.*

Notice that paying dividends is an option not a legal requirement. Instead of paying dividends, a business may retain the assets it generates through operations. If a business retains the assets, it commits to use those assets for the benefit of the stockholders. This increase in the business's commitments to its stockholders is normally called **retained earnings.** Also, note that earnings that have been retained in the past can be used to pay dividends in the future. However, a company that does not have current or prior retained earnings cannot pay dividends.

As a result of providing assets to a business the creditors and investors are entitled to make potential **claims**[3] on the assets owned by the business. The relationship between a business's assets and the claims on its assets is frequently expressed in an equality called the **accounting equation.** Based on the relationships described above the accounting equation can be developed as follows:

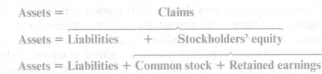

$$Assets = Claims$$
$$Assets = Liabilities + Stockholders'\ equity$$
$$Assets = Liabilities + Common\ stock + Retained\ earnings$$

☑ CHECK YOURSELF 1.2

Gupta Company has $250,000 of assets, $60,000 of liabilities, and $90,000 of common stock. What percentage of the assets was provided by retained earnings?

Answer   First, using algebra, determine the dollar amount of retained earnings:

Assets = Liabilities + Common stock + Retained earnings
Retained earnings = Assets − Liabilities − Common stock
Retained earnings = $250,000 − $60,000 − $90,000
Retained earnings = $100,000

---

[3]A claim is a legal action to obtain money, property, or the enforcement of a right against another party.

Second, determine the percentage:

Percentage of assets provided by retained earnings = Retained earnings/Total assets

Percentage of assets provided by retained earnings = $100,000/$250,000 = 40%

RECORDING BUSINESS EVENTS UNDER THE ACCOUNTING EQUATION

An **accounting event** is an economic occurrence that changes an enterprise's assets, liabilities, or stockholders' equity. A **transaction** is a particular kind of event that involves transferring something of value between two entities. Examples of transactions include acquiring assets from owners, borrowing money from creditors, and purchasing or selling goods and services. The following section of the text explains how several different types of accounting events affect a company's accounting equation.

Asset Source Transactions

As previously mentioned, businesses obtain assets (resources) from three sources. They acquire assets from owners (stockholders); they borrow assets from creditors; and they earn assets through profitable operations. Asset source transactions increase total assets and total claims. A more detailed discussion of the effects of asset source transactions is provided below:

EVENT 1 Rustic Camp Sites (RCS) was formed on January 1, 2014, when it acquired $120,000 cash from issuing common stock.

When RCS issued stock, it received cash and gave each investor (owner) a stock certificate as a receipt. Since this transaction provided $120,000 of assets (cash) to the business, it is an **asset source transaction.** It increases the business's assets (cash) and its stockholders' equity (common stock).

	Assets		=	Liab.	+	Stockholders' Equity		
	Cash	+ Land	=	N. Pay.	+	Com. Stk.	+	Ret. Earn.
Acquired cash through stock issue	120,000	+ NA	=	NA	+	120,000	+	NA

Notice the elements have been divided into accounts. For example, the element *assets* is divided into a Cash account and a Land account. Do not be concerned if some of these account titles are unfamiliar. They will be explained as new transactions are presented. Recall that the number of accounts a company uses depends on the nature of its business and the level of detail management needs to operate the business. For example, Sears would have an account called Cost of Goods Sold although GEICO Insurance would not. Why? Because Sears sells goods (merchandise) but GEICO does not.

Also, notice that a stock issue transaction affects the accounting equation in two places, both under an asset (cash) and also under the source of that asset (common stock). All transactions affect the accounting equation in at least two places. It is from this practice that the **double-entry bookkeeping** system derives its name.

EVENT 2 RCS acquired an additional $400,000 of cash by borrowing from a creditor.

This transaction is also an asset source transaction. It increases assets (cash) and liabilities (notes payable). The account title Notes Payable is used because the borrower

(RCS) is required to issue a promissory note to the creditor (a bank). A promissory note describes, among other things, the amount of interest RCS will pay and for how long it will borrow the money.[4] The effect of the borrowing transaction on the accounting equation is indicated below.

	Assets			=	Liab.	+	Stockholders' Equity		
	Cash	+	Land	=	N. Pay.	+	Com. Stk.	+	Ret. Earn.
Beginning balances	120,000	+	NA	=	NA	+	120,000	+	NA
Acquired cash by issuing note	400,000	+	NA	=	400,000	+	NA	+	NA
Ending balances	520,000	+	NA	=	400,000	+	120,000	+	NA

The beginning balances above came from the ending balances produced by the prior transaction. This practice is followed throughout the illustration.

Asset Exchange Transactions

Businesses frequently trade one asset for another asset. In such cases, the amount of one asset decreases and the amount of the other asset increases. Total assets are unaffected by asset exchange transactions. Event 3 is an asset exchange transaction.

EVENT 3 RCS paid $500,000 cash to purchase land.

This asset exchange transaction reduces the asset account Cash and increases the asset account Land. The amount of total assets is not affected. An **asset exchange transaction** simply reflects changes in the composition of assets. In this case, the company traded cash for land. The amount of cash decreased by $500,000 and the amount of land increased by the same amount.

	Assets			=	Liab.	+	Stockholders' Equity		
	Cash	+	Land	=	N. Pay.	+	Com. Stk.	+	Ret. Earn.
Beginning balances	520,000	+	NA	=	400,000	+	120,000	+	NA
Paid cash to buy land	(500,000)	+	500,000	=	NA	+	NA	+	NA
Ending balances	20,000	+	500,000	=	400,000	+	120,000	+	NA

Another Asset Source Transaction

EVENT 4 RCS obtained $85,000 cash by leasing camp sites to customers.

Revenue represents an economic benefit a company obtains by providing customers with goods and services. In this example the economic benefit is an increase in the asset cash. Revenue transactions can therefore be viewed as *asset source transactions*. The asset increase is balanced by an increase in the retained earnings section of stockholders' equity because producing revenue increases the amount of earnings that can be retained in the business.

---

[4]For simplicity, the computation of interest is ignored in this chapter. Interest computation is discussed in the appendix to Chapter 2 and in subsequent chapters.

	Assets			=	Liab.	+	Stockholders' Equity			
	Cash	+	Land	=	N. Pay.	+	Com. Stk.	+	Ret. Earn.	Acct. Title
Beginning balances	20,000	+	500,000	=	400,000	+	120,000	+	NA	
Acquired cash by earning revenue	85,000	+	NA	=	NA	+	NA	+	85,000	Revenue
Ending balances	105,000	+	500,000	=	400,000	+	120,000	+	85,000	

Note carefully that the $85,000 ending balance in the retained earnings column is *not* in the Retained Earnings account. It is in the Revenue account. It will be transferred to the Retained Earnings account at the end of the accounting period. Transferring the Revenue account balance to the Retained Earnings account is part of a process called *closing the accounts.*

Asset Use Transactions

Businesses use assets for a variety of purposes. For example, assets may be used to pay off liabilities or they may be transferred to owners. Assets may also be used in the process of generating earnings. All **asset use transactions** decrease the total amount of assets and the total amount of claims on assets (liabilities or stockholders' equity).

EVENT 5 **RCS paid $50,000 cash for operating expenses such as salaries, rent, and interest. (RCS could establish a separate account for each type of expense. However, the management team does not currently desire this level of detail. Remember, the number of accounts a business uses depends on the level of information managers need to make decisions.)**

In the normal course of generating revenue, a business consumes various assets and services. The assets and services consumed to generate revenue are called **expenses.** Revenue results from providing goods and services to customers. In exchange, the business acquires assets from its customers. Since the owners bear the ultimate risk and reap the rewards of operating the business, revenues increase stockholders' equity (retained earnings), and expenses decrease retained earnings. In this case, the asset account, Cash, decreased. This decrease is balanced by a decrease in the retained earnings section of stockholders' equity because expenses decrease the amount of earnings retained in the business.

	Assets			=	Liab.	+	Stockholders' Equity			
	Cash	+	Land	=	N. Pay.	+	Com. Stk.	+	Ret. Earn.	Acct. Title
Beginning balances	105,000	+	500,000	=	400,000	+	120,000	+	85,000	
Used cash to pay expenses	(50,000)	+	NA	=	NA	+	NA	+	(50,000)	Expense
Ending balances	55,000	+	500,000	=	400,000	+	120,000	+	35,000	

Like revenues, expenses are not recorded directly into the Retained Earnings account. The $50,000 of expense is recorded in the Expense account. It will be transferred to the Retained Earnings account at the end of the accounting period as part of the closing process. The $35,000 ending balance in the retained earnings column shows what would be in the Retained Earnings account after the balances in the Revenue and Expense accounts have been closed. The current balance in the Retained Earnings account is zero.

EVENT 6   RCS paid $4,000 in cash dividends to its owners.

To this point the enterprise's total assets and equity have increased by $35,000 ($85,000 of revenue − $50,000 of expense) as a result of its earnings activities. RCS can keep the additional assets in the business or transfer them to the owners. If a business transfers some or all of its earned assets to owners, the transfer is frequently called a **dividend.** Since assets distributed to stockholders are not used for the purpose of generating revenue, *dividends are not expenses.* Furthermore, dividends are a transfer of *earnings,* not a return of the assets acquired from the issue of common stock.

	Assets			=	Liab.	+			Stockholders' Equity			
	Cash	+	Land	=	N. Pay.	+	Com. Stk.	+	Ret. Earn.	Acct. Title
Beginning balances	55,000	+	500,000	=	400,000	+	120,000	+	35,000	
Used cash to pay dividends	(4,000)	+	NA	=	NA	+	NA	+	(4,000)	Dividends
Ending balances	51,000	+	500,000	=	400,000	+	120,000	+	31,000	

Like revenues and expenses, dividends are not recorded directly into the Retained Earnings account. The $4,000 dividend is recorded in the Dividends account. It will be transferred to retained earnings at the end of the accounting period as part of the closing process. The $31,000 ending balance in the retained earnings column shows what would be in the Retained Earnings account after the balances in the Revenue, Expense, and Dividend accounts have been closed. The current balance in the Retained Earnings account is zero.

EVENT 7   The land that RCS paid $500,000 to purchase had an appraised market value of $525,000 on December 31, 2014.

Although the appraised value of the land is higher than the original cost, RCS will not increase the amount recorded in its accounting records above the land's $500,000 historical cost. In general, accountants do not recognize changes in market value. The **historical cost concept** requires that most assets be reported at the amount paid for them (their historical cost) regardless of increases in market value.

Surely investors would rather know what an asset is worth instead of how much it originally cost. So why do accountants maintain records and report financial information based on historical cost? Accountants rely heavily on verification. Information is considered to be more useful if it can be independently verified. For example, two people looking at the legal documents associated with RCS's land purchase will both conclude that RCS paid $500,000 for the land. That historical cost is a verifiable fact. The appraised value, in contrast, is an opinion. Even two persons who are experienced appraisers are not likely to come up with the same amount for the land's market value. Accountants do not report market values in financial statements because such values are not reliable.

There are exceptions to the application of the historical cost rule. When market value can be clearly established, GAAP not only permits but requires its use. For example, securities that are traded on the New York Stock Exchange must be shown at market value rather than historical cost. We will discuss other notable exceptions to the historical cost principle later in the text. However, as a general rule you should assume that assets shown in a company's financial statements are valued at historical cost.

Summary of Transactions

The complete collection of a company's accounts is called the **general ledger.** A summary of the accounting events and the general ledger account information for RCS's 2014 accounting period is shown in Exhibit 1.4. The Revenue, Expense, and Dividend account data appear in the retained earnings column. These account titles are shown immediately to the right of the dollar amounts listed in the retained earnings column.

EXHIBIT 1.4

Accounting Events

1.	RCS issued common stock, acquiring $120,000 cash from its owners.
2.	RCS borrowed $400,000 cash.
3.	RCS paid $500,000 cash to purchase land.
4.	RCS received $85,000 cash from earning revenue.
5.	RCS paid $50,000 cash for expenses.
6.	RCS paid dividends of $4,000 cash to the owners.
7.	The land that RCS paid $500,000 to purchase had an appraised market value of $525,000 on December 31, 2014.

General Ledger Accounts Organized under the Accounting Equation

Event No.	Assets			=	Liabilities	+	Stockholders' Equity			Other Account Titles
	Cash	+	Land	=	Notes Payable	+	Common Stock	+	Retained Earnings	
Beg. bal.	0		0		0		0		0	
1.	120,000						120,000			
2.	400,000				400,000					
3.	(500,000)		500,000							
4.	85,000								85,000	Revenue
5.	(50,000)								(50,000)	Expense
6.	(4,000)								(4,000)	Dividend
7.	NA		NA		NA		NA		NA	
	51,000	+	500,000	=	400,000	+	120,000	+	31,000	

INTERPRETING INFORMATION SHOWN IN THE ACCOUNTING EQUATION

In the United States, the amounts shown in an accounting equation are normally expressed in dollars. However, the dollar amounts shown on the right side of the equation are not related to the amount of actual cash a company has on hand.

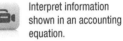

LO 1-3

Interpret information shown in an accounting equation.

The Left versus the Right Side of the Accounting Equation

To illustrate the relationship between the left and right sides of the accounting equation, assume Educate Inc. acquires $600 cash from creditors, $300 cash from investors, and $100 cash from operations. This information can be organized under an accounting equation as follows:

Assets = Liabilities + Common stock + Retained earnings
$1,000 Cash = $600 + $300 + $100

Now assume that Educate Inc. uses its cash to purchase land. Immediately after this purchase, the company's accounting equation is a follows:

Assets = Liabilities + Common stock + Retained earnings
$1,000 Land = $600 + $300 + $100

At this point the company has zero cash. This highlights the fact that the amounts in liabilities, common stock, and retained earnings do not represent cash. Instead they represent the original sources of the company's assets. Indeed, the right side of the accounting equation could be expressed as percentages instead of dollars. Specifically, the equation could be written as:

$$\text{Assets} = \text{Liabilities} + \text{Common stock} + \text{Retained earnings}$$
$$\$1{,}000 \text{ Land} = 60\% + 30\% + 10\%$$

This equation suggests 60 percent of Educate's assets came from creditors, 30 percent came from owner's, and 10 percent from its earnings. However, this does not explain what has happened to the company's assets since they were acquired. Specifically, the right side of the equation does not show that the company acquired cash and then used the cash to purchase land. The right side identifies the sources of assets, not their composition.

Two Views of the Right Side of the Accounting Equation

Another important point to recognize is that there are two views of the right side of the accounting equation. In the above case the right side is viewed as sources of assets. Clearly, when a company borrows money from a bank the business receives an asset, cash. Therefore, we say creditors are a source of assets. However, borrowing money creates an obligation for the business to return the amount borrowed to creditors. Thus, we can view the liabilities of a company as its obligations to return assets to its creditors. In summary, liabilities can be viewed as sources of assets or, alternatively, as obligations of the business.

Similarly, a business may acquire assets from its owners by issuing stock or it may earn assets through its operations. Therefore, common stock and retained earnings can be viewed as sources of assets. However, the business has a **stewardship** function, which means that it has a duty to protect and use the assets for the benefit of the owners. As a result, common stock and retained earnings can be viewed as sources of assets or, alternatively, as commitments to the investors. In summary, the right side of the accounting equation can be viewed either as sources of assets or as obligations and commitments of the business.

Cash and Retained Earnings

While the amount of retained earnings does not represent the amount of cash a company has on hand, it does limit the amount of cash that can be used to pay dividends. To illustrate, we assume that Educate Inc. earns an additional $150 of cash. This event would cause assets and retained earnings to increase, thereby resulting in the following accounting equation:

$$\text{Assets} = \text{Liabilities} + \text{Common stock} + \text{Retained earnings}$$
$$\$150 \text{ Cash} + \$1{,}000 \text{ Land} = \$600 + \$300 + \$250$$

Given that the company has $250 in retained earnings, can the company pay a $200 cash dividend? The answer is no. Remember, there is no cash in retained earnings. The only cash the company has is listed on the left side of the equation. In this case, the maximum cash dividend that can be paid is $150 because that is all the cash the company has. Suppose Educate decides it no longer needs the land and sells it for $1,000 cash. After this event, the accounting equation appears as follows:

$$\text{Assets} = \text{Liabilities} + \text{Common stock} + \text{Retained earnings}$$
$$\$1{,}150 \text{ Cash} = \$600 + \$300 + \$250$$

Given that Educate now has $1,150 in cash, can the company pay a $400 dividend? The answer is no. Based on the information in the accounting equation,

Educate has only increased its assets by $250 as a result of its operations. Since dividends are a distribution of assets that were generated through earnings, the maximum dividend Educate can distribute at this time is $250. In summary, the payment of dividends is limited by both the amount of cash and the amount of retained earnings. In other words, to pay a cash dividend a company must have both cash and retained earnings.

Distributions in Business Liquidations

If a business ceases to operate, its remaining assets are sold and the sale proceeds are returned to the creditors and investors through a process called business **liquidation.** Creditors have priority in business liquidations. This means the business uses its assets first to settle the obligations to the creditors. Any assets remaining after the creditors have been paid are then distributed to the investors.

To illustrate, suppose Cruz Company acquired $100 cash from investors and $200 cash from creditors. Also assume Cruz had a net operating loss of $75. After these events, Cruz's accounting equation is as follows:

Assets	=	Liabilities	+	Common stock	+	Retained earnings
$225 Cash =		$200	+	$100	+	$(75)

If Cruz is forced to liquidate at this point the creditors would receive $200 and the owners (investors) would receive only $25.

Return to the original scenario where Cruz acquires $100 cash from investors and $200 cash from creditors. Now suppose instead of experiencing a $75 loss Cruz experiences a $120 loss. In this scenario, Cruz's accounting equation would be:

Assets	=	Liabilities	+	Common stock	+	Retained earnings
$180 Cash =		$200	+	$100	+	$(120)

If Cruz is forced to liquidate at this point the investors would receive zero and the creditors would receive only $180 even though the business owes them $200. Simply stated, Cruz cannot distribute assets that it does not have. This case shows that creditors as well as investors are at risk to lose some or all of the resources they provide to businesses.

It is interesting to note that even profitable companies can be forced to liquidate. For example, return to the illustration where Cruz Company acquires $100 cash from investors and $200 cash from creditors. Now assume that Cruz earns a net income of $75 cash instead of experiencing a net loss. Also assume Cruz pays $350 to purchase land. After these events, Cruz would have the following accounting equation.

Assets		=	Liabilities	+	Common stock	+	Retained earnings
$25 Cash + $350 Land =			$200	+	$100	+	$75

At this point, if the liabilities come due and the creditors demand payment, Cruz could be forced into bankruptcy because it has only $25 cash to settle a $200 debt. A company must properly manage its assets as well as its liabilities and stockholders' equity in order to remain a **going concern.** The going concern doctrine assumes that a business is able to continue its operations into the foreseeable future. Many procedures and practices used by accountants are based on a going concern assumption. If a company's going concern status becomes uncertain, accountants are required to notify creditors and investors.

In practice, the relationships between a business and its creditors and investors are determined by complex legal documents that may conflict with the general conditions described above. We will discuss some of these details in later chapters. However, it is important to clearly establish the basic guidelines before we begin discussing the refinements.

RECAP: TYPES OF TRANSACTIONS

LO 1-4

Classify business events as asset source, use, or exchange transactions.

The transactions described above have each been classified into one of three categories: (1) asset source transactions; (2) asset exchange transactions; and (3) asset use transactions. A fourth category, claims exchange transactions, is introduced in a later chapter. In summary:

- *Asset source transactions* increase the total amount of assets and increase the total amount of claims. In its first year of operation, RCS acquired assets from three sources: first, from owners (Event 1); next, by borrowing (Event 2); and finally, through earnings activities (Event 4).

- *Asset exchange transactions* decrease one asset and increase another asset. The total amount of assets is unchanged by asset exchange transactions. RCS experienced one asset exchange transaction; it used cash to purchase land (Event 3).

- *Asset use transactions* decrease the total amount of assets and the total amount of claims. RCS used assets to pay expenses (Event 5) and to pay dividends (Event 6).

As you proceed through this text, practice classifying transactions into one of the four categories. Businesses engage in thousands of transactions every day. It is far more effective to learn how to classify the transactions into meaningful categories than to attempt to memorize the effects of thousands of transactions.

The Curious Accountant

The RCS case includes only seven business events, one of which is not recognized in the ledger accounts. These events are assumed to have taken place over the course of a year. In contrast, real-world companies engage in thousands, even millions, of transactions in a single day. For example, think of the number of sales events Walmart processes in a day or how many tickets Delta Airlines sells. Presenting this many events in accounting equation format would produce such a volume of data that users would be overwhelmed with details. To facilitate communication, accountants summarize and organize the transaction data into reports called financial statements. This section discusses the information contained in financial statements and explains how they are prepared. While the RCS illustration contains only a few transactions, the financial statements prepared for this company contain the same basic content as those of much larger companies.

SECTION 2:

REPORTING INFORMATION

As indicated earlier, accounting information is normally presented to external users in four general-purpose financial statements. The information in the ledger accounts is used to prepare these financial statements. The data in the ledger accounts in Exhibit 1.4 are color coded to help you understand the source of information in the financial statements. The numbers in *green* are used in the *statement of cash flows*. The numbers in *red* are used to prepare the *balance sheet*. Finally, the numbers in *blue* are used to prepare the *income statement*. The numbers reported in the statement of changes in stockholders' equity have not been color coded because they appear in more than one statement. The next section explains how the information in the accounts is presented in financial statements.

PREPARING FINANCIAL STATEMENTS

The financial statements for RCS are shown in Exhibit 1.5. The information used to prepare these statements was drawn from the ledger accounts shown in Exhibit 1.4. Information in one statement may relate to information in another statement. For example, the amount of net income reported on the income statement also appears on the statement of changes in stockholders' equity. Accountants use the term **articulation** to describe the interrelationships among the various elements of the financial statements. The key articulated relationships in RCS's financial statements are highlighted with arrows (Exhibit 1.5). A description of each statement follows.

LO 1-5

Use general ledger account information to prepare four financial statements.

Income Statement and the Matching Concept

A business must make sacrifices in order to obtain benefits. For example, RCS must sacrifice cash to pay for employee salaries, rent, and interest. In turn, RCS receives a benefit when it collects cash from its customers. As this example implies, sacrifices are defined as decreases in assets; and benefits are increases in assets. In accounting terms sacrifices are called expenses; and benefits are called revenues. *Therefore, expenses are decreases in assets; and revenues are increases in assets.*[5]

The **income statement** matches the expenses with the revenues that occur during a period when operating a business. If revenues exceed expenses, the difference is called **net income.** If expenses are greater than revenues, the difference is called **net loss.** The practice of pairing revenues with expenses on the income statement is called the **matching concept.**

The income statement in Exhibit 1.5 indicates that RCS has earned more assets than it has used. The statement shows that RCS has increased its assets by $35,000 (net

[5]The definitions for revenue and expense are expanded in subsequent chapters as additional relationships among the elements of financial statements are introduced.

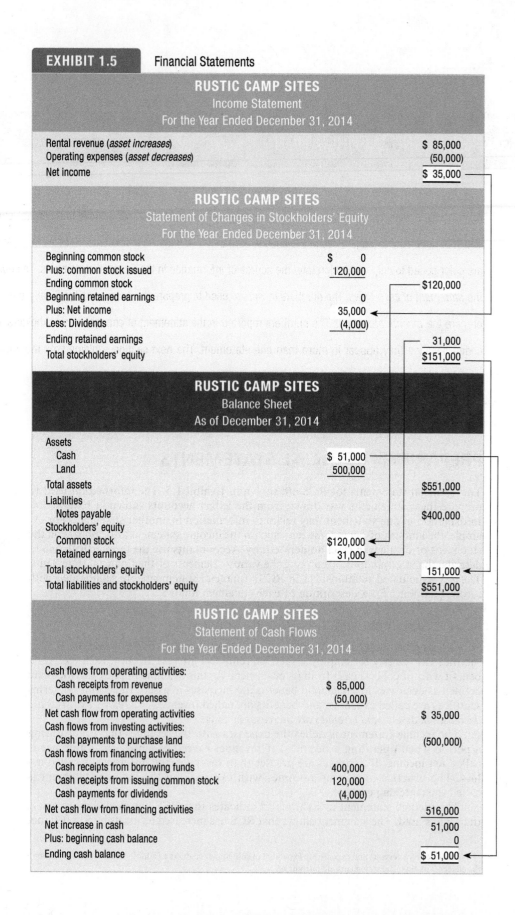

EXHIBIT 1.5   Financial Statements

RUSTIC CAMP SITES
Income Statement
For the Year Ended December 31, 2014

Rental revenue (*asset increases*)	$ 85,000
Operating expenses (*asset decreases*)	(50,000)
Net income	$ 35,000

RUSTIC CAMP SITES
Statement of Changes in Stockholders' Equity
For the Year Ended December 31, 2014

Beginning common stock	$ 0	
Plus: common stock issued	120,000	
Ending common stock		$120,000
Beginning retained earnings	0	
Plus: Net income	35,000	
Less: Dividends	(4,000)	
Ending retained earnings		31,000
Total stockholders' equity		$151,000

RUSTIC CAMP SITES
Balance Sheet
As of December 31, 2014

Assets		
Cash	$ 51,000	
Land	500,000	
Total assets		$551,000
Liabilities		
Notes payable		$400,000
Stockholders' equity		
Common stock	$120,000	
Retained earnings	31,000	
Total stockholders' equity		151,000
Total liabilities and stockholders' equity		$551,000

RUSTIC CAMP SITES
Statement of Cash Flows
For the Year Ended December 31, 2014

Cash flows from operating activities:		
Cash receipts from revenue	$ 85,000	
Cash payments for expenses	(50,000)	
Net cash flow from operating activities		$ 35,000
Cash flows from investing activities:		
Cash payments to purchase land		(500,000)
Cash flows from financing activities:		
Cash receipts from borrowing funds	400,000	
Cash receipts from issuing common stock	120,000	
Cash payments for dividends	(4,000)	
Net cash flow from financing activities		516,000
Net increase in cash		51,000
Plus: beginning cash balance		0
Ending cash balance		$ 51,000

income) as a result of operating its business. Observe the phrase *For the Year Ended December 31, 2014,* in the heading of the income statement. Income is measured for a span of time called the **accounting period.** While accounting periods of one year are normal for external financial reporting, income can be measured weekly, monthly, quarterly, semiannually, or over any other desired time period. Notice that the cash RCS paid to its stockholders (dividends) is not reported as expense. The decrease in assets for dividend payments is not incurred for the purpose of generating revenue. Instead, dividends are transfers of wealth to the owners of the business. Dividend payments are not reported on the income statement.

☑ CHECK YOURSELF 1.3

Mahoney, Inc., was started when it issued common stock to its owners for $300,000. During its first year of operation Mahoney received $523,000 cash for services provided to customers. Mahoney paid employees $233,000 cash. Advertising costs paid in cash amounted to $102,000. Other cash operating expenses amounted to $124,000. Finally, Mahoney paid a $25,000 cash dividend to its stockholders. What amount of net income would Mahoney's report on its earnings statement?

Answer   The amount of net income is $64,000 ($523,000 Revenue − $233,000 Salary Expense − $102,000 Advertising Expense − $124,000 Other Operating Expenses). The cash received from issuing stock is not revenue because it was not acquired from earnings activities. In other words, Mahoney did not work (perform services) for this money; it was contributed by owners of the business. The dividends are not expenses because the decrease in cash was not incurred for the purpose of generating revenue. Instead, the dividends represent a transfer of wealth to the owners.

Statement of Changes in Stockholders' Equity

The **statement of changes in stockholders' equity** explains the effects of transactions on stockholders' equity during the accounting period. It starts with the beginning balance in the common stock account. In the case of RCS, the beginning balance in the common stock account is zero because the company did not exist before the 2014 accounting period. The $120,000 of stock issued during the accounting period is added to the beginning balance to determine the ending balance in the common stock account.

In addition to reporting the changes in common stock, the statement describes the changes in retained earnings for the accounting period. RCS had no beginning balance in retained earnings. During the period, the company earned $35,000 and paid $4,000 in dividends to the stockholders, producing an ending retained earnings balance of $31,000 ($0 + $35,000 − $4,000). Since equity consists of common stock and retained earnings, the ending total equity balance is $151,000 ($120,000 + $31,000). This statement is also dated with the phrase *For the Year Ended December 31, 2014,* because it describes what happened to stockholders' equity during 2014.

Balance Sheet

The **balance sheet** draws its name from the accounting equation. Total assets balance with (equal) liabilities and stockholders' equity. The balance sheet for RCS is shown in Exhibit 1.5. In this case, total assets equals total liabilities plus stockholders' equity ($551,000 = $551,000).

Note the order of the assets in the balance sheet. Cash appears first, followed by land. Assets are displayed in the balance sheet based on their level of **liquidity.** This means that assets are listed in the order of how rapidly they can be converted into cash. Finally, note that the balance sheet is dated with the phrase *As of December 31, 2014,* indicating that it describes the company's financial condition on the last day of the accounting period.

☑ **CHECK YOURSELF 1.4**

To gain a clear understanding of the balance sheet, try to create one that describes your personal financial condition. First list your assets, then your liabilities. Determine the amount of your equity by subtracting your liabilities from your assets.

Answer   Answers for this exercise will vary depending on the particular assets and liabilities each student identifies. Common student assets include automobiles, computers, stereos, TVs, phones, MP3 players, clothes, and textbooks. Common student liabilities include car loans, mortgages, student loans, and credit card debt. The difference between the assets and the liabilities is the equity.

Statement of Cash Flows

The **statement of cash flows** explains how a company obtained and used *cash* during the accounting period. Receipts of cash are called *cash inflows,* and payments are *cash outflows.* The statement classifies cash receipts (inflows) and payments (outflows) into three categories: financing activities, investing activities, and operating activities.

Businesses normally start with an idea. Implementing the idea usually requires cash. For example, suppose you decide to start an apartment rental business. First, you would need cash to finance acquiring the apartments. Acquiring cash to start a business is a financing activity. **Financing activities** include obtaining cash (inflow) from owners or paying cash (outflow) to owners (dividends). Financing activities also include borrowing cash (inflow) from creditors and repaying the principal (outflow) to creditors. Because interest on borrowed money is an expense, however, cash paid to creditors for interest is reported in the operating activities section of the statement of cash flows.

After obtaining cash from financing activities, you would invest the money by building or buying apartments. **Investing activities** involve paying cash (outflow) to purchase long-term assets or receiving cash (inflow) from selling long-term assets. Long-term assets are normally used for more than one year. Cash outflows to purchase land or cash inflows from selling a building are examples of investing activities.

After investing in the productive assets (apartments), you would engage in operating activities. **Operating activities** involve receiving cash (inflow) from revenue and paying cash (outflow) for expenses. Note that cash spent to purchase short-term assets such as office supplies is reported in the operating activities section because the office supplies would likely be used (expensed) within a single accounting period.

EXHIBIT 1.6
Classification Scheme for Statement of Cash Flows

Cash flows from operating activities:
Cash receipts (inflows) from customers
Cash payments (outflows) to suppliers

Cash flows from investing activities:
Cash receipts (inflows) from the sale of long-term assets
Cash payments (outflows) for the purchase of long-term assets

Cash flows from financing activities:
Cash receipts (inflows) from borrowing funds
Cash receipts (inflows) from issuing common stock
Cash payments (outflows) to repay borrowed funds
Cash payments (outflows) for dividends

The primary cash inflows and outflows related to the types of business activity introduced in this chapter are summarized in Exhibit 1.6. The exhibit will be expanded as additional types of events are introduced in subsequent chapters.

The statement of cash flows for Rustic Camp Sites in Exhibit 1.5 shows that the amount of cash increased by $51,000 during the year. The beginning balance in the Cash account was zero; adding the $51,000 increase to the beginning balance results in a $51,000 ending balance. Notice that the $51,000 ending cash balance on the statement of cash flows is the same as the amount of cash reported in the asset section on the December 31 year-end balance sheet. Also, note that the statement of cash flows is dated with the phrase *For the Year Ended December 31, 2014,* because it describes what happened to cash over the span of the year.

☑ CHECK YOURSELF 1.5

Classify each of the following cash flows as an operating activity, investing activity, or financing activity.

1. Acquired cash from owners.
2. Borrowed cash from creditors.
3. Paid cash to purchase land.
4. Earned cash revenue.
5. Paid cash for salary expenses.
6. Paid cash dividend.
7. Paid cash for interest.

Answer   (1) financing activity; (2) financing activity; (3) investing activity; (4) operating activity; (5) operating activity; (6) financing activity; (7) operating activity.

The Closing Process

As previously indicated, transaction data are recorded in the Revenue, Expense, and Dividend accounts during the accounting period. At the end of the accounting period the data in these accounts are transferred to the Retained Earnings account. The process of transferring the balances is called **closing.** Since the Revenue, Expense, and Dividend accounts are closed each period, they are called **temporary accounts.** At the beginning of each new accounting period, the temporary accounts have zero balances. The Retained Earnings account carries forward from one accounting period to the next. Since this account is not closed, it is called a **permanent account.**

Since RCS started operations on January 1, 2014, the beginning Retained Earnings account balance was zero. In other words, there were no previous earnings available to be retained by the business. During 2014, amounts were recorded in the Revenue, Expense, and Dividend accounts. Since the Retained Earnings account is separate from the Revenue, Expense, and Dividend accounts, the entries in these temporary accounts did not affect the Retained Earnings balance. Specifically, the *before closing* balance in the Retained Earnings account on December 31, 2014, is still zero. In contrast, the Revenue account has a balance of $85,000; the Expense account has a balance of $50,000; and the Dividends account has a balance of $4,000. The closing process transfers the balances in the Revenue, Expense, and Dividend accounts to the Retained Earnings account. Therefore, *after closing* the balance in the Retained Earnings account is $31,000 ($85,000 − $50,000 − $4,000) and the Revenue, Expense, and Dividend accounts have zero balances.

Since the asset, liability, common stock, and retained earnings accounts are permanent accounts, they are not closed at the end of the accounting period. After the closing account process, RCS's general ledger will contain the following account balances as of December 31, 2014.

LO 1-6

Explain the closing process.

Cash	+	Land	=	Notes Payable	+	Common Stock	+	Retained Earnings
51,000	+	500,000	=	400,000	+	120,000	+	31,000

Take note that the December 31, 2014, ending account balances become the January 1, 2015, beginning account balances. So, RCS will start the 2015 accounting period with these same account balances. In other words, the current period's after closing ending balances become the next period's beginning balances.

> ☑ **CHECK YOURSELF 1.6**
>
> After closing on December 31, 2014, Walston Company had $4,600 of assets, $2,000 of liabilities, and $700 of common stock. During January of 2015, Walston earned $750 of revenue and incurred $300 of expense. Walston closes its books each year on December 31.
>
> 1. Determine the balance in the Retained Earnings account as of December 31, 2014.
> 2. Determine the balance in the Retained Earnings account as of January 1, 2015.
> 3. Determine the balance in the Retained Earnings account as of January 31, 2015.
>
> **Answer**
>
> 1. Assets = Liabilities + Common Stock + Retained Earnings
>
> $4,600 = $2,000 + $700 + Retained Earnings
>
>   Retained Earnings = $1,900
>
> 2. The balance in the Retained Earnings account on January 1, 2015, is the same as it was on December 31, 2014. This year's ending balance becomes next year's beginning balance. Therefore, the balance in the Retained Earnings account on January 1, 2015, is $1,900.
>
> 3. The balance in the Retained Earnings account on January 31, 2015, is still $1,900. The revenue earned and expenses incurred during January are not recorded in the Retained Earnings account. Revenue is recorded in a Revenue account and expenses are recorded in an Expense account during the accounting period. The balances in the Revenue and Expense accounts are transferred to the Retained Earnings account during the closing process at the end of the accounting period (December 31, 2015).

THE HORIZONTAL FINANCIAL STATEMENTS MODEL

LO 1-7

Record business events using a horizontal financial statements model.

Financial statements are the scorecard for business activity. If you want to succeed in business, you must know how your business decisions affect your company's financial statements. This text uses a **horizontal statements model** to help you understand how business events affect financial statements. This model shows a set of financial statements horizontally across a single page of paper. The balance sheet is displayed first, adjacent to the income statement, and then the statement of cash flows. Because the effects of equity transactions can be analyzed by referring to certain balance sheet columns, and because of limited space, the statement of changes in stockholders' equity is not shown in the horizontal statements model.

The model frequently uses abbreviations. For example, activity classifications in the statement of cash flows are identified using OA for operating activities, IA for investing activities, and FA for financing activities. NC designates the net change in cash. The statements model uses "NA" when an account is not affected by an event. The background of the *balance sheet* is red, the *income statement* is blue, and the *statement of cash flows* is green. To demonstrate the usefulness of the horizontal statements model, we use it to display the seven accounting events that RCS experienced during its first year of operation (2014).

1. RCS acquired $120,000 cash from the issuance of common stock.
2. RCS borrowed $400,000 cash.
3. RCS paid $500,000 cash to purchase land.
4. RCS received $85,000 cash from earning revenue.
5. RCS paid $50,000 cash for expenses.
6. RCS paid $4,000 of cash dividends to the owners.
7. The market value of the land owned by RCS was appraised at $525,000 on December 31, 2014.

Event No.	Balance Sheet										Income Statement					Statement of Cash Flows	
	Assets			=	Liab.	+	Stockholders' Equity										
	Cash	+	Land	=	N. Pay.	+	Com. Stk.	+	Ret. Earn.		Rev.	–	Exp.	=	Net Inc.		
Beg. bal.	0 +		0	=	0 +		0	+	0		0	–	0	=	0	NA	
1.	120,000 +		NA	=	NA +		120,000	+	NA		NA	–	NA	=	NA	120,000	FA
2.	400,000 +		NA	=	400,000 +		NA	+	NA		NA	–	NA	=	NA	400,000	FA
3.	(500,000) +		500,000	=	NA +		NA	+	NA		NA	–	NA	=	NA	(500,000)	IA
4.	85,000 +		NA	=	NA +		NA	+	85,000		85,000	–	NA	=	85,000	85,000	OA
5.	(50,000) +		NA	=	NA +		NA	+	(50,000)		NA	–	50,000	=	(50,000)	(50,000)	OA
6.	(4,000) +		NA	=	NA +		NA	+	(4,000)		NA	–	NA	=	NA	(4,000)	FA
7.	NA +		NA	=	NA +		NA	+	NA		NA	–	NA	=	NA	NA	
Totals	51,000 +		500,000	=	400,000 +		120,000	+	31,000		85,000	–	50,000	=	35,000	51,000	NC

Recognize that statements models are learning tools. Because they are helpful in understanding how accounting events affect financial statements, they are used extensively in this book. However, the models omit many of the details used in published financial statements. For example, the horizontal model shows only a partial set of statements. Also, since the statements are presented in aggregate, the description of dates (i.e., "as of" versus "for the period ended") does not distinguish periodic from cumulative data.

Real-World Financial Reports

As previously indicated, organizations exist in many different forms, including *business* entities and *not-for-profit* entities. Business entities are typically service, merchandising, or manufacturing companies. **Service businesses,** which include doctors, attorneys, accountants, dry cleaners, and housekeepers, provide services to their customers. **Merchandising businesses,** sometimes called *retail* or *wholesale companies,* sell goods to customers that other entities make. **Manufacturing businesses** make the goods that they sell to their customers.

Some business operations include combinations of these three categories. For example, an automotive repair shop might change oil (service function), sell parts such as oil filters (retail function), and rebuild engines (manufacturing function). The nature of the reporting entity affects the form and content of the information reported in an entity's financial statements. For example, governmental entities provide statements of activities while business entities provide income statements. Similarly, income statements of retail companies show an expense item called *cost of goods sold,* but service companies that do not sell goods have no such item in their income statements. You should expect some diversity when reviewing real-world financial statements.

Throughout this book we usually present income statements that end with "Net income." Due to an accounting rule that became effective at the end of 2009, income statements of large, real-world companies often appear to have three lines for net income. The partial income statements for Merck & Company, a large pharmaceutical company, shown in Exhibit 1.7, illustrate this issue. Notice that the third line from the bottom of the statement is called "Net income." However, "Net income attributable to noncontrolling interest" is subtracted from this first net income to arrive at "Net income attributable to Merck & Co., Inc." The illustrations in this text always assume that there is no net income attributable to noncontrolling interests, therefore our examples simply end with the term "Net income."

Some real-world companies with complex operations report information related to *comprehensive income.* Comprehensive income is determined by adding or subtracting certain items to or from net income. A description of the items used to determine

EXHIBIT 1.7	Real-World Financial Reporting

MERCK & CO., INC. AND SUBSIDIARIES
Consolidated Statement of Income (partial)
Years Ended December 31
($ in millions except per share amounts)

	2012	2011	2010
Sales	$47,267	$48,047	$45,987
Costs, expenses, and other			
Materials and production	16,446	16,871	18,396
Marketing and administrative	12,776	13,733	13,125
Research and development	8,168	8,467	11,111
Restructuring costs	664	1,306	985
Equity income from affiliates	(642)	(610)	(587)
Other (income) expense, net	1,116	946	1,304
	38,528	40,713	44,334
Income before taxes	8,739	7,334	1,653
Taxes on income	2,440	942	671
Net income	6,299	6,392	982
Less: Net income attributable to noncontrolling interests	131	120	121
Net income attributable to Merck & Co., Inc.	$ 6,168	$ 6,272	$ 861

comprehensive income is complex and beyond the scope of this course. Even so, the reader should be aware that, as of 2011, companies that must report comprehensive income may do so in one of two ways. First, comprehensive income items can be added to the bottom of the primary statement of earnings. Alternatively, a separate statement showing the determination of comprehensive income can be presented immediately following the primary statement of earnings. If a company chooses to report comprehensive income in a separate statement, the company's annual report will contain five financial statements. This text limits coverage to the four financial statements that traditionally appear in real-world annual reports. The optional statement of comprehensive income is not covered.

Annual Report for Target Corporation

Organizations normally provide information, including financial statements, to *stakeholders* yearly in a document known as an **annual report.** The annual report for Target Corporation is referred to in some of the end-of-chapter assignments, and it is worth your while to review it as an example of a real-world annual report. This report can be found online at http://investors.target.com. On the webpage that appears, under the "Investors" link, click on "sec filings." Next, under "filter by form type," select "annual filings" and then select the most recent "10-k" form from the list that appears. The pdf format is the easiest to work with. This report includes the company's financial statements (see pages 33–37 of the 2012 annual report). Immediately following the statements are a set of notes that

REALITY BYTES

On April 19, 2010, the stock of BP, Plc. (formally known as British Petroleum) was trading at $59.48 per share. On that same day the stock of Chevron Corp. was trading at $81.32 and the stock of Exxon Mobil Corp. was trading at $68.23. About six weeks later, on June 4, 2010, these companies' stocks had fallen to $37.16, $71.28, and $59.53 per share, respectively. Why did this happen? Did the companies report a large drop in their net earnings during these six weeks? No. What happened was that on April 20, 2010, the Deepwater Horizon oil well, owned by BP, failed and began discharging 60,000 barrels of oil daily into the Gulf of Mexico.

While it is easy to see why this event could cause BP's stock to lose 38 percent of its value, why would this cause Chevron's stock to fall 12 percent and Exxon's stock to fall 13 percent? These two companies did not have any oil spills during this time. One reason that the stock price of most oil companies declined significantly after BP's problems was that investors were concerned the failure would result in tighter regulation of all oil companies. Additionally, there was the concern that the government would ban, or seriously reduce, all future deepwater drilling. More regulations, and certainly a ban on future drilling, could drastically reduce the future earnings potential of all oil companies, not just BP.

As this situation illustrates, investors frequently use information not yet reported in a company's annual report. The annual report focuses on historical data, but investors are more concerned about the future. The historical information contained in the annual report is important because the past is frequently a strong predictor of what will occur in the future. However, current negative news, such as an oil spill, may give investors more information about a company's future than last year's annual report. For example, while the oil spill was bad news for the oil companies, it was, in financial terms, good news for companies that manufacture the oil-booms used to prevent oil from reaching the beaches. Similarly, a new company that has never earned a profit may have such an innovative idea that investors rush to buy its stock, even though they expect it to be a few years before the company has positive earnings. Also, investors and creditors may be motivated by nonfinancial considerations such as social consciousness, humanitarian concerns, or personal preferences. While accounting information is critically important, it is only one dimension of the information pool that investors and creditors use to make decisions.

provide additional details about the items described in the statements (see pages 38–64 of the 2012 annual report). The annual report contains the *auditors' report,* which is discussed in Chapter 4. Annual reports also include written commentary describing management's assessment of significant events that affected the company during the reporting period. This commentary is called *management's discussion and analysis* (MD&A).

The U.S. Securities and Exchange Commission (SEC) requires public companies to file an annual report in a document known as a 10-K. The SEC is discussed in more detail later. Even though the annual report is usually flashier (contains more color and pictures) than the 10-K, the 10-K is normally more comprehensive with respect to content. As a result, the 10-K report frequently substitutes for the annual report, but the annual report cannot substitute for the 10-K. In an effort to reduce costs, many companies now use the 10-K report as their annual report.

Special Terms in Real-World Reports

The financial statements of real-world companies include numerous items relating to advanced topics that are not covered in introductory accounting textbooks, especially the first chapter of an introductory accounting textbook. Do not, however, be discouraged from browsing through real-world annual reports. You will significantly enhance your learning if you look at many annual reports and attempt to identify as many items as you can. As your accounting knowledge grows, you will likely experience increased interest in real-world financial reports and the businesses they describe.

We encourage you to look for annual reports in the library or ask your employer for a copy of your company's report. The Internet is another excellent source for obtaining annual reports. Most companies provide links to their annual reports on their home pages. Look for links labeled "about the company" or "investor relations" or other phrases that logically lead to the company's financial reports. The best way to learn accounting is to use it. Accounting is the language of business. Learning the language will serve you well in almost any area of business that you pursue.

<< A Look Back

This chapter introduced the role of accounting in society and business: to provide information helpful to operating and evaluating the performance of organizations. Accounting is a measurement discipline. To communicate effectively, users of accounting must agree on the rules of measurement. *Generally accepted accounting principles (GAAP)* constitute the rules used by the accounting profession in the United States to govern financial reporting. GAAP is a work in progress that continues to evolve.

This chapter has discussed eight elements of financial statements: *assets, liabilities, equity, common stock (contributed capital), revenue, expenses, dividends (distributions),* and *net income.* The elements represent broad classifications reported on financial statements. Four basic financial statements appear in the reports of public companies: the *balance sheet,* the *income statement,* the *statement of changes in stockholders' equity,* and the *statement of cash flows.* The chapter discussed the form and content of each statement as well as the interrelationships among the statements.

This chapter introduced a *horizontal financial statements model* as a tool to help you understand how business events affect a set of financial statements. This model is used throughout the text. You should carefully study this model before proceeding to Chapter 2.

>> A Look Forward

To keep matters as simple as possible and to focus on the interrelationships among financial statements, this chapter considered only cash events. Obviously, many real-world events do not involve an immediate exchange of cash. For example, customers use telephone service throughout the month without paying for it until the next month. Such phone usage represents an expense in one month with a cash exchange in the following month. Events such as this are called *accruals.* Understanding the effects that accrual events have on the financial statements is included in Chapter 2.

 Video lectures and accompanying self-assessment quizzes are available for all learning objectives through McGraw-Hill *Connect®* Accounting.

SELF-STUDY REVIEW PROBLEM

During 2015 Rustic Camp Sites experienced the following transactions.

1. RCS acquired $32,000 cash by issuing common stock.
2. RCS received $116,000 cash for providing services to customers (leasing camp sites).
3. RCS paid $13,000 cash for salaries expense.
4. RCS paid a $9,000 cash dividend to the owners.
5. RCS sold land that had cost $100,000 for $100,000 cash.
6. RCS paid $47,000 cash for other operating expenses.

Required

a. Record the transaction data in a horizontal financial statements model like the following one. In the Cash Flow column, classify the cash flows as operating activities (OA), investing activities (IA), or financing activities (FA). The beginning balances have been recorded as an example. They are the ending balances shown on RCS's December 31, 2014, financial statements illustrated in the chapter. Note that the revenue and expense accounts have a zero beginning balance. Amounts in these accounts apply only to a single accounting period.

Revenue and expense account balances are not carried forward from one accounting period to the next.

Event No.	Balance Sheet										Income Statement					Statement of Cash Flows
	Assets			=	Liab.	+	Stockholders' Equity									
	Cash	+	Land	=	N. Pay.	+	Com. Stk.	+	Ret. Earn.		Rev.	−	Exp.	=	Net Inc.	
Beg. bal.	51,000	+	500,000	=	400,000	+	120,000	+	31,000		NA	−	NA	=	NA	NA

b. Explain why there are no beginning balances in the Income Statement columns.
c. What amount of net income will RCS report on the 2015 income statement?
d. What amount of total assets will RCS report on the December 31, 2015, balance sheet?
e. What amount of retained earnings will RCS report on the December 31, 2015, balance sheet?
f. What amount of net cash flow from operating activities will RCS report on the 2015 statement of cash flows?

Solution

a.

Event No.	Balance Sheet										Income Statement					Statement of Cash Flows	
	Assets			=	Liab.	+	Stockholders' Equity										
	Cash	+	Land	=	N. Pay.	+	Com. Stk.	+	Ret. Earn.		Rev.	−	Exp.	=	Net Inc.		
Beg. bal.	51,000	+	500,000	=	400,000	+	120,000	+	31,000		NA	−	NA	=	NA	NA	
1.	32,000	+	NA	=	NA	+	32,000	+	NA		NA	−	NA	=	NA	32,000	FA
2.	116,000	+	NA	=	NA	+	NA	+	116,000		116,000	−	NA	=	116,000	116,000	OA
3.	(13,000)	+	NA	=	NA	+	NA	+	(13,000)		NA	−	13,000	=	(13,000)	(13,000)	OA
4.	(9,000)	+	NA	=	NA	+	NA	+	(9,000)		NA	−	NA	=	NA	(9,000)	FA
5.	100,000	+	(100,000)	=	NA	+	NA	+	NA		NA	−	NA	=	NA	100,000	IA
6.	(47,000)	+	NA	=	NA	+	NA	+	(47,000)		NA	−	47,000	=	(47,000)	(47,000)	OA
Totals	230,000	+	400,000	=	400,000	+	152,000	+	78,000		116,000	−	60,000	=	56,000	179,000	NC*

*The letters NC on the last line of the column designate the net change in cash.

b. The revenue and expense accounts are temporary accounts used to capture data for a single accounting period. They are closed (amounts removed from the accounts) to retained earnings at the end of the accounting period and therefore always have zero balances at the beginning of the accounting cycle.

c. RCS will report net income of $56,000 on the 2015 income statement. Compute this amount by subtracting the expenses from the revenue ($116,000 Revenue − $13,000 Salaries expense − $47,000 Other operating expense).

d. RCS will report total assets of $630,000 on the December 31, 2015, balance sheet. Compute total assets by adding the cash amount to the land amount ($230,000 Cash + $400,000 Land).

e. RCS will report retained earnings of $78,000 on the December 31, 2015, balance sheet. Compute this amount using the following formula: Beginning retained earnings + Net income − Dividends = Ending retained earnings. In this case, $31,000 + $56,000 − $9,000 = $78,000.

f. Net cash flow from operating activities is the difference between the amount of cash collected from revenue and the amount of cash spent for expenses. In this case, $116,000 cash inflow from revenue − $13,000 cash outflow for salaries expense − $47,000 cash outflow for other operating expenses = $56,000 net cash inflow from operating activities.

32   Chapter 1

KEY TERMS

Accounting 3
Accounting equation 12
Accounting event 13
Accounting period 23
Accounts 11
Annual report 28
Articulation 21
Asset exchange transaction 14
Asset source transaction 13
Asset use transaction 15
Assets 11
Balance sheet 23
Claims 12
Closing 25
Common stock 12
Creditors 4
Dividend 16
Double-entry bookkeeping 13
Earnings 4

Elements 10
Expenses 15
Financial accounting 6
Financial Accounting
   Standards Board
   (FASB) 8
Financial resources 4
Financial statements 10
Financing activities 24
General ledger 16
Generally accepted accounting
   principles (GAAP) 8
Going concern 19
Historical cost concept 16
Horizontal statements
   model 26
Income 4
Income statement 21
Interest 4

International Accounting
   Standards Board
   (IASB) 9
International Financial
   Reporting Standards
   (IFRS) 9
Investing activities 24
Investors 4
Labor resources 5
Liabilities 12
Liquidation 19
Liquidity 23
Managerial accounting 6
Manufacturing businesses 27
Market 4
Matching concept 21
Merchandising businesses 27
Net income 21
Net loss 21

Not-for-profit entities 6
Operating activities 24
Permanent accounts 25
Physical resources 5
Profit 4
Reporting entities 9
Retained earnings 12
Revenue 14
Service businesses 27
Stakeholders 5
Statement of cash flows 24
Statement of changes in
   stockholders' equity 23
Stewardship 18
Stockholders 12
Stockholders' equity 12
Temporary accounts 25
Transaction 13
Users 5

QUESTIONS

1. Explain the term *stake-holder*. Distinguish between stakeholders with a direct versus an indirect interest in the companies that issue financial reports.

2. Why is accounting called the *language of business*?

3. What is the primary mechanism used to allocate resources in the United States?

4. In a business context, what does the term *market* mean?

5. What market trilogy components are involved in the process of transforming resources into finished products?

6. Give an example of a financial resource, a physical resource, and a labor resource.

7. What type of income or profit does an investor expect to receive in exchange for providing financial resources to a business? What type of income does a creditor

expect from providing financial resources to an organization or business?

8. How do financial and managerial accounting differ?

9. Describe a not-for-profit or nonprofit enterprise. What is the motivation for this type of entity?

10. What are the U.S. rules of accounting information measurement called?

11. Explain how a career in public accounting differs from a career in private accounting.

12. Distinguish between elements of financial statements and accounts.

13. What role do assets play in business profitability?

14. To whom do the assets of a business belong?

15. Describe the differences between creditors and investors.

16. Name the accounting term used to describe a business's obligations to creditors.

17. What is the accounting equation? Describe each of its three components.

18. Who ultimately bears the risk and collects the rewards associated with operating a business?

19. What does a *double-entry bookkeeping system* mean?

20. How does acquiring capital from owners affect the accounting equation?

21. What is the difference between assets that are acquired by issuing common stock and those that are acquired using retained earnings?

22. How does earning revenue affect the accounting equation?

23. What are the three primary sources of assets?

24. What is the source of retained earnings?

25. How does distributing assets (paying dividends) to owners affect the accounting equation?

26. What are the similarities and differences between dividends and expenses?

27. What four general-purpose financial statements do business enterprises use?

28. Which of the general-purpose financial statements provides information about the enterprise at a specific designated date?

29. What causes a net loss?

30. What three categories of cash receipts and cash payments do businesses report on the statement of cash flows? Explain the types of cash flows reported in each category.

31. How are asset accounts usually arranged in the balance sheet?

32. Discuss the term *articulation* as it relates to financial statements.

33. How do temporary accounts differ from permanent accounts? Name three temporary accounts. Is retained earnings a temporary or a permanent account?

34. What is the historical cost concept and how does it relate to verifiability?
35. Identify the three types of accounting transactions discussed in this chapter. Provide an example of each type of transaction, and explain how it affects the accounting equation.
36. What type of information does a business typically include in its annual report?
37. What is U.S. GAAP? What is IFRS?

MULTIPLE-CHOICE QUESTIONS

Multiple-choice questions are provided on the text website at www.mhhe.com/edmondssurvey4e.

SECTION 1 EXERCISES

connect |ACCOUNTING All applicable Exercises are available with McGraw-Hill's *Connect® Accounting.*

Exercise 1-1   *The role of accounting in society*   LO 1-1

Resource owners provide three types of resources to conversion agents that transform the resources into products or services that satisfy consumer demands.

Required

Identify the three types of resources. Write a brief memo explaining how resource owners select the particular conversion agents to which they will provide resources. Your memo should include answers to the following questions: If you work as a private accountant, what role would you play in the allocation of resources? Which professional certification would be most appropriate to your career?

Exercise 1-2   *Careers in accounting*   LO 1-1

Accounting is commonly divided into two sectors. One sector is called public accounting. The other sector is called private accounting.

Required

a. Identify three areas of service provided by public accountants.
b. Describe the common duties performed by private accountants.

Exercise 1-3   *Identifying the reporting entities*   LO 1-1

Ray Steen recently started a business. During the first few days of operation, Mr. Steen transferred $100,000 from his personal account into a business account for a company he named Steen Enterprises. Steen Enterprises borrowed $60,000 from First Bank. Mr. Steen's father-in-law, Stan Rhoades, invested $75,000 into the business for which he received a 25 percent ownership interest. Steen Enterprises purchased a building from Zoro Realty Company. The building cost $150,000 cash. Steen Enterprises earned $56,000 in revenue from the company's customers and paid its employees $31,000 for salaries expense.

Required

Identify the entities that were mentioned in the scenario and explain what happened to the cash accounts of each entity that you identify.

Exercise 1-4   *Missing information in the accounting equation*   LO 1-2

Required

Calculate the missing amounts in the following table.

Company	Assets	=	Liabilities	+	Common Stock	+	Retained Earnings
A	$?		$30,000		$ 50,000		$62,000
B	50,000		?		10,000		25,000
C	85,000		20,000		?		40,000
D	215,000		60,000		100,000		?

Stockholders' Equity

LO 1-2

Exercise 1-5   *Effect of events on the accounting equation*

Hansen Enterprises experienced the following events during 2014:

1. Acquired cash from the issue of common stock.
2. Provided services to clients for cash.
3. Paid utilities expenses with cash.
4. Paid cash to reduce the principal on a bank note.
5. Sold land for cash at an amount equal to its cost.
6. Paid a cash dividend to the stockholders.

Required

Explain how each of the events would affect the accounting equation by writing the letter I for increase, the letter D for decrease, and NA for does not affect under each of the components of the accounting equation. The first event is shown as an example.

Event Number	Assets	= Liabilities	+ Common Stock	+ Retained Earnings
			Stockholders' Equity	
1	I	NA	I	NA

LO 1-2

Exercise 1-6   *Effect of transactions on general ledger accounts*

At the beginning of 2014, Foster Corp.'s accounting records had the following general ledger accounts and balances.

FOSTER CORP. **Accounting Equation**							
Event	Assets		=	Liabilities	+	Stockholders' Equity		Acct. Titles for RE
	Cash	Land		Notes Payable		Common Stock	Retained Earnings	
Balance 1/1/2014	30,000	16,000		10,000		20,000	16,000	

Foster Corp. completed the following transactions during 2014:

1. Purchased land for $20,000 cash.
2. Acquired $10,000 cash from the issue of common stock.
3. Received $90,000 cash for providing services to customers.
4. Paid cash operating expenses of $65,000.
5. Borrowed $20,000 cash from the bank.
6. Paid a $5,000 cash dividend to the stockholders.
7. Determined that the market value of the land purchased in event 1 is $30,000.

Required

a. Record the transactions in the appropriate general ledger accounts. Record the amounts of revenue, expense, and dividends in the Retained Earnings column. Provide the appropriate titles for these accounts in the last column of the table.
b. As of December 31, 2014, determine the total amount of assets, liabilities, and stockholder's equity and present this information in the form of an accounting equation.
c. What is the amount of total assets, liabilities, and stockholders' equity as of January 1, 2015?

Exercise 1-7   *Missing information and recording events*   LO 1-2

As of December 31, 2014, Post Company had total cash of $156,000, notes payable of $85,600, and common stock of $52,400. During 2015, Post earned $36,000 of cash revenue, paid $20,000 for cash expenses, and paid a $3,000 cash dividend to the stockholders.

Required

a. Determine the amount of retained earnings as of December 31, 2014.
b. Create an accounting equation and record the beginning account balances under the appropriate elements.
c. Record the revenue, expense, and dividend events under the appropriate elements of the accounting equation created in Requirement *b*.
d. Prove the equality of the accounting equation as of December 31, 2015.
e. Identify the beginning and ending balances in the Cash and Common Stock accounts. Explain why the beginning and ending balances in the Cash account are different, but the beginning and ending balances in the Common Stock account remain the same.

Exercise 1-8   *Account titles and the accounting equation*   LO 1-2

The following account titles were drawn from the general ledger of Gutter Control, Incorporated (GCI): Cash, Notes Payable, Land, Accounts Payable, Office Furniture, Salaries Expense, Common Stock, Service Revenue, Interest Expense, Utilities Payable, Utilities Expense, Trucks, Supplies, Operating Expenses, Rent Revenue, Dividends, Computers, Building, Supplies Expense, Gasoline Expense, Retained Earnings, Dividends.

Required

a. Create an accounting equation using the elements assets, liabilities, and stockholders' equity. List each account title under the element of the accounting equation to which it belongs.
b. Will all businesses have the same number of accounts? Explain your answer.

Exercise 1-9   *Components of the accounting equation*   LO 1-3

Lang Enterprises was started when it acquired $4,000 cash from creditors and $6,000 from owners. The company immediately purchased land that cost $9,000.

Required

a. Record the events under an accounting equation.
b. After all events have been recorded, Lang's obligations to creditors represent what percent of total assets?
c. After all events have been recorded, Lang's stockholder's equity represents what percent of total assets?
d. Assume the debt is due. Given that Lang has $6,000 in stockholders' equity, can the company repay the creditors at this point? Why or why not?

Exercise 1-10   *Components of the accounting equation*   LO 1-3

The financial condition of GreyCo Inc. is expressed in the following accounting equation:

$$\text{Assets} = \text{Liabilities} + \text{Common stock} + \text{Retained earnings}$$
$$\$800 \text{ Cash} + \$9,200 \text{ Land} = \$7,000 + \$2,000 + \$1,000$$

Required

a. Are dividends paid to creditors or investors? Explain why.
b. How much cash is in the Retained Earnings account?
c. Determine the maximum dividend GreyCo can pay.
d. If the obligation to creditors is due, can GreyCo repay the loan? Why or why not?
e. Suppose the land sinks into the sea as a result of an earthquake and a resulting tsunami. The business is then liquidated. How much cash will creditors receive? How much cash will investors receive? (Assume there are no legal fees or other costs of liquidation.)

LO 1-3

Exercise 1-11 *Differences between interest and dividends*

The following account balances were drawn from the financial records of Crystal Company (CC) as of January 1, 2014. Assets, $14,000; Liabilities, $4,000; Common Stock, $7,000; and Retained Earnings, $3,000. CC has agreed to pay the creditors $400 of interest per year. Further, CC agrees that for the 2014 fiscal year any annual earnings remaining after the interest charges will be paid out as dividends to the owners.

Required

a. Assuming CC earns a before interest expense recognition profit of $900 during 2014, determine the amount of interest and dividends paid.

b. Assuming CC earns a before interest expense recognition profit of $500 during 2014, determine the amount of interest and dividends paid.

c. Assuming CC earns a before interest expense recognition profit of $100 during 2014, determine the amount of interest and dividends paid.

LO 1-3

Exercise 1-12 *Distribution in a business liquidation*

Assume that Clinton Company acquires $1,200 cash from creditors and $1,700 cash from investors.

Required

a. Explain the primary differences between investors and creditors.

b. If Clinton has net income of $800 and then liquidates, what amount of cash will the creditors receive? What amount of cash will the investors receive?

c. If Clinton has a net loss of $800 cash and then liquidates, what amount of cash will the creditors receive? What amount of cash will the investors receive?

d. If Clinton has a net loss of $1,900 cash and then liquidates, what amount of cash will the creditors receive? What amount of cash will the investors receive?

LO 1-4

Exercise 1-13 *Classifying events as asset source, use, or exchange*

Dale's Business Services experienced the following events during its first year of operations:

1. Acquired $20,000 cash from the issue of common stock.
2. Borrowed $12,000 cash from First Bank.
3. Paid $5,000 cash to purchase land.
4. Received $25,000 cash for providing boarding services.
5. Acquired an additional $5,000 cash from the issue of common stock.
6. Purchased additional land for $4,000 cash.
7. Paid $10,000 cash for salary expense.
8. Signed a contract to provide additional services in the future.
9. Paid $1,200 cash for rent expense.
10. Paid a $1,000 cash dividend to the stockholders.
11. Determined the market value of the land to be $18,000 at the end of the accounting period.

Required

Classify each event as an asset source, use, or exchange transaction or as not applicable (NA).

SECTION 2 EXERCISES

LO 1-5

Exercise 1-14 *Missing information for determining net income*

The December 31, 2013, balance sheet for Thomas Company showed total stockholders' equity of $156,000. Total stockholders' equity increased by $65,000 between December 31, 2013, and December 31, 2014. During 2014 Thomas Company acquired $20,000 cash from the issue of common stock. Thomas Company paid a $5,000 cash dividend to the stockholders during 2014.

Required

Determine the amount of net income or loss Thomas reported on its 2014 income statement. (*Hint:* Remember that stock issues, net income, and dividends all change total stockholders' equity.)

Exercise 1-15   *Preparing an income statement and a balance sheet*   LO 1-5

Topez Company was started on January 1, 2014. During 2014, the company experienced the following three accounting events: (1) earned cash revenues of $14,500, (2) paid cash expenses of $9,200, and (3) paid a $500 cash dividend to its stockholders. These were the only events that affected the company during 2014.

Required

a. Create an accounting equation and record the effects of each accounting event under the appropriate general ledger account headings.
b. Prepare an income statement, statement of changes in stockholder's equity, and a balance sheet dated December 31, 2014, for Topez Company.
c. Explain why the income statement uses different terminology to date the income statement than is used to date the balance sheet.

Exercise 1-16   *Historical cost versus market value*   LO 1-5

Mountain View, Inc., purchased land in January 2009 at a cost of $250,000. The estimated market value of the land is $425,000 as of December 31, 2014.

Required

a. Name the December 31, 2014, financial statement(s) on which the land will be shown.
b. At what dollar amount will the land be shown in the financial statement(s)?
c. Name the key concept that will be used in determining the dollar amount that will be reported for land that is shown in the financial statement(s).

Exercise 1-17   *Statement of cash flows*   LO 1-5

On January 1, 2014, Palmetto, a fast-food company, had a balance in its Cash account of $32,000. During the 2014 accounting period, the company had (1) net cash inflow from operating activities of $15,600, (2) net cash outflow for investing activities of $23,000, and (3) net cash outflow from financing activities of $4,500.

Required

a. Prepare a statement of cash flows.
b. Provide a reasonable explanation as to what may have caused the net cash inflow from operating activities.
c. Provide a reasonable explanation as to what may have caused the net cash outflow from investing activities.
d. Provide a reasonable explanation as to what may have caused the net cash outflow from financing activities.

Exercise 1-18   *Prepare a statement of cash flows*   LO 1-5

American General Company experienced the following accounting events during 2014:

1. Paid $4,000 cash for salary expense.
2. Borrowed $8,000 cash from State Bank.
3. Received $30,000 cash from the issue of common stock.
4. Purchased land for $8,000 cash.
5. Performed services for $14,000 cash.
6. Paid $4,200 cash for utilities expense.
7. Sold land for $7,000 cash.
8. Paid a cash dividend of $1,000 to the stockholders.
9. Hired an accountant to keep the books.
10. Paid $3,000 cash on the loan from State Bank.

Required

a. Indicate how each of the events would be classified on the statement of cash flows as operating activities (OA), investing activities (IA), financing activities (FA), or not applicable (NA).

b. Prepare a statement of cash flows for 2014. Assume American General had a beginning cash balance of $9,000 on January 1, 2014.

LO 1-3, 1-5

Exercise 1-19 *Preparing financial statements*

Carolina Company experienced the following events during 2014.

1. Acquired $50,000 cash from the issue of common stock.
2. Paid $15,000 cash to purchase land.
3. Borrowed $25,000 cash.
4. Provided services for $60,000 cash.
5. Paid $12,000 cash for rent expense.
6. Paid $22,000 cash for other operating expenses.
7. Paid a $5,000 cash dividend to the stockholders.
8. Determined that the market value of the land purchased in Event 2 is now $16,500.

Required

a. The January 1, 2014, general ledger account balances are shown in the following accounting equation. Record the eight events in the appropriate general ledger accounts. Record the amounts of revenue, expense, and dividends in the Retained Earnings column. Provide the appropriate titles for these accounts in the last column of the table. The first event is shown as an example.

CAROLINA COMPANY Accounting Equation							
Event	Assets		=	Liabilities	+	Stockholders' Equity		Acct. Titles for RE
	Cash	Land		Notes Payable		Common Stock	Retained Earnings	
Balance 1/1/2014	15,000	10,000		0		20,000	5,000	
1.	50,000					50,000		

b. Prepare an income statement, statement of changes in equity, year-end balance sheet, and statement of cash flows for the 2014 accounting period.

c. Determine the percentage of assets that were provided by retained earnings. How much cash is in the retained earnings account?

LO 1-4, 1-5

Exercise 1-20 *Relating accounting events to entities*

Pandora Company paid $40,000 cash to purchase land from Donnelley Company. Donnelley originally paid $40,000 for the land.

Required

a. Was this event an asset source, use, or exchange transaction for Pandora Company?

b. Was this event an asset source, use, or exchange transaction for Donnelley Company?

c. Was the cash flow an operating, investing, or financing activity on Pandora Company's 2014 statement of cash flows?

d. Was the cash flow an operating, investing, or financing activity on Donnelley Company's 2014 statement of cash flows?

Exercise 1-21   *Preparing financial statements—retained earnings emphasis*   LO 1-3, 1-4, 1-5

On January 1, 2014, the following information was drawn from the accounting records of Wilson Company: cash of $200; land of $1,800; notes payable of $600; and common stock of $1,000.

Required

a. Determine the amount of retained earnings as of January 1, 2014.

b. After looking at the amount of retained earnings, the chief executive officer (CEO) wants to pay a $300 cash dividend to the stockholders. Can the company pay this dividend? Why or why not?

c. As of January 1, 2014, what percent of the assets were acquired from creditors?

d. As of January 1, 2014, what percent of the assets were acquired from investors?

e. As of January 1, 2014, what percent of the assets were acquired from retained earnings?

f. Create an accounting equation using percentages instead of dollar amounts on the right side of the equation.

g. During 2014, Wilson Company earned cash revenue of $500, paid cash expenses of $300, and paid a cash dividend of $50. Prepare an income statement, statement of changes in stockholders' equity, a balance sheet, and a statement of cash flows dated December 31, 2014. (*Hint:* It is helpful to record these events under an accounting equation before preparing the statements.)

h. Comment on the terminology used to date each statement.

i. An appraiser determines that as of December 31, 2014, the market value of the land is $2,000. How will this fact change the financial statements?

j. What is the balance in the Revenue account on January 1, 2015?

Exercise 1-22   *Preparing financial statements—cash flow emphasis*   LO 1-5

As of January 1, 2014, Concepts Inc. had a balance of $4,500 in Cash, $2,500 in Common Stock, and $2,000 in Retained Earnings. These were the only accounts with balances in the ledger on January 1, 2014. Further analysis of the company's cash account indicated that during the 2014 accounting period, the company had (1) net cash inflow from operating activities of $5,100, (2) net cash outflow for investing activities of $13,000, and (3) net cash inflow from financing activities of $7,600. All revenue and expense events were cash events. The following accounts and balances represent the general ledger of Concepts Inc. as of December 31, 2014, before closing.

CONCEPTS INC.
General Ledger

Assets	=	Liabilities	+	Stockholders' Equity		
Cash		**Notes Payable**		**Common Stock**	**Revenue**	
Bal. 4,200		Bal. 3,000		Bal. 8,000	Bal. 9,900	
Land				**Retained Earnings**	**Expenses**	
Bal. 13,000				Bal. 2,000	Bal. 4,800	
					Dividends	
					Bal. 900	

Required

a. Assume that the net cash inflow from financing activities of $7,600 was caused by three events. Based on the information above, identify these events and determine the cash flow associated with each event.

b. What did the company purchase that resulted in the cash outflow from investing activities?

c. Prepare an income statement, statement of changes in stockholders' equity, balance sheet, and statement of cash flows.

LO 1-5, 1-6

Exercise 1-23 *Retained earnings and the closing process*

As of December 31, 2014, Blue Haven Company had total assets of $100,000, total liabilities of $30,000, and common stock of $50,000. The company's 2014 income statement contained revenue of $16,000 and expenses of $11,000. The 2014 statement of changes in stockholder's equity stated that $2,000 of dividends were paid to investors.

Required

a. Determine the before-closing balance in the Retained Earnings account on December 31, 2014.

b. Determine the after-closing balance in the Retained Earnings account on December 31, 2014.

c. Determine the before-closing balances in the Revenue, Expense, and Dividend accounts on December 31, 2014.

d. Determine the after-closing balances in the Revenue, Expense, and Dividend accounts on December 31, 2014.

e. Explain the difference between common stock and retained earnings.

f. On January 1, 2015, Blue Haven Company raised $40,000 by issuing additional common stock. Immediately after the additional capital was raised. Blue Haven reported total equity of $110,000. Are the stockholders of Blue Haven in a better financial position than they were on December 31, 2014?

LO 1-6

Exercise 1-24 *The closing process*

Sammy's Pizza opened on January 1, 2014. Sammy's reported the following for cash revenues and cash expenses for the years 2014 to 2016:

	Cash Revenues	Cash Expenses
2014	$20,000	$11,000
2015	$30,000	$14,000
2016	$40,000	$22,000

Required

a. What would Sammy's Pizza report for net income and retained earnings for the years 2014, 2015, and 2016?

b. Explain the difference between net income and retained earnings.

c. Assume that Sammy's Pizza paid a $5,000 dividend to stockholders in 2015. What would Sammy's Pizza report for net income and retained earnings for 2015 and 2016?

LO 1-6

Exercise 1-25 *Retained earnings and the closing process*

Davis Company was started on January 1, 2014. During the month of January, Davis earned $4,600 of revenue and incurred $3,000 of expenses. During the remainder of 2014, Davis earned $52,000 and incurred $42,000 of expenses. Davis closes its books on December 31 of each year.

Required

a. Determine the balance in the Retained Earnings account as of January 31, 2014.

b. Determine the balance in the Revenue and Expense accounts as of January 31, 2014.

c. Determine the balance in the Retained Earnings account as of December 31, 2014, before closing.

d. Determine the balances in the Revenue and Expense accounts as of December 31, 2014, before closing.

e. Determine the balance in the Retained Earnings account as of January 1, 2015.

f. Determine the balance in the Revenue and Expense accounts as of January 1, 2015.

Exercise 1-26 *Types of transactions and the horizontal statements model*   LO 1-4, 1-7

Happy Pet Store experienced the following events during its first year of operations, 2014:

1. Acquired cash by issuing common stock.
2. Borrowed cash from a bank.
3. Signed a contract to provide services in the future.
4. Purchased land with cash.
5. Paid cash for operating expenses.
6. Paid a cash dividend to the stockholders.
7. Determined that the market value of the land is higher than the historical cost.

Required

a. Indicate whether each event is an asset source, use, or exchange transaction.
b. Use a horizontal statements model to show how each event affects the balance sheet, income statement, and statement of cash flows. Indicate whether the event increases (I), decreases (D), or does not affect (NA) each element of the financial statements. Also, in the Cash Flows column, classify the cash flows as operating activities (OA), investing activities (IA), or financing activities (FA). The first transaction is shown as an example.

Event No.	Balance Sheet								Income Statement					Statement of Cash Flows
	Cash	+	Land	=	N. Pay	+	C. Stock.	+	Ret. Ear.	Rev.	−	Exp.	=	Net Inc.	
1.	I	+	NA	=	NA	+	I	+	NA	NA	−	NA	=	NA	I FA

Exercise 1-27 *International Financial Reporting Standards*   LO IFRS

Corrugated Boxes Inc. is a U.S.–based company that develops its financial statements under GAAP. The total amount of the company's assets shown on its December 31, 2014, balance sheet was approximately $305 million. The president of Corrugated is considering the possibility of relocating the company to a country that practices accounting under IFRS. The president has hired an international accounting firm to determine what the company's statements would look like if they were prepared under IFRS. One striking difference is that under IFRS the assets shown on the balance sheet would be valued at approximately $345 million.

Required

a. Would Corrugated Boxes' assets really be worth $40 million more if it moves its headquarters?
b. Discuss the underlying conceptual differences between U.S. GAAP and IFRS that cause the difference in the reported asset values.

SECTIONS 1 AND 2 PROBLEMS

connect | ACCOUNTING   **All applicable Problems are available with McGraw-Hill's** *Connect® Accounting.*

Problem 1-28 *Accounting's role in not-for-profits*   LO 1-1

Karen White is struggling to pass her introductory accounting course. Karen is intelligent but she likes to party. Studying is a low priority for Karen. When one of her friends tells her that she is going to have trouble in business if she doesn't learn accounting, Karen responds that she doesn't plan to go into business. She says that she is arts oriented and plans someday to be a director of a museum. She is in the school of business to develop her social skills, not her quantitative skills. Karen says she won't have to worry about accounting, since museums are not intended to make a profit.

Required

a. Write a brief memo explaining whether you agree or disagree with Karen's position regarding accounting and not-for-profit organizations.
b. Distinguish between financial accounting and managerial accounting.
c. Identify some of the stakeholders of not-for-profit institutions that would expect to receive financial accounting reports.
d. Identify some of the stakeholders of not-for-profit institutions that would expect to receive managerial accounting reports.

LO 1-1

Problem 1-29 *Accounting entities*

The following business scenarios are independent from one another:

1. Chris Hann purchased an automobile from Classic Auto Sales for $10,000.
2. Sal Pearl loaned $15,000 to the business in which he is a stockholder.
3. First State Bank paid interest to Strong Co. on a certificate of deposit that Strong Co. has invested at First State Bank.
4. Cindy's Restaurant paid the current utility bill of $135 to Midwest Utilities.
5. Sun Corp. borrowed $50,000 from City National Bank and used the funds to purchase land from Carriage Realty.
6. Sue Wang purchased $10,000 of common stock of International Sales Corporation from the corporation.
7. Chris Gordon loaned $6,000 cash to his daughter.
8. Motor Service Co. earned $20,000 in cash revenue.
9. Poy Imports paid $4,000 for salaries to each of its four employees.
10. Borg Inc. paid a cash dividend of $4,000 to its sole shareholder, Mark Borg.

Required

a. For each scenario, create a list of all of the entities that are mentioned in the description.
b. Describe what happens to the cash account of each entity that you identified in Requirement *a.*

LO 1-4

Problem 1-30 *Classifying events as asset source, use, or exchange*

The following unrelated events are typical of those experienced by business entities:

1. Pay cash for operating expenses.
2. Pay an office manager's salary with cash.
3. Receive cash for services that have been performed.
4. Pay cash for utilities expense.
5. Acquire land by accepting a liability (financing the purchase).
6. Pay cash to purchase a new office building.
7. Discuss plans for a new office building with an architect.
8. Repay part of a bank loan.
9. Acquire cash by issuing common stock.
10. Purchase land with cash.
11. Purchase equipment with cash.
12. Pay monthly rent on an office building.
13. Hire a new office manager.
14. Borrow cash from a bank.
15. Pay a cash dividend to stockholders.

Required

Identify each of the events as an asset source, use, or exchange transaction. If an event would not be recorded under generally accepted accounting principles, identify it as not applicable (NA).

Also indicate for each event whether total assets would increase, decrease, or remain unchanged. Organize your answer according to the following table. The first event is shown in the table as an example.

Event No.	Type of Event	Effect on Total Assets
1	Asset use	Decrease

Problem 1-31   *Relating titles and accounts to financial statements*   LO 1-5

Required

Identify the financial statements on which each of the following items (titles, date descriptions, and accounts) appears by placing a check mark in the appropriate column. If an item appears on more than one statement, place a check mark in every applicable column.

Item	Income Statement	Statement of Changes in Stockholders' Equity	Balance Sheet	Statement of Cash Flows
For the period ended (date)				
Net income				
Investing activities				
Net loss				
Ending cash balance				
Salary expense				
Consulting revenue				
Dividends				
Financing activities				
Ending common stock				
Interest expense				
As of (date)				
Land				
Beginning cash balance				
Notes payable				
Beginning common stock				
Service revenue				
Utility expense				
Stock issue				
Operating activities				

Problem 1-32   *Preparing financial statements for two complete accounting cycles*   LO 1-2, 1-3, 1-5, 1-6

Susan's Consulting experienced the following transactions for 2014, its first year of operations, and 2015. *Assume that all transactions involve the receipt or payment of cash.*

Transactions for 2014

1. Acquired $50,000 by issuing common stock.
2. Received $100,000 cash for providing services to customers.
3. Borrowed $15,000 cash from creditors.
4. Paid expenses amounting to $60,000.
5. Purchased land for $40,000 cash.

Transactions for 2015

Beginning account balances for 2015 are:

Cash	$65,000
Land	40,000
Notes payable	15,000
Common stock	50,000
Retained earnings	40,000

1. Acquired an additional $20,000 from the issue of common stock.
2. Received $130,000 for providing services.
3. Paid $10,000 to creditors to reduce loan.
4. Paid expenses amounting to $75,000.
5. Paid a $15,000 dividend to the stockholders.
6. Determined that the market value of the land is $50,000.

Required

a. Write an accounting equation, and record the effects of each accounting event under the appropriate headings for each year. Record the amounts of revenue, expense, and dividends in the Retained Earnings column. Provide appropriate titles for these accounts in the last column of the table.

b. Prepare an income statement, statement of changes in stockholders' equity, year-end balance sheet, and statement of cash flows for each year.

c. Determine the amount of cash that is in the Retained Earnings account at the end of 2014 and 2015.

d. Examine the balance sheets for the two years. How did assets change from 2014 to 2015?

e. Determine the balance in the Retained Earnings account immediately after Event 2 in 2014 and in 2015 are recorded.

Problem 1-33 *Interrelationships among financial statements*

Crawford Enterprises started the 2014 accounting period with $75,000 of assets (all cash), $15,000 of liabilities, and $25,000 of common stock. During the year, Crawford earned cash revenues of $46,000, paid cash expenses of $26,000, and paid a cash dividend to stockholders of $5,000. Crawford also acquired $15,000 of additional cash from the sale of common stock and paid $10,000 cash to reduce the liability owed to a bank.

Required

a. Prepare an income statement, statement of changes in stockholders' equity, period-end balance sheet, and statement of cash flows for the 2014 accounting period. (*Hint:* Determine the amount of beginning retained earnings before considering the effects of the current period events. It also might help to record all events under an accounting equation before preparing the statements.)

b. Determine the percentage of total assets that were provided by creditors, investors, and earnings.

c. Determine the balance in the Revenue, Expense, and Dividends accounts as of January 1, 2015.

Problem 1-34 *Recording events in a horizontal statements model*

Davidson Company was started on January 1, 2014, and experienced the following events during its first year of operation:

1. Acquired $52,000 cash from the issue of common stock.
2. Borrowed $20,000 cash from National Bank.

3. Earned cash revenues of $42,000 for performing services.
4. Paid cash expenses of $23,000.
5. Paid a $6,000 cash dividend to the stockholders.
6. Acquired an additional $10,000 cash from the issue of common stock.
7. Paid $10,000 cash to reduce the principal balance of the bank note.
8. Paid $45,000 cash to purchase land.
9. Determined that the market value of the land is $55,000.

Required

a. Record the preceding transactions in the horizontal statements model. Also, in the Cash Flows column, classify the cash flows as operating activities (OA), investing activities (IA), or financing activities (FA). The first event is shown as an example.

Event No.	Balance Sheet										Income Statement					Statement of Cash Flows
	Cash	+	Land	=	N. Pay	+	C. Stock.	+	Ret. Ear.		Rev.	−	Exp.	=	Net Inc.	
1.	52,000	+	NA	=	NA	+	52,000	+	NA		NA	−	NA	=	NA	52,000 FA

b. Determine the amount of total assets that Davidson would report on the December 31, 2014, balance sheet.
c. Identify the asset source transactions and related amounts for 2014.
d. Determine the net income that Davidson would report on the 2014 income statement. Explain why dividends do not appear on the income statement.
e. Determine the net cash flows from operating activities, financing activities, and investing activities that Davidson would report on the 2014 statement of cash flows.
f. Determine the percentage of assets that were provided by investors, creditors, and earnings.
g. What is the balance in the Retained Earnings account immediately after Event 3 is recorded?

ANALYZE, THINK, COMMUNICATE

ATC 1-1   Business Applications Case   *Understanding real-world annual reports*

Required

Use the Target Corporation's Form 10-K to answer the following questions related to Target's 2012 fiscal year (year ended February 2, 2013). Target's Form 10-K is available on the company's website or through the SEC's EDGAR database. Appendix A provides instructions for using the EDGAR database.

a. What was Target's net income for 2012 (the year ended February 2, 2013)?
b. Did Target's net income increase or decrease from 2011 to 2012, and by how much?
c. What was Target's accounting equation for 2012?
d. Which of the following had the largest percentage change from 2011 to 2012: net sales; cost of sales; or selling, general, and administrative expenses? Show all computations.

ATC 1-2   Group Assignment   *Missing information*

The following selected financial information is available for HAS, Inc. Amounts are in millions of dollars.

Income Statements	2017	2016	2015	2014
Revenue	$ 860	$1,520	$ (a)	$1,200
Cost and expenses	(a)	(a)	(2,400)	(860)
Income from continuing operations	(b)	450	320	(a)
Unusual items	-0-	175	(b)	(b)
Net income	$ 20	$ (b)	$ 175	$ 300

(continued)

Balance Sheets	2017	2016	2015	2014
Assets				
Cash and marketable securities	$ 350	$1,720	$ (c)	$ 940
Other assets	1,900	(c)	2,500	(c)
Total assets	2,250	$2,900	$ (d)	$3,500
Liabilities	$ (c)	$ (d)	$1,001	$ (d)
Stockholders' equity				
Common stock	880	720	(e)	800
Retained earnings	(d)	(e)	800	(e)
Total stockholders' equity	1,520	1,345	(f)	2,200
Total liabilities and stockholders' equity	$2,250	$ (f)	$3,250	$3,500

Required

a. Divide the class into groups of four or five students each. Organize the groups into four sections. Assign Task 1 to the first section of groups, Task 2 to the second section, Task 3 to the third section, and Task 4 to the fourth section.

Group Tasks

(1) Fill in the missing information for 2014.

(2) Fill in the missing information for 2015.

(3) Fill in the missing information for 2016.

(4) Fill in the missing information for 2017.

b. Each section should select two representatives. One representative is to put the financial statements assigned to that section on the board, underlining the missing amounts. The second representative is to explain to the class how the missing amounts were determined.

c. Each section should list events that could have caused the unusual items category on the income statement.

ATC 1-3   Research Assignment   *Finding real-world accounting information*

This chapter introduced the basic four financial statements companies use annually to keep their stakeholders informed of their accomplishments and financial situation. Complete the requirements below using the most recent (20xx) financial statements available on the McDonald's Corporation's website. Obtain the statements on the Internet by following the steps below. (The formatting of the company's website may have changed since these instructions were written.)

1. Go to www.mcdonalds.com.

2. Click on the "Corporate" link at the bottom of the page. (Most companies have a link titled "investors relations" that leads to their financial statements; McDonald's uses "corporate" instead.)

3. Click on the "INVESTORS" link at the top of the page.

4. Click on "*Annual Reports*" and then on "*20xx Financial Report.*"

5. Go to the company's financial statements that begin on page 45 of the annual report.

Required

a. What was the company's net income in each of the last three years?

b. What amount of total assets did the company have at the end of the most recent year?

c. How much retained earnings did the company have at the end of the most recent year?

d. For the most recent year, what was the company's cash flow from operating activities, cash flow from investing activities, and cash flow from financing activities?

ATC 1-4   Writing Assignment   *Elements of financial statements defined*

Sam and his sister Blair both attend the state university. As a reward for their successful completion of the past year (Sam had a 3.2 GPA in business, and Blair had a 3.7 GPA in art), their father gave each of them 100 shares of The Walt Disney Company stock. They have just received their first annual report. Blair does not understand what the information means and has asked Sam to explain it to her. Sam is currently taking an accounting course, and she knows he will understand the financial statements.

Required

Assume that you are Sam. Write Blair a memo explaining the following financial statement items to her. In your explanation, describe each of the two financial statements and explain the financial information each contains. Also define each of the elements listed for each financial statement and explain what it means.

Balance Sheet
Assets
Liabilities
Stockholders' equity
Income Statement
Revenue
Expense
Net income

CHAPTER 2

Accounting for Accruals and Deferrals

LEARNING OBJECTIVES

After you have mastered the material in this chapter, you will be able to:

SECTION 1: SHOW HOW ACCRUALS AFFECT FINANCIAL STATEMENTS

LO 2-1   Show how receivables affect financial statements.

LO 2-2   Show how payables affect financial statements.

SECTION 2: SHOW HOW DEFERRALS AFFECT FINANCIAL STATEMENTS

LO 2-3   Show how supplies affect financial statements.

LO 2-4   Show how prepaid items affect financial statements.

LO 2-5   Show how unearned revenues affect financial statements.

LO 2-6   Explain the accounting cycle including adjustments and the closing process.

LO 2-7   Prepare financial statements based on accrual accounting.

LO 2-8   Classify accounting events into one of four categories.

 Video lectures and accompanying self-assessment quizzes are available for all learning objectives through McGraw-Hill Connect® Accounting.

SECTION 1:

ACCOUNTING FOR ACCRUALS

Users of financial statements must distinguish between the terms *recognition* and *realization*. **Recognition** means formally *reporting* an economic item or event in the financial statements. **Realization** refers to collecting money, generally from the sale of products or services. Companies may recognize (report) revenue in the income statement in a different accounting period from the period in which they collect the cash related to the revenue. Furthermore, companies frequently make cash payments for expenses in accounting periods other than the periods in which the expenses are recognized in the income statement.

To illustrate assume Johnson Company provides services to customers in 2014 but collects cash for those services in 2015. In this case, realization occurs in 2015. When should Johnson recognize the services revenue?

Users of *cash basis* accounting recognize (report) revenues and expenses in the period in which cash is collected or paid. Under cash basis accounting Johnson would recognize the revenue in 2015 when it collects the cash. In contrast, users of **accrual accounting** recognize revenues and expenses in the period in which they occur, regardless of when cash is collected or paid. Under accrual accounting Johnson would recognize the revenue in 2014 (the period in which it performed the services) even though it does not collect (realize) the cash until 2015.

Accrual accounting is required by generally accepted accounting principles. Virtually all major companies operating in the United States use it. Its two distinguishing features are called *accruals* and *deferrals*.

- The term **accrual** describes a revenue or an expense event that is recognized ***before*** cash is exchanged. Johnson's recognition of revenue in 2014 related to cash realized in 2015 is an example of an accrual.
- The term **deferral** describes a revenue or an expense event that is recognized ***after*** cash has been exchanged. Suppose Johnson pays cash in 2014 to purchase office supplies it uses in 2015. In this case the cash payment occurs in 2014 although supplies expense is recognized in 2015. This example is a deferral.

The Curious Accountant

On September 15, 2014, Janet McGeorge purchased a subscription to *Better Homes and Gardens* magazine for her mother's birthday. She paid $12 for a one-year subscription to the Meredith Corporation, the company that publishes *Fitness, American Baby, Better Homes and Gardens, The Ladies Home Journal,* and several other magazines. The company also owns 12 television stations. Janet's mother will receive her first issue of the magazine in October.

How should Meredith Corporation account for the receipt of this cash? How would this event be reported on its December 31, 2014, financial statements? (Answer on page 64.)

ACCRUAL ACCOUNTING

LO 2-1

 Show how receivables affect financial statements.

This section of the text describes seven events experienced by Cato Consultants, a training services company that uses accrual accounting.

EVENT 1 Cato Consultants was started on January 1, 2014, when it acquired $5,000 cash by issuing common stock.

The issue of stock for cash is an **asset source transaction.** It increases the company's assets (cash) and its equity (common stock). The transaction does not affect the income statement. The cash inflow is classified as a financing activity (acquisition from owners). These effects are shown in the following financial statements model:

Assets	=	Liab.	+	Stockholders' Equity			Rev.	−	Exp.	=	Net Inc.	Cash Flow
Cash	=			Com. Stk.	+	Ret. Earn.						
5,000	=	NA	+	5,000	+	NA	NA	−	NA	=	NA	5,000 FA

Accounting for Accounts Receivable

EVENT 2 During 2014 Cato Consultants provided $84,000 of consulting services to its clients. The business has completed the work and sent bills to the clients, but not yet collected any cash. This type of transaction is frequently described as providing services *on account.*

Accrual accounting requires companies to recognize revenue in the period in which the work is done regardless of when cash is collected. In this case, revenue is recognized in 2014 even though cash has not been realized (collected). Recall that revenue represents the economic benefit that results in an increase in assets from providing goods and services to customers. The specific asset that increases is called **Accounts Receivable.** The balance in Accounts Receivable represents the amount of cash the company expects to collect in the future. Since the revenue recognition causes assets (accounts receivable) to increase, it is classified as an asset source transaction. Its effect on the financial statements follows:

Assets		=	Liab.	+	Stockholders' Equity							
Cash	+	Accts. Rec.	=		Com. Stk.	+	Ret. Earn.	Rev.	–	Exp.	=	Net Inc.	Cash Flow
NA	+	84,000	=	NA	+	NA	+	84,000	84,000	–	NA	=	84,000	NA

Notice that the event affects the income statement but not the statement of cash flows. The statement of cash flows will be affected in the future when cash is collected.

EVENT 3 Cato collected $60,000 cash from customers in partial settlement of its accounts receivable.

The collection of an account receivable is an **asset exchange transaction.** One asset account (Cash) increases and another asset account (Accounts Receivable) decreases. The amount of total assets is unchanged. The effect of the $60,000 collection of receivables on the financial statements is as follows:

Assets		=	Liab.	+	Stockholders' Equity							
Cash	+	Accts. Rec.	=		Com. Stk.	+	Ret. Earn.	Rev.	–	Exp.	=	Net Inc.	Cash Flow
60,000	+	(60,000)	=	NA	+	NA	+	NA	NA	–	NA	=	NA	60,000 OA

Notice that collecting the cash did not affect the income statement. The revenue was recognized when the work was done (see Event 2). Revenue would be double counted if it were recognized again when the cash is collected. The statement of cash flows reflects a cash inflow from operating activities.

Other Events

EVENT 4 Cato paid the instructor $10,000 for teaching training courses (salary expense).

Cash payment for salary expense is an **asset use transaction.** Both the asset account Cash and the equity account Retained Earnings decrease by $10,000. Recognizing the expense decreases net income on the income statement. Since Cato paid cash for the expense, the statement of cash flows reflects a cash outflow from operating activities. These effects on the financial statements follow:

Assets		=	Liab.	+	Stockholders' Equity							
Cash	+	Accts. Rec.	=		Com. Stk.	+	Ret. Earn.	Rev.	–	Exp.	=	Net Inc.	Cash Flow
(10,000)	+	NA	=	NA	+	NA	+	(10,000)	NA	–	10,000	=	(10,000)	(10,000) OA

EVENT 5   Cato paid $2,000 cash for advertising costs. The advertisements appeared in 2014.

Cash payments for advertising expenses are asset use transactions. Both the asset account Cash and the equity account Retained Earnings decrease by $2,000. Recognizing the expense decreases net income on the income statement. Since the expense was paid with cash, the statement of cash flows reflects a cash outflow from operating activities. These effects on the financial statements follow:

Assets			=	Liab.	+	Stockholders' Equity								
Cash	+	Accts. Rec.	=			Com. Stk.	+	Ret. Earn.	Rev.	–	Exp.	=	Net Inc.	Cash Flow
(2,000)	+	NA	=	NA	+	NA	+	(2,000)	NA	–	2,000	=	(2,000)	(2,000) OA

EVENT 6   Cato signed contracts for $42,000 of consulting services to be performed in 2015.

The $42,000 for consulting services to be performed in 2015 is not recognized in the 2014 financial statements. Revenue is recognized for work actually completed, *not* work expected to be completed. This event does not affect any of the financial statements.

Assets			=	Liab.	+	Stockholders' Equity								
Cash	+	Accts. Rec.	=			Com. Stk.	+	Ret. Earn.	Rev.	–	Exp.	=	Net Inc.	Cash Flow
NA	+	NA	=	NA	+	NA	+	NA	NA	–	NA	=	NA	NA

Accounting for Accrued Salary Expense (Adjusting Entry)

It is impractical to record many business events as they occur. For example, Cato incurs salary expense continually as the instructor teaches courses. Imagine the impossibility of trying to record salary expense second by second! Companies normally record transactions when it is most convenient. The most convenient time to record many expenses is when they are paid. Often, however, a single business transaction pertains to more than one accounting period. To provide accurate financial reports in such cases, companies may need to recognize some expenses before paying cash for them. Expenses that are recognized before cash is paid are called **accrued expenses.** The accounting for Event 7 illustrates the effect of recognizing accrued salary expense.

EVENT 7   At the end of 2014 Cato recorded accrued salary expense of $6,000 (the salary expense is for courses the instructor taught in 2014 that Cato will pay cash for in 2015).

Accrual accounting requires that companies recognize expenses in the period in which they are incurred regardless of when cash is paid. Cato must recognize all salary expense in the period in which the instructor worked (2014) even though Cato will not pay the instructor again until 2015. Cato must also recognize the obligation (liability) it has to pay the instructor. To accurately report all 2014 salary expense and year-end obligations, Cato must record the unpaid salary expense and salary liability before preparing its financial statements. The entry to recognize the accrued salary expense is called an **adjusting entry.** Like all adjusting entries, it is only to update the accounting records; it does not affect cash.

   This adjusting entry decreases stockholders' equity (Retained Earnings) and increases a liability account called **Salaries Payable.** The balance in the Salaries Payable account represents the amount of cash the company is obligated to pay the instructor in the future. The effect of the expense recognition on the financial statements follows:

Assets			=	Liab.	+	Stockholders' Equity									
Cash	+	Accts. Rec.	=	Sal. Pay.	+	Com. Stk.	+	Ret. Earn.	Rev.	−	Exp.	=	Net Inc.	Cash Flow
NA	+	NA	=	6,000	+	NA	+	(6,000)	NA	−	6,000	=	(6,000)	NA

This event is a **claims exchange transaction.** The claims of creditors (liabilities) increase and the claims of stockholders (retained earnings) decrease. Total claims remain unchanged. The salary expense is reported on the income statement. The statement of cash flows is not affected.

Be careful not to confuse liabilities with expenses. Although liabilities may increase when a company recognizes expenses, liabilities are not expenses. Liabilities are obligations. They can arise from acquiring assets as well as recognizing expenses. For example, when a business borrows money from a bank, it recognizes an increase in assets (cash) and liabilities (notes payable). The borrowing transaction does not affect expenses.

☑ CHECK YOURSELF 2.1

During 2014, Anwar Company earned $345,000 of revenue on account and collected $320,000 cash from accounts receivable. Anwar paid cash expenses of $300,000 and cash dividends of $12,000. Determine the amount of net income Anwar should report on the 2014 income statement and the amount of cash flow from operating activities Anwar should report on the 2014 statement of cash flows.

Answer Net income is $45,000 ($345,000 revenue − $300,000 expenses). The cash flow from operating activities is $20,000, the amount of revenue collected in cash from customers (accounts receivable) minus the cash paid for expenses ($320,000 − $300,000). Dividend payments are classified as financing activities and do not affect the determination of either net income or cash flow from operating activities.

Summary of Events and General Ledger

The previous section of this chapter described seven events Cato Consultants experienced during the 2014 accounting period. These events are summarized in Exhibit 2.1. The associated general ledger accounts are also shown in the exhibit. The information in these accounts is used to prepare the financial statements. The revenue and expense items appear in the Retained Earnings column with their account titles immediately to the right of the dollar amounts. The amounts are color coded to help you trace the data to the financial statements. Data in red appear on the balance sheet, data in blue on the income statement, and data in green on the statement of cash flows.

Vertical Statements Model

The financial statements for Cato Consultants' 2014 accounting period are represented in a vertical statements model in Exhibit 2.2. A vertical statements model arranges a set of financial statement information vertically on a single page. Like horizontal statements models, vertical statements models are learning tools. They illustrate interrelationships among financial statements. The models do not, however, portray the full, formal presentation formats companies use in published financial statements. For example, statements models may use summarized formats with abbreviated titles and dates. As you read the following explanations of each financial statement, trace the color-coded financial data from Exhibit 2.1 to Exhibit 2.2.

EXHIBIT 2.1

Transaction Data for 2013 Recorded in General Ledger Accounts

1	Cato Consultants acquired $5,000 cash by issuing common stock.
2	Cato provided $84,000 of consulting services on account.
3	Cato collected $60,000 cash from customers in partial settlement of its accounts receivable.
4	Cato paid $10,000 cash for salary expense.
5	Cato paid $2,000 cash for 2014 advertising costs.
6	Cato signed contracts for $42,000 of consulting services to be performed in 2015.
7	Cato recognized $6,000 of accrued salary expense.

	Assets			=	Liabilities	+		Stockholders' Equity		
Event No.	Cash	+	Accounts Receivable	=	Salaries Payable	+	Common Stock	+	Retained Earnings	Other Account Titles
Beg. bal.	0		0		0		0		0	
1	5,000						5,000			
2			84,000						84,000	Consulting revenue
3	60,000		(60,000)							
4	(10,000)								(10,000)	Salary expense
5	(2,000)								(2,000)	Advertising expense
6										
7					6,000				(6,000)	Salary Expense
End bal.	53,000	+	24,000	=	6,000	+	5,000	+	66,000	

Income Statement

The income statement reflects accrual accounting. Consulting revenue represents the price Cato charged for all the services it performed in 2014, even though Cato had not by the end of the year received cash for some of the services performed. Expenses include all costs incurred to produce revenue, whether paid for by year-end or not. We can now expand the definition of expenses introduced in Chapter 1. Expenses were previously defined as assets consumed in the process of generating revenue. Cato's adjusting entry to recognize accrued salaries expense did not reflect consuming assets. Instead of a decrease in assets, Cato recorded an increase in liabilities (salaries payable). An **expense** can therefore be more precisely defined as *a decrease in assets or an increase in liabilities resulting from operating activities undertaken to generate revenue.*

Statement of Changes in Stockholders' Equity

The statement of changes in stockholders' equity reports the effects on equity of issuing common stock, earning net income, and paying dividends to stockholders. It identifies how an entity's equity increased and decreased during the period as a result of transactions with stockholders and operating the business. In the Cato case, the statement shows that equity increased when the business acquired $5,000 cash by issuing common stock. The statement also reports that equity increased by $66,000 from earning income and that none of the $66,000 of net earnings was distributed to owners (no dividends were paid). Equity at the end of the year is $71,000 ($5,000 + $66,000).

Balance Sheet

The balance sheet discloses an entity's assets, liabilities, and stockholders' equity at a particular point in time. As of December 31, 2014, Cato Consultants had total assets of $77,000 ($53,000 cash + $24,000 accounts receivable). These assets are equal to the

| EXHIBIT 2.2 | Vertical Statements Model |

CATO CONSULTANTS
Financial Statements*
Income Statement
For the Year Ended December 31, 2014

Consulting revenue	$84,000
Salary expense	(16,000)
Advertising expense	(2,000)
Net income	$66,000

Statement of Changes in Stockholders' Equity
For the Year Ended December 31, 2014

Beginning common stock	$ 0	
Plus: Common stock issued	5,000	
Ending common stock		$ 5,000
Beginning retained earnings	0	
Plus: Net income	66,000	
Less: Dividends	0	
Ending retained earnings		66,000
Total stockholders' equity		$71,000

Balance Sheet
As of December 31, 2014

Assets		
Cash	$53,000	
Accounts receivable	24,000	
Total assets		$77,000
Liabilities		
Salaries payable		$ 6,000
Stockholders' equity		
Common stock	$ 5,000	
Retained earnings	66,000	
Total stockholders' equity		71,000
Total liabilities and stockholders' equity		$77,000

Statement of Cash Flows
For the Year Ended December 31, 2014

Cash flows from operating activities		
Cash receipts from customers	$60,000	
Cash payments for salary expense	(10,000)	
Cash payments for advertising expenses	(2,000)	
Net cash flow from operating activities		$48,000
Cash flow from investing activities		0
Cash flows from financing activities		
Cash receipt from issuing common stock	5,000	
Net cash flow from financing activities		5,000
Net change in cash		53,000
Plus: Beginning cash balance		0
Ending cash balance		$53,000

*In real-world annual reports, financial statements are normally presented separately with appropriate descriptions of the date to indicate whether the statement applies to the entire accounting period or a specific point in time.

obligations and commitments Cato has to its creditors and investors. Specifically, Cato has a $6,000 obligation (liability) to creditors, with the remaining $71,000 of assets available to support commitments (stockholders' equity) to stockholders.

Statement of Cash Flows

The statement of cash flows explains the change in cash from the beginning to the end of the accounting period. It can be prepared by analyzing the Cash account. Since Cato Consultants was established in 2014, its beginning cash balance was zero. By the end of the year, the cash balance was $53,000. The statement of cash flows explains this increase. The Cash account increased because Cato collected $60,000 from customers and decreased because Cato paid $12,000 for expenses. As a result, Cato's net cash inflow from operating activities was $48,000. Also, the business acquired $5,000 cash through the financing activity of issuing common stock, for a cumulative cash increase of $53,000 ($48,000 + $5,000) during 2014.

Comparing Cash Flow from Operating Activities with Net Income

The amount of net income measured using accrual accounting differs from the amount of cash flow from operating activities. For Cato Consulting in 2014, the differences are summarized below.

	Accrual Accounting	Cash Flow
Consulting revenue	$84,000	$60,000
Salary expense	(16,000)	(10,000)
Advertising expense	(2,000)	(2,000)
Net income	$66,000	$48,000

Many students begin their first accounting class with the misconception that revenue and expense items are cash equivalents. The Cato illustration demonstrates that a company may recognize a revenue or expense without a corresponding cash collection or payment in the same accounting period.

The Closing Process

Recall that the temporary accounts (revenue, expense, and dividend) are closed prior to the start of the next accounting cycle. The closing process transfers the amount in each of these accounts to the Retained Earnings account, leaving each temporary account with a zero balance.

Exhibit 2.3 shows the general ledger accounts for Cato Consultants after the revenue and expense accounts have been closed to retained earnings. The closing entry labeled C1.1 transfers the balance in the Consulting Revenue account to the Retained Earnings account. Closing entries C1.2 and C1.3 transfer the balances in the expense accounts to retained earnings.

Steps in an Accounting Cycle

An accounting cycle, which is represented graphically in Exhibit 2.4, involves several steps. The four steps identified to this point are (1) recording transactions; (2) adjusting the accounts; (3) preparing financial statements; and (4) closing the temporary accounts. The first step occurs continually throughout the accounting period. Steps 2, 3, and 4 normally occur at the end of the accounting period.

The Matching Concept

Cash basis accounting can distort reported net income because it sometimes fails to match expenses with the revenues they produce. To illustrate, consider the $6,000 of accrued salary expense that Cato Consultants recognized at the end of 2014. The instructor's teaching produced revenue in 2014. If Cato waited until 2015 (when it paid

EXHIBIT 2.3

General Ledger Accounts for Cato Consultants

Assets		=	Liabilities		+	Stockholders' Equity	
Cash			**Salaries Payable**			**Common Stock**	
(1)	5,000		(7)	6,000		(1)	5,000
(3)	60,000		Bal.	6,000			
(4)	(10,000)					**Retained Earnings**	
(5)	(2,000)						
Bal.	53,000					Cl.1	84,000
						Cl.2	(16,000)
Accounts Receivable						Cl.3	(2,000)
(2)	84,000					Bal.	66,000
(3)	(60,000)						
Bal.	24,000					**Consulting Revenue**	
						(2)	84,000
						Cl.1	(84,000)
						Bal.	0
						Salary Expense	
						(4)	(10,000)
						(7)	(6,000)
						Cl.2	16,000
						Bal.	0
						Advertising Expense	
						(5)	(2,000)
						Cl.3	2,000
						Bal.	0

the instructor) to recognize $6,000 of the total $16,000 salary expense, then $6,000 of the expense would not be matched with the revenue it generated. By using accrual accounting, Cato recognized all the salary expense in the same accounting period in which the consulting revenue was recognized. A primary goal of accrual accounting is to appropriately match expenses with revenues, the **matching concept.**

Appropriately matching expenses with revenues can be difficult even when using accrual accounting. For example, consider Cato's advertising expense. Money spent on advertising may generate revenue in future accounting periods as well as in the current period. A prospective customer could save an advertising brochure for several years before calling Cato for training services. It is difficult to know when and to what extent advertising produces revenue. When the connection between an expense and the corresponding revenue is vague, accountants commonly match the expense with the period in which it is incurred. Cato matched (recognized) the entire $2,000 of advertising cost with the 2013 accounting period even though some of that cost might generate revenue in future accounting periods. Expenses that are matched with the period in which they are incurred are frequently called **period costs.**

Matching is not perfect. Although it would be more accurate to match expenses with revenues than with periods, there is sometimes no obvious direct connection between expenses and revenue.

EXHIBIT 2.4

The Accounting Cycle

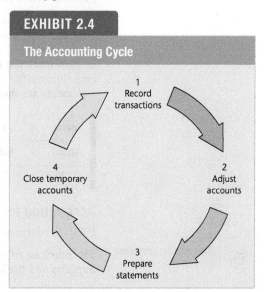

1 Record transactions

2 Adjust accounts

3 Prepare statements

4 Close temporary accounts

Accountants must exercise judgment to select the accounting period in which to recognize revenues and expenses. The concept of conservatism influences such judgment calls.

The Conservatism Principle

When faced with a recognition dilemma, **conservatism** guides accountants to select the alternative that produces the lowest amount of net income. In uncertain circumstances, accountants tend to delay revenue recognition and accelerate expense recognition. The conservatism principle holds that it is better to understate net income than to overstate it. If subsequent developments suggest that net income should have been higher, investors will respond more favorably than if they learn it was really lower. This practice explains why Cato recognized all of the advertising cost as expense in 2014 even though some of that cost may generate revenue in future accounting periods.

SECTION 2:

ACCOUNTING FOR DEFERRALS

As previously discussed cash may be exchanged before revenue or expense is recognized. In this case the business defers recognition. This section introduces three common deferrals.

SECOND ACCOUNTING CYCLE

The effects of Cato Consultants' 2015 events are as follows:

EVENT 1   Cato paid $6,000 to the instructor to settle the salaries payable obligation.

Cash payments to creditors are *asset use transactions.* When Cato pays the instructor, both the asset account Cash and the liability account Salaries Payable decrease. The cash payment does not affect the income statement. The salary expense was recognized in 2014 when the instructor taught the classes. The statement of cash flows reflects a cash outflow from operating activities. The effects of this transaction on the financial statements are shown here.

Assets	=	Liab.	+	Stk. Equity					
Cash	=	Sal. Pay.			Rev.	–	Exp.	=	Net Inc.	Cash Flow
(6,000)	=	(6,000)	+	NA	NA	–	NA	=	NA	(6,000) OA

Accounting for Supplies Purchase

EVENT 2   Cato purchased $800 of supplies on account.

The purchase of supplies on account is an *asset source transaction.* The asset account Supplies and the liability account Accounts Payable increase. The income statement is unaffected. Expense recognition is deferred until the supplies are used. The statement of cash flows is not affected. The effects of this transaction on the financial statements are shown here.

Assets	=	Liab.	+	Stk. Equity		Rev.	–	Exp.	=	Net Inc.	Cash Flow
Supplies	=	Accts. Pay.				Rev.	–	Exp.	=	Net Inc.	Cash Flow
800	=	800	+	NA		NA	–	NA	=	NA	NA

Prepaid Items (Cost versus Expense)

EVENT 3 On March 1, 2015, Cato signed a one-year lease agreement and paid $12,000 cash in advance to rent office space. The one-year lease term began on March 1.

Accrual accounting draws a distinction between the terms *cost* and *expense*. A **cost** *might be either an asset or an expense.* If a company has already consumed a purchased resource in the process of earning revenue, the cost of the resource is an *expense*. For example, companies normally pay for electricity the month after using it. The cost of electric utilities is therefore usually recorded as an expense. In contrast, if a company purchases a resource it will use in the future to generate revenue, the cost of the resource represents an *asset*. Accountants record such a cost in an asset account and *defer* recognizing an expense until the resource is used to produce revenue. Deferring the expense recognition provides more accurate *matching* of revenues and expenses.

The cost of the office space Cato leased in Event 2 is an asset. It is recorded in the asset account *Prepaid Rent*. Cato expects to benefit from incurring this cost for the next twelve months. Expense recognition is deferred until Cato uses the office space to help generate revenue. Other common deferred expenses include *prepaid insurance* and *prepaid taxes*. As these titles imply, deferred expenses are frequently called **prepaid items.** Exhibit 2.5 illustrates the relationship between costs, assets, and expenses.

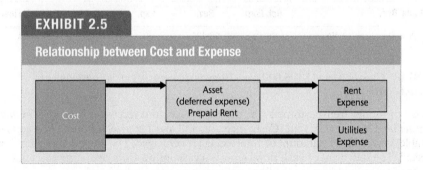

EXHIBIT 2.5

Relationship between Cost and Expense

Purchasing prepaid rent is an asset exchange transaction. The asset account Cash decreases and the asset account Prepaid Rent increases. The amount of total assets is unaffected. The income statement is unaffected. Expense recognition is deferred until the office space is used. The statement of cash flows reflects a cash outflow from operating activities. The effects of this transaction on the financial statements are shown here.

Assets			=	Liab.	+	Stk. Equity		Rev.	–	Exp.	=	Net Inc.	Cash Flow
Cash	+	Prep. Rent						Rev.	–	Exp.	=	Net Inc.	Cash Flow
(12,000)	+	12,000	=	NA	+	NA		NA	–	NA	=	NA	(12,000) OA

LO 2-5

Show how unearned revenues affect financial statements.

Accounting for Receipt of Unearned Revenue

EVENT 4   Cato received **$18,000 cash in advance from Westberry Company for consulting services Cato agreed to perform over a one-year period beginning June 1, 2015.**

Cato must defer (delay) recognizing any revenue until it performs (does the work) the consulting services for Westberry. From Cato's point of view, the deferred revenue is a liability because Cato is obligated to perform services in the future. The liability is called **unearned revenue.** The cash receipt is an *asset source transaction.* The asset account Cash and the liability account Unearned Revenue both increase. Collecting the cash has no effect on the income statement. The revenue will be reported on the income statement after Cato performs the services. The statement of cash flows reflects a cash inflow from operating activities. The effects of this transaction on the financial statements are shown here.

Assets	=	Liab.	+	Stk. Equity		Rev.	–	Exp.	=	Net Inc.	Cash Flow
Cash	=	Unearn. Rev.				Rev.	–	Exp.	=	Net Inc.	Cash Flow
18,000	=	18,000	+	NA		NA	–	NA	=	NA	18,000 OA

Other 2015 Events

EVENT 5   Cato provided **$96,400 of consulting services on account.**

Providing services on account is an *asset source transaction.* The asset account Accounts Receivable and the stockholders' equity account Retained Earnings increase. Revenue and net income increase. The statement of cash flows is not affected. The effects of this transaction on the financial statements are shown here.

Assets	=	Liab.	+	Stk. Equity		Rev.	–	Exp.	=	Net Inc.	Cash Flow
Accts. Rec.	=			Ret. Earn.		Rev.	–	Exp.	=	Net Inc.	Cash Flow
96,400	=	NA	+	96,400		96,400	–	NA	=	96,400	NA

EVENT 6   Cato collected **$105,000 cash from customers as partial settlement of accounts receivable.**

Collecting money from customers who are paying accounts receivable is an *asset exchange transaction.* One asset account (Cash) increases and another asset account (Accounts Receivable) decreases. The amount of total assets is unchanged. The income statement is not affected. The statement of cash flows reports a cash inflow from operating activities. The effects of this transaction on the financial statements are shown here.

Assets			=	Liab.	+	Stk. Equity		Rev.	–	Exp.	=	Net Inc.	Cash Flow
Cash	+	Accts. Rec.						Rev.	–	Exp.	=	Net Inc.	Cash Flow
105,000	+	(105,000)	=	NA	+	NA		NA	–	NA	=	NA	105,000 OA

EVENT 7   Cato paid **$32,000 cash for salary expense.**

Cash payments for salary expense are *asset use transactions.* Both the asset account Cash and the equity account Retained Earnings decrease by $32,000. Recognizing the expense decreases net income on the income statement. The statement of cash flows reflects a cash outflow from operating activities. The effects of this transaction on the financial statements are shown here.

Assets	=	Liab.	+	Stk. Equity						
Cash	=			Ret. Earn.	Rev.	–	Exp.	=	Net Inc.	Cash Flow
(32,000)	=	NA	+	(32,000)	NA	–	32,000	=	(32,000)	(32,000) OA

EVENT 8   Cato incurred $21,000 of other operating expenses on account.

Recognizing expenses incurred on account are *claims exchange transactions.* One claims account (Accounts Payable) increases and another claims account (Retained Earnings) decreases. The amount of total claims is not affected. Recognizing the expenses decreases net income. The statement of cash flows is not affected. The effects of this transaction on the financial statements are shown here.

Assets	=	Liab.	+	Stk. Equity						
		Accts. Pay.	+	Ret. Earn.	Rev.	–	Exp.	=	Net Inc.	Cash Flow
NA	=	21,000	+	(21,000)	NA	–	21,000	=	(21,000)	NA

EVENT 9   Cato paid $18,200 in partial settlement of accounts payable.

Paying accounts payable is an *asset use transaction.* The asset account Cash and the liability account Accounts Payable decrease. The statement of cash flows reports a cash outflow for operating activities. The income statement is not affected. The effects of this transaction on the financial statements are shown here.

Assets	=	Liab.	+	Stk. Equity						
Cash	=	Accts. Pay.			Rev.	–	Exp.	=	Net Inc.	Cash Flow
(18,200)	=	(18,200)	+	NA	NA	–	NA	=	NA	(18,200) OA

EVENT 10   Cato paid $79,500 to purchase land it planned to use in the future as a building site for its home office.

Purchasing land with cash is an *asset exchange transaction.* One asset account, Cash, decreases and another asset account, Land, increases. The amount of total assets is unchanged. The income statement is not affected. The statement of cash flows reports a cash outflow for investing activities. The effects of this transaction on the financial statements are shown here.

Assets			=	Liab.	+	Stk. Equity					
Cash	+	Land	=	Liab.	+		Rev.	–	Exp.	=	Net Inc.	Cash Flow
(79,500)	+	79,500	=	NA	+	NA	NA	–	NA	=	NA	(79,500) IA

EVENT 11   Cato paid $21,000 in cash dividends to its stockholders.

Cash payments for dividends are *asset use transactions.* Both the asset account Cash and the equity account Retained Earnings decrease. Recall that dividends are wealth transfers from the business to the stockholders, not expenses. They are not incurred in the process of generating revenue. They do not affect the income statement. The statement of cash flows reflects a cash outflow from financing activities. The effects of this transaction on the financial statements are shown here.

Assets	=	Liab.	+	Stk. Equity						
Cash	=			Ret. Earn.	Rev.	–	Exp.	=	Net Inc.	Cash Flow
(21,000)	=	NA	+	(21,000)	NA	–	NA	=	NA	(21,000) FA

EVENT 12   Cato acquired $2,000 cash from issuing additional shares of common stock.

Issuing common stock is an *asset source transaction.* The asset account Cash and the stockholders' equity account Common Stock increase. The income statement is unaffected. The statement of cash flows reports a cash inflow from financing activities. The effects of this transaction on the financial statements are shown here.

Assets	=	Liab.	+	Stk. Equity						
Cash	=			Com. Stk.	Rev.	−	Exp.	=	Net Inc.	Cash Flow
2,000	=	NA	+	2,000	NA	−	NA	=	NA	2,000 FA

Adjusting Entries

LO 2-6

Explain the accounting cycle including adjustments and the closing process.

Recall that companies make adjusting entries at the end of an accounting period to update the account balances before preparing the financial statements. Adjusting entries ensure that companies report revenues and expenses in the appropriate accounting period; adjusting entries never affect the Cash account.

Accounting for Supplies (Adjusting Entry)

EVENT 13   After determining through a physical count that it had $150 of unused supplies on hand as of December 31, Cato recognized supplies expense.

Companies would find the cost of recording supplies expense each time a pencil, piece of paper, envelope, or other supply item is used to far outweigh the benefit derived from such tedious recordkeeping. Instead, accountants transfer to expense the total cost of all supplies used during the entire accounting period in a single year-end adjusting entry. The cost of supplies used is determined as follows:

Beginning supplies balance + Supplies purchased = Supplies available for use

Supplies available for use − Ending supplies balance = Supplies used

Companies determine the ending supplies balance by physically counting the supplies on hand at the end of the period. Cato used $650 of supplies during the year (zero beginning balance + $800 supplies purchase = $800 available for use; $800 available for use − $150 ending balance = $650). Recognizing Cato's supplies expense is an *asset use transaction.* The asset account Supplies and the stockholders' equity account Retained Earnings decrease. Recognizing supplies expense reduces net income. The statement of cash flows is not affected. The effects of this transaction on the financial statements are shown here.

Assets	=	Liab.	+	Stk. Equity						
Supplies	=			Ret. Earn.	Rev.	−	Exp.	=	Net Inc.	Cash Flow
(650)	=	NA	+	(650)	NA	−	650	=	(650)	NA

Accounting for Prepaid Rent (Adjusting Entry)

EVENT 14   Cato recognized rent expense for the office space used during the accounting period.

Recall that Cato paid $12,000 on March 1, 2015, to rent office space for one year (see Event 3). The portion of the lease cost that represents using office space from March 1 through December 31 is computed as follows:

$12,000 Cost of annual lease ÷ 12 Months = $1,000 Cost per month

$1,000 Cost per month × 10 Months used = $10,000 Rent expense

Recognizing the rent expense decreases the asset account Prepaid Rent and the stockholders' equity account Retained Earnings. Recognizing rent expense reduces net income. The statement of cash flows is not affected. The cash flow effect was recorded in the March 1 event. These effects on the financial statements follow:

Assets	=	Liab.	+	Stk. Equity					
Prep. Rent	=			Ret. Earn.	Rev.	−	Exp.	=	Net Inc.	Cash Flow
(10,000)	=	NA	+	(10,000)	NA	−	10,000	=	(10,000)	NA

☑ CHECK YOURSELF 2.2

Rujoub Inc. paid $18,000 cash for one year of insurance coverage that began on November 1, 2014. Based on this information alone, determine the cash flow from operating activities that Rujoub would report on the 2014 and 2015 statements of cash flows. Also, determine the amount of insurance expense Rujoub would report on the 2014 income statement and the amount of prepaid insurance (an asset) that Rujoub would report on the December 31, 2014, balance sheet.

Answer   Since Rujoub paid all of the cash in 2014, the 2014 statement of cash flows would report an $18,000 cash outflow from operating activities. The 2015 statement of cash flows would report zero cash flow from operating activities. The expense would be recognized in the periods in which the insurance is used. In this case, insurance expense is recognized at the rate of $1,500 per month ($18,000 ÷ 12 months). Rujoub used two months of insurance coverage in 2014 and therefore would report $3,000 (2 months × $1,500) of insurance expense on the 2014 income statement. Rujoub would report a $15,000 (10 months × $1,500) asset, prepaid insurance, on the December 31, 2014, balance sheet. The $15,000 of prepaid insurance would be recognized as insurance expense in 2015 when the insurance coverage is used.

Accounting for Unearned Revenue (Adjusting Entry)

EVENT 15   Cato recognized the portion of the unearned revenue it earned during the accounting period.

Recall that Cato received an $18,000 cash advance from Westberry Company to provide consulting services from June 1, 2015, to May 31, 2016 (see Event 4). By December 31, Cato had earned 7 months (June 1 through December 31) of the revenue related to this contract. Rather than recording the revenue continuously as it performed the consulting services, Cato can simply recognize the amount earned in a single adjustment to the accounting records at the end of the accounting period. The amount of the adjustment is computed as follows:

$$\$18,000 \div 12 \text{ months} = \$1,500 \text{ revenue earned per month}$$

$$\$1,500 \times 7 \text{ months} = \$10,500 \text{ revenue to be recognized in 2015}$$

The adjusting entry moves $10,500 from the Unearned Revenue account to the Consulting Revenue account. This entry is a *claims exchange transaction.* The liability account Unearned Revenue decreases and the equity account Retained Earnings increases. The effects of this transaction on the financial statements are shown here.

Assets	=	Liab.	+	Stk. Equity					
		Unearn. Rev.	+	Ret. Earn.	Rev.	−	Exp.	=	Net Inc.	Cash Flow
NA	=	(10,500)	+	10,500	10,500	−	NA	=	10,500	NA

Recall that revenue was previously defined as an economic benefit a company obtains by providing customers with goods and services. In this case the economic benefit is a decrease in the liability account Unearned Revenue. **Revenue** can therefore be more precisely defined as *an increase in assets or a decrease in liabilities that a company obtains by providing customers with goods or services.*

☑ CHECK YOURSELF 2.3

Sanderson & Associates received a $24,000 cash advance as a retainer to provide legal services to a client. The contract called for Sanderson to render services during a one-year period beginning October 1, 2014. Based on this information alone, determine the cash flow from operating activities Sanderson would report on the 2014 and 2015 statements of cash flows. Also determine the amount of revenue Sanderson would report on the 2014 and 2015 income statements.

Answer   Since Sanderson collected all of the cash in 2014, the 2014 statement of cash flows would report a $24,000 cash inflow from operating activities. The 2015 statement of cash flows would report zero cash flow from operating activities. Revenue is recognized in the period in which it is earned. In this case revenue is earned at the rate of $2,000 per month ($24,000 ÷ 12 months = $2,000 per month). Sanderson rendered services for three months in 2014 and nine months in 2015. Sanderson would report $6,000 (3 months × $2,000) of revenue on the 2014 income statement and $18,000 (9 months × $2,000) of revenue on the 2015 income statement.

Answers to The Curious Accountant

Because the Meredith Corporation receives cash from customers before actually sending any magazines to them, the company has not earned any revenue when it receives the cash. Meredith has a liability called *unearned revenue.* If Meredith closed its books on December 31, then $3 of Janet's subscription would be recognized as revenue in 2014. The remaining $9 would appear on the balance sheet as a liability.

Meredith actually ends its accounting year on June 30 each year. The actual June 30, 2012, balance sheet for the company is presented in Exhibit 2.6. The liability for unearned revenue was $322.3 million ($180.9 + $141.4)—which represented about 26.4 percent of total liabilities!

Will Meredith need cash to pay these subscription liabilities? Not exactly. The liabilities will not be paid directly with cash. Instead, they will be satisfied by providing magazines to the subscribers. However, Meredith will need cash to pay for producing and distributing the magazines supplied to the customers. Even so, the amount of cash required to provide magazines will probably differ significantly from the amount of unearned revenues. In most cases, subscription fees do not cover the cost of producing and distributing magazines. By collecting significant amounts of advertising revenue, publishers can provide magazines to customers at prices well below the cost of publication. The amount of unearned revenue is not likely to coincide with the amount of cash needed to cover the cost of satisfying the company's obligation to produce and distribute magazines. Even though the association between unearned revenues and the cost of providing magazines to customers is not direct, a knowledgeable financial analyst can use the information to make estimates of future cash flows and revenue recognition.

EXHIBIT 2.6	Balance Sheet for Meredith Corporation

MEREDITH CORPORATION AND SUBSIDIARIES
Consolidated Balance Sheets
As of June 30 (amounts in thousands)

	2012	2011
Assets		
Current assets		
Cash and cash equivalents	$ 25,820	$ 27,721
Accounts receivable		
(net of allowances of $13,436 in 2012 and $10,823 in 2011)	215,526	212,365
Inventories	22,559	21,529
Current portion of subscription acquisition costs	75,446	54,581
Current portion of broadcast rights	3,408	3,974
Other current assets	16,677	13,568
Total current assets	359,436	333,738
Property, plant, and equipment		
Land	19,517	19,619
Buildings and improvements	129,688	127,916
Machinery and equipment	290,866	289,045
Leasehold improvements	14,816	14,468
Construction in progress	384	8,209
Total property, plant, and equipment	455,271	459,257
Less accumulated depreciation	(260,967)	(272,819)
Net property, plant, and equipment	194,304	186,438
Subscription acquisition costs	75,368	54,286
Broadcast rights	943	1,292
Other assets	66,858	66,940
Intangible assets, net	586,263	545,101
Goodwill	733,127	525,034
Total assets	$2,016,299	$1,712,829
Liabilities and Shareholders' Equity,		
Current liabilities		
Current portion of long-term debt	$ 105,000	$ 50,000
Current portion of long-term broadcast rights payable	6,752	8,548
Accounts payable	72,911	82,878
Accrued expenses		
Compensation and benefits	52,402	53,593
Distribution expenses	12,029	13,937
Other taxes and expenses	52,640	48,205
Total accrued expenses	117,071	115,735
Current portion of unearned subscription revenues	180,852	151,831
Total current liabilities	482,586	408,992
Long-term debt	275,000	145,000
Long-term broadcast rights payable	3,695	5,431
Unearned subscription revenues	141,408	120,024
Deferred income taxes	204,054	160,709
Other noncurrent liabilities	112,111	97,688
Total liabilities	1,218,854	937,844
Shareholders' equity		
Series preferred stock, par value $1 per share	—	—
Common stock, par value $1 per share	35,791	36,282
Class B stock, par value $1 per share, convertible to common stock	8,716	8,776
Additional paid-in capital	53,275	58,274
Retained earnings	722,778	687,816
Accumulated other comprehensive income (loss)	(23,115)	(16,163)
Total shareholders' equity	797,445	74,985
Total liabilities and shareholders' equity	$2,016,299	$1,712,829

Accounting for Accrued Salary Expense (Adjusting Entry)

EVENT 16   Cato recognized $4,000 of accrued salary expense.

The adjusting entry to recognize the accrued salary expense is a *claims exchange transaction.* One claims account, Retained Earnings, decreases and another claims account, Salaries Payable, increases. The expense recognition reduces net income. The statement of cash flows is not affected. The effects of this transaction on the financial statements are shown here.

Assets	=	Liab.	+	Stk. Equity						
		Sal. Pay.	+	Ret. Earn.	Rev.	−	Exp.	=	Net Inc.	Cash Flow
NA	=	4,000	+	(4,000)	NA	−	4,000	=	(4,000)	NA

Summary of Events and General Ledger

The previous section of this chapter described sixteen events Cato Consultants experienced the during the 2015 accounting period. These events are summarized in Exhibit 2.7 on page 67. The associated general ledger accounts are also shown in the exhibit. The account balances at the end of 2014, shown in Exhibit 2.3, become the beginning balances for the 2015 accounting period. The 2015 transaction data are referenced to the accounting events with numbers in parentheses. The information in the ledger accounts is the basis for the financial statements in Exhibit 2.8 on pages 68 and 69. Before reading further, trace each event shown in Exhibit 2.7 to the related accounts that are also shown in that exhibit.

Vertical Statements Model

LO 2-7

Prepare financial statements based on accrual accounting.

Financial statement users obtain helpful insights by analyzing company trends over multiple accounting cycles. Exhibit 2.8 presents for Cato Consultants a multicycle **vertical statements model** of 2014 and 2015 accounting data. To conserve space, we have combined all the expenses for each year into single amounts labeled "Operating Expenses," determined as follows:

	2014	2015
Other operating expenses	$ 0	$21,000
Salary expense	16,000	36,000
Rent expense	0	10,000
Advertising expense	2,000	0
Supplies expense	0	650
Total operating expenses	$18,000	$67,650

Similarly, we combined the cash payments for operating expenses on the statement of cash flows as follows:

	2014	2015
Supplies and other operating expenses	$ 0	$18,200*
Salary expense	10,000	38,000
Rent expense	0	12,000
Advertising expense	2,000	0
Total cash payments for operating expenses	$12,000	$68,200

*Amount paid in partial settlement of accounts payable

Recall that the level of detail reported in financial statements depends on user information needs. Most real-world companies combine many account balances together to report highly summarized totals under each financial statement caption. Before

EXHIBIT 2.7

Ledger Accounts with 2015 Transaction Data

1. Cato paid $6,000 to the instructor to settle the salaries payable obligation.
2. Cato purchased $800 of supplies on account.
3. On March 1, Cato paid $12,000 cash to lease office space for one year.
4. Cato received $18,000 cash in advance from Westberry Company for consulting services to be performed for one year beginning June 1.
5. Cato provided $96,400 of consulting services on account.
6. Cato collected $105,000 cash from customers as partial settlement of accounts receivable.
7. Cato paid $32,000 cash for salary expense.
8. Cato incurred $21,000 of other operating expenses on account.
9. Cato paid $18,200 in partial settlement of accounts payable.
10. Cato paid $79,500 to purchase land it planned to use in the future as a building site for its home office.
11. Cato paid $21,000 in cash dividends to its stockholders.
12. Cato acquired $2,000 cash from issuing additional shares of common stock.

The year-end adjustments are:

13. After determining through a physical count that it had $150 of unused supplies on hand as of December 31, Cato recognized supplies expense.
14. Cato recognized rent expense for the office space used during the accounting period.
15. Cato recognized the portion of the unearned revenue it earned during the accounting period.
16. Cato recognized $4,000 of accrued salary expense.

Assets				=	Liabilities		+		Stockholders' Equity	

Cash		**Prepaid Rent**		**Accounts Payable**		**Common Stock**		**Retained Earnings**	
Bal.	53,000	Bal.	0	Bal.	0	Bal.	5,000	Bal.	66,000
(1)	(6,000)	(3)	12,000	(2)	800	(12)	2,000	**Dividends**	
(3)	(12,000)	(14)	(10,000)	(8)	21,000	Bal.	7,000		
(4)	18,000	Bal.	2,000	(9)	(18,200)			Bal.	0
(6)	105,000			Bal.	3,600			(11)	(21,000)
(7)	(32,000)	**Land**						Bal.	(21,000)
(9)	(18,200)	Bal.	0	**Unearned Revenue**				**Consulting Revenue**	
(10)	(79,500)	(10)	79,500	Bal.	0				
(11)	(21,000)	Bal.	79,500	(4)	18,000			Bal.	0
(12)	2,000			(15)	(10,500)			(5)	96,400
Bal.	9,300			Bal.	7,500			(15)	10,500
								Bal.	106,900
Accounts Receivable				**Salaries Payable**				**Other Operating Expenses**	
Bal.	24,000			Bal.	6,000				
(5)	96,400			(1)	(6,000)			Bal.	0
(6)	(105,000)			(16)	4,000			(8)	(21,000)
Bal.	15,400			Bal.	4,000			Bal.	(21,000)
Supplies								**Salary Expense**	
Bal.	0							Bal.	0
(2)	800							(7)	(32,000)
(13)	(650)							(16)	(4,000)
Bal.	150							Bal.	(36,000)
								Rent Expense	
								Bal.	0
								(14)	(10,000)
								Bal.	(10,000)
								Supplies Expense	
								Bal.	0
								(13)	(650)
								Bal.	(650)

EXHIBIT 2.8	Vertical Statements Model

CATO CONSULTANTS
Financial Statements
Income Statements
For the Years Ended December 31

	2014	2015
Consulting revenue	$84,000	$106,900
Operating expenses	(18,000)	(67,650)
Net income	$66,000	$ 39,250

Statements of Changes in Stockholders' Equity
For the Years Ended December 31

	2014	2015
Beginning common stock	$ 0	$ 5,000
Plus: Common stock issued	5,000	2,000
Ending common stock	5,000	7,000
Beginning retained earnings	0	66,000
Plus: Net income	66,000	39,250
Less: Dividends	0	(21,000)
Ending retained earnings	66,000	84,250
Total stockholders' equity	$71,000	$ 91,250

Balance Sheets
As of December 31

	2014	2015
Assets		
Cash	$53,000	$ 9,300
Accounts receivable	24,000	15,400
Supplies	0	150
Prepaid rent	0	2,000
Land	0	79,500
Total assets	$77,000	$106,350
Liabilities		
Accounts payable	$ 0	$ 3,600
Unearned revenue	0	7,500
Salaries payable	6,000	4,000
Total liabilities	6,000	15,100
Stockholders' equity		
Common stock	5,000	7,000
Retained earnings	66,000	84,250
Total stockholders' equity	71,000	91,250
Total liabilities and stockholders' equity	$77,000	$106,350

continued

EXHIBIT 2.8	*Concluded*

Statements of Cash Flows
For the Years Ended December 31

	2014	2015
Cash Flows from Operating Activities		
Cash receipts from customers	$60,000	$123,000
Cash payments for operating expenses	(12,000)	(68,200)
Net cash flow from operating activities	48,000	54,800
Cash Flows from Investing Activities		
Cash payment to purchase land	0	(79,500)
Cash Flows from Financing Activities		
Cash receipts from issuing common stock	5,000	2,000
Cash payments for dividends	0	(21,000)
Net cash flow from financing activities	5,000	(19,000)
Net change in cash	53,000	(43,700)
Plus: Beginning cash balance	0	53,000
Ending cash balance	$53,000	$ 9,300

reading further, trace the remaining financial statement items from the ledger accounts in Exhibit 2.7 to where they are reported in Exhibit 2.8.

The vertical statements model in Exhibit 2.8 shows significant interrelationships among the financial statements. For each year, trace the amount of net income from the income statement to the statement of changes in stockholders' equity. Next, trace the ending balances of common stock and retained earnings reported on the statement of changes in stockholders' equity to the stockholders' equity section of the balance sheet. Also, confirm that the amount of cash reported on the balance sheet equals the ending cash balance on the statement of cash flows.

Other relationships connect the two accounting periods. For example, trace the ending retained earnings balance from the 2014 statement of stockholders' equity to the beginning retained earnings balance on the 2015 statement of stockholders' equity. Also, trace the ending cash balance on the 2014 statement of cash flows to the beginning cash balance on the 2015 statement of cash flows. Finally, confirm that the change in cash between the 2014 and 2015 balance sheets ($53,000 − $9,300 = $43,700 decrease) agrees with the net change in cash reported on the 2014 statement of cash flows.

☑ CHECK YOURSELF 2.4

Treadmore Company started the 2014 accounting period with $580 of supplies on hand. During 2014 the company paid cash to purchase $2,200 of supplies. A physical count of supplies indicated that there was $420 of supplies on hand at the end of 2014. Treadmore pays cash for supplies at the time they are purchased. Based on this information alone, determine the amount of supplies expense to be recognized on the income statement and the amount of cash flow to be shown in the operating activities section of the statement of cash flows.

Answer   The amount of supplies expense recognized on the income statement is the amount of supplies that were used during the accounting period. This amount is computed below:

$580 Beginning balance + $2,200 Supplies purchases = $2,780 Supplies available for use

$2,780 Supplies available for use − $420 Ending supplies balance = $2,360 supplies used

The cash flow from operating activities is the amount of cash paid for supplies during the accounting period. In this case, Treadmore paid $2,200 cash to purchase supplies. This amount would be shown as a cash outflow.

REALITY BYTES

REVENUE VERSUS CASH FLOW: THE GAMES PEOPLE PLAY

Most banks have a sign on their door that says "FDIC Insured." The FDIC on the sign refers to the Federal Deposit Insurance Corporation. Insurance provided by the FDIC protects the bank's depositors up to $250,000 per account in the event the bank should fail. To pay for this insurance, the FDIC charges participating banks a fee.

After 164 banks failed during the economic and banking crisis of 2007 and 2008 the FDIC was concerned that its reserves available to pay potential claims were running low. To address this, it required banks to prepay three years of premiums in 2009, rather than pay them in 2009, 2010, and 2011. Although such measures improved the FDIC's cash reserves, it does not mean they earned three year's worth of revenue in 2009, and it did not change the fact that cash payments would still have to be made over the next three years with moneys collected in 2009. And, even though the banks paid three years of premiums in 2009, they spread the expense recognition over 2009, 2010, and 2011.

The FDIC was not the first entity to use such tactics. State and local governments have sometimes delayed payments due near the end of their fiscal year into the next year so as not to show a deficit in the current year.

Near the end of their fiscal year, business entities sometimes try to convince customers to buy more goods and services than they need immediately. The company tells the customer that they can always return the goods next year if they do not need them. The goal is to increase this year's revenues, and profits, and executive bonuses. This tactic, called "trade loading" is at best a violation of GAAP, and in some situations may be illegal.

The problems these tactics create are rather obvious. Cash collected in advance in 2009 by the FDIC means less cash will be collected in 2010 and 2011. Expenses deferred into the next fiscal year by a state government means that next year will have higher expenses to pay than it otherwise would have. These schemes are sometimes referred to as, "kicking the can down the road." Such plans are seldom successful in the long run.

Source of FDIC information: *Birmingham Business Journal*, October 2, 2009.

TRANSACTION CLASSIFICATION

LO 2-8

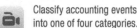

Classify accounting events into one of four categories.

Chapters 1 and 2 introduced four types of transactions. Although businesses engage in an infinite number of different transactions, all transactions fall into one of four types. By learning to identify transactions by type, you can understand how unfamiliar events affect financial statements. The four types of transactions are

1. *Asset source transactions:* An asset account increases, and a corresponding claims account increases.

2. *Asset use transactions:* An asset account decreases, and a corresponding claims account decreases.

3. *Asset exchange transactions:* One asset account increases, and another asset account decreases.

4. *Claims exchange transactions:* One claims account increases, and another claims account decreases.

◄◄ A Look Back

This chapter introduced the *accrual accounting* concept. Accrual accounting causes the amount of revenues and expenses reported on the income statement to differ significantly from the amount of cash flow from operating activities reported on the statement of cash flows because of timing differences. These differences are readily apparent when relevant events are recorded in a horizontal financial statements model. To review, study the following transactions and the corresponding statements model. Set up a statements model on a piece of paper and try to record the effects of each event before reading the explanation.

Events

1. Provided $600 of services on account.
2. Collected $400 cash from accounts receivable.
3. Accrued $350 of salary expense.
4. Paid $225 cash in partial settlement of salaries payable.

Event No.	Balance Sheet								Income Statement						Statement of Cash Flows	
	Cash	+	Accts. Rec.	=	Sal. Pay.	+	Ret. Earn.		Rev.	–	Exp.	=	Net Inc.			
1	NA	+	600	=	NA	+	600		600	–	NA	=	600		NA	
2	400	+	(400)	=	NA	+	NA		NA	–	NA	=	NA		400	OA
3	NA	+	NA	=	350	+	(350)		NA	–	350	=	(350)		NA	
4	(225)	+	NA	=	(225)	+	NA		NA	–	NA	=	NA		(225)	OA
Totals	175	+	200	=	125	+	250		600	–	350	=	250		175	NC

Notice the $250 of net income differs from the $175 cash flow from operating activities. The entries in the statements model demonstrate the reasons for the difference. Although $600 of revenue is recognized, only $400 of cash was collected. The remaining $200 will be collected in the future and is currently shown on the balance sheet as Accounts Receivable. Also, although $350 of salary expense is recognized, only $225 was paid in cash. The remaining $125 will be paid in the future. This obligation is shown as Salaries Payable on the balance sheet. Study these relationships carefully to develop a clear understanding of how accrual accounting affects financial reporting.

Also, the definitions of revenue and expense have been expanded. The complete definitions of these two elements are as follows:

1. **Revenue:** Revenue is the *economic benefit* derived from operating the business. Its recognition is accompanied by an increase in assets or a decrease in liabilities resulting from providing products or services to customers.
2. **Expense:** An expense is an *economic sacrifice* incurred in the process of generating revenue. Its recognition is accompanied by a decrease in assets or an increase in liabilities resulting from consuming assets and services in an effort to produce revenue.

A Look Forward

Chapters 1 and 2 focused on businesses that generate revenue by providing services to their customers. Examples of these types of businesses include consulting, real estate sales, medical services, and legal services. The next chapter introduces accounting practices for businesses that generate revenue by selling goods. Examples of these companies include Wal-Mart, Radio Shack, Office Depot, and Lowes.

Video lectures and accompanying self-assessment quizzes are available for all learning objectives through McGraw-Hill *Connect® Accounting*.

SELF-STUDY REVIEW PROBLEM

Gifford Company experienced the following accounting events during 2014:

1. Started operations on January 1 when it acquired $20,000 cash by issuing common stock.
2. Earned $18,000 of revenue on account.
3. On March 1 collected $36,000 cash as an advance for services to be performed in the future.
4. Paid cash operating expenses of $17,000.
5. Paid a $2,700 cash dividend to stockholders.
6. On December 31, 2014, adjusted the books to recognize the revenue earned by providing services related to the advance described in Event 3. The contract required Gifford to provide services for a one-year period starting March 1.
7. Collected $15,000 cash from accounts receivable.

Gifford Company experienced the following accounting events during 2015:

1. Recognized $38,000 of cash revenue.
2. On April 1 paid $12,000 cash for an insurance policy that provides coverage for one year beginning immediately.
3. Collected $2,000 cash from accounts receivable.
4. Paid cash operating expenses of $21,000.
5. Paid a $5,000 cash dividend to stockholders.
6. On December 31, 2015, adjusted the books to recognize the remaining revenue earned by providing services related to the advance described in Event 3 of 2014.
7. On December 31, 2015, Gifford adjusted the books to recognize the amount of the insurance policy used during 2015.

Required

a. Record the events in a financial statements model like the following one. The first event is recorded as an example.

Event No.	Assets			=	Liab.	+	Stockholders' Equity						
	Cash +	Accts. Rec. +	Prep. Ins.	=	Unearn. Rev. +		Com. Stk. +	Ret. Earn.	Rev. −	Exp. =	Net Inc.	Cash Flow
1	20,000 +	NA +	NA	=	NA	+	20,000 +	NA	NA −	NA =	NA	20,000 FA

b. What amount of revenue would Gifford report on the 2014 income statement?
c. What amount of cash flow from customers would Gifford report on the 2014 statement of cash flows?
d. What amount of unearned revenue would Gifford report on the 2014 and 2015 year-end balance sheets?
e. What are the 2015 opening balances for the revenue and expense accounts?
f. What amount of total assets would Gifford report on the December 31, 2014 balance sheet?
g. What obligations and commitments would Gifford report on the December 31, 2015 balance sheet?

Solution to Requirement a

The financial statements model follows:

Event No.	Cash	+	Accts. Rec.	+	Prep. Ins.	=	Unearn. Rev.	+	Com. Stk.	+	Ret. Earn.	Rev.	−	Exp.	=	Net Inc.	Cash Flow	
						Assets = **Liab.** + **Stockholders' Equity**												
2013																		
1	20,000	+	NA	+	NA	=	NA	+	20,000	+	NA	NA	−	NA	=	NA	20,000	FA
2	NA	+	18,000	+	NA	=	NA	+	NA	+	18,000	18,000	−	NA	=	18,000	NA	
3	36,000	+	NA	+	NA	=	36,000	+	NA	+	NA	NA	−	NA	=	NA	36,000	OA
4	(17,000)	+	NA	+	NA	=	NA	+	NA	+	(17,000)	NA	−	17,000	=	(17,000)	(17,000)	OA
5	(2,700)	+	NA	+	NA	=	NA	+	NA	+	(2,700)	NA	−	NA	=	NA	(2,700)	FA
6*	NA	+	NA	+	NA	=	(30,000)	+	NA	+	30,000	30,000	−	NA	=	30,000	NA	
7	15,000	+	(15,000)	+	NA	=	NA	+	NA	+	NA	NA	−	NA	=	NA	15,000	OA
Bal.	51,300	+	3,000	+	NA	=	6,000	+	20,000	+	28,300	48,000	−	17,000	=	31,000	51,300	NC
		Asset, liability, and equity account balances carry forward											Rev. & exp. accts. are closed					
2014																		
Bal.	51,300	+	3,000	+	NA	=	6,000	+	20,000	+	28,300	NA	−	NA	=	NA	NA	
1	38,000	+	NA	+	NA	=	NA	+	NA	+	38,000	38,000	−	NA	=	38,000	38,000	OA
2	(12,000)	+	NA	+	12,000	=	NA	+	NA	+	NA	NA	−	NA	=	NA	(12,000)	OA
3	2,000	+	(2,000)	+	NA	=	NA	+	NA	+	NA	NA	−	NA	=	NA	2,000	OA
4	(21,000)	+	NA	+	NA	=	NA	+	NA	+	(21,000)	NA	−	21,000	=	(21,000)	(21,000)	OA
5	(5,000)	+	NA	+	NA	=	NA	+	NA	+	(5,000)	NA	−	NA	=	NA	(5,000)	FA
6*	NA	+	NA	+	NA	=	(6,000)	+	NA	+	6,000	6,000	−	NA	=	6,000	NA	
7†	NA	+	NA	+	(9,000)	=	NA	+	NA	+	(9,000)	NA	−	9,000	=	(9,000)	NA	
Bal.	53,300	+	1,000	+	3,000	=	0	+	20,000	+	37,300	44,000	−	30,000	=	14,000	2,000	NC

*Revenue is earned at the rate of $3,000 ($36,000 ÷ 12 months) per month. Revenue recognized in 2014 is $30,000 ($3,000 × 10 months). Revenue recognized in 2015 is $6,000 ($3,000 × 2 months).

†Rent expense is incurred at the rate of $1,000 ($12,000 ÷ 12 months) per month. Rent expense recognized in 2015 is $9,000 ($1,000 × 9 months).

Solutions to Requirements b–g

b. Gifford would report $48,000 of revenue in 2014 ($18,000 revenue on account plus $30,000 of the $36,000 of unearned revenue).

c. The cash inflow from customers in 2014 is $51,000 ($36,000 when the unearned revenue was received plus $15,000 collection of accounts receivable).

d. The December 31, 2014, balance sheet will report $6,000 of unearned revenue, which is the amount of the cash advance less the amount of revenue recognized in 2014 ($36,000 − $30,000). The December 31, 2015, unearned revenue balance is zero.

e. Since revenue and expense accounts are closed at the end of each accounting period, the beginning balances in these accounts are always zero.

f. Assets on the December 31, 2014, balance sheet are $54,300 [Gifford's cash at year-end plus the balance in accounts receivable ($51,300 + $3,000)].

g. Since all unearned revenue would be recognized before the financial statements were prepared at the end of 2015, there would be no liabilities on the 2015 balance sheet. In this case, all of the assets are committed to the investors.

KEY TERMS

Accounts receivable 51	Asset source transaction 50	Deferral 49	Recognition 49
Accrual 49	Asset use transaction 51	Expense 54	Revenue 64
Accrual accounting 49	Claims exchange	Matching concept 57	Salaries payable 52
Accrued expenses 52	transaction 53	Period costs 57	Unearned revenue 60
Adjusting entry 52	Conservatism 58	Prepaid items 59	Vertical statements
Asset exchange transaction 51	Cost 59	Realization 49	model 66

QUESTIONS

1. What does accrual accounting attempt to accomplish?
2. Define *recognition*. How is it independent of collecting or paying cash?
3. What does the term *deferral* mean?
4. If cash is collected in advance of performing services, when is the associated revenue recognized?
5. What does the term *asset source transaction* mean?
6. What effect does the issue of common stock have on the accounting equation?
7. How does the recognition of revenue on account (accounts receivable) affect the income statement compared to its effect on the statement of cash flows?
8. Give an example of an asset source transaction. What is the effect of this transaction on the accounting equation?
9. When is revenue recognized under accrual accounting?
10. Give an example of an asset exchange transaction. What is the effect of this transaction on the accounting equation?
11. What is the effect on the right side of the accounting equation when cash is collected in advance of performing services?
12. What does the term *unearned revenue* mean?
13. What effect does expense recognition have on the accounting equation?
14. What does the term *claims exchange transaction* mean?
15. What type of transaction is a cash payment to creditors? How does this type of transaction affect the accounting equation?
16. When are expenses recognized under accrual accounting?
17. Why may net cash flow from operating activities on the cash flow statement be different from the amount of net income reported on the income statement?
18. What is the relationship between the income statement and changes in assets and liabilities?
19. How does net income affect the stockholders' claims on the business's assets?
20. What is the difference between a cost and an expense?
21. When does a cost become an expense? Do all costs become expenses?
22. How and when is the cost of the *supplies used* recognized in an accounting period?
23. What does the term *expense* mean?
24. What does the term *revenue* mean?
25. What is the purpose of the statement of changes in stockholders' equity?
26. What is the main purpose of the balance sheet?
27. Why is the balance sheet dated *as of* a specific date when the income statement, statement of changes in stockholders'
equity, and statement of cash flows are dated with the phrase *for the period ended*?
28. In what order are assets listed on the balance sheet?
29. What does the statement of cash flows explain?
30. What does the term *adjusting entry* mean? Give an example.
31. What types of accounts are closed at the end of the accounting period? Why is it necessary to close these accounts?
32. Give several examples of period costs.
33. Give an example of a cost that can be directly matched with the revenue produced by an accounting firm from preparing a tax return.
34. List and describe the four stages of the accounting cycle discussed in Chapter 2.

MULTIPLE-CHOICE QUESTIONS

Multiple-choice questions are provided on the text website at www.mhhe.com/edmondssurvey4e.

SECTION 1 EXERCISES

connect | ACCOUNTING   **All applicable Exercises are available with McGraw-Hill's *Connect® Accounting.***

Where applicable in all exercises, round computations to the nearest dollar.

LO 2-1

Exercise 2-1   *Effect of collecting accounts receivable on the accounting equation and financial statements*

Burke Company earned $12,000 of service revenue on account during 2014. The company collected $9,800 cash from accounts receivable during 2014.

Required

Based on this information alone, determine the following for Burke Company. (*Hint:* Record the events in general ledger accounts under an accounting equation before satisfying the requirements.)

a. The balance of the accounts receivable that Burke would report on the December 31, 2014, balance sheet.
b. The amount of net income that Burke would report on the 2014 income statement.

c. The amount of net cash flow from operating activities that would be reported on the 2014 statement of cash flows.
d. The amount of retained earnings that would be reported on the 2014 balance sheet.
e. Why are the answers to Requirements *b* and *c* different?

Exercise 2-2 *Effect of accrued expenses on the accounting equation and financial statements*

LO 2-2

During 2014, Crest Corporation earned $5,000 of cash revenue and accrued $3,000 of salaries expense.

Required

(*Hint:* Record the events in general ledger accounts under an accounting equation before satisfying the requirements.) Based on this information alone:

a. Prepare the December 31, 2014, balance sheet.
b. Determine the amount of net income that Crest would report on the 2014 income statement.
c. Determine the amount of net cash flow from operating activities that Crest would report on the 2014 statement of cash flows.
d. Why are the answers to Requirements *b* and *c* different?

Exercise 2-3 *Effect of accruals on the financial statements*

LO 2-1, 2-2

Coates Inc. experienced the following events in 2014, in its first year of operation:

1. Received $20,000 cash from the issue of common stock.
2. Performed services on account for $38,000.
3. Paid the utility expense of $2,500.
4. Collected $21,000 of the accounts receivable.
5. Recorded $15,000 of accrued salaries at the end of the year.
6. Paid a $2,000 cash dividend to the shareholders.

Required

a. Record the events in general ledger accounts under an accounting equation. In the last column of the table, provide appropriate account titles for the Retained Earnings amounts. The first transaction has been recorded as an example.

	COATES INC. General Ledger Accounts							
Event	Assets		=	Liabilities	+	Stockholders' Equity		Acct. Titles for Ret. Earn.
	Cash	Accounts Receivable		Salaries Payable		Common Stock	Retained Earnings	
1.	20,000					20,000		

b. Prepare the income statement, statement of changes in stockholders' equity, balance sheet, and statement of cash flows for the 2014 accounting period.
c. Why is the amount of net income different from the amount of net cash flow from operating activities?

Exercise 2-4 *Effect of accounts receivable and accounts payable transactions on financial statements*

LO 2-1, 2-2

The following events apply to Brown and Birgin, a public accounting firm, for the 2014 accounting period:

1. Performed $96,000 of services for clients on account.
2. Performed $65,000 of services for cash.

3. Incurred $45,000 of other operating expenses on account.
4. Paid $26,000 cash to an employee for salary.
5. Collected $70,000 cash from accounts receivable.
6. Paid $38,000 cash on accounts payable.
7. Paid a $10,000 cash dividend to the stockholders.
8. Accrued salaries were $3,000 at the end of 2014.

Required

a. Show the effects of the events on the financial statements using a horizontal statements model like the following one. In the Cash Flow column, use OA to designate operating activity, IA for investment activity, FA for financing activity, and NC for net change in cash. Use NA to indicate the element is not affected by the event. The first event is recorded as an example.

Event No.	Assets		=	Liabilities		+	Equity		Rev.	–	Exp.	=	Net Inc.	Cash Flow
	Cash	+ Accts. Rec.	=	Accts. Pay.	+ Sal. Pay	+	Ret. Earn.							
1	NA	+ 96,000	=	NA	+ NA	+	96,000		96,000	–	NA	=	96,000	NA

b. What is the amount of total assets at the end of 2014?
c. What is the balance of accounts receivable at the end of 2014?
d. What is the balance of accounts payable at the end of 2014?
e. What is the difference between accounts receivable and accounts payable?
f. What is net income for 2014?
g. What is the amount of net cash flow from operating activities for 2014?

LO 2-1, 2-2

Exercise 2-5   *Missing information related to accruals*

Panoramic Inc. had a beginning balance of $2,000 in its Accounts Receivable account. The ending balance of Accounts Receivable was $2,400. During the period, Panoramic recognized $40,000 of revenue on account. Panoramic's Salaries Payable account has a beginning balance of $1,300 and an ending balance of $900. During the period, the company recognized $35,000 of accrued salaries expense.

Required

a. Based on the information provided, determine the amount of net income.
b. Based on the information provided, determine the amount of net cash flow from operating activities.

LO 2-1, 2-2, 2-6

Exercise 2-6   *Effect of accruals on the financial statements*

Valmont Inc. experienced the following events in 2014, its first year of operation:

1. Received $50,000 cash from the issue of common stock.
2. Performed services on account for $67,000.
3. Paid a $5,000 cash dividend to the stockholders.
4. Collected $45,000 of the accounts receivable.
5. Paid $49,000 cash for other operating expenses.
6. Performed services for $10,000 cash.
7. Recognized $2,000 of accrued utilities expense at the end of the year.

Required

a. Identify the events that result in revenue or expense recognition.
b. Based on your response to Requirement *a*, determine the amount of net income reported on the 2014 income statement.
c. Identify the events that affect the statement of cash flows.

d. Based on your response to Requirement *c*, determine the amount of cash flow from operating activities reported on the 2014 statement of cash flows.

e. What is the before- and after-closing balance in the service revenue account? What other accounts would be closed at the end of the accounting cycle?

f. What is the balance of the retained earnings account that appears on the 2014 balance sheet?

Exercise 2-7   *Net income versus changes in cash*   LO 2-1, 2-2

In 2014, Zoe Inc. billed its customers $62,000 for services performed. The company collected $51,000 of the amount billed. Zoe incurred $39,000 of other operating expenses on account. Zoe paid $31,000 of the accounts payable. Zoe acquired $40,000 cash from the issue of common stock. The company invested $21,000 cash in the purchase of land.

Required

(*Hint:* Identify the six events described in the paragraph and record them in general ledger accounts under an accounting equation before attempting to answer the questions.) Use the preceding information to answer the following questions:

a. What amount of revenue will Zoe report on the 2014 income statement?

b. What amount of cash flow from revenue will Zoe report on the statement of cash flows?

c. What is the net income for the period?

d. What is the net cash flow from operating activities for the period?

e. Why is the amount of net income different from the net cash flow from operating activities for the period?

f. What is the amount of net cash flow from investing activities?

g. What is the amount of net cash flow from financing activities?

h. What amounts of total assets, liabilities, and equity will Zoe report on the year-end balance sheet?

SECTION 2 EXERCISES

Exercise 2-8   *Supplies and the financial statements model*   LO 2-2, 2-3

Copy Express Inc. began the 2014 accounting period with $9,000 cash, $5,000 of common stock, and $4,000 of retained earnings. Copy Express was affected by the following accounting events during 2014:

1. Purchased $9,500 of paper and other supplies on account.

2. Earned and collected $32,500 of cash revenue.

3. Paid $7,200 cash on accounts payable.

4. Adjusted the records to reflect the use of supplies. A physical count indicated that $1,700 of supplies was still on hand on December 31, 2014.

Required

a. Show the effects of the events on the financial statements using a horizontal statements model like the following one. In the Cash Flows column, use OA to designate operating activity, IA for investing activity, FA for financing activity, and NC for net change in cash. Use NA to indicate accounts not affected by the event. The beginning balances are entered in the following example:

Event No.	Cash	+	Supplies	=	Accts. Pay.	+	Com. Stk.	+	Ret. Earn.	Rev.	−	Exp.	=	Net Inc.	Cash Flows
	Assets			**=**	**Liab.**	**+**	**Stockholders' Equity**								
Beg. bal.	9,000	+	0	=	0	+	5,000	+	4,000	0	−	0	=	0	0

b. Explain the difference between the amount of net income and amount of net cash flow from operating activities.

LO 2-3, 2-6

Exercise 2-9 *Supplies on financial statements*

Accounting Professionals Inc. experienced the following events in 2014, its first year of operation:

1. Performed services for $20,000 cash.
2. Purchased $4,000 of supplies on account.
3. A physical count on December 31, 2014, found that there was $1,000 of supplies on hand.

Required

Based on this information alone

a. Record the events under an accounting equation.
b. Prepare an income statement, balance sheet, and statement of cash flows for the 2014 accounting period.
c. What is the balance in the Supplies account as of January 1, 2015?
d. What is the balance in the Supplies Expense account as of January 1, 2015?

LO 2-3, 2-4

Exercise 2-10 *Asset versus expense*

A cost can be either an asset or an expense.

Required

a. Distinguish between a cost that is an asset and a cost that is an expense.
b. List three costs that are assets.
c. List three costs that are expenses.

LO 2-4

Exercise 2-11 *Prepaid items on financial statements*

Therapy Inc. experienced the following events in 2014, its first year of operation:

1. Performed counseling services for $18,000 cash.
2. On February 1, 2014, paid $12,000 cash to rent office space for the coming year.
3. Adjusted the accounts to reflect the amount of rent used during the year.

Required

Based on this information alone

a. Record the events under an accounting equation.
b. Prepare an income statement, balance sheet, and statement of cash flows for the 2014 accounting period.
c. Ignoring all other future events, what is the amount of rent expense that would be recognized in 2015?

LO 2-4, 2-6

Exercise 2-12 *Effect of an error on financial statements*

On June 1, 2014, Cole Corporation paid $8,400 to purchase a 24-month insurance policy. Assume that Cole records the purchase as an asset and that the books are closed on December 31.

Required

a. Show the purchase of the insurance policy and the related adjusting entry to recognize insurance expense in the accounting equation.
b. Assume that Cole Corporation failed to record the adjusting entry to reflect the expiration of insurance. How would the error affect the company's 2014 income statement and balance sheet?

LO 2-5

Exercise 2-13 *Unearned items on financial statements*

Interior Design Consultants (IDC) experienced the following events in 2014, its first year of operation:

1. On October 1, 2014, IDC collected $24,000 for consulting services it agreed to provide during the coming year.
2. Adjusted the accounts to reflect the amount of consulting service revenue recognized in 2014.

Required

Based on this information alone

a. Record the events under an accounting equation.
b. Prepare an income statement, balance sheet, and statement of cash flows for the 2014 accounting period.
c. Ignoring all other future events, what is the amount of service revenue that would be recognized in 2015?

Exercise 2-14   *Unearned revenue defined as a liability*

LO 2-5

Kim Wong received $800 in advance for tutoring fees when she agreed to help Joe Pratt with his introductory accounting course. Upon receiving the cash, Kim mentioned that she would have to record the transaction as a liability on her books. Joe asked, "Why a liability? You don't owe me any money, do you?"

Required

Respond to Joe's question regarding Wong's liability.

Exercise 2-15   *Supplies, unearned revenue, and the financial statements model*

LO 2-3, 2-5

Ross, Attorney at Law, experienced the following transactions in 2014, the first year of operations:

1. Purchased $1,500 of office supplies on account.
2. Accepted $36,000 on February 1, 2014, as a retainer for services to be performed evenly over the next 12 months.
3. Performed legal services for cash of $84,000.
4. Paid cash for salaries expense of $32,000.
5. Paid a cash dividend to the stockholders of $8,000.
6. Paid $1,200 of the amount due on accounts payable.
7. Determined that at the end of the accounting period, $150 of office supplies remained on hand.
8. On December 31, 2014, recognized the revenue that had been earned for services performed in accordance with Transaction 2.

Required

Show the effects of the events on the financial statements using a horizontal statements model like the following one. In the Cash Flow column, use the initials OA to designate operating activity, IA for investing activity, FA for financing activity, and NC for net change in cash. Use NA to indicate accounts not affected by the event. The first event has been recorded as an example.

Event No.	Assets		=	Liabilities			+	Stk. Equity						
	Cash	+ Supplies	=	Accts. Pay.	+	Unearn. Rev.	+	Ret. Earn.	Rev.	− Exp.	=	Net Inc.	Cash Flow	
1	NA	+ 1,500	=	1,500	+	NA	+	NA	NA	− NA	=	NA	NA	

Exercise 2-16   *Unearned revenue and the financial statements model*

LO 2-5

Ed Arnold started a personal financial planning business when he accepted $120,000 cash as advance payment for managing the financial assets of a large estate. Arnold agreed to manage the estate for a one-year period beginning May 1, 2014.

Required

a. Show the effects of the advance payment and revenue recognition on the 2014 financial statements using a horizontal statements model like the following one. In the Cash Flows column, use OA to designate operating activity, IA for investing activity, FA for financing activity, and NC for net change in cash. Use NA if the account is not affected.

Event	Assets	=	Liab.	+	Stockholders' Equity	Rev.	−	Exp.	=	Net Inc.	Cash Flows
	Cash	=	Unearn. Rev.	+	Ret. Earn.						

    b. How much revenue would Ed recognize on the 2015 income statement?

    c. What is the amount of cash flow from operating activities in 2015?

LO 2-4, 2-5

Exercise 2-17 *Prepaid vs. unearned, the entity concept*

On October 1, 2014, Caldonia Company paid East Alabama Rentals $4,800 for a 12-month lease on warehouse space.

Required

a. Record the deferral and the related December 31, 2014, adjustment for Caldonia Company in the accounting equation.

b. Record the deferral and the related December 31, 2014, adjustment for East Alabama Rentals in the accounting equation.

LO 2-1, 2-2, 2-3, 2-4, 2-5

Exercise 2-18 *Identifying deferral and accrual events*

Required

Identify each of the following events as an accrual, deferral, or neither:

a. Incurred other operating expenses on account.

b. Recorded expense for salaries owed to employees at the end of the accounting period.

c. Paid a cash dividend to the stockholders.

d. Paid cash to purchase supplies to be used over the next several months.

e. Paid cash to purchase land.

f. Provided services on account.

g. Collected accounts receivable.

h. Paid one year's rent in advance.

i. Paid cash for utilities expense.

j. Collected $2,400 in advance for services to be performed over the next 12 months.

k. Recorded interest revenue earned for the period.

LO 2-1, 2-2, 2-3, 2-4, 2-5

Exercise 2-19 *Revenue and expense recognition*

Required

a. Describe a revenue recognition event that results in an increase in assets.

b. Describe a revenue recognition event that results in a decrease in liabilities.

c. Describe an expense recognition event that results in an increase in liabilities.

d. Describe an expense recognition event that results in a decrease in assets.

LO 2-6

Exercise 2-20 *Closing entries*

Rollins Company's accounting records show an after-closing balance of $19,400 in its Retained Earnings account on December 31, 2014. During the 2014 accounting cycle, Rollins earned $15,100 of revenue, incurred $9,200 of expense, and paid $1,500 of dividends. Revenues and expenses were recognized evenly throughout the accounting period.

Required

a. Determine the balance in the Retained Earnings account as of January 1, 2015.

b. Determine the balance in the temporary accounts as of January 1, 2014.

c. Determine the after-closing balance in the Retained Earnings account as of December 31, 2013.

d. Determine the balance in the Retained Earnings account as of June 30, 2014.

LO 2-6

Exercise 2-21 *Adjusting the accounts*

Mikita Inc. experienced the following accounting events during its 2014 accounting period:

1. Paid cash to settle an account payable.

2. Collected a cash advance for services that will be provided during the coming year.

3. Paid a cash dividend to the stockholders.

4. Paid cash for a one-year lease to rent office space.
5. Collected cash from accounts receivable.
6. Recognized cash revenue.
7. Issued common stock.
8. Paid cash to purchase land.
9. Paid cash to purchase supplies.
10. Recognized operating expenses on account.

Required

a. Identify the events that would require a year-end adjusting entry.
b. Are adjusting or closing entries recorded first? Why?

Exercise 2-22 *Closing the accounts*   LO 2-6

The following information was drawn from the accounting records of Swanson Company as of December 31, 2014, before the temporary accounts had been closed. The Cash balance was $6,000, and Notes Payable amounted to $3,000. The company had revenues of $7,000 and expenses of $4,200. The company's Land account had a $4,000 balance. Dividends amounted to $1,000. There was $2,000 of common stock issued.

Required

a. Identify which accounts would be classified as permanent and which accounts would be classified as temporary.
b. Assuming that Swanson's beginning balance (as of January 1, 2014) in the Retained Earnings account was $5,200, determine its balance after the temporary accounts were closed at the end of 2014.
c. What amount of net income would Swanson Company report on its 2014 income statement?
d. Explain why the amount of net income differs from the amount of the ending Retained Earnings balance.
e. What are the balances in the revenue, expense, and dividend accounts on January 1, 2015?

Exercise 2-23 *Closing accounts and the accounting cycle*   LO 2-6

Required

a. Identify which of the following accounts are temporary (will be closed to Retained Earnings at the end of the year) and which are permanent:
   (1) Service Revenue
   (2) Dividends
   (3) Common Stock
   (4) Notes Payable
   (5) Cash
   (6) Rent Expense
   (7) Accounts Receivable
   (8) Utilities Expense
   (9) Prepaid Insurance
   (10) Retained Earnings
b. List and explain the four stages of the accounting cycle. Which stage must be first? Which stage is last?

Exercise 2-24 *Matching concept*   LO 2-7

Companies make sacrifices known as *expenses* to obtain benefits called *revenues.* The accurate measurement of net income requires that expenses be matched with revenues. In some circumstances, matching a particular expense directly with revenue is difficult or impossible. In these circumstances, the expense is matched with the period in which it is incurred.

Required

Distinguish the following items that could be matched directly with revenues from the items that would be classified as period expenses:

a. Sales commissions paid to employees.
b. Advertising expense.
c. Supplies.
d. The cost of land that has been sold.

LO 2-7

Exercise 2-25   *Classifying events on the statement of cash flows*

The following transactions pertain to the operations of Blair Company for 2014:

1. Acquired $30,000 cash from the issue of common stock.
2. Performed services for $12,000 cash.
3. Paid a $7,200 cash advance for a one-year contract to rent equipment.
4. Recognized $15,000 of accrued salary expense.
5. Accepted a $21,000 cash advance for services to be performed in the future.
6. Provided $60,000 of services on account.
7. Incurred $28,000 of other operating expenses on account.
8. Collected $51,000 cash from accounts receivable.
9. Paid a $5,000 cash dividend to the stockholders.
10. Paid $22,000 cash on accounts payable.

Required

a. Classify the cash flows from these transactions as operating activities (OA), investing activities (IA), or financing activities (FA). Use NA for transactions that do not affect the statement of cash flows.

b. Prepare a statement of cash flows. (There is no beginning cash balance.)

LO 2-7

Exercise 2-26   *Relationship of accounts to financial statements*

Required

Identify whether each of the following items would appear on the income statement (IS), statement of changes in stockholders' equity (SE), balance sheet (BS), or statement of cash flows (CF). Some items may appear on more than one statement; if so, identify all applicable statements. If an item would not appear on any financial statement, label it NA.

a. Consulting Revenue
b. Market Value of Land
c. Supplies Expense
d. Salaries Payable
e. Notes Payable
f. Ending Common Stock
g. Beginning Cash Balance
h. Prepaid Rent
i. Net Change in Cash
j. Land
k. Operating Expenses
l. Total Liabilities
m. "As of" Date Notation
n. Salaries Expense
o. Net Income
p. Service Revenue
q. Cash Flow from Operating Activities
r. Operating Income
s. Interest Receivable
t. Interest Revenue

u. Rent Expense
v. Salary Expense
w. Total Stockholders' Equity
x. Unearned Revenue
y. Cash Flow from Investing Activities
z. Insurance Expense
aa. Ending Retained Earnings
bb. Interest Revenue
cc. Supplies
dd. Beginning Retained Earnings
ee. Utilities Payable
ff. Cash Flow from Financing Activities
gg. Accounts Receivable
hh. Prepaid Insurance
ii. Ending Cash Balance
jj. Utilities Expense
kk. Accounts Payable
ll. Beginning Common Stock
mm. Dividends
nn. Total Assets

Exercise 2-27 *Identifying transaction type and effect on the financial statements*   LO 2-7, 2-8

Required

Identify whether each of the following transactions is an asset source (AS), asset use (AU), asset exchange (AE), or claims exchange (CE). Also show the effects of the events on the financial statements using the horizontal statements model. Indicate whether the event increases (I), decreases (D), or does not affect (NA) each element of the financial statements. In the Cash Flows column, designate the cash flows as operating activities (OA), investing activities (IA), or financing activities (FA). The first two transactions have been recorded as examples.

Event No.	Type of Event	Assets	=	Liabilities	+	Common Stock	+	Retained Earnings	Rev.	−	Exp.	=	Net Inc.	Cash Flows
a	AE	I/D		NA		NA		NA	NA		NA		NA	D IA
b	AS	I		NA		I		NA	NA		NA		NA	I FA

a. Purchased land for cash.
b. Acquired cash from the issue of common stock.
c. Collected cash from accounts receivable.
d. Paid cash for operating expenses.
e. Recorded accrued salaries.
f. Purchased supplies on account.
g. Performed services on account.
h. Paid cash in advance for rent on office space.
i. Adjusted the books to record supplies used during the period.
j. Performed services for cash.
k. Paid cash for salaries accrued at the end of a prior period.
l. Paid a cash dividend to the stockholders.
m. Adjusted books to reflect the amount of prepaid rent expired during the period.
n. Incurred operating expenses on account.
o. Paid cash on accounts payable.
p. Received cash advance for services to be provided in the future.
q. Recorded accrued interest revenue earned at the end of the accounting period.

Exercise 2-28 *Effect of accounting events on the income statement and statement of cash flows*   LO 2-1, 2-2, 2-3, 2-4, 2-5, 2-6, 2-7

Required

Explain how each of the following events or series of events and the related adjusting entry will affect the amount of *net income* and the amount of *cash flow from operating activities* reported on the year-end financial statements. Identify the direction of change (increase, decrease, or NA) and the amount of the change. Organize your answers according to the following table. The first event is recorded as an example. If an event does not have a related adjusting entry, record only the effects of the event.

	Net Income		Cash Flows from Operating Activities	
Event	Direction of Change	Amount of Change	Direction of Change	Amount of Change
a	NA	NA	NA	NA

a. Acquired $60,000 cash from the issue of common stock.
b. Earned $20,000 of revenue on account. Collected $15,000 cash from accounts receivable.
c. Paid $4,800 cash on October 1 to purchase a one-year insurance policy.

d. Collected $12,000 in advance for services to be performed in the future. The contract called for services to start on August 1 and to continue for one year.
e. Accrued salaries amounting to $5,000.
f. Sold land that cost $15,000 for $15,000 cash.
g. Provided services for $9,200 cash.
h. Purchased $2,000 of supplies on account. Paid $1,500 cash on accounts payable. The ending balance in the Supplies account, after adjustment, was $800.
i. Paid cash for other operating expenses of $2,200.

LO 2-8

Exercise 2-29   *Transactions that affect the elements of financial statements*

Required

Give an example of a transaction that will

a. Increase an asset and decrease another asset (asset exchange event).
b. Increase an asset and increase a liability (asset source event).
c. Decrease an asset and decrease a liability (asset use event).
d. Decrease an asset and decrease equity (asset use event).
e. Increase a liability and decrease equity (claims exchange event).
f. Increase an asset and increase equity (asset source event).
g. Decrease a liability and increase equity (claims exchange event).

LO 2-8

Exercise 2-30   *Identifying source, use, and exchange transactions*

Required

Indicate whether each of the following transactions is an asset source (AS), asset use (AU), asset exchange (AE), or claims exchange (CE) transaction:

a. Performed services for clients on account.
b. Paid cash for salary expense.
c. Acquired cash from the issue of common stock.
d. Incurred other operating expenses on account.
e. Performed services for cash.
f. Paid cash on accounts payable.
g. Collected cash from accounts receivable.
h. Paid a cash dividend to the stockholders.
i. Received cash for services to be performed in the future.
j. Purchased land with cash.

LO 2-8

Exercise 2-31   *Identifying asset source, use, and exchange transactions*

Required

a. Name an asset use transaction that will affect the income statement.
b. Name an asset use transaction that will *not* affect the income statement.
c. Name an asset exchange transaction that will *not* affect the statement of cash flows.
d. Name an asset exchange transaction that will affect the statement of cash flows.
e. Name an asset source transaction that will *not* affect the income statement.

SECTIONS 1 AND 2 PROBLEMS

≣ connect |ACCOUNTING   **All applicable Problems are available with McGraw-Hill's *Connect*® Accounting.**

LO 2-1, 2-2, 2-3, 2-4, 2-5

Problem 2-32   *Recording events in a horizontal statements model*

CHECK FIGURES
Net Income: $15,200
Ending Cash Balance: $24,600

The following events pertain to James Cleaning Company:

1. Acquired $15,000 cash from the issue of common stock.
2. Provided services for $6,000 cash.

3. Provided $18,000 of services on account.

4. Collected $11,000 cash from the account receivable created in Event 3.

5. Paid $1,400 cash to purchase supplies.

6. Had $100 of supplies on hand at the end of the accounting period.

7. Received $3,600 cash in advance for services to be performed in the future.

8. Performed one-half of the services agreed to in Event 7.

9. Paid $6,500 for salaries expense.

10. Incurred $2,800 of other operating expenses on account.

11. Paid $2,100 cash on the account payable created in Event 10.

12. Paid a $1,000 cash dividend to the stockholders.

Required

Show the effects of the events on the financial statements using a horizontal statements model like the following one. In the Cash Flows column, use the letters OA to designate operating activity, IA for investing activity, FA for financing activity, and NC for net change in cash. Use NA to indicate accounts not affected by the event. The first event is recorded as an example.

			Assets			=	Liabilities			+	Stockholders' Equity								
Event No.	Cash	+	Accts. Rec.	+	Supp.	=	Accts. Pay.	+	Unearn. Rev.	+	Com. Stk.	+	Ret. Earn.	Rev.	−	Exp.	=	Net Inc.	Cash Flows
1	15,000	+	NA	+	NA	=	NA	+	NA	+	15,000	+	NA	NA	−	NA	=	NA	15,000 FA

Problem 2-33   *Effect of adjusting entries on the accounting equation*

LO 2-1, 2-2, 2-3, 2-4, 2-5, 2-6

Required

Each of the following independent events requires a year-end adjusting entry. Show how each event and its related adjusting entry affect the accounting equation. Assume a December 31 closing date. The first event is recorded as an example.

	Total Assets						**Stockholders Equity**		
Event/ Adjustment	Cash	+	Other Assets	=	Liabilities	+	Common Stock	+	Retained Earnings
a	−6,000	+	+6,000	=	NA	+	NA	+	NA
Adj.	NA		−4,500		NA		NA		−4,500

a. Paid $6,000 cash in advance on April 1 for a one-year insurance policy.

b. Purchased $2,400 of supplies on account. At year's end, $200 of supplies remained on hand.

c. Paid $7,200 cash in advance on March 1 for a one-year lease on office space.

d. Received an $18,000 cash advance for a contract to provide services in the future. The contract required a one-year commitment starting September 1.

Problem 2-34   *Closing the accounts*

LO 2-6

The following selected accounts and account balances were taken from the records of Bates Company. Except as otherwise indicated, all balances are as of December 31, 2014, before the closing entries were recorded.

Cash received from common stock issued during 2013	$ 4,500
Cash	10,500
Revenue	18,000
Salary expense	13,000
Cash flow from operating activities	4,500
Notes payable	6,000
Utility expense	1,800
Dividends	1,000
Cash flow from financing activities	5,000
Rent expense	1,600
Land	25,000
Retained earnings, January 1, 2014	19,700
Common stock, December 31, 2014	20,000

Required

a. Prepare the income statement Black would include in its 2014 annual report.

b. Identify the accounts that should be closed to the Retained Earnings account.

c. Determine the Retained Earnings account balance at December 31, 2014. Identify the reasons for the difference between net income and the ending balance in Retained Earnings.

d. What are the balances in the Revenue, Expense, and Dividend accounts on January 1, 2015? Explain.

LO 2-1, 2-2, 2-3, 2-4, 2-5, 2-6

Problem 2-35   *Effect of events on financial statements*

Davis Company had the following balances in its accounting records as of December 31, 2013:

Assets		Liabilities and Equity	
Cash	$ 60,000	Accounts Payable	$ 32,000
Accounts Receivable	45,000	Common Stock	60,000
Land	35,000	Retained Earnings	48,000
Totals	$140,000		$140,000

The following accounting events apply to Davis for 2014:

Jan.	1	Acquired an additional $30,000 cash from the issue of common stock.
April	1	Paid $7,200 cash in advance for a one-year lease for office space.
June	1	Paid a $5,000 cash dividend to the stockholders.
July	1	Purchased additional land that cost $40,000 cash.
Aug.	1	Made a cash payment on accounts payable of $21,000.
Sept.	1	Received $9,600 cash in advance as a retainer for services to be performed monthly during the next eight months.
Sept.	30	Sold land for $20,000 cash that had originally cost $20,000.
Oct.	1	Purchased $1,200 of supplies on account.
Dec.	31	Earned $75,000 of service revenue on account during the year.
	31	Received $62,000 cash collections from accounts receivable.
	31	Incurred $27,000 other operating expenses on account during the year.
	31	Recognized accrued salaries expense of $18,000.
	31	Had $100 of supplies on hand at the end of the period.
	31	The land purchased on July 1 had a market value of $56,000.
	31	Recognized $120 of accrued interest revenue.

Required

Based on the preceding information for Davis Company answer the following questions. All questions pertain to the 2014 financial statements. (*Hint:* Record the events in general ledger accounts under an accounting equation before answering the questions.)

a. What two additional adjusting entries need to be made at the end of the year?

b. What amount would be reported for land on the balance sheet?

c. What amount of net cash flow from operating activities would be reported on the statement of cash flows?

d. What amount of rent expense would be reported in the income statement?
e. What amount of total liabilities would be reported on the balance sheet?
f. What amount of supplies expense would be reported on the income statement?
g. What amount of unearned revenue would be reported on the balance sheet?
h. What amount of net cash flow from investing activities would be reported on the statement of cash flows?
i. What amount of total expenses would be reported on the income statement?
j. What total amount of service revenue would be reported on the income statement?
k. What amount of cash flows from financing activities would be reported on the statement of cash flows?
l. What amount of net income would be reported on the income statement?
m. What amount of retained earnings would be reported on the balance sheet?

Problem 2-36 Identifying and arranging elements on financial statements

LO 2-7

The following accounts and balances were drawn from the records of Dawkins Company at December 31, 2014:

CHECK FIGURES
a. Total Assets $91,700
b. Net Income $20,000

Cash	$22,100	Accounts receivable	$21,000
Land	43,000	Cash flow from operating act.	8,600
Insurance expense	2,500	Beginning retained earnings	47,200
Dividends	5,000	Beginning common stock	5,500
Prepaid insurance	3,500	Service revenue	86,000
Accounts payable	15,000	Cash flow from financing act.	9,000
Supplies	2,100	Ending common stock	14,500
Supplies expense	1,000	Cash flow from investing act.	(6,000)
Rent expense	3,500	Other operating expenses	59,000

Required

Use the accounts and balances from Dawkins Company to construct an income statement, statement of changes in stockholders' equity, balance sheet, and statement of cash flows (show only totals for each activity on the statement of cash flows).

Problem 2-37 Missing information in financial statements

LO 2-7

Required

Fill in the blanks (indicated by the alphabetic letters in parentheses) in the following financial statements. Assume the company started operations January 1, 2014, and all transactions involve cash.

	For the Years		
	2014	2015	2016
Income Statements			
Revenue	$ 400	$ 500	$ 800
Expense	(250)	(l)	(425)
Net income	$ (a)	$ 100	$ 375
Statement of Changes in Stockholders' Equity			
Beginning common stock	$ 0	$ (m)	$ 9,100
Plus: Common stock issued	(b)	1,100	310
Ending common stock	$8,000	9,100	(s)
Beginning retained earnings	0	25	75
Plus: Net income	(c)	100	375
Less: Dividends	(d)	(50)	(150)
Ending retained earnings	25	(n)	300
Total stockholders' equity	$ (e)	$ 9,175	$ (t)

continued

Balance Sheets						
Assets						
Cash	$	(f)	$	(o)	$	(u)
Land		0		(p)		2,500
Total assets		$11,000		$11,650		$10,550
Liabilities	$	(g)	$	(q)	$	840
Stockholders' equity						
Common stock		(h)		(r)		9,410
Retained earnings		(i)		75		300
Total stockholders' equity		8,025		9,175		9,710
Total liabilities and stockholders' equity		$11,000		$11,650		$10,550

Statements of Cash Flows						
Cash flows from operating activities						
Cash receipts from customers	$	(j)	$	500	$	(v)
Cash payments for expenses		(k)		(400)		(w)
Net cash flows from operating activities		150		100		375
Cash flows from investing activities						
Cash payments for land		0		(5,000)		0
Cash receipt from sale of land		0		0		2,500
Net cash flows from investing activities		0		(5,000)		2,500
Cash flows from financing activities						
Cash receipts from borrowed funds		2,975		0		0
Cash payments to reduce debt		0		(500)		(x)
Cash receipts from stock issue		8,000		1,100		(y)
Cash payments for dividends		(125)		(50)		(z)
Net cash flows from financing activities		10,850		550		(1,475)
Net change in cash		11,000		(4,350)		1,400
Plus: Beginning cash balance		0		11,000		6,650
Ending cash balance		$11,000		$ 6,650		$ 8,050

LO 2-1, 2-2, 2-3, 2-4, 2-5, 2-6, 2-7, 2-8

CHECK FIGURES
Net Income, 2014: $16,800
Net Income, 2015: $6,300

Problem 2-38 *Events for two complete accounting cycles*

Alabama Service Company was formed on January 1, 2014.

Events Affecting the 2014 Accounting Period

1. Acquired cash of $60,000 from the issue of common stock.
2. Purchased $1,200 of supplies on account.
3. Purchased land that cost $18,000 cash.
4. Paid $800 cash to settle accounts payable created in Event 2.
5. Recognized revenue on account of $42,000.
6. Paid $21,000 cash for other operating expenses.
7. Collected $38,000 cash from accounts receivable.

Information for 2014 Adjusting Entries

8. Recognized accrued salaries of $3,200 on December 31, 2014.
9. Had $200 of supplies on hand at the end of the accounting period.

Events Affecting the 2015 Accounting Period

1. Acquired an additional $20,000 cash from the issue of common stock.
2. Paid $3,200 cash to settle the salaries payable obligation.

3. Paid $3,600 cash in advance for a lease on office facilities.
4. Sold land that had cost $15,000 for $15,000 cash.
5. Received $4,800 cash in advance for services to be performed in the future.
6. Purchased $1,000 of supplies on account during the year.
7. Provided services on account of $32,000.
8. Collected $33,000 cash from accounts receivable.
9. Paid a cash dividend of $5,000 to the stockholders.
10. Paid other operating expenses of $19,500.

Information for 2015 Adjusting Entries

11. The advance payment for rental of the office facilities (see Event 3) was made on March 1 for a one-year lease term.
12. The cash advance for services to be provided in the future was collected on October 1 (see Event 5). The one-year contract started October 1.
13. Had $300 of supplies on hand at the end of the period.
14. Recognized accrued salaries of $3,900 at the end of the accounting period.
15. Recognized $400 of accrued interest revenue.

Required

a. Identify each event affecting the 2014 and 2015 accounting periods as asset source (AS), asset use (AU), asset exchange (AE), or claims exchange (CE). Record the effects of each event under the appropriate general ledger account headings of the accounting equation.

b. Prepare an income statement, statement of changes in stockholders' equity, balance sheet, and statement of cash flows for 2014 and 2015, using the vertical statements model.

ANALYZE, THINK, COMMUNICATE

ATC 2-1   Business Applications Case   *Understanding real-world annual reports*

Required

Use the Target Corporation's Form 10-K to answer the following questions related to Target's 2012 fiscal year (year ended February 2, 2013). Target's Form 10-K is available on the company's website or through the SEC's EDGAR database. Appendix A provides instructions for using the EDGAR database.

a. Which accounts on Target's balance sheet are accrual-type accounts?
b. Which accounts on Target's balance sheet are deferral-type accounts?
c. Compare Target's 2012 *net earnings* (the year ended February 2, 2013) to its 2012 *cash provided by operating activities.* Which is larger?
d. First, compare Target's 2011 net income to its 2012 net income. Next, compare Target's 2011 cash provided by operating activities to its 2012 cash provided by operating activities. Which changed the most from 2011 to 2012, net earnings or cash provided by operating activities?

ATC 2-2   Group Assignment   *Financial reporting and market evaluation*

The following financial highlights were drawn from the 2012 annual reports of Exxon Mobil Corporation and Apple Inc.

	Exxon	Apple
Revenue	$482.3 Billion	$156.5 Billion
Net income	$ 44.9 Billion	$ 41.7 Billion
Cash and short-term investments	$ 38.1 Billion	$ 29.1 Billion

Even so, as of February 28, 2013, Wall Street valued Exxon Mobil at $402.9 billion and Apple at $418.6 billion.

Divide the class into groups of four or five students.

Required

Have the members of each group reach a consensus response for each of the following tasks. Each group should elect a spokesperson to represent the group.

Group Tasks

(1) Determine the amount of expenses incurred by each company.

(2) Comment on how the concept of conservatism applies to the information presented in this case.

(3) Speculate as to why investors would be willing to pay more for Apple than Exxon Mobil.

ATC 2-3 Research Assignment *Identifying accruals and deferrals at Netflix*

This chapter defined and discussed accrual and deferral transactions. Complete the requirements below using the most recent financial statements available on the Internet for Netflix, Inc. Obtain the statements by following the steps below. (Be aware that the formatting of the company's website may have changed since these instructions were written.)

1. Go to www.netflix.com.
2. Click on "Investor Relations," which is at the bottom of the page in very small print.
3. Click on the "Annual Reports and Proxies" link at the left side of the page.
4. Click on the "20xx Annual Report." Use the pdf. version of the annual report.
5. Find the company's balance sheet and complete the requirements below. In recent years this has been shown toward the end of the Form 10-K section of the company's annual report, on page 48. The "Index" near the beginning of the report can help you locate the financial statements.

Required

a. Make a list of all the accounts on the balance sheet that you believe are accrual-type accounts.

b. Make a list of all the accounts on the balance sheet that you believe are deferral-type accounts.

ATC 2-4 Writing Assignment *Conservatism and Matching*

Glenn's Cleaning Services Company is experiencing cash flow problems and needs a loan. Glenn has a friend who is willing to lend him the money he needs provided she can be convinced that he will be able to repay the debt. Glenn has assured his friend that his business is viable, but his friend has asked to see the company's financial statements. Glenn's accountant produced the following financial statements.

Income Statement		Balance Sheet	
Service Revenue	$ 38,000	Assets	$85,000
Operating Expenses	(70,000)	Liabilities	$35,000
Net Loss	$(32,000)	Stockholders' Equity	
		Common Stock	82,000
		Retained Earnings	(32,000)
		Total Liabilities and	
		Stockholders' Equity	$85,000

Glenn made the following adjustments to these statements before showing them to his friend. He recorded $82,000 of revenue on account from Barrymore Manufacturing Company for a contract to clean its headquarters office building that was still being negotiated for the next month. Barrymore had scheduled a meeting to sign a contract the following week, so Glenn was sure that he would get the job. Barrymore was a reputable company, and Glenn was confident that he could ultimately collect the $82,000. Also, he subtracted $30,000 of accrued salaries expense and the corresponding liability. He reasoned that since he had not paid the employees, he had not incurred any expense.

Required

a. Reconstruct the income statement and balance sheet as they would appear after Glenn's adjustments.
b. Write a brief memo explaining how Glenn's treatment of the expected revenue from Barrymore violated the conservatism concept.
c. Write a brief memo explaining how Glenn's treatment of the accrued salaries expense violates the matching concept.

CHAPTER 3

Accounting for Merchandising Businesses

LEARNING OBJECTIVES

After you have mastered the material in this chapter, you will be able to:

LO 3-1	Record and report on inventory transactions using the perpetual system.
LO 3-2	Show how transportation costs, cash discounts, returns and allowances, and inventory shrinkage affect financial statements.
LO 3-3	Explain how gains, losses, and other items are shown on a multistep income statement.
LO 3-4	Determine the amount of net sales.
LO 3-5	Use common size financial statements to evaluate managerial performance.
LO 3-6	Identify the primary features of the periodic inventory system. (Appendix)

Video lectures and accompanying self-assessment quizzes are available for all learning objectives through McGraw-Hill Connect® Accounting.

CHAPTER OPENING

Previous chapters have discussed accounting for service businesses. These businesses obtain revenue by providing some kind of service such as medical or legal advice to their customers. Other examples of service companies include dry cleaning companies, maid service companies, and car washes. This chapter introduces accounting practices for merchandising businesses. **Merchandising businesses** generate revenue by selling goods. They buy the merchandise they sell from companies called suppliers. The goods purchased for resale are called **merchandise inventory.** Merchandising businesses include **retail companies** (companies that sell goods to the final consumer) and **wholesale companies** (companies that sell to other businesses). Sears, JCPenney, Target, and Sam's Club are real-world merchandising businesses.

The Curious Accountant

Richard recently purchased a new Ford automobile from a dealer near his home. When he told his friend Jeff that he was able to purchase the car for $1,000 less than the sticker price, Jeff told Richard he had gotten a lousy deal. "Everybody knows there is a huge markup on cars," Jeff said. "You could have gotten a much lower price if you'd shopped around."

Richard responded, "If there is such a big profit margin on cars, why did so many of the car manufacturers get into financial trouble?" Jeff told him that he was confusing the maker of the car with the dealer. Jeff argued that although the manufacturers may not have high profit margins, the dealers do, and told him again that he had paid too much.

Exhibit 3.1 presents the income statements for AutoNation, Inc., and Ford Motor Company. Based on these statements, do you think either of these guys is correct? For example, if you pay $20,000 for a vehicle from a dealership operated by AutoNation, the largest auto retailer in the United States, how much did the car cost the company? Also, how much did the car cost the Ford Motor Company to manufacture? (Answers on page 110.)

EXHIBIT 3.1	Comparative Income Statements

AUTONATION, INC.
Consolidated Statements of Operations (partial)
For the Years Ended December 31,
(In millions, except per share data)

	2012	2011	2010
Revenue:			
New vehicle	$ 8,906.9	$ 7,498.9	$ 6,669.1
Used vehicle	3,714.7	3,512.8	3,116.1
Parts and service	2,399.2	2,293.1	2,209.1
Finance and insurance, net	571.2	474.5	418.9
Other	76.8	53.0	47.8
Total revenue	15,668.8	13,832.3	12,461.0
Cost of Sales:			
New vehicle	8,327.4	6,951.2	6,217.9
Used vehicle	3,415.4	3,228.0	2,849.4
Parts and service	1,391.3	1,323.0	1,245.9
Other	48.3	26.1	20.3
Total cost of sales	13,182.4	11,528.3	10,333.5
Gross Profit:			
New vehicle	579.5	547.7	451.2
Used vehicle	299.3	284.8	266.7
Parts and service	1,007.9	970.1	963.2
Finance and insurance	571.2	474.5	418.9
Other	28.5	26.9	27.5
Total gross profit	2,486.4	2,304.0	2,127.5
Selling, general, and administrative expenses	1,749.5	1,649.4	1,552.1
Depreciation and amortization	87.3	83.7	76.8
Franchise rights impairment	4.2	—	—
Other expenses (income), net	0.1	(1.1)	2.0
Operating income	645.3	572.0	496.6
Floorplan interest expense	(45.5)	(42.7)	(42.5)
Other interest expense	(86.9)	(66.0)	(56.1)
Loss on debt extinguishment	—	(2.2)	(19.6)
Interest income	0.3	0.7	1.4
Other gains (losses), net	3.6	(0.5)	1.5
Income (loss) from continuing operations before income taxes	516.8	461.3	381.3
Income tax provision	199.5	177.1	146.0
Net income from continuing operations	317.3	284.2	235.3
Loss from discontinued operations, net of income taxes	(0.9)	(2.8)	(8.7)
Net income	$ 316.4	$ 281.4	$ 226.6

FORD MOTOR COMPANY AND SUBSIDIARIES
Consolidated Statement of Operations (Partial)
For the Years Ended December 31, 2012, 2011, and 2010
(in millions, except per share amounts)

	2012	2011	2010
Sales and revenues			
Automotive sales	$126,567	$128,168	$119,280
Financial Services revenues	7,685	8,096	9,674
Total sales and revenues	134,252	136,264	128,954

(continued)

	2012	2011	2010
Costs and expenses			
Automotive cost of sales	112,578	113,345	104,451
Selling, administrative, and other expenses	12,182	11,578	11,909
Interest expense	3,115	3,614	4,345
Financial Services provision for credit and insurance losses	86	(33)	(216)
Total costs and expenses	127,961	128,504	120,489
Automotive interest expense	(713)	(817)	(1,807)
Automotive interest income, expense, and other non-operating income/(expense), net	1,185	825	(362)
Financial Services other income/(loss), net	369	413	315
Equity in net income/(loss) of affiliated companies	588	500	538
Income before income taxes	7,720	8,681	7,149
Provision for/(Benefit from) income taxes	2,056	(11,541)	592
Net income	5,664	20,222	6,557
Less: Income/(Loss) attributable to noncontrolling interests	(1)	9	(4)
Net income/attributable to Ford Motor Company	$ 5,665	$ 20,213	$ 6,561

PRODUCT COSTS VERSUS SELLING AND ADMINISTRATIVE COSTS

Companies report inventory costs on the balance sheet in the asset account Merchandise Inventory. All costs incurred to acquire merchandise and ready it for sale are included in the inventory account. Examples of inventory costs include the price of goods purchased, shipping and handling costs, transit insurance, and storage costs. Since inventory items are referred to as products, inventory costs are frequently called **product costs.**

Costs that are not included in inventory are usually called **selling and administrative costs.** Examples of selling and administrative costs include advertising, administrative salaries, sales commissions, insurance, and interest. Since selling and administrative costs are usually recognized as expenses *in the period* in which they are incurred, they are sometimes called **period costs.** In contrast, product costs are expensed when inventory is sold regardless of when it was purchased. In other words, product costs are matched directly with sales revenue, while selling and administrative costs are matched with the period in which they are incurred.

ALLOCATING INVENTORY COST BETWEEN ASSET AND EXPENSE ACCOUNTS

The cost of inventory that is available for sale during a specific accounting period is determined as follows.

Beginning inventory balance + Inventory purchased during the period = Cost of goods available for sale

The **cost of goods available for sale** is allocated between the asset account Merchandise Inventory and an expense account called **Cost of Goods Sold.** The cost of inventory items that have not been sold (Merchandise Inventory) is reported as an asset on the balance sheet, and the cost of the items sold (Cost of Goods Sold) is expensed on the income statement. This allocation is depicted graphically as follows.

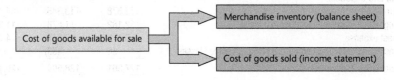

The difference between the sales revenue and the cost of goods sold is called **gross margin** or **gross profit**. The selling and administrative expenses (period costs) are subtracted from gross margin to obtain the net income.

Exhibit 3.1 displays income statements from the annual reports of AutoNation and Ford. For each company, review the most current income statement and determine the amount of gross margin. You should find a gross profit of $2,486.4 for AutoNation and a gross margin of $6,291 ($134,252 − $127,961) for Ford.

PERPETUAL INVENTORY SYSTEM

LO 3-1

Record and report on inventory transactions using the perpetual system.

Most modern companies maintain their inventory records using the **perpetual inventory system,** so-called because the inventory account is adjusted perpetually (continually) throughout the accounting period. Each time merchandise is purchased, the inventory account is increased; each time it is sold, the inventory account is decreased. The following illustration demonstrates the basic features of the perpetual inventory system.

June Gardener loved plants and grew them with such remarkable success that she decided to open a small retail plant store. She started June's Plant Shop (JPS) on January 1, 2014. The following discussion explains and illustrates the effects of the five events the company experienced during its first year of operation.

Effects of 2014 Events on Financial Statements

EVENT 1   JPS acquired $15,000 cash by issuing common stock.

This event is an asset source transaction. It increases both assets (cash) and stockholders' equity (common stock). The income statement is not affected. The statement of cash flows reflects an inflow from financing activities. These effects are shown here.

Assets			=	Liab.	+	Stockholders' Equity							
Cash	+ Inventory	+ Land	=	Accts. Pay.	+	Com. Stk.	+ Ret. Earn.	Rev.	−	Exp.	=	Net Inc.	Cash Flow
15,000	+ NA	+ NA	=	NA	+	15,000	+ NA	NA	−	NA	=	NA	15,000 FA

EVENT 2   JPS purchased merchandise inventory for $14,000 cash.

This event is an asset exchange transaction. One asset, cash, decreases and another asset, merchandise inventory, increases; total assets remain unchanged. Because product costs are expensed when inventory is sold, not when it is purchased, the event does not affect the income statement. The cash outflow, however, is reported in the operating activities section of the statement of cash flows. These effects are illustrated below.

Assets			=	Liab.	+	Stockholders' Equity							
Cash	+ Inventory	+ Land	=	Accts. Pay.	+	Com. Stk.	+ Ret. Earn.	Rev.	−	Exp.	=	Net Inc.	Cash Flow
(14,000)	+ 14,000	+ NA	=	NA	+	NA	+ NA	NA	−	NA	=	NA	(14,000) OA

EVENT 3A   JPS recognized sales revenue from selling inventory for $12,000 cash.

The revenue recognition is the first part of a two-part transaction. The *sales part* represents a source of assets (cash increases from earning sales revenue). Both assets (cash) and stockholders' equity (retained earnings) increase. Sales revenue on the income statement increases. The $12,000 cash inflow is reported in the operating activities section of the statement of cash flows. These effects are shown in the following financial statements model.

Assets			=	Liab.	+	Stockholders' Equity						
Cash	+ Inventory	+ Land	=	Accts. Pay.	+	Com. Stk.	+ Ret. Earn.	Rev.	− Exp.	= Net Inc.	Cash Flow
12,000 +	NA	+ NA	=	NA	+	NA	+ 12,000	12,000	− NA	= 12,000	12,000 OA

EVENT 3B   JPS recognized $8,000 of cost of goods sold.

The expense recognition is the second part of the two-part transaction. The *expense part* represents a use of assets. Both assets (merchandise inventory) and stockholders' equity (retained earnings) decrease. An expense account, Cost of Goods Sold, is reported on the income statement. This part of the transaction does not affect the statement of cash flows. A cash outflow occurred when the goods were bought, not when they were sold. These effects are shown here.

Assets			=	Liab.	+	Stockholders' Equity						
Cash	+ Inventory	+ Land	=	Accts. Pay.	+	Com. Stk.	+ Ret. Earn.	Rev.	− Exp.	= Net Inc.	Cash Flow
NA	+ (8,000)	+ NA	=	NA	+	NA	+ (8,000)	NA	− 8,000	= (8,000)	NA

EVENT 4   JPS paid $1,000 cash for selling and administrative expenses.

This event is an asset use transaction. The payment decreases both assets (cash) and stockholders' equity (retained earnings). The increase in selling and administrative expenses decreases net income. The $1,000 cash payment is reported in the operating activities section of the statement of cash flows. These effects are illustrated below.

Assets			=	Liab.	+	Stockholders' Equity						
Cash	+ Inventory	+ Land	=	Accts. Pay.	+	Com. Stk.	+ Ret. Earn.	Rev.	− Exp.	= Net Inc.	Cash Flow
(1,000) +	NA	+ NA	=	NA	+	NA	+ (1,000)	NA	− 1,000	= (1,000)	(1,000) OA

EVENT 5   JPS paid $5,500 cash to purchase land for a place to locate a future store.

Buying the land increases the Land account and decreases the Cash account on the balance sheet. The income statement is not affected. The statement of cash flow shows a cash outflow to purchase land in the investing activities section of the statement of cash flows. These effects are shown below.

Assets			=	Liab.	+	Stockholders' Equity						
Cash	+ Inventory	+ Land	=	Accts. Pay.	+	Com. Stk.	+ Ret. Earn.	Rev.	− Exp.	= Net Inc.	Cash Flow
(5,500) +	NA	+ 5,500	=	NA	+	NA	+ NA	NA	− NA	= NA	(5,500) IA

EXHIBIT 3.2

Financial Statements

2014 Income Statement		12/31/14 Balance Sheet			2014 Statement of Cash Flows	
Sales revenue	$12,000	Assets			Operating activities	
Cost of goods sold	(8,000)	Cash	$ 6,500		Inflow from customers	$12,000
Gross margin	4,000	Merchandise inventory	6,000		Outflow for inventory	(14,000)
Less: Operating exp.		Land	5,500		Outflow for selling	
Selling and		Total assets		$18,000	& admin. exp.	(1,000)
admin. exp.	(1,000)	Liabilities		$ 0	Net cash outflow for	
Net income	$ 3,000	Stockholders' equity			operating activities	$ (3,000)
		Common stock	$15,000		Investing activities	
		Retained earnings	3,000		Outflow to purchase land	(5,500)
		Total stockholders' equity		18,000	Financing activities	
		Total liab. and stk. equity		$18,000	Inflow from stock issue	15,000
					Net change in cash	6,500
					Plus: Beginning cash balance	0
					Ending cash balance	$ 6,500

Financial Statements for 2014

JPS's financial statements for 2014 are shown in Exhibit 3.2. JPS had no beginning inventory in its first year, so the cost of merchandise inventory available for sale was $14,000 (the amount of inventory purchased during the period). Recall that JPS must allocate the *Cost of Goods (Inventory) Available for Sale* between the *Cost of Goods Sold* ($8,000) and the ending balance ($6,000) in the *Merchandise Inventory* account. The cost of goods sold is reported as an expense on the income statement and the ending balance of merchandise inventory is reported as an asset on the balance sheet. The difference between the sales revenue ($12,000) and the cost of goods sold ($8,000) is labeled *gross margin* ($4,000) on the income statement.

☑ CHECK YOURSELF 3.1

Phambroom Company began 2014 with $35,600 in its Inventory account. During the year, it purchased inventory costing $356,800 and sold inventory that had cost $360,000 for $520,000. Based on this information alone, determine (1) the inventory balance as of December 31, 2014, and (2) the amount of gross margin Phambroom would report on its 2014 income statement.

Answer

1. $35,600 Beginning inventory + $356,800 Purchases = $392,400 Goods available for sale
   $392,400 Goods available for sale − $360,000 Cost of goods sold = $32,400 Ending inventory

2. Sales revenue − Cost of goods sold = Gross margin
   $520,000 − $360,000 = $160,000

Transportation Cost, Purchase Returns and Allowances, and Cash Discounts Related to Inventory Purchases

LO 3-2

Show how transportation costs, cash discounts, returns and allowances, and inventory shrinkage affect financial statements.

Purchasing inventory often involves: (1) incurring transportation costs, (2) returning inventory or receiving purchase allowances (cost reductions), and (3) taking cash discounts (also cost reductions). During its second accounting cycle, JPS encountered these kinds of events. The final account balances at the end of the 2014 fiscal year become the beginning balances for 2015: Cash, $6,500; Merchandise Inventory, $6,000; Land, 5,500; Common Stock, $15,000; and Retained Earnings, $3,000.

Effects of 2015 Events on Financial Statements

JPS experienced the following events during its 2015 accounting period. The effects of each of these events are explained and illustrated in the following discussion.

EVENT 1   JPS borrowed $4,000 cash by issuing a note payable.

JPS borrowed the money to enable it to purchase a plot of land for a site for a store it planned to build in the near future. Borrowing the money increases the Cash account and the Note Payable account on the balance sheet. The income statement is not affected. The statement of cash flow shows a cash flow from financing activities. These effects are shown below.

		Assets			=	Liabilities		+	Stockholders' Equity						
Cash +	Accts. Rec.	+ Inventory	+ Land	=	Accts. Pay.	+ Notes Pay.	+	Com. Stk.	+ Ret. Earn.		Rev.	− Exp.	= Net Inc.		Cash Flow
4,000 +	NA	+ NA	+ NA	=	NA	+ 4,000	+	NA	+ NA		NA	− NA	= NA		4,000 FA

EVENT 2   JPS purchased on account merchandise inventory with a list price of $11,000.

The inventory purchase increases both assets (merchandise inventory) and liabilities (accounts payable) on the balance sheet. The income statement is not affected until later, when inventory is sold. Since the inventory was purchased on account, there was no cash outflow. These effects are shown here.

		Assets			=	Liab.		+	Stockholders' Equity						
Cash +	Accts. Rec.	+ Inventory	+ Land	=	Accts. Pay.	+ Notes Pay.	+	Com. Stk.	+ Ret. Earn.		Rev.	− Exp.	= Net Inc.		Cash Flow
NA +	NA	+ 11,000	+ NA	=	11,000	+ NA	+	NA	+ NA		NA	− NA	= NA		NA

Accounting for Purchase Returns and Allowances

EVENT 3   JPS returned some of the inventory purchased in Event 2. The list price of the returned merchandise was $1,000.

To promote customer satisfaction, many businesses allow customers to return goods for reasons such as wrong size, wrong color, wrong design, or even simply because the purchaser changed his mind. The effect of a purchase return is the *opposite* of the original purchase. For JPS the **purchase return** decreases both assets (merchandise inventory) and liabilities (accounts payable). There is no effect on either the income statement or the statement of cash flows. These effects are shown below.

		Assets			=	Liab.		+	Stockholders' Equity						
Cash +	Accts. Rec.	+ Inventory	+ Land	=	Accts. Pay.	+ Notes Pay.	+	Com. Stk.	+ Ret. Earn.		Rev.	− Exp.	= Net Inc.		Cash Flow
NA +	NA	+ (1,000)	+ NA	=	(1,000)	+ NA	+	NA	+ NA		NA	− NA	= NA		NA

Sometimes dissatisfied buyers will agree to keep goods instead of returning them if the seller offers to reduce the price. Such reductions are called allowances. **Purchase allowances** affect the financial statements the same way purchase returns do.

Purchase Discounts

EVENT 4 **JPS received a cash discount on goods purchased in Event 2. The credit terms were 2/10, n/30.**

To encourage buyers to pay promptly, sellers sometimes offer **cash discounts.** To illustrate, assume JPS purchased the inventory in Event 2 under terms **2/10, n/30** (two-ten, net thirty). These terms mean the seller will allow a 2 percent cash discount if the purchaser pays cash within 10 days from the date of purchase. The amount not paid within the first 10 days is due at the end of 30 days from date of purchase. Recall that JPS returned $1,000 of the inventory purchased in Event 1 leaving a $10,000 balance ($11,000 list price − $1,000 purchase return). If JPS pays for the inventory within 10 days, the amount of the discount is $200 ($10,000 × .02).

When cash discounts are applied to purchases they are called **purchases discounts.** When they are applied to sales, they are called sales discounts. Sales discounts will be discussed later in the chapter. A *purchase discount* reduces the cost of the inventory and the associated account payable on the balance sheet. A purchase discount does not directly affect the income statement or the statement of cash flow. These effects are shown here.

		Assets			=	Liab.		+	Stockholders' Equity						
Cash	+	Accts. Rec.	+ Inventory	+ Land =		Accts. Pay.	+ Notes Pay.	+	Com. Stk.	+ Ret. Earn.	Rev.	− Exp.	= Net Inc.		Cash Flow
NA	+	NA	+ (200)	+ NA =		(200)	+ NA	+	NA	+ NA	NA	− NA	= NA		NA

If JPS paid the account payable after 10 days, there would be no purchase discount. In this case the balances in the Inventory and Account Payable accounts would remain at $10,000.

EVENT 5 **JPS paid the $9,800 balance due on the account payable.**

The remaining balance in the accounts payable is $9,800 ($10,000 list price − $200 purchase discount). Paying cash to settle the liability reduces cash and accounts payable on the balance sheet. The income statement is not affected. The cash outflow is shown in the operating section of the statement of cash flows. These effects are shown below.

		Assets			=	Liab.		+	Stockholders' Equity						
Cash	+	Accts. Rec.	+ Inventory	+ Land =		Accts. Pay.	+ Notes Pay.	+	Com. Stk.	+ Ret. Earn.	Rev.	− Exp.	= Net Inc.		Cash Flow
(9,800)	+	NA	+ NA	+ NA =		(9,800)	+ NA	+	NA	+ NA	NA	− NA	= NA		(9,800) OA

The Cost of Financing Inventory

Suppose you buy inventory this month and sell it next month. Where do you get the money to pay for the inventory at the time you buy it? One way to finance the purchase is to buy it on account and withhold payment until the last day of the term for the account payable. For example, suppose you buy inventory under terms 2/10, net/30. Under these circumstances you could delay payment for 30 days after the day of purchase. This way you may be able to collect enough money from the inventory you sell

REALITY BYTES

Many real-world companies have found it more effective to impose a penalty for late payment than to use a cash discount to encourage early payment. The invoice from Arley Water Works is an example of the penalty strategy. Notice that the amount due, if paid by the due date, is $18.14. A $1.88 late charge is imposed if the bill is paid after the due date. The $1.88 late charge is in fact interest. If Arley Water Works collects the payment after the due date, the utility will receive cash of $20.02. The collection will increase cash ($20.02), reduce accounts receivable ($18.14), and increase interest revenue ($1.88).

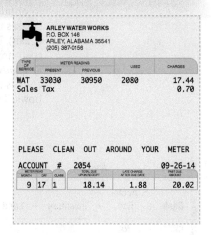

to pay for the inventory you purchased. Refusing the discount allows you the time needed to generate the cash necessary to pay off the liability (account payable). Unfortunately, this is usually a very expensive way to finance the purchase of inventory.

While the amount of a cash discount may appear small, the discount period is short. Consider the terms 2/10, net/30. Since you can pay on the tenth day and still receive the discount, you obtain financing for only 20 days (30-day full credit term − 10-day discount term). In other words, you must forgo a 2 percent discount to obtain a loan with a 20-day term. What is the size of the discount in annual terms? The answer is determined by the following formula.

$$\text{Annual rate} = \text{Discount rate} \times (365 \text{ days} \div \text{term of the loan})$$

$$\text{Annual rate} = 2\% \times (365 \div 20)$$

$$\text{Annual rate} = 36.5\%$$

This means that a 2 percent discount rate for 20 days is equivalent to a 36.5 percent annual rate of interest. So, if you do not have the money to pay the account payable, but can borrow money from a bank at less than 36.5 percent annual interest, you should borrow the money and pay off the account payable within the discount period.

Accounting for Transportation Costs

EVENT 6   The shipping terms for the inventory purchased in Event 2 were FOB shipping point. JPS paid the freight company $300 cash for delivering the merchandise.

The terms **FOB shipping point** and **FOB destination** identify whether the buyer or the seller is responsible for transportation costs. If goods are delivered FOB shipping point, the buyer is responsible for the freight cost. If goods are delivered FOB destination, the seller is responsible. When the buyer is responsible, the freight cost is called **transportation-in.** When the seller is responsible, the cost is called **transportation-out.** The following table summarizes freight cost terms.

Responsible Party	Buyer	Seller
Freight terms	FOB shipping point	FOB destination
Account title	Merchandise inventory	Transportation-out

Event 6 indicates the inventory was delivered FOB shipping point, so JPS (the buyer) is responsible for the $300 freight cost. Since incurring transportation-in costs is necessary to obtain inventory, these costs are added to the inventory account. The freight cost increases one asset account (Merchandise Inventory) and decreases another asset account (Cash). The income statement is not affected by this transaction because transportation-in costs are not expensed when they are incurred. Instead they are expensed as part of *cost of goods sold* when the inventory is sold. However, the cash paid for transportation-in costs is reported as an outflow in the operating activities section of the statement of cash flows. The effects of *transportation-in costs* are shown here.

Assets				=	Liab.		+	Stockholders' Equity							
Cash	+	Accts. Rec.	+ Inventory + Land	=	Accts. Pay.	+ Notes Pay.	+	Com. Stk.	+ Ret. Earn.		Rev.	− Exp.	= Net Inc.		Cash Flow
(300)	+	NA	+ 300 + NA	=	NA	+ NA	+	NA	+ NA		NA	− NA	= NA		(300) OA

EVENT 7A   JPS recognized $24,750 of revenue on the cash sale of merchandise that cost $11,500.

The sale increases assets (cash) and stockholders' equity (retained earnings). The revenue recognition increases net income. The $24,750 cash inflow from the sale is reported in the operating activities section of the statement of cash flows. These effects are shown below.

Assets				=	Liab.		+	Stockholders' Equity							
Cash	+	Accts. Rec.	+ Inventory + Land	=	Accts. Pay.	+ Notes Pay.	+	Com. Stk.	+ Ret. Earn.		Rev.	− Exp.	= Net Inc.		Cash Flow
24,750	+	NA	+ NA + NA	=	NA	+ NA	+	NA	+ 24,750		24,750	− NA	= 24,750		24,750 OA

EVENT 7B   JPS recognized $11,500 of cost of goods sold.

When goods are sold, the product cost—*including a proportionate share of transportation-in and adjustments for purchase returns and allowances*—is transferred from the Merchandise Inventory account to the expense account, Cost of Goods Sold. Recognizing cost of goods sold decreases both assets (merchandise inventory) and stockholders' equity (retained earnings). The expense recognition for cost of goods sold decreases net income. Cash flow is not affected. These effects are shown here.

Assets				=	Liab.		+	Stockholders' Equity							
Cash	+	Accts. Rec.	+ Inventory + Land	=	Accts. Pay.	+ Notes Pay.	+	Com. Stk.	+ Ret. Earn.		Rev.	− Exp.	= Net Inc.		Cash Flow
NA	+	NA	+ (11,500) + NA	=	NA	+ NA	+	NA	+ (11,500)		NA	− 11,500	= (11,500)		NA

EVENT 8   JPS paid $450 cash for freight costs on inventory delivered to customers.

Assume the merchandise sold in Event 7A was shipped FOB destination. Also assume JPS paid the freight cost in cash. FOB destination means the seller is responsible for the freight cost, which is called transportation-out. Transportation-out is reported on the income statement as an operating expense in the section below gross margin. The cost of freight on goods shipped to customers is incurred *after* the goods are sold. It is not part of the costs to obtain goods or ready them for sale. Recognizing the expense of transportation-out reduces assets (cash) and stockholders' equity (retained earnings). Operating expenses increase and net income decreases. The cash outflow is reported in the operating activities section of the statement of cash flows. These effects are shown below.

	Assets			=	Liab.		+	Stockholders' Equity						
Cash +	Accts. Rec. +	Inventory +	Land =		Accts. Pay. +	Notes Pay. +		Com. Stk. +	Ret. Earn.	Rev. −	Exp. =	Net Inc.	Cash Flow	
(450) +	NA +	NA +	NA =		NA +	NA +		NA +	(450)	NA −	450 =	(450)	(450) OA	

If the terms had been FOB shipping point, the customer would have been responsible for the transportation cost and JPS would not have recorded an expense.

EVENT 9   JPS paid $5,000 cash for selling and administrative expenses.

The effect on the balance sheet is to decrease both assets (cash) and stockholders' equity (retained earnings). Recognizing the selling and administrative expenses decreases net income. The $5,000 cash outflow is reported in the operating activities section of the statement of cash flows. These effects are shown below.

	Assets			=	Liab.		+	Stockholders' Equity						
Cash +	Accts. Rec. +	Inventory +	Land =		Accts. Pay. +	Notes Pay. +		Com. Stk. +	Ret. Earn.	Rev. −	Exp. =	Net Inc.	Cash Flow	
(5,000) +	NA +	NA +	NA =		NA +	NA +		NA +	(5,000)	NA −	5,000 =	(5,000)	(5,000) OA	

EVENT 10   JPS paid $360 cash for interest expense on the note described in Event 1.

The effect on the balance sheet is to decrease both assets (cash) and stockholders' equity (retained earnings). Recognizing the interest expense decreases net income. The $360 cash outflow is reported in the operating activities section of the statement of cash flows. These effects are shown below.

	Assets			=	Liab.		+	Stockholders' Equity						
Cash +	Accts. Rec. +	Inventory +	Land =		Accts. Pay. +	Notes Pay. +		Com. Stk. +	Ret. Earn.	Rev. −	Exp. =	Net Inc.	Cash Flow	
(360) +	NA +	NA +	NA =		NA +	NA +		NA +	(360)	NA −	360 =	(360)	(360) OA	

Adjustment for Lost, Damaged, or Stolen Inventory

EVENT 11   **JPS took a physical count of its inventory and found $4,100 of inventory on hand.**

Most merchandising companies experience some level of inventory **shrinkage,** a term that reflects decreases in inventory for reasons other than sales to customers. Inventory may be stolen by shoplifters, damaged by customers or employees, or even simply lost or misplaced. Since the *perpetual* inventory system is designed to record purchases and sales of inventory as they occur, the balance in the merchandise inventory account represents the amount of inventory that *should* be on hand at any given time. For example, based on the previous transactions the book balance of the JPS's Inventory account can be computed as follows:

Beginning balance	$ 6,000
Purchases	11,000
Purchase returns	(1,000)
Purchase discounts	(200)
Transportation in	300
Goods available for sale	16,100
Cost of goods sold	(11,500)
Ending balance	$ 4,600

Assume that JPS takes a physical count of its inventory on hand and finds that it has only $4,100 of inventory. By comparing the $4,600 book balance in the Merchandise Inventory account with the $4,100 of actual inventory counted, we determine that the Company has experienced $500 of shrinkage. Under these circumstances JPS must make an adjusting entry to write down the Inventory account so the amount reported on the financial statements agrees with the amount actually on hand at the end of the period. The write-down decreases both assets (inventory) and stockholders' equity (retained earnings). The write-down increases expenses and decreases net income. Cash flow is not affected. The effects on the statements are as follows.

Assets	=	Liab.	+	Equity	Rev.	−	Exp.	=	Net Inc.	Cash Flow
(500)	=	NA	+	(500)	NA	−	500	=	(500)	NA

Theoretically, inventory losses are operating expenses. However, because such losses are normally immaterial in amount, they are usually added to cost of goods sold for external reporting purposes.

REALITY BYTES

"Closed for Inventory Count" is a sign you frequently see on retail stores sometime during the month of January. Even if companies use a perpetual inventory system, the amount of inventory on hand may be unknown because of lost, damaged, or stolen goods. The only way to determine the amount of inventory on hand is to count it. Why count it in January? Christmas shoppers and many after-Christmas sales shoppers are satiated by mid-January, leaving the stores low on both merchandise and customers. Accordingly, stores have less merchandise to count and "lost sales" are minimized during January. Companies that do not depend on seasonal sales (e.g., a plumbing supplies wholesale business) may choose to count inventory at some other time during the year. Counting inventory is not a revenue-generating activity; it is a necessary evil that should be conducted when it least disrupts operations.

RECOGNIZING GAINS AND LOSSES

EVENT 12   JPS sold the land that had cost $5,500 for $6,200 cash.

When JPS sells merchandise inventory for more than it cost, the difference between the sales revenue and the cost of the goods sold is called the *gross margin.* In contrast, when JPS sells land for more than it cost, the difference between the sales price and the cost of the land is called a **gain.** Why is one called *gross margin* and the other a *gain*? The terms are used to alert financial statement users to the fact that the nature of the underlying transactions is different.

JPS's primary business is selling inventory, not land. The term *gain* indicates profit resulting from transactions that are not likely to regularly recur. Similarly, had the land sold for less than cost the difference would have been labeled **loss** rather than expense. This term also indicates the underlying transaction is not from normal, recurring operating activities. Gains and losses are shown separately on the income statement to communicate the expectation that they are nonrecurring.

The presentation of gains and losses in the income statement is discussed in more detail in a later section of the chapter. At this point note that the sale increases cash, decreases land, and increases retained earnings on the balance sheet. The income statement shows a gain on the sale of land and net income increases. The $6,200 cash inflow is shown as an investing activity on the statement of cash flows. These effects are shown below:

> **LO 3-3**
>
> Explain how gains, losses, and other items are shown on a multistep income statement.

	Assets				=	Liab.			+	Stockholders' Equity								
Cash	+	Accts. Rec.	+	Inventory	+	Land	=	Accts. Pay.	+	Notes Pay.	+	Com. Stk.	+	Ret. Earn.	Gain	−	Exp.	=	Net Inc.	Cash Flow
6,200	+	NA	+	NA	+	(5,500)	=	NA	+	NA	+	NA	+	700	700	−	NA	=	700	6,200 IA

☑ CHECK YOURSELF 3.2

Tsang Company purchased $32,000 of inventory on account with payment terms of 2/10, n/30 and freight terms FOB shipping point. Freight costs were $1,100. Tsang obtained a $2,000 purchase allowance because the inventory was damaged upon arrival. Tsang paid for the inventory within the discount period. Based on this information alone, determine the balance in the inventory account.

Answer

List price of inventory	$32,000
Plus: Transportation-in costs	1,100
Less: Purchase returns and allowances	(2,000)
Less: Purchase discount [($32,000 − $2,000) × .02]	(600)
Balance in inventory account	$30,500

Multistep Income Statement

JPS's 2015 income statement is shown in Exhibit 3.3. Observe the form of this statement carefully. It is more informative than one which simply subtracts expenses from revenues. First, it compares sales revenue with the cost of the goods that were sold to produce that revenue. The difference between the sales revenue and the cost of goods sold is called *gross margin.* Next, the operating expenses are subtracted from the gross margin to determine the *operating income.* **Operating income** is the amount of income that is generated from the normal recurring operations of a business. Items that are not expected to recur on a regular basis are subtracted from the operating income to determine the amount of *net income.*[1]

EXHIBIT 3.3	
JUNE'S PLANT SHOP	
Income Statement	
For the Period Ended December 31, 2015	
Sales revenue	$ 24,750
Cost of goods sold*	(12,000)
Gross margin	12,750
Less: Operating expenses	
Selling and administrative expense	(5,000)
Transportation-out	(450)
Operating income	7,300
Nonoperating items	
Interest expense	(360)
Gain on the sale of land	700
Net income	$ 7,640

*$11,500 inventory sold + $500 shrinkage.

EXHIBIT 3.4

Income Statement Format Used by U.S. Companies

Data Source: AICPA, *Accounting Trends and Techniques.*

Income statements that show these additional relationships are called **multistep income statements.** Income statements that display a single comparison of all revenues minus all expenses are called **single-step income statements.** To this point in the text we have shown only single-step income statements to promote simplicity. However, the multistep form is used more frequently in practice. Exhibit 3.4 shows the percentage of companies that use the multistep versus the single-step format. Go to Exhibit 3.1 and identify the company that presents its income statement in the multistep format. You should have identified AutoNation as the company using the multistep format. Ford's statement is shown in the single-step format.

Note that interest is reported as a *nonoperating* item on the income statement in Exhibit 3.3. In contrast, it is shown in the *operating* activities section of the statement of cash flows in Exhibit 3.6. When the FASB issued Statement of Financial Accounting Standard (SFAS) 95, it required interest to be reported in the operating activities section of the statement of cash flows. There was no corresponding requirement for the treatment of interest on the income statement. Prior to SFAS 95, interest was considered to be a nonoperating item. Most companies continued to report interest as a nonoperating item on their income statements even though they were required to change how it was reported on the statement of cash flows. As a result, there is frequent inconsistency in the way interest is reported on the two financial statements.

Also note that while the gain on the sale of land is shown on the income statement, it is not included in the operating activities section of the statement of cash flows. Since the gain is a nonoperating item, it is included in the cash inflow from the sale of land shown in the investing activities section. In this case the full cash inflow from the sale of

[1] Revenue and expense items with special characteristics may be classified as discontinued or extraordinary items. These items are shown separately just above net income regardless of whether a company uses a single-step or multistep format. Further discussion of these items is beyond the scope of this text.

EXHIBIT 3.5

JUNE'S PLANT SHOP Balance Sheet As of December 31, 2015		
Assets		
Cash	$25,540	
Merchandise inventory	4,100	
Total assets		$29,640
Liabilities		
Notes payable		$ 4,000
Stockholders' equity		
Common stock	$15,000	
Retained earnings	10,640	
Total stockholders' equity		25,640
Total liabilities and stockholders' equity		$29,640

EXHIBIT 3.6

JUNE'S PLANT SHOP Statement of Cash Flows For the Period Ended December 31, 2015		
Operating activities		
Inflow from customers	$ 24,750	
Outflow for inventory*	(10,100)	
Outflow for transportation-out	(450)	
Outflow for selling and administrative expense	(5,000)	
Outflow for interest expense	(360)	
Net cash outflow for operating activities		$ 8,840
Investing activities		
Inflow from sale of land		6,200
Financing activities		
Inflow from issue of note payable		4,000
Net change in cash		19,040
Plus beginning cash balance		6,500
Ending cash balance		$25,540

*Net cost on inventory $9,800 + transportation-in $300 = $10,100

land ($6,200) is shown in the investing activities section of the statement of cash flows in Exhibit 3.6. Finally, note that the ending inventory balance is shown on the balance sheet in Exhibit 3.5.

EVENTS AFFECTING SALES

To this point we assumed JPS did not offer cash discounts to its customers. However, sales, as well as purchases of inventory, can be affected by returns, allowances, and discounts. **Sales discounts** are price reductions offered by sellers to encourage buyers to pay promptly. To illustrate, assume JPS engaged in the following selected events during January 2016.

LO 3-4

Determine the amount of net sales.

EVENT 1A   JPS sold on account merchandise with a list price of $8,500. Payment terms were 1/10, n/30. The merchandise had cost JPS $4,000.

The sale increases both assets (accounts receivable) and shareholders' equity (retained earnings). Recognizing revenue increases net income. The statement of cash flows is not affected. The effects on the financial statements follow.

Assets			=	Liab.	+	Stockholders' Equity		Rev.	−	Exp.	=	Net Inc.	Cash Flow
Cash	+	Accts. Rec.	+	Inventory	=	Note Pay.	+	Com. Stk.	+	Retained Earnings			
NA	+	8,500	+	NA	=	NA	+	NA	+	8,500	8,500	−	NA	=	8,500	NA

EVENT 1B   JPS recognized $4,000 of cost of goods sold.

Recognizing the expense decreases assets (merchandise inventory) and stockholders' equity (retained earnings). Cost of goods sold increases and net income decreases. Cash flow is not affected. The effects on the financial statements follow.

Assets			=	Liab.	+	Stockholders' Equity		Rev.	−	Exp.	=	Net Inc.	Cash Flow
Cash	+	Accts. Rec.	+	Inventory	=	Note Pay.	+	Com. Stk.	+	Retained Earnings			
NA	+	NA	+	(4,000)	=	NA	+	NA	+	(4,000)	NA	−	4,000	=	(4,000)	NA

Accounting for Sales Returns and Allowances

EVENT 2A   A customer from Event 1A returned inventory with a $1,000 list price. The merchandise had cost JPS $450.

The sales return decreases both assets (accounts receivable) and stockholders' equity (retained earnings) on the balance sheet. Sales and net income decrease. Cash flow is not affected. The effects on the financial statements follow.

Assets			=	Liab.	+	Stockholders' Equity		Rev.	−	Exp.	=	Net Inc.	Cash Flow
Cash	+	Accts. Rec.	+	Inventory	=	Note Pay.	+	Com. Stk.	+	Retained Earnings			
NA	+	(1,000)	+	NA	=	NA	+	NA	+	(1,000)	(1,000)	−	NA	=	(1,000)	NA

EVENT 2B   The cost of the goods ($450) is returned to the inventory account.

Since JPS got the inventory back, the sales return increases both assets (merchandise inventory) and stockholders' equity (retained earnings). The expense (cost of goods sold) decreases and net income increases. Cash flow is not affected. The effects on the financial statements follow.

Assets			=	Liab.	+	Stockholders' Equity		Rev.	−	Exp.	=	Net Inc.	Cash Flow
Cash	+	Accts. Rec.	+	Inventory	=	Note Pay.	+	Com. Stk.	+	Retained Earnings			
NA	+	NA	+	450	=	NA	+	NA	+	450	NA	−	(450)	=	450	NA

Accounting for Sales Discounts

EVENT 3 JPS collected the balance of the accounts receivable generated in Event 1A. Recall the goods were sold under terms 1/10, net/30.

ALTERNATIVE 1 The collection occurs before the discount period has expired (within 10 days from the date of the sale).

JPS would give the buyer a 1 percent discount. Given the original sales amount of $8,500 and a sales return of $1,000, the amount of the discount is $75 [($8,500 − $1,000) × .01]. The sales discount reduces the amount of accounts receivable and retained earnings on the balance sheet. It also reduces the amount of revenue and the net income shown on the balance sheet. It does not affect the statement of cash flows. The effects on the financial statements follow.

Assets					=	Liab.	+	Stockholders' Equity			Rev.	−	Exp.	=	Net Inc.	Cash Flow
Cash	+	Accts. Rec.	+	Inventory	=	Note Pay.	+	Com. Stk.	+	Retained Earnings						
NA	+	(75)	+	NA	=	NA	+	NA	+	(75)	(75)	−	NA	=	(75)	NA

The balance due on the account receivable is $7,425 ($8,500 original sales − $1,000 sales return − $75 discount). The collection increases the Cash account and decreases the Accounts Receivable account. The income statement is not affected. The cash inflow is shown in the operating activities section of the statement of cash flows. The effects on the financial statements follow.

Assets					=	Liab.	+	Stockholders' Equity			Rev.	−	Exp.	=	Net Inc.	Cash Flow
Cash	+	Accts. Rec.	+	Inventory	=	Accts. Pay.	+	Com. Stk.	+	Retained Earnings						
7,425	+	(7,425)	+	NA	=	NA	+	NA	+	NA	NA	−	NA	=	NA	7,425 OA

Net Sales

The gross amount of sales minus **sales returns and allowance** and sales discounts is commonly called **net sales.** Companies are not required by GAAP to show sales returns and allowance and sales discount on their income statement. Indeed, most companies show only the amount of *net sales* on the income statement. In this case the net sales amount to $7,425 ($8,500 original sales − $1,000 sales return − $75 discount).

ALTERNATIVE 2 The collection occurs after the discount period has expired (after 10 days from the date of the sale).

Under these circumstances there is no sales discount. The amount collected is $7,500 ($8,500 original sale − $1,000 sales return). Net sales shown on the income statement would also be $7,500.

COMMON SIZE FINANCIAL STATEMENTS

How good is a $1,000,000 increase in net income? The answer is not clear because there is no indication as to the size of the company. A million dollar increase may be excellent for a small company but would be virtually meaningless for a company the size of Exxon. To enable meaningful comparisons analysts prepare **common size financial statements.** Common size statements display information in percentages as well as absolute dollar amounts.

To illustrate, we expand the income statements for JPS to include percentages. The results are shown in Exhibit 3.7. The percentage data are computed by defining net

LO 3-5

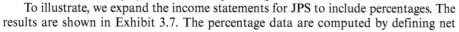 Use common size financial statements to evaluate managerial performance.

Answers to The Curious Accountant

As data from the income statement for AutoNation show, automobile dealers do not have big markups on the cars they sell. The new vehicles the company sold for $8,906.9 million in 2012 cost the company $8,327.4 to purchase, resulting in a gross margin of $579.5, or 6.5 percent. In other words, if you bought an "average" car from AutoNation for $20,000, the company's gross profit on it was only $1,300 ($20,000 × .065), meaning it paid Ford $18,700 ($20,000 − $1,300). Furthermore, the company still had to pay other expenses besides its cost of goods sold. In 2012, only 2.0 percent of each dollar of AutoNation's sales was net profit ($316.4 ÷ $15,668.8) Remember, the amount shown for sales on AutoNation's income statement is based on what customers actually paid for the cars the company sold, not the "sticker price."

Meanwhile, if Ford sold the car to AutoNation for $18,700, it earned a gross margin on the sale of 11.1 percent, or $2,076 [$13,989 ÷ $126,567 = 11.1%; ($126,567 − $112,578 = $13,989)] [$18,700 × .111 = $2.076]. Like AutoNation, Ford still had other expenses to pay for besides the cost of goods sold. In 2012 Ford earned 4.3 percent of net profit on each dollar of sales ($5,665 ÷ $134,252).

Most consumers significantly overestimate the profit margins of the companies from which they buy goods. Retailers, especially, operate with small profit margins, so inventory management is very important to their success.

sales as the base figure, or 100 percent. The other amounts on the statements are then shown as a percentage of net sales. For example, the *cost of goods sold percentage* is the dollar amount of *cost of goods sold* divided by the dollar amount of *net sales,* which produces a percentage of 66.7 percent ($8,000 ÷ $12,000) for 2014 and 48.5 percent ($12,000 ÷ $24,750) for 2015. Other income statement items are computed using the same approach.

EXHIBIT 3.7   Common Size Financial Statements

JUNE'S PLANT SHOP
Income Statement
For the Period Ended

	2014		2015	
Net sales*	$12,000	100.0%	$24,750	100.0%
Cost of goods sold	(8,000)	66.7	(12,000)	48.5
Gross margin	4,000	33.3	12,750	51.5
Less: Operating expenses				
Selling and administrative expense	(1,000)	8.3	(5,000)	20.2
Transportation-out			(450)	1.8
Operating income	3,000	25.0	7,300	29.5
Nonoperating items				
Interest expense			(360)	(1.5)
Gain on the sale of land			700	2.8
Net income	$ 3,000	25.0	$ 7,640	30.9

*Since JPS did not offer sales discounts or have sales returns and allowances during 2014 or 2015, the amount of sales revenue is equal to the amount of net sales. We use the term *net sales* here because it is more commonly used in business practice. Percentages do not add exactly because they have been rounded.

These common size statements provide insight into the company's operating strategy. For example, assume JPS relocated its store in an upscale mall in early 2015. Management realized that the company would have to pay more for operating expenses but believed those expenses could be offset by charging significantly higher prices. The common size income statement confirms that the company's goals were accomplished. Note that the gross margin increased from 33.3 percent of sales to 51.5 percent, confirming that the company was able to increase prices. Also, note that operating expenses increased. Selling and administrative expense increased from 8.3 percent of sales to 20.2 percent. Also, the company experienced a new expense, transportation out, for delivering merchandise to its customers. These increases in expenses confirm the fact that JPS is paying more for rental space and providing additional services to its customers. The common size statements, therefore, support the conclusion that JPS's increase in net income from $3,000 to $7,640 was a result of management's new operating strategy. As a side note, the new operating strategy may also explain why JPS sold its land in late 2015. Considering the success the company experienced at the new location, there was no motive to build a store on the land.

A Look Back

Merchandising companies earn profits by selling inventory at prices that are higher than the cost paid for the goods. Merchandising companies include *retail companies* (companies that sell goods to the final consumer) and *wholesale companies* (companies that sell to other merchandising companies). The products sold by merchandising companies are called *inventory.* The costs to purchase inventory, to receive it, and to ready it for sale are *product costs,* which are first accumulated in an inventory account (balance sheet asset account) and then recognized as cost of goods sold (income statement expense account) in the period in which goods are sold. Purchases and sales of inventory can be recorded continually as goods are bought and sold (perpetual system) or at the end of the accounting period (periodic system, discussed in the chapter appendix).

Accounting for inventory includes the treatment of cash discounts, transportation costs, and returns and allowances. The cost of inventory is the list price less any purchase returns and allowances and purchase discounts, plus transportation-in costs. The cost of freight paid to acquire inventory (*transportation-in*) is considered a product cost. The cost of freight paid to deliver inventory to customers (*transportation-out*) is a selling expense. *Sales returns and allowances* and *sales discounts* are subtracted from sales revenue to determine the amount of *net sales* reported on the income statement. Purchase returns and allowances reduce product cost. Theoretically, the cost of lost, damaged, or stolen inventory is an operating expense. However, because these costs are usually immaterial in amount they are typically included as part of cost of goods sold on the income statement.

Some companies use a *multistep income statement* which reports product costs separately from selling and administrative costs. Cost of goods sold is subtracted from sales revenue to determine *gross margin.* Selling and administrative expenses are subtracted from gross margin to determine income from operations. Other companies report income using a *single-step format* in which the cost of goods sold is listed along with selling and administrative items in a single expense category that is subtracted in total from revenue to determine income from operations.

Managers of merchandising businesses operate in a highly competitive environment. They must manage company operations carefully to remain profitable. *Common size financial statements* (statements presented on a percentage basis) and ratio analysis are useful monitoring tools. Common size financial statements permit ready comparisons among different-size companies. Although a $1 million increase in sales may be good for a small company and bad for a large company, a 10 percent increase can apply to any size company.

>> A Look Forward

To this point, the text has explained the basic accounting cycle for service and merchandising businesses. Future chapters more closely address specific accounting issues. For example, in Chapter 5 you will learn how to deal with inventory items that are purchased at differing prices. Other chapters will discuss a variety of specific practices that are widely used by real-world companies.

APPENDIX

LO 3-6

Identify the primary features of the periodic inventory system.

Periodic Inventory System

Under certain conditions, it is impractical to record inventory sales transactions as they occur. Consider the operations of a fast-food restaurant. To maintain perpetual inventory records, the restaurant would have to transfer from the Inventory account to the Cost of Goods Sold account the *cost* of each hamburger, order of fries, soft drink, or other food items as they were sold. Obviously, recording the cost of each item at the point of sale would be impractical without using highly sophisticated computer equipment (recording the selling price the customer pays is captured by cash registers; the difficulty lies in capturing inventory cost).

The **periodic inventory system** offers a practical solution for recording inventory transactions in a low-technology, high-volume environment. Inventory costs are recorded in a Purchases account at the time of purchase. Purchase returns and allowances and transportation-in are recorded in separate accounts. No entries for the cost of merchandise purchases or sales are recorded in the Inventory account during the period. The cost of goods sold is determined at the end of the period as shown in Exhibit 3.8.

The perpetual and periodic inventory systems represent alternative procedures for recording the same information. The amounts of cost of goods sold and ending inventory reported in the financial statements will be the same regardless of the method used.

The **schedule of cost of goods sold** presented in Exhibit 3.8 is used for internal reporting purposes. It is normally not shown in published financial statements. The amount of cost of goods sold is reported as a single line item on the income statement. The income statement in Exhibit 3.3 will be the same whether JPS maintains perpetual or periodic inventory records.

EXHIBIT 3.8

Schedule of Cost of Goods Sold for 2015

Beginning inventory	$ 6,000
Purchases	11,000
Purchase returns and allowances	(1,000)
Purchase discounts	(200)
Transportation-in	300
Cost of goods available for sale	16,100
Ending inventory	4,600
Cost of goods sold	$11,500

Advantages and Disadvantages of the Periodic System versus the Perpetual System

The chief advantage of the periodic method is recording efficiency. Recording inventory transactions occasionally (periodically) requires less effort than recording them continually (perpetually). Historically, practical limitations offered businesses like fast-food restaurants or grocery stores no alternative to using the periodic system. The sheer volume of transactions made recording individual decreases to the Inventory account balance as each item was sold impossible. Imagine the number of transactions a grocery store would have to record every business day to maintain perpetual records.

Although the periodic system provides a recordkeeping advantage over the perpetual system, perpetual inventory records provide significant control advantages over periodic records. With perpetual records, the book balance in the Inventory account should agree with the amount of inventory in stock at any given time. By comparing that book balance with the results of a physical inventory count, management can determine the amount of lost, damaged, destroyed, or stolen inventory. Perpetual records also permit more timely and accurate reorder decisions and profitability assessments.

When a company uses the *periodic* inventory system, lost, damaged, or stolen merchandise is automatically included in cost of goods sold. Because such goods are not included in the year-end physical count, they are treated as sold regardless of the reason for their absence. Since the periodic system does not separate the cost of lost, damaged, or stolen merchandise from the cost of goods sold, the amount of any inventory shrinkage is unknown. This feature is a major disadvantage of the periodic system. Without knowing the amount of inventory losses, management cannot weigh the costs of various security systems against the potential benefits.

Advances in such technology as electronic bar code scanning and increased computing power have eliminated most of the practical constraints that once prevented merchandisers with high-volume, low dollar-value inventories from recording inventory transactions on a continual basis. As a result, use of the perpetual inventory system has expanded rapidly in recent years and continued growth can be expected. This text, therefore, concentrates on the perpetual inventory system.

 Video lectures and accompanying self-assessment quizzes are available for all learning objectives through McGraw-Hill *Connect® Accounting.*

SELF-STUDY REVIEW PROBLEM

Academy Sales Company (ASC) started the 2014 accounting period with the balances given in the financial statements model shown below. During 2014 ASC experienced the following business events.

1. Purchased $16,000 of merchandise inventory on account, terms 2/10, n/30.
2. The goods that were purchased in Event 1 were delivered FOB shipping point. Freight costs of $600 were paid in cash by the responsible party.
3. Returned $500 of goods purchased in Event 1.
4a. Recorded the cash discount on the goods purchased in Event 1.
4b. Paid the balance due on the account payable within the discount period.
5a. Recognized $21,000 of cash revenue from the sale of merchandise.
5b. Recognized $15,000 of cost of goods sold.
6. The merchandise in Event 5a was sold to customers FOB destination. Freight costs of $950 were paid in cash by the responsible party.
7. Paid cash of $4,000 for selling and administrative expenses.
8. Sold the land for $5,600 cash.

Required

a. Record the above transactions in a financial statements model like the one shown below.

Event No.	Cash	+	Inventory	+	Land	=	Accts. Pay.	+	Com. Stk.	+	Ret. Earn.	Rev./ Gain	−	Exp.	=	Net Inc.	Cash Flow
Bal.	25,000	+	3,000	+	5,000	=	–0–	+	18,000	+	15,000	NA	−	NA	=	NA	NA

b. Prepare a schedule of cost of goods sold. (Appendix)
c. Prepare a multistep income statement. Include common size percentages on the income statement.

d. ASC's gross margin percentage in 2013 was 22 percent. Based on the common size data in the income statement, did ASC raise or lower its prices in 2014? (Appendix)

e. Assuming a 10 percent rate of growth, what is the amount of net income expected for 2015?

Solution

a.

Event No.	Cash	+	Inventory	+	Land	=	Accts. Pay.	+	Com. Stk.	+	Ret. Earn.	Rev./ Gain	−	Exp.	=	Net Inc.	Cash Flow	
Bal.	25,000	+	3,000	+	5,000	=	–0–	+	18,000	+	15,000	NA	−	NA	=	NA	NA	
1		+	16,000			=	16,000	+		+			−		=			
2	(600)	+	600			=		+		+			−		=		(600)	OA
3		+	(500)			=	(500)	+		+			−		=			
4a		+	(310)			=	(310)	+		+			−		=			
4b	(15,190)	+				=	(15,190)	+		+			−		=		(15,190)	OA
5a	21,000	+				=		+		+	21,000	21,000	−		=	21,000	21,000	OA
5b		+	(15,000)			=		+		+	(15,000)		−	15,000	=	(15,000)		
6	(950)	+				=		+		+	(950)		−	950	=	(950)	(950)	OA
7	(4,000)	+				=		+		+	(4,000)		−	4,000	=	(4,000)	(4,000)	OA
8	5,600	+			(5,000)	=		+		+	600	600	−		=	600	5,600	IA
Bal.	30,860	+	3,790		–0–	=	–0–	+	18,000	+	16,650	21,600	−	19,950	=	1,650	5,860	NC

b.

ACADEMY SALES COMPANY
Schedule of Cost of Goods Sold
For the Period Ended December 31, 2014

Beginning inventory	$ 3,000
Plus purchases	16,000
Less: Purchase returns and allowances	(500)
Less: Purchases discounts	(310)
Plus: Transportation-in	600
Goods available for sale	18,790
Less: Ending inventory	3,790
Cost of goods sold	$15,000

c.

ACADEMY SALES COMPANY
Income Statement*
For the Period Ended December 31, 2014

Net sales	$21,000	100.0%
Cost of goods sold	(15,000)	71.4
Gross margin	6,000	28.6
Less: Operating expenses		
Selling and administrative expense	(4,000)	19.0
Transportation-out	(950)	4.5
Operating income	1,050	5.0
Nonoperating items		
Gain on the sale of land	600	2.9
Net income	$ 1,650	7.9

*Percentages do not add exactly because they have been rounded.

d. All other things being equal, the higher the gross margin percentage, the higher the sales prices. Since the gross margin percentage increased from 22 percent to 28.6 percent, the data suggest that Academy raised its sales prices.

e. $1,155 [$1,050 + (.10 × $1,050)]. Note that the gain is not expected to recur.

KEY TERMS

Cash discount 100
Common size financial
  statements 109
Cost of goods available for
  sale 95
Cost of Goods Sold 95
FOB (free on board)
  destination 101
FOB (free on board) shipping
  point 101
Gain 105
Gross margin 96

Gross profit 96
Loss 105
Merchandise inventory 92
Merchandising businesses 92
Multistep income
  statement 106
Net sales 109
Operating income
  (or loss) 106
Period costs 95
Periodic inventory
  system 112

Perpetual inventory system 96
Product costs 95
Purchase discount 100
Purchase returns and
  allowances 99
Retail companies 92
Sales discounts 107
Sales returns and
  allowances 109
Schedule of cost of goods
  sold 112

Selling and administrative
  costs 95
Shrinkage 104
Single-step income
  statement 106
Transportation-in
  (freight-in) 101
Transportation-out
  (freight-out) 101
2/10, n/30 100
Wholesale companies 92

QUESTIONS

1. Define *merchandise inventory*. What types of costs are included in the Merchandise Inventory account?

2. What is the difference between a product cost and a selling and administrative cost?

3. How is the cost of goods available for sale determined?

4. What portion of cost of goods available for sale is shown on the balance sheet? What portion is shown on the income statement?

5. When are period costs expensed? When are product costs expensed?

6. If PetCo had net sales of $600,000, goods available for sale of $450,000, and cost of goods sold of $375,000, what is its gross margin? What amount of inventory will be shown on its balance sheet?

7. Describe how the perpetual inventory system

works. What are some advantages of using the perpetual inventory system? Is it necessary to take a physical inventory when using the perpetual inventory system?

8. What are the effects of the following types of transactions on the accounting equation? Also identify the financial statements that are affected. (Assume that the perpetual inventory system is used.)
   a. Acquisition of cash from the issue of common stock.
   b. Contribution of inventory by an owner of a company.
   c. Purchase of inventory with cash by a company.
   d. Sale of inventory for cash.

9. Northern Merchandising Company sold inventory that cost $12,000 for $20,000 cash. How does

this event affect the accounting equation? What financial statements and accounts are affected? (Assume that the perpetual inventory system is used.)

10. If goods are shipped FOB shipping point, which party (buyer or seller) is responsible for the shipping costs?

11. Define *transportation-in*. Is it a product or a period cost?

12. Quality Cellular Co. paid $80 for freight on merchandise that it had purchased for resale to customers (transportation-in) and paid $135 for freight on merchandise delivered to customers (transportation-out). The $80 payment is added to what account? The $135 payment is added to what account?

13. Why would a seller grant an allowance to a buyer of his merchandise?

14. Dyer Department Store purchased goods with the terms 2/10, n/30. What do these terms mean?

15. Eastern Discount Stores incurred a $5,000 cash cost. How does the accounting for this cost differ if the cash were paid for inventory versus commissions to sales personnel?

16. What is the purpose of giving a cash discount to charge customers?

17. Define *transportation-out*. Is it a product cost or a period cost for the seller?

18. Ball Co. purchased inventory with a list price of $4,000 with the terms 2/10, n/30. What amount will be added to the Merchandise Inventory account?

19. Explain the difference between purchase returns and sales returns. How do

116   Chapter 3

purchase returns affect the financial statements of both buyer and seller? How do sales returns affect the financial statements of both buyer and seller?

20. Explain the difference between gross margin and a gain.

21. What is the difference between a multistep income statement and a single-step income statement?

22. What is the advantage of using common size income statements to present financial information for several accounting periods?

23. What is the purpose of preparing a schedule of cost of goods sold?

24. Explain how the periodic inventory system works. What are some advantages of using the periodic inventory system? What are some disadvantages of using the periodic inventory system? Is it necessary to take a physical inventory when using the periodic inventory system?

25. Why does the periodic inventory system impose a major disadvantage for management in accounting for lost, stolen, or damaged goods?

MULTIPLE-CHOICE QUESTIONS

Multiple-choice questions are provided on the text website at www.mhhe.com/edmondssurvey4e.

EXERCISES

connect
|ACCOUNTING| All applicable Exercises are available with McGraw-Hill's *Connect® Accounting.*

When the instructions for *any* exercise or problem call for the preparation of an income statement, use the *multistep format* unless otherwise indicated.

LO 3-1

Exercise 3-1   *Determining the cost of financing inventory*

On January 1, 2014, Laura started a small flower merchandising business that she named Laura's Flowers. The company experienced the following events during the first year of operation.

1. Started the business by issuing common stock for $20,000 cash.
2. Paid $14,000 cash to purchase inventory.
3. Sold merchandise that cost $8,000 for $18,000 on account.
4. Collected $15,000 cash from accounts receivable.
5. Paid $3,750 for operating expenses.

Required

a. Organize ledger accounts under an accounting equation and record the events in the accounts.

b. Prepare an income statement, a balance sheet, and a statement of cash flows.

c. Since Laura sold inventory for $18,000, she will be able to recover more than half of the $20,000 she invested in the stock. Do you agree with this statement? Why or why not?

LO 3-1

Exercise 3-2   *Comparing a merchandising company with a service company*

The following information is available for two different types of businesses for the 2014 accounting period. Lewis CPAs is a service business that provides accounting services to small businesses. Casual Clothing is a merchandising business that sells sports clothing to college students.

Data for Lewis CPAs

1. Borrowed $80,000 from the bank to start the business.
2. Provided $60,000 of services to clients and collected $60,000 cash.
3. Paid salary expense of $40,000.

Data for Casual Clothing

1. Borrowed $80,000 from the bank to start the business.
2. Purchased $50,000 inventory for cash.
3. Inventory costing $32,000 was sold for $60,000 cash.
4. Paid $7,200 cash for operating expenses.

Required

a. Prepare an income statement, a balance sheet, and a statement of cash flows for each of the companies.
b. Which of the two businesses would have product costs? Why?
c. Why does Lewis CPAs not compute gross margin on its income statement?
d. Compare the assets of both companies. What assets do they have in common? What assets are different? Why?

Exercise 3-3   *Effect of inventory transactions on financial statements: Perpetual system*   LO 3-1

Justin Swords started a small merchandising business in 2014. The business experienced the following events during its first year of operation. Assume that Swords uses the perpetual inventory system.

1. Acquired $70,000 cash from the issue of common stock.
2. Purchased inventory for $60,000 cash.
3. Sold inventory costing $48,000 for $82,000 cash.

Required

a. Record the events in a statements model like the one shown below.

Assets			=	Equity			Rev.	−	Exp.	=	Net Inc.	Cash Flow
Cash	+	Inv.	=	Com. Stk.	+	Ret. Earn.						

b. Prepare an income statement for 2014 (use the multistep format).
c. What is the amount of total assets at the end of the period?

Exercise 3-4   *Effect of inventory transactions on the income statement and statement of cash flows: Perpetual system*   LO 3-1

During 2014, King Merchandising Company purchased $30,000 of inventory on account. King sold inventory on account that cost $22,500 for $31,000. Cash payments on accounts payable were $18,000. There was $22,000 cash collected from accounts receivable. King also paid $4,200 cash for operating expenses. Assume that King started the accounting period with $18,000 in both cash and common stock.

Required

a. Identify the events described in the preceding paragraph and record them in a horizontal statements model like the following one:

Assets						=	Liab.	+	Equity				Rev.	−	Exp.	=	Net inc.	Cash Flow
Cash	+	Accts. Rec.	+	Inv.	=		Accts. Pay.	+	Com. Stk.	+	Ret. Earn.							
14,000	+	NA	+	NA	=		NA	+	14,000	+	NA		NA	−	NA	=	NA	NA

b. What is the balance of accounts receivable at the end of 2014?

c. What is the balance of accounts payable at the end of 2014?

d. What are the amounts of gross margin and net income for 2014?

e. Determine the amount of net cash flow from operating activities.

f. Explain why net income and retained earnings are the same for King. Normally would these amounts be the same? Why or why not?

LO 3-1

Exercise 3-5   *Recording inventory transactions in a financial statements model*

Hilo Clothing experienced the following events during 2014, its first year of operation:

1. Acquired $25,000 cash from the issue of common stock.
2. Purchased inventory for $12,000 cash.
3. Sold inventory costing $8,000 for $15,000 cash.
4. Paid $1,200 for advertising expense.

Required

Record the events in a statements model like the one shown below.

Assets			=	Equity			Rev.	−	Exp.	=	Net Inc.	Cash Flow
Cash	+	Inv.	=	Com. Stk.	+	Ret. Earn.						

LO 3-2

Exercise 3-6   *Understanding the freight terms FOB shipping point and FOB destination*

Required

Determine which party, buyer or seller, is responsible for freight charges in each of the following situations:

a. Sold merchandise, freight terms, FOB shipping point.

b. Sold merchandise, freight terms, FOB destination.

c. Purchased merchandise, freight terms, FOB shipping point.

d. Purchased merchandise, freight terms, FOB destination.

LO 3-2

Exercise 3-7   *Effect of purchase returns and allowances and freight costs on the financial statements: Perpetual system*

The beginning account balances for Austin's Auto Shop as of January 1, 2014, follows:

Account Titles	Beginning Balances
Cash	$14,000
Inventory	7,000
Common stock	18,000
Retained earnings	3,000

The following events affected the company during the 2014 accounting period:

1. Purchased merchandise on account that cost $12,000.
2. The goods in Event 1 were purchased FOB shipping point with freight cost of $800 cash.
3. Returned $2,600 of damaged merchandise for credit on account.
4. Agreed to keep other damaged merchandise for which the company received an $1,100 allowance.
5. Sold merchandise that cost $12,000 for $21,500 cash.
6. Delivered merchandise to customers in Event 5 under terms FOB destination with freight costs amounting to $500 cash.
7. Paid $8,000 on the merchandise purchased in Event 1.

Required

a. Organize appropriate ledger accounts under an accounting equation. Record the beginning balances and the transaction data in the accounts.
b. Prepare an income statement and a statement of cash flows for 2014.
c. Explain why a difference does or does not exist between net income and net cash flow from operating activities.

Exercise 3-8   *Accounting for product costs: Perpetual inventory system*   LO 3-2

Which of the following would be *added* to the Inventory account for a merchandising business using the perpetual inventory system?

Required

a. Purchase of a new computer to be used by the business.
b. Purchase of inventory.
c. Allowance received for damaged inventory.
d. Transportation-out.
e. Purchase discount.
f. Transportation-in.

Exercise 3-9   *Effect of product cost and period cost: Horizontal statements model*   LO 3-2

The Sports Store experienced the following events for the 2014 accounting period:

1. Acquired $40,000 cash from the issue of common stock.
2. Purchased $78,000 of inventory on account.
3. Received goods purchased in Event 2 FOB shipping point; freight cost of $900 paid in cash.
4. Sold inventory on account that cost $46,000 for $72,000.
5. Freight cost on the goods sold in Event 4 was $560. The goods were shipped FOB destination. Cash was paid for the freight cost.
6. Customer in Event 4 returned $5,100 worth of goods that had a cost of $2,950.
7. Collected $61,500 cash from accounts receivable.
8. Paid $66,100 cash on accounts payable.
9. Paid $2,600 cash for advertising expense.
10. Paid $3,100 cash for insurance expense.

Required

a. Which of these events affect period (selling and administrative) costs? Which result in product costs? If neither, label the transaction NA.
b. Record each event in a horizontal statements model like the following one. The first event is recorded as an example.

Assets			=	Liab.	+	Equity			Rev.	−	Exp.	=	Net Inc.	Cash Flow	
Cash	+ Accts. Rec.	+ Inv.	=	Accts. Pay.	+	C. Stk.	+	Ret. Earn.							
40,000	+ NA	+ NA	=	NA	+	40,000	+	NA	NA	−	NA	=	NA	40,000	FA

Exercise 3-10   *Cash discounts and purchase returns*   LO 3-3

On April 6, 2014, Fashion Furnishings purchased $24,800 of merchandise from James's Imports, terms 2/10, n/45. On April 8, Fashion returned $2,400 of the merchandise to James's Imports for credit. Fashion paid cash for the merchandise on April 15, 2014.

Required

a. What is the amount that Fashion must pay James's Imports on April 15?

b. Record the events in a horizontal statements model like the following one.

Assets			=	Liab.	+	Equity			Rev.	−	Exp.	=	Net Inc.	Cash Flow
Cash	+	Inv.	=	Accts. Pay.	+	C. Stock.	+	Ret. Earn.						

c. How much must Fashion pay for the merchandise purchased if the payment is not made until April 20, 2014?

d. Record the payment in event (c) in a horizontal statements model like the one above.

e. Why would Fashion want to pay for the merchandise by April 15?

LO 3-2

Exercise 3-11 *Determining the effect of inventory transactions on the horizontal statements model: Perpetual system*

Mario Company experienced the following events:

1. Purchased merchandise inventory for cash.
2. Sold merchandise inventory on account. Label the revenue recognition 2a and the expense recognition 2b.
3. Returned merchandise purchased on account.
4. Purchased merchandise inventory on account.
5. Paid cash on accounts payable within the discount period.
6. Paid cash for selling and administrative expenses.
7. Sold merchandise inventory for cash. Label the revenue recognition 7a and the expense recognition 7b.
8. Paid cash for transportation-out.
9. Paid cash for transportation-in.
10. Collected cash from accounts receivable not within the discount period.

Required

Identify each event as asset source (AS), asset use (AU), asset exchange (AE), or claims exchange (CE). Also explain how each event affects the financial statements by placing a + for increase, − for decrease, or NA for not affected under each of the components in the following statements model. Assume the company uses the perpetual inventory system. The first event is recorded as an example.

Event No.	Event Type	Assets	=	Liab.	+	Equity	Rev.	−	Exp.	=	Net Inc.	Cash Flow
1	AE	+−	=	NA	+	NA	NA	−	NA	=	NA	−OA

LO 3-2

Exercise 3-12 *Inventory financing costs*

Nichole Jordan comes to you for advice. She has just purchased a large amount of inventory with the terms 2/10, n/30. The amount of the invoice is $270,000. She is currently short of cash but has decent credit. She can borrow the money needed to settle the account payable at an annual interest rate of 7 percent. Nichole is sure she will have the necessary cash by the due date of the invoice but not by the last day of the discount period.

Required

a. Convert the discount rate into an annual interest rate.

b. Make a recommendation regarding whether Jordan should borrow the money and pay off the account payable within the discount period.

Exercise 3-13   *Effect of shrinkage: Perpetual system*

LO 3-2

Royal Sales experienced the following events during 2014, its first year of operation:

1. Started the business when it acquired $80,000 cash from the issue of common stock.
2. Paid $35,000 cash to purchase inventory.
3. Sold inventory costing $21,000 for $40,500 cash.
4. Physically counted inventory showing $13,500 inventory was on hand at the end of the accounting period.

Required

a. Determine the amount of the difference between book balance and the actual amount of inventory as determined by the physical count.
b. Explain how differences between the book balance and the physical count of inventory could arise. Why is being able to determine whether differences exist useful to management?

Exercise 3-14   *Comparing gross margin and gain on sale of land*

LO 3-3

Phillips Sales Company had the following balances in its accounts on January 1, 2014.

Cash	$35,000
Merchandise Inventory	25,000
Land	60,000
Common Stock	50,000
Retained Earnings	70,000

Phillips experienced the following events during 2014.

1. Sold merchandise inventory that cost $20,000 for $37,500.
2. Sold land that cost $25,000 for $40,000.

Required

a. Determine the amount of gross margin recognized by Phillips.
b. Determine the amount of the gain on the sale of land recognized by Phillips.
c. Comment on how the gross margin versus the gain will be recognized on the income statement.
d. Comment on how the gross margin versus the gain will be recognized on the statement of cash flows.

Exercise 3-15   *Single-step and multistep income statements*

LO 3-3

The following information was taken from the accounts of Healthy Eats, a delicatessen, at December 31, 2014. The accounts are listed in alphabetical order, and each has a normal balance.

Accounts payable	$1,200
Accounts receivable	800
Advertising expense	400
Cash	820
Common stock	400
Cost of goods sold	1,200
Interest expense	140
Merchandise inventory	900
Prepaid rent	80
Retained earnings	1,000
Sales revenue	2,000
Salaries expense	260
Rent expense	220
Loss on sale of land	50

Required

First, prepare an income statement for the year using the single-step approach. Then prepare another income statement using the multistep approach.

LO 3-4

Exercise 3-16 *Effect of sales returns and allowances and freight costs on the financial statements: Perpetual system*

Poole Company began the 2014 accounting period with $36,000 cash, $80,000 inventory, $70,000 common stock, and $46,000 retained earnings. During the 2014 accounting period, Poole experienced the following events:

1. Sold merchandise costing $51,500 for $92,900 on account to Mable's General Store.
2. Delivered the goods to Mable's under terms FOB destination. Freight costs were $500 cash.
3. Received returned goods from Mable's. The goods cost Poole Company $3,200 and were sold to Mable's for $4,700.
4. Granted Mable's a $1,500 allowance for damaged goods that Mable's agreed to keep.
5. Collected partial payment of $71,000 cash from accounts receivable.

Required

a. Record the events in a statements model like the one shown below.

Assets			=	Equity			Rev.	−	Exp.	=	Net Inc.	Cash Flow
Cash	+ Accts. Rec.	+ Inv.	=	Com. Stk.	+	Ret. Earn.						

b. Prepare an income statement, a balance sheet, and a statement of cash flows.
c. Why would Poole grant the $1,500 allowance to Mable's? Who benefits more?

LO 3-4

Exercise 3-17 *Effect of cash discounts on financial statements: Perpetual system*

Clayton Computers was started in 2014. The company experienced the following accounting events during its first year of operation.

1. Started business when it acquired $25,000 cash from the issue of common stock.
2. Purchased merchandise with a list price of $23,000 on account, terms 2/10, n/30.
3. Paid off one-half of the accounts payable balance within the discount period.
4. Sold merchandise on account that had a list price of $24,000. Credit terms were 1/20, n/30. The merchandise had cost Clayton Computers $14,000.
5. Collected cash from the account receivable within the discount period.
6. Paid $1,700 cash for operating expenses.
7. Paid the balance due on accounts payable. The payment was not made within the discount period.

Required

a. Record the events in a horizontal statements model like the following one.

Assets			=	Liab.	+	Equity			Rev.	−	Exp.	=	Net Inc.	Cash Flow
Cash	+ Accts. Rec.	+ Inv.	=	Accts. Pay.	+ Com. Stk.	+ Ret. Earn.								

b. What is the amount of gross margin for the period? What is the net income for the period?
c. Why would Clayton Computers sell merchandise with the terms 1/20, n/30?
d. What do the terms 2/10, n/30 in Event 2 mean to Clayton Computers?

Exercise 3-18   *Using common size statements and ratios to make comparisons*   LO 3-5

At the end of 2014 the following information is available for Fargo and Huston companies:

	Fargo	Huston
Sales	$2,000,000	$2,000,000
Cost of goods sold	1,600,000	1,200,000
Operating expenses	300,000	640,000
Total assets	2,500,000	2,500,000
Stockholders' equity	700,000	1,500,000

Required

a. Prepare common size income statements for each company.

b. One company is a high-end retailer, and the other operates a discount store. Which is the discounter? Support your selection by referring to the common size statements.

Exercise 3-19   *Effect of inventory transactions on the income statement and balance sheet: Periodic system (Appendix)*   LO 3-6

Edd Gant owns Edd's Sporting Goods. At the beginning of the year, Edd's had $16,000 in inventory. During the year, Edd's purchased inventory that cost $65,000. At the end of the year, inventory on hand amounted to $26,300.

Required

Calculate the following:

a. Cost of goods available for sale during the year.

b. Cost of goods sold for the year.

c. Amount of inventory Edd's would report on the year-end balance sheet.

Exercise 3-20   *Determining cost of goods sold: Periodic system (Appendix)*   LO 3-6

Belk Antiques uses the periodic inventory system to account for its inventory transactions. The following account titles and balances were drawn from Belk's records for the year 2014: beginning balance in inventory, $42,000; purchases, $128,000; purchase returns and allowances, $12,000; sales, $520,000; sales returns and allowances, $3,900; freight-in, $1,000; and operating expenses, $130,000. A physical count indicated that $26,000 of merchandise was on hand at the end of the accounting period.

Required

a. Prepare a schedule of cost of goods sold.

b. Prepare a multistep income statement.

PROBLEMS

≡ connect   **All applicable Problems are available with McGraw-Hill's**
|ACCOUNTING   ***Connect® Accounting.***

Problem 3-21   *Identifying product and period costs*   LO 3-2

Required

Indicate whether each of the following costs is a product cost or a period (selling and administrative) cost.

CHECK FIGURE
a. Period cost

a. Cleaning supplies for the office.

b. Freight on goods purchased for resale.

c. Salary of the marketing director.

d. Freight on goods sold to customer with terms FOB destination.

e. Utilities expense incurred for office building.

f. Advertising expense.

g. Insurance on vans used to deliver goods to customers.

h. Salaries of sales supervisors.

i. Monthly maintenance expense for a copier.

j. Goods purchased for resale.

LO 3-2

CHECK FIGURE
Event (b): NA Cost: $0

Problem 3-22   *Identifying freight costs*

Required

For each of the following events, determine the amount of freight paid by Tom's Part House. Also indicate whether the freight cost would be classified as a product or period (selling and administrative) cost.

a. Purchased inventory with freight costs of $500. The goods were shipped FOB shipping point.

b. Sold merchandise to a customer. Freight costs were $800. The goods were shipped FOB shipping point.

c. Purchased merchandise inventory with freight costs of $1,400. The merchandise was shipped FOB destination.

d. Shipped merchandise to customers, freight terms FOB destination. The freight costs were $300.

LO 3-2

CHECK FIGURES
a. Ending Cash: $29,245
b. Net Income: $6,550

Problem 3-23   *Effect of purchase returns and allowances and purchase discounts on the financial statements: Perpetual system*

The following events were completed by Yang's Imports in September 2014.

Sept.	1	Acquired $30,000 cash from the issue of common stock.
	1	Purchased $18,000 of merchandise on account with terms 2/10, n/30.
	5	Paid $400 cash for freight to obtain merchandise purchased on September 1.
	8	Sold merchandise that cost $10,000 to customers for $19,000 on account, with terms 2/10, n/30.
	8	Returned $750 of defective merchandise from the September 1 purchase to the supplier.
	10	Paid cash for the balance due on the merchandise purchased on September 1.
	20	Received cash from customers of September 8 sale in settlement of the account balances, but not within the discount period.
	30	Paid $2,450 cash for selling expenses.

Required

a. Record each event in a statements model like the following one. The first event is recorded as an example.

Assets			=	Liab.	+	Equity			Rev.	–	Exp.	=	Net Inc.	Cash Flow
Cash	+ Accts. Rec.	+ Inv.	=	Accts. Pay.	+	Com. Stk.	+ Ret. Earn.							
30,000	+ NA	+ NA	=	NA	+	30,000	+ NA		NA	– NA	=	NA		30,000 FA

b. Prepare an income statement for the month ending September 30.

c. Prepare a statement of cash flows for the month ending September 30.

d. Explain why there is a difference between net income and cash flow from operating activities.

Problem 3-24 *Preparing a schedule of cost of goods sold and multistep and single-step income statements: Periodic system (Appendix)*

The following account titles and balances were taken from the adjusted trial balance of Omar Farm Co. for 2014. The company uses the periodic inventory system.

Account Title	Balance
Sales returns and allowances	$ 6,500
Miscellaneous expense	800
Transportation-out	1,400
Sales	139,500
Advertising expense	5,500
Salaries expense	17,000
Transportation-in	3,450
Purchases	84,000
Interest expense	720
Merchandise inventory, January 1	12,400
Rent expense	10,000
Merchandise inventory, December 31	8,100
Purchase returns and allowances	2,500
Loss on sale of land	6,800
Utilities expense	1,420

Required

a. Prepare a schedule to determine the amount of cost of goods sold.
b. Prepare a multistep income statement.
c. Prepare a single-step income statement.

Problem 3-25 *Basic transactions for three accounting cycles: prepetual system*

Amber's Flower Company was started in 2014 when it acquired $80,000 cash from the issue of common stock. The following data summarize the company's first three years' operating activities. Assume that all transactions were cash transactions.

	2014	2015	2016
Purchases of inventory	$40,000	$55,000	$ 95,000
Sales	75,000	88,000	146,000
Cost of goods sold	38,000	49,000	82,000
Selling and administrative expenses	29,000	35,000	42,000

Required

Prepare an income statement (use multistep format) and balance sheet for each fiscal year. (*Hint:* Record the transaction data for each accounting period in the accounting equation before preparing the statements for that year.)

Problem 3-26 *Comprehensive cycle problem: Perpetual system*

At the beginning of 2013, the Bradley Company had the following balances in its accounts:

Cash	$ 8,600
Inventory	18,000
Common stock	20,000
Retained earnings	6,600

During 2014, the company experienced the following events:

1. Purchased inventory that cost $4,400 on account from Bivins Company under terms 1/10, n/30. The merchandise was delivered FOB shipping point. Freight costs of $190 were paid in cash.
2. Returned $400 of the inventory that it had purchased because the inventory was damaged in transit. The seller agreed to pay the return freight cost.
3. Paid the amount due on its account payable to Bivins Company within the cash discount period.
4. Sold inventory that had cost $6,000 for $11,000 on account, under terms 2/10, n/45.
5. Received merchandise returned from a customer. The merchandise originally cost $800 and was sold to the customer for $1,450 cash. The customer was paid $1,450 cash for the returned merchandise.
6. Delivered goods FOB destination in Event 4. Freight costs of $120 were paid in cash.
7. Collected the amount due on the account receivable within the discount period.
8. Took a physical count indicating that $15,500 of inventory was on hand at the end of the accounting period.

Required

a. Identify these events as asset source (AS), asset use (AU), asset exchange (AE), or claims exchange (CE).

b. Record each event in a statements model like the following one.

Event	Balance Sheet									Income Statement					Statement of Cash Flows
	Assets			=	Liab.	=		Equity		Rev.	−	Exp.	=	Net Inc.	
	Cash	+	Accts. Rec.	+	Mdse. Inv.	=	Accts. Pay.	+	Ret. Earn.						

c. Prepare a multistep income statement, a statement of changes in stockholders' equity, a balance sheet, and a statement of cash flows.

LO 3-5

Problem 3-27 *Using common size income statements to make comparisons*

The following income statements were drawn from the annual reports of Harper Sales Company.

	2014*	2015*
Net sales	$200,000	$250,000
Cost of goods sold	(140,000)	(170,000)
Gross margin	60,000	80,000
Less: Operating expense		
Selling and administrative expenses	(28,000)	(32,000)
Net income	$ 32,000	$ 48,000

*All dollar amounts are reported in thousands.

The president's message in the company's annual report stated that the company had implemented a strategy to increase market share by spending more on advertising. The president indicated that prices held steady and sales grew as expected. Write a memo indicating whether you agree with the president's statements. How has the strategy affected profitability? Support your answer by measuring growth in sales and selling expenses. Also prepare common size income statements and make appropriate references to the differences between 2014 and 2015.

Problem 3-28   *Comprehensive cycle problem: Periodic system (Appendix)*   LO 3-6

The following trial balance pertains to Cal's Grocery as of January 1, 2014:

Account Title	Beginning Balances
Cash	$ 52,000
Accounts receivable	8,000
Merchandise inventory	100,000
Accounts payable	8,000
Common stock	86,000
Retained earnings	66,000

The following events occurred in 2014. Assume that Cal's uses the periodic inventory method.

1. Purchased land for $40,000 cash.
2. Purchased merchandise on account for $252,000, terms 1/10, n/45.
3. Paid freight of $2,000 cash on merchandise purchased FOB shipping point.
4. Returned $7,200 of defective merchandise purchased in Event 2.
5. Sold merchandise for $172,000 cash.
6. Sold merchandise on account for $240,000, terms 2/10, n/30.
7. Paid cash within the discount period on accounts payable due on merchandise purchased in Event 2.
8. Paid $23,200 cash for selling expenses.
9. Collected $95,000 of the accounts receivable from Event 6 within the discount period.
10. Collected $62,000 of the accounts receivable but not within the discount period.
11. Paid $13,200 of other operating expenses.
12. A physical count indicated that $53,100 of inventory was on hand at the end of the accounting period.

Required

a. Record the above transactions in a horizontal statements model like the following one.

	Balance Sheet								Income Statement			
Event	**Assets**				**=**	**Equity**			**Rev. − Exp. = Net Inc.**			**Statement of Cash Flows**
	Cash +	Accts. Rec. +	Mdse. Inv. +	Land	=	Accts. Pay. +	Com. Stock +	Ret. Earn.				

b. Prepare a schedule of cost of goods sold and an income statement.

ANALYZE, THINK, COMMUNICATE

ATC 3-1   Business Application Case   *Understanding real world annual reports*

Use the Target Corporation's Form 10-K to answer the following questions related to Target's 2012 fiscal year (year ended February 2, 2013). Target's Form 10-K is available on the company's website or through the SEC's EDGAR database. Appendix A provides instructions for using the EDGAR database.

Required

a. What percentage of Target's *total revenues* end up as net earnings?
b. What percentage of Target's *sales* go to pay for the costs of the goods being sold?

c. What costs does Target include in its Cost of Sales account?

d. When does Target recognize revenue from the sale of gift cards?

ATC 3-2   Group Exercise   *Multistep income statement*

The following quarterly information is given for Raybon for the year ended 2014 (amounts shown are in millions).

	First Quarter	Second Quarter	Third Quarter	Fourth Quarter
Net Sales	$736.0	$717.4	$815.2	$620.1
Gross Margin	461.9	440.3	525.3	252.3
Net Income	37.1	24.6	38.6	31.4

Required

a. Divide the class into groups and organize the groups into four sections. Assign each section financial information for one of the quarters.

   (1) Each group should compute the cost of goods sold and operating expenses for the specific quarter assigned to its section and prepare a multistep income statement for the quarter.

   (2) Each group should compute the gross margin percentage and cost of goods sold percentage for its specific quarter.

   (3) Have a representative of each group put that quarter's sales, cost of goods sold percentage, and gross margin percentage on the board.

Class Discussion

b. Have the class discuss the change in each of these items from quarter to quarter and explain why the change might have occurred. Which was the best quarter and why?

ATC 3-3   Research Assignment   *Analyzing Amazon.com's income statement*

Complete the requirements below using the most recent financial statements available [20xx] on Amazon.com's corporate website. Obtain the statements on the Internet by following the steps below. (Be aware that the formatting of the company's website may have changed since these instructions were written.)

■ Go to www.amazon.com.

■ At the bottom of the screen, under "Get to Know Us," click on "Investor Relations."

■ Annual Reports and Proxies.

■ Click on "20xx Annual Report" (the most recent year).

Read the following sections of the annual report:

■ The income statement, which Amazon.com calls the "Consolidated Statement of Operations."

■ In the footnotes section, "Note 1—Description of Business and Accounting Policies," read the subsections titled "*Revenues*" and "*Cost of Sales.*"

Required

a. What percentage of Amazon's sales end up as net income?

b. What percentage of Amazon's sales go to pay for the costs of the goods being sold?

c. What specific criteria are necessary before Amazon will recognize a sale as having been completed and record the related revenue?

d. How does Amazon account for (report on its income statement) the shipping costs it incurs to ship goods to its customers?

ATC 3-4   Written Assignment, Critical Thinking   *Effect of sales returns on financial statements*

Bell Farm and Garden Equipment reported the following information for 2014:

Net Sales of Equipment	$2,450,567
Other Income	6,786
Cost of Goods Sold	1,425,990
Selling, General, and Administrative Expense	325,965
Net Operating Income	$ 705,398

Selected information from the balance sheet as of December 31, 2014, follows.

Cash and Marketable Securities	$113,545
Inventory	248,600
Accounts Receivable	82,462
Property, Plant, and Equipment—Net	335,890
Other Assets	5,410
Total Assets	$785,907

Assume that a major customer returned a large order to Bell on December 31, 2014. The amount of the sale had been $146,800 with a cost of sales of $94,623. The return was recorded in the books on January 1, 2015. The company president does not want to correct the books. He argues that it makes no difference as to whether the return is recorded in 2014 or 2015. Either way, the return has been duly recognized.

Required

a. Assume that you are the CFO for Bell Farm and Garden Equipment Co. Write a memo to the president explaining how omitting the entry on December 31, 2014, could cause the financial statements to be misleading to investors and creditors. Explain how omitting the return from the customer would affect net income and the balance sheet.

b. Why might the president want to record the return on January 1, 2015, instead of December 31, 2014?

CHAPTER 4

Internal Controls, Accounting for Cash, and Ethics

LEARNING OBJECTIVES

After you have mastered the material in this chapter, you will be able to:

LO 4-1   Identify the key elements of a strong system of internal control.

LO 4-2   Prepare a bank reconciliation.

LO 4-3   Discuss the role of ethics in the accounting profession.

LO 4-4   Describe the auditor's role in financial reporting.

 Video lectures and accompanying self-assessment quizzes are available for all learning objectives through McGraw-Hill Connect® Accounting.

CHAPTER OPENING

In the first three chapters, we covered the basics of the accounting system. By now you should understand how basic business events affect financial statements and how the accounting cycle works. Accounting is an elegant system that when implemented correctly provides meaningful information to investors and other stakeholders. However, without effective control, the accounting system can be manipulated in ways that may overstate business performance. This can lead investors to make bad decisions, which can result in huge losses when the true performance is revealed. This chapter discusses the importance of internal control systems. The chapter also discusses accounting for cash, an area where good internal controls are critical. The chapter concludes with a discussion on the importance of ethical conduct in the accounting profession.

The Curious Accountant

On December 11, 2008, Bernard Madoff was arrested on suspicion of having defrauded the clients of his investment company, Bernard L. Madoff Investments (BMI), of $50 billion. Later estimates would put the losses at over $60 billion. Although his clients believed the money they sent to BMI was being invested in the stock market, it was actually just being deposited into bank accounts.

Mr. Madoff was accused of operating the largest Ponzi scheme in history. Clients were sent monthly statements falsely showing that their investments were earning income and growing at a steady rate, even when the overall stock market was falling. When individual investors asked to withdraw their funds, they were simply given money that had been deposited by other investors.

This fraudulent system works as long as more new money is being deposited than is being withdrawn. Unfortunately for BMI, with the severe stock-market decline of 2008 too many clients got nervous and asked to withdraw their money, including the gains they believed they had earned over the years. At this point the Ponzi scheme failed.

How could such a pervasive fraud go undetected for so long? (Answer on page 142.)

KEY FEATURES OF INTERNAL CONTROL SYSTEMS

LO 4-1

Identify the key elements of a strong system of internal control.

During the early 2000s a number of accounting-related scandals cost investors billions. In 2001, Enron's share price went from $85 to $0.30 after it was revealed that the company had billions of dollars in losses that were not reported on the financial statements. Several months later, WorldCom reported an $11 billion accounting fraud, which included hundreds of millions in personal loans to then CEO, Bernie Ebbers.

The Enron and WorldCom accounting scandals had such devastating effects that they led Congress to pass the Sarbanes-Oxley Act of 2002 (SOX). SOX requires public companies to evaluate their *internal control* and to publish those findings with their SEC filings. **Internal control** is the process designed to ensure reliable financial reporting, effective and efficient operations, and compliance with applicable laws and regulations. Safeguarding assets against theft and unauthorized use, acquisition, or disposal is also part of internal control.

Section 404 of Sarbanes-Oxley requires a statement of management's responsibility for establishing and maintaining adequate internal control over financial reporting by public companies. This section includes an assessment of the controls and the identification of the framework used for the assessment. The framework established by The Committee of Sponsoring Organizations of the Treadway Commission (COSO) in 1992 is the de facto standard by which SOX compliance is judged. COSO's framework titled *Internal Control—An Integrated Framework* recognizes five interrelated components including:

1. *Control Environment.* The integrity and ethical values of the company, including its code of conduct, involvement of the board of directors, and other actions that set the tone of the organization.

2. *Risk Assessment.* Management's process of identifying potential risks that could result in misstated financial statements and developing actions to address those risks.

3. *Control Activities.* These are the activities usually thought of as "the internal controls." They include such things as segregation of duties, account reconciliations, and information processing controls that are designed to safeguard assets and enable an organization to timely prepare reliable financial statements.

4. *Information and Communication.* The internal and external reporting process, and includes an assessment of the technology environment.

5. *Monitoring.* Assessing the quality of a company's internal control over time and taking actions as necessary to ensure it continues to address the risks of the organization.

In 2004 COSO updated the framework to help entities design and implement effective enterprise-wide approaches to risk management. The updated document is titled *Enterprise Risk Management (ERM)—An Integrated Framework.* The ERM framework introduces an enterprise-wide approach to risk management as well as concepts such as risk appetite, risk tolerance, and portfolio view. While SOX applies only to U.S. public companies, the ERM framework has been adopted by both public and private organizations around the world.

The ERM framework does not replace the internal control framework. Instead, it incorporates the internal control framework within it. Accordingly, companies may decide to look to the ERM framework both to satisfy their internal control needs and to move toward a fuller risk management process.

While a detailed discussion of the COSO documents is beyond the scope of this text, the following overview of the more common *control activities* of the internal control framework is insightful.

Separation of Duties

The likelihood of fraud or theft is reduced if collusion is required to accomplish it. Clear **separation of duties** is frequently used as a deterrent to corruption. When duties are separated, the work of one employee can act as a check on the work of another employee. For example, a person selling seats to a movie may be tempted to steal money received from customers who enter the theater. This temptation is reduced if the person staffing the box office is required to issue tickets that a second employee collects as people enter the theater. If ticket stubs collected by the second employee are compared with the cash receipts from ticket sales, any cash shortages would become apparent. Furthermore, friends and relatives of the ticket agent could not easily enter the theater without paying. Theft or unauthorized entry would require collusion between the ticket agent and the usher who collects the tickets. Both individuals would have to be dishonest enough to steal, yet trustworthy enough to convince each other they would keep the embezzlement secret. Whenever possible, the functions of *authorization, recording,* and *custody of assets* should be performed by separate individuals.

Quality of Employees

A business is only as good as the people it employs. Cheap labor is not a bargain if the employees are incompetent. Employees should be properly trained. In fact, they should be trained to perform a variety of tasks. The ability of employees to substitute for one another prevents disruptions when co-workers are absent because of illnesses, vacations, or other commitments. The capacity to rotate jobs also relieves boredom and increases respect for the contributions of other employees. Every business should strive to maximize the productivity of every employee. Ongoing training programs are essential to a strong system of internal control.

Bonded Employees

The best way to ensure employee honesty is to hire individuals with *high levels of personal integrity.* Employers should screen job applicants using interviews, background checks, and recommendations from prior employers or educators. Even so, screening programs may fail to identify character weaknesses. Further, unusual circumstances may cause honest employees to go astray. Therefore, employees in positions of trust should be bonded. A **fidelity bond** provides insurance that protects a company from losses caused by employee dishonesty.

Required Absences

Employees should be required to take regular vacations and their duties should be rotated periodically. Employees may be able to cover up fraudulent activities if they are always present at work. Consider the case of a parking meter collection agent who covered the same route for several years with no vacation. When the agent became sick, a substitute collected more money each day than the regular reader usually reported. Management checked past records and found that the ill meter reader had been understating the cash receipts and pocketing the difference. If management had required vacations or rotated the routes, the embezzlement would have been discovered much earlier.

Procedures Manual

Appropriate accounting procedures should be documented in a **procedures manual.** The manual should be routinely updated. Periodic reviews should be conducted to ensure that employees are following the procedures outlined in the manual.

Authority and Responsibility

Employees are motivated by clear lines of authority and responsibility. They work harder when they have the authority to use their own judgment and they exercise reasonable caution when they are held responsible for their actions. Businesses should prepare an **authority manual** that establishes a definitive *chain of command.* The authority manual should guide both specific and general authorizations. **Specific authorizations** apply to specific positions within the organization. For example, investment decisions are authorized at the division level while hiring decisions are authorized at the departmental level. In contrast, **general authority** applies across different levels of management. For example, employees at all levels may be required to fly coach or to make purchases from specific vendors.

Prenumbered Documents

How would you know if a check were stolen from your check book? If you keep a record of your check numbers, the missing number would tip you off immediately. Businesses also use prenumbered checks to avoid the unauthorized use of their bank accounts. In fact, prenumbered forms are used for all important documents such as purchase orders, receiving reports, invoices, and checks. To reduce errors, prenumbered forms should be as simple and easy to use as possible. Also, the documents should allow for authorized signatures. For example, credit sales slips should be signed by the customer to clearly establish who made the purchase, reducing the likelihood of unauthorized transactions.

Physical Control

Employees walk away with billions of dollars of business assets each year. To limit losses, companies should establish adequate physical control over valuable assets. For example, inventory should be kept in a storeroom and not released without proper authorization. Serial numbers on equipment should be recorded along with the name of the individual who is responsible for the equipment. Unannounced physical counts should be conducted randomly to verify the presence of company-owned equipment. Certificates of deposit and marketable securities should be kept in fireproof vaults. Access to these vaults should be limited to authorized personnel. These procedures protect the documents from fire and limit access to only those individuals who have the appropriate security clearance to handle the documents.

In addition to safeguarding assets, there should be physical control over the accounting records. The accounting journals, ledgers, and supporting documents should be kept in a fireproof safe. Only personnel responsible for recording transactions in the journals should have access to them. With limited access, there is less chance that someone will change the records to conceal fraud or embezzlement.

Performance Evaluations

Because few people can evaluate their own performance objectively, internal controls should include independent verification of employee performance. For example, someone other than the person who has control over inventory should take a physical count of inventory. Internal and external audits serve as independent verification of performance. Auditors should evaluate the effectiveness of the internal control system as well as verify the accuracy of the accounting records. In addition, the external auditors attest to the company's use of generally accepted accounting principles in the financial statements.

Limitations

A system of internal controls is designed to prevent or detect errors and fraud. However, no control system is foolproof. Internal controls can be circumvented by collusion among employees. Two or more employees working together can hide embezzlement by covering for each other. For example, if an embezzler goes on vacation, fraud will not be reported by a replacement who is in collusion with the embezzler. No system can prevent all fraud. However, a good system of internal controls minimizes illegal or unethical activities by reducing temptation and increasing the likelihood of early detection.

✓ CHECK YOURSELF 4.1

What are nine features of an internal control system?

Answer

The nine features follow.

1. Separating duties so that fraud or theft requires collusion.
2. Hiring and training competent employees.

3. Bonding employees to recover losses through insurance.

4. Requiring employees to be absent from their jobs so that their replacements can discover errors or fraudulent activity that might have occurred.

5. Establishing proper procedures for processing transactions.

6. Establishing clear lines of authority and responsibility.

7. Using prenumbered documents.

8. Implementing physical controls such as locking cash in a safe.

9. Conducting performance evaluations through independent internal and external audits.

ACCOUNTING FOR CASH

For financial reporting purposes, **cash** generally includes currency and other items that are payable *on demand,* such as checks, money orders, bank drafts, and certain savings accounts. Savings accounts that impose substantial penalties for early withdrawal should be classified as *investments* rather than cash. Postdated checks or IOUs represent *receivables* and should not be included in cash. As illustrated in Exhibit 4.1, most companies combine currency and other payable on demand items in a single balance sheet account with varying titles.

Companies must maintain a sufficient amount of cash to pay employees, suppliers, and other creditors. When a company fails to pay its legal obligations, its creditors can force the company into bankruptcy. Even so, management should avoid accumulating more cash than is needed. The failure to invest excess cash in earning assets reduces profitability. Cash inflows and outflows must be managed to prevent a shortage or surplus of cash.

Controlling Cash

Controlling cash, more than any other asset, requires strict adherence to internal control procedures. Cash has universal appeal. A relatively small suitcase filled with high-denomination currency can represent significant value. Furthermore, the rightful owner of currency is difficult to prove. In most cases, possession constitutes ownership. As a result, cash is highly susceptible to theft and must be carefully protected. Cash is most susceptible to embezzlement when it is received or disbursed. The following controls should be employed to reduce the likelihood of theft.

Cash Receipts

A record of all cash collections should be prepared immediately upon receipt. The amount of cash on hand should be counted regularly. Missing amounts of money can be detected by comparing the actual cash on hand with the book balance. Employees who receive cash should give customers a copy of a written receipt. Customers usually review their receipts to ensure they have gotten credit for the amount paid and call any errors to the receipts clerk's attention. This not only reduces errors but also provides a control on the clerk's honesty. Cash receipts should be deposited in a bank on a timely basis. Cash collected late in the day should be deposited in a night depository. Every effort should be made to minimize the amount of cash on hand. Keeping large amounts of cash on hand not only increases the risk of loss from theft but also places employees in danger of being harmed by criminals who may be tempted to rob the company.

Cash Payments

To effectively control cash, a company should make all disbursements using checks, thereby providing a record of cash payments. All checks should be prenumbered, and unused checks should be locked up. Using prenumbered checks allows companies to easily identify lost or stolen checks by comparing the numbers on unused and canceled checks with the numbers used for legitimate disbursements.

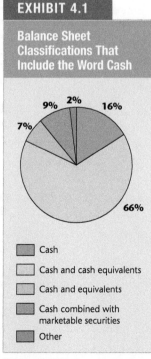

EXHIBIT 4.1

Balance Sheet Classifications That Include the Word Cash

- Cash
- Cash and cash equivalents
- Cash and equivalents
- Cash combined with marketable securities
- Other

Data Source: AICPA, *Accounting Trends and Techniques.*

REALITY BYTES

THE COST OF PROTECTING CASH

Could you afford to buy a safe like the one shown here? The vault is only one of many expensive security devices used by banks to safeguard cash. By using checking accounts, companies are able to avoid many of the costs associated with keeping cash safe. In addition to providing physical control, checking accounts enable companies to maintain a written audit trail of cash receipts and payments. Checking accounts represent the most widely used internal control device in modern society. It is difficult to imagine a business operating without the use of checking accounts.

The duties of approving disbursements, signing checks, and recording transactions should be separated. If one person is authorized to approve, sign, and record checks, he or she could falsify supporting documents, write an unauthorized check, and record a cover-up transaction in the accounting records. By separating these duties, the check signer reviews the documentation provided by the approving individual before signing the check. Likewise, the recording clerk reviews the work of both the approving person and the check signer when the disbursement is recorded in the accounting records. Thus writing unauthorized checks requires trilevel collusion.

Supporting documents with authorized approval signatures should be required when checks are presented to the check signer. For example, a warehouse receiving order should be matched with a purchase order before a check is approved to pay a bill from a supplier. Before payments are approved, invoice amounts should be checked and payees verified as valid vendors. Matching supporting documents with proper authorization discourages employees from creating phony documents for a disbursement to a friend or fictitious business. Also, the approval process serves as a check on the accuracy of the work of all employees involved.

Supporting documents should be marked *Paid* when the check is signed. If the documents are not indelibly marked, they could be retrieved from the files and resubmitted for a duplicate, unauthorized payment. A payables clerk could collude with the payee to split extra cash paid out by submitting the same supporting documents for a second payment.

All spoiled and voided checks should be defaced and retained. If defaced checks are not retained, an employee could steal a check and then claim that it was written incorrectly and thrown away. The clerk could then use the stolen check to make an unauthorized payment.

Checking Account Documents

The previous section explained the need for businesses to use checking accounts. A description of four main types of forms associated with a bank checking account follows.

Signature Card

A bank **signature card** shows the bank account number and the signatures of the people authorized to sign checks. The card is retained in the bank's files. If a bank employee is unfamiliar with the signature on a check, he or she can refer to the signature card to verify the signature before cashing the check.

Deposit Ticket

Each deposit of cash or checks is accompanied by a **deposit ticket,** which normally identifies the account number and the name of the account. The depositor lists the individual amounts of currency, coins, and checks, as well as the total deposited, on the deposit ticket.

Bank Check

A written check affects three parties: (1) the person or business writing the check (the *payer*); (2) the bank on which the check is drawn; and (3) the person or business to whom the check is payable (the *payee*). Companies often write **checks** using multicopy, prenumbered forms, with the name of the issuing business preprinted on the face of each check. A remittance notice is usually attached to the check forms. This portion of the form provides the issuer space to record what the check is for (e.g., what invoices are being paid), the amount being disbursed, and the date of payment. When signed by the person whose signature is on the signature card, the check authorizes the bank to transfer the face amount of the check from the payer's account to the payee.

Bank Statement

Periodically, the bank sends the depositor a **bank statement.** The bank statement is presented from the bank's point of view. Checking accounts are liabilities to a bank because the bank is obligated to pay back the money that customers have deposited in their accounts. Therefore, in the bank's accounting records a customer's checking account has a *credit* balance. As a result, **bank statement debit memos** describe transactions that reduce the customer's account balance (the bank's liability). **Bank statement credit memos** describe activities that increase the customer's account balance (the bank's liability). Since a checking account is an asset (cash) to the depositor, a *bank statement debit memo* requires a *credit entry* to the cash account on the depositor's books. Likewise, when a bank tells you that it has credited your account, you will debit your cash account in response.

Bank statements normally report (a) the balance of the account at the beginning of the period; (b) additions for customer deposits made during the period; (c) other additions described in credit memos (e.g., for interest earned); (d) subtractions for the payment of checks drawn on the account during the period; (e) other subtractions described in debit memos (e.g., for service charges); (f) a running balance of the account; and (g) the balance of the account at the end of the period. The sample bank statement in Exhibit 4.2 on the next page illustrates these items. Normally, the canceled checks or copies of them are enclosed with the bank statement.

RECONCILING THE BANK ACCOUNT

Usually the ending balance reported on the bank statement differs from the balance in the depositor's cash account as of the same date. The discrepancy is normally attributable to timing differences. For example, a depositor deducts the amount of a check from its cash account when it writes the check. However, the bank does not deduct the amount of the check from the depositor's account until the payee presents it for payment, which may be days, weeks, or even months after the check is written. As a result, the balance on the depositor's books is lower than the balance on the bank's books. Companies prepare a **bank reconciliation** to explain the differences between the cash balance reported on the bank statement and the cash balance recorded in the depositor's accounting records.

Prepare a bank reconciliation.

Determining True Cash Balance

A bank reconciliation normally begins with the cash balance reported by the bank which is called the **unadjusted bank balance.** The adjustments necessary to determine the amount of cash that the depositor actually owns as of the date of the bank statement are then added to and subtracted from the unadjusted bank balance. The final total is the **true cash balance.** The true cash balance is independently reached a second time by making adjustments to the **unadjusted book balance.** The bank account is

FIRST STATE BANK

of Frisco County

2121 Westbury Drive • Harrison, Nevada • 54269 - 0001

Green Shades Resorts, Inc

1439 Lazy Lane
Harrison, Nevada 54275 - 0023

Account Number
53-9872-3

Checking Account Summary	On This Date	Your Balance Was	Deposits Added	No. Deposits	Checks Paid	No. Checks
	8/31/2014	4,779.86	3,571.72	5	4,537.22	22
	Other Debits	Resulting in a Balance of			On This Date	Enclosures
	297.91	3,516.45			9/30/2014	29

Checks and Debits			Deposits and Credits	Date	Balance
15.82	24.85		600.25	9/3	5,339.44
249.08	497.00			9/5	4,593.36
42.53	124.61			9/7	4,426.22
79.87	859.38			9/8	3,486.97
685.00	742.59		711.43	9/9	2,770.81
25.75	38.98			9/12	2,706.08
36.45	59.91			9/14	2,609.72
	8.40 DM		940.00 CM	9/15	3,541.32
61.40			689.47	9/18	4,169.39
289.51 NS				9/19	3,879.88
71.59	82.00			9/21	3,726.29
312.87				9/24	3,413.42
25.00			630.57	9/27	4,018.99
227.00				9/28	3,791.99
95.06	180.48			9/30	3,516.45

LEGEND – NS Nonsufficient Funds • DM Debit Memo • CM Credit Memo

FIRST STATE BANK OF FRISCO COUNTY

reconciled when the true cash balance determined from the perspective of the unadjusted *bank* balance agrees with the true cash balance determined from the perspective of the unadjusted *book* balance. The procedures a company uses to determine the *true cash balance* from the two different perspectives are outlined here.

Adjustments to the Bank Balance

A typical format for determining the true cash balance beginning with the unadjusted bank balance is

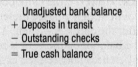

```
  Unadjusted bank balance
+ Deposits in transit
− Outstanding checks
= True cash balance
```

Deposits in transit. Companies frequently leave deposits in the bank's night depository or make them on the day following the receipt of cash. Such deposits are called **deposits in transit.** Because these deposits have been recorded in the depositor's accounting records but have not yet been added to the depositor's account by the bank, they must be added to the unadjusted bank balance.

Outstanding checks. These are disbursements that have been properly recorded as cash deductions on the depositor's books. However, the bank has not deducted the amounts from the depositor's bank account because the checks have not yet been presented by the payee to the bank for payment; that is, the checks have not cleared the bank. **Outstanding checks** must be subtracted from the unadjusted bank balance to determine the true cash balance.

Adjustments to the Book Balance

A typical format for determining the true cash balance beginning with the unadjusted book balance is as follows.

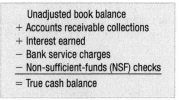

Unadjusted book balance
+ Accounts receivable collections
+ Interest earned
− Bank service charges
− Non-sufficient-funds (NSF) checks
= True cash balance

Accounts receivable collections. To collect cash as quickly as possible, many companies have their customers send payments directly to the bank. The bank adds the collection directly to the depositor's account and notifies the depositor about the collection through a credit memo that is included on the bank statement. The depositor adds the amount of the cash collections to the unadjusted book balance in the process of determining the true cash balance.

Interest earned. Banks pay interest on certain checking accounts. The amount of the interest is added directly to the depositor's bank account. The bank notifies the depositor about the interest through a credit memo that is included on the bank statement. The depositor adds the amount of the interest revenue to the unadjusted book balance in the process of determining the true cash balance.

Service charges. Banks frequently charge depositors fees for services performed. They may also charge a penalty if the depositor fails to maintain a specified minimum cash balance throughout the period. Banks deduct such fees and penalties directly from the depositor's account and advise the depositor of the deduction through a debit memo that is included on the bank statement. The depositor deducts such **service charges** from the unadjusted book balance to determine the true cash balance.

Non-sufficient-funds (NSF) checks. **NSF checks** are checks that a company obtains from its customers and deposits in its checking account. However, when the checks are submitted to the customers' banks for payment, the banks refuse payment because there is insufficient money in the customers' accounts. When such checks are returned, the amounts of the checks are deducted from the company's bank account balance. The company is advised of NSF checks through debit memos that appear on the bank statement. The depositor deducts the amounts of the NSF checks from the unadjusted book balance in the process of determining the true cash balance.

Correction of Errors

In the course of reconciling the bank statement with the cash account, the depositor may discover errors in the bank's records, the depositor's records, or both. If an error is found on the bank statement, an adjustment for it is made to the unadjusted bank balance to determine the true cash balance, and the bank should be notified immediately to correct its records. Errors made by the depositor require adjustments to the book balance to arrive at the true cash balance.

Certified Checks

A **certified check** is guaranteed for payment by a bank. Whereas a regular check is deducted from the customer's account when it is presented for payment, a certified check is deducted from the customer's account when the bank certifies that the check is good.

Certified checks, therefore, *have* been deducted by the bank in determining the unadjusted bank balance, whether they have cleared the bank or remain outstanding as of the date of the bank statement. Since certified checks are deducted both from bank and depositor records immediately, they do not cause differences between the depositor and bank balances. As a result, certified checks are not included in a bank reconciliation.

Illustrating a Bank Reconciliation

The following example illustrates preparing the bank reconciliation for Green Shades Resorts, Inc. (GSRI). The bank statement for GSRI is displayed in Exhibit 4.2. Exhibit 4.3 illustrates the completed bank reconciliation. The items on the reconciliation are described below.

Adjustments to the Bank Balance

As of September 30, 2014, the bank statement showed an unadjusted balance of $3,516.45. A review of the bank statement disclosed three adjustments that had to be made to the unadjusted bank balance to determine GSRI's true cash balance.

1. Comparing the deposits on the bank statement with deposits recorded in GSRI's accounting records indicated there was $724.11 of deposits in transit.

2. An examination of the returned checks disclosed that the bank had erroneously deducted a $25 check written by Green Valley Resorts from GSRI's bank account. This amount must be added back to the unadjusted bank balance to determine the true cash balance.

3. The checks returned with the bank statement were sorted and compared to the cash records. Three checks with amounts totaling $235.25 were outstanding.

After these adjustment are made GSRI's true cash balance is determined to be $4,030.31.

EXHIBIT 4.3

GREEN SHADES RESORTS, INC.
Bank Reconciliation
September 30, 2014

Unadjusted bank balance, September 30, 2014		$3,516.45
Add: Deposits in transit		724.11
Bank error: Check drawn on Green Valley Resorts charged to GSRI		25.00
Less: Outstanding checks		

Check No.	Date	Amount
639	Sept. 18	$ 13.75
646	Sept. 20	29.00
672	Sept. 27	192.50

Total		(235.25)
True cash balance, September 30, 2014		$4,030.31
Unadjusted book balance, September 30, 2014		$3,361.22
Add: Receivable collected by bank		940.00
Error made by accountant (Check no. 633 recorded as $63.45 instead of $36.45)		27.00
Less: Bank service charges		(8.40)
NSF check		(289.51)
True cash balance, September 30, 2014		$4,030.31

Adjustments to the Book Balance

As indicated in Exhibit 4.3, GSRI's unadjusted book balance as of September 30, 2014, was $3,361.22. This balance differs from GSRI's true cash balance because of four unrecorded accounting events:

1. The bank collected a $940 account receivable for GSRI.
2. GSRI's accountant made a $27 recording error.
3. The bank charged GSRI an $8.40 service fee.
4. GSRI had deposited a $289.51 check from a customer who did not have sufficient funds to cover the check.

Two of these four adjustments increase the unadjusted cash balance. The other two decrease the unadjusted cash balance. After the adjustments have been recorded, the cash account reflects the true cash balance of $4,030.31 ($3,361.22 unadjusted cash balance + $940.00 receivable collection + $27.00 recording error − $8.40 service charge − $289.51 NSF check). Because the true balance determined from the perspective of the bank statement agrees with the true balance determined from the perspective of GSRI's books, the bank statement has been successfully reconciled with the accounting records.

Updating GSRI's Accounting Records

Each of the adjustments to the book balance must be recorded in GSRI's financial records. The effects of each adjustment on the financial statements are as follows.

ADJUSTMENT 1 *Recording the $940 receivable collection increases cash and reduces accounts receivable.*

The event is an asset exchange transaction. The effect of the collection on GSRI's financial statements is

Assets			=	Liab.	+	Equity	Rev.	−	Exp.	=	Net Inc.	Cash Flow
Cash	+	Accts. Rec.										
940	+	(940)	=	NA	+	NA	NA	−	NA	=	NA	940 OA

ADJUSTMENT 2 *Assume the $27 recording error occurred because GSRI's accountant accidentally transposed two numbers when recording check no. 633 for utilities expense.*

The check was written to pay utilities expense of $36.45 but was recorded as a $63.45 disbursement. Since cash payments are overstated by $27.00 ($63.45 − $36.45), this amount must be added back to GSRI's cash balance and deducted from the utilities expense account, which increases net income. The effects on the financial statements are

Assets	=	Liab.	+	Equity	Rev.	−	Exp.	=	Net Inc.	Cash Flow
Cash	=			Ret. Earn.						
27	=	NA	+	27	NA	−	(27)	=	27	27 OA

ADJUSTMENT 3   *The $8.40 service charge is an expense that reduces assets, stockholders' equity, net income, and cash.*

The effects are

Assets	=	Liab.	+	Equity	Rev.	−	Exp.	=	Net Inc.	Cash Flow
Cash	=			Ret. Earn.						
(8.40)	=	NA	+	(8.40)	NA	−	8.40	=	(8.40)	(8.40) OA

ADJUSTMENT 4   *The $289.51 NSF check reduces GSRI's cash balance.*

When it originally accepted the customer's check, GSRI increased its cash account. Because there is not enough money in the customer's bank account to pay the check, GSRI didn't actually receive cash so GSRI must reduce its cash account. GSRI will still try to collect the money from the customer. In the meantime, it will show the amount of the NSF check as an account receivable. The adjusting entry to record the NSF check is an asset exchange transaction. Cash decreases and accounts receivable increases. The effect on GSRI's financial statements is

Assets			=	Liab.	+	Equity	Rev.	−	Exp.	=	Net Inc.	Cash Flow
Cash	+	Accts. Rec.										
(289.51)	+	289.51	=	NA	+	NA	NA	−	NA	=	NA	(289.51) OA

Answers to The Curious Accountant

As this chapter explains, separation of duties is one of the primary features of a good system of internal controls. However, separation of duties is not designed to detect fraud at the very top level of management. Mr. Madoff ran BMI with almost complete control; he had no boss.

Even with a good system of internal controls, there is always some level of trust required in business. Mr. Madoff had an excellent reputation in the investment community. He had even been the president of the NASDAQ. His investors trusted him and assumed they could depend on his independent auditor to detect any major problems with the way BMI was investing, or not investing, their money.

On March 12, 2009, the 70-year-old Mr. Madoff pled guilty to 11 felony charges. He entered his guilty pleas without the benefit of a plea bargain, and will spend the remainder of his life in prison. In 2012, Peter Madoff, Bernard's 67-year-old brother, pled guilty to several crimes related to the scandal, including falsifying documents. In December 2012, he was sentenced to 10 years in prison.

Federal prosecutors accused BMI's auditor, David Friehling, with improperly auditing BMI's books. On March 18, 2009, he also was arrested and charged with falsely certifying BMI's financial statements. He pled guilty to several charges related to the fraud and is cooperating with federal prosecutors. His sentencing has been scheduled and postponed several times pending the outcome of his cooperation.

Prison terms and financial fines are not the only price people pay as a result of their fraud. On Saturday, December 11, 2010, exactly two years after Bernard Madoff's arrest, his oldest son committed suicide. His death was attributed to personal problems related to his father's scandal. In November of 2012, the 23-year-old son of David Friehling also committed suicide.

☑ CHECK YOURSELF 4.2

The following information was drawn from Reliance Company's October bank statement. The unadjusted bank balance on October 31 was $2,300. The statement showed that the bank had collected a $200 account receivable for Reliance. The statement also included $20 of bank service charges for October and a $100 check payable to Reliance that was returned NSF. A comparison of the bank statement with company accounting records indicates that there was a $500 deposit in transit and $1,800 of checks outstanding at the end of the month. Based on this information, determine the true cash balance on October 31.

Answer   Since the unadjusted book balance is not given, start with the unadjusted bank balance to determine the true cash balance. The collection of the receivable, the bank service charges, and the NSF check are already recognized in the unadjusted bank balance, so these items are not used to determine the true cash balance. Determine the true cash balance by adding the deposit in transit to and subtracting the outstanding checks from the unadjusted bank balance. The true cash balance is $1,000 ($2,300 unadjusted bank balance + $500 deposit in transit − $1,800 outstanding checks).

IMPORTANCE OF ETHICS

The chapter began with a discussion of the importance of internal control systems in preventing accounting scandals. After the Enron and WorldCom scandals and the passage of the Sarbanes-Oxley Act, much more attention has been paid to establishing effective internal control systems. However, despite this increase in legislation and awareness, accounting scandals continue to occur. In 2008, Lehman Brothers declared bankruptcy after it was discovered that the company had kept more than $50 billion in loans off the balance sheet by classifying them as sales. Several months later, Bernie Madoff used a Ponzi scheme to leave his investors with more than $21.2 billion in cash losses. These examples illustrate that legislation alone will not prevent accounting scandals. To prevent a scandal it is necessary to develop a culture that fosters and promotes ethical conduct.

LO 4-3

Discuss the role of ethics in the accounting profession.

The accountant's role in society requires trust and credibility. Accounting information is worthless if the accountant is not trustworthy. Similarly, tax and consulting advice is useless if it comes from an incompetent person. The high ethical standards required by the profession state "a certified public accountant assumes an obligation of self-discipline above and beyond requirements of laws and regulations." The **American Institute of Certified Public Accountants** requires its members to comply with the **Code of Professional Conduct.** Section I of the Code includes six articles that are summarized in Exhibit 4.4. The importance of ethical conduct is universally recognized across a broad spectrum of accounting organizations. The Institute of Management Accountants requires its members to follow a set of Standards of Ethical Conduct. The Institute of Internal Auditors also requires its members to subscribe to the organization's Code of Ethics.

Common Features of Criminal and Ethical Misconduct

Unfortunately, it takes more than a code of conduct to stop fraud. People frequently engage in activities that they know are unethical or even criminal. The auditing profession has identified three elements that are typically present when fraud occurs.

1. The availability of an opportunity.
2. The existence of some form of pressure leading to an incentive.
3. The capacity to rationalize.

EXHIBIT 4.4

Articles of AICPA Code of Professional Conduct

Article I Responsibilities
In carrying out their responsibilities as professionals, members should exercise sensitive professional and moral judgments in all their activities.

Article II The Public Interest
Members should accept the obligation to act in a way that will serve the public interest, honor the public trust, and demonstrate commitment to professionalism.

Article III Integrity
To maintain and broaden public confidence, members should perform all professional responsibilities with the highest sense of integrity.

Article IV Objectivity and Independence
A member should maintain objectivity and be free of conflicts of interest in discharging professional responsibilities. A member in public practice should be independent in fact and appearance when providing auditing and other attestation services.

Article V Due Care
A member should observe the profession's technical and ethical standards, strive continually to improve competence and the quality of services, and discharge professional responsibility to the best of the member's ability.

Article VI Scope and Nature of Services
A member in public practice should observe the principles of the Code of Professional Conduct in determining the scope and nature of services to be provided.

The three elements are frequently arranged in the shape of a triangle as shown in Exhibit 4.5.

Opportunity is shown at the head to the triangle because without opportunity fraud could not exist. The most effective way to reduce opportunities for ethical or criminal misconduct is to implement an effective set of internal controls. *Internal controls* are policies and procedures that a business implements to reduce opportunities

EXHIBIT 4.5

The Fraud Triangle

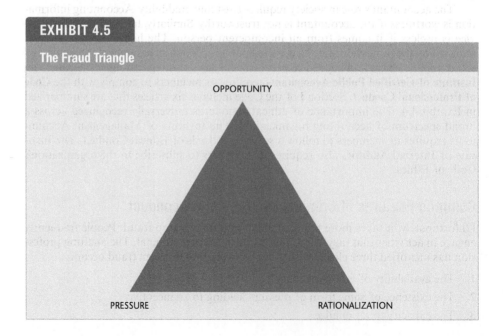

for fraud and to assure that its objectives will be accomplished. Specific controls are tailored to meet the individual needs of particular businesses. For example, banks use elaborate vaults to protect cash and safety deposit boxes, but universities have little use for this type of equipment. Even so, many of the same procedures are used by a wide variety of businesses. The internal control policies and procedures that have gained widespread acceptance are discussed in a subsequent chapter.

Only a few employees turn to the dark side even when internal control is weak and opportunities abound. So, what causes one person to commit fraud and another to remain honest? The second element of the fraud triangle recognizes **pressure** as a key ingredient of misconduct. A manager who is told "either make the numbers or you are fired" is more likely to cheat than one who is told to "tell it like it is." Pressure can come from a variety of sources.

- Personal vices such as drug addiction, gambling, and promiscuity.
- Intimidation from superiors.
- Personal debt from credit cards, consumer and mortgage loans, or poor investments.
- Family expectations to provide a standard of living that is beyond one's capabilities.
- Business failure caused by poor decision making or temporary factors such as a poor economy.
- Loyalty or trying to be agreeable.

The third and final element of the fraud triangle is **rationalization.** Few individuals think of themselves as evil. They develop rationalizations to justify their misconduct. Common rationalizations include the following.

- Everybody does it.
- They are not paying me enough. I'm only taking what I deserve.
- I'm only borrowing the money. I'll pay it back.
- The company can afford it. Look what they are paying the officers.
- I'm taking what my family needs to live like everyone else.

Most people are able to resist pressure and the tendency to rationalize ethical or legal misconduct. However, some people will yield to temptation. What can accountants do to protect themselves and their companies from unscrupulous characters? The answer lies in personal integrity. The best indicator of personal integrity is past performance. Accordingly, companies must exercise due care in performing appropriate background investigations before hiring people to fill positions of trust.

Ethical misconduct is a serious offense in the accounting profession. A single mistake can destroy an accounting career. If you commit a white-collar crime, you normally lose the opportunity to hold a white-collar job. Second chances are rarely granted; it is extremely important that you learn how to recognize and avoid the common features of ethical misconduct. To help you prepare for the real-world situations you are likely to encounter, we include ethical dilemmas in the end-of-chapter materials. When working with these dilemmas, try to identify the (1) opportunity, (2) pressure, and (3) rationalization associated with the particular ethical situation described. If you are not an ethical person, accounting is not the career for you.

ROLE OF THE INDEPENDENT AUDITOR

As previously explained, financial statements are prepared in accordance with certain rules called *generally accepted accounting principles (GAAP).* Thus, when General Electric publishes its financial statements, it is saying, "here are our financial statements prepared according to GAAP." How can a financial analyst know that a company really did follow GAAP? Analysts and other statement users rely on **audits** conducted by **certified public accountants (CPAs).**

LO 4-4

Describe the auditor's role in financial reporting.

The primary roles of an independent auditor (CPA) are summarized below:

1. Conducts a financial audit (a detailed examination of a company's financial statements and underlying accounting records).

2. Assumes both legal and professional responsibilities to the public as well as to the company paying the auditor.

3. Determines if financial statements are *materially* correct rather than *absolutely* correct.

4. Presents conclusions in an audit report that includes an opinion as to whether the statements are prepared in conformity with GAAP. In rare cases, the auditor issues a disclaimer.

5. Maintains professional confidentiality of client records. The auditor is not, however, exempt from legal obligations such as testifying in court.

The Financial Statement Audit

What is an audit? There are several types of audits. The type most relevant to this course is a **financial statement audit,** often referred to as simply a financial audit. The financial audit is a detailed examination of a company's financial statements and the documents that support those statements. It also tests the reliability of the accounting system used to produce the financial reports. A financial audit is conducted by an **independent auditor.**

The term *independent auditor* typically refers to a *firm* of certified public accountants. CPAs are licensed by state governments to provide services to the public. They are to be as independent of the companies they audit as is reasonably possible. To help assure independence, CPAs may not be employees of the companies they audit. Further, they cannot have investments in the companies they audit. Although CPAs are paid by the companies they audit, the audit fee may not be based on the outcome of the audit.

Although the independent auditors are chosen by, paid by, and can be fired by their client companies, the auditors are primarily responsible to *the public.* In fact, auditors have a legal responsibility to those members of the public who have a financial interest in the company being audited. If investors in a company lose money, they sometimes sue the independent auditors in an attempt to recover their losses, especially if the losses were related to financial failure. A lawsuit against auditors will succeed only if the auditors failed in their professional responsibilities when conducting the audit. Auditors are not responsible for the success or failure of a company. Instead, they are responsible for the appropriate reporting of that success or failure. While recent debacles such as Bernard Madoff Investments produce spectacular headlines, auditors are actually not sued very often, considering the number of audits they perform.

Materiality and Financial Audits

Auditors do not guarantee that financial statements are absolutely correct—only that they are free from *material* misstatements. This is where things get a little fuzzy. What is a *material misstatement*? The concept of materiality is very subjective. If ExxonMobil inadvertently overstated its sales by $1 million, would this be material? In 2012, ExxonMobil had approximately $453 billion of sales! A $1 million error in computing sales at ExxonMobil is like a $1 error in computing the pay of a person who makes $453,000 per year—not material at all! An error, or other reporting problem, is **material** if knowing about it would influence the decisions of an *average prudent investor.*

Financial audits are not directed toward the discovery of fraud. Auditors are, however, responsible for providing *reasonable assurance* that statements are free from material misstatements, whether caused by errors or fraud. Also, auditors are responsible for evaluating whether internal control procedures are in place to help prevent material misstatements due to fraud. If fraud is widespread in a company, normal audit procedures should detect it.

Accounting majors take at least one and often two or more courses in auditing to understand how to conduct an audit. An explanation of auditing techniques is beyond the scope of this course, but at least be aware that auditors do not review how the company accounted for every transaction. Along with other methods, auditors use statistics to choose representative samples of transactions to examine.

Types of Audit Opinions

Once an audit is complete, the auditors present their conclusions in a report that includes an *audit opinion*. There are three basic types of audit opinions.

An **unqualified opinion,** despite its negative-sounding name, is the most favorable opinion auditors can express. It means the auditor believes the financial statements are in compliance with GAAP without qualification, reservation, or exception. Most audits result in unqualified opinions because companies correct any reporting deficiencies the auditors find before the financial statements are released.

The most negative report an auditor can issue is an **adverse opinion.** An adverse opinion means that one or more departures from GAAP are so material that the financial statements do not present a fair picture of the company's status. The auditor's report explains the unacceptable accounting practice(s) that resulted in the adverse opinion being issued. Adverse opinions are very rare because public companies are required by law to follow GAAP.

A **qualified opinion** falls between an unqualified and an adverse opinion. A qualified opinion means that for the most part, the company's financial statements are in compliance with GAAP, but the auditors have reservations about something in the statements. The auditors' report explains why the opinion is qualified. A qualified opinion usually does not imply a serious accounting problem, but users should read the auditors' report and draw their own conclusions.

If an auditor is unable to perform the audit procedures necessary to determine whether the statements are prepared in accordance with GAAP, the auditor cannot issue an opinion on the financial statements. Instead, the auditor issues a **disclaimer of opinion.** A disclaimer means that the auditor is unable to obtain enough information to confirm compliance with GAAP.

Regardless of the type of report they issue, auditors are only expressing their judgment about whether the financial statements present a fair picture of a company. They do not provide opinions regarding the investment quality of a company.

The ultimate responsibility for financial statements rests with the executives of the reporting company. Just like auditors, managers can be sued by investors who believe they lost money due to improper financial reporting. This is one reason all business persons should understand accounting fundamentals.

Confidentiality

The **confidentiality** rules in the AICPA's code of ethics for CPAs prohibits auditors from *voluntarily disclosing* information they have acquired as a result of their accountant-client relationships. However, accountants may be required to testify in a court of law. In general, federal law does not recognize an accountant-client privilege as it does with attorneys and clergy. Some federal courts have taken exception to this position, especially as it applies to tax cases. State law varies with respect to accountant-client privilege. Furthermore, if auditors terminate a client relationship because of ethical or legal disagreements and they are subsequently contacted by a successor auditor, they may be required to inform the successor of the reasons for the termination. In addition, auditors must consider the particular circumstances of a case when assessing the appropriateness of disclosing confidential information. Given the diverse legal positions governing accountant-client confidentiality, auditors should seek legal counsel prior to disclosing any information obtained in an accountant-client relationship.

To illustrate, assume that Joe Smith, CPA, discovers that his client Jane Doe is misrepresenting information reported in her financial statements. Smith tries to convince Doe to correct the misrepresentations, but she refuses to do so. Smith is required by the code of ethics to terminate his relationship with Doe. However, Smith is not permitted to disclose Doe's dishonest reporting practices unless he is called on to testify in a legal hearing or to respond to an inquiry by Doe's successor accountant.

With respect to the discovery of significant fraud, the auditor is required to inform management at least one level above the position of the employee who is engaged in the fraud and to notify the board of directors of the company. Suppose that Joe Smith, CPA, discovers that Jane Doe, employee of Western Company, is embezzling money from Western. Smith is required to inform Doe's supervisor and to notify Western's board of directors. However, Smith is prohibited from publicly disclosing the fraud.

<< A Look Back

The policies and procedures used to provide reasonable assurance that the objectives of an enterprise will be accomplished are called *internal controls*. While the mechanics of internal control systems vary from company to company, the more prevalent features include the following.

1. *Separation of duties.* Whenever possible, the functions of authorization, recording, and custody should be exercised by different individuals.

2. *Quality of employees.* Employees should be qualified to competently perform the duties that are assigned to them. Companies must establish hiring practices to screen out unqualified candidates. Furthermore, procedures should be established to ensure that employees receive appropriate training to maintain their competence.

3. *Bonded employees.* Employees in sensitive positions should be covered by a fidelity bond that provides insurance to reimburse losses due to illegal actions committed by employees.

4. *Required absences.* Employees should be required to take extended absences from their jobs so that they are not always present to hide unscrupulous or illegal activities.

5. *Procedures manual.* To promote compliance, the procedures for processing transactions should be clearly described in a manual.

6. *Authority and responsibility.* To motivate employees and promote effective control, clear lines of authority and responsibility should be established.

7. *Prenumbered documents.* Prenumbered documents minimize the likelihood of missing or duplicate documents. Prenumbered forms should be used for all important documents such as purchase orders, receiving reports, invoices, and checks.

8. *Physical control.* Locks, fences, security personnel, and other physical devices should be employed to safeguard assets.

9. *Performance evaluations.* Because few people can evaluate their own performance objectively, independent performance evaluations should be performed. Substandard performance will likely persist unless employees are encouraged to take corrective action.

Because cash is such an important business asset and because it is tempting to steal, much of the discussion of internal controls in this chapter focused on cash controls. Special procedures should be employed to control the receipts and payments of cash. One of the most common control policies is to use *checking accounts* for all payments except petty cash disbursements.

A *bank reconciliation* should be prepared each month to explain differences between the bank statement and a company's internal accounting records. A common reconciliation format determines the true cash balance based on both bank and book records. Items that typically appear on a bank reconciliation include the following:

Unadjusted bank balance	xxx	Unadjusted book balance	xxx
Add		Add	
Deposits in transit	xxx	Interest revenue	xxx
		Collection of receivables	xxx
Subtract		Subtract	
Outstanding checks	xxx	Bank service charges	xxx
		NSF checks	xxx
True cash balance	xxx	True cash balance	xxx

Agreement of the two true cash balances provides evidence that accounting for cash transactions has been accurate.

The chapter discussed the importance of ethics in the accounting profession. The *American Institute of Public Accountants* requires all of its members to comply with the *Code of Professional Conduct*. Situations where *opportunity, pressure,* and *rationalization* exist can lead employees to conduct unethical acts, which, in cases like Enron, have destroyed the organization. Finally, the chapter discussed the auditor's role in financial reporting, including the materiality concept and the types of audit opinions that may be issued.

A Look Forward >>

The next chapter focuses on more specific issues related to accounts receivables and inventory. Accounting for receivables and payables was introduced in Chapter 2, using relatively simple illustrations. For example, we assumed that customers who purchased services on account always paid their bills. In real business practice, some customers do not pay their bills. Among other topics, Chapter 5 examines how companies account for uncollectible accounts receivable.

Accounting for inventory was discussed in Chapter 3. However, we assumed that all inventory items were purchased at the same price. This is unrealistic given that the price of goods is constantly changing. Chapter 5 discusses how to account for inventory items that are purchased at different times and different prices.

Video lectures and accompanying self-assessment quizzes are available for all learning objectives through McGraw-Hill *Connect®* Accounting.

SELF-STUDY REVIEW PROBLEM

The following information pertains to Terry's Pest Control Company (TPCC) for July:

1. The unadjusted bank balance at July 31 was $870.
2. The bank statement included the following items:
   (a) A $60 credit memo for interest earned by TPCC.
   (b) A $200 NSF check made payable to TPCC.
   (c) A $110 debit memo for bank service charges.
3. The unadjusted book balance at July 31 was $1,400.

4. A comparison of the bank statement with company accounting records disclosed the following:

(a) A $400 deposit in transit at July 31.

(b) Outstanding checks totaling $120 at the end of the month.

Required

Prepare a bank reconciliation.

Solution

TERRY'S PEST CONTROL COMPANY
Bank Reconciliation
July 31

Unadjusted bank balance	$ 870
Add: Deposits in transit	400
Less: Outstanding checks	(120)
True cash balance	$1,150
Unadjusted book balance	$1,400
Add: Interest revenue	60
Less: NSF check	(200)
Less: Bank service charges	(110)
True cash balance	$1,150

KEY TERMS

Adverse opinion 147	Cash 135	Financial statement audit 146	Qualified opinion 147
American Institute of Certified Public Accountants 143	Certified check 139 Certified public accountants (CPAs) 145	General authority 133 Independent auditor 146	Rationalization 145 Separation of duties 132 Service charges 139
Audits 145	Checks 137	Internal controls 132	Signature card 136
Authority manual 133	Code of Professional	Material 146	Specific authorizations 133
Bank reconciliation 137	Conduct 143	Non-sufficient-funds (NSF)	True cash balance 137
Bank statement 137	Confidentiality 147	checks 139	Unadjusted bank
Bank statement credit memo 137	Deposits in transit 138 Deposit ticket 137	Opportunity 144 Outstanding checks 139	balance 137 Unadjusted book
Bank statement debit memo 137	Disclaimer of opinion 147 Fidelity bond 133	Pressure 145 Procedures manual 133	balance 137 Unqualified opinion 147

QUESTIONS

1. What motivated Congress to pass the Sarbanes-Oxley Act (SOX) of 2002?

2. Define the term *internal control*.

3. Explain the relationship between SOX and COSO.

4. Name and briefly define the five components of COSO's internal control framework.

5. Explain how COSO's *Enterprise Risk Management—An Integrated Framework* project relates to COSO's *Internal Control—An Integrated Framework* project.

6. List several control activities of an effective internal control system.

7. What is meant by *separation of duties*? Give an illustration.

8. What are the attributes of a high-quality employee?

9. What is a fidelity bond? Explain its purpose.

10. Why is it important that every employee periodically take a leave of absence or vacation?

11. What are the purpose and importance of a procedures manual?

12. What is the difference between specific and general authorizations?

13. Why should documents (checks, invoices, receipts) be prenumbered?

14. What procedures are important in the physical

control of assets and accounting records?

15. What is the purpose of independent verification of performance?

16. What items are considered cash?

17. Why is cash more susceptible to theft or embezzlement than other assets?

18. Giving written copies of receipts to customers can help prevent what type of illegal acts?

19. What procedures can help to protect cash receipts?

20. What procedures can help protect cash disbursements?

21. What effect does a debit memo in a bank statement have on the Cash account? What effect does a credit memo in a bank statement have on the Cash account?

22. What information is normally included in a bank statement?

23. Why might a bank statement reflect a balance that is larger than the balance recorded in the depositor's books? What could cause the bank balance to be smaller than the book balance?

24. What is the purpose of a bank reconciliation?

25. What is an outstanding check?

26. What is a deposit in transit?

27. What is a certified check?

28. How is an NSF check accounted for in the accounting records?

29. Name and comment on the three elements of the fraud triangle.

30. What are the six articles of ethical conduct set out under section I of the AICPA's Code of Professional Conduct?

MULTIPLE-CHOICE QUESTIONS

Multiple-choice questions are provided on the text website at www.mhhe.com/edmondssurvey4e.

EXERCISES

connect |ACCOUNTING All applicable Exercises are available with McGraw-Hill's *Connect® Accounting.*

Exercise 4-1 *SOX and COSO's internal control frameworks* LO 4-1

Required

a. Explain what the acronym SOX refers to.
b. Define the acronym COSO and explain how it relates to SOX.
c. Name and briefly define the five components of COSO's internal control framework.
d. Define the acronym ERM and explain how it relates to COSO's internal control framework.

Exercise 4-2 *Control activities of a strong internal control system* LO 4-1

Required

List and describe nine control activities of a strong internal control system discussed in this chapter.

Exercise 4-3 *Internal controls for small businesses* LO 4-1

Dick Haney is opening a new business that will sell sporting goods. It will initially be a small operation, and he is concerned about the security of his assets. He will not be able to be at the business all of the time and will have to rely on his employees and internal control procedures to ensure that transactions are properly accounted for and assets are safeguarded. He will have a store manager and two other employees who will be sales personnel and stock personnel and who will also perform any other duties necessary. Dick will be in the business on a regular basis. He has come to you for advice.

Required

Write a memo to Dick outlining the procedures that he should implement to ensure that his store assets are protected and that the financial transactions are properly recorded.

Exercise 4-4 *Internal controls for cash* LO 4-1

Required

List and discuss effective internal control procedures that apply to cash.

LO 4-1

Exercise 4-5 *Internal controls to prevent theft*

Rhonda Cox worked as the parts manager for State Line Automobiles, a local automobile dealership. Rhonda was very dedicated and never missed a day of work. Since State Line was a small operation, she was the only employee in the parts department. Her duties consisted of ordering parts for stock and as needed for repairs, receiving the parts and checking them in, distributing them as needed to the shop or to customers for purchase, and keeping track of and taking the year-end inventory of parts. State Line decided to expand and needed to secure additional financing. The local bank agreed to a loan contingent on an audit of the dealership. One requirement of the audit was to oversee the inventory count of both automobiles and parts on hand. Rhonda was clearly nervous, explaining that she had just inventoried all parts in the parts department. She supplied the auditors with a detailed list. The inventory showed parts on hand worth $225,000. The auditors decided they needed to verify a substantial part of the inventory. When the auditors began their counts, a pattern began to develop. Each type of part seemed to be one or two items short when the actual count was taken. This raised more concern. Although Rhonda assured the auditors the parts were just misplaced, the auditors continued the count. After completing the count of parts on hand, the auditors could document only $155,000 of actual parts. Suddenly, Rhonda quit her job and moved to another state.

Required

a. What do you suppose caused the discrepancy between the actual count and the count that Rhonda had supplied?

b. What procedures could be put into place to prevent this type of problem?

LO 4-1

Exercise 4-6 *Internal control procedures to prevent embezzlement*

Jane Jones was in charge of the returns department at The Software Company. She was responsible for evaluating returned merchandise. She sent merchandise that was reusable back to the warehouse, where it was restocked in inventory. Jones was also responsible for taking the merchandise that she determined to be defective to the city dump for disposal. She had agreed to buy a tax planning program for one of her friends at a discount through her contacts at work. That is when the idea came to her. She could simply classify one of the reusable returns as defective and bring it home instead of taking it to the dump. She did so and made a quick $150. She was happy, and her friend was ecstatic; he was able to buy a $400 software package for only $150. He told his friends about the deal, and soon Jones had a regular set of customers. She was caught when a retail store owner complained to the marketing manager that his pricing strategy was being undercut by The Software Company's direct sales to the public. The marketing manager was suspicious because The Software Company had no direct marketing program. When the outside sales were ultimately traced back to Jones, the company discovered that it had lost over $10,000 in sales revenue because of her criminal activity.

Required

Identify an internal control procedure that could have prevented the company's losses. Explain how the procedure would have stopped the embezzlement.

LO 4-2

Exercise 4-7 *Treatment of NSF check*

Montgomery Stationery's bank statement contained a $260 NSF check that one of its customers had written to pay for supplies purchased.

Required

a. Show the effects of recognizing the NSF check on the financial statements by recording the appropriate amounts in a horizontal statements model like the following one:

Assets			=	Liab.	+	Equity	Rev.	−	Exp.	=	Net Inc.	Cash Flow
Cash	+	Accts. Rec.										

b. Is the recognition of the NSF check on Montgomery's books an asset source, use, or exchange transaction?

c. Suppose the customer redeems the check by giving Montgomery $290 cash in exchange for the bad check. The additional $30 was a service fee charged by Montgomery. Show the effects on the financial statements in the horizontal statements model in Requirement *a*.

d. Is the receipt of cash referenced in Requirement *c* an asset source, use, or exchange transaction?

Exercise 4-8   *Adjustments to the balance per books*

LO 4-2

Required

Identify which of the following items are added to or subtracted from the unadjusted *book balance* to arrive at the true cash balance. Distinguish the additions from the subtractions by placing a + beside the items that are added to the unadjusted book balance and a − beside those that are subtracted from it. The first item is recorded as an example.

Reconciling Items	Book Balance Adjusted?	Added or Subtracted?
Charge for checks	Yes	−
NSF check from customer		
Note receivable collected by the bank		
Outstanding checks		
Credit memo		
Interest revenue		
Deposits in transit		
Debit memo		
Service charge		

Exercise 4-9   *Adjustments to the balance per bank*

LO 4-2

Required

Identify which of the following items are added to or subtracted from the unadjusted *bank balance* to arrive at the true cash balance. Distinguish the additions from the subtractions by placing a + beside the items that are added to the unadjusted bank balance and a − beside those that are subtracted from it. The first item is recorded as an example.

Reconciling Items	Bank Balance Adjusted?	Added or Subtracted?
Certified checks	No	NA
Petty cash voucher		
NSF check from customer		
Interest revenue		
Bank service charge		
Outstanding checks		
Deposits in transit		
Debit memo		
Credit memo		

Exercise 4-10   *Adjusting the cash account*

LO 4-2

As of May 31, 2014, the bank statement showed an ending balance of $26,100. The unadjusted Cash account balance was $27,350. The following information is available:

1. Deposit in transit, $6,981.
2. Credit memo in bank statement for interest earned in May, $36.
3. Outstanding check, $5,720.
4. Debit memo for service charge, $25.

Required

Determine the true cash balance by preparing a bank reconciliation as of May 31, 2014, using the preceding information.

LO 4-2

Exercise 4-11   *Determining the true cash balance, starting with the unadjusted bank balance*

The following information is available for Sharder Company for the month of June:

1. The unadjusted balance per the bank statement on June 30 was $71,230.
2. Deposits in transit on June 30 were $2,350.
3. A debit memo was included with the bank statement for a service charge of $25.
4. A $5,611 check written in June had not been paid by the bank.
5. The bank statement included a $930 credit memo for the collection of a note. The principal of the note was $900, and the interest collected amounted to $30.

Required

Determine the true cash balance as of June 30. (*Hint:* It is not necessary to use all of the preceding items to determine the true balance.)

LO 4-2

Exercise 4-12   *Determining the true cash balance, starting with the unadjusted book balance*

Henderson Company had an unadjusted cash balance of $7,215 as of May 31. The company's bank statement, also dated May 31, included a $68 NSF check written by one of Henderson's customers. There were $750 in outstanding checks and $930 in deposits in transit as of May 31. According to the bank statement, service charges were $50, and the bank collected a $500 note receivable for Henderson. The bank statement also showed $13 of interest revenue earned by Henderson.

Required

Determine the true cash balance as of May 31. (*Hint:* It is not necessary to use all of the preceding items to determine the true balance.)

LO 4-3

Exercise 4-13   *AICPA Code of Professional Conduct*

Mark Miller owns and operates Miller Enterprises. Mark's sister, Jessica, is the independent public accountant for Miller Enterprises. Jessica worked for Miller Enterprises for five years before she started her independent CPA practice. Mark considered hiring a different accounting firm but ultimately decided that no one knew his business as well as his sister.

Required

Use the AICPA Code of Professional Conduct to evaluate the appropriateness of Jessica's client relationship with Miller Enterprises.

LO 4-3

Exercise 4-14   *AICPA Code of Professional Conduct*

Raula Kato discovered a material reporting error in the accounting records of Sampoon, Inc. (SI), during the annual audit. The error was so significant that it will certainly have an adverse effect on the price of the client's stock, which is actively traded on the Western stock exchange. After talking to his close friend and president of SI, Kato agreed to withhold the information until the president had time to sell his SI stock. Kato leaked the information to his parents so that they could sell their shares of stock as well. The reporting matter was a relatively complex issue that involved recently issued reporting standards. Kato told himself that if he were caught he would simply plead ignorance. He would simply say that he did not have time to keep up with the rapidly changing standards and he would be off the hook.

Required

a. Write a memo that identifies specific articles of the AICPA Code of Professional Conduct that were violated by Kato.
b. Would pleading ignorance relieve Kato from his audit responsibilities?

Exercise 4-15 *Fraud triangle*

Jacob Perry is a CPA with a secret. His secret is that he gambles on sports. Jacob knows that his profession disapproves of gambling, but considers the professional standards to be misguided in his case. Jacob really doesn't consider his bets to be gambling because he spends a lot of time studying sports facts. He believes that he is simply making educated decisions based on facts. He argues that using sports facts to place bets is no different than using accounting information to buy stock.

Required

Use the fraud triangle as a basis to comment on Jacob Perry's gambling activities.

Exercise 4-16 *Materiality and the auditor*

Melissa Moore is an auditor. Her work at two companies disclosed inappropriate recognition of revenue. Both cases involved dollar amounts in the $200,000 range. In one case, Moore considered the item material and required her client to restate earnings. In the other case, Moore dismissed the misstatement as being immaterial.

Required

Write a memo that explains how a $200,000 misstatement of revenue is acceptable for one company but unacceptable for a different company.

PROBLEMS

 **All applicable Problems are available with McGraw-Hill's**
Connect® Accounting.

Problem 4-17 *Types of audit reports*

Ellen Norman is a partner of a regional accounting firm. Ms. Norman was hired by a client to audit the company's books. After extensive work, Ms. Norman determined that she was unable to perform the appropriate audit procedures.

Required

a. Name the type of audit report that Ms. Norman should issue with respect to the work that she did accomplish.

b. If Ms. Norman had been able to perform the necessary audit procedures, there are three types of audit reports that she could have issued depending on the outcome of the audit. Name and describe these three types of audit reports.

Problem 4-18 *Using internal controls to restrict illegal or unethical behavior*

Required

For each of the following fraudulent acts, describe one or more internal control procedures that could have prevented (or helped prevent) the problems.

a. Nina Wells, the administrative assistant in charge of payroll, created a fictitious employee, wrote weekly checks to the fictitious employee, and then personally cashed the checks for her own benefit.

b. Noel Rand, the receiving manager of Southern Lumber, created a fictitious supplier named F&M Building Supply. F&M regularly billed Southern Lumber for supplies purchased. Rand had printed shipping slips and billing invoices with the name of the fictitious company and opened a post office box as the mailing address. Rand simply prepared a receiving report and submitted it for payment to the accounts payable department. The accounts payable clerk then paid the invoice when it was received because Rand acknowledged receipt of the supplies.

c. Patty Smith works at a local hobby shop and usually operates the cash register. She has developed a way to give discounts to her friends. When they come by, she rings a lower price or does not charge the friend for some of the material purchased. At first, Smith thought she would get caught, but no one seemed to notice. Indeed, she has become so sure that there is no way for the owner to find out that she has started taking home some supplies for her own personal use.

LO 4-2

Problem 4-19 *Preparing a bank reconciliation*

Hank Brock owns a card shop, Four Aces. The following cash information is available for the month of August 2014.

As of August 31, the bank statement shows a balance of $15,320. The August 31 unadjusted balance in the Cash account of Four Aces is $13,910. A review of the bank statement revealed the following information:

1. A deposit of $4,295 on August 31, 2014, does not appear on the August bank statement.
2. It was discovered that a check to pay for baseball cards was correctly written and paid by the bank for $3,650 but was recorded on the books as $4,400.
3. When checks written during the month were compared with those paid by the bank, three checks amounting to $5,030 were found to be outstanding.
4. A debit memo for $75 was included in the bank statement for the purchase of a new supply of checks.

Required

Prepare a bank reconciliation at the end of August showing the true cash balance.

LO 4-2

Problem 4-20 *Missing information in a bank reconciliation*

The following data apply to Larry's Auto Supply Inc. for May 2014:

1. Balance per the bank on May 31, $8,250.
2. Deposits in transit not recorded by the bank, $1,230.
3. Bank error; check written by L7 Auto Supply was charged to Larry's Auto Supply's account, $720.
4. The following checks written and recorded by Larry's Auto Supply were not included in the bank statement:

3013	$ 420
3054	650
3056	1,830

5. Note collected by the bank, $400.
6. Service charge for collection of note, $15.
7. The bookkeeper recorded a check written for $230 to pay for the May utilities expense as $430 in the cash disbursements journal.
8. Bank service charge in addition to the note collection fee, $35.
9. Customer checks returned by the bank as NSF, $275.

Required

Determine the amount of the unadjusted cash balance per Larry's Auto Supply's books.

LO 4-2

Problem 4-21 *Adjustments to the cash account based on the bank reconciliation*

Required

Determine whether the following items included in Sung Company's bank reconciliation will require adjusting or correcting entries on Sung's books.

a. Service charges of $30 for the month of January were listed on the bank statement.
b. The bank charged a $350 check drawn on Yung Restaurant to Sung's account. The check was included in Sung's bank statement.
c. A check of $62 was returned to the bank because of insufficient funds and was noted on the bank statement. Sung received the check from a customer and thought that it was good when it was deposited into the account.

d. A $982 deposit was recorded by the bank as $928.

e. Four checks totaling $725 written during the month of January were not included with the January bank statement.

f. A $65 check written to Office Max for office supplies was recorded in the general journal as $56.

g. The bank statement indicated that the bank had collected a $450 note for Sung.

h. Sung recorded $700 of receipts on January 31, 2014, which was deposited in the night depository of the bank. These deposits were not included in the bank statement.

Problem 4-22 *Bank reconciliation and adjustments to the cash account*

The following information is available for Sunset Valley Hotel for July 2014:

LO 4-2

CHECK FIGURE
a. True Cash Balance, July 31, 2014: $16,234

Bank Statement

STATE BANK

Bolta Vista, NV 10001

Sunset Valley Hotel   Account number
10 Main Street   12-4567
Bolta Vista, NV 10001   July 31, 2014

Beginning balance 6/30/2014	$ 9,031
Total deposits and other credits	29,800
Total checks and other debits	23,902
Ending balance 7/31/2014	14,929

Checks and Debits		Deposits and Credits		
Check No.	Amount	Date		Amount
2350	$3,761	July	1	$1,102
2351	1,643	July	10	6,498
2352	8,000	July	15	4,929
2354	2,894	July	21	6,174
2355	1,401	July	26	5,963
2357	6,187	July	30	2,084
DM	16	CM		3,050

The following is a list of checks and deposits recorded on the books of the Sunset Valley Hotel for July 2014:

Date		Check No.	Amount of Check	Date		Amount of Deposit
July	2	2351	$1,643	July	8	$6,498
July	4	2352	8,000	July	14	4,929
July	10	2353	1,500	July	21	6,174
July	10	2354	2,894	July	26	5,963
July	15	2355	1,401	July	29	2,084
July	20	2356	745	July	30	3,550
July	22	2357	6,187			

Other Information

1. Check no. 2350 was outstanding from June.
2. The credit memo was for collection of notes receivable.
3. All checks were paid at the correct amount.
4. The debit memo was for printed checks.
5. The June 30 bank reconciliation showed a deposit in transit of $1,102.
6. The unadjusted Cash account balance at July 31 was $13,200.

Required

a. Prepare the bank reconciliation for Sunset Valley Hotel at the end of July.

b. Explain how the adjustments described above affect the cash account.

LO 4-1, 4-2

CHECK FIGURE

a. True Cash Balance, May 31, 2014: $21,650

Problem 4-23   *Bank reconciliation and internal control*

Following is a bank reconciliation for Pizza Express for May 31, 2014:

	Cash Account	Bank Statement
Balance as of 5/31/2014	$25,000	$22,000
Deposit in transit		4,250
Outstanding checks		(465)
Note collected by bank	1,815	
Bank service charge	(30)	
Automatic payment on loan	(1,000)	
Adjusted cash balance as of 5/31/2014	$25,785	$25,785

Because of limited funds, Pizza Express employed only one accountant who was responsible for receiving cash, recording receipts and disbursements, preparing deposits, and preparing the bank reconciliation. The accountant left the company on June 8, 2014, after preparing the May 31 bank reconciliation. His replacement compared the checks returned with the bank statement to the cash disbursements journal and found the total of outstanding checks to be $4,600.

Required

a. Prepare a corrected bank reconciliation.

b. What is the total amount of cash missing, and how was the difference between the "true cash" per the bank and the "true cash" per the books hidden on the reconciliation prepared by the former employee?

c. What could Pizza Express do to avoid cash theft in the future?

LO 4-3

Problem 4-24   *Fraud Triangle*

Robert Stroup is an accountant with a shady past. Suffice it to say that he owes some very unsavory characters a lot of money. Despite his past, Robert works hard at keeping up a strong professional image. He is a manager at Smith and Associates, a fast-growing CPA firm. Robert is highly regarded around the office because he is a strong producer of client revenue. Indeed, on several occasions he exceeded his authority in establishing prices with clients. This is typically a partner's job but who could criticize Robert, who is most certainly bringing in the business. Indeed, Robert is so good that he is able to pull off the following scheme. He bills clients at inflated rates and then reports the ordinary rate to his accounting firm. Say, for example, the normal charge for a job is $2,500. Robert will smooth talk the client, then charge him $3,000. He reports the normal charge of $2,500 to his firm and keeps the extra $500 for himself. He knows it isn't exactly right. Even so, his firm gets its regular charges and the client willingly pays for the services rendered. He thinks to himself, as he pockets his ill-gotten gains, who is getting hurt anyway?

Required

The text discusses three common features (conditions) that motivate ethical misconduct. Identify and explain each of the three features as they appear in the above scenario.

LO 4-4

Problem 4-25   *Confidentiality and the auditor*

West Aston discovered a significant fraud in the accounting records of a high profile client. The story has been broadcast on national airways. Aston was unable to resolve his remaining concerns with the company's management team and ultimately resigned from the audit engagement.

Aston knows that he will be asked by several interested parties, including his friends and relatives, the successor auditor, and prosecuting attorneys in a court of law, to tell what he knows. He has asked you for advice.

Required

Write a memo that explains Aston's disclosure responsibilities to each of the interested parties.

Problem 4-26   *Auditor responsibilities*   LO 4-4

You have probably heard it is unwise to bite the hand that feeds you. Independent auditors are chosen by, paid by, and can be fired by the companies they audit. What keeps the auditor independent? In other words, what stops an auditor from blindly following the orders of a client?

Required

Write a memo that explains the reporting responsibilities of an independent auditor.

ANALYZE, THINK, COMMUNICATE

ATC 4-1   Business Application Case   *Understanding real-world annual reports*

Use the Target Corporation's Form 10-K to answer the following questions related to Target's 2012 fiscal year (year ended February 2, 2013). Target's Form 10-K is available on the company's website or through the SEC's EDGAR database. Appendix A provides instructions for using the EDGAR database.

Required

a. Instead of "Cash," the company's balance sheet uses the account name "Cash and cash equivalents." How does the company define cash equivalents?

b. The annual report has two reports in which management is clearly identified as having responsibility for the company's financial reporting and internal controls. What are the names of these reports and on what pages are they located?

ATC 4-2   Group Assignment   *Bank reconciliations*

The following cash and bank information is available for three companies on June 30, 2014.

Cash and Adjustment Information	Peach Co.	Apple Co.	Pear Co.
Unadjusted cash balance per books, 6/30	$45,620	$32,450	$23,467
Outstanding checks	1,345	2,478	2,540
Service charge	50	75	35
Balance per bank statement, 6/30	48,632	37,176	24,894
Credit memo for collection of notes receivable	4,500	5,600	3,800
NSF check	325	145	90
Deposits in transit	2,500	3,200	4,800
Credit memo for interest earned	42	68	12

Required

a. Organize the class into three sections and divide each section into groups of three to five students. Assign Peach Co. to section 1, Apple Co. to section 2, and Pear Co. to section 3.

Group Tasks

(1) Prepare a bank reconciliation for the company assigned to your group.

(2) Select a representative from a group in each section to put the bank reconciliation on the board.

Class Discussion:

b. Discuss the cause of the difference between the unadjusted cash balance and the ending balance for the bank statement. Also, discuss types of adjustment that are commonly made to the bank balance and types of adjustment that are commonly made to the unadjusted book balance.

ATC 4-3   Research Assignment   *Investigating cash and management issues at Smucker's*

Using the most current Form 10-K available on EDGAR, or the company's website, answer the following questions about the J. M. Smucker Company. Instructions for using EDGAR are in Appendix A. *Note: In some years the financial statements, footnotes, etc., portion of Smucker's annual report have been located at the end of the Form 10-K, in or just after "Item 15."*

Required

a. Instead of "Cash," the company's balance sheet uses the account name "Cash and cash equivalents." How does the company define cash equivalents?

b. The annual report has two reports in which management clearly acknowledges its responsibility for the company's financial reporting and internal controls. What are the names of these reports and on what pages are they located?

ATC 4-4   Writing Assignment   *Internal control procedures*

Sarah Johnson was a trusted employee of Evergreen Trust Bank. She was involved in everything. She worked as a teller, she accounted for the cash at the other teller windows, and she recorded many of the transactions in the accounting records. She was so loyal that she never would take a day off, even when she was really too sick to work. She routinely worked late to see that all the day's work was posted into the accounting records. She would never take even a day's vacation because they might need her at the bank. Adam and Jammie, CPAs, were hired to perform an audit, the first complete audit that had been done in several years. Johnson seemed somewhat upset by the upcoming audit. She said that everything had been properly accounted for and that the audit was a needless expense. When Adam and Jammie examined some of the bank's internal control procedures, it discovered problems. In fact, as the audit progressed, it became apparent that a large amount of cash was missing. Numerous adjustments had been made to customer accounts with credit memorandums, and many of the transactions had been posted several days late. In addition, there were numerous cash payments for "office expenses." When the audit was complete, it was determined that more than $100,000 of funds was missing or improperly accounted for. All fingers pointed to Johnson. The bank's president, who was a close friend of Johnson, was bewildered. How could this type of thing happen at this bank?

Required

Prepare a written memo to the bank president, outlining the procedures that should be followed to prevent this type of problem in the future.

ATC 4-5   Ethical Dilemma   *I need just a little extra money*

John Riley, a certified public accountant, has worked for the past eight years as a payroll clerk for Southeast Industries, a small furniture manufacturing firm in the Northeast. John recently experienced unfortunate circumstances. His teenage son required major surgery and the medical bills not covered by John's insurance have financially strained John's family.

John works hard and is a model employee. Although he received regular performance raises during his first few years with Southeast, John's wages have not increased in three years. John asked his supervisor, Bill Jameson, for a raise. Bill agreed that John deserved a raise, but told him he could not currently approve one because of sluggish sales.

A disappointed John returned to his duties while the financial pressures in his life continued. Two weeks later, Larry Tyler, an assembly worker at Southwest, quit over a dispute with management. John conceived an idea. John's duties included not only processing employee terminations but also approving time cards before paychecks were issued and then distributing the paychecks to firm personnel. John decided to delay processing Mr. Tyler's termination, to forge timecards for Larry Tyler for the next few weeks, and to cash the checks himself. Since he distributed paychecks, no one would find out, and John reasoned that he was really entitled to the extra money anyway. In fact, no one did discover his maneuver and John stopped the practice after three weeks.

Required

a. Does John's scheme affect Southeast's balance sheet? Explain your answer.

b. Review the AICPA's Articles of Professional Conduct and comment on any of the standards that have been violated.

c. Identify the three elements of unethical and criminal conduct recognized in the fraud triangle.

CHAPTER 5

Accounting for Receivables and Inventory Cost Flow

LEARNING OBJECTIVES

After you have mastered the material in this chapter, you will be able to:

LO 5-1   Explain how the allowance method of accounting for uncollectible accounts affects financial statements.

LO 5-2   Use the percent of revenue method to estimate the uncollectible accounts expense.

LO 5-3   Use the percent of receivables method to estimate the uncollectible accounts expense.

LO 5-4   Explain how accounting for notes receivable and accrued interest affects financial statements.

LO 5-5   Explain how accounting for credit card sales affects financial statements.

LO 5-6   Explain how different inventory cost flow methods (specific identification, FIFO, LIFO, and weighted average) affect financial statements.

 Video lectures and accompanying self-assessment quizzes are available for all learning objectives through McGraw-Hill Connect® Accounting.

CHAPTER OPENING

Many people buy on impulse. If they must wait, the desire to buy wanes. To take advantage of impulse buyers, most merchandising companies offer customers credit because it increases their sales. A disadvantage of this strategy occurs when some customers are unable or unwilling to pay their bills. Nevertheless, the widespread availability of credit suggests that the advantages of increased sales outweigh the disadvantages of some uncollectible accounts.

When a company allows a customer to "buy now and pay later," the company's right to collect cash in the future is called an **account receivable.** Typically, amounts due from individual accounts receivable are relatively small and the collection period is short. Most accounts receivable are collected within 30 days. When a longer credit term is needed or when a receivable is large, the seller usually requires the buyer to issue a note reflecting a credit agreement between the parties. The note specifies the maturity date, interest rate, and other credit terms. Receivables evidenced by such notes are called **notes receivable.** Accounts and notes receivable are reported as assets on the balance sheet.

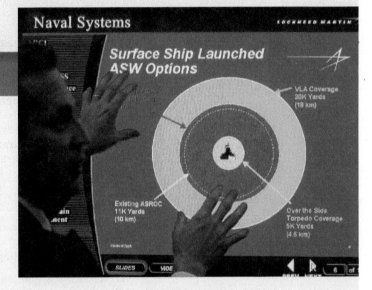

The Curious Accountant

Lockheed Martin develops and maintains various types of technology related to security. Its biggest customer, by far, is the U.S. government for whom it provides aeronautics and space-system products and services. In 2012, 82 percent of its revenue came from sales to the U.S. government, and another 17 percent came from sales to governments of other countries. Suppose the U.S. government contracted with Lockheed Martin Corporation to provide management services related to a governmental hardware and software system, and that the cost of these services will be $10 million per month. Assume the government offers to pay for the services on the day they are provided (a cash purchase) or 30 days later (a purchase on account).

Assume that Lockheed Martin is absolutely sure the government will pay its account when due. Do you think the company should care whether the government pays for the services upon delivery or 30 days later? Why? (Answer on page 165.)

ALLOWANCE METHOD OF ACCOUNTING FOR UNCOLLECTIBLE ACCOUNTS

LO 5-1

Explain how the allowance method of accounting for uncollectible accounts affects financial statements.

Most companies do not expect to collect the full amount (face value) of their accounts receivable. Even carefully screened credit customers sometimes don't pay their bills. The **net realizable value** of accounts receivable represents the amount of receivables a company estimates it will actually collect. The net realizable value is the *face value* less an *allowance for doubtful accounts*.

The **allowance for doubtful accounts** represents a company's estimate of the amount of uncollectible receivables. To illustrate, assume a company with total accounts receivable of $50,000 estimates that $2,000 of its receivables will not be collected. The net realizable value of receivables is computed as follows.

Accounts receivable	$50,000
Less: Allowance for doubtful accounts	(2,000)
Net realizable value of receivables	$48,000

A company cannot know today, of course, the exact amount of the receivables it will not be able to collect in the future. The *allowance for doubtful accounts* and the *net realizable value* are necessarily *estimated amounts*. The net realizable value, however, more closely measures the cash that will ultimately be collected than does the face value. To avoid overstating assets, companies usually report receivables on their balance sheets at the net realizable value.

Reporting accounts receivable in the financial statements at net realizable value is commonly called the **allowance method of accounting for uncollectible accounts.** The following section illustrates using the allowance method for Allen's Tutoring Services (ATS).

Accounting Events Affecting the 2014 Period

Allen's Tutoring Services is a small company that provides tutoring services to college students. Allen's started operations on January 1, 2014. During 2014, Allen's experienced three types of accounting events. These events are discussed below.

EVENT 1   Revenue Recognition
Allen's Tutoring Services recognized $14,000 of service revenue earned on account during 2014.

This is an asset source transaction. Allen's Tutoring Services obtained assets (accounts receivable) by providing services to customers. Both assets and stockholders' equity (retained earnings) increase. The event increases revenue and net income. Cash flow is not affected. These effects follow.

Event No.	Assets	=	Liab.	+	Equity	Rev.	−	Exp.	=	Net Inc.	Cash Flow
	Accts. Rec.	=			Ret. Earn.						
1	14,000	=	NA	+	14,000	14,000	−	NA	=	14,000	NA

EVENT 2   Collection of Receivables
Allen's Tutoring Services collected $12,500 cash from accounts receivable in 2014.

This event is an asset exchange transaction. The asset cash increases; the asset accounts receivable decreases. Total assets remains unchanged. Net income is not affected

Answers to The Curious Accountant

Lockheed Martin would definitely prefer to make the sale to the government in cash rather than on account. Even though it may be certain to collect its accounts receivable, the sooner the company gets its cash the sooner the cash can be reinvested.

The interest cost related to a small account receivable of $50 that takes 30 days to collect may seem immaterial; at 6 percent the lost interest amounts to $.25. However, when one considers that Lockheed Martin had approximately $6.6 billion of accounts receivable on December 31, 2012, and took an average of 51 days to collect them, the cost of financing receivables for a real-world company becomes apparent. At 6 percent the cost of waiting 51 days to collect $6.6 billion of cash is $55.3 million ($6.6 billion × .06 × 51/365). For a full year, the cost to Lockheed Martin would be $396 million ($6.6 billion × .06). In 2012 the weighted-average interest rate on Lockheed Martin's debt was approximately 6 percent.

because the revenue was recognized in the previous transaction. The cash inflow is reported in the operating activities section of the statement of cash flows.

Event No.	Assets			=	Liab.	+	Equity	Rev.	−	Exp.	=	Net Inc.	Cash Flow
	Cash	+	Accts. Rec.										
2	12,500	+	(12,500)	=	NA	+	NA	NA	−	NA	=	NA	12,500 OA

Accounting for Uncollectible Accounts Expense

EVENT 3 Recognizing Uncollectible Accounts Expense

Allen's Tutoring Services recognized uncollectible accounts expense for accounts expected to be uncollectible in the future.

The year-end balance in the Accounts Receivable account is $1,500 ($14,000 of revenue on account − $12,500 of collections). Although Allen's Tutoring Services has the legal right to receive this $1,500 in 2015, the company is not likely to collect the entire amount because some of its customers may not pay the amounts due. Allen's will not know the actual amount of uncollectible accounts until some future time when the customers default (fail to pay). However, the company can *estimate* the amount of receivables that will be uncollectible.

Suppose Allen's Tutoring Services estimates that $75 of the receivables is uncollectible. To improve financial reporting, the company can recognize the estimated expense in 2014. In this way, uncollectible accounts expense and the related revenue will be recognized in the same accounting period (2014). Recognizing an estimated expense is more useful than recognizing no expense. The *matching* of revenues and expenses is improved and the statements are, therefore, more accurate.

The estimated amount of **uncollectible accounts expense** is recognized in a year-end adjusting entry. The adjusting entry reduces the book value of total assets, reduces stockholders' equity (retained earnings), and reduces the amount of reported net income. The statement of cash flows is not affected. The effects of recognizing uncollectible accounts expense are shown here.

Event No.	Assets			=	Liab.	+	Equity	Rev.	−	Exp.	=	Net Inc.	Cash Flow
	Accts. Rec.	−	Allow.	=			Ret. Earn.						
3	NA	−	75	=	NA	+	(75)	NA	−	75	=	(75)	NA

Instead of decreasing the receivables account directly, the asset reduction is recorded in the **contra asset account,** Allowance for Doubtful Accounts. Recall that the contra account is subtracted from the accounts receivable balance to determine the net realizable value of receivables, as follows for ATS.

Accounts receivable	$1,500
Less: Allowance for doubtful accounts	(75)
Net realizable value of receivables	$1,425

Generally accepted accounting principles require disclosure of both the net realizable value and the amount of the allowance account. Many companies disclose these amounts directly in the balance sheet in a manner similar to that shown in the text box above. Other companies disclose this information in the footnotes to the financial statements.

Financial Statements

The financial statements for Allen's Tutoring Services' 2014 accounting period are shown in Exhibit 5.1. As previously indicated, estimating uncollectible accounts improves the usefulness of the 2014 financial statements in two ways. First, the balance sheet reports the amount of cash ($1,500 − $75 = $1,425) the company actually expects to collect (net realizable value of accounts receivable). Second, the income statement provides a clearer picture of managerial performance because it better *matches* the uncollectible accounts expense with the revenue it helped produce. The statements in Exhibit 5.1 show that the cash flow from operating activities ($12,500)

EXHIBIT 5.1

Financial Statements for 2014

Income Statement		Balance Sheet			Statement of Cash Flows	
Service revenue	$14,000	Assets			Operating Activities	
Uncollectible accts. exp.	(75)	Cash		$12,500	Inflow from customers	$12,500
Net income	$13,925	Accounts receivable	$1,500		Investing Activities	0
		Less: Allowance	(75)		Financing Activities	0
		Net realizable value		1,425	Net change in cash	12,500
		Total assets		$13,925	Plus: Beginning cash balance	0
		Stockholders' equity			Ending cash balance	$12,500
		Retained earnings		$13,925		

differs from net income ($13,925). The statement of cash flows reports only cash collections, whereas the income statement reports revenues earned on account less the estimated amount of uncollectible accounts expense.

Accounting Events Affecting the 2015 Period

To further illustrate accounting for uncollectible accounts, we discuss six accounting events affecting Allen's Tutoring Services during 2015.

Accounting for Write-Off of Uncollectible Accounts Receivable
EVENT 1   Write-Off of Uncollectible Accounts Receivable
Allen's Tutoring Services wrote off $70 of uncollectible accounts receivable.

This is an asset exchange transaction. The amount of the uncollectible accounts is removed from the Accounts Receivable account and from the Allowance for Doubtful Accounts account. Because the balances in both the Accounts Receivable and the Allowance accounts decrease, the net realizable value of receivables—and therefore total assets—remains unchanged. The write-off does not affect the income statement. Because the uncollectible accounts expense was recognized in the previous year, the expense would be double counted if it were recognized again at the time an uncollectible account is written off. Finally, the statement of cash flows is not affected by the write-off. These effects are shown in the following statements model.

Event No.	Assets			=	Liab.	+	Equity	Rev.	−	Exp.	=	Net Inc.	Cash Flow
	Accts. Rec.	−	Allow.										
1	(70)	−	(70)	=	NA	+	NA	NA	−	NA	=	NA	NA

The computation of the *net realizable value,* before and after the write-off, is shown below.

	Before Write-Off	After Write-Off
Accounts receivable	$1,500	$1,430
Less: Allowance for doubtful accounts	(75)	(5)
Net realizable value	$1,425	$1,425

EVENT 2   Revenue Recognition
Allen's Tutoring Services provided $10,000 of tutoring services on account during 2015.

Assets (accounts receivable) and stockholders' equity (retained earnings) increase. Recognizing revenue increases net income. Cash flow is not affected. These effects are illustrated below.

Event No.	Assets	=	Liab.	+	Equity	Rev.	−	Exp.	=	Net Inc.	Cash Flow
	Accts. Rec.	=			Ret. Earn.						
2	10,000	=	NA	+	10,000	10,000	−	NA	=	10,000	NA

EVENT 3   Collection of Accounts Receivable
Allen's Tutoring Services collected $8,430 cash from accounts receivable.

The balance in the Cash account increases, and the balance in the Accounts Receivable account decreases. Total assets are unaffected. Net income is not affected because revenue was recognized previously. The cash inflow is reported in the operating activities section of the statement of cash flows.

Event No.	Assets			=	Liab.	+	Equity	Rev.	−	Exp.	=	Net Inc.	Cash Flow
	Cash	+	Accts. Rec.										
3	8,430	+	(8,430)	=	NA	+	NA	NA	−	NA	=	NA	8,430 OA

Accounting for Recovery of an Uncollectible Account Receivable

EVENT 4   Recovery of an Uncollectible Account: Reinstate Receivable
Allen's Tutoring Services recovered a receivable that it had previously written off.

Occasionally, a company receives payment from a customer whose account was previously written off. In such cases, the customer's account should be reinstated and the cash received should be recorded the same way as any other collection on account. The account receivable is reinstated because a complete record of the customer's payment history may be useful if the customer requests credit again at some future date. To illustrate, assume that Allen's Tutoring Services received a $10 cash payment from a customer whose account had previously been written off. The first step is to **reinstate** the account receivable by reversing the previous write-off. The balances in the Accounts Receivable and the Allowance accounts increase. Since Allowance is a contra asset account, the increase in it offsets the increase in the Accounts Receivable account, and total assets are unchanged. Net income and cash flow are unaffected. These effects are shown here.

Event No.	Assets			=	Liab.	+	Equity	Rev.	−	Exp.	=	Net Inc.	Cash Flow
	Accts. Rec.	−	Allow.										
4	10	−	10	=	NA	+	NA	NA	−	NA	=	NA	NA

EVENT 5   Recovery of an Uncollectible Account: Collection of Receivable
Allen's Tutoring Services recorded collection of the reinstated receivable.

The collection of $10 is recorded like any other collection of a receivable account. Cash increases, and accounts receivable decreases.

Event No.	Assets			=	Liab.	+	Equity	Rev.	–	Exp.	=	Net Inc.	Cash Flow
	Cash	+	Accts. Rec.										
5	10	+	(10)	=	NA	+	NA	NA	–	NA	=	NA	10 OA

ESTIMATING UNCOLLECTIBLE ACCOUNTS EXPENSE USING THE PERCENT OF REVENUE (SALES) METHOD

Companies recognize the estimated amount of uncollectible accounts expense in a period-end adjusting entry. Since Allen's Tutoring Service began operations in 2014, it had no previous credit history upon which to base its estimate. After consulting trade publications and experienced people in the same industry, ATS made an educated guess as to the amount of expense it should recognize for its first year. In its second year of operation, however, ATS can use its first-year experience as a starting point for estimating the second year (2015) uncollectible accounts expense.

At the end of 2014 ATS estimated uncollectible accounts expense to be $75 on service revenue of $14,000. In 2015 ATS actually wrote off $70 of which $10 was later recovered. ATS therefore experienced actual uncollectible accounts of $60 on service revenue of $14,000 for an uncollectible accounts rate of approximately .43 percent of service revenue. ATS could apply this percentage to the 2015 service revenue to estimate the 2015 uncollectible accounts expense. In practice, many companies determine the percentage estimate of uncollectible accounts on a three- or five-year moving average.

Companies adjust the historical percentage for anticipated future circumstances. For example, they reduce it if they adopt more rigorous approval standards for new credit applicants. Alternatively, they may increase the percentage if economic forecasts signal an economic downturn that would make future defaults more likely. A company will also increase the percentage if it has specific knowledge one or more of its customers is financially distressed. Multiplying the service revenue by the percentage estimate of uncollectible accounts is commonly called the **percent of revenue method** of estimating uncollectible accounts expense.

LO 5-2

Use the percent of revenue method to estimate the uncollectible accounts expense.

EVENT 6   Adjustment for Recognition of Uncollectible Accounts Expense
Using the percent of revenue method, Allen's Tutoring Services recognized uncollectible accounts expense for 2015.

ATS must record this adjustment as of December 31, 2015, to update its accounting records before preparing the 2015 financial statements. After reviewing its credit history, economic forecasts, and correspondence with customers, management estimates uncollectible accounts expense to be 1.35 percent of service revenue, or $135 ($10,000 service revenue × .0135). Recognizing the $135 uncollectible accounts expense decreases both assets (net realizable of receivables) and stockholders' equity (retained earnings). The expense recognition decreases net income. The statement of cash flows is not affected. The financial statements are affected as shown here.

Event No.	Assets			=	Liab.	+	Equity	Rev.	–	Exp.	=	Net Inc.	Cash Flow
	Accts. Rec.	–	Allow.	=			Ret. Earn.						
6	NA	–	135	=	NA	+	(135)	NA	–	135	=	(135)	NA

Analysis of Financial Statements

Exhibit 5.2 displays the 2015 financial statements. The amount of uncollectible accounts expense ($135) differs from the ending balance of the Allowance account ($150). The balance in the Allowance account was $15 before the 2015 adjusting entry for

EXHIBIT 5.2

Financial Statements for 2015

Income Statement		Balance Sheet			Statement of Cash Flows	
Service revenue	$10,000	Assets			Operating Activities	
Uncollectible accts. exp.	(135)	Cash		$20,940	Inflow from customers	$ 8,440
Net income	$ 9,865	Accounts receivable	$3,000		Investing Activities	0
		Less: Allowance	(150)		Financing Activities	0
		Net realizable value		2,850	Net change in cash	8,440
		Total assets		$23,790	Plus: Beginning cash balance	12,500
		Stockholders' equity			Ending cash balance	$20,940
		Retained earnings		$23,790		

uncollectible accounts expense was recorded. At the end of 2014, Allen's Tutoring Services estimated there would be $75 of uncollectible accounts as a result of 2014 revenue earned on account. Actual write-offs, however, amounted to $70 and $10 of that amount was recovered, indicating the actual uncollectible accounts expense for 2014 was only $60. Hindsight shows the expense for 2014 was overstated by $15. However, if no estimate had been made, the amount of uncollectible accounts expense would have been understated by $60. In some accounting periods estimated uncollectible accounts expense will likely be overstated; in others it may be understated. The allowance method cannot produce perfect results, but it does improve the accuracy of the financial statements.

Because no dividends were paid, retained earnings at the end of 2015 equals the December 31, 2014, retained earnings plus 2015 net income (that is, $13,925 + $9,865 = $23,790). Again, the cash flow from operating activities ($8,440) differs from net income ($9,865) because the statement of cash flows does not include the effects of revenues earned on account and the recognition of uncollectible accounts expense.

☑ CHECK YOURSELF 5.2

Maher Company had beginning balances in Accounts Receivable and Allowance for Doubtful Accounts of $24,200 and $2,000, respectively. During the accounting period Maher earned $230,000 of revenue on account and collected $232,500 of cash from receivables. The company also wrote off $1,950 of uncollectible accounts during the period. Maher estimates uncollectible accounts expense will be 1 percent of credit sales. Based on this information, what is the net realizable value of receivables at the end of the period?

Answer   The balance in the Accounts Receivable account is $19,750 ($24,200 + $230,000 − $232,500 − $1,950). The amount of uncollectible accounts expense for the period is $2,300 ($230,000 × 0.01). The balance in Allowance for Doubtful Accounts is $2,350 ($2,000 − $1,950 + $2,300). The net realizable value of receivables is therefore $17,400 ($19,750 − $2,350).

ESTIMATING UNCOLLECTIBLE ACCOUNTS EXPENSE USING THE PERCENT OF RECEIVABLES METHOD

LO 5-3

Use the percent of receivables method to estimate the uncollectible accounts expense.

As an alternative to the percent of revenue method, which focuses on estimating the *expense* of uncollectible accounts, companies may estimate the amount of the adjusting entry to record uncollectible accounts expense using the **percent of receivables method.** The percent of receivables method focuses on estimating the most accurate amount for the balance sheet *Allowance for Doubtful Accounts* account.

EXHIBIT 5.3

PYRAMID CORPORATION
Accounts Receivable Aging Schedule
December 31, 2015

Customer Name	Total Balance	Current	Number of Days Past Due			
			0–30	31–60	61–90	Over 90
J. Davis	$ 6,700	$ 6,700				
B. Diamond	4,800	2,100	$ 2,700			
K. Eppy	9,400	9,400				
B. Gilman	2,200				$1,000	$1,200
A. Kelly	7,300	7,300				
L. Niel	8,600	1,000	6,000	$ 1,600		
L. Platt	4,600			4,600		
J. Turner	5,500			3,000	2,000	500
H. Zachry	6,900		3,000	3,900		
Total	$56,000	$26,500	$11,700	$13,100	$3,000	$1,700

The longer an account receivable remains outstanding, the less likely it is to be collected. Companies using the percent of receivables method typically determine the age of their individual accounts receivable accounts as part of estimating the allowance for doubtful accounts. An **aging of accounts receivable** schedule classifies all receivables by their due date. Exhibit 5.3 shows an aging schedule for Pyramid Corporation as of December 31, 2015.

A company estimates the required Allowance for Doubtful Accounts balance by applying different percentages to each category in the aging schedule. The percentage for each category is based on a company's previous collection experience for each of the categories. The percentages become progressively higher as the accounts become older. Exhibit 5.4 illustrates computing the allowance balance Pyramid Corporation requires.

The computations in Exhibit 5.4 mean the *ending balance* in the Allowance for Doubtful Accounts account should be $3,760. This balance represents the amount Pyramid will subtract from total accounts receivable to determine the net realizable value of receivables. To determine the amount of the adjusting entry to recognize uncollectible accounts expense, Pyramid must take into account any existing balance in the allowance account *before* recording the adjustment. For example, if Pyramid Corporation had a $500 balance in the Allowance account before the year-end adjustment, the

EXHIBIT 5.4

Balance Required in the Allowance for Doubtful Accounts at December 31, 2015

Number of Days Past Due	Receivables Amount	Percentage Likely to Be Uncollectible	Required Allowance Account Balance
Current	$26,500	.01	$ 265
0–30	11,700	.05	585
31–60	13,100	.10	1,310
61–90	3,000	.25	750
Over 90	1,700	.50	850
Total	$56,000		$3,760

adjusting entry would need to add $3,260 ($3,760 − $500) to the account. The effects on the financial statements are shown below.

Assets			= Liab.	+	Equity	Rev.	−	Exp.	=	Net Inc.	Cash Flow
Accts. Rec.	−	Allow. =			Ret. Earn.						
NA	−	3,260 =	NA	+	(3,260)	NA	−	3,260	=	3,260	NA

Matching Revenues and Expenses versus Asset Measurement

The *percent of revenue* method, with its focus on determining the uncollectible accounts expense, is often called the income statement approach. The *percent of receivables* method, focused on determining the best estimate of the allowance balance, is frequently called the balance sheet approach. Which estimating method is better? In any given year, the results will vary slightly between approaches. In the long run, however, the percentages used in either approach are based on a company's actual history of uncollectible accounts. Accountants routinely revise their estimates as more data become available, using hindsight to determine if the percentages should be increased or decreased. Either approach provides acceptable results.

ACCOUNTING FOR NOTES RECEIVABLE (PROMISSORY NOTES)

LO 5-4

Explain how accounting for notes receivable and accrued interest affects financial statements.

Companies typically do not charge their customers interest on accounts receivable that are not past due. When a company extends credit for a long time or when the amount of credit it extends is large, however, the cost of granting free credit and the potential for disputes about payment terms both increase. To address these concerns, the parties frequently enter into a credit agreement, the terms of which are legally documented in a **promissory note.**

To illustrate, assume Allen's Tutoring Services (ATS) loans some of its idle cash to an individual, Stanford Cummings, so Cummings can buy a car. ATS and Cummings agree that Cummings will repay the money borrowed plus interest at the end of one year. They also agree that ATS will hold the title to the car to secure the debt. Exhibit 5.5 illustrates a promissory note that outlines this credit agreement. For ATS, the credit arrangement represents a *note receivable*.

EXHIBIT 5.5

Promissory Note

Promissory Note

$15,000 (3)   November 1, 2014

Amount   **Date**

For consideration received, Stanford Cummings **hereby promises to pay to the order of:**

Allen's Tutoring Services (2)

Fifteen thousand and no/100   **Dollars**

payable on   October 31, 2015 (5)

plus interest thereon at the rate of 6 **percent per year.** (4)

Collateral Description   Automobile title (6)

Signature   *Stanford Cummings* (1)

Features of this note are discussed below. Each feature is cross-referenced with a number that corresponds to an item on the promissory note in Exhibit 5.5. Locate each feature in Exhibit 5.5 and read the corresponding description of the feature below.

1. Maker—The person responsible for making payment on the due date is the **maker** of the note. The maker may also be called the *borrower* or *debtor.*

2. Payee—The person to whom the note is made payable is the **payee.** The payee may also be called the *creditor* or *lender.* The payee loans money to the maker and expects the return of the principal and the interest due.

3. Principal—The amount of money loaned by the payee to the maker of the note is the **principal.**

4. Interest—The economic benefit earned by the payee for loaning the principal to the maker is **interest,** which is normally expressed as an annual percentage of the principal amount. For example, a note with a 6 percent interest rate requires interest payments equal to 6 percent of the principal amount every year the loan is outstanding.

5. Maturity Date—The date on which the maker must repay the principal and make the final interest payment to the payee is the **maturity date.**

6. Collateral—Assets belonging to the maker that are assigned as security to ensure that the principal and interest will be paid when due are called **collateral.** In this example, if Cummings fails to pay ATS the amount due, ownership of the car Cummings purchased will be transferred to ATS.

How Accounting for Notes Receivable Affects Financial Statements

We illustrate accounting for notes receivable using the credit agreement evidenced by the promissory note in Exhibit 5.5. Allen's Tutoring Services engaged in many transactions during 2014; we discuss here only transactions directly related to the note receivable.

EVENT 1   Loan of Money

The note shows that ATS loaned $15,000 to Stanford Cummings on November 1, 2014. This event is an asset exchange. The asset account Cash decreases and the asset account Notes Receivable increases. The income statement is not affected. The statement of cash flows shows a cash outflow for investing activities. The effects on the financial statements are shown below.

Date	Assets				=	Liab.	+	Equity	Rev.	–	Exp.	=	Net Inc.	Cash Flow
	Cash	+	Notes Rec.	+	Int. Rec.	=			Ret. Earn.						
11/01/12	(15,000)	+	15,000	+	NA	=	NA	+	NA	NA	–	NA	=	NA	(15,000) IA

EVENT 2   Accrual of Interest

For ATS, loaning money to the maker of the note, Stanford Cummings, represents investing in the note receivable. Cummings will repay the principal ($15,000) plus interest of 6 percent of the principal amount (0.06 × $15,000 = $900), or a total of $15,900, on October 31, 2015, one year from the date he borrowed the money from ATS.

Conceptually, lenders *earn* interest continually even though they do not *collect* cash payment for it every day. Each day, the amount of interest due, called **accrued interest,** is greater than the day before. Companies would find it highly impractical to attempt to record (recognize) accrued interest continually as the amount due increased.

Businesses typically solve the record-keeping problem by only recording accrued interest when it is time to prepare financial statements or when it is due. At such times, the accounts are *adjusted* to reflect the amount of interest currently due. For example, ATS recorded the asset exchange immediately upon investing in the note receivable on November 1, 2014. ATS did not, however, recognize any interest earned on the note until the balance sheet date, December 31, 2014. At year-end ATS made an entry to recognize the interest it had earned during the previous two months (November 1 through December 31). This entry is an **adjusting entry** because it adjusts (updates) the account balances prior to preparing financial statements.

ATS computed the amount of accrued interest by multiplying the principal amount of the note by the annual interest rate and by the length of time for which the note has been outstanding.

Principal × Annual interest rate × Time outstanding = Interest revenue

$15,000 ×   0.06   ×   (2/12)   = $150

ATS recognized the $150 of interest revenue in 2014 although ATS will not collect the cash until 2015. This practice illustrates the **matching concept.** Interest revenue is recognized in (matched with) the period in which it is earned regardless of when the related cash is collected. The adjustment is an asset source transaction. The asset account Interest Receivable increases, and the stockholders' equity account Retained Earnings increases. The income statement reflects an increase in revenue and net income. The statement of cash flows is not affected because ATS will not collect cash until the maturity date (October 31, 2015). The effects on the financial statements are shown below.

	Assets				=	Liab.	+	Equity	Rev.	–	Exp.	=	Net Inc.	Cash Flow
Date	Cash	+	Notes Rec.	+	Int. Rec.	=			Ret. Earn.					
12/31/12	NA	+	NA	+	150	=	NA	+	150	150	–	NA	=	150	NA

EVENT 3 Collection of Principal and Interest on the Maturity Date

ATS collected $15,900 cash on the maturity date. The collection included $15,000 for the principal plus $900 for the interest. Recall that ATS previously accrued interest in the December 31, 2014, adjusting entry for the two months in 2014 that the note was outstanding. Since year-end, ATS has earned an additional 10 months of interest revenue. ATS must recognize this interest revenue before recording the cash collection. The amount of interest earned in 2015 is computed as follows.

Principal × Annual interest rate × Time outstanding = Interest revenue

$15,000 ×   0.06   ×   (10/12)   = $750

The effects on the financial statements are shown below.

	Assets				=	Liab.	+	Equity	Rev.	–	Exp.	=	Net Inc.	Cash Flow
Date	Cash	+	Notes Rec.	+	Int. Rec.	=			Ret. Earn.					
10/31/13	NA	+	NA	+	750	=	NA	+	750	750	–	NA	=	750	NA

The total amount of accrued interest is now $900 ($150 accrued in 2014 plus $750 accrued in 2015). The $15,900 cash collection is an asset exchange transaction. The asset account Cash increases and two asset accounts, Notes Receivable and Interest Receivable, decrease. The income statement is not affected. The statement of cash flows shows a $15,000 inflow from investing activities (recovery of principal) and a $900 inflow from operating activities (interest collection). The effects on the financial statements are shown below.

Date	Assets					= Liab.	+	Equity	Rev.	−	Exp.	=	Net Inc.	Cash Flow	
	Cash	+	Notes Rec.	+	Int. Rec. =			Ret. Earn.							
10/31/13	15,900	+	(15,000)	+	(900) =	NA	+	NA	NA	−	NA	=	NA	15,000	IA
														900	OA

Financial Statements

The financial statements reveal key differences between the timing of revenue recognition and the exchange of cash. These differences are highlighted below.

	2014	2015	Total
Interest revenue recognized	$150	$750	$900
Cash inflow from operating activities	0	900	900

Accrual accounting calls for recognizing revenue in the period in which it is earned regardless of when cash is collected.

Income Statement

Although generally accepted accounting principles require reporting receipts of or payments for interest on the statement of cash flows as operating activities, they do not specify how to classify interest on the income statement. In fact, companies traditionally report interest on the income statement as a nonoperating item. Interest is therefore frequently reported in two different categories within the same set of financial statements.

Balance Sheet

As with other assets, companies report interest receivable and notes receivable on the balance sheet in order of their liquidity. **Liquidity** refers to how quickly assets are expected to be converted to cash during normal operations. In the preceding example, ATS expects to convert its accounts receivable to cash before it collects the interest receivable and note receivable. Companies commonly report interest and notes receivable after accounts receivable. Exhibit 5.6 shows a partial balance sheet for Southern Company to illustrate the presentation of receivables.

EXHIBIT 5.6

Typical Balance Sheet Presentation of Receivables

SOUTHERN COMPANY
Partial Balance Sheet
As of December 31, 2014

Cash		$xxxx
Accounts receivable	$xxxx	
Less: Allowance for doubtful accounts	(xxxx)	
Net realizable value of accounts receivable		xxxx
Interest receivable		xxxx
Notes receivable		xxxx

> ☑ **CHECK YOURSELF 5.3**
>
> On October 1, 2014, Mei Company accepted a promissory note for a loan it made to the Asia Pacific Company. The note had a $24,000 principal amount, a four-month term, and an annual interest rate of 4 percent. Determine the amount of interest revenue and the cash inflow from operating activities Mei will report in its 2014 and 2015 financial statements.
>
> **Answer**   The computation of accrued interest revenue is shown below. The interest rate is stated in annual terms even though the term of the note is only four months. Interest rates are commonly expressed as an annual percentage regardless of the term of the note. The *time outstanding* in the following formulas is therefore expressed as a fraction of a year. Mei charged annual interest of 4 percent, but the note was outstanding for only 3/12 of a year in 2014 and 1/12 of a year in 2015.
>
>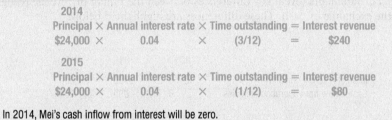
>
> 2014
> Principal × Annual interest rate × Time outstanding = Interest revenue
> $24,000 ×   0.04   ×   (3/12)   = $240
>
> 2015
> Principal × Annual interest rate × Time outstanding = Interest revenue
> $24,000 ×   0.04   ×   (1/12)   = $80
>
> In 2014, Mei's cash inflow from interest will be zero.
>   In 2015, Mei will report a $320 ($240 + $80) cash inflow from operating activities for interest.

ACCOUNTING FOR CREDIT CARD SALES

LO 5-5

📷 Explain how accounting for credit card sales affects financial statements.

Maintaining accounts and notes receivable is expensive. In addition to uncollectible accounts expense, companies extending credit to their customers incur considerable costs for such clerical tasks as running background checks and maintaining customer records. Many businesses find it more efficient to accept third-party credit cards instead of offering credit directly to their customers. Credit card companies service the merchant's credit sales for a fee that typically ranges between 2 and 8 percent of gross sales.

The credit card company provides customers with plastic cards that permit cardholders to charge purchases at various retail outlets. When a sale takes place, the seller records the transaction on a receipt the customer signs. The receipt is forwarded to the credit card company, which immediately pays the merchant.

The credit card company deducts its service fee from the gross amount of the sale and pays the merchant the net balance (gross amount of sale less credit card fee) in cash. The credit card company collects the gross sale amount directly from the customer. The merchant avoids the risk of uncollectible accounts as well as the cost of maintaining customer credit records. To illustrate, assume that Allen's Tutoring Service experiences the following events.

EVENT 1   Recognition of Revenue and Expense on Credit Card Sales
ATS accepts a credit card payment for $1,000 of services rendered.

Assume the credit card company charges a 5 percent fee for handling the transaction ($1,000 × 0.05 = $50). ATS's income increases by the amount of revenue ($1,000) and decreases by the amount of the credit card expense ($50). Net income increases by $950. The event increases an asset, accounts receivable, due from the credit card company, and stockholders' equity (retained earnings) by $950 ($1,000 revenue − $50 credit card expense). Cash flow is not affected. These effects are shown here.

Event No.	Assets	= Liab. +	Equity	Rev.	− Exp.	= Net Inc.	Cash Flow
	Accts. Rec. =		Ret. Earn.				
1	950	= NA +	950	1,000	− 50	= 950	NA

EVENT 2   Collection of Credit Card Receivable

The collection of the receivable due from the credit card company is recorded like any other receivable collection.

When ATS collects the net amount of $950 ($1,000 − $50) from the credit card company, one asset account (Cash) increases and another asset account (Accounts Receivable) decreases. Total assets are not affected. The income statement is not affected. A $950 cash inflow is reported in the operating activities section of the statement of cash flows. These effects are illustrated below.

Event No.	Assets		= Liab. + Equity	Rev.	− Exp.	= Net Inc.	Cash Flow
	Cash +	Accts. Rec.					
2	950 +	(950)	= NA + NA	NA	− NA	= NA	950 OA

As mentioned earlier, two costs of extending credit to customers are bad debts expense and record-keeping costs. These costs can be significant. Large companies spend literally millions of dollars to buy the equipment and pay the staff necessary to operate entire departments devoted to managing accounts receivable. Further, there is an implicit interest charge associated with extending credit. When a customer is permitted to delay payment, the creditor forgoes the opportunity to invest the amount the customer owes.

INVENTORY COST FLOW METHODS

In Chapter 3, we used the simplifying assumption that identical inventory items cost the same amount. In practice, businesses often pay different amounts for identical items. Suppose The Mountain Bike Company (TMBC) sells high-end Model 201 helmets. Even though all Model 201 helmets are identical, the price TMBC pays for each helmet frequently changes.

Assume TMBC purchases one Model 201 helmet at a cost of $100. Two weeks later, TMBC purchases a second Model 201 helmet. Because the supplier has raised prices, the second helmet costs $110. If TMBC sells one of its two helmets, should it record $100 or $110 as cost of goods sold? The following section of this chapter discusses several acceptable alternative methods for determining the amount of cost of goods sold under generally accepted accounting principles.

Recall that when goods are sold, product costs flow (are transferred) from the Inventory account to the Cost of Goods Sold account. Four acceptable methods for determining the amount of cost to transfer are (1) specific identification; (2) first-in, first-out (FIFO); (3) last-in, first-out (LIFO); and (4) weighted average.

LO 5-6

Explain how different inventory cost flow methods (specific identification, FIFO, LIFO, and weighted average) affect financial statements.

Specific Identification

Suppose TMBC tags inventory items so that it can identify which one is sold at the time of sale. TMBC could then charge the actual cost of the specific item sold to cost of goods sold. Recall that the first inventory item TMBC purchased cost $100 and the second item cost $110. Using **specific identification,** cost of goods sold would be $100 if the first item purchased were sold or $110 if the second item purchased were sold.

When a company's inventory consists of many low-priced, high-turnover goods, the record keeping necessary to use specific identification isn't practical. Imagine the difficulty of recording the cost of each specific food item in a grocery store. Another disadvantage of the specific identification method is the opportunity for managers to manipulate the income statement. For example, TMBC can report a lower cost of goods sold by selling the first instead of the second item. Specific identification is, however, frequently used for high-priced, low-turnover inventory items such as automobiles. For big-ticket items like cars, customer demands for specific products limit management's ability to select which merchandise is sold and volume is low enough to manage the record keeping.

First-In, First-Out (FIFO)

The **first-in, first-out (FIFO) cost flow method** requires that the cost of the items purchased *first* be assigned to cost of goods sold. Using FIFO, TMBC's cost of goods sold is $100.

Last-In, First-Out (LIFO)

The **last-in, first-out (LIFO) cost flow method** requires that the cost of the items purchased *last* be charged to cost of goods sold. Using LIFO, TMBC's cost of goods sold is $110.

Weighted Average

To use the **weighted-average cost flow method,** first calculate the average cost per unit by dividing the *total cost* of the inventory available by the *total number* of units available. In the case of TMBC, the average cost per unit of the inventory is $105 ([$100 + $110] ÷ 2). Cost of goods sold is then calculated by multiplying the average cost per unit by the number of units sold. Using weighted average, TMBC's cost of goods sold is $105 ($105 × 1).

Physical Flow

The preceding discussion pertains to the flow of *costs* through the accounting records, *not* the actual **physical flow of goods.** Goods usually move physically on a FIFO basis, which means that the first items of merchandise acquired by a company (first-in) are the first items sold to its customers (first-out). The inventory items on hand at the end of the accounting period are typically the last items in (the most recently acquired goods). If companies did not sell their oldest inventory items first, inventories would include dated, less marketable merchandise. *Cost flow,* however, can differ from *physical flow.* For example, a company may use LIFO or weighted average for financial reporting even if its goods flow physically on a FIFO basis.

EFFECT OF COST FLOW ON FINANCIAL STATEMENTS

Effect on Income Statement

The cost flow method a company uses can significantly affect the gross margin reported in the income statement. To demonstrate, assume that TMBC sold the inventory item discussed previously for $120. The amounts of gross margin using the FIFO, LIFO, and weighted-average cost flow assumptions are shown in the following table.

	FIFO	LIFO	Weighted Average
Sales	$120	$120	$120
Cost of goods sold	(100)	(110)	(105)
Gross margin	$ 20	$ 10	$ 15

Even though the physical flow is assumed to be identical for each method, the gross margin reported under FIFO is double the amount reported under LIFO. Companies experiencing identical economic events (same units of inventory purchased and sold) can report significantly different results in their financial statements. Meaningful financial analysis requires an understanding of financial reporting practices.

Effect on Balance Sheet

Because total product costs are allocated between cost of goods sold and ending inventory, the cost flow method a company uses affects its balance sheet as well as its income statement. Because FIFO transfers the first cost to the income statement, it leaves the last cost on the balance sheet. Similarly, by transferring the last cost to the income statement, LIFO leaves the first cost in ending inventory. The weighted-average method bases both cost of goods sold and ending inventory on the average cost per unit. To illustrate, the ending inventory TMBC would report on the balance sheet using each of the three cost flow methods is shown in the following table.

EXHIBIT 5.7

Use of Inventory Cost Flow Methods

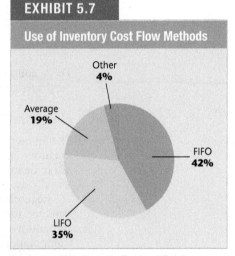

Data Source: AICPA, *Accounting Trends and Techniques.*

	FIFO	LIFO	Weighted Average
Ending inventory	$110	$100	$105

The FIFO, LIFO, and weighted-average methods are all used extensively in business practice. The same company may even use one cost flow method for some of its products and different cost flow methods for other products. Exhibit 5.7 illustrates the relative use of the different cost flow methods among U.S. companies.

☑ **CHECK YOURSELF 5.4**

Nash Office Supply (NOS) purchased two Model 303 copiers at different times. The first copier purchased cost $400 and the second copier purchased cost $450. NOS sold one of the copiers for $600. Determine the gross margin on the sale and the ending inventory balance assuming NOS accounts for inventory using (1) FIFO, (2) LIFO, and (3) weighted average.

Answer

	FIFO	LIFO	Weighted Average
Sales	$600	$600	$600
Cost of goods sold	(400)	(450)	(425)
Gross margin	$200	$150	$175
Ending inventory	$450	$400	$425

Multiple Layers with Multiple Quantities

The previous example illustrates different **inventory cost flow methods** using only two cost layers ($100 and $110) with only one unit of inventory in each layer. Actual business inventories are considerably more complex. Most real-world inventories are composed of multiple cost layers with different quantities of inventory in each layer. The underlying allocation concepts, however, remain unchanged.

For example, a different inventory item The Mountain Bike Company (TMBC) carries in its stores is a bike called the Eraser. TMBC's beginning inventory and two purchases of Eraser bikes are described below.

Jan. 1	Beginning inventory	10 units @ $200	=	$ 2,000
Mar. 18	First purchase	20 units @ $220	=	4,400
Aug. 21	Second purchase	25 units @ $250	=	6,250
Total cost of the 55 bikes available for sale				$12,650

The accounting records for the period show that TMBC paid cash for all Eraser bike purchases and that it sold 43 bikes at a cash price of $350 each.

Allocating Cost of Goods Available for Sale

The following discussion shows how to determine the cost of goods sold and ending inventory amounts under FIFO, LIFO, and weighted average. We show all three methods to demonstrate how they affect the financial statements differently; TMBC would actually use only one of the methods.

Regardless of the cost flow method chosen, TMBC must allocate the cost of goods available for sale ($12,650) between cost of goods sold and ending inventory. The amounts assigned to each category will differ depending on TMBC's cost flow method. Computations for each method are shown below.

FIFO Inventory Cost Flow

Recall that TMBC sold 43 Eraser bikes during the accounting period. The FIFO method transfers to the Cost of Goods Sold account the *cost of the first 43 bikes* TMBC had available to sell. The first 43 bikes acquired by TMBC were the 10 bikes in the beginning inventory (these were purchased in the prior period) plus the 20 bikes purchased in March and 13 of the bikes purchased in August. The expense recognized for the cost of these bikes ($9,650) is computed as follows.

Jan. 1	Beginning inventory	10 units @ $200	=	$2,000
Mar. 18	First purchase	20 units @ $220	=	4,400
Aug. 21	Second purchase	13 units @ $250	=	3,250
Total cost of the 43 bikes sold				$9,650

Because TMBC had 55 bikes available for sale it would have 12 bikes (55 available − 43 sold) in ending inventory. The cost assigned to these 12 bikes (the ending balance in the Inventory account) equals the cost of goods available for sale minus the cost of goods sold as shown below.

Cost of goods available for sale	$12,650
Cost of goods sold	(9,650)
Ending inventory balance	$ 3,000

We show the allocation of the cost of goods available for sale between cost of goods sold and ending inventory graphically below.

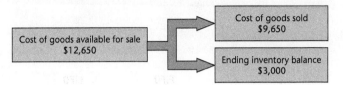

LIFO Inventory Cost Flow

Under LIFO, the cost of goods sold is the cost of the last 43 bikes acquired by TMBC, computed as follows.

Aug. 21	Second purchase	25 units @ $250	=	$ 6,250
Mar. 18	First purchase	18 units @ $220	=	3,960
Total cost of the 43 bikes sold				$10,210

The LIFO cost of the 12 bikes in ending inventory is computed as shown below.

Cost of goods available for sale	$12,650
Cost of goods sold	(10,210)
Ending inventory balance	$ 2,440

We show the allocation of the cost of goods available for sale between cost of goods sold and ending inventory graphically below.

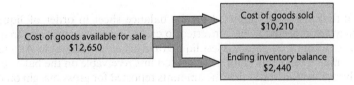

Weighted-Average Cost Flow

The weighted-average cost per unit is determined by dividing the *total cost of goods available for sale* by the *total number of units* available for sale. For TMBC, the weighted-average cost per unit is $230 ($12,650 ÷ 55). The weighted-average cost of goods sold is determined by multiplying the average cost per unit by the number of units sold ($230 × 43 = $9,890). The cost assigned to the 12 bikes in ending inventory is $2,760 (12 × $230).

We show the allocation of the cost of goods available for sale between cost of goods sold and ending inventory graphically below.

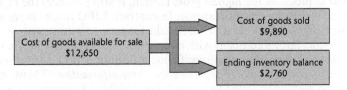

Effect of Cost Flow on Financial Statements

Exhibit 5.8 displays partial financial statements for The Mountain Bike Company (TMBC). This exhibit includes only information pertaining to the Eraser bikes inventory item described above. Other financial statement data are omitted.

EXHIBIT 5.8

TMBC COMPANY
Comparative Financial Statements
Partial Income Statements

	FIFO	LIFO	Weighted Average
Sales	$15,050	$15,050	$15,050
Cost of goods sold	(9,650)	(10,210)	(9,890)
Gross margin	5,400	4,840	5,160

Partial Balance Sheets

	FIFO	LIFO	Weighted Average
Assets			
Cash	$ xx	$ xx	$ xx
Accounts receivable	xx	xx	xx
Inventory	3,000	2,440	2,760

Partial Statements of Cash Flows

	FIFO	LIFO	Weighted Average
Operating Activities			
Cash inflow from customers	$15,050	$15,050	$15,050
Cash outflow for inventory	(10,650)	(10,650)	(10,650)

Recall that assets are reported on the balance sheet in order of liquidity (how quickly they are expected to be converted to cash). Because companies frequently sell inventory on account, inventory is less liquid than accounts receivable. As a result, companies commonly report inventory below accounts receivable on the balance sheet.

Exhibit 5.8 demonstrates that the amounts reported for gross margin on the income statement and inventory on the balance sheet differ significantly. The cash flow from operating activities on the statement of cash flows, however, is identical under all three methods. Regardless of cost flow reporting method, TMBC paid $10,650 cash ($4,400 first purchase + $6,250 second purchase) to purchase inventory and received $15,050 cash for inventory sold.

The Impact of Income Tax

Based on the financial statement information in Exhibit 5.8, which cost flow method should TMBC use? Most people initially suggest FIFO because FIFO reports the highest gross margin and the largest balance in ending inventory. However, other factors are relevant. FIFO produces the highest gross margin; it also produces the highest net income and the highest income tax expense. In contrast, LIFO results in recognizing the lowest gross margin, lowest net income, and the lowest income tax expense.

Will investors favor a company with more assets and higher net income or one with lower tax expense? Recognize that specific identification, FIFO, LIFO, and weighted average are *different methods of reporting the same information.* TMBC experienced only one set of events pertaining to Eraser bikes. Exhibit 5.8 reports those same events three different ways. However, if the FIFO reporting method causes TMBC to pay more taxes than the LIFO method, using FIFO will cause a real reduction in the value of the company. Paying more money in taxes leaves less money in the company. Knowledgeable investors would be more attracted to TMBC if it uses LIFO because the lower tax payments allow the company to keep more value in the business.

Research suggests that, as a group, investors are knowledgeable. They make investment decisions based on economic substance regardless of how information is reported in financial statements.

The Income Statement versus the Tax Return

In some instances companies may use one accounting method for financial reporting and a different method to compute income taxes (the tax return must explain any differences). With respect to LIFO, however, the Internal Revenue Service requires that companies using LIFO for income tax purposes must also use LIFO for financial reporting. A company could not, therefore, get both the lower tax benefit provided by LIFO and the financial reporting advantage offered under FIFO.

Inflation versus Deflation

Our illustration assumes an inflationary environment (rising inventory prices). In a deflationary environment, the impact of using LIFO versus FIFO is reversed. LIFO produces tax advantages in an inflationary environment, while FIFO produces tax advantages in a deflationary environment. Companies operating in the computer industry where prices are falling would obtain a tax advantage by using FIFO. In contrast, companies that sell medical supplies in an inflationary environment would obtain a tax advantage by using LIFO.

Full Disclosure and Consistency

Generally accepted accounting principles allow each company to choose the inventory cost flow method best suited to its reporting needs. Because results can vary considerably among methods, however, the GAAP principle of **full disclosure** requires that financial statements disclose the method chosen. In addition, so that a company's financial statements are comparable from year to year, the GAAP principle of **consistency** generally requires that companies use the same cost flow method each period. The limited exceptions to the consistency principle are described in more advanced accounting courses.

☑ CHECK YOURSELF 5.5

The following information was drawn from the inventory records of Fields, Inc.

Beginning inventory	200 units @ $20
First purchase	400 units @ $22
Second purchase	600 units @ $24

Assume that Fields sold 900 units of inventory.

1. Determine the amount of cost of goods sold using FIFO.

2. Would using LIFO produce a higher or lower amount of cost of goods sold? Why?

Answer

1. Cost of goods sold using FIFO

Beginning inventory	200 units @ $20	=	$ 4,000
First purchase	400 units @ $22	=	8,800
Second purchase	300 units @ $24	=	7,200
Total cost of goods sold			$20,000

2. The inventory records reflect an inflationary environment of steadily rising prices. Since LIFO charges the latest costs (in this case the highest costs) to the income statement, using LIFO would produce a higher amount of cost of goods sold than would using FIFO.

REALITY BYTES

To avoid spoilage or obsolescence, most companies use the first-in, first-out (FIFO) approach for the flow of physical goods. The older goods (first units purchased) are sold before the newer goods are sold. For example, Kroger's and other food stores stack older merchandise at the front of the shelf where customers are more likely to pick it up first. As a result, merchandise is sold before it becomes dated. However, when timing is not an issue, convenience may dictate the use of the last-in, first-out (LIFO) method. Examples of products that frequently move on a LIFO basis include rock, gravel, dirt, or other nonwasting assets. Indeed, rock, gravel, and dirt are normally stored in piles that are unprotected from weather. New inventory is simply piled on top of the old. Inventory that is sold is taken from the top of the pile because it is convenient to do so. Accordingly, the last inventory purchased is the first inventory sold. For example, Vulcan Materials Co., which claims to be the nation's largest producer of construction aggregates (stone and gravel), uses LIFO. Regardless of whether the flow of physical goods occurs on a LIFO or FIFO basis, costs can flow differently. The flow of inventory through the physical facility is a separate issue from the flow of costs through the accounting system.

FOCUS ON INTERNATIONAL ISSUES

LIFO IN OTHER COUNTRIES

This chapter introduced a rather strange inventory cost flow assumption called LIFO. As explained, the primary advantage of LIFO is to reduce a company's income taxes. Given the choice, companies that use LIFO to reduce their taxes would probably prefer to use another method when preparing their GAAP–based financial statements, but the IRS does not permit this. Thus, they are left with no choice but to use the seemingly counterintuitive LIFO assumption for GAAP as well as tax reporting.

What happens in countries other than the United States? International Financial Reporting Standards (IFRS) do not allow the use of LIFO. Most industrialized nations are now using IFRS. You can see the impact of this disparity if you review the annual report of a U.S. company that uses LIFO *and* has significant operations in other countries. Very often it will explain that LIFO is used to calculate inventory (and cost of goods sold) for domestic operations, but another method is used for activities outside the United States.

For example, here is an excerpt from General Electric's 2012 Form 10-K, Note 1.

All inventories are stated at the lower of cost or realizable values. Cost for a significant portion of GE U.S. inventories is determined on a last-in, first-out (LIFO) basis. Cost of other GE inventories is determined on a first-in, first-out (FIFO) basis. LIFO was used for 37% and 38% of GE inventories at December 31, 2012 and 2011, respectively.

If the company has its headquarters in the United States, why not simply use LIFO in its foreign operations? In addition to having to prepare financial statements for the United States, the company probably has to prepare statements for its local operations using the reporting standards of the local country.

Prior to the establishment of IFRS each country was responsible for issuing its own, local GAAP. Even then, most countries did not allow for the use of LIFO.

A Look Back

We first introduced accounting for receivables in Chapter 2. This chapter presented additional complexities related to accounts receivable, such as the *allowance method of accounting for uncollectible accounts*. The allowance method improves matching of expenses with revenues. It also provides a more accurate measure of the value of accounts receivable on the balance sheet.

Under the allowance method, estimated uncollectible accounts expense is recorded in an adjusting entry at the end of the period in which a company has made credit sales. There are two methods commonly used to estimate the amount of uncollectible accounts expense: the percent of revenue method and the percent of receivables method. With the percent of revenue method, uncollectible accounts expense is measured as a percent of the period's sales. With the percent of receivables method, a company analyzes its accounts receivable at the end of the period, usually classifying them by age, to estimate the amount of the accounts receivable balance that is likely to be uncollectible. The balance in the Allowance for Doubtful Accounts account is then adjusted to equal the estimated amount of uncollectible accounts. Uncollectible accounts expense decreases the net realizable value of receivables (accounts receivable − allowance for doubtful accounts), stockholders' equity, and net income.

The allowance method of accounting for uncollectible accounts is conceptually superior to the *direct write-off method,* in which uncollectible accounts expense is recognized when an account is determined to be uncollectible. The direct write-off method fails to match revenues with expenses and overstates accounts receivable on the balance sheet. It is easier to use, however, and is permitted by generally accepted accounting principles if the amount of uncollectible accounts expense is immaterial.

The chapter also introduced notes receivable and accounting for *accrued interest.* When the term of a promissory note extends over more than one accounting period, companies must record adjusting entries to recognize interest in the appropriate accounting period, even if the cash exchange of interest occurs in a different accounting period.

We also discussed accounting for credit card sales, a vehicle that shifts uncollectible accounts expense to the credit card issuer. Many companies find the benefits of accepting major credit cards to be worth the credit card expense consequently incurred. Finally, we addressed the costs of making credit sales. In addition to uncollectible accounts expense, interest is a major cost of financing receivables.

This chapter also discussed the inventory cost flow methods of first-in, first-out (FIFO); last-in, first-out (LIFO); weighted average; and specific identification. Under FIFO, the cost of the items purchased first is reported on the income statement, and the cost of the items purchased last is reported on the balance sheet. Under the weighted-average method, the average cost of inventory is reported on both the income statement and the balance sheet. Finally, under specific identification the actual cost of goods is reported on the income statement and the balance sheet.

A Look Forward >>

Chapter 6 discusses accounting for long-term assets such as buildings and equipment. As with inventory cost flow, GAAP allows companies to use different accounting methods to report on similar types of business events. Life would be easier for accounting students if all companies used the same accounting methods. However, the business world is complex. For the foreseeable future, people are likely to continue to have diverse views as to the best way to account for a variety of business transactions. To function effectively in today's business environment, it is important for you to be able to recognize differences in reporting practices.

> Video lectures and accompanying self-assessment quizzes are available for all learning objectives through McGraw-Hill *Connect®* *Accounting.*

SELF-STUDY REVIEW PROBLEM 1

During 2014 Calico Company experienced the following accounting events.

1. Provided $120,000 of services on account.
2. Collected $85,000 cash from accounts receivable.
3. Wrote off $1,800 of accounts receivable that were uncollectible.
4. Loaned $3,000 to an individual, Emma Gardner, in exchange for a note receivable.
5. Paid $90,500 cash for operating expenses.
6. Estimated that uncollectible accounts expense would be 2 percent of revenue earned on account. Recorded the year-end adjusting entry.
7. Recorded the year-end adjusting entry for accrued interest on the note receivable (see Event 4). Calico made the loan on August 1. It had a six-month term and a 6 percent rate of interest.

Calico's ledger balances on January 1, 2014, were as follows.

Event No.	Cash	+	Accts. Rec.	−	Allow.	+	Notes Rec.	+	Int. Rec.	=	Liab.	+	Com. Stk.	+	Ret. Earn.
													Equity		
Bal.	12,000		18,000		2,200	+	NA	+	NA	=	NA	+	20,000	+	7,800

Required

a. Record the 2014 events in ledger accounts using the horizontal format shown above.
b. Determine net income for 2014.
c. Determine net cash flow from operating activities for 2014.
d. Determine the net realizable value of accounts receivable at December 31, 2014.
e. What amount of interest revenue will Calico recognize on its note receivable in 2015?

Solution to Requirement *a.*

Event No.	Cash	+	Accts. Rec.	−	Allow.	+	Notes Rec.	+	Int. Rec.	=	Liab.	+	Com. Stk.	+	Ret. Earn.
Bal.	12,000	+	18,000	−	2,200	+	NA	+	NA	=	NA	+	20,000	+	7,800
1	NA	+	120,000	−	NA	+	NA	+	NA	=	NA	+	NA	+	120,000
2	85,000	+	(85,000)	−	NA	+	NA	+	NA	=	NA	+	NA	+	NA
3	NA	+	(1,800)	−	(1,800)	+	NA	+	NA	=	NA	+	NA	+	NA
4	(3,000)	+	NA	−	NA	+	3,000	+	NA	=	NA	+	NA	+	NA
5	(90,500)	+	NA	−	NA	+	NA	+	NA	=	NA	+	NA	+	(90,500)
6	NA	+	NA	−	2,400	+	NA	+	NA	=	NA	+	NA	+	(2,400)
7	NA	+	NA	−	NA	+	NA	+	75*	=	NA	+	NA	+	75
Totals	3,500	+	51,200	−	2,800	+	3,000	+	75	=	NA	+	20,000	+	34,975

*$3,000 × .06 × 5/12 = $75.

Solution to Requirements *b–e.*

b. Net income is $27,175 ($120,000 − $90,500 − $2,400 + $75).
c. Net cash flow from operating activities is an outflow of $5,500 ($85,000 − $90,500).
d. The net realizable value of accounts receivable is $48,400 ($51,200 − $2,800).
e. In 2015, Calico will recognize interest revenue for one month: $3,000 × .06 × 1/12 = $15.

Video lectures and accompanying self-assessment quizzes are available for all learning objectives through McGraw-Hill *Connect®* *Accounting.*

SELF-STUDY REVIEW PROBLEM 2

Erie Jewelers sells gold earrings. Its beginning inventory of Model 407 gold earrings consisted of 100 pairs of earrings at $50 per pair. Erie purchased two batches of Model 407 earrings during the year. The first batch purchased consisted of 150 pairs at $53 per pair; the second batch consisted of 200 pairs at $56 per pair. During the year, Erie sold 375 pairs of Model 407 earrings.

Required

Determine the amount of product cost Erie would allocate to cost of goods sold and ending inventory assuming that Erie uses (a) FIFO, (b) LIFO, and (c) weighted average.

Solution to Requirements *a–c*

Goods Available for Sale				
Beginning inventory	100	@	$50	=	$ 5,000
First purchase	150	@	53	=	7,950
Second purchase	200	@	56	=	11,200
Goods available for sale	450				$24,150

a. FIFO

Cost of Goods Sold	Pairs		Cost per Pair		Cost of Goods Sold
From beginning inventory	100	@	$50	=	$ 5,000
From first purchase	150	@	53	=	7,950
From second purchase	125	@	56	=	7,000
Total pairs sold	375				$19,950

Ending inventory = Goods available for sale − Cost of goods sold
Ending inventory = $24,150 − $19,950 = $4,200

b. LIFO

Cost of Goods Sold	Pairs		Cost per Pair		Cost of Goods Sold
From second purchase	200	@	$56	=	$11,200
From first purchase	150	@	53	=	7,950
From beginning inventory	25	@	50	=	1,250
Total pairs sold	375				$20,400

Ending inventory = Goods available for sale − Cost of goods sold
Ending inventory = $24,150 − $20,400 = $3,750

c. Weighted average

Goods available for sale ÷ Total pairs = Cost per pair
$24,150   ÷   450   = $53.6667

Cost of goods sold   375 units @ $53.6667 = $20,125
Ending inventory   75 units @ $53.6667 = $4,025

188   Chapter 5

KEY TERMS

Account receivable 162	Consistency 183	Maker 173	Principal 173
Accrued interest 173	Contra asset account 166	Matching concept 174	Promissory note 172
Adjusting entry 174	First-in, first-out (FIFO) cost	Maturity date 173	Reinstate 168
Aging of accounts	flow method 178	Net realizable value 164	Specific identification 178
receivable 171	Full disclosure 183	Notes receivable 165	Uncollectible accounts
Allowance for doubtful	Interest 173	Payee 173	expense 165
accounts 164	Inventory cost flow	Percent of receivables	Weighted-average cost flow
Allowance method of	methods 180	method 170	method 178
accounting for uncollectible	Last-in, first-out (LIFO) cost	Percent of revenue	
accounts 164	flow method 178	method 169	
Collateral 173	Liquidity 175	Physical flow of goods 178	

QUESTIONS

1. What is the difference between accounts receivable and notes receivable?

2. What is the *net realizable value* of receivables?

3. What type of account is the Allowance for Doubtful Accounts?

4. What are two ways in which estimating uncollectible accounts improves the accuracy of the financial statements?

5. When using the allowance method, why is uncollectible accounts expense an estimated amount?

6. What is the most common format for reporting accounts receivable on the balance sheet? What information does this method provide beyond showing only the net amount?

7. Why is it necessary to reinstate a previously written off account receivable before the collection is recorded?

8. What are some factors considered in estimating the amount of uncollectible accounts receivable?

9. What is the effect on the accounting equation of recognizing uncollectible accounts expense?

10. What is the effect on the accounting equation of writing off an uncollectible account receivable when the allowance method is used?

11. How does the recovery of a previously written-off account affect the income statement when the allowance method is used? How does the recovery of a previously written-off account affect the statement of cash flows when the allowance method is used?

12. What is the advantage of using the allowance method of accounting for uncollectible accounts?

13. How do companies determine the percentage estimate of uncollectible accounts when using the percent of revenue method?

14. What is an advantage of using the percent of receivables method of estimating uncollectible accounts expense?

15. What is "aging of accounts receivable"?

16. What is a promissory note?

17. Define the following terms:
    a. Maker
    b. Payee
    c. Principal

    d. Interest
    e. Maturity date
    f. Collateral

18. What is the formula for computing interest revenue?

19. What is accrued interest?

20. How does the accrual of interest revenue or expense illustrate the matching concept?

21. Assets are listed on the balance sheet in the order of their liquidity. Explain this statement.

22. When is an adjusting entry for accrued interest generally recorded?

23. Assume that on July 1, 2014, Big Corp. loaned Little Corp. $12,000 for a period of one year at 6 percent interest. What amount of interest revenue will Big report for 2014? What amount of cash will Big receive upon maturity of the note?

24. In which section of the statement of cash flows will Big report the cash collected in Question 23?

25. Why is it generally beneficial for a business to accept major credit cards as payment for goods and services even when the fee charged by the credit card company is substantial?

26. What types of costs do businesses avoid when they accept major credit cards as compared with handling credit sales themselves?

27. Name and describe the four cost flow methods discussed in this chapter.

28. What are some advantages and disadvantages of the specific identification method of accounting for inventory?

29. What are some advantages and disadvantages of using the FIFO method of inventory valuation?

30. What are some advantages and disadvantages of using the LIFO method of inventory valuation?

31. In an inflationary period, which inventory cost flow method will produce the highest net income? Explain.

32. In an inflationary period, which inventory cost flow method will produce the largest amount of total assets on the balance sheet? Explain.

33. What is the difference between the flow of costs and the physical flow of goods?

34. Does the choice of cost flow method (FIFO, LIFO, or weighted average) affect the statement of cash flows? Explain.

35. Assume that Key Co. purchased 1,000 units of merchandise in its first year of operations for $25 per unit. The company sold 850 units for

$40. What is the amount of cost of goods sold using FIFO? LIFO? Weighted average?

36. Assume that Key Co. purchased 1,500 units of merchandise in its second year of operation for $27 per unit. Its beginning inventory was determined in Question 35.

Assuming that 1,500 units are sold, what is the amount of cost of goods sold using FIFO? LIFO? Weighted average?

37. Refer to Questions 35 and 36. Which method might be preferable for financial statements? For income tax reporting? Explain.

38. In an inflationary period, which cost flow method, FIFO or LIFO, produces the larger cash flow? Explain.

39. Which inventory cost flow method produces the highest net income in a deflationary period?

MULTIPLE-CHOICE QUESTIONS

Multiple-choice questions are provided on the text website at www.mhhe.com/edmondssurvey4e.

EXERCISES

connect
|ACCOUNTING All applicable Exercises are available with McGraw-Hill's *Connect® Accounting.*

Exercise 5-1   *Accounting for bad debts: Allowance method*   LO 5-1

Michelle's Accounting Service began operation on January 1, 2014. The company experienced the following events for its first year of operations:

Events Affecting 2014:

1. Provided $96,000 of accounting services on account.
2. Collected $80,000 cash from accounts receivable.
3. Paid salaries of $32,000 for the year.
4. Adjusted the accounts to reflect management's expectations that uncollectible accounts expense would be $1,600.

Required

a. Organize the transaction data in accounts under on accounting equation.

b. Prepare an income statement, a balance sheet, and a statement of cash flows for 2014.

Exercise 5-2   *Analysis of financial statement effects of accounting for uncollectible*   LO 5-1
                 accounts under the allowance method

Businesses using the allowance method for the recognition of uncollectible accounts expense commonly experience four accounting events.

1. Recognition of revenue on account.
2. Collection of cash from accounts receivable.
3. Recognition of uncollectible accounts expense through a year-end adjusting entry.
4. Write-off of uncollectible accounts.

Required

Show the effect of each event on the elements of the financial statements, using a horizontal statements model like the one shown here. Use the following coding scheme to record your answers: increase is +, decrease is −, not affected is NA. In the cash flow column, indicate whether the item is an operating activity (OA), investing activity (IA), or financing activity (FA). The first transaction is entered as an example.

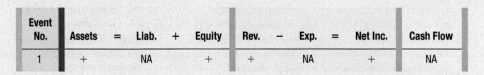

Event No.	Assets	=	Liab.	+	Equity	Rev.	−	Exp.	=	Net Inc.	Cash Flow
1	+		NA		+	+		NA		+	NA

LO 5-1

Exercise 5-3   *Analyzing account balances for a company using the allowance method of accounting for uncollectible accounts*

The following account balances come from the records of King Company:

	Beginning Balance	Ending Balance
Accounts Receivable	$4,000	$4,500
Allowance for Doubtful Accounts	150	250

During the accounting period, King recorded $21,000 of service revenue on account. The company also wrote off a $180 account receivable.

Required

a. Determine the amount of cash collected from receivables.

b. Determine the amount of uncollectible accounts expense recognized during the period.

LO 5-2

Exercise 5-4   *Effect of recognizing uncollectible accounts expense on financial statements: Percent of revenue allowance method*

Bulldog Auto Service was started on January 1, 2014. The company experienced the following events during its first two years of operation:

Events Affecting 2014

1. Provided $45,000 of repair services on account.
2. Collected $32,000 cash from accounts receivable.
3. Adjusted the accounting records to reflect the estimate that uncollectible accounts expense would be 1 percent of the service revenue on account.

Events Affecting 2015

1. Wrote off a $320 account receivable that was determined to be uncollectible.
2. Provided $65,000 of repair services on account.
3. Collected $66,000 cash from accounts receivable.
4. Adjusted the accounting records to reflect the estimate that uncollectible accounts expense would be 1 percent of the service revenue on account.

Required

a. Organize the transaction data in accounts under an accounting equation.

b. Determine the following amounts:

(1) Net income for 2014.

(2) Net cash flow from operating activities for 2014.

(3) Balance of accounts receivable at the end of 2014.

(4) Net realizable value of accounts receivable at the end of 2014.

c. Repeat Requirement *b* for the 2015 accounting period.

Exercise 5-5 *Analyzing financial statement effects of accounting for uncollectible*   LO 5-2
accounts using the percent of revenue allowance method

Pate Bros. uses the allowance method to account for uncollectible accounts expense. Pate experienced the following four events in 2014:

1. Recognized $68,000 of revenue on account.
2. Collected $62,000 cash from accounts receivable.
3. Determined that $500 of accounts receivable were not collectible and wrote them off.
4. Recognized uncollectible accounts expense for the year. Pate estimates that uncollectible accounts expense will be 2 percent of its sales.

Required

Show the effect of each of these events on the elements of the financial statements, using a horizontal statements model like the following one. Use + for increase, − for decrease, and NA for not affected. In the Cash Flow column, indicate whether the item is an operating activity (OA), investing activity (IA), or financing activity (FA).

Event No.	Assets				=	Liab.	+	Equity	Rev.	−	Exp.	=	Net Inc.	Cash Flow
	Cash	+	Accts. Rec.	− Allow.	=			Ret. Earn.						

Exercise 5-6 *Effect of recovering a receivable previously written off*   LO 5-1, 5-2

The accounts receivable balance for Don's Shoe Repair at December 31, 2014, was $76,000. Also on that date, the balance in Allowance for Doubtful Accounts was $3,200. During 2015, $2,900 of accounts receivable were written off as uncollectible. In addition, Don's Shoe Repair unexpectedly collected $200 of receivables that had been written off in a previous accounting period. Sales on account during 2015 were $210,000, and cash collections from receivables were $215,000. Uncollectible accounts expense was estimated to be 1 percent of the sales on account for the period.

Required

a. Organize the information in accounts under an accounting equation.
b. Based on the preceding information, compute (after year-end adjustment):
   (1) Balance of Allowance for Doubtful Accounts at December 31, 2015.
   (2) Balance of Accounts Receivable at December 31, 2015.
   (3) Net realizable value of Accounts Receivable at December 31, 2015.
c. What amount of uncollectible accounts expense will Don's Shoe Repair report for 2015?
d. Explain how the $200 recovery of receivables affected the accounting equation.

Exercise 5-7 *Accounting for uncollectible accounts: Percent of revenue*   LO 5-2
allowance method

Bing Auto Parts sells new and used auto parts. Although a majority of its sales are cash sales, it makes a significant amount of credit sales. During 2014, its first year of operations, Bing Auto Parts experienced the following:

Sales on account	$320,000
Cash sales	680,000
Collections of accounts receivable	295,000
Uncollectible accounts charged off during the year	1,400

Required

Assume that Bing Auto Parts uses the allowance method of accounting for uncollectible accounts and estimates that 1 percent of its sales on account will not be collected. Answer the following questions:

a. What is the Accounts Receivable balance at December 31, 2014?
b. What is the ending balance of Allowance for Doubtful Accounts at December 31, 2014, after all entries and adjusting entries are posted?
c. What is the amount of uncollectible accounts expense for 2014?
d. What is the net realizable value of accounts receivable at December 31, 2014?

LO 5-2

Exercise 5-8   *Determining account balances: Allowance method of accounting for uncollectible accounts*

During the first year of operation, 2014, Clayton Repair Co. recognized $500,000 of service revenue on account. At the end of 2014, the accounts receivable balance was $72,000. For this first year in business, the owner believes uncollectible accounts expense will be about 1 percent of sales on account.

Required

a. What amount of cash did Clayton collect from accounts receivable during 2014?
b. Assuming Clayton uses the allowance method to account for uncollectible accounts, what amount should Clayton record as uncollectible accounts expense for 2014?
c. What is the net realizable value of receivables at the end of 2014?
d. Show the effects of the above transactions on the financial statements by recording the appropriate amounts in a horizontal statements model like the one shown here. In the Cash Flow column, indicate whether the item is an operating activity (OA), investing activity (IA), or financing activity (FA). Use NA for not affected.

Assets			=	Liab.	+	Equity	Rev.	−	Exp.	=	Net Inc.	Cash Flow
Cash	+	Accts. Rec.	−	Allow.								

LO 5-3

Exercise 5-9   *Accounting for uncollectible accounts: Percent of receivables allowance method*

Tyler Service Co. experienced the following transactions for 2014, its first year of operations:

1. Provided $86,000 of services on account.
2. Collected $72,000 cash from accounts receivable.
3. Paid $39,000 of salaries expense for the year.
4. Tyler adjusted the accounts using the following information from an accounts receivable aging schedule:

Number of Days Past Due	Amount	Percent Likely to Be Uncollectible	Allowance Balance
Current	$7,500	.01	
0–30	2,000	.05	
31–60	1,500	.10	
61–90	1,000	.30	
Over 90 days	2,000	.50	

Required

a. Organize the information in accounts under an accounting equation.
b. Prepare the income statement for Tyler Service Co. for 2014.
c. What is the net realizable value of the accounts receivable at December 31, 2014?

Exercise 5-10 *Effect of recognizing uncollectible accounts on the financial statements: Percent of receivables allowance method*   LO 5-3

Faello Inc. experienced the following events for the first two years of its operations:

2014:

1. Provided $80,000 of services on account.
2. Provided $22,000 of services and received cash.
3. Collected $65,000 cash from accounts receivable.
4. Paid $24,000 of salaries expense for the year.
5. Adjusted the accounting records to reflect uncollectible accounts expense for the year. Faello estimates that 5 percent of the ending accounts receivable balance will be uncollectible.

2015:

1. Wrote off an uncollectible account of $620.
2. Provided $95,000 of services on account.
3. Provided $15,000 of services and collected cash.
4. Collected $90,000 cash from accounts receivable.
5. Paid $35,000 of salaries expense for the year.
6. Adjusted the accounts to reflect uncollectible accounts expense for the year. Faello estimates that 5 percent of the ending accounts receivable balance will be uncollectible.

Required

a. Organize the transaction data in accounts under an accounting equation.
b. Prepare the income statement, statement of changes in stockholders' equity, balance sheet, and statement of cash flows for 2014.
c. What is the net realizable value of the accounts receivable at December 31, 2014?
d. Repeat Requirements *a, b,* and *c* for 2015.

Exercise 5-11 *Accounting for notes receivable*   LO 5-4

Poole Enterprises loaned $30,000 to Boyd Co. on September 1, 2014, for one year at 6 percent interest.

Required

Show the effects of the following transactions in a horizontal statements model like the one shown below.

(1) The loan to Boyd Co.
(2) The adjusting entry at December 31, 2014.
(3) The adjusting entry and collection of the note on September 1, 2015.

	Assets					=	Liab.	+	Equity	Rev.	−	Exp.	=	Net Inc.	Cash Flow
Date	Cash	+	Notes Rec.	+	Int. Rec.	=			Ret. Earn.						

Exercise 5-12 *Notes receivable—accrued interest*   LO 5-4

On March 1, 2014, Peppers Deli loaned $18,000 to Simms Supply for one year at 5 percent interest.

Required

Answer the following questions.

a. What is Peppers interest income for 2014?
b. What is Peppers total amount of receivables at December 31, 2014?
c. What amounts will be reported on Peppers 2014 statement of cash flows?
d. What is Peppers interest income for 2015?
e. What is the total amount of cash that Peppers will collect in 2015 from Simms Supply?

f. What amounts will be reported on Peppers's 2015 statement of cash flows?

g. What is the total amount of interest Peppers Deli earned from the loan to Simms Supply?

LO 5-2, 5-4

Exercise 5-13   *Comprehensive single-cycle problem*

The following post-closing trial balance was drawn from the accounts of Hardwood Timber Co. as of December 31, 2013:

	Debit	Credit
Cash	$16,000	
Accounts receivable	18,000	
Allowance for doubtful accounts		$ 2,000
Inventory	25,000	
Accounts payable		9,200
Common stock		30,000
Retained earnings		17,800
Totals	$59,000	$59,000

Transactions for 2014

1. Acquired an additional $20,000 cash from the issue of common stock.
2. Purchased $80,000 of inventory on account.
3. Sold inventory that cost $61,000 for $98,000. Sales were made on account.
4. Wrote off $1,500 of uncollectible accounts.
5. On September 1, Hardwood loaned $10,000 to Pine Co. The note had a 6 percent interest rate and a one-year term.
6. Paid $24,500 cash for salaries expense.
7. Collected $99,000 cash from accounts receivable.
8. Paid $78,000 cash on accounts payable.
9. Paid a $5,000 cash dividend to the stockholders.
10. Estimated uncollectible accounts expense to be 1 percent of sales on account.
11. Recorded the accrued interest at December 31, 2014.

Required

a. Organize the transaction data in accounts under an accounting equation.

b. Prepare an income statement, a statement of changes in stockholders' equity, a balance sheet, and a statement of cash flows for 2014.

LO 5-5

Exercise 5-14   *Effect of credit card sales on financial statements*

Superior Carpet Cleaning provided $76,000 of services during 2014, its first year of operations. All customers paid for the services with major credit cards. Superior submitted the credit card receipts to the credit card company immediately. The credit card company paid Superior cash in the amount of face value less a 3 percent service charge.

Required

a. Record the credit card sales and the subsequent collection of accounts receivable in a horizontal statements model like the one shown below. In the Cash Flow column, indicate whether the item is an operating activity (OA), investing activity (IA), or financing activity (FA). Use NA to indicate that an element is not affected by the event.

Assets			=	Liab.	+	Equity	Rev.	−	Exp.	=	Net Inc.	Cash Flow
Cash	+	Accts. Rec.										

b. Answer the following questions:

   (1) What is the amount of total assets at the end of the accounting period?

   (2) What is the amount of revenue reported on the income statement?

   (3) What is the amount of cash flow from operating activities reported on the statement of cash flows?

   (4) Why would Superior Carpet Cleaning accept credit cards instead of providing credit directly to its customers? In other words, why would Superior be willing to pay 3 percent of sales to have the credit card company handle its sales on account?

Exercise 5-15   *Recording credit card sales*   LO 5-5

Cassell Company accepted credit cards in payment for $8,650 of services performed during March 2014. The credit card company charged Cassell a 4 percent service fee. The credit card company paid Cassell as soon as it received the invoices.

Required

Based on this information alone, what is the amount of net income earned during the month of March?

Exercise 5-16   *Effect of inventory cost flow assumption on financial statements*   LO 5-6

Required

For each of the following situations, fill in the blank with *FIFO, LIFO*, or *weighted average:*

a. _____ would produce the highest amount of net income in an inflationary environment.

b. _____ would produce the highest amount of assets in an inflationary environment.

c. _____ would produce the lowest amount of net income in a deflationary environment.

d. _____ would produce the same unit cost for assets and cost of goods sold in an inflationary environment.

e. _____ would produce the lowest amount of net income in an inflationary environment.

f. _____ would produce an asset value that was the same regardless of whether the environment was inflationary or deflationary.

g. _____ would produce the lowest amount of assets in an inflationary environment.

h. _____ would produce the highest amount of assets in a deflationary environment.

Exercise 5-17   *Allocating product cost between cost of goods sold and ending inventory*   LO 5-6

Adams Co. started the year with no inventory. During the year, it purchased two identical inventory items at different times. The first purchase cost $950 and the other, $1,250. Adams sold one of the items during the year.

Required

Based on this information, how much product cost would be allocated to cost of goods sold and ending inventory on the year-end financial statements, assuming use of

a. FIFO?

b. LIFO?

c. Weighted average?

Exercise 5-18   *Allocating product cost between cost of goods sold and ending inventory: Multiple purchases*   LO 5-6

Suggs Company sells coffee makers used in business offices. Its beginning inventory of coffee makers was 400 units at $50 per unit. During the year, Suggs made two batch purchases of coffee makers. The first was a 500-unit purchase at $55 per unit; the second was a 600-unit purchase at $58 per unit. During the period, Suggs sold 1,200 coffee makers.

Required

Determine the amount of product costs that would be allocated to cost of goods sold and ending inventory, assuming that Suggs uses

a. FIFO.
b. LIFO.
c. Weighted average.

LO 5-6

Exercise 5-19 *Effect of inventory cost flow (FIFO, LIFO, and weighted average) on gross margin*

The following information pertains to Baxter Company for 2014.

Beginning inventory	90 units @ $15
Units purchased	320 units @ $19

Ending inventory consisted of 40 units. Baxter sold 370 units at $30 each. All purchases and sales were made with cash.

Required

a. Compute the gross margin for Baxter Company using the following cost flow assumptions: (1) FIFO, (2) LIFO, and (3) weighted average.
b. What is the dollar amount of difference in net income between using FIFO versus LIFO? (Ignore income tax considerations.)
c. Determine the cash flow from operating activities, using each of the three cost flow assumptions listed in Requirement *a.* Ignore the effect of income taxes. Explain why these cash flows have no differences.

LO 5-6

Exercise 5-20 *Effect of inventory cost flow on ending inventory balance and gross margin*

Dugan Sales had the following transactions for jackets in 2014, its first year of operations:

Jan. 20	Purchased 80 units @ $15	= $1,200
Apr. 21	Purchased 420 units @ $16	= 6,720
July 25	Purchased 250 units @ $20	= 5,000
Sept. 19	Purchased 150 units @ $22	= 3,300

During the year, Dugan Sales sold 830 jackets for $40 each.

Required

a. Compute the amount of ending inventory Dugan would report on the balance sheet, assuming the following cost flow assumptions: (1) FIFO, (2) LIFO, and (3) weighted average.
b. Compute the difference in gross margin between the FIFO and LIFO cost flow assumptions.

LO 5-6

Exercise 5-21 *Income tax effect of shifting from FIFO to LIFO*

The following information pertains to the inventory of the Windjammer Company:

Jan. 1	Beginning Inventory	300 units @ $25
Apr. 1	Purchased	2,800 units @ $30
Oct. 1	Purchased	1,000 units @ $32

During the year, Windjammer sold 3,500 units of inventory at $50 per unit and incurred $21,000 of operating expenses. Windjammer currently uses the FIFO method but is considering a change to LIFO. All transactions are cash transactions. Assume a 30 percent income tax rate. Windjammer started the period with cash of $36,000, inventory of $7,500, common stock of $20,000, and retained earnings of $23,500.

Required

a. Prepare income statements using FIFO and LIFO.

b. Determine the amount of income taxes Windjammer would save if it changed cost flow methods.

c. Determine the cash flow from operating activities under FIFO and LIFO.

d. Explain why cash flow from operating activities is lower under FIFO when that cost flow method produced the higher gross margin.

Exercise 5-22 *Effect of FIFO versus LIFO on income tax expense*   LO 5-6

Garden Gifts Inc. had cash sales of $112,500 for 2014, its first year of operation. On April 2, the company purchased 150 units of inventory at $180 per unit. On September 1, an additional 200 units were purchased for $200 per unit. The company had 50 units on hand at the end of the year. The company's income tax rate is 40 percent. All transactions are cash transactions.

Required

a. The preceding paragraph describes five accounting events: (1) a sales transaction, (2) the first purchase of inventory, (3) the second purchase of inventory, (4) the recognition of cost of goods sold expense, and (5) the payment of income tax expense. Record the amounts of each event in horizontal statements models like the following ones, assuming first a FIFO and then a LIFO cost flow.

Effect of Events on Financial Statements													
Panel 1: FIFO Cost Flow													
Event No.	**Balance Sheet**							**Income Statement**					**Statement of Cash Flows**
	Cash	+	Inventory	=	C. Stk.	+	Ret. Earn.	Rev.	−	Exp.	=	Net Inc.	
Panel 2: LIFO Cost Flow													
Event No.	**Balance Sheet**							**Income Statement**					**Statement of Cash Flows**
	Cash	+	Inventory	=	C. Stk.	+	Ret. Earn.	Rev.	−	Exp.	=	Net Inc.	

b. Compute net income using FIFO.

c. Compute net income using LIFO.

d. Explain the difference, if any, in the amount of income tax expense incurred using the two cost flow assumptions.

e. How does the use of the FIFO versus the LIFO cost flow assumptions affect the statement of cash flows?

PROBLEMS

connect | **All applicable Problems are available with McGraw-Hill's**
ACCOUNTING | ***Connect® Accounting.***

Problem 5-23 *Accounting for uncollectible accounts—two cycles using the percent of revenue allowance method*   LO 5-2

The following transactions apply to Expert Consulting for 2014, the first year of operation:

1. Recognized $70,000 of service revenue earned on account.

2. Collected $62,000 from accounts receivable.

3. Adjusted accounts to recognize uncollectible accounts expense. Expert uses the allowance method of accounting for uncollectible accounts and estimates that uncollectible accounts expense will be 2 percent of sales on account.

The following transactions apply to Expert Consulting for 2015:

1. Recognized $84,000 of service revenue on account.
2. Collected $70,000 from accounts receivable.
3. Determined that $1,100 of the accounts receivable were uncollectible and wrote them off.
4. Collected $200 of an account that had been previously written off.
5. Paid $51,200 cash for operating expenses.
6. Adjusted accounts to recognize uncollectible accounts expense for 2015. Expert estimates that uncollectible accounts expense will be 1 percent of sales on account.

Required

Complete all the following requirements for 2014 and 2015. Complete all requirements for 2014 prior to beginning the requirements for 2015.

a. Identify the type of each transaction (asset source, asset use, asset exchange, or claims exchange).
b. Show the effect of each transaction on the elements of the financial statements, using a horizontal statements model like the one shown here. Use + for increase, − for decrease, and NA for not affected. Also, in the Cash Flow column, indicate whether the item is an operating activity (OA), investing activity (IA), or financing activity (FA). The first transaction is entered as an example.

Event No.	Assets	=	Liab.	+	Equity	Rev.	−	Exp.	=	Net Inc.	Cash Flow
1	+		NA		+	+		NA		+	NA

c. Organize the transaction data in accounts under an accounting equation.
d. Prepare the income statement, statement of changes in stockholders' equity, balance sheet, and statement of cash flows.

LO 5-2

Problem 5-24   Determining account balances: Percent of revenue allowance method of accounting for uncollectible accounts

CHECK FIGURE
a. Net Realizable Value: $97,320

The following information pertains to CJ's Cabinet Company's sales on account and accounts receivable:

Accounts Receivable Balance, January 1, 2014	$ 96,200
Allowance for Doubtful Accounts, January 1, 2014	6,250
Sales on Account, 2014	726,000
Cost of Goods Sold, 2014	473,000
Collections of Accounts Receivable, 2014	715,000

After several collection attempts, CJ's Cabinet Company wrote off $3,100 of accounts that could not be collected. CJ's estimates that uncollectible accounts expense will be 0.5 percent of sales on account.

Required

a. Compute the following amounts.
   (1) Using the allowance method, the amount of uncollectible accounts expense for 2014.
   (2) Net realizable value of receivables at the end of 2014.
b. Explain why the uncollectible accounts expense amount is different from the amount that was written off as uncollectible.

LO 5-3

Problem 5-25   Accounting for uncollectible accounts: Percent of receivables allowance method

CHECK FIGURES
b. Net Income: $34,898
Total Assets: $114,898

Frankel Inc. experienced the following transactions for 2014, its first year of operations:

1. Issued common stock for $60,000 cash.
2. Purchased $210,000 of merchandise on account.
3. Sold merchandise that cost $165,000 for $310,000 on account.
4. Collected $278,000 cash from accounts receivable.

5. Paid $190,000 on accounts payable.
6. Paid $46,000 of salaries expense for the year.
7. Paid other operating expenses of $62,000.
8. Frankel adjusted the accounts using the following information from an accounts receivable aging schedule.

Number of Days Past Due	Amount	Percent Likely to Be Uncollectible	Allowance Balance
Current	$15,700	.01	
0–30	8,500	.05	
31–60	4,000	.10	
61–90	2,600	.20	
Over 90 days	1,200	.50	

Required

a. Organize the transaction data in accounts under an accounting equation.
b. Prepare the income statement, statement of changes in stockholders' equity, balance sheet, and statement of cash flows for Frankel Inc. for 2014.
c. What is the net realizable value of the accounts receivable at December 31, 2014?

Problem 5-26   *Determination of account balances—percent of receivables allowance method of accounting for uncollectible accounts*

LO 5-2

CHECK FIGURE
c. Net Realizable Value: $44,448

During the first year of operation, 2014, Ferrell's Appliance recognized $261,000 of service revenue on account. At the end of 2014, the accounts receivable balance was $46,300. Even though this is his first year in business, the owner believes he will collect all but about 4 percent of the ending balance.

Required

a. What amount of cash was collected by Ferrell's during 2014?
b. Assuming the use of an allowance system to account for uncollectible accounts, what amount should Ferrell record as uncollectible accounts expense in 2014?
c. What is the net realizable value of receivables at the end of 2014?
d. Show the effect of the above transactions on the financial statements by recording the appropriate amounts in a horizontal statements model like the one shown here. When you record amounts in the Cash Flow column, indicate whether the item is an operating activity (OA), investing activity (IA), or financing activity (FA). The letters NA indicate that an element is not affected by the event.

Assets			=	Liab.	+	Equity	Rev.	−	Exp.	=	Net Inc.	Cash Flow
Cash	+	Accts. Rec.	−	Allow.								

Problem 5-27   *Accounting for notes receivable and uncollectible accounts using the percent of sales allowance method*

LO 5-2, 5-4

CHECK FIGURE
b. Net Income: $26,560

The following transactions apply to Brooks Co. for 2014, its first year of operations.

1. Issued $60,000 of common stock for cash.
2. Provided $74,000 of services on account.
3. Collected $62,000 cash from accounts receivable.
4. Loaned $15,000 to Horne Co. on October 1, 2014. The note had a one-year term to maturity and an 8 percent interest rate.
5. Paid $47,000 of salaries expense for the year.
6. Paid a $2,500 dividend to the stockholders.
7. Recorded the accrued interest on December 31, 2014 (see item 4).
8. Uncollectible accounts expense is estimated to be 1 percent of service revenue on account.

Required

a. Show the effects of the above transactions in a horizontal statements model like the one shown below.

	Assets				Equity		Rev. − Exp. = Net Inc.	Cash Flows
Event	Cash +	Accts. Rec. − Allow. for Doubtful Accts.	+ Notes Rec.	+ Int. Rec. =	Com. Stk. +	Ret. Earn.		

b. Prepare the income statement, balance sheet, and statement of cash flows for 2014.

LO 5-1, 5-4

Problem 5-28 *Multistep income statement and balance sheet*

Required

Use the following information to prepare a multistep income statement and a classified balance sheet for Webb Equipment Co. for 2014. (*Hint:* Some of the items will *not* appear on either statement, and ending retained earnings must be calculated.)

Salaries expense	$ 61,200	Interest receivable (short term)	$ 2,100
Common stock	70,000	Beginning retained earnings	120,100
Notes receivable (long term)	15,000	Operating expenses	45,000
Allowance for doubtful accounts	6,500	Cash flow from investing activities	(91,600)
Accumulated depreciation	12,000	Prepaid rent	16,100
Notes payable (long term)	26,000	Land	45,000
Salvage value of equipment	6,000	Cash	16,700
Interest payable (short term)	1,900	Inventory	105,000
Uncollectible accounts expense	9,600	Accounts payable	48,000
Supplies	4,500	Interest expense	1,300
Office equipment	47,000	Salaries payable	14,500
Interest revenue	12,000	Unearned revenue	42,000
Sales revenue	350,000	Cost of goods sold	225,000
Dividends	10,000	Accounts receivable	92,000
Rent expense	7,500		

LO 5-2, 5-4

Problem 5-29 *Missing information*

The following information comes from the accounts of Sawyer Company:

Account Title	Beginning Balance	Ending Balance
Accounts Receivable	$36,000	$32,000
Allowance for Doubtful Accounts	2,000	2,200
Notes Receivable	50,000	50,000
Interest Receivable	2,000	5,000

Required

a. There were $160,000 in sales on account during the accounting period. Write-offs of uncollectible accounts were $1,200. What was the amount of cash collected from accounts receivable? What amount of uncollectible accounts expense was reported on the income statement? What was the net realizable value of receivables at the end of the accounting period?

b. The note has a 6 percent interest rate and 24 months to maturity. What amount of interest revenue was recognized during the period? How much cash was collected for interest?

Problem 5-30 *Accounting for credit card sales and uncollectible accounts: Percent of receivables allowance method*

LO 5-3, 5-5

Iupe Supply Company had the following transactions in 2014:

1. Acquired $50,000 cash from the issue of common stock.
2. Purchased $120,000 of merchandise for cash in 2014.
3. Sold merchandise that cost $95,000 for $180,000 during the year under the following terms:

$ 50,000	Cash sales
115,000	Credit card sales (The credit card company charges a 3 percent service fee.)
15,000	Sales on account

4. Collected all the amount receivable from the credit card company.
5. Collected $11,300 of accounts receivable.
6. Paid selling and administrative expenses of $51,500.
7. Determined that 5 percent of the ending accounts receivable balance would be uncollectible.

Required

a. Record the above events in a horizontal statements model like the following one. When you record amounts in the Cash Flow column, indicate whether the item is an operating activity (OA), an investing activity (IA), or a financing activity (FA). The letters NA indicate that an element is not affected by the event.

Event	Balance Sheet									Income Statement						Statemt. of Cash Flows
	Assets					=	Equity			Rev.	−	Exp.	=	Net Inc.		
	Cash	+	Accts. Rec.	−	Allow	+	Mdse. Inv.	=	Com. Stk.	+	Ret. Earn.					

b. Prepare an income statement, a statement of changes in stockholders' equity, a balance sheet, and a statement of cash flows for 2014.

Problem 5-31 *Effect of transactions on the elements of financial statements*

LO 5-1, 5-4, 5-5

Required

Identify each of the following independent transactions as asset source (AS), asset use (AU), asset exchange (AE), or claims exchange (CE). Also explain how each event affects assets, liabilities, stockholders' equity, net income, and cash flow by placing a + for increase, − for decrease, or NA for not affected under each of the categories. The first event is recorded as an example.

Event	Type of Event	Assets	Liabilities	Common Stock	Retained Earnings	Net Income	Cash Flow
a	AS/AU	+/−	NA	NA	+	+	NA

a. Sold merchandise at a price above cost. Accepted payment by credit card. The credit card company charges a service fee. The receipts have not yet been forwarded to the credit card company.
b. Sold land for cash at its cost.
c. Paid cash to satisfy salaries payable.
d. Submitted receipts to the credit card company (see *a* above) and collected cash.

e. Loaned Carl Maddox cash. The loan had a 5 percent interest rate and a one-year term to maturity.

f. Paid cash to creditors on accounts payable.

g. Accrued three months' interest on the note receivable (see *e* above).

h. Provided services for cash.

i. Paid cash for salaries expense.

j. Provided services on account.

k. Wrote off an uncollectible account (use direct write-off method).

l. Collected cash from customers paying their accounts.

m. Recovered an uncollectible account that was previously written off (assume direct write-off method was used).

n. Paid cash for land.

o. Paid cash for other operating expenses.

LO 5-2, 5-4, 5-5

Problem 5-32   *Comprehensive accounting cycle problem (uses percent of revenue allowance method)*

The following trial balance was prepared for Village Cycle Sales and Service on December 31, 2013, after the closing entries were posted:

Account Title	Debit	Credit
Cash	$ 46,200	
Accounts Receivable	21,300	
Allowance for Doubtful Accounts		$ 1,350
Inventory	85,600	
Accounts Payable		28,000
Common Stock		80,000
Retained Earnings		43,750
Totals	$153,100	$153,100

Village Cycle had the following transactions in 2014:

1. Purchased merchandise on account for $260,000.

2. Sold merchandise that cost $243,000 on account for $340,000.

3. Performed $80,000 of services for cash.

4. Sold merchandise for $60,000 to credit card customers. The merchandise cost $41,250. The credit card company charges a 5 percent fee.

5. Collected $348,000 cash from accounts receivable.

6. Paid $265,000 cash on accounts payable.

7. Paid $115,000 cash for selling and administrative expenses.

8. Collected cash for the full amount due from the credit card company (see item 4).

9. Loaned $50,000 to Lee Supply. The note had a 9 percent interest rate and a one-year term to maturity.

10. Wrote off $830 of accounts as uncollectible.

11. Made the following adjusting entries:

   (a) Recorded three months' interest on the note at December 31, 2014 (see item 9).

   (b) Estimated uncollectible accounts expense to be .5 percent of sales on account.

Required

a. Organize the transaction data in accounts under an accounting equation.

b. Prepare an income statement, a statement of changes in stockholders' equity, a balance sheet, and a statement of cash flows for 2014.

Problem 5-33   *Effect of different inventory cost flow methods on financial statements*   **LO 5-6**

The accounting records of Carrol's Lamp Shop reflected the following balances as of January 1, 2014:

Cash	$90,500
Beginning inventory	28,000 (200 units @ $140)
Common stock	40,000
Retained earnings	78,500

The following five transactions occurred in 2014:

1. First purchase (cash)   120 units @ $150
2. Second purchase (cash)   140 units @ $160
3. Sales (all cash)   400 units @ $320
4. Paid $40,000 cash for salaries expense.
5. Paid cash for income tax at the rate of 25 percent of income before taxes.

Required

a. Compute the cost of goods sold and ending inventory, assuming (1) FIFO cost flow, (2) LIFO cost flow, and (3) weighted-average cost flow.

b. Use a vertical model to prepare the 2014 income statement, balance sheet, and statement of cash flows under FIFO, LIFO, and weighted average. (*Hint:* Record the events under an accounting equation before preparing the statements.)

ANALYZE, THINK, COMMUNICATE

ATC 5-1   Business Application Case   *Understanding real-world annual reports*

Use the Target Corporation's Form 10-K to answer the following questions related to Target's 2012 fiscal year (year ended February 2, 2013). Target's Form 10-K is available on the company's website or through the SEC's EDGAR database. Appendix A provides instructions for using the EDGAR database. Round answers to one decimal place.

Required

a. What percentage of Target's total assets was comprised of credit card receivables?
b. Approximately what percentage of credit card receivables did the company think will not be collected in 2012 and 2013?
c. What is Target's policy regarding when to write off credit card receivables?
d. What percentage of Target's total assets was comprised of inventory?
e. What cost flow method did Target use to account for its inventory?
f. Target had arrangements with some of its vendors such that it does not purchase or pay for merchandise inventory until the merchandise is sold to outside customers. Was the cost of these goods ever included in the Inventory account?

ATC 5-2   Group Assignment   *Inventory cost flow*

The accounting records of Robin Co. showed the following balances at January 1, 2014:

Cash	$30,000
Beginning inventory (100 units @ $50, 70 units @ $55)	8,850
Common stock	20,000
Retained earnings	18,850

Transactions for 2014 were as follows:

> Purchased 100 units @ $54 per unit.
> Purchased 250 units @ $58 per unit.
> Sold 220 units @ $80 per unit.
> Sold 200 units @ $90 per unit.
> Paid operating expenses of $3,200.
> Paid income tax expense. The income tax rate is 30%.

Required

a. Organize the class into three sections, and divide each section into groups of three to five students. Assign each section one of the cost flow methods, FIFO, LIFO, or weighted average. The company uses the perpetual inventory system.

Group Tasks

Determine the amount of ending inventory, cost of goods sold, gross margin, and net income after income tax for the cost flow method assigned to your section. Also prepare an income statement using that cost flow assumption.

Class Discussion

b. Have a representative of each section put its income statement on the board. Discuss the effect that each cost flow method has on assets (ending inventory), net income, and cash flows. Which method is preferred for tax reporting? For financial reporting? What restrictions are placed on the use of LIFO for tax reporting?

ATC 5-3   Research Assignment   *Analyzing two real-world companies' accounts receivable*

Using the most current annual reports or the Forms 10-K for Starbucks, the world's largest coffee houses, and Whirlpool, which manufactures appliances, complete the requirements below. To obtain the Forms 10-K, use either the EDGAR system following the instructions in Appendix A or the companies' websites. The annual reports can be found on the companies' websites.

Required

a. For each company, compute accounts receivable as a percentage of revenue. Show your computations.
b. Which company appears to be making more of its sales on account? Explain your answer.
c. Try to provide a logical explanation as to why one of these companies is making more of its sales on account than the other.

ATC 5-4   Writing Assignment   *Cost of charge sales*

Paul Smith is opening a plumbing supply store in University City. He plans to sell plumbing parts and materials to both wholesale and retail customers. Since contractors (wholesale customers) prefer to buy parts and materials and pay at the end of the month, Paul expects he will have to offer charge accounts. He plans to offer charge sales to the wholesale customers only and to require retail customers to pay with either cash or credit cards. Paul wondered what expenses his business would incur relative to the charge sales and the credit cards.

Required

a. What issues will Paul need to consider if he allows wholesale customers to buy plumbing supplies on account?
b. Write a memo to Paul Smith outlining the potential cost of accepting charge customers. Discuss the difference between the allowance method for uncollectible accounts and the direct write-off method. Also discuss the cost of accepting credit cards.

ATC 5-5   Ethical Dilemma   *How bad can it be?*

Alonzo Saunders owns a small training services company that is experiencing growing pains. The company has grown rapidly by offering liberal credit terms to its customers. Although his competitors require payment for services within 30 days, Saunders permits his customers to delay payment for up to 90 days. Saunders's customers thereby have time to fully evaluate the training that employees receive before they must pay for that training. Saunders guarantees satisfaction. If a customer is unhappy, the customer does not have to pay. Saunders works with reputable companies, provides top-quality training, and rarely encounters dissatisfied customers.

The long collection period, however, has created a cash flow problem. Saunders has a $100,000 accounts receivable balance, but needs cash to pay current bills. He has recently negotiated a loan agreement with National Bank of Brighton County that should solve his cash flow problems. The loan agreement requires that Saunders pledge the accounts receivable as collateral for the loan. The bank agreed to loan Saunders 70 percent of the receivables balance, thereby giving him access to $70,000 cash. Saunders is satisfied with this arrangement because he estimates he needs approximately $60,000.

On the day Saunders was to execute the loan agreement, he heard a rumor that his biggest customer was experiencing financial problems and might declare bankruptcy. The customer owed Saunders $45,000. Saunders promptly called the customer's chief accountant and learned "off the record" that the rumor was true. The accountant told Saunders that the company's net worth was negative and most of its assets were pledged as collateral for bank loans. In his opinion, Saunders was unlikely to collect the balance due. Saunders's immediate concern was the impact the circumstances would have on his loan agreement with the bank.

Saunders uses the direct write-off method to recognize uncollectible accounts expense. Removing the $45,000 receivable from the collateral pool would leave only $55,000 of receivables, reducing the available credit to $38,500 ($55,000 × 0.70). Even worse, recognizing the uncollectible accounts expense would so adversely affect his income statement that the bank might further reduce the available credit by reducing the percentage of receivables allowed under the loan agreement. Saunders will have to attest to the quality of the receivables at the date of the loan but reasons that since the information he obtained about the possible bankruptcy was "off the record" he is under no obligation to recognize the uncollectible accounts expense until the receivable is officially uncollectible.

Required

a. How are income and assets affected by the decision not to act on the bankruptcy information?

b. Review the AICPA's Articles of Professional Conduct (see Chapter 4) and comment on any of the standards that would be violated by the actions Saunders is contemplating.

c. How do the elements of the fraud triangle (see Chapter 4) apply to this case?

CHAPTER 6

Accounting for Long-Term Operational Assets

LEARNING OBJECTIVES

After you have mastered the material in this chapter, you will be able to:

LO 6-1   Identify different types of long-term operational assets.

LO 6-2   Determine the cost of long-term operational assets.

LO 6-3   Explain how different depreciation methods affect financial statements.

LO 6-4   Determine how gains and losses on disposals of long-term operational assets affect financial statements.

LO 6-5   Show how revising estimates affects financial statements.

LO 6-6   Explain how continuing expenditures for operational assets affect financial statements.

LO 6-7   Explain how expense recognition for natural resources (depletion) affects financial statements.

LO 6-8   Explain how expense recognition for intangible assets (amortization) affects financial statements.

LO 6-9   Explain how expense recognition choices and industry characteristics affect financial performance measures.

 Video lectures and accompanying self-assessment quizzes are available for all learning objectives through McGraw-Hill Connect® Accounting.

CHAPTER OPENING

Companies use assets to produce revenue. Some assets, like inventory or office supplies, are called **current assets** because they are used relatively quickly (within a single accounting period). Other assets, like equipment or buildings, are used for extended periods of time (two or more accounting periods). These assets are called **long-term operational assets.**[1] Accounting for long-term assets raises several questions. For example, what is the cost of the asset? Is it

[1]Classifying assets as current versus long term is explained in more detail in Chapter 7.

the list price only or should the cost of transportation, transit insurance, setup, and so on be added to the list price? Should the cost of a long-term asset be recognized as expense in the period the asset is purchased or should the cost be expensed over the useful life of the asset? What happens in the accounting records when a long-term asset is retired from use? This chapter answers these questions. It explains accounting for long-term operational assets from the date of purchase through the date of disposal.

The Curious Accountant

Most companies have various types of long-term assets that they use to operate their business. Common types of long-term assets include buildings, machinery, and equipment. But there are other types as well. A major category of long-term assets for a mining company is the mineral reserves from which they extract ore.

Freeport-McMoRan Copper & Gold, Inc. (referred to as FCX) is one of the largest mining operations in the world. It produces copper, gold, and molybdenum from 12 major mines located on four continents. As of December 31, 2012, it owned proven mineral reserves that cost $4.6 billion, and buildings, machinery, and equipment that cost $16.7 billion.

How do you think the way a mining company uses its buildings and equipment differs from the way it uses its mineral reserves, and how will these differences affect the way these assets are accounted for? (Answer on page 211.)

Identify different types of long-term operational assets.

TANGIBLE VERSUS INTANGIBLE ASSETS

Long-term assets may be tangible or intangible. **Tangible assets** have a physical presence; they can be seen and touched. Tangible assets include equipment, machinery, natural resources, and land. In contrast, intangible assets have no physical form. Although they may be represented by physical documents, **intangible assets** are, in fact, rights or privileges. They cannot be seen or touched. For example, a patent represents an exclusive legal *privilege* to produce and sell a particular product. It protects inventors by making it illegal for others to profit by copying their inventions. Although a patent may be represented by legal documents, the privilege is the actual asset. Because the privilege cannot be seen or touched, the patent is an intangible asset.

Tangible Long-Term Assets

Tangible long-term assets are classified as (1) property, plant, and equipment; (2) natural resources; or (3) land.

Property, Plant, and Equipment

Property, plant, and equipment is sometimes called *plant assets* or *fixed assets.* Examples of property, plant, and equipment include furniture, cash registers, machinery, delivery trucks, computers, mechanical robots, and buildings. The level of detail used to account for these assets varies. One company may include all office equipment in one account, whereas another company might divide office equipment into computers, desks, chairs, and so on. The term used to recognize expense for property, plant, and equipment is **depreciation.**

Natural Resources

Mineral deposits, oil and gas reserves, timber stands, coal mines, and stone quarries are examples of **natural resources.** Conceptually, natural resources are inventories. When sold, the cost of these assets is frequently expensed as *cost of goods sold.* Although inventories are usually classified as short-term assets, natural resources are normally classified as long term because the resource deposits generally have long lives. For example, it may take decades to extract all of the diamonds from a diamond mine. The term used to recognize expense for natural resources is **depletion.**

Land

Land is classified separately from other property because land is not subject to depreciation or depletion. Land has an infinite life. It is not worn out or consumed as it is used. When buildings or natural resources are purchased simultaneously with land, the amount paid must be divided between the land and the other assets because of the non-depreciable nature of the land.

Intangible Assets

Intangible assets fall into two categories, those with *identifiable useful lives* and those with *indefinite useful lives.*

Intangible Assets with Identifiable Useful Lives

Intangible assets with identifiable useful lives include patents and copyrights. These assets may become obsolete (a patent may become worthless if new technology provides a superior product) or may reach the end of their legal lives. The term used when recognizing expense for intangible assets with identifiable useful lives is called **amortization.**

Intangible Assets with Indefinite Useful Lives

The benefits of some intangible assets may extend so far into the future that their useful lives cannot be estimated. For how many years will the Coca-Cola trademark attract customers? When will the value of a McDonald's franchise end? There are no answers to these questions. Intangible assets such as renewable franchises, trademarks, and goodwill have indefinite useful lives. The costs of such assets are not expensed unless the value of the assets becomes impaired.

DETERMINING THE COST OF LONG-TERM ASSETS

The **historical cost concept** requires that an asset be recorded at the amount paid for it. This amount includes the purchase price plus any costs necessary to get the asset in the location and condition for its intended use. Common cost components are:

LO 6-2

Determine the cost of long-term operational assets.

- **Buildings:** (1) purchase price, (2) sales taxes, (3) title search and transfer document costs, (4) realtor's and attorney's fees, and (5) remodeling costs.
- **Land:** (1) purchase price, (2) sales taxes, (3) title search and transfer document costs, (4) realtor's and attorney's fees, (5) costs for removal of old buildings, and (6) grading costs.
- **Equipment:** (1) purchase price (less discounts), (2) sales taxes, (3) delivery costs, (4) installation costs, and (5) costs to adapt for intended use.

The cost of an asset does not include payments for fines, damages, and so on that could have been avoided.

☑ CHECK YOURSELF 6.1

Sheridan Construction Company purchased a new bulldozer that had a $260,000 list price. The seller agreed to allow a 4 percent cash discount in exchange for immediate payment. The bulldozer was delivered FOB shipping point at a cost of $1,200. Sheridan hired a new employee to operate the dozer for an annual salary of $36,000. The employee was trained to operate the dozer for a one-time training fee of $800. The cost of the company's theft insurance policy increased by $300 per year as a result of adding the dozer to the policy. The dozer had a five-year useful life and an expected salvage value of $26,000. Determine the asset's cost.

Answer

List price	$260,000
Less: Cash discount ($260,000 × 0.04)	(10,400)
Shipping cost	1,200
Training cost	800
Total asset cost (amount capitalized)	$251,600

Basket Purchase Allocation

Acquiring a group of assets in a single transaction is known as a **basket purchase.** The total price of a basket purchase must be allocated among the assets acquired. Accountants commonly allocate the purchase price using the **relative fair market value method.** To illustrate, assume that Beatty Company purchased land and a building for $240,000 cash. A real estate appraiser determined the fair market value of each asset to be

Building	$270,000
Land	90,000
Total	$360,000

The appraisal indicates that the land is worth 25 percent ($90,000 ÷ $360,000) of the total value and the building is worth 75 percent ($270,000 ÷ $360,000). Using these percentages, the actual purchase price is allocated as follows.

Building	0.75 × $240,000 =	$180,000
Land	0.25 × $240,000 =	60,000
Total		$240,000

METHODS OF RECOGNIZING DEPRECIATION EXPENSE

LO 6-3

Explain how different depreciation methods affect financial statements.

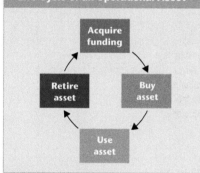
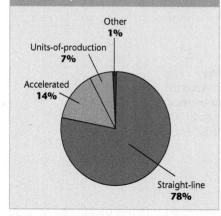
The life cycle of an operational asset involves (1) acquiring the funds to buy the asset, (2) purchasing the asset, (3) using the asset, and (4) retiring (disposing of) the asset. These stages are illustrated in Exhibit 6.1. The stages involving (1) acquiring funds and (2) purchasing assets have been discussed previously. This section of the chapter describes how accountants recognize the *use* of assets (Stage 3). As they are used, assets suffer from wear and tear called *depreciation.* Ultimately, assets depreciate to the point that they are no longer useful in the process of earning revenue. This process usually takes several years. The amount of an asset's cost that is allocated to expense during an accounting period is called **depreciation expense.**

An asset that is fully depreciated by one company may still be useful to another company. For example, a rental car that is no longer useful to Hertz may still be useful to a local delivery company. As a result, companies are frequently able to sell their fully depreciated assets to other companies or individuals. The expected market value of a fully depreciated asset is called its **salvage value.** The total amount of depreciation a company recognizes for an asset, its **depreciable cost,** is the difference between its original cost and its salvage value.

For example, assume a company purchases an asset for $5,000. The company expects to use the asset for 5 years (the **estimated useful life**) and then to sell it for $1,000 (salvage value). The depreciable cost of the asset is $4,000 ($5,000 − $1,000). The portion of the depreciable cost ($4,000) that represents its annual usage is recognized as depreciation expense.

Accountants must exercise judgment to estimate the amount of depreciation expense to recognize each period. For example, suppose you own a personal computer. You know how much the computer cost, and you know you will eventually need to replace it. How would you determine the amount the computer depreciates each year you use it? Businesses may use any of several acceptable methods to estimate the amount of depreciation expense to recognize each year.

The method used to recognize depreciation expense should match the asset's usage pattern. More expense should be recognized in periods when the asset is used more and less in periods when the asset is used less. Because assets are used to produce revenue, matching expense recognition with asset usage also matches expense recognition with revenue recognition. Three alternative methods for recognizing depreciation expense are (1) straight-line, (2) double-declining-balance, and (3) units-of-production.

The *straight-line* method produces the same amount of depreciation expense each accounting period. *Double-declining-balance,* an accelerated method, produces more depreciation expense in the early years of an asset's life, with a declining amount of expense in later years. *Units-of-production* produces varying amounts of depreciation expense in different accounting periods (more in some accounting periods and less in others). Exhibit 6.2 shows the relative use of different depreciation methods by U.S. companies.

Answers to The Curious Accountant

As assets lose their productive capacity, either from being used or due to obsolescence, the asset account is reduced and an expense account is increased. Assets such as buildings and equipment may decline faster if they are used, but, due to obsolescence, they usually continue to decline even if they are not used. For this reason, a time-based depreciation method, such as straight-line or double-declining-balance, is almost always used for buildings and more often than not for equipment. In contrast, a mineral reserve does not lose its capacity unless ore is extracted. After all, the gold the FCX is mining today has been in the earth for millions of years. For this reason, companies typically use the units-of-production method to calculate depletion on mineral reserves. In both cases, the objective should be to achieve the best matching of expenses incurred with the revenues they generate.

Dryden Enterprises Illustration

To illustrate the different depreciation methods, consider a van purchased by Dryden Enterprises. Dryden plans to use the van as rental property. The van had a list price of $23,500. Dryden obtained a 10 percent cash discount from the dealer. The van was delivered FOB shipping point, and Dryden paid an additional $250 for transportation costs. Dryden also paid $2,600 for a custom accessory package to increase the van's appeal as a rental vehicle. The cost of the van is computed as follows.

List price	$23,500	
Less: Cash discount	(2,350)	$23,500 × 0.10
Plus: Transportation costs	250	
Plus: Cost of customization	2,600	
Total	$24,000	

The van has an estimated *salvage value* of $4,000 and an *estimated useful life* of four years. The following section examines three different patterns of expense recognition for this van.

Straight-Line Depreciation

The first scenario assumes the van is used evenly over its four-year life. The revenue from renting the van is assumed to be $8,000 per year. The matching concept calls for the expense recognition pattern to match the revenue stream. Because the same amount of revenue is recognized in each accounting period, Dryden should use **straight-line depreciation** because it produces equal amounts of depreciation expense each year.

Life Cycle Phase 1

The first phase of the asset life cycle is to acquire funds to purchase the asset. Assume Dryden acquired $25,000 cash on January 1, 2014, by issuing common stock. The effects on the financial statements follow.

Assets					=	Equity			Rev.	−	Exp.	=	Net Inc.	Cash Flow
Cash	+	Van	−	Acc. Dep.	=	Com. Stk.	+	Ret. Earn.						
25,000	+	NA	−	NA	=	25,000	+	NA	NA	−	NA	=	NA	25,000 FA

Life Cycle Phase 2

The second phase of the life cycle is to purchase the van. Assume Dryden bought the van on January 1, 2014, using funds from the stock issue. The cost of the van, previously computed, was $24,000 cash. The effects on the financial statements are:

Assets			=	Equity			Rev.	–	Exp.	=	Net Inc.	Cash Flow
Cash	+ Van	– Acc. Dep.	=	Com. Stk.	+	Ret. Earn.						
(24,000)	+ 24,000	– NA	=	NA	+	NA	NA	–	NA	=	NA	(24,000) IA

Life Cycle Phase 3

Dryden used the van by renting it to customers. The rent revenue each year is $8,000 cash. The effects on the financial statements are shown next.

Assets			=	Equity			Rev.	–	Exp.	=	Net Inc.	Cash Flow
Cash	+ Van	– Acc. Dep.	=	Com. Stk.	+	Ret. Earn.						
8,000	+ NA	– NA	=	NA	+	8,000	8,000	–	NA	=	8,000	8,000 OA

Although illustrated only once, these effects occur four times—once for each year Dryden earns revenue by renting the van.

At the end of each year, Dryden adjusts its accounts to recognize depreciation expense. The amount of depreciation recognized using the straight-line method is calculated as follows.

$$(\text{Asset cost} - \text{Salvage value}) \div \text{Useful life} = \text{Depreciation expense}$$

$$(\$24,000 - \$4,000) \div 4 \text{ years} = \$5,000 \text{ per year}$$

Recognizing depreciation expense is an asset use transaction that reduces assets and equity. The asset reduction is reported using a **contra asset account** called **Accumulated Depreciation**. Recognizing depreciation expense *does not affect cash flow*. The entire cash outflow for this asset occurred in January 2014 when Dryden purchased the van. Depreciation reflects *using* tangible assets, not spending cash to purchase them. The effects on the financial statements are as follows.

Assets			=	Equity			Rev.	–	Exp.	=	Net Inc.	Cash Flow
Cash	+ Van	– Acc. Dep.	=	Com. Stk.	+	Ret. Earn.						
NA	+ NA	– 5,000	=	NA	+	(5,000)	NA	–	5,000	=	(5,000)	NA

The Depreciation *Expense* account, like other expense accounts, is closed to the Retained Earnings account at the end of each year. The *Accumulated* Depreciation account, in contrast, increases each year, *accumulating* the total amount of depreciation recognized on the asset to date.

LO 6-4

Determine how gains and losses on disposals of long-term operational assets affect financial statements.

Life Cycle Phase 4

The final stage in the life cycle of a tangible asset is its disposal and removal from the company's records. Dryden retired the van from service on January 1, 2018, selling it for $4,500 cash. The van's **book value** (cost − accumulated depreciation) when it was sold was $4,000 ($24,000 cost − $20,000 accumulated depreciation), so Dryden recognized a $500 gain ($4,500 − $4,000) on the sale.

Gains are *like* revenues in that they increase assets or decrease liabilities. Gains are *unlike* revenues in that gains result from peripheral (incidental) transactions rather than routine operating activities. Dryden is not in the business of selling vans. Dryden's normal business activity is renting vans. Because selling vans is incidental to Dryden's normal operations, gains are reported separately, after operating income, on the income statement.

If Dryden had sold the asset for less than book value, the company would have recognized a loss on the asset disposal. Losses are similar to expenses in that they decrease assets or increase liabilities. However, like gains, losses result from peripheral transactions. Losses are reported as nonoperating items on the income statement.

The effects of the asset disposal on the financial statements are shown next.

Assets				=	Equity			Rev. or Gain	−	Exp. or Loss	=	Net Inc.	Cash Flow
Cash	+	Van	−	Acc. Dep.	=	Com. Stk.	+	Ret. Earn.					
4,500	+	(24,000)	−	(20,000)	=	NA	+	500	500	−	NA	=	500	4,500 IA

Although the gain reported on the 2018 income statement is $500, the cash inflow from selling the van is $4,500. Gains and losses are not reported on the statement of cash flows. Instead they are included in the total amount of cash collected from the sale of the asset. In this case, the entire $4,500 is shown in the cash flow from investing activities section of the 2018 statement of cash flows.

Financial Statements

Exhibit 6.3 displays a vertical statements model that shows the financial results for the Dryden illustration from 2014 through 2018. Study the exhibit until you understand how all the figures were derived. The amount of depreciation expense ($5,000) reported on the income statement is constant each year from 2014 through 2017. The amount of accumulated depreciation reported on the balance sheet grows from $5,000 to $10,000, to $15,000, and finally to $20,000. The Accumulated Depreciation account is a *contra asset account* that is subtracted from the Van account in determining total assets.

Study the timing differences between cash flow and net income. Dryden spent $24,000 cash to acquire the van. Over the van's life cycle, Dryden collected $36,500 [($8,000 revenue × 4 years = $32,000) plus ($4,500 from the asset disposal) = $36,500]. The $12,500 difference between the cash collected and the cash paid ($36,500 − $24,000) equals the total net income earned during the van's life cycle.

Although the amounts are the same, the timing of the cash flows and the income recognition are different. For example, in 2014 there was a $24,000 cash outflow to purchase the van and an $8,000 cash inflow from customers. In contrast, the income statement reports net income of $3,000. In 2018, Dryden reported a $500 gain on the asset disposal, but the amount of operating income and the cash flow from operating activities is zero for that year. The gain is only indirectly related to cash flows. The $4,500 of cash received on disposal is reported as a cash inflow from investing activities. Because gains and losses result from peripheral transactions, they do not affect operating income or cash flow from operating activities.

Double-Declining-Balance Depreciation

For the second scenario, assume demand for the van is strong when it is new, but fewer people rent the van as it ages. As a result, the van produces smaller amounts of revenue

EXHIBIT 6.3	Financial Statements under Straight-Line Depreciation

DRYDEN ENTERPRISES
Financial Statements

	2014	2015	2016	2017	2018
Income Statements					
Rent revenue	$ 8,000	$ 8,000	$ 8,000	$ 8,000	$ 0
Depreciation expense	(5,000)	(5,000)	(5,000)	(5,000)	0
Operating income	3,000	3,000	3,000	3,000	0
Gain on sale of van	0	0	0	0	500
Net income	$ 3,000	$ 3,000	$ 3,000	$ 3,000	$ 500
Balance Sheets					
Assets					
Cash	$ 9,000	$17,000	$25,000	$33,000	$37,500
Van	24,000	24,000	24,000	24,000	0
Accumulated depreciation	(5,000)	(10,000)	(15,000)	(20,000)	0
Total assets	$28,000	$31,000	$34,000	$37,000	$37,500
Stockholders' equity					
Common stock	$25,000	$25,000	$25,000	$25,000	$25,000
Retained earnings	3,000	6,000	9,000	12,000	12,500
Total stockholders' equity	$28,000	$31,000	$34,000	$37,000	$37,500
Statements of Cash Flows					
Operating Activities					
Inflow from customers	$ 8,000	$ 8,000	$ 8,000	$ 8,000	$ 0
Investing Activities					
Outflow to purchase van	(24,000)				
Inflow from sale of van					4,500
Financing Activities					
Inflow from stock issue	25,000				
Net Change in Cash	9,000	8,000	8,000	8,000	4,500
Beginning cash balance	0	9,000	17,000	25,000	33,000
Ending cash balance	$ 9,000	$17,000	$25,000	$33,000	$37,500

as time goes by. To match expenses with revenues, it is reasonable to recognize more depreciation expense in the van's early years and less as it ages.

Double-declining-balance depreciation produces a large amount of depreciation in the first year of an asset's life and progressively smaller levels of expense in each succeeding year. Because the double-declining-balance method recognizes depreciation expense more rapidly than the straight-line method does, it is called an **accelerated depreciation method.** Depreciation expense recognized using double-declining-balance is computed in three steps.

1. *Determine the straight-line rate.* Divide one by the asset's useful life. Because the estimated useful life of Dryden's van is four years, the straight-line rate is 25 percent $(1 \div 4)$ per year.

2. *Determine the double-declining-balance rate.* Multiply the straight-line rate by 2 (*double* the rate). The double-declining-balance rate for the van is 50 percent (25 percent × 2).

3. *Determine the depreciation expense.* Multiply the double-declining-balance rate by the book value of the asset *at the beginning of the period* (recall that book value is historical cost minus *accumulated depreciation*). The following table shows the amount of depreciation expense Dryden will recognize over the van's useful life (2014–2017).

Year	Book Value at Beginning of Period	×	Double the Straight-Line Rate	=	Annual Depreciation Expense	
2014	($24,000 − $ 0) ×		0.50	=	$12,000	
2015	(24,000 − 12,000) ×		0.50	=	6,000	
2016	(24,000 − 18,000) ×		0.50	=	~~3,000~~	2,000
2017	(24,000 − 20,000) ×		0.50	=	~~2,000~~	0

Regardless of the depreciation method used, *an asset cannot be depreciated below its salvage value.* This restriction affects depreciation computations for the third and fourth years. Because the van had a cost of $24,000 and a salvage value of $4,000, the total amount of depreciable cost (historical cost − salvage value) is $20,000 ($24,000 − $4,000). Because $18,000 ($12,000 + $6,000) of the depreciable cost is recognized in the first two years, only $2,000 ($20,000 − $18,000) remains to be recognized after the second year. Depreciation expense recognized in the third year is therefore $2,000 even though double-declining-balance computations suggest that $3,000 should be recognized. Similarly, zero depreciation expense is recognized in the fourth year even though the computations indicate a $2,000 charge.

☑ CHECK YOURSELF 6.2

Olds Company purchased an asset that cost $36,000 on January 1, 2016. The asset had an expected useful life of five years and an estimated salvage value of $5,000. Assuming Olds uses the double-declining-balance method, determine the amount of depreciation expense and the amount of accumulated depreciation Olds would report on the 2018 financial statements.

Answer

Year	Book Value at Beginning of Period ×	Double the Straight-Line Rate* =	Annual Depreciation Expense
2016	($36,000 − $ 0) ×	0.40 =	$14,400
2017	(36,000 − 14,400) ×	0.40 =	8,640
2018	(36,000 − 23,040) ×	0.40 =	5,184
Total accumulated depreciation at December 31, 2018			$28,224

*Double-declining-balance rate = 2 × Straight-line rate = 2 × (1 ÷ 5 years) = 0.40

Effects on the Financial Statements

Exhibit 6.4 displays financial statements for the life of the asset assuming Dryden uses double-declining-balance depreciation. The illustration assumes a cash revenue stream of $15,000, $9,000, $5,000, and $3,000 for the years 2014, 2015, 2016, and 2017, respectively. Trace the depreciation expense from the table above to the income statements. Reported depreciation expense is greater in the earlier years and smaller in the later years of the asset's life.

| EXHIBIT 6.4 | Financial Statements under Double-Declining-Balance Depreciation |

DRYDEN ENTERPRISES
Financial Statements

	2014	2015	2016	2017	2018
Income Statements					
Rent revenue	$15,000	$ 9,000	$ 5,000	$ 3,000	$ 0
Depreciation expense	(12,000)	(6,000)	(2,000)	0	0
Operating income	3,000	3,000	3,000	3,000	0
Gain on sale of van	0	0	0	0	500
Net income	$ 3,000	$ 3,000	$ 3,000	$ 3,000	$ 500
Balance Sheets					
Assets					
Cash	$16,000	$25,000	$30,000	$33,000	$37,500
Van	24,000	24,000	24,000	24,000	0
Accumulated depreciation	(12,000)	(18,000)	(20,000)	(20,000)	0
Total assets	$28,000	$31,000	$34,000	$37,000	$37,500
Stockholders' equity					
Common stock	$25,000	$25,000	$25,000	$25,000	$25,000
Retained earnings	3,000	6,000	9,000	12,000	12,500
Total stockholders' equity	$28,000	$31,000	$34,000	$37,000	$37,500
Statements of Cash Flows					
Operating Activities					
Inflow from customers	$15,000	$ 9,000	$ 5,000	$ 3,000	$ 0
Investing Activities					
Outflow to purchase van	(24,000)				
Inflow from sale of van					4,500
Financing Activities					
Inflow from stock issue	25,000				
Net Change in Cash	16,000	9,000	5,000	3,000	4,500
Beginning cash balance	0	16,000	25,000	30,000	33,000
Ending cash balance	$16,000	$25,000	$30,000	$33,000	$37,500

The double-declining-balance method smooths the amount of net income reported over the asset's useful life. In the early years, when heavy asset use produces higher revenue, depreciation expense is also higher. Similarly, in the later years, lower levels of revenue are matched with lower levels of depreciation expense. Net income is constant at $3,000 per year.

The depreciation method a company uses *does not* affect how it acquires the financing, invests the funds, and retires the asset. For Dryden's van, the accounting effects of these life cycle phases are the same as under the straight-line approach. Similarly, the *recording procedures* are not affected by the depreciation method. Different depreciation methods affect only the amount of depreciation expense recorded each year, not which accounts are used.

Units-of-Production Depreciation

Suppose rental demand for Dryden's van depends on general economic conditions. In a robust economy, travel increases, and demand for renting vans is high. In a stagnant economy, demand for van rentals declines. In such circumstances, revenues fluctuate from year to year. To accomplish the matching objective, depreciation should also fluctuate from year to year. A method of depreciation known as **units-of-production depreciation** accomplishes this goal by basing depreciation expense on actual asset usage.

Computing depreciation expense using units-of-production begins with identifying a measure of the asset's productive capacity. For example, the number of miles Dryden expects its van to be driven may be a reasonable measure of its productive capacity. If the depreciable asset were a saw, an appropriate measure of productive capacity could be the number of board feet the saw was expected to cut during its useful life. In other words, the basis for measuring production depends on the nature of the depreciable asset.

To illustrate computing depreciation using the units-of-production depreciation method, assume that Dryden measures productive capacity based on the total number of miles the van will be driven over its useful life. Assume Dryden estimates this productive capacity to be 100,000 miles. The first step in determining depreciation expense is to compute the cost per unit of production. For Dryden's van, this amount is total depreciable cost (historical cost − salvage value) divided by total units of expected productive capacity (100,000 miles). The depreciation cost per mile is therefore $0.20 ([$24,000 cost − $4,000 salvage] ÷ 100,000 miles). Annual depreciation expense is computed by multiplying the cost per mile by the number of miles driven. Odometer readings indicate the van was driven 40,000 miles, 20,000 miles, 30,000 miles, and 15,000 miles in 2014, 2015, 2016, and 2017, respectively. Dryden developed the following schedule of depreciation charges.

Year	Cost per Mile (a)	Miles Driven (b)	Depreciation Expense (a × b)
2014	$.20	40,000	$8,000
2015	.20	20,000	4,000
2016	.20	30,000	6,000
2017	.20	15,000	~~3,000~~ 2,000

As pointed out in the discussion of the double-declining-balance method, an asset cannot be depreciated below its salvage value. Because $18,000 of the $20,000 ($24,000 cost − $4,000 salvage) depreciable cost is recognized in the first three years of using the van, only $2,000 ($20,000 − $18,000) remains to be charged to depreciation in the fourth year, even though the depreciation computations suggest the charge should be $3,000. As the preceding table indicates, the general formula for computing units-of-production depreciation is

$$\frac{\text{Cost} - \text{Salvage value}}{\text{Total estimated units of production}} \times \begin{matrix} \text{Units of production} \\ \text{in current} \\ \text{year} \end{matrix} = \begin{matrix} \text{Annual} \\ \text{depreciation} \\ \text{expense} \end{matrix}$$

Exhibit 6.5 displays financial statements that assume Dryden uses units-of-production depreciation. The exhibit assumes a cash revenue stream of $11,000, $7,000, $9,000, and $5,000 for 2014, 2015, 2016, and 2017, respectively. Trace the depreciation expense from the schedule above to the income statements. Depreciation expense is greater in years the van is driven more and smaller in years the van is driven less, providing a reasonable matching of depreciation expense with revenue produced. Net income is again constant at $3,000 per year.

Comparing the Depreciation Methods

The total amount of depreciation expense Dryden recognized using each of the three methods was $20,000 ($24,000 cost − $4,000 salvage value). The different methods affect the *timing,* but not the *total amount,* of expense recognized. The different methods simply assign the $20,000 to different accounting periods. Exhibit 6.6

EXHIBIT 6.5	Financial Statements under Units-of-Production Depreciation

DRYDEN ENTERPRISES
Financial Statements

	2014	2015	2016	2017	2018
Income Statements					
Rent revenue	$11,000	$ 7,000	$ 9,000	$ 5,000	$ 0
Depreciation expense	(8,000)	(4,000)	(6,000)	(2,000)	0
Operating income	3,000	3,000	3,000	3,000	0
Gain on sale of van	0	0	0	0	500
Net income	$ 3,000	$ 3,000	$ 3,000	$ 3,000	$ 500
Balance Sheets					
Assets					
Cash	$12,000	$19,000	$28,000	$33,000	$37,500
Van	24,000	24,000	24,000	24,000	0
Accumulated depreciation	(8,000)	(12,000)	(18,000)	(20,000)	0
Total assets	$28,000	$31,000	$34,000	$37,000	$37,500
Stockholders' equity					
Common stock	$25,000	$25,000	$25,000	$25,000	$25,000
Retained earnings	3,000	6,000	9,000	12,000	12,500
Total stockholders' equity	$28,000	$31,000	$34,000	$37,000	$37,500
Statements of Cash Flows					
Operating Activities					
Inflow from customers	$11,000	$ 7,000	$ 9,000	$ 5,000	$ 0
Investing Activities					
Outflow to purchase van	(24,000)				
Inflow from sale of van					4,500
Financing Activities					
Inflow from stock issue	25,000				
Net Change in Cash	12,000	7,000	9,000	5,000	4,500
Beginning cash balance	0	12,000	19,000	28,000	33,000
Ending cash balance	$12,000	$19,000	$28,000	$33,000	$37,500

EXHIBIT 6.6

Depreciation Expense under Different Depreciation Methods

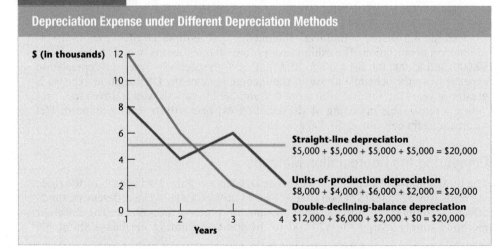

Straight-line depreciation
$5,000 + $5,000 + $5,000 + $5,000 = $20,000

Units-of-production depreciation
$8,000 + $4,000 + $6,000 + $2,000 = $20,000

Double-declining-balance depreciation
$12,000 + $6,000 + $2,000 + $0 = $20,000

presents graphically the differences among the three depreciation methods discussed above. A company should use the method that most closely matches expenses with revenues.

REVISION OF ESTIMATES

In order to report useful financial information on a timely basis, accountants must make many estimates of future results, such as the salvage value and useful life of depreciable assets and uncollectible accounts expense. Estimates are frequently revised when new information surfaces. Because revisions of estimates are common, generally accepted accounting principles call for incorporating the revised information into present and future calculations. Prior reports are not corrected.

LO 6-5

Show how revising estimates affects financial statements.

To illustrate, assume that McGraw Company purchased a machine on January 1, 2016, for $50,000. McGraw estimated the machine would have a useful life of 8 years and a salvage value of $3,000. Using the straight-line method, McGraw determined the annual depreciation charge as follows:

$$(\$50,000 - \$3,000) \div 8 \text{ years} = \$5,875 \text{ per year}$$

At the beginning of the fifth year, accumulated depreciation on the machine is $23,500 ($5,875 × 4). The machine's book value is $26,500 ($50,000 − $23,500). At this point, what happens if McGraw changes its estimates of useful life or the salvage value? Consider the following revision examples independently of each other.

Revision of Life

Assume McGraw revises the expected life to 14, rather than 8, years. The machine's *remaining* life would then be 10 more years instead of 4 more years. Assume salvage value remains $3,000. Depreciation for each remaining year is:

$$(\$26,500 \text{ book value} - \$3,000 \text{ salvage}) \div 10\text{-year remaining life} = \$2,350$$

Revision of Salvage

Alternatively, assume the original expected life remained 8 years, but McGraw revised its estimate of salvage value to $6,000. Depreciation for each of the remaining four years would be

$$(\$26,500 \text{ book value} - \$6,000 \text{ salvage}) \div 4\text{-year remaining life} = \$5,125$$

The revised amounts are determined for the full year, regardless of when McGraw revised its estimates. For example, if McGraw decides to change the estimated useful life on October 1, 2021, the change would be effective as of January 1, 2021. The year-end adjusting entry for depreciation would include a full year's depreciation calculated on the basis of the revised estimated useful life.

CONTINUING EXPENDITURES FOR PLANT ASSETS

Most plant assets require additional expenditures for maintenance or improvement during their useful lives. Accountants must determine if these expenditures should be expensed or capitalized (recorded as assets).

LO 6-6

Explain how continuing expenditures for operational assets affect financial statements.

Costs That Are Expensed

The costs of routine maintenance and minor repairs that are incurred to *keep* an asset in good working order are expensed in the period in which they are incurred. Because they reduce net income when incurred, accountants often call repair and maintenance costs **revenue expenditures** (companies subtract them from revenue).

With respect to the previous example, assume McGraw spent $500 for routine lubrication and to replace minor parts. The effects on the financial statements follow.

Assets	=	Equity			Rev.	–	Exp.	=	Net Inc.	Cash Flow
Cash	=	Com. Stk.	+	Ret. Earn.						
(500)	=	NA	+	(500)	NA	–	500	=	(500)	(500) OA

Costs That Are Capitalized

Substantial amounts spent to improve the quality or extend the life of an asset are described as **capital expenditures.** Capital expenditures are accounted for in one of two ways, depending on whether the cost incurred *improves the quality* or *extends the life* of the asset.

Improving Quality

Expenditures such as adding air conditioning to an existing building or installing a trailer hitch on a vehicle improve the quality of service these assets provide. If a capital expenditure improves an asset's quality, the amount is added to the historical cost of the asset. The additional cost is expensed through higher depreciation charges over the asset's remaining useful life.

To demonstrate, return to the McGraw Company example. Recall that the machine originally cost $50,000, had an estimated salvage of $3,000, and had a predicted life of 8 years. Recall further that accumulated depreciation at the beginning of the fifth year is $23,500 ($5,875 × 4) so the book value is $26,500 ($50,000 − $23,500). Assume McGraw makes a major expenditure of $4,000 in the machine's fifth year to improve its productive capacity. The effects on the financial statements follow.

Assets					=	Equity			Rev.	–	Exp.	=	Net Inc.	Cash Flow
Cash	+	Mach.	–	Acc. Dep.	=	Com. Stk.	+	Ret. Earn.						
(4,000)	+	4,000	–	NA	=	NA	+	NA	NA	–	NA	=	NA	(4,000) IA

After recording the expenditure, the machine account balance is $54,000 and the asset's book value is $30,500 ($54,000 − $23,500). The depreciation charges for each of the remaining four years are

$$(\$30{,}500 \text{ book value} - \$3{,}000 \text{ salvage}) \div 4\text{-year remaining life} = \$6{,}875$$

Extending Life

Expenditures such as replacing the roof of an existing building or putting a new engine in an old vehicle extend the useful life of these assets. If a capital expenditure extends the life of an asset rather than improving the asset's quality of service, accountants view the expenditure as canceling some of the depreciation previously charged to expense. The event is still an asset exchange; cash decreases, and the book value of the machine increases. However, the increase in the book value of the machine results from reducing the balance in the contra asset account, Accumulated Depreciation.

To illustrate, assume that instead of increasing productive capacity, McGraw's $4,000 expenditure had extended the useful life of the machine by two years. The effects of the expenditure on the financial statements follow.

Assets					=	Equity			Rev.	–	Exp.	=	Net Inc.	Cash Flow
Cash	+	Mach.	–	Acc. Dep.	=	Com. Stk.	+	Ret. Earn.						
(4,000)	+	NA	–	(4,000)	=	NA	+	NA	NA	–	NA	=	NA	(4,000) IA

After the expenditure is recognized, the book value is the same as if the $4,000 had been added to the Machine account ($50,000 cost − $19,500 adjusted balance in Accumulated Depreciation = $30,500). Depreciation expense for each of the remaining six years follows.

($30,500 book value − $3,000 salvage) ÷ 6-year remaining life = $4,583

☑ CHECK YOURSELF 6.3

On January 1, 2016, Dager Inc. purchased an asset that cost $18,000. It had a five-year useful life and a $3,000 salvage value. Dager uses straight-line depreciation. On January 1, 2018, it incurred a $1,200 cost related to the asset. With respect to this asset, determine the amount of expense and accumulated depreciation Dager would report in the 2018 financial statements under each of the following assumptions.

1. The $1,200 cost was incurred to repair damage resulting from an accident.
2. The $1,200 cost improved the operating capacity of the asset. The total useful life and salvage value remained unchanged.
3. The $1,200 cost extended the useful life of the asset by one year. The salvage value remained unchanged.

Answer

1. Dager would report the $1,200 repair cost as an expense. Dager would also report depreciation expense of $3,000 ([$18,000 − $3,000] ÷ 5). Total expenses related to this asset in 2018 would be $4,200 ($1,200 repair expense + $3,000 depreciation expense). Accumulated depreciation at the end of 2018 would be $9,000 ($3,000 depreciation expense × 3 years).

2. The $1,200 cost would be capitalized in the asset account, increasing both the book value of the asset and the annual depreciation expense.

	After Effects of Capital Improvement
Amount in asset account ($18,000 + $1,200)	$19,200
Less: Salvage value	(3,000)
Accumulated depreciation on January 1, 2018	(6,000)
Remaining depreciable cost before recording 2018 depreciation	$10,200
Depreciation for 2018 ($10,200 ÷ 3 years)	$ 3,400
Accumulated depreciation at December 31, 2018 ($6,000 + $3,400)	$ 9,400

3. The $1,200 cost would be subtracted from the Accumulated Depreciation account, increasing the book value of the asset. The remaining useful life would increase to four years, which would decrease the depreciation expense.

	After Effects of Capital Improvement
Amount in asset account	$18,000
Less: Salvage value	(3,000)
Accumulated depreciation on January 1, 2018 ($6,000 − $1,200)	(4,800)
Remaining depreciable cost before recording 2018 depreciation	$10,200
Depreciation for 2018 ($10,200 ÷ 4 years)	$ 2,550
Accumulated depreciation at December 31, 2018 ($4,800 + $2,550)	$ 7,350

NATURAL RESOURCES

LO 6-7

Explain how expense recognition for natural resources (depletion) affects financial statements.

The cost of natural resources includes not only the purchase price but also related items such as the cost of exploration, geographic surveys, and estimates. The process of expensing natural resources is commonly called depletion.[2] The most common method used to calculate depletion is units-of-production.

To illustrate, assume Apex Coal Mining paid $4,000,000 cash to purchase a mine with an estimated 16,000,000 tons of coal. The unit depletion charge is

$$\$4,000,000 \div 16,000,000 \text{ tons} = \$0.25 \text{ per ton}$$

If Apex mines 360,000 tons of coal in the first year, the depletion charge is:

$$360,000 \text{ tons} \times \$0.25 \text{ per ton} = \$90,000$$

The depletion of a natural resource has the same effect on the accounting equation as other expense recognition events. Assets (in this case, a *coal mine*) and stockholders' equity decrease. The depletion expense reduces net income. The effects on the financial statements follow.

Assets			=	Equity			Rev.	−	Exp.	=	Net Inc.	Cash Flow	
Cash	+	Coal Mine	=	Com. Stk.	+	Ret. Earn.							
(4,000,000)	+	4,000,000	=	NA	+	NA	NA	−	NA	=	NA	(4,000,000)	IA
NA	+	(90,000)	=	NA	+	(90,000)	NA	−	90,000	=	(90,000)	NA	

INTANGIBLE ASSETS

LO 6-8

Explain how expense recognition for intangible assets (amortization) affects financial statements.

Intangible assets provide rights, privileges, and special opportunities to businesses. Common intangible assets include trademarks, patents, copyrights, franchises, and goodwill. Some of the unique characteristics of these intangible assets are described in the following sections.

Trademarks

A **trademark** is a name or symbol that identifies a company or a product. Familiar trademarks include the Polo emblem, the name *Coca-Cola*, and the Nike slogan, "Just do it." Trademarks are registered with the federal government and have an indefinite legal lifetime.

The costs incurred to design, purchase, or defend a trademark are capitalized in an asset account called Trademarks. Companies want their trademarks to become familiar but also face the risk of a trademark being used as the generic name for a product. To protect a trademark, companies in this predicament spend large sums on legal fees and extensive advertising programs to educate consumers. Well-known trademarks that have been subject to this problem include Coke, Xerox, Kleenex, and Vaseline.

Patents

A **patent** grants its owner an exclusive legal right to produce and sell a product that has one or more unique features. Patents issued by the U.S. Patent Office have a legal life of 20 years. Companies may obtain patents through purchase, lease, or internal development. The costs capitalized in the Patent account are usually limited to the purchase price and legal fees to obtain and defend the patent. The research and development

[2]In practice, the depletion charge is considered a product cost and allocated between inventory and cost of goods sold. This text uses the simplifying assumption that all resources are sold in the same accounting period in which they are extracted. The full depletion charge is therefore expensed in the period in which the resources are extracted.

FOCUS ON INTERNATIONAL ISSUES

As you have learned, U.S. GAAP requires companies to use historical cost when accounting for property, plant, and equipment (PPE). Once a company begins depreciating its buildings and equipment, expenses increase (due to depreciation expense), which causes net income and retained earnings to decrease. This, of course, ignores the revenue the company hopes to generate by using the asset.

Under IFRS a company has two options regarding accounting of PPE. First, it can use a historical cost accounting method that is virtually identical to that required by U.S. GAAP. Second, it can use the "revaluation model," which reports PPE at its fair value. There can be different ways of determining fair value, but the preferred approach is to base fair value on a market-based appraisal, performed by professional appraisers. These revaluations must be conducted frequently enough that the fair value of an asset is not materially different from its recorded book value.

Basically, the revaluation model works as follows. The company periodically compares the current book value of its PPE to the fair value at that same date. This fair value relates to the value of the used asset, not the amount required to replace it with a new asset. If the fair value of an asset is higher than its currently recorded book value, the recorded amount for the asset is increased, which increases total assets. However, the increase in the asset's fair value is *not* reported on the company's income statement, as would a gain from selling the asset. Rather, the increase is reported in a special section of stockholders' equity, which balances the increase that was recorded for assets. However, if the new fair value is *lower* than the asset's current book value, the decrease is charged to net income, as well as to assets. This is another example of the conservatism principle at work. Not surprisingly, there are exceptions to these rules. Once a new fair value is established, future depreciation expense is based on these values.

One concern might be that companies, hoping to manipulate earnings, would pick and choose some assets to account for under historical costs and others to account for under the revaluation model. This is not permitted. Although a company does not have to use a single method for all its assets, it must use a single method for all the assets in a given class of assets. For example, historical costs could be used for all factory equipment, and the revaluation model used for all its buildings.

As significant as the difference between the historical cost method and the fair value approach might be, the majority of companies continue to use historical costs. Professors H.B. Christensen and V. Nikolaev conducted a study of the use of revaluation accounting for nonfinancial assets by companies in Germany and the United Kingdom. Their research found that only 3.2 percent of the 1,539 companies surveyed used the revaluation model for property, plant, and equipment.*

*Source: Christensen, H.B. and Nikolaev, V., "Who Uses Fair Value Accounting for Nonfinancial Assets after IFRS Adoption?" The University of Chicago Booth School of Business Working Paper No. 09-12, February 2009.

costs that are incurred to develop patentable products are usually expensed in the period in which they are incurred.

Copyrights

A **copyright** protects writings, musical compositions, works of art, and other intellectual property for the exclusive benefit of the creator or persons assigned the right by the creator. The cost of a copyright includes the purchase price and any legal costs associated with obtaining and defending the copyright. Copyrights granted by the federal government extend for the life of the creator plus 70 years. A radio commercial could legally use a Bach composition as background music; it could not, however, use the theme song from the movie, *The Matrix,* without obtaining permission from the copyright owner. The cost of a copyright is often expensed early because future royalties may be uncertain.

Franchises

Franchises grant exclusive rights to sell products or perform services in certain geographic areas. Franchises may be granted by governments or private businesses.

REALITY BYTES

For its fiscal year ended April 30, 2010, Jackson-Hewitt Tax Services, Inc. wrote off $274 million of its $419 million of goodwill due to "goodwill impairment." Without this write-off, the company would have reported positive earnings before taxes of $2.7 million. Because of the write-off, it reported a negative loss before taxes of $271.4 million. Below is an excerpt from the notes to its financial statements explaining the goodwill impairment.

GOODWILL AND OTHER INTANGIBLE ASSETS

Goodwill is the excess of the purchase price over the fair value assigned to the net assets acquired in a business combination. Goodwill is not amortized, but instead is subject to periodic testing for impairment. The Company assesses goodwill for impairment by comparing the carrying values of its reporting units to their estimated fair values. . . .

Due to the loss of approximately 50% of the Company's RAL [*refund anticipation loans*] program in the third quarter of fiscal 2010, the Company concluded that a goodwill impairment triggering event had occurred. . . .

Significant management judgment is required in assessing whether goodwill is impaired.

Franchises granted by governments include federal broadcasting licenses. Private business franchises include fast-food restaurant chains and brand labels such as Healthy Choice. The legal and useful lives of a franchise are frequently difficult to determine. Judgment is often crucial to establishing the estimated useful life for franchises.

Goodwill

Goodwill is the value attributable to favorable factors such as reputation, location, and superior products. Consider the most popular restaurant in your town. If the owner sells the restaurant, do you think the purchase price would be simply the total value of the chairs, tables, kitchen equipment, and building? Certainly not, because much of the restaurant's value lies in its popularity; in other words, its ability to generate a high return is based on the goodwill (reputation) of the business.

Calculating goodwill can be complex; here we present a simple example to illustrate how it is determined. Suppose the accounting records of a restaurant named Bendigo's show

$$\text{Assets} = \text{Liabilities} + \text{Stockholders' Equity}$$

$$\$200,000 = \$50,000 + \$150,000$$

Assume a buyer agrees to purchase the restaurant by paying the owner $300,000 cash and assuming the existing liabilities. In other words, the restaurant is purchased at a price of $350,000 ($300,000 cash + $50,000 assumed liabilities). Now assume that the assets of the business (tables, chairs, kitchen equipment, etc.) have a fair market value of only $280,000. Why would the buyer pay $350,000 to purchase assets with a market value of $280,000? Obviously, the buyer is purchasing more than just the assets. The buyer is purchasing the business's goodwill. The amount of the goodwill is the difference between the purchase price and the fair market value of the assets. In this case, the goodwill is $70,000 ($350,000 − $280,000). The effects of the purchase on the financial statements of the buyer follow.

Assets					=	Liab.	+	Equity	Rev.	−	Exp.	=	Net Inc.	Cash Flow
Cash	+	Rest. Assets	+	Goodwill										
(300,000)	+	280,000	+	70,000	=	50,000	+	NA	NA	−	NA	=	NA	(300,000) IA

The fair market value of the restaurant assets represents the historical cost to the new owner. It becomes the basis for future depreciation charges.

EXPENSE RECOGNITION FOR INTANGIBLE ASSETS

As mentioned earlier, intangible assets fall into two categories, those with *identifiable useful lives* and those with *indefinite useful lives*. Expense recognition for intangible assets depends on which classification applies.

Expensing Intangible Assets with Identifiable Useful Lives

The costs of intangible assets with identifiable useful lives are normally expensed on a straight-line basis using a process called *amortization*. An intangible asset should be amortized over the shorter of two possible time periods: (1) its legal life or (2) its useful life.

To illustrate, assume that Flowers Industries purchased a newly granted patent for $44,000 cash. Although the patent has a legal life of 20 years, Flowers estimates that it will be useful for only 11 years. The annual amortization charge is therefore $4,000 ($44,000 ÷ 11 years). The effects on the financial statements follow.

Assets			=	Equity			Rev.	–	Exp.	=	Net Inc.	Cash Flow	
Cash	+	Patent	=	Com. Stk.	+	Ret. Earn.							
(44,000)	+	44,000	=	NA	+	NA	NA	–	NA	=	NA	(44,000)	IA
NA	+	(4,000)	=	NA	+	(4,000)	NA	–	4,000	=	(4,000)	NA	

Impairment Losses for Intangible Assets with Indefinite Useful Lives

Intangible assets with indefinite useful lives must be tested for impairment annually. The impairment test consists of comparing the fair value of the intangible asset to its carrying value (book value). If the fair value is less than the book value, an impairment loss must be recognized.

To illustrate, return to the example of the Bendigo's restaurant purchase. Recall that the buyer of Bendigo's paid $70,000 for goodwill. Assume the restaurant experiences a significant decline in revenue because many of its former regular customers are dissatisfied with the food prepared by the new chef. Suppose the decline in revenue is so substantial that the new owner believes the Bendigo's name is permanently impaired. The owner decides to hire a different chef and change the name of the restaurant. In this case, the business has suffered a permanent decline in value of goodwill. The company must recognize an impairment loss.

The restaurant's name has lost its value, but the owner believes the location continues to provide the opportunity to produce above-average earnings. Some, but not all, of the goodwill has been lost. Assume the fair value of the remaining goodwill is determined to be $40,000. The impairment loss to recognize is $30,000 ($70,000 − $40,000). The loss reduces the intangible asset (goodwill), stockholder's equity (retained earnings), and net income. The statement of cash flows would not be affected. The effects on the financial statements follow.

Assets	=	Liab.	+	Equity	Rev.	–	Exp./Loss	=	Net Inc.	Cash Flow
Goodwill	=			Ret. Earn.						
(30,000)	=	NA	+	(30,000)	NA	–	30,000	=	(30,000)	NA

BALANCE SHEET PRESENTATION

This chapter has explained accounting for the acquisition, expense recognition, and disposal of a wide range of long-term assets. Exhibit 6.7 illustrates typical balance sheet presentation of many of the assets discussed.

EXHIBIT 6.7			
Balance Sheet Presentation of Operational Assets			
Partial Balance Sheet			
Long-Term Assets			
Plant and equipment			
Buildings	$4,000,000		
Less: Accumulated depreciation	(2,500,000)	$1,500,000	
Equipment	1,750,000		
Less: Accumulated depreciation	(1,200,000)	550,000	
Total plant and equipment			$2,050,000
Land			850,000
Natural resources			
Mineral deposits (Less: Depletion)		2,100,000	
Oil reserves (Less: Depletion)		890,000	
Total natural resources			2,990,000
Intangibles			
Patents (Less: Amortization)		38,000	
Goodwill		175,000	
Total intangible assets			213,000
Total long-term assets			$6,103,000

EFFECT OF JUDGMENT AND ESTIMATION

Explain how expense recognition choices and industry characteristics affect financial performance measures.

Managers may have differing opinions about which allocation method (straight-line, accelerated, or units-of-production) best matches expenses with revenues. As a result, one company may use straight-line depreciation while another company in similar circumstances uses double-declining-balance. Because the allocation method a company uses affects the amount of expense it recognizes, analysts reviewing financial statements must consider the accounting procedures companies use in preparing the statements.

Assume that two companies, Alpha and Zeta, experience identical economic events in 2015 and 2016. Both generate revenue of $50,000 and incur cost of goods sold of $30,000 during each year. In 2015, each company pays $20,000 for an asset with an expected useful life of five years and no salvage value. How will the companies' financial statements differ if one uses straight-line depreciation and the other uses the double-declining-balance method? To answer this question, first compute the depreciation expense for both companies for 2015 and 2016.

If Alpha Company uses the straight-line method, depreciation for 2015 and 2016 is

$$(\text{Cost} - \text{Salvage}) \div \text{Useful life} = \text{Depreciation expense per year}$$

$$(\$20,000 - \$0) \div 5 \text{ years} = \$4,000$$

In contrast, if Zeta Company uses the double-declining-balance method, Zeta recognizes the following amounts of depreciation expense for 2015 and 2016.

(Cost − Accumulated Depreciation)	×	2 × (Straight-Line Rate)	=	Depreciation Expense
2015	($20,000 − $ 0) ×	[2 × (1 ÷ 5)]	=	$8,000
2016	($20,000 − $8,000) ×	[2 × (1 ÷ 5)]	=	$4,800

Based on these computations, the income statements for the two companies are:

	Income Statements			
	2015		**2016**	
	Alpha Co.	Zeta Co.	Alpha Co.	Zeta Co.
Sales	$50,000	$50,000	$50,000	$50,000
Cost of goods sold	(30,000)	(30,000)	(30,000)	(30,000)
Gross margin	20,000	20,000	20,000	20,000
Depreciation expense	(4,000)	(8,000)	(4,000)	(4,800)
Net income	$16,000	$12,000	$16,000	$15,200

The relevant sections of the balance sheets are

	Plant Assets			
	2015		**2016**	
	Alpha Co.	Zeta Co.	Alpha Co.	Zeta Co.
Assets	$20,000	$20,000	$20,000	$20,000
Accumulated depreciation	(4,000)	(8,000)	(8,000)	(12,800)
Book value	$16,000	$12,000	$12,000	$ 7,200

The depreciation method is not the only aspect of expense recognition that can vary between companies. Companies may also make different assumptions about the useful lives and salvage values of long-term operational assets. Thus, even if the same depreciation method is used, depreciation expense may still differ.

Because the depreciation method and the underlying assumptions regarding useful life and salvage value affect the determination of depreciation expense, they also affect the amounts of net income, retained earnings, and total assets.

To promote meaningful analysis, public companies are required to disclose all significant accounting policies used to prepare their financial statements. This disclosure is usually provided in the notes that accompany the financial statements.

EFFECT OF INDUSTRY CHARACTERISTICS

As indicated in previous chapters, industry characteristics affect financial performance measures. For example, companies in manufacturing industries invest heavily in machinery while insurance companies rely more on human capital. Manufacturing companies therefore have relatively higher depreciation charges than insurance companies. To illustrate how the type of industry affects financial reporting, examine Exhibit 6.8. This exhibit compares the ratio of sales to property, plant, and equipment for two companies in each of three different industries.

EXHIBIT 6.8		
Industry Data Reflecting the Use of Long-Term Tangible Assets		
Industry	**Company**	**Sales ÷ Property, Plant, and Equipment**
Cable Companies	Comcast Corporation	2.30
	Verizon Communications	1.31
Airlines	Alaska Air Group	1.29
	Southwest Airlines	1.34
Employment Agencies	Kelly Services	60.63
	Manpower, Inc.	111.89

The table indicates that for every $1.00 invested in property, plant, and equipment, Kelly Services produced $60.63 of sales. In contrast, Verizon Communications and Alaska Air Group produced only $1.31 and $1.29, respectively, for each $1.00 they invested in operational assets. Does this mean the management of Kelly is doing a better job than the management of Verizon Communications or Alaska Air Group? Not necessarily. It means that these companies operate in different economic environments. In other words, it takes significantly more equipment to operate a cable company or an airline than it takes to operate an employment agency.

<< A Look Back

This chapter explains that the primary objective of recognizing depreciation is to match the cost of a long-term tangible asset with the revenues the asset is expected to generate. The matching concept also applies to natural resources (depletion) and intangible assets (amortization). The chapter explains how alternative methods can be used to account for the same event (e.g., straight-line versus double-declining-balance depreciation). Companies experiencing exactly the same business events could produce different financial statements. The alternative accounting methods for depreciating, depleting, or amortizing assets include the (1) straight-line, (2) double-declining-balance, and (3) units-of-production methods.

The *straight-line method* produces equal amounts of expense in each accounting period. The amount of the expense recognized is determined using the formula [(cost − salvage) ÷ number of years of useful life]. The *double-declining-balance method* produces proportionately larger amounts of expense in the early years of an asset's useful life and increasingly smaller amounts of expense in the later years of the asset's useful life. The formula for calculating double-declining-balance depreciation is [book value at beginning of period × (2 × the straight-line rate)]. The *units-of-production method* produces expense in direct proportion to the number of units produced during an accounting period. The formula for the amount of expense recognized each period is [(cost − salvage) ÷ total estimated units of production = allocation rate × units of production in current accounting period].

This chapter showed how to account for *changes in estimates* such as the useful life or the salvage value of a depreciable asset. Changes in estimates do not affect the amount of depreciation recognized previously. Instead, the remaining book value of the asset is expensed over its remaining useful life.

After an asset has been placed into service, companies typically incur further costs for maintenance, quality improvement, and extensions of useful life. *Maintenance costs are expensed in the period in which they are incurred. Costs that improve the quality* of an asset are added to the cost of the asset, increasing the book value and the amount of future depreciation charges. *Costs that extend the useful life* of an asset are subtracted from the asset's Accumulated Depreciation account thereby increasing the book value of the asset.

A Look Forward

In Chapter 7 we move from the assets section of the balance sheet to issues in accounting for liabilities.

 Video lectures and accompanying self-assessment quizzes are available for all learning objectives through McGraw-Hill *Connect*® *Accounting*.

SELF-STUDY REVIEW PROBLEM

The following information pertains to a machine purchased by Bakersfield Company on January 1, 2016.

Purchase price	$ 63,000
Delivery cost	$ 2,000
Installation charge	$ 3,000
Estimated useful life	8 years
Estimated units the machine will produce	130,000
Estimated salvage value	$ 3,000

The machine produced 14,400 units during 2016 and 17,000 units during 2017.

Required

Determine the depreciation expense Bakersfield would report for 2016 and 2017 using each of the following methods.

a. Straight-line.
b. Double-declining-balance.
c. Units-of-production.

Solution to Requirements a–c.

a. Straight-line

Purchase price	$63,000
Delivery cost	2,000
Installation charge	3,000
Total cost of machine	68,000
Less: Salvage value	(3,000)
	$65,000 ÷ 8 = $8,125 Depreciation per year
2016	$ 8,125
2017	$ 8,125

b. Double-declining-balance

Year	Cost	−	Accumulated Depreciation at Beginning of Year	×	2 × S-L Rate	=	Annual Depreciation
2016	$68,000	−	$ 0	×	(2 × 0.125)	=	$17,000
2017	68,000	−	17,000	×	(2 × 0.125)	=	12,750

c. Units-of-production

(1) (Cost − Salvage value) ÷ Estimated units of production = Depreciation cost per unit produced

$$\frac{\$68,000 - \$3,000}{130,000} = \$0.50 \text{ per unit}$$

(2) Cost per unit × Annual units produced = Annual depreciation expense

2016 $0.50 × 14,400 = $7,200
2017   0.50 × 17,000 = 8,500

KEY TERMS

Accelerated depreciation method 214
Accumulated Depreciation 212
Amortization 208
Basket purchase 209
Book value 212
Capital expenditures 220
Contra asset account 212
Copyright 223

Current assets 206
Depletion 208
Depreciable cost 210
Depreciation 208
Depreciation expense 210
Double-declining-balance depreciation 214
Estimated useful life 210
Franchise 223

Goodwill 224
Historical cost concept 209
Intangible assets 208
Long-term operational assets 206
Natural resources 208
Patent 222
Property, plant, and equipment 208

Relative fair market value method 209
Revenue expenditures 219
Salvage value 210
Straight-line depreciation 211
Tangible assets 208
Trademark 222
Units-of-production depreciation 217

QUESTIONS

1. What is the difference between the functions of long-term operational assets and investments?

2. What is the difference between tangible and intangible assets? Give an example of each.

3. What is the difference between goodwill and specifically identifiable intangible assets?

4. Define *depreciation*. What kind of asset depreciates?

5. Why are natural resources called *wasting assets*?

6. Is land a depreciable asset? Why or why not?

7. Define *amortization*. What kind of assets are *amortized*?

8. Explain the historical cost concept as it applies to long-term operational assets. Why is the book value of an asset likely to be different from the current market value of the asset?

9. What different kinds of expenditures might be included in the recorded cost of a building?

10. What is a basket purchase of assets? When a basket purchase is made, how is cost assigned to individual assets?

11. What are the stages in the life cycle of a long-term operational asset?

12. Explain straight-line, units-of-production, and double-declining-balance depreciation. When is it appropriate to use each of these depreciation methods?

13. What effect does the recognition of depreciation expense have on total assets? On total equity?

14. Does the recognition of depreciation expense affect cash flows? Why or why not?

15. MalMax purchased a depreciable asset. What would be the difference in total assets at the end of the first year if MalMax chooses straight-line depreciation versus double-declining-balance depreciation?

16. John Smith mistakenly expensed the cost of a long-term tangible fixed asset. Specifically, he charged the cost of a truck to a delivery expense account. How will this error affect the income statement and the balance sheet in the year in which the mistake is made?

17. What is *salvage value*?

18. What type of account (classification) is Accumulated Depreciation?

19. How is the book value of an asset determined?

20. Why is depreciation that has been recognized over the life of an asset shown in a contra account? Why not just reduce the asset account?

21. Assume that a piece of equipment cost $5,000 and had accumulated depreciation of $3,000. What is the book value of the equipment? Is the book value equal to the fair market value of the equipment? Explain.

22. Why would a company choose to depreciate one piece of equipment using the double-declining-balance method and another piece of equipment using straight-line depreciation?

23. Why may it be necessary to revise the estimated life of a plant asset? When the estimated life is revised, does it affect the amount of depreciation per year? Why or why not?

24. How are capital expenditures made to improve the

quality of a capital asset accounted for? Would the answer change if the expenditure extended the life of the asset but did not improve quality? Explain.

25. When a long-term operational asset is sold at a gain, how is the balance sheet affected? Is the statement of cash flows affected? If so, how?

26. Define *depletion*. What is the most commonly used method of computing depletion?

27. List several common intangible assets. How is the life determined that is to be used to compute amortization?

28. List some differences between U.S. GAAP and GAAP of other countries with respect to amortization and accounting for intangibles.

29. How can judgment and estimation affect information reported in the financial statements?

MULTIPLE-CHOICE QUESTIONS

Multiple-choice questions are provided on the text website at www.mhhe.com/edmondssurvey4e.

EXERCISES

≣ connect **All applicable Exercises are available with McGraw-Hill's**
|ACCOUNTING   ***Connect® Accounting.***

Unless specifically included, ignore income tax considerations in all exercises and problems.

Exercise 6-1   *Long-term operational assets used in a business*   LO 6-1

Required

Give some examples of long-term operational assets that each of the following companies is likely to own: *(a)* Freds, *(b)* Princess Cruise Lines, *(c)* Southwest Airlines, and *(d)* Harley-Davidson Co.

Exercise 6-2   *Identifying long-term operational assets*   LO 6-1

Required

Which of the following items should be classified as long-term operational assets?

a. Inventory
b. Patent
c. Tract of timber
d. Land
e. Computer
f. Goodwill

g. Cash
h. Buildings
i. Production machinery
j. Accounts receivable
k. Prepaid rent
l. Franchise

Exercise 6-3   *Classifying tangible and intangible assets*   LO 6-1

Required

Identify each of the following long-term operational assets as either tangible (T) or intangible (I).

a. 18-wheel truck
b. Timber
c. Log loader
d. Dental chair
e. Goodwill
f. Computer software

g. Retail store building
h. Shelving for inventory
i. Trademark
j. Gas well
k. Drilling rig
l. FCC license for TV station

Exercise 6-4   *Determining the cost of an asset*   LO 6-2

Louisiana Logging Co. purchased an electronic saw to cut various types and sizes of logs. The saw had a list price of $160,000. The seller agreed to allow a 5 percent discount because

Louisiana paid cash. Delivery terms were FOB shipping point. Freight cost amounted to $3,200. Louisiana had to hire an individual to operate the saw. Louisiana had to build a special platform to mount the saw. The cost of the platform was $2,500. The saw operator was paid an annual salary of $50,000. The cost of the company's theft insurance policy increased by $1,800 per year as a result of acquiring the saw. The saw had a five-year useful life and an expected salvage value of $25,000.

Required

Determine the amount to be capitalized in the asset account for the purchase of the saw.

LO 6-2

Exercise 6-5 *Allocating costs on the basis of relative market values*

Carolina Company purchased a building and the land on which the building is situated for a total cost of $800,000 cash. The land was appraised at $300,000 and the building at $700,000.

Required

a. What is the accounting term for this type of acquisition?
b. Determine the amount of the purchase cost to allocate to the land and the amount to allocate to the building.
c. Would the company recognize a gain on the purchase? Why or why not?
d. Record the purchase in a statements model like the following one.

Assets			=	Liab.	+	Equity	Rev.	−	Exp.	=	Net Inc.	Cash Flow
Cash	+ Land	+ Building										

LO 6-2

Exercise 6-6 *Allocating costs for a basket purchase*

Sneathen Company purchased a restaurant building, land, and equipment for $600,000 cash. The appraised value of the assets was as follows:

Land	$200,000
Building	480,000
Equipment	120,000
Total	$800,000

Required

a. Compute the amount to be recorded on the books for each of the assets.
b. Record the purchase in a horizontal statements model like the following one.

Assets				=	Liab.	+	Equity	Rev.	−	Exp.	=	Net Inc.	Cash Flow
Cash	+ Land	+ Building	+ Equip.										

LO 6-3

Exercise 6-7 *Effect of depreciation on the accounting equation and financial statements*

The following events apply to The Ice Cream Parlor for the 2014 fiscal year:

1. The company started when it acquired $20,000 cash from the issue of common stock.
2. Purchased a new ice cream machine that cost $20,000 cash.
3. Earned $36,000 in cash revenue.
4. Paid $21,000 cash for salaries expense.
5. Paid $6,000 cash for operating expenses.

6. Adjusted the records to reflect the use of the ice cream machine. The machine, purchased on January 1, 2014, has an expected useful life of five years and an estimated salvage value of $5,000. Use straight-line depreciation. The adjusting entry was made as of December 31, 2014.

Required

a. Record the above transactions in a horizontal statements model like the following one.

Event	Balance Sheet							Income Statement					Statemt. of Cash Flows
	Assets				=	Equity		Rev.	−	Exp.	=	Net Inc.	
	Cash	+	Equip.	−	A. Depr.	=	Com. Stock	+	Ret. Earn.				

b. What amount of depreciation expense would The Ice Cream Parlor report on the 2014 income statement?

c. What amount of accumulated depreciation would The Ice Cream Parlor report on the December 31, 2014, balance sheet?

d. Would the cash flow from operating activities be affected by depreciation in 2014?

Exercise 6-8   *Effect of double-declining-balance depreciation on financial statements*   LO 6-3

Posey Company started operations by acquiring $120,000 cash from the issue of common stock. On January 1, 2014, the company purchased equipment that cost $110,000 cash. The equipment had an expected useful life of five years and an estimated salvage value of $10,000. Posey Company earned $85,000 and $72,000 of cash revenue during 2014 and 2015, respectively. Posey Company uses double-declining-balance depreciation.

Required

a. Record the above transactions in a horizontal statements model like the following one.

Event	Balance Sheet							Income Statement					Statemt. of Cash Flows
	Assets				=	Equity		Rev.	−	Exp.	=	Net Inc.	
	Cash	+	Equip.	−	A. Depr.	=	Com. Stock	+	Ret. Earn.				

b. Prepare income statements, balance sheets, and statements of cash flows for 2014 and 2015. Use a vertical statements format.

Exercise 6-9   *Computing and recording straight-line versus double-declining-balance depreciation*   LO 6-3

At the beginning of 2014, Metal Manufacturing purchased a new computerized drill press for $75,000. It is expected to have a five-year life and a $15,000 salvage value.

Required

a. Compute the depreciation for each of the five years, assuming that the company uses
  (1) Straight-line depreciation.
  (2) Double-declining-balance depreciation.

b. Record the purchase of the drill press and the depreciation expense for the first year under the straight-line and double-declining-balance methods in a financial statements model like the following one:

Assets					=	Equity	Rev.	−	Exp.	=	Net Inc.	Cash Flow
Cash	+	Drill Press	−	Acc. Dep.	=	Ret. Earn						

LO 6-3, 6-4

Exercise 6-10   *Double-declining-balance and units-of-production depreciation: Gain or loss on disposal*

Graphics Service Co. purchased a new color copier at the beginning of 2014 for $47,000. The copier is expected to have a five-year useful life and a $7,000 salvage value. The expected copy production was estimated at 2,000,000 copies. Actual copy production for the five years was as follows:

2014	560,000
2015	490,000
2016	430,000
2017	350,000
2018	210,000
Total	2,040,000

The copier was sold at the end of 2018 for $7,600.

Required

a. Compute the depreciation expense for each of the five years, using double-declining-balance depreciation.
b. Compute the depreciation expense for each of the five years, using units-of-production depreciation. (Round cost per unit to three decimal places.)
c. Calculate the amount of gain or loss from the sale of the asset under each of the depreciation methods.

LO 6-3, 6-4

Exercise 6-11   *Events related to the acquisition, use, and disposal of a tangible plant asset: Straight-line depreciation*

Sam's Subs purchased a delivery van on January 1, 2014, for $35,000. In addition, Sam's paid sales tax and title fees of $1,500 for the van. The van is expected to have a four-year life and a salvage value of $6,500.

Required

a. Using the straight-line method, compute the depreciation expense for 2014 and 2015.
b. Assume the van was sold on January 1, 2017, for $21,000. Determine the amount of gain or loss that would be recognized on the asset disposal.

LO 6-4

Exercise 6-12   *Effect of the disposal of plant assets on the financial statements*

A plant asset with a cost of $50,000 and accumulated depreciation of $41,000 is sold for $10,000.

Required

a. What is the book value of the asset at the time of sale?
b. What is the amount of gain or loss on the disposal?
c. How would the sale affect net income (increase, decrease, no effect) and by how much?
d. How would the sale affect the amount of total assets shown on the balance sheet (increase, decrease, no effect) and by how much?
e. How would the event affect the statement of cash flows (inflow, outflow, no effect) and in what section?

LO 6-4

Exercise 6-13   *Effect of gains and losses on the accounting equation and financial statements*

On January 1, 2014, Liken Enterprises purchased a parcel of land for $20,000 cash. At the time of purchase, the company planned to use the land for future expansion. In 2015, Liken Enterprises changed its plans and sold the land.

Required

a. Assume that the land was sold for $22,500 in 2015.
   (1) Show the effect of the sale on the accounting equation.
   (2) What amount would Liken report on the income statement related to the sale of the land?
   (3) What amount would Liken report on the statement of cash flows related to the sale of the land?

b. Assume that the land was sold for $18,500 in 2015.
   (1) Show the effect of the sale on the accounting equation.
   (2) What amount would Liken report on the income statement related to the sale of the land?
   (3) What amount would Liken report on the statement of cash flows related to the sale of the land?

Exercise 6-14   *Revision of estimated useful life*   LO 6-5

On January 1, 2014, Muoy Machining Co. purchased a compressor and related installation equipment for $72,500. The equipment had a three-year estimated life with a $12,500 salvage value. Straight-line depreciation was used. At the beginning of 2016, Muoy revised the expected life of the asset to four years rather than three years. The salvage value was revised to $2,500.

Required

Compute the depreciation expense for each of the four years.

Exercise 6-15   *Distinguishing between revenue expenditures and capital expenditures*   LO 6-6

Houston's Shredding Service has just completed a minor repair on a shredding machine. The repair cost was $1,900, and the book value prior to the repair was $6,000. In addition, the company spent $12,000 to replace the roof on a building. The new roof extended the life of the building by five years. Prior to the roof replacement, the general ledger reflected the Building account at $110,000 and related Accumulated Depreciation account at $30,000.

Required

After the work was completed, what book value should Houston's report on the balance sheet for the shredding machine and the building?

Exercise 6-16   *Effect of revenue expenditures versus capital expenditures on financial statements*   LO 6-6

Apac Construction Company purchased a forklift for $150,000 cash. It had an estimated useful life of four years and a $10,000 salvage value. At the beginning of the third year of use, the company spent an additional $9,000 that was related to the forklift. The company's financial condition just prior to this expenditure is shown in the following statements model:

Assets			=	Equity			Rev.	−	Exp.	=	Net Inc.	Cash Flow
Cash	+	Forklift	Acc. Depr.	=	Com. Stk.	+	Ret. Earn.						
15,000	+	150,000	70,000	=	45,000	+	50,000	NA	−	NA	=	NA	NA

Required

Record the $9,000 expenditure in the statements model under each of the following *independent* assumptions:

a. The expenditure was for routine maintenance.
b. The expenditure extended the forklift's life.
c. The expenditure improved the forklift's operating capacity.

LO 6-6

Exercise 6-17 *Effect of revenue expenditures versus capital expenditures on financial statements*

On January 1, 2014, Plains Power Company overhauled four turbine engines that generate power for customers. The overhaul resulted in a slight increase in the capacity of the engines to produce power. Such overhauls occur regularly at two-year intervals and have been treated as maintenance expense in the past. Management is considering whether to capitalize this year's $22,000 cash cost in the Engine asset account or to expense it as a maintenance expense. Assume that the engines have a remaining useful life of two years and no expected salvage value. Assume straight-line depreciation.

Required

a. Determine the amount of additional depreciation expense Plains would recognize in 2014 and 2015 if the cost were capitalized in the Engine account.
b. Determine the amount of expense Plains would recognize in 2014 and 2015 if the cost were recognized as maintenance expense.
c. Determine the effect of the overhaul on cash flow from operating activities for 2014 and 2015 if the cost were capitalized and expensed through depreciation charges.
d. Determine the effect of the overhaul on cash flow from operating activities for 2014 and 2015 if the cost were recognized as maintenance expense.

LO 6-7

Exercise 6-18 *Computing and recording depletion expense*

Tishimingo Sand and Gravel paid $800,000 to acquire 1,200,000 cubic yards of sand reserves. The following statements model reflects Tishimingo's financial condition just prior to purchasing the sand reserves. The company extracted 650,000 cubic yards of sand in year 1 and 450,000 cubic yards in year 2.

Assets			=	Equity			Rev.	–	Exp.	=	Net Inc.	Cash Flow
Cash	+	Sand Res.	=	Com. Stk.	+	Ret. Earn.						
900,000	+	NA	=	900,000	+	NA	NA	–	NA	=	NA	NA

Required

a. Compute the depletion charge per unit.
b. Record the acquisition of the sand reserves and the depletion expense for years 1 and 2 in a financial statements model like the preceding one.

LO 6-8

Exercise 6-19 *Computing and recording the amortization of intangibles*

Pacart Manufacturing paid cash to acquire the assets of an existing company. Among the assets acquired were the following items:

Patent with 5 remaining years of legal life	$48,000
Goodwill	35,000

Pacart's financial condition just prior to the purchase of these assets is shown in the following statements model:

Assets					=	Liab.	+	Equity	Rev.	–	Exp.	=	Net Inc.	Cash Flow
Cash	+	Patent	+	Goodwill										
94,000	+	NA	+	NA	=	NA	+	94,000	NA	–	NA	=	NA	NA

Required

a. Compute the annual amortization expense for these items if applicable.
b. Record the purchase of the intangible assets and the related amortization expense for year 1 in a horizontal statements model like the preceding one.

Exercise 6-20   *Computing and recording goodwill*   LO 6-8

Bill Yeates acquired the business Sun Supply Co. for $275,000 cash and assumed all liabilities at the date of acquisition. Sun's books showed tangible assets of $250,000, liabilities of $10,000, and equity of $240,000. An appraiser assessed the fair market value of the tangible assets at $265,000 at the date of acquisition. Yeates's financial condition just prior to the acquisition is shown in the following statements model:

Assets			=	Liab.	+	Equity	Rev.	−	Exp.	=	Net Inc.	Cash Flow
Cash	+	Assets	+	Goodwill								
450,000	+	NA	+	NA	=	NA	+	450,000	NA	−	NA	=	NA	NA

Required

a. Compute the amount of goodwill purchased.
b. Record the purchase in a financial statements model like the preceding one.

Exercise 6-21   *Performing ratio analysis using real-world data*   LO 6-9

American Greetings Corporation manufactures and sells greeting cards and related items such as gift wrapping paper. CSX Corporation is one of the largest railway networks in the nation. The following data were taken from one of the companies' December 28, 2012, annual report and from the other's February 29, 2012, annual report. Revealing which data relate to which company was intentionally omitted. For one company, the dollar amounts are in thousands, while for the other they are in millions.

	Company 1	Company 2
Sales	$1,695,144	$11,756
Depreciation costs	34,210	1,059
Net earnings	57,198	1,859
Current assets	640,959	2,801
Property, plant, and equipment	277,597	24,974
Total assets	1,549,464	30,571

Required

a. Calculate depreciation costs as a percentage of sales for each company.
b. Calculate property, plant, and equipment as a percentage of total assets for each company.
c. Based on the information now available to you, decide which data relate to which company. Explain the rationale for your decision.
d. Which company appears to be using its assets most efficiently? Explain your answer.

PROBLEMS

connect
|ACCOUNTING   All applicable Problems are available with McGraw-Hill's *Connect® Accounting.*

Problem 6-22   *Accounting for acquisition of assets including a basket purchase*   LO 6-2

Shay Company made several purchases of long-term assets in 2014. The details of each purchase are presented here.

New Office Equipment

1. List price: $50,000; terms: 1/10, n/30; paid within the discount period.
2. Transportation-in: $1,200.
3. Installation: $1,000.
4. Cost to repair damage during unloading: $700.
5. Routine maintenance cost after eight months: $240.

Basket Purchase of Office Furniture, Copier, Computers, and Laser Printers for $70,000 with Fair Market Values

1. Office furniture, $48,000.
2. Copier, $12,000.
3. Computers and printers, $20,000.

Land for New Headquarters with Old Barn Torn Down

1. Purchase price, $100,000.
2. Demolition of barn, $7,000.
3. Lumber sold from old barn, $2,000.
4. Grading in preparation for new building, $11,000.
5. Construction of new building, $310,000.

Required

In each of these cases, determine the amount of cost to be capitalized in the asset accounts.

LO 6-3

Problem 6-23 *Calculating depreciation expense using four different methods*

Weir Service Company purchased a copier on January 1, 2014, for $25,000 and paid an additional $500 for delivery charges. The copier was estimated to have a life of four years or 1,000,000 copies. Salvage was estimated at $1,500. The copier produced 250,000 copies in 2014 and 270,000 copies in 2015.

Required

Compute the amount of depreciation expense for the copier for calendar years 2014 and 2015, using these methods:

a. Straight-line.
b. Units-of-production.
c. Double-declining-balance.

LO 6-3

Problem 6-24 *Determining the effect of depreciation expense on financial statements*

Three different companies each purchased a machine on January 1, 2014, for $64,000. Each machine was expected to last five years or 200,000 hours. Salvage value was estimated to be $4,000. All three machines were operated for 50,000 hours in 2014, 55,000 hours in 2015, 40,000 hours in 2016, 44,000 hours in 2017, and 31,000 hours in 2018. Each of the three companies earned $30,000 of cash revenue during each of the five years. Company A uses straight-line depreciation, company B uses double-declining-balance depreciation, and company C uses units-of-production depreciation.

Required

Answer each of the following questions. Ignore the effects of income taxes.

a. Which company will report the highest amount of net income for 2014?
b. Which company will report the lowest amount of net income for 2016?
c. Which company will report the highest book value on the December 31, 2016, balance sheet?

d. Which company will report the highest amount of retained earnings on the December 31, 2017, balance sheet?

e. Which company will report the lowest amount of cash flow from operating activities on the 2016 statement of cash flows?

Problem 6-25   *Accounting for depreciation over multiple accounting cycles: Straight-line depreciation*

LO 6-3, 6-4

CHECK FIGURES
Net Income, 2014: $500
Total Assets, 2017: $42,500

Zhao Company began operations when it acquired $40,000 cash from the issue of common stock on January 1, 2014. The cash acquired was immediately used to purchase equipment for $40,000 that had a $4,000 salvage value and an expected useful life of four years. The equipment was used to produce the following revenue stream (assume all revenue transactions are for cash). At the beginning of the fifth year, the equipment was sold for $4,500 cash. Zhao uses straight-line depreciation.

	2014	2015	2016	2017	2018
Revenue	$9,500	$10,000	$10,500	$8,500	$0

Required

Prepare income statements, statements of changes in stockholders' equity, balance sheets, and statements of cash flows for each of the five years.

Problem 6-26   *Effect of straight-line versus double-declining-balance depreciation on the recognition of expense and gains or losses*

LO 6-3, 6-4

CHECK FIGURES
a. Depreciation Expense, Year 2: $8,000
b. Depreciation Expense, Year 2: $10,080

One Day Laundry Services purchased a new steam press on January 1, for $42,000. It is expected to have a five-year useful life and a $2,000 salvage value. One Day expects to use the steam press more extensively in the early years of its life.

Required

a. Calculate the depreciation expense for each of the five years, assuming the use of straight-line depreciation.

b. Calculate the depreciation expense for each of the five years, assuming the use of double-declining-balance depreciation.

c. Would the choice of one depreciation method over another produce a different amount of cash flow for any year? Why or why not?

d. Assume that One Day Laundry Services sold the steam press at the end of the third year for $22,000. Compute the amount of gain or loss using each depreciation method.

Problem 6-27   *Computing and recording units-of-production depreciation*

LO 6-3, 6-4

Renner Corporation purchased a delivery van for $28,500 in 2014. The firm's financial condition immediately prior to the purchase is shown in the following horizontal statements model:

Assets			=	Equity			Rev.	−	Exp.	=	Net Inc.	Cash Flow
Cash	+	Book Value of Van	=	Com. Stk.	+	Ret. Earn.						
50,000	+	NA	=	50,000	+	NA	NA	−	NA	=	NA	NA

The van was expected to have a useful life of 200,000 miles and a salvage value of $2,500. Actual mileage was as follows:

CHECK FIGURES
a. Depreciation Expense, 2014: $7,800
c. Gain on Sale: $950

2014	60,000
2015	50,000
2016	55,000

Required

a. Compute the depreciation for each of the three years, assuming the use of units-of-production depreciation.

b. Assume that Renner earns $26,000 of cash revenue during 2014. Record the purchase of the van and the recognition of the revenue and the depreciation expense for the first year in a financial statements model like the preceding one.

c. Assume that Renner sold the van at the end of the third year for $8,000. Calculate the amount of gain or loss from the sale.

LO 6-2, 6-3, 6-5, 6-6

CHECK FIGURES
b. Net Income, 2014: $48,520
Total Assets, 2016: $242,591

Problem 6-28   *Purchase and use of tangible asset: Three accounting cycles, double-declining-balance depreciation*

The following transactions pertain to Engineering Solutions Inc. Assume the transactions for the purchase of the computer and any capital improvements occur on January 1 each year.

2014

1. Acquired $80,000 cash from the issue of common stock.
2. Purchased a computer system for $35,000. It has an estimated useful life of five years and a $5,000 salvage value.
3. Paid $2,450 sales tax on the computer system.
4. Collected $65,000 in fees from clients.
5. Paid $1,500 in fees to service the computers.
6. Recorded double-declining-balance depreciation on the computer system for 2014.

2015

1. Paid $1,000 for repairs to the computer system.
2. Bought off-site backup services to maintain the computer system, $1,500.
3. Collected $68,000 in fees from clients.
4. Paid $1,500 in fees to service the computers.
5. Recorded double-declining-balance depreciation for 2015.

2016

1. Paid $6,000 to upgrade the computer system, which extended the total life of the system to six years. The salvage value did not change.
2. Paid $1,200 in fees to service the computers.
3. Collected $70,000 in fees from clients.
4. Recorded double-declining-balance depreciation for 2016.

Required

a. Record the above transactions in a horizontal statements model like the following one.

Event	Balance Sheet							Income Statement					Statemt. of Cash Flows
	Assets				=	Equity		Rev.	−	Exp.	=	Net Inc.	
	Cash	+	Equip.	−	A. Depr.	=	Com. Stock	+	Ret. Earn.				

b. Use a vertical model to present financial statements for 2014, 2015, and 2016.

Problem 6-29   *Recording continuing expenditures for plant assets*

LO 6-3, 6-4, 6-5, 6-6

Seaside Inc. recorded the following transactions over the life of a piece of equipment purchased in 2014:

Jan. 1, 2014	Purchased the equipment for $38,000 cash. The equipment is estimated to have a five-year life and $3,000 salvage value and was to be depreciated using the straight-line method.
Dec. 31, 2014	Recorded depreciation expense for 2014.
May 5, 2015	Undertook routine repairs costing $900.
Dec. 31, 2015	Recorded depreciation expense for 2015.
Jan. 1, 2016	Made an adjustment costing $4,000 to the equipment. It improved the quality of the output but did not affect the life and salvage value estimates.
Dec. 31, 2016	Recorded depreciation expense for 2016.
Mar. 1, 2017	Incurred $410 cost to oil and clean the equipment.
Dec. 31, 2017	Recorded depreciation expense for 2017.
Jan. 1, 2018	Had the equipment completely overhauled at a cost of $9,000. The overhaul was estimated to extend the total life to seven years and revised the salvage value to $2,500.
Dec. 31, 2018	Recorded depreciation expense for 2018.
July 1, 2019	Sold the equipment for $8,500 cash.

CHECK FIGURES
b. 2016 Depreciation Expense: $8,333
d. Loss on Sale: $2,916

Required

a. Use a horizontal statements model like the following one to show the effects of these transactions on the elements of the financial statements. Use + for increase, − for decrease, and NA for not affected. The first event is recorded as an example.

Date	Assets	=	Liabilities	+	Equity	Net Inc.	Cash Flow
Jan. 1, 2011	+ −		NA		NA	NA	− IA

b. Determine the amount of depreciation expense Seaside will report on the income statements for the years 2014 through 2018.

c. Determine the book value (cost − accumulated depreciation) Seaside will report on the balance sheets at the end of the years 2014 through 2018.

d. Determine the amount of the gain or loss Seaside will report on the disposal of the equipment on July 1, 2019.

Problem 6-30   *Accounting for depletion*

LO 6-7

Cohen Exploration Corporation engages in the exploration and development of many types of natural resources. In the last two years, the company has engaged in the following activities:

Jan. 1, 2014	Purchased a coal mine estimated to contain 300,000 tons of coal for $900,000.
July 1, 2014	Purchased for $2,000,000 a tract of timber estimated to yield 3,000,000 board feet of lumber and to have a residual land value of $200,000.
Feb. 1, 2014	Purchased a silver mine estimated to contain 30,000 tons of silver for $850,000.
Aug. 1, 2014	Purchased for $875,000 oil reserves estimated to contain 270,000 barrels of oil, of which 20,000 would be unprofitable to pump.

CHECK FIGURES
a. Coal Mine Depletion, 2014: $204,000
b. Total Natural Resources: $2,126,030

Required

a. Determine the amount of depletion expense that would be recognized on the 2014 income statement for each of the four reserves, assuming 68,000 tons of coal, 1,200,000 board feet of lumber, 9,000 tons of silver, and 80,000 barrels of oil are extracted.

b. Prepare the portion of the December 31, 2014, balance sheet that reports natural resources.

LO 6-5, 6-6, 6-7

CHECK FIGURE
Depreciation Expense: $9,000

Problem 6-31   *Accounting for continuing expenditures*

Bird Manufacturing paid $62,000 to purchase a computerized assembly machine on January 1, 2014. The machine had an estimated life of eight years and a $2,000 salvage value. Bird's financial condition as of January 1, 2017, is shown in the following financial statements model. Bird uses the straight-line method for depreciation.

Assets					Equity			Rev.	–	Exp.	=	Net Inc.	Cash Flow
Cash	+	Mach.	–	Acc. Dep.	=	Com. Stk.	+	Ret. Earn.					
15,000	+	62,000	–	22,500	=	10,500	+	44,000	NA	–	NA	=	NA NA

Bird Manufacturing made the following expenditures on the computerized assembly machine in 2017.

Jan. 2   Added an overdrive mechanism for $8,000 that would improve the overall quality of the performance of the machine but would not extend its life. The salvage value was revised to $2,500.

Aug. 1   Performed routine maintenance, $1,250.

Oct. 2   Replaced some computer chips (considered routine), $800.

Dec. 31   Recognized 2017 depreciation expense.

Required

Record the 2017 transactions in a statements model like the preceding one.

LO 6-8

CHECK FIGURE
Goodwill Purchased: $120,000

Problem 6-32   *Accounting for intangible assets*

Cafe Olé Company acquired a fast-food restaurant for $1,500,000. The fair market values of the assets acquired were as follows. No liabilities were assumed.

Equipment	$380,000
Land	200,000
Building	680,000
Franchise (5-year life)	120,000

Required

Calculate the amount of goodwill purchased.

LO 6-8

CHECK FIGURE
Impairment Loss: $100,000

Problem 6-33   *Accounting for goodwill*

Tri-State Co. acquired the assets of Riley Co. for $1,200,000 in 2014. The estimated fair market value of the assets at the acquisition date was $1,000,000. Goodwill of $200,000 was recorded at acquisition. In 2015, because of negative publicity, one-half of the goodwill acquired from Riley Co. was judged to be permanently impaired.

Required

Explain how the recognition of the impairment of the goodwill will affect the 2015 balance sheet, income statement, and statement of cash flows.

LO 6-9

Problem 6-34   *Performing ratio analysis using real-world data*

Companies in the coal mining business use a lot of property, plant, and equipment. Not only is there the significant investment they must make in the equipment used to extract and process the coal, but they must also purchase the rights to the coal reserves themselves.

Goodyear Tire & Rubber Company, Inc. is the largest tire manufacturer in North America. Cloud Peak Energy Corporation claims to be the largest private-sector coal company in the world. The following information was taken from these companies' December 31, 2012, annual reports. All dollar amounts are in millions.

	Cloud Peak Energy, Inc.	Goodyear Tire
Sales	$1,517	$20,992
Depreciation and depletion costs	95	684
Property, plant, and equipment (net of accumulated depreciation)	1,678	6,956
Total assets	2,351	16,973
Depreciation method	Straight-line or units of production	Straight-line
Estimated life of assets:		
Buildings	5 to 25 years	5 to 45 years
Machinery and equipment	3 to 20 years	3 to 30 years

Required

a. Calculate depreciation costs as a percentage of sales for each company.

b. Calculate buildings, property, plant, and equipment as a percentage of total assets for each company.

c. Based only on the percentages calculated in Requirements a and b, which company appears to be using its assets most efficiently? Explain your answer.

d. Identify some of the problems a financial analyst encounters when trying to compare the used of long-term assets of Cloud Peak versus Goodyear.

ANALYZE, THINK, COMMUNICATE

ATC 6-1   Business Applications Case   *Understanding real-world annual reports*

Required

Use the Target Corporation's Form 10-K to answer the following questions related to Target's 2012 fiscal year (year ended February 2, 2013). Target's Form 10-K is available on the company's website or through the SEC's EDGAR database. Appendix A provides instructions for using the EDGAR database.

a. What method of depreciation does Target use?

b. What types of intangible assets does Target have?

c. What are the estimated lives that Target uses for the various types of long-term assets?

d. As of February 2, 2013, what is the original cost of Target's: Land; Buildings and improvements; and Fixtures and equipment (see the footnotes)?

e. What was Target's depreciation expense and amortization expense for 2012 (see the footnotes)?

ATC 6-2   Group Assignment   *Different depreciation methods*

Sweet's Bakery makes cakes, pies, and other pastries that it sells to local grocery stores. The company experienced the following transactions during 2014.

1. Started business by acquiring $60,000 cash from the issue of common stock.

2. Purchased bakery equipment for $46,000 with a four-year life and a $6,000 salvage value.

3. Had cash sales in 2014 amounting to $42,000.

4. Paid $8,200 of cash for supplies which were all used during the year to make baked goods.

5. Paid other operating expenses of $12,000 for 2014.

Required

a. Organize the class into two sections and divide each section into groups of three to five students. Assign each section a depreciation method: straight-line or double-declining-balance.

Group Task

Prepare an income statement and a balance sheet using the preceding information and the depreciation method assigned to your group.

Class Discussion

b. Have a representative of each section put its income statement on the board. Are there differences in net income? How will these differences in the amount of depreciation expense change over the life of the equipment?

ATC 6-3   Research Assignment   *Comparing Microsoft's and Intel's operational assets*

Companies in different industries often use different proportions of current versus long-term assets to accomplish their business objective. The technology revolution resulting from the silicon microchip has often been led by two well-known companies: Microsoft and Intel. Although often thought of together, these companies are really very different. Using either the most current Forms 10-K or annual reports for Microsoft Corporation and Intel Corporation, complete the requirements below. To obtain the Forms 10-K, use either the EDGAR system following the instructions in Appendix A or the company's website. Microsoft's annual report is available on its website; Intel's annual report is its Form 10-K.

Required

a. Fill in the missing data in the following table. The percentages must be computed; they are not included in the companies' 10-Ks. (*Note:* The percentages for current assets and property, plant, and equipment will not sum to 100.)

	Current Assets	Property, Plant, and Equipment	Total Assets
Microsoft			
Dollar Amount	$	$	$
% of Total Assets	%	%	100%
Intel			
Dollar Amount	$	$	$
% of Total Assets	%	%	100%

b. Briefly explain why these two companies have different percentages of their assets in current assets versus property, plant, and equipment.

ATC 6-4   Writing Assignment   *Impact of historical cost on asset presentation on the balance sheet*

Assume that you are examining the balance sheets of two companies and note the following information.

	Company A	Company B
Equipment	$1,130,000	$900,000
Accumulated Depreciation	(730,000)	(500,000)
Book Value	$ 400,000	$400,000

Maxie Smith, a student who has had no accounting courses, remarks that Company A and Company B have the same amount of equipment.

Required

In a short paragraph, explain to Maxie that the two companies do not have equal amounts of equipment. You may want to include in your discussion comments regarding the possible age of each company's equipment, the impact of the historical cost concept on balance sheet information, and the impact of different depreciation methods on book value.

ATC 6-5   Ethical Dilemma   *What's an expense?*

Several years ago, Wilson Blowhard founded a communications company. The company became successful and grew by expanding its customer base and acquiring some of its competitors. In fact, most of its growth resulted from acquiring other companies. Mr. Blowhard is adamant about continuing the company's growth and increasing its net worth. To achieve these goals, the business's net income must continue to increase at a rapid pace.

If the company's net worth continues to rise, Mr. Blowhard plans to sell the company and retire. He is, therefore, focused on improving the company's profit any way he can.

In the communications business, companies often use the lines of other communications companies. This line usage is a significant operating expense for Mr. Blowhard's company. Generally accepted accounting principles require operating costs like line use to be expensed as they are incurred each year. Each dollar of line cost reduces net income by a dollar.

After reviewing the company's operations, Mr. Blowhard concluded that the company did not currently need all of the line use it was paying for. It was really paying the owner of the lines now so that the line use would be available in the future for all of Mr. Blowhard's expected new customers. Mr. Blowhard instructed his accountant to capitalize all of the line cost charges and depreciate them over 10 years. The accountant reluctantly followed Mr. Blowhard's instructions and the company's net income for the current year showed a significant increase over the prior year's net income. Mr. Blowhard had found a way to report continued growth in the company's net income and increase the value of the company.

Required

a. How does Mr. Blowhard's scheme affect the amount of income that the company would otherwise report in its financial statements and how does the scheme affect the company's balance sheet? Explain your answer.

b. Review the AICPA's Articles of Professional Conduct (see Chapter 4) and comment on any of the standards that were violated.

c. Review the fraud triangle discussed in Chapter 4 and comment on the features of the fraud triangle that are evident in this case.

CHAPTER 8

Proprietorships, Partnerships, and Corporations

LEARNING OBJECTIVES

After you have mastered the material in this chapter, you will be able to:

LO 8-1	Identify the primary characteristics of sole proprietorships, partnerships, and corporations.
LO 8-2	Analyze financial statements to identify the different types of business organizations.
LO 8-3	Explain the characteristics of major types of stock issued by corporations.
LO 8-4	Explain how to account for different types of stock issued by corporations.
LO 8-5	Show how treasury stock transactions affect a company's financial statements.
LO 8-6	Explain the effects of declaring and paying cash dividends on a company's financial statements.
LO 8-7	Explain the effects of stock dividends and stock splits on a company's financial statements.
LO 8-8	Show how the appropriation of retained earnings affects financial statements.
LO 8-9	Explain some uses of accounting information in making stock investment decisions.

 Video lectures and accompanying self-assessment quizzes are available for all learning objectives through McGraw-Hill Connect® Accounting.

CHAPTER OPENING

You want to start a business. How should you structure it? Should it be a sole proprietorship, partnership, or corporation? Each form of business structure presents advantages and disadvantages. For example, a sole proprietorship allows maximum independence and control while partnerships and corporations allow individuals to pool resources and talents with other people. This chapter discusses these and other features of the three primary forms of business structure.

The Curious Accountant

Imagine your rich uncle rewarded you for doing well in your first accounting course by giving you $10,000 to invest in the stock of one company. After reviewing many recent annual reports, you narrowed your choice to two companies with the following characteristics:

Mystery Company A: This company began operations in 2003, but did not begin selling its stock to the public until June 28, 2010. It has lost money every year it has been in existence, and by December 31, 2012, it had total life-time losses of approximately $1 billion. Even so, its products have received lots of attention from the media and celebrities. At its current price of $35 you could buy 286 shares. A friend told you that a status-conscious person like you should at least buy this company's stock, since you cannot afford its products.

Mystery Company B: This company has been in existence since 1883 and has made a profit most years. In its 2012 fiscal year alone its net earnings were $1.5 billion, and it paid dividends of $267 million. Unlike Company A, Company B sells items that everyone needs and can afford. Its stock is selling for about $32 per share, so you can buy around 312 shares. Your friend said that buying this company's stock would be the most boring investment you would ever make.

The names of the real-world companies described above are disclosed later. Based on the information provided, which company's stock would you buy? (Answer on page 296.)

FORMS OF BUSINESS ORGANIZATIONS

LO 8-1

Identify the primary characteristics of sole proprietorships, partnerships, and corporations.

Sole proprietorships are owned by a single individual who is responsible for making business and profit distribution decisions. If you want to be the absolute master of your destiny, you should organize your business as a proprietorship. Establishing a sole proprietorship is usually as simple as obtaining a business license from local government authorities. Usually no legal ownership agreement is required.

Partnerships allow persons to share their talents, capital, and the risks and rewards of business ownership. Because two or more individuals share ownership, partnerships require clear agreements about how authority, risks, and profits will be shared. Prudent partners minimize misunderstandings by hiring attorneys to prepare a **partnership agreement** which defines the responsibilities of each partner and describes how income or losses will be divided. Because the measurement of income affects the distribution of profits, partnerships frequently hire accountants to ensure that records are maintained in accordance with generally accepted accounting principles (GAAP). Partnerships (and sole proprietorships) also may need professional advice to deal with tax issues.

A **corporation** is a separate legal entity created by the authority of a state government. The paperwork to start a corporation is complex. For most laypersons, engaging professional attorneys and accountants to assist with the paperwork is well worth the fees charged.

Each state has separate laws governing establishing corporations. Many states follow the standard provisions of the Model Business Corporation Act. All states require the initial application to provide **articles of incorporation,** which normally include the following information: (1) the corporation's name and proposed date of incorporation; (2) the purpose of the corporation; (3) the location of the business and its expected life (which can be *perpetuity,* meaning *endless*); (4) provisions for capital stock; and (5) the names and addresses of the members of the first board of directors, the individuals with the ultimate authority for operating the business. If the articles are in order, the state establishes the legal existence of the corporation by issuing a charter of incorporation. The charter and the articles are public documents.

ADVANTAGES AND DISADVANTAGES OF DIFFERENT FORMS OF BUSINESS ORGANIZATION

Each form of business organization presents a different combination of advantages and disadvantages. Persons wanting to start a business or invest in one should consider the characteristics of each type of business structure.

Regulation

Few laws specifically affect the operations of proprietorships and partnerships. Corporations, however, are usually heavily regulated. The extent of government regulation depends on the size and distribution of a company's ownership interests. Ownership interests in corporations are normally evidenced by **stock certificates.**

Ownership of corporations can be transferred from one individual to another through exchanging stock certificates. As long as the exchanges (buying and selling of shares of stock, often called *trading*) are limited to transactions between individuals, a company is defined as a **closely held corporation.** However, once a corporation reaches a certain size, it may list its stock on a stock exchange such as the New York Stock Exchange or the NASDAQ. Trading on a stock exchange is limited to the stockbrokers who are members of the exchange. These brokers represent buyers and sellers who are willing to pay the brokers commissions for exchanging stock certificates on their behalf. Although closely held corporations are relatively free from government regulation, companies whose stock is publicly traded on the exchanges by brokers are subject to extensive regulation.

The extensive regulation of trading on stock exchanges began in the 1930s. The stock market crash of 1929 and the subsequent Great Depression led Congress to pass the **Securities Act of 1933** and the **Securities Exchange Act of 1934** to regulate issuing stock and to govern the exchanges. The 1934 act also created the Securities and Exchange Commission (SEC) to enforce the securities laws. Congress gave the SEC legal authority to establish accounting principles for corporations that are registered on the exchanges. However, the SEC has generally deferred its rule-making authority to private sector accounting bodies such as the Financial Accounting Standards Board (FASB), effectively allowing the accounting profession to regulate itself.

A number of high-profile business failures around the turn of the last century raised questions about the effectiveness of self-regulation and the usefulness of audits to protect the public. The Sarbanes-Oxley Act of 2002 was adopted to address these concerns. The act creates a five-member Public Company Accounting Oversight Board (PCAOB) with the authority to set and enforce auditing, attestation, quality control, and ethics standards for auditors of public companies. The PCAOB is empowered to impose disciplinary and remedial sanctions for violations of its rules, securities laws, and professional auditing and accounting standards. Public corporations operate in a complex regulatory environment that requires the services of attorneys and professional accountants.

Double Taxation

Corporations pay income taxes on their earnings and then owners pay income taxes on distributions (dividends) received from corporations. As a result, distributed corporate profits are taxed twice—first when income is reported on the corporation's income tax return and a second time when distributions are reported on individual owners' tax returns. This phenomenon is commonly called **double taxation** and is a significant disadvantage of the corporate form of business organization.

To illustrate, assume Glide Corporation earns pretax income of $100,000. Glide is in a 30 percent tax bracket. The corporation itself will pay income tax of $30,000 ($100,000 × 0.30). If the corporation distributes the after-tax income of $70,000 ($100,000 − $30,000) to individual stockholders in 15 percent tax brackets, the $70,000 dividend will be reported on the individual tax returns, requiring tax payments of $10,500 ($70,000 × .15). Total income tax of $40,500 ($30,000 + $10,500) is due on $100,000 of earned income. In contrast, consider a proprietorship that is owned by an individual in a 30 percent tax bracket. If the proprietorship earns and distributes $100,000 profit, the total tax would be only $30,000 ($100,000 × .30).

Double taxation can be a burden for small companies. To reduce that burden, tax laws permit small closely held corporations to elect "S Corporation" status. S Corporations are taxed as proprietorships or partnerships. Also, many states have recently enacted laws permitting the formation of **limited liability companies (LLCs),** which offer many of the benefits of corporate ownership yet are in general taxed as partnerships. Because proprietorships and partnerships are not separate legal entities, company earnings are taxable to the owners rather than the company itself.

Limited Liability

Given the disadvantages of increased regulation and double taxation, why would anyone choose the corporate form of business structure over a partnership or proprietorship? A major reason is that the corporate form limits an investor's potential liability as an owner of a business venture. Because a corporation is legally separate from its owners, creditors cannot claim owners' personal assets as payment for the company's debts. Also, plaintiffs must sue the corporation, not its owners. The most that owners of a

Answers to The Curious Accountant

Mystery Company A is Tesla Motors, Inc., as of March 20, 2013. The company's original product was the Tesla Roadster. The Roadster is an electric-only sports car that can go from 0 to 60 miles per hour in under 4 seconds; reach a top speed of 125 MPH, and go up to 245 miles before having to recharge its batteries. It cost over $100,000. The company sold its first car in 2008, and had sold around 2,500 cars by the end of 2012, the year in which it ended production of the Roadster. In 2012 it began selling a second model of car named the Model S, 2,700 units of which had been sold by the end of that year. Tesla also supplies electric car components to Daimler and Toyota.

Mystery Company B is Kroger Company, as of March 20, 2013. Of course, only the future will tell which company will be the better investment.

corporation can lose is the amount they have invested in the company (the value of the company's stock).

Unlike corporate stockholders, the owners of proprietorships and partnerships are *personally liable* for actions they take in the name of their companies. In fact, partners are responsible not only for their own actions but also for those taken by any other partner on behalf of the partnership. The benefit of **limited liability** is one of the most significant reasons the corporate form of business organization is so popular.

Continuity

Unlike partnerships or proprietorships, which terminate with the departure of their owners, a corporation's life continues when a shareholder dies or sells his or her stock. Because of **continuity** of existence, many corporations formed in the 1800s still thrive today.

Transferability of Ownership

The **transferability** of corporate ownership is easy. An investor simply buys or sells stock to acquire or give up an ownership interest in a corporation. Hundreds of millions of shares of stock are bought and sold on the major stock exchanges each day.

Transferring the ownership of proprietorships is much more difficult. To sell an ownership interest in a proprietorship, the proprietor must find someone willing to purchase the entire business. Because most proprietors also run their businesses, transferring ownership also requires transferring management responsibilities. Consider the difference in selling $1 million of ExxonMobil stock versus selling a locally owned gas station. The stock could be sold on the New York Stock Exchange within minutes. In contrast, it could take years to find a buyer who is financially capable of and interested in owning and operating a gas station.

Transferring ownership in partnerships can also be difficult. As with proprietorships, ownership transfers may require a new partner to make a significant investment and accept management responsibilities in the business. Further, a new partner must accept and be accepted by the other partners. Personality conflicts and differences in management style can cause problems in transferring ownership interests in partnerships.

Management Structure

Partnerships and proprietorships are usually managed by their owners. Corporations, in contrast, have three tiers of management authority. The *owners* (**stockholders**) represent the highest level of organizational authority. The stockholders *elect* a **board of directors** to oversee company operations. The directors then *hire* professional executives to manage the company on a daily basis. Because large corporations can offer high salaries and challenging career opportunities, they can often attract superior managerial talent.

While the management structure used by corporations is generally effective, it sometimes complicates dismissing incompetent managers. The chief executive officer (CEO) is usually a member of the board of directors and is frequently influential in choosing other board members. The CEO is also in a position to reward loyal board members. As a result, board members may be reluctant to fire the CEO or other top executives even if the individuals are performing poorly. Corporations operating under such conditions are said to be experiencing **entrenched management.**

Ability to Raise Capital

Because corporations can have millions of owners (shareholders), they have the opportunity to raise huge amounts of capital. Few individuals have the financial means to build and operate a telecommunications network such as AT&T or a marketing distribution system such as Walmart. However, by pooling the resources of millions of owners through public stock and bond offerings, corporations generate the billions of dollars of capital needed for such massive investments. In contrast, the capital resources of proprietorships and partnerships are limited to a relatively small number of private owners. Although proprietorships and partnerships can also obtain resources by borrowing, the amount creditors are willing to lend them is usually limited by the size of the owners' net worth.

APPEARANCE OF CAPITAL STRUCTURE IN FINANCIAL STATEMENTS

The ownership interest (equity) in a business is composed of two elements: (1) owner/investor contributions and (2) retained earnings. The way these two elements are reported in the financial statements differs for each type of business structure (proprietorship, partnership, or corporation).

LO 8-2

Analyze financial statements to identify the different types of business organizations.

Presentation of Equity in Proprietorships

Owner contributions and retained earnings are combined in a single capital account on the balance sheets of proprietorships. To illustrate, assume that Worthington Sole Proprietorship was started on January 1, 2014, when it acquired a $5,000 capital contribution from its owner, Phil Worthington. During the first year of operation, the company generated $4,000 of cash revenues, incurred $2,500 of cash expenses, and distributed $1,000 cash to the owner. Exhibit 8.1 displays 2012 financial statements for Worthington's company. Note on the *capital statement* that distributions are called **withdrawals.** Verify that the $5,500 balance in the capital account on the balance sheet includes the $5,000 owner contribution and the retained earnings of $500 ($1,500 net income − $1,000 withdrawal).

EXHIBIT 8.1

WORTHINGTON SOLE PROPRIETORSHIP
Financial Statements
As of December 31, 2014

Income Statement		Capital Statement		Balance Sheet	
Revenue	$4,000	Beginning capital balance	$ 0	Assets	
Expenses	2,500	Plus: Investment by owner	5,000	Cash	$5,500
Net income	$1,500	Plus: Net income	1,500	Equity	
		Less: Withdrawal by owner	(1,000)	Worthington, capital	$5,500
		Ending capital balance	$5,500		

☑ **CHECK YOURSELF 8.1**

Weiss Company was started on January 1, 2014, when it acquired $50,000 cash from its owner(s). During 2014 the company earned $72,000 of net income. Explain how the equity section of Weiss's December 31, 2014, balance sheet would differ if the company were a proprietorship versus a corporation.

Answer   *Proprietorship* records combine capital acquisitions from the owner and earnings from operating the business in a single capital account. In contrast, *corporation* records separate capital acquisitions from the owners and earnings from operating the business. If Weiss were a proprietorship, the equity section of the year-end balance sheet would report a single capital component of $122,000. If Weiss were a corporation, the equity section would report two separate equity components, most likely common stock of $50,000 and retained earnings of $72,000.

Presentation of Equity in Partnerships

The financial statement format for reporting partnership equity is similar to that used for proprietorships. Contributed capital and retained earnings are combined. However, a separate capital account is maintained for each partner in the business to reflect each partner's ownership interest.

To illustrate, assume that Sara Slater and Jill Johnson formed a partnership on January 1, 2014. The partnership acquired $2,000 of capital from Slater and $4,000 from Johnson. The partnership agreement called for each partner to receive an annual distribution equal to 10 percent of her capital contribution. Any further earnings were to be retained in the business and divided equally between the partners. During 2014, the company earned $5,000 of cash revenue and incurred $3,000 of cash expenses, for net income of $2,000 ($5,000 − $3,000). As specified by the partnership agreement, Slater received a $200 ($2,000 × 0.10) cash withdrawal and Johnson received $400 ($4,000 × 0.10). The remaining $1,400 ($2,000 − $200 − $400) of income was retained in the business and divided equally, adding $700 to each partner's capital account.

Exhibit 8.2 displays financial statements for the Slater and Johnson partnership. Again, note that distributions are called *withdrawals*. Also find on the balance sheet a *separate capital account* for each partner. Each capital account includes the amount of the partner's contributed capital plus her proportionate share of the retained earnings.

EXHIBIT 8.2

SLATER AND JOHNSON PARTNERSHIP
Financial Statements
As of December 31, 2014

Income Statement		Capital Statement		Balance Sheet	
Revenue	$5,000	Beginning capital balance	$ 0	Assets	
Expenses	3,000	Plus: Investment by owners	6,000	Cash	$7,400
Net income	$2,000	Plus: Net income	2,000	Equity	
		Less: Withdrawal by owners	(600)	Slater, capital	$2,700
		Ending capital balance	$7,400	Johnson, capital	4,700
				Total capital	$7,400

Presentation of Equity in Corporations

Corporations have more complex capital structures than proprietorships and partnerships. Explanations of some of the more common features of corporate capital structures and transactions follow.

CHARACTERISTICS OF CAPITAL STOCK

Stock issued by corporations may have a variety of different characteristics. For example, a company may issue different classes of stock that grant owners different rights and privileges. Also, the number of shares a corporation can legally issue may differ from the number it actually has issued. Further, a corporation can even buy back its own stock. Finally, a corporation may assign different values to the stock it issues. Accounting for corporate equity transactions is discussed in the next section of the text.

LO 8-3

Explain the characteristics of major types of stock issued by corporations.

Par Value

Many states require assigning a **par value** to stock. Historically, par value represented the maximum liability of the investors. Par value multiplied by the number of shares of stock issued represents the minimum amount of assets that must be retained in the company as protection for creditors. This amount is known as **legal capital.** To ensure that the amount of legal capital is maintained in a corporation, many states require that purchasers pay at least the par value for a share of stock initially purchased from a corporation. To minimize the amount of assets that owners must maintain in the business, many corporations issue stock with very low par values, often $1 or less. Therefore, *legal capital* as defined by par value has come to have very little relevance to investors or creditors. As a result, many states allow corporations to issue no-par stock.

Stated Value

No-par stock may have a stated value. Like par value, **stated value** is an arbitrary amount assigned by the board of directors to the stock. It also has little relevance to investors and creditors. Stock with a par value and stock with a stated value are accounted for exactly the same way. When stock has no par or stated value, accounting for it is slightly different. These accounting differences are illustrated later in this chapter.

Other Valuation Terminology

The price an investor must pay to purchase a share of stock is the **market value.** The sales price of a share of stock may be more or less than the par value. Another term analysts frequently associate with stock is *book value*. **Book value per share** is calculated by dividing total stockholders' equity (assets − liabilities) by the number of shares of stock owned by investors. Book value per share differs from market value per share because equity is measured in historical dollars and market value reflects investors' estimates of a company's current value.

Stock: Authorized, Issued, and Outstanding

As part of the regulatory function, states approve the maximum number of shares of stock corporations are legally permitted to issue. This maximum number is called **authorized stock.** Authorized stock that has been sold to the public is called **issued stock.** When a corporation buys back some of its issued stock from the public, the repurchased stock is called **treasury stock.** Treasury stock is still considered to be issued stock, but it is no longer outstanding. **Outstanding stock** (total issued stock minus treasury stock) is stock owned by investors outside the corporation. For example, assume a company that is authorized to issue 150 shares of stock issues 100 shares to investors,

FOCUS ON INTERNATIONAL ISSUES

PICKY, PICKY, PICKY ...

Considering the almost countless number of differences that could exist between U.S. GAAP and IFRS, it is not surprising that some of those that do exist relate to very specific issues. Consider the case of the timing of stock splits.

Assume a company that ends its fiscal year on December 31, 2014, declares a 2-for-1 stock split on January 15, 2015, before it has issued its 2014 annual report. Should the company apply the effects of the stock split retroactively to its 2014 financial statements, or begin showing the effects of the split on its 2015 statements? Under U.S. GAAP the split must be applied retroactively to the 2014 statements since they had not been issued at the time of the split. Under IFRS the 2014 statements would not show the effects of the split, but the 2015 statements would. By the way, an event that occurs between a company's fiscal year-end and the date its annual report is released is called a *subsequent event* by accountants.

Obviously no one can know every GAAP rule, much less all of the differences between GAAP and IFRS. This is why it is important to learn how to find answers to specific accounting questions as well as to develop an understanding of the basic accounting rules. Most important, if you are not sure you know the answer, do not assume you do.

and then buys back 20 shares of treasury stock. There are 150 shares authorized, 100 shares issued, and 80 shares outstanding.

Classes of Stock

The corporate charter defines the number of shares of stock authorized, the par value or stated value (if any), and the classes of stock that a corporation can issue. Most stock issued is either *common* or *preferred*.

Common Stock

All corporations issue **common stock.** Common stockholders bear the highest risk of losing their investment if a company is forced to liquidate. On the other hand, they reap the greatest rewards when a corporation prospers. Common stockholders generally enjoy several rights, including: (1) the right to buy and sell stock, (2) the right to share in the distribution of profits, (3) the right to share in the distribution of corporate assets in the case of liquidation, (4) the right to vote on significant matters that affect the corporate charter, and (5) the right to participate in the election of directors.

Preferred Stock

Many corporations issue **preferred stock** in addition to common stock. Holders of preferred stock receive certain privileges relative to holders of common stock. In exchange for special privileges in some areas, preferred stockholders give up rights in other areas. Preferred stockholders usually have no voting rights and the amount of their dividends is usually limited. Preferences granted to preferred stockholders include the following.

1. *Preference as to assets.* Preferred stock often has a liquidation value. In case of bankruptcy, preferred stockholders must be paid the liquidation value before any assets are distributed to common stockholders. However, preferred stockholder claims still fall behind creditor claims.

2. *Preference as to dividends.* Preferred shareholders are frequently guaranteed the right to receive dividends before common stockholders. The amount of the preferred dividend is normally stated on the stock certificate. It may be stated as a

dollar value (say, $5) per share or as a percentage of the par value. Most preferred stock has **cumulative dividends,** meaning that if a corporation is unable to pay the preferred dividend in any year, the dividend is not lost but begins to accumulate. Cumulative dividends that have not been paid are called **dividends in arrears.** When a company pays dividends, any preferred stock arrearages must be paid before any other dividends are paid. Noncumulative preferred stock is not often issued because preferred stock is much less attractive if missed dividends do not accumulate.

To illustrate the effects of preferred dividends, consider Dillion, Incorporated, which has the following shares of stock outstanding.

> Preferred stock, 4%, $10 par, 10,000 shares
> Common stock, $10 par, 20,000 shares

Assume the preferred stock dividend has not been paid for two years. If Dillion pays $22,000 in dividends, how much will each class of stock receive? It depends on whether the preferred stock is cumulative.

Allocation of Distribution for Cumulative Preferred Stock

	To Preferred	To Common
Dividends in arrears	$ 8,000	$ 0
Current year's dividends	4,000	10,000
Total distribution	$12,000	$10,000

Allocation of Distribution for Noncumulative Preferred Stock

	To Preferred	To Common
Dividends in arrears	$ 0	$ 0
Current year's dividends	4,000	18,000
Total distribution	$4,000	$18,000

The total annual dividend on the preferred stock is $4,000 (0.04 × $10 par × 10,000 shares). If the preferred stock is cumulative, the $8,000 in arrears must be paid first. Then $4,000 for the current year's dividend is paid next. The remaining $10,000 goes to common stockholders. If the preferred stock is noncumulative, the $8,000 of dividends from past periods is ignored. This year's $4,000 preferred dividend is paid first, with the remaining $18,000 going to common.

Other features of preferred stock may include the right to participate in distributions beyond the established amount of the preferred dividend, the right to convert preferred stock to common stock or to bonds, and the potential for having the preferred stock called (repurchased) by the corporation. Detailed discussion of these topics is left to more advanced courses. Exhibit 8.3 indicates that roughly 25 percent of U.S. companies have preferred shares outstanding.

EXHIBIT 8.3

Presence of Preferred Stock in the Capital Structure of U.S. Companies

With preferred stock **25%**

Without preferred stock **75%**

Data Source: AICPA, *Accounting Trends and Techniques,* 2006.

ACCOUNTING FOR STOCK TRANSACTIONS ON THE DAY OF ISSUE

LO 8-4

Explain how to account for different types of stock issued by corporations.

Issuing stock with a par or stated value is accounted for differently from issuing no-par stock. For stock with either a par or stated value, the total amount acquired from the owners is divided between two separate equity accounts. The amount of the par or stated value is recorded in the stock account. Any amount received above the par or stated value is recorded in an account called **Paid-in Capital in Excess of Par** (or **Stated**) **Value.**

Issuing Par Value Stock

To illustrate the issue of common stock with a par value, assume that Nelson Incorporated is authorized to issue 250 shares of common stock. During 2014, Nelson issued 100 shares of $10 par common stock for $22 per share. The event increases assets and stockholders' equity by $2,200 ($22 × 100 shares). The increase in stockholders' equity is divided into two parts, $1,000 of par value ($10 per share × 100 shares) and $1,200 ($2,200 − $1,000) received in excess of par value. The income statement is not affected. The $2,200 cash inflow is reported in the financing activities section of the statement of cash flows. The effects on the financial statements follow.

Assets	=	Liab.	+		Equity			Rev.	−	Exp.	=	Net Inc.		Cash Flow
Cash	=			Com. Stk.	+	PIC in Excess								
2,200	=	NA	+	1,000	+	1,200		NA	−	NA	=	NA		2,200 FA

The *legal capital* of the corporation is $1,000, the total par value of the issued common stock. The number of shares issued can be easily verified by dividing the total amount in the common stock account by the par value ($1,000 ÷ $10 = 100 shares).

Stock Classification

Assume Nelson Incorporated obtains authorization to issue 400 shares of Class B, $20 par value common stock. The company issues 150 shares of this stock at $25 per share. The event increases assets and stockholders' equity by $3,750 ($25 × 150 shares). The increase in stockholders' equity is divided into two parts, $3,000 of par value ($20 per share × 150 shares) and $750 ($3,750 − $3,000) received in excess of par value. The income statement is not affected. The $3,750 cash inflow is reported in the financing activities section of the statement of cash flows. The effects on the financial statements follow.

Assets	=	Liab.	+		Equity			Rev.	−	Exp.	=	Net Inc.		Cash Flow
Cash	=			Com. Stk.	+	PIC in Excess								
3,750	=	NA	+	3,000	+	750		NA	−	NA	=	NA		3,750 FA

As the preceding event suggests, companies can issue numerous classes of common stock. The specific rights and privileges for each class are described in the individual stock certificates.

Stock Issued at Stated Value

Assume Nelson is authorized to issue 300 shares of a third class of stock, 7 percent cumulative preferred stock with a stated value of $10 per share. Nelson issued 100 shares of the preferred stock at a price of $22 per share. The effects on the financial statements are identical to those described for the issue of the $10 par value common stock.

Assets	=	Liab.	+		Equity			Rev.	–	Exp.	=	Net Inc.	Cash Flow
Cash	=			Pfd. Stk.	+	PIC in Excess							
2,200	=	NA	+	1,000	+	1,200		NA	–	NA	=	NA	2,200 FA

Stock Issued with No Par Value

Assume that Nelson Incorporated is authorized to issue 150 shares of a fourth class of stock. This stock is no-par common stock. Nelson issues 100 shares of this no-par stock at $22 per share. The entire amount received ($22 × 100 = $2,200) is recorded in the stock account. The effects on the financial statements follow.

Assets	=	Liab.	+		Equity			Rev.	–	Exp.	=	Net Inc.	Cash Flow
Cash	=			Com. Stk.	+	PIC in Excess							
2,200	=	NA	+	2,200	+	NA		NA	–	NA	=	NA	2,200 FA

Financial Statement Presentation

Exhibit 8.4 displays Nelson Incorporated's balance sheet after the four stock issuances described above. The exhibit assumes that Nelson earned and retained $5,000 of cash income during 2014. The stock accounts are presented first, followed by the paid-in capital in excess of par (or stated) value accounts. A wide variety of reporting formats is used in practice. For example, another popular format is to group accounts by stock class, with the paid-in capital in excess accounts listed with their associated stock accounts. Alternatively, many companies combine the different classes of stock into a single amount and provide the detailed information in notes to the financial statements.

EXHIBIT 8.4

NELSON INCORPORATED
Balance Sheet
As of December 31, 2014

Assets	
Cash	$15,350
Stockholders' equity	
Preferred stock, $10 stated value, 7% cumulative, 300 shares authorized, 100 issued and outstanding	$ 1,000
Common stock, $10 par value, 250 shares authorized, 100 issued and outstanding	1,000
Common stock, class B, $20 par value, 400 shares authorized, 150 issued and outstanding	3,000
Common stock, no par, 150 shares authorized, 100 issued and outstanding	2,200
Paid-in capital in excess of stated value—preferred	1,200
Paid-in capital in excess of par value—common	1,200
Paid-in capital in excess of par value—class B common	750
Total paid-in capital	10,350
Retained earnings	5,000
Total stockholders' equity	$15,350

STOCKHOLDERS' EQUITY TRANSACTIONS AFTER THE DAY OF ISSUE

Treasury Stock

LO 8-5

Show how treasury stock transactions affect a company's financial statements.

When a company buys its own stock, the stock purchased is called *treasury stock*. Why would a company buy its own stock? Common reasons include (1) to have stock available to give employees pursuant to stock option plans, (2) to accumulate stock in preparation for a merger or business combination, (3) to reduce the number of shares outstanding in order to increase earnings per share, (4) to keep the price of the stock high when it appears to be falling, and (5) to avoid a hostile takeover (removing shares from the open market reduces the opportunity for outsiders to obtain enough voting shares to gain control of the company).

Conceptually, purchasing treasury stock is the reverse of issuing stock. When a business issues stock, the assets and equity of the business increase. When a business buys treasury stock, the assets and equity of the business decrease. To illustrate, return to the Nelson Incorporated example. Assume that in 2015 Nelson paid $20 per share to buy back 50 shares of the $10 par value common stock that it originally issued at $22 per share. The purchase of treasury stock is an asset use transaction. Assets and stockholders' equity decrease by the cost of the purchase ($20 × 50 shares = $1,000). The income statement is not affected. The cash outflow is reported in the financing activities section of the statement of cash flows. The effects on the financial statements follow.

Assets	=	Liab.	+	Equity			Rev.	−	Exp.	=	Net Inc.	Cash Flow
Cash	=			Other Equity Accts.	−	Treasury Stk.						
(1,000)	=	NA	+	NA	−	1,000	NA	−	NA	=	NA	(1,000) FA

The Treasury Stock account is a contra equity account. It is deducted from the other equity accounts in determining total stockholders' equity. In this example, the Treasury Stock account contains the full amount paid ($1,000). The original issue price and the par value of the stock have no effect on the Treasury Stock account. Recognizing the full amount paid in the treasury stock account is called the **cost method of accounting for treasury stock** transactions. Although other methods could be used, the cost method is the most common.

Assume Nelson reissues 30 shares of treasury stock at a price of $25 per share. As with any other stock issue, the sale of treasury stock is an asset source transaction. In this case, assets and stockholders' equity increase by $750 ($25 × 30 shares). The income statement is not affected. The cash inflow is reported in the financing activities section of the statement of cash flows. The effects on the financial statements follow.

Assets	=	Liab.	+	Equity					Rev.	−	Exp.	=	Net Inc.	Cash Flow
Cash	=			Other Equity Accounts	−	Treasury Stock	+	PIC from Treasury Stk.						
750	=	NA	+	NA	−	(600)	+	150	NA	−	NA	=	NA	750 FA

The decrease in the Treasury Stock account increases stockholders' equity. The $150 difference between the cost of the treasury stock ($20 per share × 30 shares = $600) and the sales price ($750) is *not* reported as a gain. The sale of treasury stock is a capital acquisition, not a revenue transaction. The $150 is additional paid-in capital. *Corporations do not recognize gains or losses on the sale of treasury stock.*

After selling 30 shares of treasury stock, 20 shares remain in Nelson's possession. These shares cost $20 each, so the balance in the Treasury Stock account is now $400 ($20 × 20 shares). Treasury stock is reported on the balance sheet directly below retained earnings. Although this placement suggests that treasury stock reduces retained earnings, the reduction actually applies to the entire stockholders' equity section. Exhibit 8.5 on page 308 shows the presentation of treasury stock in the balance sheet.

☑ CHECK YOURSELF 8.2

On January 1, 2014, Janell Company's Common Stock account balance was $20,000. On April 1, 2014, Janell paid $12,000 cash to purchase some of its own stock. Janell resold this stock on October 1, 2014, for $14,500. What is the effect on the company's cash and stockholders' equity from both the April 1 purchase and the October 1 resale of the stock?

Answer   The April 1 purchase would reduce both cash and stockholders' equity by $12,000. The treasury stock transaction represents a return of invested capital to those owners who sold stock back to the company.

The sale of the treasury stock on October 1 would increase both cash and stockholders' equity by $14,500. The difference between the sales price of the treasury stock and its cost ($14,500 − $12,000) represents additional paid-in capital from treasury stock transactions. The stockholders' equity section of the balance sheet would include Common Stock, $20,000, and Additional Paid-in Capital from Treasury Stock Transactions, $2,500.

Cash Dividend

Cash dividends are affected by three significant dates: *the declaration date, the date of record,* and *the payment date.* Assume that on October 15, 2015, the board of Nelson Incorporated declared a 7 percent cash dividend on the 100 outstanding shares of its $10 stated value preferred stock. The dividend will be paid to stockholders of record as of November 15, 2015. The cash payment will be made on December 15, 2015.

LO 8-6

Explain the effects of declaring and paying cash dividends on a company's financial statements.

Declaration Date

Although corporations are not required to declare dividends, they are legally obligated to pay dividends once they have been declared. They must recognize a liability on the **declaration date** (in this case, October 15, 2015). The increase in liabilities is accompanied by a decrease in retained earnings. The income statement and statement of cash flows are not affected. The effects on the financial statements of *declaring* the $70 (0.07 × $10 × 100 shares) dividend follow.

Assets	=	Liab.	+		Equity		Rev.	−	Exp.	=	Net Inc.	Cash Flow
Cash	=	Div. Pay.	+	Com. Stk.	+	Ret. Earn.						
NA	=	70	+	NA	+	(70)	NA	−	NA	=	NA	NA

Date of Record

Cash dividends are paid to investors who owned the preferred stock on the **date of record** (in this case November 15, 2015). Any stock sold after the date of record but

REALITY BYTES

As you have learned, dividends, unlike interest on bonds, do not have to be paid. In fact, a company's board of directors must vote to pay dividends before they can be paid. Even so, once a company establishes a practice of paying a dividend of a given amount each period, usually quarterly, the company is reluctant to not pay the dividend. The amount of dividends that companies pay, relative to their earnings, varies widely.

Large, well-established companies usually do pay dividends, while young, growing companies often do not. Consider the 30 companies that make up the Dow Jones Industrials Average group. In 2012, 29 of these companies paid dividends. The only one that did not was General Motors, and it was still trying to repay money it received from the U.S. government during the recession of 2008–2009. Of the remaining 29 companies, UnitedHealth Group paid the lowest percentage of its earnings out in

dividends (14.8 percent). At the other extreme, in 2012 Verizon Communications paid $5.98 of dividends for every $1.00 it had in earnings. The average percentage of earnings paid out as dividends for all 30 companies in the Dow was 60.9 percent.

For comparison, consider two large, relatively young, technology companies: Google and Facebook. Although both of these companies have had positive earnings in recent years—Google alone had $10.7 billion of earnings in 2012—neither has ever paid a dividend to its common shareholders. They are using their cash to grow their businesses, often by purchasing other companies.

---

before the payment date (in this case December 15, 2015) is traded **ex-dividend,** meaning the buyer will not receive the upcoming dividend. The date of record is merely a cutoff date. It does not affect the financial statements.

Payment Date

Nelson actually paid the cash dividend on the **payment date.** This event has the same effect as paying any other liability. Assets (cash) and liabilities (dividends payable) both decrease. The income statement is not affected. The cash outflow is reported in the financing activities section of the statement of cash flows. The effects of the cash payment on the financial statements follow.

Assets	=	Liab.	+	Equity			Rev.	−	Exp.	=	Net Inc.	Cash Flow
Cash	=	Div. Pay.	+	Com. Stk.	+	Ret. Earn.						
(70)	=	(70)	+	NA	+	NA	NA	−	NA	=	NA	(70) FA

Stock Dividend

LO 8-7

Explain the effects of stock dividends and stock splits on a company's financial statements.

Dividends are not always paid in cash. Companies sometimes choose to issue **stock dividends,** wherein they distribute additional shares of stock to the stockholders. To illustrate, assume that Nelson Incorporated decided to issue a 10 percent stock dividend on its class B, $20 par value common stock. Because dividends apply to outstanding shares only, Nelson will issue 15 (150 outstanding shares × 0.10) additional shares of class B stock.

Assume the new shares are distributed when the market value of the stock is $30 per share. As a result of the stock dividend, Nelson will transfer $450 ($30 × 15 new shares) from retained earnings to paid-in capital.[1] The stock dividend is an equity exchange

---

[1] The accounting here applies to small stock dividends. Accounting for large stock dividends is explained in a more advanced course.

transaction. The income statement and statement of cash flows are not affected. The effects of the stock dividend on the financial statements follow.

Assets	=	Liab.	+	Equity						Rev.	−	Exp.	=	Net Inc.	Cash Flow
				Com. Stk.	+	PIC in Excess	+	Ret. Earn.							
NA	=	NA	+	300	+	150	+	(450)		NA	−	NA	=	NA	NA

Stock dividends have no effect on assets. They merely increase the number of shares of stock outstanding. Because a greater number of shares represents the same ownership interest in the same amount of assets, the market value per share of a company's stock normally declines when a stock dividend is distributed. A lower market price makes the stock more affordable and may increase demand for the stock, which benefits both the company and its stockholders.

Stock Split

A corporation may also reduce the market price of its stock through a **stock split.** A stock split replaces existing shares with a greater number of new shares. Any par or stated value of the stock is proportionately reduced to reflect the new number of shares outstanding. For example, assume Nelson Incorporated declared a 2-for-1 stock split on the 165 outstanding shares (150 originally issued + 15 shares distributed in a stock dividend) of its $20 par value, class B common stock. Nelson notes in the accounting records that the 165 old $20 par shares are replaced with 330 new $10 par shares. Investors who owned the 165 shares of old common stock would now own 330 shares of the new common stock.

Stock splits have no effect on the dollar amounts of assets, liabilities, and stockholders' equity. They only affect the number of shares of stock outstanding. In Nelson's case, the ownership interest that was previously represented by 165 shares of stock is now represented by 330 shares. Because twice as many shares now represent the same ownership interest, the market value per share should be one-half as much as it was prior to the split. However, as with a stock dividend, the lower market price will probably stimulate demand for the stock. As a result, doubling the number of shares will likely reduce the market price to slightly more than one-half of the pre-split value. For example, if the stock were selling for $30 per share before the 2-for-1 split, it might sell for $15.50 after the split.

Appropriation of Retained Earnings

The board of directors may restrict the amount of retained earnings available to distribute as dividends. The restriction may be required by credit agreements, or it may be discretionary. A retained earnings restriction, often called an *appropriation,* is an equity exchange event. It transfers a portion of existing retained earnings to **Appropriated Retained Earnings.** Total retained earnings remains unchanged. To illustrate, assume that Nelson appropriates $1,000 of retained earnings for future expansion. The income statement and the statement of cash flows are not affected. The effects on the financial statements of appropriating $1,000 of retained earnings follow.

LO 8-8

Show how the appropriation of retained earnings affects financial statements.

Assets	=	Liab.	+	Equity						Rev.	−	Exp.	=	Net Inc.	Cash Flow
				Com. Stk.	+	Ret. Earn.	+	App. Ret. Earn.							
NA	=	NA	+	NA	+	(1,000)	+	1,000		NA	−	NA	=	NA	NA

FINANCIAL STATEMENT PRESENTATION

The 2014 and 2015 events for Nelson Incorporated are summarized below. Events 1 through 8 are cash transactions. The results of the 2014 transactions (nos. 1–5) are reflected in Exhibit 8.4. The results of the 2015 transactions (nos. 6–9) are shown in Exhibit 8.5.

1. Issued 100 shares of $10 par value common stock at a market price of $22 per share.
2. Issued 150 shares of class B, $20 par value common stock at a market price of $25 per share.
3. Issued 100 shares of $10 stated value, 7 percent cumulative preferred stock at a market price of $22 per share.
4. Issued 100 shares of no-par common stock at a market price of $22 per share.
5. Earned and retained $5,000 cash from operations.
6. Purchased 50 shares of $10 par value common stock as treasury stock at a market price of $20 per share.
7. Sold 30 shares of treasury stock at a market price of $25 per share.
8. Declared and paid a $70 cash dividend on the preferred stock.
9. Issued a 10 percent stock dividend on the 150 shares of outstanding class B, $20 par value common stock (15 additional shares). The additional shares were issued when the market price of the stock was $30 per share. There are 165 (150 + 15) class B common shares outstanding after the stock dividend.
10. Issued a 2-for-1 stock split on the 165 shares of class B, $20 par value common stock. After this transaction, there are 330 shares outstanding of the class B common stock with a $10 par value.
11. Appropriated $1,000 of retained earnings.

EXHIBIT 8.5

NELSON INCORPORATED
Balance Sheet
As of December 31, 2015

Assets		
Cash		$21,030
Stockholders' equity		
Preferred stock, $10 stated value, 7% cumulative, 300 shares authorized, 100 issued and outstanding	$1,000	
Common stock, $10 par value, 250 shares authorized, 100 issued, and 80 outstanding	1,000	
Common stock, class B, $10 par, 800 shares authorized, 330 issued and outstanding	3,300	
Common stock, no par, 150 shares authorized, 100 issued and outstanding	2,200	
Paid-in capital in excess of stated value—preferred	1,200	
Paid-in capital in excess of par value—common	1,200	
Paid-in capital in excess of par value—class B common	900	
Paid-in capital in excess of cost of treasury stock	150	
Total paid-in capital		$10,950
Retained earnings		
Appropriated	1,000	
Unappropriated	9,480	
Total retained earnings		10,480
Less: Treasury stock, 20 shares @ $20 per share		(400)
Total stockholders' equity		$21,030

The illustration assumes that Nelson earned net income of $6,000 in 2015. The ending retained earnings balance is determined as follows: Beginning Balance $5,000 − $70 Cash Dividend − $450 Stock Dividend + $6,000 Net Income = $10,480.

INVESTING IN CAPITAL STOCK

Stockholders may benefit in two ways when a company generates earnings. The company may distribute the earnings directly to the stockholders in the form of dividends. Alternatively, the company may retain some or all of the earnings to finance growth and increase its potential for future earnings. If the company retains earnings, the market value of its stock should increase to reflect its greater earnings prospects. How can analysts use financial reporting to help assess the potential for dividend payments or growth in market value?

LO 8-9

 Explain some uses of accounting information in making stock investment decisions.

Receiving Dividends

Is a company likely to pay dividends in the future? The financial statements can help answer this question. They show if dividends were paid in the past. Companies with a history of paying dividends usually continue to pay dividends. Also, to pay dividends in the future, a company must have sufficient cash and retained earnings. These amounts are reported on the balance sheet and the statement of cash flows.

Increasing the Price of Stock

Is the market value (price) of a company's stock likely to increase? Increases in a company's stock price occur when investors believe the company's earnings will grow. Financial statements provide information that is useful in predicting the prospects for earnings growth. Here also, a company's earnings history is an indicator of its growth potential. However, because published financial statements report historical information, investors must recognize their limitations. Investors want to know about the future. Stock prices are therefore influenced more by forecasts than by history.

For example:

- On February 12, 2013, Blue Nile, Inc., announced that earnings for the fourth quarter of 2012 were 30 percent higher than they had been for the same quarter of 2011. In reaction to this seemingly good news, the price of Blue Nile's stock *fell* by almost 7 percent. Why did the stock market respond in this way? Because financial analysts who follow the company closely had expected the company's fourth quarter earnings to be 21 percent higher than they were.

- On February 12, 2013, Avon Products, Inc., announced that earnings for the fourth quarter of 2012 were about 5 percent lower than they had been for the fourth quarter of 2011. The stock market's reaction to the news was to *increase* the price of Avon's stock by a little over 23 percent. The market reacted this way because even though earnings were down from the previous year, they were 37 percent higher than analysts had expected them to be.

In each case, investors reacted to the potential for earnings growth rather than the historical earnings reports. Because investors find forecasted statements more relevant to decision making than historical financial statements, most companies provide forecasts in addition to historical financial statements.

The value of a company's stock is also influenced by nonfinancial information that financial statements cannot provide. For example, suppose ExxonMobil announced in the middle of its fiscal year that it had just discovered substantial oil reserves on property to which it held drilling rights. Consider the following questions:

- What would happen to the price of ExxonMobil's stock on the day of the announcement?

- What would happen to ExxonMobil's financial statements on that day?

The price of ExxonMobil's stock would almost certainly increase as soon as the discovery was made public. However, nothing would happen to its financial statements on that day. There would probably be very little effect on its financial statements for that year. Only after the company begins to develop the oil field and sell the oil will its financial statements reflect the discovery. Changes in financial statements tend to lag behind the announcements companies make regarding their earnings potential.

Stock prices are also affected by general economic conditions and consumer confidence as well as the performance measures reported in financial statements. For example, the stock prices of virtually all companies declined sharply immediately after the September 11, 2001, terrorist attacks on the World Trade Center and the Pentagon. Historically based financial statements are of little benefit in predicting general economic conditions or changes in consumer confidence.

Exercising Control through Stock Ownership

The more influence an investor has over the operations of a company, the more the investor can benefit from owning stock in the company. For example, consider a power company that needs coal to produce electricity. The power company may purchase some common stock in a coal mining company to ensure a stable supply of coal. What percentage of the mining company's stock must the power company acquire to exercise significant influence over the mining company? The answer depends on how many investors own stock in the mining company and how the number of shares is distributed among the stockholders.

The greater its number of stockholders, the more *widely held* a company is. If stock ownership is concentrated in the hands of a few persons, a company is *closely held*. Widely held companies can generally be controlled with smaller percentages of ownership than closely held companies. Consider a company in which no existing investor owns more than 1 percent of the voting stock. A new investor who acquires a 5 percent interest would immediately become, by far, the largest shareholder and would likely be able to significantly influence board decisions. In contrast, consider a closely held company in which one current shareholder owns 51 percent of the company's stock. Even if another investor acquired the remaining 49 percent of the company, that investor could not control the company.

Financial statements contain some, but not all, of the information needed to help an investor determine ownership levels necessary to permit control. For example, the financial statements disclose the total number of shares of stock outstanding, but they normally contain little information about the number of shareholders and even less information about any relationships between shareholders. Relationships between shareholders are critically important because related shareholders, whether bound by family or business interests, might exercise control by voting as a block. For publicly traded companies, information about the number of shareholders and the identity of some large shareholders is disclosed in reports filed with the Securities and Exchange Commission.

<< A Look Back

Starting a business requires obtaining financing; it takes money to make money. Although some money may be borrowed, lenders are unlikely to make loans to businesses that lack some degree of owner financing. Equity financing is therefore critical to virtually all profit-oriented businesses. This chapter has examined some of the issues related to accounting for equity transactions.

The idea that a business must obtain financing from its owners was one of the first events presented in this textbook. This chapter discussed the advantages and disadvantages of organizing a business as a sole proprietorship versus a partnership versus a corporation. These advantages and disadvantages include the following.

1. *Double taxation*—Income of corporations is subject to double taxation, but that of proprietorships and partnerships is not.

2. *Regulation*—Corporations are subject to more regulation than are proprietorships and partnerships.

3. *Limited liability*—An investor's personal assets are not at risk as a result of owning corporate securities. The investor's liability is limited to the amount of the investment. In general, proprietorships and partnerships do not offer limited liability. However, laws in some states permit the formation of limited liability companies, which operate like proprietorships and partnerships yet place some limits on the personal liability of their owners.

4. *Continuity*—Proprietorships and partnerships dissolve when one of the owners leaves the business. Corporations are separate legal entities that continue to exist regardless of changes in ownership.

5. *Transferability*—Ownership interests in corporations are easier to transfer than those of proprietorships or partnerships.

6. *Management structure*—Corporations are more likely to have independent professional managers than are proprietorships or partnerships.

7. *Ability to raise capital*—Because they can be owned by millions of investors, corporations have the opportunity to raise more capital than proprietorships or partnerships.

Corporations issue different classes of common stock and preferred stock as evidence of ownership interests. In general, *common stock* provides the widest range of privileges including the right to vote and participate in earnings. *Preferred stockholders* usually give up the right to vote in exchange for preferences such as the right to receive dividends or assets upon liquidation before common stockholders. Stock may have a *par value* or *stated value,* which relates to legal requirements governing the amount of capital that must be maintained in the corporation. Corporations may also issue *no-par stock,* avoiding some of the legal requirements that pertain to par or stated value stock.

Stock that a company issues and then repurchases is called *treasury stock.* Purchasing treasury stock reduces total assets and stockholders' equity. Reselling treasury stock represents a capital acquisition. The difference between the reissue price and the cost of the treasury stock is recorded directly in the equity accounts. Treasury stock transactions do not result in gains or losses on the income statement.

Companies may issue *stock splits* or *stock dividends.* These transactions increase the number of shares of stock without changing the net assets of a company. The per share market value usually drops when a company issues stock splits or dividends.

A Look Forward

Financial statement analysis is so important that Chapter 9 is devoted solely to a detailed discussion of this subject. The chapter covers vertical analysis (analyzing relationships within a specific statement) and horizontal analysis (analyzing relationships across accounting periods). Finally, the chapter discusses limitations associated with financial statement analysis.

312   Chapter 8

 Video lectures and accompanying self-assessment quizzes are available for all learning objectives through McGraw-Hill *Connect*® *Accounting*.

SELF-STUDY REVIEW PROBLEM

Edwards Inc. experienced the following events:

1. Issued common stock for cash.
2. Declared a cash dividend.
3. Issued noncumulative preferred stock for cash.
4. Appropriated retained earnings.
5. Distributed a stock dividend.
6. Paid cash to purchase treasury stock.
7. Distributed a 2-for-1 stock split.
8. Issued cumulative preferred stock for cash.
9. Paid a cash dividend that had previously been declared.
10. Sold treasury stock for cash at a higher amount than the cost of the treasury stock.

Required

Show the effect of each event on the elements of the financial statements using a horizontal statements model like the one shown here. Use + for increase, − for decrease, and NA for not affected. In the Cash Flow column, indicate whether the item is an operating activity (OA), investing activity (IA), or a financing activity (FA). The first transaction is entered as an example.

Event	Assets	=	Liab.	+	Equity	Rev.	−	Exp.	=	Net Inc.	Cash Flow
1	+		NA		+	NA		NA		NA	+ FA

Solution to Self-Study Review Problem

Event	Assets	=	Liab.	+	Equity	Rev.	−	Exp.	=	Net Inc.	Cash Flow
1	+		NA		+	NA		NA		NA	+ FA
2	NA		+		−	NA		NA		NA	NA
3	+		NA		+	NA		NA		NA	+ FA
4	NA		NA		− +	NA		NA		NA	NA
5	NA		NA		− +	NA		NA		NA	NA
6	−		NA		−	NA		NA		NA	− FA
7	NA		NA		NA	NA		NA		NA	NA
8	+		NA		+	NA		NA		NA	+ FA
9	−		−		NA	NA		NA		NA	− FA
10	+		NA		+	NA		NA		NA	+ FA

KEY TERMS

Issued stock 299	Paid-in Capital in Excess of	Securities Act of 1933 and	Stockholders 296
Legal capital 299	Par Value 302	Securities Exchange Act of	Stock split 307
Limited liability 296	Partnership agreement 294	1934 295	Transferability 296
Limited liability companies	Partnerships 294	Sole proprietorships 294	Treasury stock 299
(LLCs) 295	Par value 299	Stated value 299	Withdrawals 297
Market value 299	Payment date 306	Stock certificates 294	
Outstanding stock 299	Preferred stock 300	Stock dividends 306	

QUESTIONS

1. What are the three major forms of business organizations? Describe each.

2. How are sole proprietorships formed?

3. Discuss the purpose of a partnership agreement. Is such an agreement necessary for partnership formation?

4. What is meant by the phrase *separate legal entity*? To which type of business organization does it apply?

5. What is the purpose of the articles of incorporation? What information do they provide?

6. What is the function of the stock certificate?

7. What prompted Congress to pass the Securities Act of 1933 and the Securities Exchange Act of 1934? What is the purpose of these laws?

8. What are the advantages and disadvantages of the corporate form of business organization?

9. What is a limited liability company? Discuss its advantages and disadvantages.

10. How does the term *double taxation* apply to corporations? Give an example of double taxation.

11. What is the difference between contributed capital and retained earnings for a corporation?

12. What are the similarities and differences in the equity structure of a sole proprietorship, a partnership, and a corporation?

13. Why is it easier for a corporation to raise large amounts of capital than it is for a partnership?

14. What is the meaning of each of the following terms with respect to the corporate form of organization?
   (a) Legal capital
   (b) Par value of stock
   (c) Stated value of stock
   (d) Market value of stock
   (e) Book value of stock
   (f) Authorized shares of stock
   (g) Issued stock
   (h) Outstanding stock
   (i) Treasury stock
   (j) Common stock
   (k) Preferred stock
   (l) Dividends

15. What is the difference between cumulative preferred stock and noncumulative preferred stock?

16. What is no-par stock? How is it recorded in the accounting records?

17. Assume that Best Co. has issued and outstanding 1,000 shares of $100 par value, 10 percent, cumulative preferred stock. What is the dividend per share? If the preferred dividend is two years in arrears, what total amount of dividends must be paid before the common shareholders can receive any dividends?

18. If Best Co. issued 10,000 shares of $20 par value common stock for $30 per share, what amount is added to the Common Stock account? What amount of cash is received?

19. What is the difference between par value stock and stated value stock?

20. Why might a company repurchase its own stock?

21. What effect does the purchase of treasury stock have on the equity of a company?

22. Assume that Day Company repurchased 1,000 of its own shares for $30 per share and sold the shares two weeks later for $35 per share. What is the amount of gain on the sale? How is it reported on the balance sheet? What type of account is Treasury Stock?

23. What is the importance of the declaration date,

record date, and payment date in conjunction with corporate dividends?

24. What is the difference between a stock dividend and a stock split?

25. Why would a company choose to distribute a stock dividend instead of a cash dividend?

26. What is the primary reason that a company would declare a stock split?

27. If Best Co. had 10,000 shares of $20 par value common stock outstanding and declared a 5-for-1 stock split, how many shares would then be outstanding and what would be their par value after the split?

28. When a company appropriates retained earnings, does the company set aside cash for a specific use? Explain.

29. What is the largest source of financing for most U.S. businesses?

30. What is meant by *equity financing*? What is meant by *debt financing*?

31. What is a widely held corporation? What is a closely held corporation?

32. What are some reasons that a corporation might not pay dividends?

MULTIPLE-CHOICE QUESTIONS

Multiple-choice questions are provided on the text website at www.mhhe.com/edmondssurvey4e.

EXERCISES

connect |ACCOUNTING **All applicable Exercises are available with McGraw-Hill's _Connect®_ Accounting.**

LO 8-1, 8-2

Exercise 8-1   *Effect of accounting events on the financial statements of a sole proprietorship*

A sole proprietorship was started on January 1, 2014, when it received $30,000 cash from Alex Ard, the owner. During 2014, the company earned $50,000 in cash revenues and paid $22,300 in cash expenses. Ard withdrew $10,000 cash from the business during 2014.

Required

Prepare the income statement, capital statement (statement of changes in equity), balance sheet, and statement of cash flows for Ard's 2014 fiscal year.

LO 8-1, 8-2

Exercise 8-2   *Effect of accounting events on the financial statements of a partnership*

Drake Cushing and Shawn Tadlock started the CT partnership on January 1, 2014. The business acquired $70,000 cash from Cushing and $140,000 from Tadlock. During 2014, the partnership earned $75,000 in cash revenues and paid $39,000 for cash expenses. Cushing withdrew $2,000 cash from the business, and Tadlock withdrew $4,000 cash. The net income was allocated to the capital accounts of the two partners in proportion to the amounts of their original investments in the business.

Required

Prepare the income statement, capital statement, balance sheet, and statement of cash flows for the CT partnership for the 2014 fiscal year.

LO 8-1, 8-2

Exercise 8-3   *Effect of accounting events on the financial statements of a corporation*

Bozeman Corporation was started with the issue of 10,000 shares of $10 par common stock for cash on January 1, 2014. The stock was issued at a market price of $16 per share. During 2014, the company earned $71,000 in cash revenues and paid $46,500 for cash expenses. Also a $5,000 cash dividend was paid to the stockholders.

Required

Prepare the income statement, statement of changes in stockholders' equity, balance sheet, and statement of cash flows for Bozeman Corporation's 2014 fiscal year.

LO 8-4

Exercise 8-4   *Effect of issuing common stock on the balance sheet*

Newly formed Electronics Services Corporation has 100,000 shares of $10 par common stock authorized. On March 1, 2014, Electronics Services issued 20,000 shares of the stock for $12 per share. On May 2 the company issued an additional 30,000 shares for $15 per share. Electronics Services was not affected by other events during 2014.

Required

a. Record the transactions in a horizontal statements model like the following one. In the Cash Flow column, indicate whether the item is an operating activity (OA), investing activity (IA), or financing activity (FA). Use NA to indicate that an element was not affected by the event.

Assets	=	Liab.	+	Equity			Rev.	−	Exp.	=	Net Inc.	Cash Flow
Cash	=		+	Com. Stk.	+	Paid-in Excess						

b. Determine the amount Electronics Services would report for common stock on the December 31, 2014, balance sheet.

c. Determine the amount Electronics Services would report for paid-in capital in excess of par.

d. What is the total amount of capital contributed by the owners?

e. What amount of total assets would Electronics Services report on the December 31, 2014, balance sheet?

Exercise 8-5 *Recording and reporting common and preferred stock transactions*

LO 8-4

Goldman Inc. was organized on June 1, 2014. It was authorized to issue 500,000 shares of $10 par common stock and 100,000 shares of 4 percent cumulative class A preferred stock. The class A stock had a stated value of $50 per share. The following stock transactions pertain to Goldman Inc.:

1. Issued 40,000 shares of common stock for $16 per share.
2. Issued 20,000 shares of the class A preferred stock for $52 per share.
3. Issued 60,000 shares of common stock for $20 per share.

Required

Prepare the stockholders' equity section of the balance sheet immediately after these transactions have been recognized.

Exercise 8-6 *Effect of no-par common and par preferred stock on the horizontal statements model*

LO 8-4

Bailey Corporation issued 10,000 shares of no-par common stock for $25 per share. Bailey also issued 3,000 shares of $40 par, 6 percent noncumulative preferred stock at $42 per share.

Required

Record these events in a horizontal statements model like the following one. In the cash flow column, indicate whether the item is an operating activity (OA), investing activity (IA), or financing activity (FA). Use NA to indicate that an element was not affected by the event.

Assets =	Equity			Rev. – Exp. = Net Inc.	Cash Flow
Cash	= Pfd. Stk.	+ Com. Stk.	+ PIC in Excess		

Exercise 8-7 *Issuing stock for assets other than cash*

LO 8-4

Hammond Corporation was formed when it issued shares of common stock to two of its shareholders. Hammond issued 10,000 shares of $5 par common stock to P. Coldwell in exchange for $80,000 cash (the issue price was $8 per share). Hammond also issued 3,500 shares of stock to M. Roberts in exchange for a one-year-old delivery van on the same day. Roberts had originally paid $39,000 for the van.

Required

a. What was the market value of the delivery van on the date of the stock issue?

b. Show the effect of the two stock issues on Hammond's books in a horizontal statements model like the following one. In the Cash Flow column, indicate whether the item is an operating activity (OA), investing activity (IA), or financing activity (FA). Use NA to indicate that an element was not affected by the event.

Assets =		Equity		Rev. – Exp. = Net Inc.	Cash Flow
Cash + Van	= Com. Stk.	+ PIC in Excess			

Exercise 8-8 *Treasury stock transactions*

LO 8-5

Moore Corporation repurchased 4,000 shares of its own stock for $30 per share. The stock has a par of $10 per share. A month later Moore resold 2,500 shares of the treasury stock for $35 per share.

Required

What is the balance of the Treasury Stock account after these transactions are recognized?

LO 8-5

Exercise 8-9   *Recording and reporting treasury stock transactions*

The following information pertains to Wise Corp. at January 1, 2014:

Common stock, $10 par, 50,000 shares authorized,	
3,000 shares issued and outstanding	$30,000
Paid-in capital in excess of par, common stock	12,000
Retained earnings	46,000

Wise Corp. completed the following transactions during 2014:

1. Issued 2,000 shares of $10 par common stock for $16 per share.
2. Repurchased 500 shares of its own common stock for $18 per share.
3. Resold 120 shares of treasury stock for $20 per share.

Required

a. How many shares of common stock were outstanding at the end of the period?
b. How many shares of common stock had been issued at the end of the period?
c. Organize the transactions data in accounts under the accounting equation.
d. Prepare the stockholders' equity section of the balance sheet reflecting these transactions. Include the number of shares authorized, issued, and outstanding in the description of the common stock.

LO 8-6

Exercise 8-10   *Effect of cash dividends on financial statements*

On October 1, 2014, Daster Corporation declared a $50,000 cash dividend to be paid on December 15 to shareholders of record on November 1.

Required

Record the events occurring on October 1 and December 15 in a horizontal statements model like the following one. In the Cash Flow column, indicate whether the item is an operating activity (OA), investing activity (IA), or financing activity (FA).

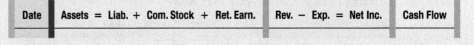

Date	Assets	=	Liab.	+	Com. Stock	+	Ret. Earn.	Rev.	−	Exp.	=	Net Inc.	Cash Flow

LO 8-6

Exercise 8-11   *Accounting for cumulative preferred dividends*

When Higdon Corporation was organized in January 2014, it immediately issued 10,000 shares of $50 par, 5 percent, cumulative preferred stock and 15,000 shares of $10 par common stock. The company's earnings history is as follows: 2014, net loss of $18,000; 2015, net income of $110,000; 2016, net income of $90,000. The corporation did not pay a dividend in 2014.

Required

a. How much is the dividend arrearage as of January 1, 2014?
b. Assume that the board of directors declares a $65,000 cash dividend at the end of 2015 (remember that the 2014 and 2015 preferred dividends are due). How will the dividend be divided between the preferred and common stockholders?

Exercise 8-12   *Cash dividends for preferred and common shareholders*

J&J Corporation had the following stock issued and outstanding at January 1, 2014:

1. 200,000 shares of $10 par common stock.
2. 8,000 shares of $100 par, 4 percent, noncumulative preferred stock.

On May 10, J&J Corporation declared the annual cash dividend on its 8,000 shares of preferred stock and a $.50 per share dividend for the common shareholders. The dividends will be paid on June 15 to the shareholders of record on May 30.

Required

Determine the total amount of dividends to be paid to the preferred shareholders and common shareholders.

Exercise 8-13   *Cash dividends: Common and preferred stock*   LO 8-6

Yan Corp. had the following stock issued and outstanding at January 1, 2014:

1. 60,000 shares of no-par common stock.
2. 15,000 shares of $100 par, 4 percent, cumulative preferred stock. (Dividends are in arrears for one year, 2013.)

   On February 1, 2014, Yan declared a $150,000 cash dividend to be paid March 31 to shareholders of record on March 10.

Required

What amount of dividends will be paid to the preferred shareholders versus the common shareholders?

Exercise 8-14   *Accounting for stock dividends*   LO 8-7

Tidwell Corporation issued a 4 percent stock dividend on 20,000 shares of its $10 par common stock. At the time of the dividend, the market value of the stock was $30 per share.

Required

a. Compute the amount of the stock dividend.
b. Show the effects of the stock dividend on the financial statements using a horizontal statements model like the following one.

Assets	=	Liab.	+	Com. Stk.	+	PIC in Excess	+	Ret. Earn.	Rev.	−	Exp.	=	Net Inc.	Cash Flow

Exercise 8-15   *Determining the effects of stock splits on the accounting records*   LO 8-7

The market value of Dylan Corporation's common stock had become excessively high. The stock was currently selling for $240 per share. To reduce the market price of the common stock, Dylan declared a 3-for-1 stock split for the 200,000 outstanding shares of its $10 par common stock.

Required

a. How will Dylan Corporation's books be affected by the stock split?
b. Determine the number of common shares outstanding and the par value after the split.
c. Explain how the market value of the stock will be affected by the stock split.

Exercise 8-16   *Corporate announcements*   LO 8-9

Super Drugs (one of the three largest drug makers) just reported that its 2014 third-quarter profits are essentially the same as the 2013 third-quarter profits. In addition to this announcement, the same day, Super Drugs also announced that the Food and Drug Administration has just approved a new drug used to treat high blood pressure that Super Drugs developed. This new drug has been shown to be extremely effective and has few or no side effects. It will also be less expensive than the other drugs currently on the market.

Required

Using the above information, answer the following questions:

a. What do you think will happen to the stock price of Super Drugs on the day these two announcements are made? Explain your answer.
b. How will the balance sheet be affected on that day by the above announcements?
c. How will the income statement be affected on that day by the above announcements?
d. How will the statement of cash flows be affected on that day by the above announcements?

PROBLEMS

connect | ACCOUNTING   All applicable Problems are available with McGraw-Hill's *Connect® Accounting.*

LO 8-1

Problem 8-17   *Different forms of business organization*

Shawn Bates was working to establish a business enterprise with four of his wealthy friends. Each of the five individuals would receive a 20 percent ownership interest in the company. A primary goal of establishing the enterprise was to minimize the amount of income taxes paid. Assume that the five investors are in a 35 percent personal tax bracket and that the corporate tax rate is 25 percent. Also assume that the new company is expected to earn $200,000 of cash income before taxes during its first year of operation. All earnings are expected to be immediately distributed to the owners.

Required

Calculate the amount of after-tax cash flow available to each investor if the business is established as a partnership versus a corporation. Write a memo explaining the advantages and disadvantages of these two forms of business organization. Explain why a limited liability company may be a better choice than either a partnership or a corporation.

LO 8-1, 8-2

CHECK FIGURES
a. Net Income: $24,000
b. Sue Moore Capital: $78,100

Problem 8-18   *Effect of business structure on financial statements*

Auto Spa Company was started on January 1, 2014, when the owners invested $120,000 cash in the business. During 2014, the company earned cash revenues of $80,000 and incurred cash expenses of $56,000. The company also paid cash distributions of $5,000.

Required

Prepare a 2014 income statement, capital statement (statement of changes in equity), balance sheet, and statement of cash flows using each of the following assumptions. (Consider each assumption separately.)

a. Auto Spa is a sole proprietorship owned by B. Burns.
b. Auto Spa is a partnership with two partners, Sue Moore and Jim Pounds. Moore invested $72,000 and Pounds invested $48,000 of the $120,000 cash that was used to start the business. Pounds was expected to assume the vast majority of the responsibility for operating the business. The partnership agreement called for Pounds to receive 60 percent of the profits and Moore the remaining 40 percent. With regard to the $5,000 distribution, Pounds withdrew $1,500 from the business and Moore withdrew $3,500.
c. Auto Spa is a corporation. The owners were issued 10,000 shares of $10 par common stock when they invested the $120,000 cash in the business.

LO 8-5

CHECK FIGURES
Total Paid-In Capital: $653,600
Total Stockholders' Equity:
$792,600

Problem 8-19   *Recording and reporting treasury stock transactions*

Quality Corporation reports the following information in its January 1, 2014, balance sheet:

Stockholders' equity	
Common stock, $10 par value, 100,000 shares authorized, 50,000	
shares issued and outstanding	$500,000
Paid-in capital in excess of par value	150,000
Retained earnings	120,000
Total stockholders' equity	$770,000

During 2014, Quality was affected by the following accounting events:

1. Purchased 2,000 shares of treasury stock at $15 per share.
2. Reissued 1,200 shares of treasury stock at $18 per share.
3. Earned $72,000 of cash revenues.
4. Paid $41,000 of cash operating expenses.

Required

Prepare the stockholders' equity section of the year-end balance sheet.

Problem 8-20   *Recording and reporting stock transactions and cash dividends across two accounting cycles*

Malard Corporation was authorized to issue 100,000 shares of $8 par common stock and 50,000 shares of $80 par, 4 percent, cumulative preferred stock. Malard Corporation completed the following transactions during its first two years of operation:

2014

Jan.	2	Issued 25,000 shares of $8 par common stock for $10 per share.
	15	Issued 2,000 shares of $80 par preferred stock for $90 per share.
Feb.	14	Issued 20,000 shares of $8 par common stock for $12 per share.
Dec.	31	During the year, earned $280,000 of cash revenues and paid $165,000 of cash operating expenses.
	31	Declared the cash dividend on outstanding shares of preferred stock for 2014. The dividend will be paid on January 31 to stockholders of record on January 15, 2015.
	31	Closed revenue, expense, and dividend accounts to the retained earnings account.

2015

Jan.	31	Paid the cash dividend declared on December 31, 2014.
Mar.	1	Issued 4,000 shares of $80 par preferred stock for $92 per share.
June	1	Purchased 1,000 shares of common stock as treasury stock at $14 per share.
Dec.	31	During the year, earned $185,000 of cash revenues and paid $110,000 of cash operating expenses.
	31	Declared the dividend on the preferred stock and a $1.00 per share dividend on the common stock.
	31	Closed revenue, expense, and dividend accounts to the retained earnings account.

Required

a. Organize the transaction data in accounts under an accounting equation.
b. Prepare the stockholders' equity section of the balance sheet at December 31, 2014.
c. Prepare the balance sheet at December 31, 2015.

Problem 8-21   *Recording and reporting treasury stock transactions*

Prairie Corp. completed the following transactions in 2014, the first year of operation:

1. Issued 15,000 shares of $10 par common stock at par.
2. Issued 5,000 shares of $50 stated value preferred stock at $52 per share.
3. Purchased 800 shares of common stock as treasury stock for $12 per share.
4. Declared a 5 percent cash dividend on preferred stock.
5. Sold 300 shares of treasury stock for $16 per share.
6. Paid the cash dividend on preferred stock that was declared in Event 4.
7. Earned revenue of $80,000 and incurred operating expenses of $48,000.
8. Appropriated $6,000 of retained earnings.

Required

a. Organize the transaction in accounts under an accounting equation.
b. Prepare the stockholders' equity section of the balance sheet as of December 31, 2014.

Problem 8-22   *Recording and reporting stock dividends*

Concord Corp. completed the following transactions in 2014, the first year of operation:

1. Issued 30,000 shares of $10 par common stock for $15 per share.
2. Issued 6,000 shares of $100 par, 5 percent, preferred stock at $101 per share.
3. Paid the annual cash dividend to preferred shareholders.
4. Issued a 5 percent stock dividend on the common stock. The market value at the dividend declaration date was $19 per share.
5. Later that year, issued a 2-for-1 split on the 31,500 shares of outstanding common stock.
6. Earned $165,000 of cash revenues and paid $98,000 of cash operating expenses.

320   Chapter 8

Required

a. Record each of these events in a horizontal statements model like the following one. In the Cash Flow column, indicate whether the item is an operating activity (OA), investing activity (IA), or financing activity (FA). Use NA to indicate that an element is not affected by the event.

Assets	=	Liab.	+	Equity					Rev.	−	Exp.	=	Net Inc.	Cash Flow
				Pfd. Stk. + Com. Stk. + PIC in Excess PS + PIC in Excess CS + Ret. Earn.										

b. Prepare the stockholders' equity section of the balance sheet at the end of 2014.

LO 8-4, 8-7

CHECK FIGURES
a. Par value per share: $10
b. Dividend per share: $.50

Problem 8-23 *Analyzing the stockholders' equity section of the balance sheet*

The stockholders' equity section of the balance sheet for Gator Company at December 31, 2014, is as follows:

Stockholders' Equity		
Paid-in capital		
Preferred stock, ? par value, 5% cumulative,		
100,000 shares authorized, 40,000 shares issued		
and outstanding	$400,000	
Common stock, $20 stated value, 150,000 shares		
authorized, 40,000 shares issued and ? outstanding	800,000	
Paid-in capital in excess of par—Preferred	30,000	
Paid-in capital in excess of stated value—Common	100,000	
Total paid-in capital		$1,330,000
Retained earnings		250,000
Treasury stock, 2,000 shares		(25,000)
Total stockholders' equity		$1,555,000

Note: The market value per share of the common stock is $40, and the market value per share of the preferred stock is $12.

Required

a. What is the par value per share of the preferred stock?
b. What is the dividend per share on the preferred stock?
c. What is the number of common stock shares outstanding?
d. What was the average issue price per share (price for which the stock was issued) of the common stock?
e. Explain the difference between the average issue price and the market price of the common stock.
f. If Gator declared a 2-for-1 stock split on the common stock, how many shares would be outstanding after the split? What amount would be transferred from the Retained Earnings account because of the stock split? Theoretically, what would be the market price of the common stock immediately after the stock split?

LO 8-4, 8-5, 8-6, 8-7, 8-8   **Problem 8-24** *Effects of equity transactions on financial statements*

The following events were experienced by Baskin, Inc.:

1. Issued cumulative preferred stock.
2. Issued common stock for cash.
3. Issued noncumulative preferred stock.
4. Paid cash to purchase treasury stock.
5. Sold treasury stock for an amount of cash that was more than the cost of the treasury stock.
6. Declared a cash dividend.
7. Declared a 2-for-1 stock split on the common stock.
8. Distributed a stock dividend.

9. Appropriated retained earnings.

10. Paid a cash dividend that was previously declared.

Required

Show the effect of each event on the elements of the financial statements using a horizontal statements model like the following one. Use + for increase, − for decrease, and NA for not affected. In the Cash Flow column indicate whether the item is an operating activity (OA), investing activity (IA), or financing activity (FA). The first transaction is entered as an example.

Event No.	Assets	=	Liab.	+	Equity	Rev.	−	Exp.	=	Net Inc.	Cash Flow
1	+		NA		+	NA		NA		NA	+ FA

ANALYZE, THINK, COMMUNICATE

ATC 8-1   Business Applications Case   *Understanding real-world annual reports*

Use the Target Corporation's Form 10-K to answer the following questions related to Target's 2012 fiscal year (year ended February 2, 2013). Target's Form 10-K is available on the company's website or through the SEC's EDGAR database. Appendix A provides instructions for using the EDGAR database.

Required

a. What is the par value per share of Target's stock?

b. How many shares of Target's common stock were *outstanding* as of February 2, 2013?

c. Target's annual report provides some details about the company's executive officers. How many are identified? What is their minimum, maximum, and average age? How many are females?

d. Target's balance sheet does not show a balance for treasury stock. Does this mean the company has not repurchased any of its own stock? Explain.

ATC 8-2   Group Assignment   *Missing information*

Listed here are the stockholders' equity sections of three public companies for years ending in 2012 and 2011:

	2012	2011
Wendy's/Arby's Group (in thousands)		
Stockholders' equity		
Common stock, ?? stated value per share, authorized:		
1,500,000; 470,424 shares issued	$ 47,042	$ 47,042
Capital in excess of stated value	2,782,765	2,779,871
Retained earnings	(467,007)	(434,999)
Acc. other comp. income (loss)	5,981	102
Treasury stock, at cost: 78,051 in 2012 and 80,700 in 2011	(382,926)	(395,947)
Coca-Cola (in millions)		
Stockholders' equity		
Common stock, ?? par value per share, authorized:		
11,200; issued: 7,040 shares in 2012 and 2011	1,760	1,760
Capital surplus	11,379	10,332
Reinvested earnings	58,045	53,621
Acc. other comp. inc. (loss)	(3,385)	(2,774)
Treasury stock, at cost: 2,571 in 2012 and 2,514 in 2011	(35,009)	(31,304)
Harley-Davidson (in thousands)		
Stockholders' equity		
Common stock, ?? par value per share, authorized: 800,000;		
issued: 341,266 in 2012 and 339,107 shares in 2011	3,412	3,391
Additional paid-in capital	1,066,069	968,392
Retained earnings	7,306,424	6,824,180
Acc. other comp. inc. (loss)	(607,678)	(476,733)
Treasury stock, at cost: 115,166 for 2012 and 108,567 for 2011	(5,210,604)	(4,898,974)

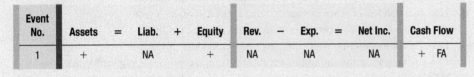

Required

a. Divide the class in three sections and divide each section into groups of three to five students. Assign each section one of the companies.

Group Tasks

Based on the company assigned to your group, answer the following questions.

b. What is the per-share par or stated value of the common stock in 2012?
c. What was the average issue price of the common stock for each year?
d. How many shares of stock are outstanding at the end of each year?
e. What is the average cost per share of the treasury stock for 2012?
f. Do the data suggest that your company was profitable in 2012?
g. Can you determine the amount of net income from the information given? What is missing?
h. What is the total stockholders' equity of your company for each year?

Class Discussion

i. Have each group select a representative to present the information about its company. Compare the share issue price and the par or stated value of the companies.

j. Compare the average issue price to the current market price for each of the companies. Speculate about what might cause the difference.

ATC 8-3   Research Assignment   *Analyzing Skechers' equity structure*

Using either Skechers USA, Inc. most current Form 10-K or the company's annual report, answer the questions below. To obtain the Form 10-K use either the EDGAR system following the instructions in Appendix A or the company's website. The company's annual report is available on its website.

Required

a. What is the *book value* of Skechers' stockholders' equity that is shown on the company's balance sheet?
b. What is the par value of Skechers common stock?
c. Does Skechers have any treasury stock? If so, how many shares of treasury stock does the company hold?
d. Why does the stock of a company such as a Skechers have a market value that is higher than its book value?

ATC 8-4   Writing Assignment   *Comparison of organizational forms*

Jim Baku and Scott Hanson are thinking about opening a new restaurant. Baku has extensive marketing experience but does not know that much about food preparation. However, Hanson is an excellent chef. Both will work in the business, but Baku will provide most of the funds necessary to start the business. At this time, they cannot decide whether to operate the business as a partnership or a corporation.

Required

Prepare a written memo to Baku and Hanson describing the advantages and disadvantages of each organizational form. Also, from the limited information provided, recommend the organizational form you think they should use.

ATC 8-5   Ethical Dilemma   *Bad news versus very bad news*

Louise Stinson, the chief financial officer of Bostonian Corporation, was on her way to the president's office. She was carrying the latest round of bad news. There would be no executive bonuses this year. Corporate profits were down. Indeed, if the latest projections held true, the company would report a small loss on the year-end income statement. Executive bonuses were tied to corporate profits. The executive compensation plan provided for 10 percent of net earnings to be set aside for bonuses. No profits meant no bonuses. While things looked bleak, Stinson had a plan that might help soften the blow.

After informing the company president of the earnings forecast, Stinson made the following suggestion: Because the company was going to report a loss anyway, why not report a big loss? She reasoned that the directors and stockholders would not be much more angry if the company reported a large loss than if it reported a small one. There were several questionable assets that could be written down in the current year. This would increase the current year's loss but would reduce expenses in subsequent accounting periods. For example, the company was carrying damaged inventory that was estimated to have a value of $2,500,000. If this estimate were revised to $500,000, the company would have to recognize a $2,000,000 loss in the current year. However, next year when the goods were sold, the expense for cost of goods sold would be $2,000,000 less and profits would be higher by that amount. Although the directors would be angry this year, they would certainly be happy next year. The strategy would also have the benefit of adding $200,000 to next year's executive bonus pool ($2,000,000 × 0.10). Furthermore, it could not hurt this year's bonus pool since there would be no pool this year because the company is going to report a loss.

Some of the other items that Stinson is considering include (1) converting from straight-line to accelerated depreciation, (2) increasing the percentage of receivables estimated to be uncollectible in the current year and lowering the percentage in the following year, and (3) raising the percentage of estimated warranty claims in the current period and lowering it in the following period. Finally, Stinson notes that two of the company's department stores have been experiencing losses. The company could sell these stores this year and thereby improve earnings next year. Stinson admits that the sale would result in significant losses this year, but she smiles as she thinks of next year's bonus check.

Required

a. Explain how each of the three numbered strategies for increasing the amount of the current year's loss would affect the stockholders' equity section of the balance sheet in the current year. How would the other elements of the balance sheet be affected?

b. If Stinson's strategy were effectively implemented, how would it affect the stockholders' equity in subsequent accounting periods?

c. Comment on the ethical implications of running the company for the sake of management (maximization of bonuses) versus the maximization of return to stockholders.

d. Formulate a bonus plan that will motivate managers to maximize the value of the firm instead of motivating them to manipulate the reporting process.

e. How would Stinson's strategy of overstating the amount of the reported loss in the current year affect the company's current P/E ratio?

CHAPTER 10

An Introduction to Management Accounting

LEARNING OBJECTIVES

After you have mastered the material in this chapter, you will be able to:

LO 10-1   Distinguish between managerial and financial accounting.

LO 10-2   Identify the cost of manufacturing a product and show how these costs affect financial statements.

LO 10-3   Prepare a schedule of cost of goods manufactured and sold.

LO 10-4   Show how just-in-time inventory can increase profitability.

LO 10-5   Identify the standards contained in IMA's Statement of Ethical Professional Practice.

LO 10-6   Identify emerging trends in accounting (Appendix).

Video lectures and accompanying self-assessment quizzes are available for all learning objectives through McGraw-Hill Connect® Accounting.

CHAPTER OPENING

Andy Grove, Senior Advisor to Executive Management of Intel Corporation, is credited with the motto, "Only the paranoid survive." Mr. Grove describes a wide variety of concerns that make him paranoid. Specifically, he declares:

> I worry about products getting screwed up, and I worry about products getting introduced prematurely. I worry about factories not performing well, and I worry about having too many factories. I worry about hiring the right people, and I worry about morale slacking off. And, of course, I worry about competitors. I worry about other people figuring out how to do what we do better or cheaper, and displacing us with our customers.

Do Intel's historically based financial statements contain the information Mr. Grove needs? No.

Financial accounting is not designed to satisfy all the information needs of business managers. Its scope is limited to the needs of external users such as investors and creditors. The field of accounting designed to meet the needs of internal users is called **managerial accounting.**

The Curious Accountant

Earlier in this course of accounting, you learned how retailers, such as Target, account for the cost of equipment that lasts more than one year. Recall that the equipment was recorded as an asset when purchased, and then it was depreciated over its expected useful life. The depreciation charge reduced the company's assets and increased its expenses. This approach was justified under the matching principle, which seeks to recognize costs as expenses in the same period that the cost (resource) is used to generate revenue.

Is depreciation always shown as an expense on the income statement? The answer may surprise you. Consider the following scenario. Bose Corporation manufactures the headphones that it sells to Target. In order to produce the headphones, Bose had to purchase a robotic machine that it expects can be used to produce 100,000 headphones.

Do you think Bose should account for depreciation on its manufacturing equipment the same way Target accounts for depreciation on its registers at the checkout counters? If not, how should Bose account for its depreciation? Remember the matching principle when thinking of your answer. (Answer on page 373.)

DIFFERENCES BETWEEN MANAGERIAL AND FINANCIAL ACCOUNTING

Distinguish between managerial and financial accounting.

While the information needs of internal and external users overlap, the needs of managers generally differ from those of investors or creditors. Some distinguishing characteristics are discussed in the following section.

Users and Types of Information

Financial accounting provides information used primarily by investors, creditors, and others *outside* a business. In contrast, managerial accounting focuses on information used by executives, managers, and employees who work *inside* the business. These two user groups need different types of information.

Internal users need information to *plan, direct,* and *control* business operations. The nature of information needed is related to an employee's job level. Lower level employees use nonfinancial information such as work schedules, store hours, and customer service policies. Moving up the organizational ladder, financial information becomes increasingly important. Middle managers use a blend of financial and nonfinancial information, while senior executives concentrate on financial data. To a lesser degree, senior executives also use general economic data and nonfinancial operating information. For example, an executive may consider the growth rate of the economy before deciding to expand the company's workforce.

External users (investors and creditors) have greater needs for general economic information than do internal users. For example, an investor debating whether to purchase stock versus bond securities might be more interested in government tax policy than financial statement data. Exhibit 10.1 summarizes the information needs of different user groups.

Level of Aggregation

External users generally desire *global information* that reflects the performance of a company as a whole. For example, an investor is not so much interested in the performance of a particular Sears store as she is in the performance of Sears Roebuck Company versus that of JC Penney Company. In contrast, internal users focus on detailed information about specific subunits of the company. To meet the needs of the different user groups, financial accounting data are more aggregated than managerial accounting data.

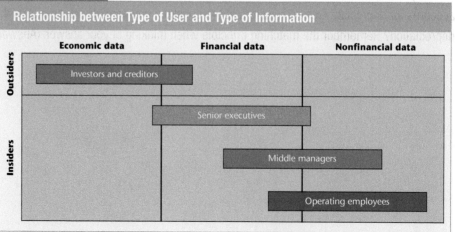

EXHIBIT 10.1

Relationship between Type of User and Type of Information

Regulation

Financial accounting is designed to generate information for the general public. In an effort to protect the public interest, Congress established the **Securities and Exchange Commission (SEC)** and gave it authority to regulate public financial reporting practices. The SEC has delegated much of its authority for developing accounting rules to the private sector **Financial Accounting Standards Board (FASB),** thereby allowing the accounting profession considerable influence over financial accounting reports. The FASB supports a broad base of pronouncements and practices known as **generally accepted accounting principles (GAAP).** GAAP severely restricts the accounting procedures and practices permitted in published financial statements.

Beyond financial statement data, much of the information generated by management accounting systems is proprietary information not available to the public. Since this information is not distributed to the public, it need not be regulated to protect the public interest. Management accounting is restricted only by the **value-added principle.** Management accountants are free to engage in any information gathering and reporting activity so long as the activity adds value in excess of its cost. For example, management accountants are free to provide forecasted information to internal users. In contrast, financial accounting as prescribed by GAAP does not permit forecasting.

Information Characteristics

While financial accounting is characterized by its objectivity, reliability, consistency, and historical nature, managerial accounting is more concerned with relevance and timeliness. Managerial accounting uses more estimates and fewer facts than financial accounting. Financial accounting reports what happened yesterday; managerial accounting reports what is expected to happen tomorrow.

Time Horizon and Reporting Frequency

Financial accounting information is reported periodically, normally at the end of a year. Management cannot wait until the end of the year to discover problems. Planning, controlling, and directing require immediate attention. Managerial accounting information is delivered on a continuous basis.

Exhibit 10.2 summarizes significant differences between financial and managerial accounting.

PRODUCT COSTING IN MANUFACTURING COMPANIES

A major focus for managerial accountants is determining **product cost.**[1] Managers need to know the cost of their products for a variety of reasons. For example, **cost-plus pricing** is a common business practice.[2] **Product costing** is also used to control business operations. It is useful in answering questions such as: Are costs higher or lower than expected? Who is responsible for the variances between expected and actual costs? What actions can be taken to control the variances?

LO 10-2

Identify the cost of manufacturing a product and show how these costs affect financial statements.

Components of Product Cost

A company normally incurs three types of costs when making products. Specifically, the company must pay for (1) the *materials* used to make the products, (2) the *labor*

---

[1]This text uses the term *product* in a generic sense to mean both goods and services.
[2]Other pricing strategies will be introduced in subsequent chapters.

EXHIBIT 10.2

Comparative Features of Managerial versus Financial Accounting Information

Features	Managerial Accounting	Financial Accounting
Users	Insiders, including executives, managers, and operators	Outsiders, including investors, creditors, government agencies, analysts, and reporters
Information type	Economic and physical data as well as financial data	Financial data
Level of aggregation	Local information on subunits of the organization	Global information on the company as a whole
Regulation	No regulation, limited only by the value-added principle	Regulation by SEC, FASB, and other determiners of GAAP
Information characteristics	Estimates that promote relevance and enable timeliness	Factual information that is characterized by objectivity, reliability, consistency, and accuracy
Time horizon	Past, present, and future	Past only, historically based
Reporting frequency	Continuous reporting	Delayed, with emphasis on annual reports

expended by the employees who transform the materials into products, and (3) the *overhead* (other resources such as utilities and equipment consumed in the process of making the products). If the company stores its products, the costs of the materials, labor, and overhead used in making the products are maintained in an inventory account until the products are sold. For a detailed explanation of how product costs flow through the financial statements, refer to the following example of Tabor Manufacturing Company.

Tabor Manufacturing Company

Tabor Manufacturing Company makes wooden tables. The company spent $1,000 cash to build four tables: $390 for materials, $470 for a carpenter's labor, and $140 for tools used in making the tables. How much is Tabor's expense? The answer is zero. The $1,000 cash has been converted into products (four tables). The cash payments for materials, labor, and tools (overhead) were *asset exchange* transactions. One asset (cash) decreased while another asset (tables) increased. Tabor will not recognize any expense until the tables are sold; in the meantime, the cost of the tables is held in an asset account called *Finished Goods Inventory*. Exhibit 10.3 illustrates how cash is transformed into inventory.

Average Cost per Unit

How much did each table made by Tabor cost? The *actual* cost of each of the four tables likely differs. The carpenter probably spent a little more time on some of the tables than others. Material and tool usage probably varied from table to table. Determining the exact cost of each table is virtually impossible. Minute details such as a second of labor time cannot be effectively measured. Even if Tabor could determine the exact cost of each table, the information would be of little use. Minor differences in the cost per table would make no difference in pricing or other decisions management needs to make. Accountants therefore normally calculate cost per unit as an *average*. In the case of Tabor Manufacturing, the **average cost** per table is $250 ($1,000 ÷ 4 units). Unless otherwise stated, assume *cost per unit* means *average cost per unit*.

EXHIBIT 10.3

Transforming the Asset Cash into the Asset Finished Goods Inventory

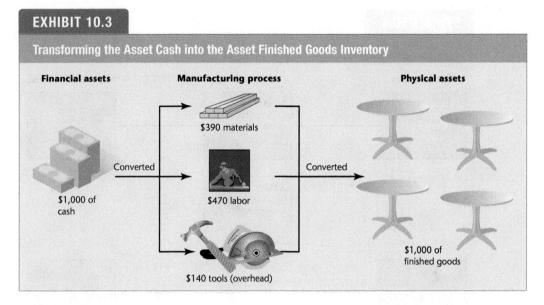

CHECK YOURSELF 10.1

All boxes of General Mills' Total Raisin Bran cereal are priced at exactly the same amount in your local grocery store. Does this mean that the actual cost of making each box of cereal was exactly the same?

Answer No, making each box would not cost exactly the same amount. For example, some boxes contain slightly more or less cereal than other boxes. Accordingly, some boxes cost slightly more or less to make than others do. General Mills uses average cost rather than actual cost to develop its pricing strategy.

Costs Can Be Assets or Expenses

It might seem odd that wages paid to production workers are recorded as inventory instead of being expensed. Remember, however, that expenses are assets used in the process of *earning revenue.* The cash paid to production workers is not used to produce revenue. Instead, the cash is used to produce inventory. Revenue will be earned when the inventory is used (sold). So long as the inventory remains on hand, all product costs (materials, labor, and overhead) remain in an inventory account.

When a table is sold, the average cost of the table is transferred from the Inventory account to the Cost of Goods Sold (expense) account. If some tables remain unsold at the end of the accounting period, part of the *product cost* is reported as an asset (inventory) on the balance sheet while the other part is reported as an expense (cost of goods sold) on the income statement.

Costs that are not classified as product costs are normally expensed in the period in which they are incurred. These costs include *general operating costs, selling and administrative costs, interest costs,* and the *cost of income taxes.*

To illustrate, return to the Tabor Manufacturing example. Recall that Tabor made four tables at an average cost per unit of $250. Assume Tabor pays an employee who sells three of the tables a $200 sales commission. The sales commission is expensed immediately. The total product cost for the three tables (3 tables × $250 each = $750) is expensed on the income statement as cost of goods sold. The portion of the total

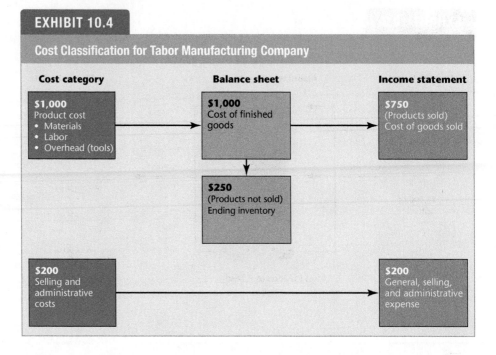

EXHIBIT 10.4

Cost Classification for Tabor Manufacturing Company

Cost category	Balance sheet	Income statement
$1,000 Product cost • Materials • Labor • Overhead (tools)	**$1,000** Cost of finished goods	**$750** (Products sold) Cost of goods sold
	$250 (Products not sold) Ending inventory	
$200 Selling and administrative costs		**$200** General, selling, and administrative expense

product cost remaining in inventory is $250 (1 table × $250). Exhibit 10.4 shows the relationship between the costs incurred and the expenses recognized for Tabor Manufacturing Company.

Effect of Product Costs on Financial Statements

We illustrate accounting for product costs in manufacturing companies with Patillo Manufacturing Company, a producer of ceramic pottery. Patillo, started on January 1, 2016, experienced the following accounting events during its first year of operations.[3] *Assume that all transactions except 6, 8, and 10 are cash transactions.*

1. Acquired $15,000 cash by issuing common stock.
2. Paid $2,000 for materials that were used to make products. All products started were completed during the period.
3. Paid $1,200 for salaries of selling and administrative employees.
4. Paid $3,000 for wages of production workers.
5. Paid $2,800 for furniture used in selling and administrative offices.
6. Recognized depreciation on the office furniture purchased in Event 5. The furniture was acquired on January 1, had a $400 estimated salvage value, and a four-year useful life. The annual depreciation charge is $600 [($2,800 − $400) ÷ 4].
7. Paid $4,500 for manufacturing equipment.
8. Recognized depreciation on the equipment purchased in Event 7. The equipment was acquired on January 1, had a $1,500 estimated salvage value, and a three-year useful life. The annual depreciation charge is $1,000 [($4,500 − $1,500) ÷ 3].
9. Sold inventory to customers for $7,500 cash.
10. The inventory sold in Event 9 cost $4,000 to make.

[3]This illustration assumes that all inventory started during the period was completed during the period. Patillo therefore uses only one inventory account, Finished Goods Inventory. Many manufacturing companies normally have three categories of inventory on hand at the end of an accounting period: Raw Materials Inventory, Work in Process Inventory (inventory of partially completed units), and Finished Goods Inventory.

EXHIBIT 10.5

Effect of Product versus Selling and Administrative Costs on Financial Statements

Event No.	Cash	+	Inventory	+	Office Furn.*	+	Manuf. Equip.*	=	Com. Stk.	+	Ret. Earn.	Rev.	−	Exp.	=	Net Inc.	Cash Flow	
1	15,000							=	15,000								15,000	FA
2	(2,000)	+	2,000														(2,000)	OA
3	(1,200)							=			(1,200)		−	1,200	=	(1,200)	(1,200)	OA
4	(3,000)	+	3,000														(3,000)	OA
5	(2,800)	+			2,800												(2,800)	IA
6					(600)			=			(600)		−	600	=	(600)		
7	(4,500)	+					4,500										(4,500)	IA
8			1,000	+			(1,000)											
9	7,500							=			7,500	7,500			=	7,500	7,500	OA
10			(4,000)					=			(4,000)		−	4,000	=	(4,000)		
Totals	9,000	+	2,000	+	2,200	+	3,500	=	15,000	+	1,700	7,500	−	5,800	=	1,700	9,000	NC

*Negative amounts in these columns represent accumulated depreciation.

The effects of these transactions on the balance sheet, income statement, and statement of cash flows are shown in Exhibit 10.5. Study each row in this exhibit, paying particular attention to how similar costs such as salaries for selling and administrative personnel and wages for production workers have radically different effects on the financial statements. The example illustrates the three elements of product costs—materials (Event 2), labor (Event 4), and overhead (Event 8). These events are discussed in more detail below.

Materials Costs (Event 2)

Materials used to make products are usually called **raw materials.** The cost of raw materials is first recorded in an asset account (Inventory). The cost is then transferred from the Inventory account to the Cost of Goods Sold account at the time the goods are sold. Remember that materials cost is only one component of total manufacturing costs. When inventory is sold, the combined cost of materials, labor, and overhead is expensed as *cost of goods sold*. The costs of materials that can be easily and conveniently traced to products are called **direct raw materials** costs.

Labor Costs (Event 4)

The salaries paid to selling and administrative employees (Event 3) and the wages paid to production workers (Event 4) are accounted for differently. Salaries paid to selling and administrative employees are expensed immediately, but the cost of production wages is added to inventory. Production wages are expensed as part of cost of goods sold at the time the inventory is sold. Labor costs that can be easily and conveniently traced to products are called **direct labor** costs. The cost flow of wages for production employees versus salaries for selling and administrative personnel is shown in Exhibit 10.6.

Overhead Costs (Event 8)

Although depreciation cost totaled $1,600 ($600 on office furniture and $1,000 on manufacturing equipment), only the $600 of depreciation on the office furniture is expensed directly on the income statement. The depreciation on the manufacturing equipment is

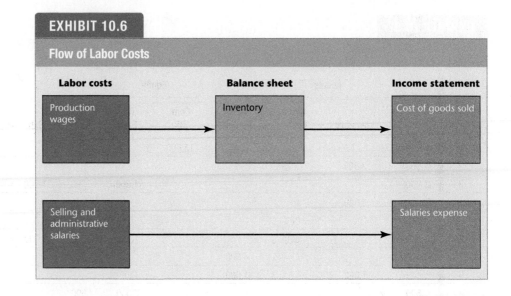

EXHIBIT 10.6

Flow of Labor Costs

Labor costs	Balance sheet	Income statement
Production wages	Inventory	Cost of goods sold
Selling and administrative salaries		Salaries expense

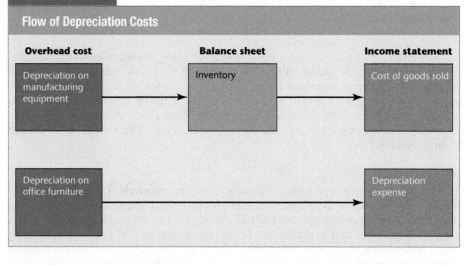

EXHIBIT 10.7

Flow of Depreciation Costs

Overhead cost	Balance sheet	Income statement
Depreciation on manufacturing equipment	Inventory	Cost of goods sold
Depreciation on office furniture		Depreciation expense

split between the income statement (cost of goods sold) and the balance sheet (inventory). The depreciation cost flow for the manufacturing equipment versus the office furniture is shown in Exhibit 10.7.

Total Product Cost. A summary of Patillo Manufacturing's total product cost is shown in Exhibit 10.8.

Financial Statements

The income statement, balance sheet, and statement of cash flows for Patillo Manufacturing are displayed in Exhibit 10.9.

Product Costs. The $4,000 cost of goods sold reported on the income statement includes a portion of the materials, labor, and overhead costs incurred by Patillo during the year. Similarly, the $2,000 of finished goods inventory on the balance sheet includes

EXHIBIT 10.8

Schedule of Inventory Costs

Materials	$ 2,000
Labor	3,000
Manufacturing overhead*	1,000
Total product costs	6,000
Less: Cost of goods sold	(4,000)
Ending inventory balance	$ 2,000

*Depreciation [($4,500 − $1,500) ÷ 3]

EXHIBIT 10.9

PATILLO MANUFACTURING COMPANY
Financial Statements
Income Statement for 2016

Sales revenue	$ 7,500
Cost of goods sold	(4,000)
Gross margin	3,500
G, S, & A expenses	
Salaries expense	(1,200)
Depreciation expense—office furniture	(600)
Net income	$ 1,700

Balance Sheet as of December 31, 2016

Cash		$ 9,000
Finished goods inventory		2,000
Office furniture	$2,800	
Accumulated depreciation	(600)	
Book value		2,200
Manufacturing equipment	4,500	
Accumulated depreciation	(1,000)	
Book value		3,500
Total assets		$16,700
Stockholders' equity		
Common stock		$15,000
Retained earnings		1,700
Total stockholders' equity		$16,700

Statement of Cash Flows for 2016

Operating Activities	
Inflow from revenue	$ 7,500
Outflow for inventory	(5,000)
Outflow for S&A salaries	(1,200)
Net inflow from operating activities	1,300
Investing Activities	
Outflow for equipment and furniture	(7,300)
Financing Activities	
Inflow from stock issue	15,000
Net change in cash	9,000
Beginning cash balance	-0-
Ending cash balance	$ 9,000

materials, labor, and overhead costs. These product costs will be recognized as an expense in the next accounting period when the goods are sold. Initially classifying a cost as a product cost delays, but does not eliminate, its recognition as an expense. All product costs are ultimately recognized as an expense (cost of goods sold). Cost classification does not affect cash flow. Cash inflows and outflows are recognized in the period that cash is collected or paid regardless of whether the cost is recorded as an asset or is expensed.

Selling, General, and Administrative Costs. Selling, general, and administrative costs (SG&A) are normally expensed *in the period* in which they are incurred. Because of this recognition pattern, nonproduct expenses are sometimes called **period costs.** In Patillo's case, the salaries expense for selling and administrative employees and the depreciation on office furniture are period costs reported directly on the income statement.

Overhead Costs: A Closer Look

Costs such as depreciation on manufacturing equipment cannot be easily traced to products. Suppose that Patillo Manufacturing makes both tables and chairs. What part of the depreciation is caused by manufacturing tables versus manufacturing chairs? Similarly, suppose a production supervisor oversees employees who work on both tables and chairs. How much of the supervisor's salary relates to tables and how much to chairs? Likewise, the cost of glue used in the production department would be difficult to trace to tables versus chairs. You could count the drops of glue used on each product, but the information would not be useful enough to merit the time and money spent collecting the data.

Costs that cannot be traced to products and services in a *cost-effective* manner are called **indirect costs.** The indirect costs incurred to make products are called **manufacturing overhead.** Some of the items commonly included in manufacturing overhead are indirect materials, indirect labor, factory utilities, rent of manufacturing facilities, and depreciation on manufacturing assets.

> **☑ CHECK YOURSELF 10.2**
>
> Lawson Manufacturing Company paid production workers wages of $100,000. It incurred materials costs of $120,000 and manufacturing overhead costs of $160,000. Selling and administrative salaries were $80,000. Lawson started and completed 1,000 units of product and sold 800 of these units. The company sets sales prices at $220 above the average per-unit production cost. Based on this information alone, determine the amount of gross margin and net income. What is Lawson's pricing strategy called?
>
> **Answer** Total product cost is $380,000 ($100,000 labor + $120,000 materials + $160,000 overhead). Cost per unit is $380 ($380,000 ÷ 1,000 units). The sales price per unit is $600 ($380 + $220). Cost of goods sold is $304,000 ($380 × 800 units). Sales revenue is $480,000 ($600 × 800 units). Gross margin is $176,000 ($480,000 revenue − $304,000 cost of goods sold). Net income is $96,000 ($176,000 gross margin − $80,000 selling and administrative salaries). Lawson's pricing strategy is called *cost-plus* pricing.

Since indirect costs cannot be effectively traced to products, they are normally assigned to products using **cost allocation,** a process of dividing a total cost into parts and assigning the parts to relevant cost objects. To illustrate, suppose that production workers spend an eight-hour day making a chair and a table. The chair requires two hours to complete and the table requires six hours. Now suppose that $120 of utilities cost is consumed during the day. How much of the $120 should be assigned to each piece of furniture? The utility cost cannot be directly traced to each specific piece of furniture, but the piece of furniture that required more labor also likely consumed more of the utility cost. Using this line of reasoning, it is rational to allocate the utility cost to the two pieces of furniture based on *direct labor hours* at a rate of $15 per hour ($120 ÷ 8 hours). The chair would be assigned $30 ($15 per hour × 2 hours) of the utility cost and the table would be assigned the remaining $90 ($15 × 6 hours) of utility cost. The allocation of the utility cost is shown in Exhibit 10.10.

We discuss the details of cost allocation in a later chapter. For now, recognize that overhead costs are normally allocated to products rather than traced directly to them.

Manufacturing Product Cost Summary

As explained, the cost of a product made by a manufacturing company is normally composed of three categories: direct materials, direct labor, and manufacturing overhead. Relevant information about these three cost components is summarized in Exhibit 10.11.

EXHIBIT 10.10

Cost Allocation

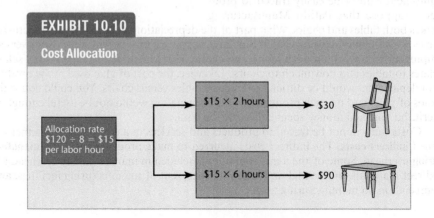

Answers to The Curious Accountant

As you have seen, accounting for depreciation related to manufacturing assets is different from accounting for depreciation for nonmanufacturing assets. Depreciation on the checkout equipment at Target is recorded as depreciation expense. Depreciation on manufacturing equipment at Bose is considered a product cost. It is included first as a part of the cost of inventory and eventually as a part of the expense, cost of goods sold. Recording depreciation on manufacturing equipment as an inventory cost is simply another example of the matching principle, because the cost does not become an expense until revenue from the product sale is recognized.

EXHIBIT 10.11

Components of Manufacturing Product Cost

Component 1—Direct Raw Materials
Sometimes called *raw materials*. In addition to basic resources such as wood or metals, it can include manufactured parts. For example, engines, glass, and car tires can be considered as raw materials for an automotive manufacturer. If the amount of a material in a product is known, it can usually be classified as a direct material. The cost of direct materials can be easily traced to specific products.

Component 2—Direct Labor
The cost of wages paid to factory workers involved in hands-on contact with the products being manufactured. If the amount of time employees worked on a product can be determined, this cost can usually be classified as direct labor. Like direct materials, labor costs must be easily traced to a specific product in order to be classified as a direct cost.

Component 3—Manufacturing Overhead
Costs that cannot be easily traced to specific products. Accordingly, these costs are called *indirect costs*. They can include but are not limited to the following:

1. Indirect materials such as glue, nails, paper, and oil. Indeed, note that indirect materials used in the production process may not appear in the finished product. An example is a chemical solvent used to clean products during the production process but not a component material found in the final product.

2. Indirect labor such as the cost of salaries paid to production supervisors, inspectors, and maintenance personnel.

3. Rental cost for manufacturing facilities and equipment.

4. Utility costs.

5. Depreciation.

6. Security.

7. The cost of preparing equipment for the manufacturing process (i.e., setup costs).

8. Maintenance cost for the manufacturing facility and equipment.

SCHEDULE OF COST OF GOODS MANUFACTURED AND SOLD

To this point, we assumed all inventory started during an accounting period was also completed during that accounting period. All product costs (materials, labor, and manufacturing overhead) were either in inventory or expensed as cost of goods sold. At the end of an accounting period, however, most real-world companies have raw materials on hand, and manufacturing companies are likely to have in inventory items

LO 10-3

Prepare a schedule of cost of goods manufactured and sold.

that have been started but are not completed. Most manufacturing companies accumulate product costs in three distinct inventory accounts: (1) **Raw Materials Inventory,** which includes lumber, metals, paints, and chemicals that will be used to make the company's products; (2) **Work in Process Inventory,** which includes partially completed products; and (3) **Finished Goods Inventory,** which includes completed products that are ready for sale.

The cost of materials is first recorded in the Raw Materials Inventory account. The cost of materials placed in production is then transferred from the Raw Materials Inventory account to the Work in Process Inventory account. The costs of labor and overhead are added to the Work in Process Inventory account. The cost of the goods completed during the period is transferred from the Work in Process Inventory account to the Finished Goods Inventory account. The cost of the goods that are sold during the accounting period is transferred from the Finished Goods Inventory account to the Cost of Goods Sold account. The balances that remain in the Raw Materials, Work in Process, and Finished Goods Inventory accounts are reported on the balance sheet. The amount of product cost transferred to the Cost of Goods Sold account is expensed on the income statement. Exhibit 10.12 shows the flow of manufacturing costs through the accounting records.

To help managers analyze manufacturing costs, companies frequently summarize product cost information in a report called a **schedule of cost of goods manufactured and sold.** To illustrate, assume that in 2017 Patillo Manufacturing Company purchased $37,950 of raw materials inventory. During 2017 Patillo used $37,000 of raw materials, incurred $34,600 of labor costs, and $26,700 of overhead costs in the process of making inventory. Also, during 2017 the company completed work on products that cost $94,600. Recall that Patillo had zero balances in its Raw Materials and Work in Process Inventory accounts at the end of 2016. It had a $2,000 balance in its Finished Goods Inventory account at the end of 2016. The 2016 ending balance becomes the 2017 beginning balance for finished goods. The 2017 ending balances for the inventory accounts were as follows: Raw Materials Inventory, $950; Work in Process Inventory, $3,700; Finished Goods Inventory, $3,200. Finally, during 2017 Patillo had sales revenue of $153,000. Patillo's schedule of cost of goods manufactured and sold for 2017 is shown in Exhibit 10.13.

The $93,400 of cost of goods sold would appear on Patillo's 2017 income statement. A partial income statement for Patillo is shown in Exhibit 10.14.

EXHIBIT 10.12

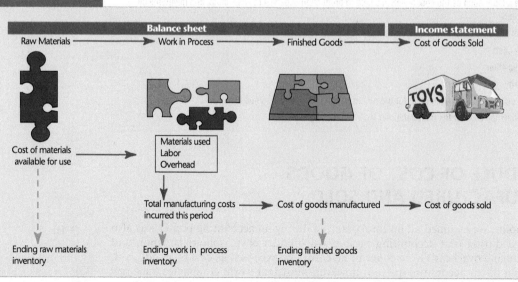

EXHIBIT 10.13

PATILLO MANUFACTURING COMPANY
Schedule of Cost of Goods Manufactured and Sold
For the Year Ended December 31, 2017

Beginning raw materials Inventory	$ 0
Plus: Raw materials purchases	37,950
Less: Ending raw materials inventory	(950)
Raw materials used	37,000
Labor	34,600
Overhead	26,700
Total manufacturing costs	98,300
Plus: Beginning work in process inventory	0
Total work in process inventory	98,300
Less: Ending work in process inventory	(3,700)
Cost of goods manufactured	94,600
Plus: Beginning finished goods inventory	2,000
Cost of goods available for sale	96,600
Less: Ending finished goods inventory	(3,200)
Cost of goods sold	$93,400

EXHIBIT 10.14

PATILLO MANUFACTURING COMPANY
Income Statement
For the Year Ended December 31, 2017

Sales revenue	$153,000
Cost of goods sold	(93,400)
Gross margin	$ 59,600

Upstream and Downstream Costs

Most companies incur product-related costs before and after, as well as during, the manufacturing process. For example, Ford Motor Company incurs significant research and development costs prior to mass producing a new car model. These **upstream costs** occur before the manufacturing process begins. Similarly, companies normally incur significant costs after the manufacturing process is complete. Examples of **downstream costs** include transportation, advertising, sales commissions, and bad debts. While upstream and downstream costs are not considered to be product costs for financial reporting purposes, profitability analysis requires that they be considered in cost-plus pricing decisions. To be profitable, a company must recover the total cost of developing, producing, and delivering its products to customers.

Product Costing in Service and Merchandising Companies

Companies are frequently classified as being service, merchandising, or manufacturing businesses. As the name implies, service organizations provide services, rather than physical products, to consumers. For example, St. Jude Children's Hospital provides treatment programs aimed at healing patient diseases. Other common service providers include public accountants, lawyers, restaurants, dry cleaning establishments, and lawn care companies. Merchandising businesses are sometimes called retail or wholesale companies; they sell goods other companies make. The Home Depot, Inc., Costco Wholesale Corporation, and Best Buy Co., Inc., are merchandising companies. Manufacturing companies make the goods they sell to their customers. Toyota Motor Corporation, Texaco, Inc., and American Standard Companies, Inc., are manufacturing businesses.

How do manufacturing companies differ from service and merchandising businesses? Do service and merchandising companies incur materials, labor, and overhead costs? Yes. For example, Ernst & Young, a large accounting firm, must pay employees (labor costs), use office supplies (material costs), and incur utilities, depreciation, and so on (overhead costs) in the process of conducting audits. ***The primary difference between*** *manufacturing entities and service companies is that the products provided by service companies are consumed immediately.* In contrast, products made by manufacturing companies can be held in the form of inventory until they are sold to consumers. Similarly, most labor and overhead costs incurred by merchandising companies result from providing assistance to customers. These costs are normally treated as selling, general, and administrative expenses rather than accumulated in inventory accounts. Indeed, merchandising companies are often viewed as service companies rather than considered a separate business category.

The important point to remember is that all business managers are expected to control costs, improve quality, and increase productivity. Like managers of manufacturing companies, managers of service and merchandising businesses can benefit from the analysis of the cost of satisfying their customers. For example, Wendy's, a service company, can benefit from knowing how much a hamburger costs in the same manner that Bayer Corporation, a manufacturing company, benefits from knowing the cost of a bottle of aspirin.

☑ CHECK YOURSELF 10.3

The cost of making a Burger King hamburger includes the cost of materials, labor, and overhead. Does this mean that Burger King is a manufacturing company?

Answer   No, Burger King is not a manufacturing company. It is a service company because its products are consumed immediately. In contrast, there may be a considerable delay between the time the product of a manufacturing company is made and the time it is consumed. For example, it could be several months between the time Ford Motor Company makes an Explorer and the time the Explorer is ultimately sold to a customer. The primary difference between service and manufacturing companies is that manufacturing companies have inventories of products and service companies do not.

JUST-IN-TIME INVENTORY

LO 10-4

Show how just-in-time inventory can increase profitability.

Companies attempt to minimize the amount of inventory they maintain because of the high cost of holding it. Many **inventory holding costs** are obvious: financing, warehouse space, supervision, theft, damage, and obsolescence. Other costs are hidden: diminished motivation, sloppy work, inattentive attitudes, and increased production time.

Many businesses have been able to simultaneously reduce their inventory holding costs and increase customer satisfaction by making products available **just in time (JIT)** for customer consumption. For example, hamburgers that are cooked to order are fresher and more individualized than those that are prepared in advance and stored until a customer places an order. Many fast-food restaurants have discovered that JIT systems lead not only to greater customer satisfaction but also to lower costs through reduced waste.

Just-in-Time Illustration

To illustrate the benefits of a JIT system, consider Paula Elliot, a student at a large urban university. She helps support herself by selling flowers. Three days each week, Paula drives to a florist, purchases 25 single-stem roses, returns to the school, and sells the flowers to individuals from a location on a local street corner. She pays $2 per rose and sells each one for $3. Some days she does not have enough flowers to meet customer demand. Other days, she must discard one or two unsold flowers; she believes quality is important and refuses to sell flowers that are not fresh. During May, she purchased 300 roses and sold 280. She calculated her driving cost to be $45. Exhibit 10.15 displays Paula's May income statement.

EXHIBIT 10.15

Income Statement for May

Sales revenue (280 units × $3 per unit)	$840
Cost of goods sold (280 units × $2 per unit)	(560)
Gross margin	280
Driving expense	(45)
Excess inventory waste (20 units × 2)	(40)
Net income	$195

EXHIBIT 10.16

Income Statement for June

Sales revenue (310 units × $3 per unit)	$930
Cost of goods sold (310 units × $2 per unit)	(620)
Gross margin	310
Driving expense	0
Net income	$310

After studying just-in-time inventory systems in her managerial accounting class, Paula decided to apply the concepts to her small business. She *reengineered* her distribution system by purchasing her flowers from a florist within walking distance of her sales location. She had considered purchasing from this florist earlier but had rejected the idea because the florist's regular selling price of $2.25 per rose was too high. After learning about *most-favored customer status,* she developed a strategy to get a price reduction. By guaranteeing that she would buy at least 30 roses per week, she was able to convince the local florist to match her current cost of $2.00 per rose. The local florist agreed that she could make purchases in batches of any size so long as the total amounted to at least 30 per week. Under this arrangement, Paula was able to buy roses *just in time* to meet customer demand. Each day she purchased a small number of flowers. When she ran out, she simply returned to the florist for additional ones.

The JIT system also enabled Paula to eliminate the cost of the *nonvalue-added activity* of driving to her former florist. Customer satisfaction actually improved because no one was ever turned away because of the lack of inventory. In June, Paula was able to buy and sell 310 roses with no waste and no driving expense. The June income statement is shown in Exhibit 10.16.

At **Ford Motor Company's** plant in Valencia, Spain, suppliers feed parts such as these bumpers just in time and in the right order directly to the assembly line.

Paula was ecstatic about her $115 increase in profitability ($310 in June − $195 in May = $115 increase), but she was puzzled about the exact reasons for the change. She had saved $40 (20 flowers × $2 each) by avoiding waste and eliminated $45 of driving expenses. These two factors explained only $85 ($40 waste + $45 driving expense) of the $115 increase. What had caused the remaining $30 ($115 − $85) increase in profitability? Paula asked her accounting professor to help her identify the remaining $30 difference.

The professor explained that May sales had suffered from *lost opportunities.* Recall that under the earlier inventory system, Paula had to turn away some prospective customers because she sold out of flowers before all customers were served. Sales increased from 280 roses in May to 310 roses in June. A likely explanation for the 30 unit difference (310 − 280) is that customers who would have purchased flowers in May were unable to do so because of a lack of availability. May's sales suffered from the lost opportunity to earn a gross margin of $1 per flower on 30 roses, a $30 **opportunity cost.** This opportunity cost is the missing link in explaining the profitability difference between May and June. The total $115 difference consists of (1) $40 savings from waste elimination, (2) $45 savings from eliminating driving expense, and (3) opportunity cost of $30. The subject of opportunity cost has widespread application and is discussed in more depth in subsequent chapters of the text.

CHECK YOURSELF 10.4

A strike at a General Motors brake plant caused an almost immediate shutdown of many of the company's assembly plants. What could have caused such a rapid and widespread shutdown?

Answer   A rapid and widespread shutdown could have occurred because General Motors uses a just-in-time inventory system. With a just-in-time inventory system, there is no stockpile of inventory to draw on when strikes or other forces disrupt inventory deliveries. This illustrates a potential negative effect of using a just-in-time inventory system.

STATEMENT OF ETHICAL PROFESSIONAL PRACTICE

LO 10-5

Identify the standards contained in IMA's Statement of Ethical Professional Practice.

There are several conflicts of interest management accountants might face. It is tempting to misclassify a cost if doing so will significantly increase a manager's bonus. Management accountants must be prepared not only to make difficult choices between legitimate alternatives but also to face conflicts of a more troubling nature, such as pressure to:

1. Undertake duties they have not been trained to perform competently.
2. Disclose confidential information.
3. Compromise their integrity through falsification, embezzlement, bribery, and so on.
4. Issue biased, misleading, or incomplete reports.

To provide management accountants with guidance for ethical conduct, the Institute of Management Accountants (IMA) issued a *Statement of Ethical Professional Practice,* which is shown in Exhibit 10.17. Management accountants are also frequently required to abide by organizational codes of ethics. Failure to adhere to professional and organizational ethical standards can lead to personal disgrace, loss of employment, or imprisonment.

FOCUS ON INTERNATIONAL ISSUES

FINANCIAL ACCOUNTING VERSUS MANAGERIAL ACCOUNTING—AN INTERNATIONAL PERSPECTIVE

This chapter has already explained some of the conceptual differences between financial and managerial accounting, but these differences have implications for international businesses as well. With respect to financial accounting, publicly traded companies in most countries must follow the generally accepted accounting principles (GAAP) for their country, but these rules can vary from country to country. Generally, companies that are audited under the auditing standards of the United States follow the standards established by the Financial Accounting Standards Board. Most companies located outside of the United States follow the standards established by the International Accounting Standards Board (IASB). For example, the United States is one of very few countries whose GAAP allow the use of the LIFO inventory cost flow assumption.

Conversely, most of the managerial accounting concepts introduced in this course can be used by businesses in any country. For example, while accrual-based earnings can differ depending on whether a company uses U.S. GAAP or IFRS, cash flow will not. As you will learn, managerial accounting decisions often focus on cash flow versus accrual-based income. Therefore, managerial accounting concepts are more universal than financial accounting rules.

EXHIBIT 10.17

Statement of Ethical Professional Practice

Members of IMA shall behave ethically. A commitment to ethical professional practice includes overarching principles that express our values, and standards that guide our conduct. IMA's overarching ethical principles include: Honesty, Fairness, Objectivity, and Responsibility. Members shall act in accordance with these principles and shall encourage others within their organizations to adhere to them. A member's failure to comply with the following standards may result in disciplinary action.

Competence Each member has a responsibility to
- Maintain an appropriate level of professional expertise by continually developing knowledge and skills.
- Perform professional duties in accordance with relevant laws, regulations, and technical standards.
- Provide decision support information and recommendations that are accurate, clear, concise, and timely.
- Recognize and communicate professional limitations or other constraints that would preclude responsible judgment or successful performance of an activity.

Confidentiality Each member has a responsibility to
- Keep information confidential except when disclosure is authorized or legally required.
- Inform all relevant parties regarding appropriate use of confidential information. Monitor subordinates' activities to ensure compliance.
- Refrain from using confidential information for unethical or illegal advantage.

Integrity Each member has a responsibility to
- Mitigate actual conflicts of interest and avoid apparent conflicts of interest. Advise all parties of any potential conflicts.
- Refrain from engaging in any conduct that would prejudice carrying out duties ethically.
- Abstain from engaging in or supporting any activity that might discredit the profession.

Credibility Each member has a responsibility to
- Communicate information fairly and objectively.
- Disclose all relevant information that could reasonably be expected to influence an intended user's understanding of the reports, analyses, or recommendations.
- Disclose delays or deficiencies in information, timeliness, processing, or internal controls in conformance with organization policy and/or applicable law.

Resolution of Ethical Conflict In applying these standards, you may encounter problems identifying unethical behavior or resolving an ethical conflict. When faced with ethical issues, follow your organization's established policies on the resolution of such conflict. If these policies do not resolve the ethical conflict, consider the following courses of action:
- Discuss the issue with your immediate supervisor except when it appears that the supervisor is involved. In that case, present the issue to the next level. If you cannot achieve a satisfactory resolution, submit the issue to the next management level. Communication of such problems to authorities or individuals not employed or engaged by the organization is not considered appropriate, unless you believe there is a clear violation of the law.
- Clarify relevant ethical issues by initiating a confidential discussion with an IMA Ethics Counselor or other impartial advisor to obtain a better understanding of possible courses of action.
- Consult your own attorney as to legal obligations and rights concerning the ethical conflict.

REALITY BYTES

Unethical behavior occurs in all types of organizations. In its **2011 National Business Ethics Survey**, the Ethics Resource Center reported its findings of the occurrences and reporting of unethical behavior in American corporations based on a survey of over 4,600 employees.

Forty-five percent of those surveyed reported having observed unethical conduct during the past year. This was the lowest level reported in the 17 years the survey has been conducted. Sixty-five percent of those who said they had observed misconduct went on to report it to their employer. However, fear of retaliation for reporting misconduct was a concern. Of respondents who said they had reported misconduct at their companies, 22 percent said they had experienced some form of retaliation, such as being excluded from decision making.

The definition of ethical misconduct used in the study was quite broad. The five most frequently reported types of misconduct were: misuse of company time, abusive behavior, abusing company resources, lying to employees, and violating the company's policies for using the Internet.

For the complete *2011 National Business Ethics Survey,* go to www.ethics.org.

<<   A Look Back

Managerial accounting focuses on the information needs of *internal* users, while *financial accounting* focuses on the information needs of *external* users. Managerial accounting uses economic, operating, and nonfinancial, as well as financial, data. Managerial accounting information is local (pertains to the company's subunits), is limited by cost/benefit considerations, is more concerned with relevance and timeliness, and is future-oriented. Financial accounting information, on the other hand, is more global than managerial accounting information. It supplies information that applies to the whole company. Financial accounting is regulated by numerous authorities, is characterized by objectivity, is focused on reliability and accuracy, and is historical in nature.

Both managerial and financial accounting are concerned with product costing. Financial accountants need product cost information to determine the amount of inventory reported on the balance sheet and the amount of cost of goods sold reported on the income statement. Managerial accountants need to know the cost of products for pricing decisions and for control and evaluation purposes. When determining unit product costs, managers use the average cost per unit. Determining the actual cost of each product requires an unreasonable amount of time and record keeping and it makes no difference in product pricing and product cost control decisions.

Product costs are the costs incurred to make products: the costs of direct materials, direct labor, and overhead. *Overhead costs* are product costs that cannot be cost effectively traced to a product; therefore, they are assigned to products using *cost allocation.* Overhead costs include indirect materials, indirect labor, depreciation, rent, and utilities for manufacturing facilities. Product costs are first accumulated in an asset account (Inventory). They are expensed as cost of goods sold in the period the inventory is sold. The difference between sales revenue and cost of goods sold is called *gross margin.*

Selling, general, and administrative costs are classified separately from product costs. They are subtracted from gross margin to determine net income. Selling, general, and administrative costs can be divided into two categories. Costs incurred before the manufacturing process begins (research and development costs) are *upstream costs.* Costs incurred after manufacturing is complete (transportation) are *downstream costs.*

Service companies, like manufacturing companies, incur materials, labor, and overhead costs, but the products provided by service companies are consumed immediately. Therefore, service company product costs are not accumulated in an Inventory account.

A *code of ethical conduct* is needed in the accounting profession because accountants hold positions of trust and face conflicts of interest. In recognition of the temptations that accountants face, the IMA has issued a *Statement of Ethical Professional Practice,* which provides accountants guidance in resisting temptations and in making difficult decisions.

Emerging trends such as *just-in-time inventory* and *activity-based management* are methods that many companies have used to reengineer their production and delivery systems to eliminate waste, reduce errors, and minimize costs. Activity-based management seeks to eliminate or reduce *nonvalue-added activities* and to create new *value-added activities.* Just-in-time inventory seeks to reduce inventory holding costs and to lower prices for customers by making inventory available just in time for customer consumption.

>>   A Look Forward

In addition to distinguishing costs by product versus SG&A classification, other classifications can be used to facilitate managerial decision making. In the next chapter, costs are classified according to the *behavior* they exhibit when the number of units of product increases or decreases (volume of activity changes). You will learn to distinguish between costs that vary with activity volume changes versus costs that remain fixed with activity volume changes. You will learn not only to recognize *cost behavior* but also how to use such recognition to evaluate business risk and opportunity.

APPENDIX

Emerging Trends in Managerial Accounting

Global competition has forced many companies to reengineer their production and delivery systems to eliminate waste, reduce errors, and minimize costs. A key ingredient of successful **reengineering** is benchmarking. **Benchmarking** involves identifying the **best practices** used by world-class competitors. By studying and mimicking these practices, a company uses benchmarking to implement highly effective and efficient operating methods. Best practices employed by world-class companies include total quality management (TQM), activity-based management (ABM), and value-added assessment.

> **LO 10-6**
>
> Identify emerging trends in accounting.

Total Quality Management

To promote effective and efficient operations, many companies practice **total quality management (TQM).** TQM is a two-dimensional management philosophy using (1) a systematic problem-solving philosophy that encourages frontline workers to achieve *zero defects* and (2) an organizational commitment to achieving *customer satisfaction.* A key component of TQM is **continuous improvement,** an ongoing process through which employees strive to eliminate waste, reduce response time, minimize defects, and simplify the design and delivery of products and services to customers.

Activity-Based Management

Simple changes in perspective can have dramatic results. For example, imagine how realizing the world is round instead of flat changed the nature of travel. A recent change in perspective developing in management accounting is the realization that an organization cannot manage *costs.* Instead, it manages the *activities* that cause costs to be incurred. **Activities** represent the measures an organization takes to accomplish its goals.

The primary goal of all organizations is to provide products (goods and services) their customers *value.* The sequence of activities used to provide products is called a **value chain. Activity-based management** assesses the value chain to create new or refine existing **value-added activities** and to eliminate or reduce *nonvalue-added activities.* A value-added activity is any unit of work that contributes to a product's ability to satisfy customer needs. For example, cooking is an activity that adds value to food served to a hungry customer. **Nonvalue-added activities** are tasks undertaken that do not contribute to a product's ability to satisfy customer needs. Waiting for the oven to preheat so that food can be cooked does not add value. Most customers value cooked food, but they do not value waiting for it.

To illustrate, consider the value-added activities undertaken by a pizza restaurant. Begin with a customer who is hungry for pizza; certain activities must occur to satisfy that hunger. These activities are pictured in Exhibit 10.18. At a minimum, the restaurant must conduct research and development (devise a recipe), obtain raw materials (acquire the ingredients), manufacture the product (combine and bake the ingredients), market the product (advertise its availability), and deliver the product (transfer the pizza to the customer).

Businesses gain competitive advantages by adding activities that satisfy customer needs. For example, Domino's Pizza grew briskly by recognizing the value customers placed on the convenience of home pizza delivery. Alternatively, Little Caesar's has been highly successful by satisfying customers who value low prices. Other restaurants capitalize on customer values pertaining to taste, ambience, or location. Businesses can

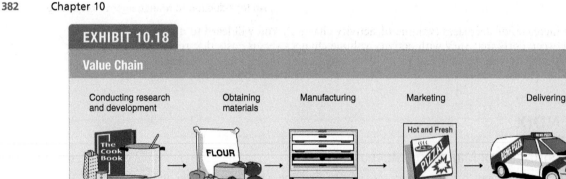

| EXHIBIT 10.18 |
| Value Chain |

Conducting research and development → Obtaining materials → Manufacturing → Marketing → Delivering

also gain competitive advantages by identifying and eliminating nonvalue-added activities, providing products of comparable quality at lower cost than competitors.

Value Chain Analysis across Companies

Comprehensive value chain analysis extends from obtaining raw materials to the ultimate disposition of finished products. It encompasses the activities performed not only by a particular organization but also by that organization's suppliers and those who service its finished products. For example, PepsiCo must be concerned with the activities of the company that supplies the containers for its soft drinks as well as the retail companies that sell its products. If cans of Pepsi fail to open properly, the customer is more likely to blame PepsiCo than the supplier of the cans. Comprehensive value chain analysis can lead to identifying and eliminating nonvalue-added activities that occur between companies. For example, container producers could be encouraged to build manufacturing facilities near Pepsi's bottling factories, eliminating the nonvalue-added activity of transporting empty containers from the manufacturer to the bottling facility. The resulting cost savings benefits customers by reducing costs without affecting quality.

 Video lectures and accompanying self-assessment quizzes are available for all learning objectives through McGraw-Hill *Connect® Accounting.*

SELF-STUDY REVIEW PROBLEM

Tuscan Manufacturing Company makes a unique headset for use with mobile phones. The company had the following amounts in its accounts at the beginning of 2015: Cash, $795,000; Raw Materials Inventory, $5,000; Work in Process Inventory, $11,000; Finished Goods Inventory, $39,000; Common Stock, $650,000; and Retained Earnings, $200,000. Tuscan experienced the following accounting events during 2015. Other than the adjusting entries for depreciation, assume that all transactions are cash transactions.

1. Paid $50,000 of research and development costs to create the headset.
2. Paid $139,000 for raw materials that will be used to make headsets.
3. Placed $141,000 of the raw materials cost into the process of manufacturing headsets.
4. Paid $82,200 for salaries of selling and administrative employees.
5. Paid $224,000 for wages of production workers.
6. Paid $48,000 to purchase furniture used in selling and administrative offices.
7. Recognized depreciation on the office furniture. The furniture was acquired January 1, 2015. It has an $8,000 salvage value and a four-year useful life. The amount of depreciation is computed as [(cost − salvage) ÷ useful life]. Specifically, ($48,000 − $8,000) ÷ 4 = $10,000.
8. Paid $65,000 to purchase manufacturing equipment.

9. Recognized depreciation on the manufacturing equipment. The equipment was acquired January 1, 2015. It has a $5,000 salvage value and a three-year useful life. The amount of depreciation is computed as [(cost − salvage) ÷ useful life]. Specifically, ($65,000 − $5,000) ÷ 3 = $20,000.

10. Paid $136,000 for rent and utility costs on the manufacturing facility.

11. Paid $41,000 for inventory holding expenses for completed headsets (rental of warehouse space, salaries of warehouse personnel, and other general storage costs).

12. Completed and transferred headsets that had a total cost of $520,000 from work in process inventory to finished goods.

13. Sold headsets for $738,200.

14. It cost Tuscan $517,400 to make the headsets sold in Event 13.

Required

a. Show how these events affect the balance sheet, income statement, and statement of cash flows by recording them in a horizontal financial statement model.

b. Explain why Tuscan's recognition of cost of goods sold expense had no impact on cash flow.

c. Prepare a schedule of costs of goods manufactured and sold, an income statement, and a balance sheet.

d. Distinguish between the product costs and the upstream and downstream costs that Tuscan incurred.

Solution to Requirement a

Event No.	Cash +	Raw Mat. Inv. +	WIP Inv. +	Finished Goods Inv. +	Office Furn.* +	Manuf. Equip.* =	Com. Stk. +	Ret. Earn.	Rev. −	Exp. = Net Inc.	Cash Flow
	795,000	5,000	11,000	39,000		=	650,000	200,000		=	
1	(50,000)					=		(50,000)		− 50,000 = (50,000)	(50,000) OA
2	(139,000)	139,000				=				=	(139,000) OA
3		(141,000)	141,000			=				=	
4	(82,200)					=		(82,200)		− 82,200 = (82,200)	(82,200) OA
5	(224,000)		224,000			=				=	(224,000) OA
6	(48,000)				48,000	=				=	(48,000) IA
7					(10,000)	=		(10,000)		− 10,000 = (10,000)	
8	(65,000)					65,000 =				=	(65,000) IA
9			20,000			(20,000) =				=	
10	(136,000)		136,000			=				=	(136,000) OA
11	(41,000)					=		(41,000)		− 41,000 = (41,000)	(41,000) OA
12			(520,000)	520,000		=				=	
13	738,200					=		738,200	738,200	= 738,200	738,200 OA
14				(517,400)		=		(517,400)		− 517,400 = (517,400)	
Totals	748,000 +	3,000 +	12,000 +	41,600 +	38,000 +	45,000 =	650,000 +	237,600	738,200 −	700,600 = 37,600	(47,000) NC

*Negative amounts in these columns represent accumulated depreciation.

Solution to Requirement b

Tuscan does not recognize a cash outflow at the time the goods are sold because the cash is paid when the materials, labor, and overhead are acquired.

Solution to Requirement *c*

TUSCAN MANUFACTURING COMPANY
Schedule of Cost of Goods Manufactured and Sold
For the Year Ended December 31, 2015

Beginning raw materials inventory	$ 5,000
Plus: Raw materials purchases	139,000
Less: Ending raw materials inventory	(3,000)
Raw materials used	141,000
Labor	224,000
Overhead	156,000
Total manufacturing costs	521,000
Plus: Beginning work in process inventory	11,000
Total work in process inventory	532,000
Less: Ending work in process inventory	(12,000)
Cost of goods manufactured	520,000
Plus: Beginning finished goods inventory	39,000
Cost of goods available for sale	559,000
Less: Ending finished goods inventory	(41,600)
Cost of goods sold	$517,400

TUSCAN MANUFACTURING COMPANY
Income Statement
For the Year Ended December 31, 2015

Sales revenue	$738,200
Cost of goods sold	(517,400)
Gross margin	220,800
Research and development expenses	(50,000)
Selling and administrative salary expense	(82,200)
Selling and administrative depreciation expense	(10,000)
Inventory holding expenses	(41,000)
Net Income	$ 37,600

TUSCAN MANUFACTURING COMPANY
Balance Sheet
As of December 31, 2015

Assets	
Cash	$748,000
Raw materials inventory	3,000
Work in process inventory	12,000
Finished goods inventory	41,600
Manufacturing equipment less accumulated depreciation	45,000
Office furniture less accumulated depreciation	38,000
Total assets	$887,600
Equity	
Common stock	$650,000
Retained earnings	237,600
Total stockholders' equity	$887,600

Solution to Requirement *d*

Inventory product costs for manufacturing companies focus on the costs necessary to make the product. The cost of research and development (Event 1) occurs before the inventory is made and is therefore an upstream cost, not an inventory (product) cost. The inventory holding costs (Event 11) are incurred after the inventory has been made and are therefore downstream costs, not product costs. Selling costs (included in Events 4 and 7) are normally incurred after products have been made and are therefore usually classified as downstream costs. Administrative costs (also included in Events 4 and 7) are not related to making products and are therefore not classified as product costs. Administrative costs may be incurred before, during, or after products are made, so they may be classified as either upstream or downstream costs. Only the costs of materials, labor, and overhead that are actually incurred for the purpose of making goods (Events 3, 5, 9, and 10) are classified as product costs.

KEY TERMS

Activities 381
Activity-based management (ABM) 381
Average cost 366
Benchmarking 381
Best practices 381
Continuous improvement 381
Cost allocation 372
Cost-plus pricing 365
Direct labor 369
Direct raw materials 369
Downstream costs 375

Financial accounting 362
Financial Accounting Standards Board (FASB) 365
Finished Goods Inventory 374
Generally acceptable accounting principles (GAAP) 365
Indirect costs 371
Inventory holding costs 376
Just in time (JIT) 376
Managerial accounting 362

Manufacturing overhead 371
Nonvalue-added activities 381
Opportunity cost 377
Overhead 366
Period costs 371
Product costing 365
Product costs 365
Raw materials 369
Raw Materials Inventory 374
Reengineering 381
Schedule of cost of goods manufactured and sold 374

Securities and Exchange Commission (SEC) 365
Selling, general, and administrative costs 371
Total quality management (TQM) 381
Upstream costs 375
Value-added activity 381
Value-added principle 365
Value chain 381
Work in Process Inventory 374

QUESTIONS

1. What are some differences between financial and managerial accounting?

2. What does the value-added principle mean as it applies to managerial accounting information? Give an example of value-added information that may be included in managerial accounting reports but is not shown in publicly reported financial statements.

3. How does product costing used in financial accounting differ from product costing used in managerial accounting?

4. What does the statement "costs can be assets or expenses" mean?

5. Why are the salaries of production workers accumulated in an inventory account instead of being directly expensed on the income statement?

6. How do product costs affect the financial statements? How does the classification of product cost (as an asset vs. an expense) affect net income?

7. What is an indirect cost? Provide examples of product costs that would be classified as indirect.

8. How does a product cost differ from a general, selling, and administrative cost? Give examples of each.

9. Why is cost classification important to managers?

10. What is cost allocation? Give an example of a cost that needs to be allocated.

11. What are some of the common ethical conflicts that accountants encounter?

12. What costs should be considered in determining the sales price of a product?

13. What is a just-in-time (JIT) inventory system? Name some inventory costs that can be eliminated or reduced by its use.

14. What are the two dimensions of a total quality management (TQM) program? Why is TQM being used in business practice? (Appendix)

15. How has the Institute of Management Accountants responded to the need for high standards of ethical conduct in the accounting profession?

16. What does the term *reengineering* mean? Name some reengineering practices. (Appendix)

17. What does the term *activity-based management* mean? (Appendix)

18. What is a value chain? (Appendix)

19. What do the terms *value-added activity* and *nonvalue-added activity* mean? Provide an example of each type of activity. (Appendix)

MULTIPLE-CHOICE QUESTIONS

Multiple-choice questions are provided on the text website at www.mhhe.com/edmondssurvey4e.

EXERCISES

connect |ACCOUNTING   All applicable Exercises are available with McGraw-Hill *Connect® Accounting.*

LO 10-1

Exercise 10-1   *Identifying financial versus managerial accounting items*

Required

Indicate whether each of the following items is representative of managerial or of financial accounting.

a. Information is based on estimates that are bounded by relevance and timeliness.
b. Information is historically based and usually reported annually.
c. Information is local and pertains to subunits of the organization.
d. Information includes economic and nonfinancial data as well as financial data.
e. Information is global and pertains to the company as a whole.
f. Information is provided to insiders, including executives, managers, and employees.
g. Information is factual and is characterized by objectivity, reliability, consistency, and accuracy.
h. Information is reported continuously and has a current or future orientation.
i. Information is provided to outsiders, including investors, creditors, government agencies, analysts, and reporters.
j. Information is regulated by the SEC, FASB, and other sources of GAAP.

LO 10-2

Exercise 10-2   *Identifying product versus general, selling, and administrative costs*

Required

Indicate whether each of the following costs should be classified as a product cost or as a selling, general, and administrative cost.

a. Interest on the mortgage for the company's corporate headquarters.
b. Indirect labor used to manufacture inventory.
c. Attorney's fees paid to protect the company from frivolous lawsuits.
d. Research and development costs incurred to create new drugs for a pharmaceutical company.
e. The cost of secretarial supplies used in a doctor's office.
f. Depreciation on the office furniture of the company president.
g. Direct materials used in a manufacturing company.
h. Indirect materials used in a manufacturing company.
i. Salaries of employees working in the accounting department.
j. Commissions paid to sales staff.

LO 10-2

Exercise 10-3   *Classifying costs: Product or SG&A cost; asset or expense*

Required

Use the following format to classify each cost as a product cost or a selling, general, and administrative (SG&A) cost. Also indicate whether the cost would be recorded as an asset or an expense. The first item is shown as an example.

Cost Category	Product/SG&A	Asset/Expense
Utilities used in manufacturing facility	Product	Asset
Cars for sales staff		
Real estate tax levied on a factory		
General office supplies		
Raw materials used in the manufacturing process		
Cost to rent office equipment		
Wages of production workers		
Advertising costs		
Promotion costs		
Production supplies		
Depreciation on administration building		
Depreciation on manufacturing equipment		
Research and development costs		
Cost to set up manufacturing equipment		

Exercise 10-4   Identifying effect of product versus selling, general, and administrative costs on financial statements

LO 10-2

Required

Ames Corporation recognized accrued compensation cost. Use the following model to show how this event would affect the company's financial statements under the following two assumptions: (1) the compensation is for office personnel and (2) the compensation is for production workers. Use pluses or minuses to show the effect on each element. If an element is not affected, indicate so by placing the letters NA under the appropriate heading.

	Assets	=	Liab.	+	Equity	Rev.	−	Exp.	=	Net Inc.	Cash Flow
1.											
2.											

Exercise 10-5   Identify effect of product versus selling, general, and administrative costs on financial statements

LO 10-2

Required

Taft Industries recognized the annual cost of depreciation on its December 31, 2015, financial statements. Using the following horizontal financial statements model, indicate how this event affected the company's financial statements under the following two assumptions: (1) the depreciation was on office furniture and (2) the depreciation was on manufacturing equipment. Indicate whether the event increases (I), decreases (D), or has no effect (NA) on each element of the financial statements. Also, in the Cash Flow column, indicate whether the cash flow is for operating activities (OA), investing activities (IA), or financing activities (FA). (Note: Show accumulated depreciation as a decrease in the book value of the appropriate asset account.)

Event No.			Assets						Equity							
	Cash	+	Inventory	+	Manuf. Equip.	+	Office Furn.	=	Com. Stk.	+	Ret. Ear.	Rev.	−	Exp.	=	Net Inc.	Cash Flow
1.																
2.																

LO 10-2

Exercise 10-6 *Identifying product costs in a manufacturing company*

Jessica Hansen was talking to another accounting student, Adam Ruud. Upon discovering that the accounting department offered an upper-level course in cost measurement, Jessica remarked to Adam, "How difficult can it be? My parents own a toy store. All you have to do to figure out how much something costs is look at the invoice. Surely you don't need an entire course to teach you how to read an invoice."

Required

a. Identify the three main components of product cost for a manufacturing entity.

b. Explain why measuring product cost for a manufacturing entity is more complex than measuring product cost for a retail toy store.

c. Assume that Jessica's parents rent a store for $7,500 per month. Different types of toys use different amounts of store space. For example, displaying a bicycle requires more store space than displaying a deck of cards. Also, some toys remain on the shelf longer than others. Fad toys sell rapidly, but traditional toys sell more slowly. Under these circumstances, how would you determine the amount of rental cost required to display each type of toy? Identify two other costs incurred by a toy store that may be difficult to allocate to individual toys.

LO 10-2

Exercise 10-7 *Identifying product versus selling, general, and administrative costs*

A review of the accounting records of Spiller Manufacturing indicated that the company incurred the following payroll costs during the month of September.

1. Salary of the company president—$40,000.
2. Salary of the vice president of manufacturing—$25,000.
3. Salary of the chief financial officer—$20,000.
4. Salary of the vice president of marketing—$18,000.
5. Salaries of middle managers (department heads, production supervisors) in manufacturing plant—$196,000.
6. Wages of production workers—$938,000.
7. Salaries of administrative secretaries—$60,000.
8. Salaries of engineers and other personnel responsible for maintaining production equipment—$178,000.
9. Commissions paid to sales staff—$252,000.

Required

a. What amount of payroll cost would be classified as selling, general, and administrative expense?

b. Assuming that Spiller made 4,000 units of product and sold 3,600 of them during the month of September, determine the amount of payroll cost that would be included in cost of goods sold.

LO 10-2

Exercise 10-8 *Recording product versus selling, general, and administrative costs in a financial statements model*

Naoki Manufacturing experienced the following events during its first accounting period.

1. Recognized depreciation on manufacturing equipment.
2. Recognized depreciation on office furniture.
3. Recognized revenue from cash sale of products.
4. Recognized cost of goods sold from sale referenced in Event 3.
5. Acquired cash by issuing common stock.
6. Paid cash to purchase raw materials that were used to make products.
7. Paid wages to production workers.
8. Paid salaries to administrative staff.

Required

Use the following horizontal financial statements model to show how each event affects the balance sheet, income statement, and the statement of cash flows. Indicate whether the event increases (I), decreases (D), or has no effect (NA) on each element of the financial statements. Also, in the Cash Flow column, indicate whether the cash flow is for operating activities (OA), investing activities (IA), or financing activities (FA). The first transaction has been recorded as an example. (*Note:* Show accumulated depreciation as a decrease in the book value of the appropriate asset account.)

Event No.			Assets					Equity							
	Cash	+	Inventory	+	Manuf. Equip.	+	Office Furn.	=	Com. Stk.	+	Ret. Ear.	Rev.	−	Exp.	=	Net Inc.	Cash Flow
1.	NA		I		D		NA		NA		NA	NA		NA		NA	NA

Exercise 10-9 *Allocating product costs between ending inventory and cost of goods sold*

LO 10-2

Santiago Manufacturing Company began operations on January 1. During the year, it started and completed 2,000 units of product. The company incurred the following costs.

1. Raw materials purchased and used—$4,700.
2. Wages of production workers—$5,100.
3. Salaries of administrative and sales personnel—$2,600.
4. Depreciation on manufacturing equipment—$3,800.
5. Depreciation on administrative equipment—$1,900.

Santiago sold 1,650 units of product.

Required

a. Determine the total product cost for the year.
b. Determine the total cost of the ending inventory.
c. Determine the total of cost of goods sold.

Exercise 10-10 *Financial statement effects for manufacturing versus service organizations*

LO 10-2

The following financial statements model shows the effects of recognizing depreciation in two different circumstances. One circumstance represents recognizing depreciation on a machine used in a factory. The other circumstance recognizes depreciation on computers used in a consulting firm. The effects of each event have been recorded using the letter (I) for increase, (D) for decrease, and (NA) for no effect.

Event No.			Assets				Equity							
	Cash	+	Inventory	+	Equip.	=	Com. Stk.	+	Ret. Ear.	Rev.	−	Exp.	=	Net Inc.	Cash Flow
1.	NA		NA		D		NA		D	NA		I		D	NA
2.	NA		I		D		NA		NA	NA		NA		NA	NA

Required

a. Identify the event that represents depreciation on the computers.
b. Explain why recognizing depreciation on equipment used in a manufacturing company affects financial statements differently than recognizing depreciation on equipment used in a service organization.

LO 10-2

Exercise 10-11 *Identifying the effect of product versus selling, general, and administrative cost on the income statement*

Each of the following events describes acquiring an asset that requires a year-end adjusting entry.

1. Paid $27,000 cash on January 1 to purchase computer equipment to be used for administrative purposes. The equipment had an estimated expected useful life of five years and a $2,000 salvage value.
2. Paid $27,000 cash on January 1 to purchase manufacturing equipment. The equipment had an estimated expected useful life of five years and a $2,000 salvage value.
3. Paid $12,000 cash in advance on May 1 for a one-year rental contract on administrative offices.
4. Paid $12,000 cash in advance on May 1 for a one-year rental contract on manufacturing facilities.
5. Paid $2,000 cash to purchase supplies to be used by the marketing department. At the end of the year, $400 of supplies was still on hand.
6. Paid $2,000 cash to purchase supplies to be used in the manufacturing process. At the end of the year, $400 of supplies was still on hand.

Required

Explain how the adjusting entry affects the amount of net income shown on the year-end financial statements. Assume a December 31 annual closing date. Also, in the Cash Flow column, indicate whether the cash flow is for operating activities (OA), investing activities (IA), or financing activities (FA). The first event has been recorded as an example. Assume that any products that have been made have not been sold.

	Net Income	Cash Flow
Event No.	**Amount of Change**	**Amount of Change**
1. Adjusting entry	$(5,000)	NA

LO 10-3

Exercise 10-12 *Missing information in a schedule of cost of goods manufactured*

Required

Supply the missing information on the following schedule of cost of goods manufactured.

FISCHER CORPORATION
Schedule of Cost of Goods Manufactured
For the Year Ended December 31, 2014

Raw materials		
Beginning inventory	$?	
Plus: Purchases	120,000	
Raw materials available for use	$148,000	
Minus: Ending raw materials inventory	?	
Cost of direct raw materials used		$124,000
Direct labor		?
Manufacturing overhead		24,000
Total manufacturing costs		324,000
Plus: Beginning work in process inventory		?
Total work in process		?
Minus: Ending work in process inventory		46,000
Cost of goods manufactured		$320,000

Exercise 10-13 *Cost of goods manufactured and sold*   LO 10-3

The following information pertains to Flaxman Manufacturing Company for March 2015. Assume actual overhead equaled applied overhead.

March 1	
Inventory balances	
Raw materials	$100,000
Work in process	120,000
Finished goods	78,000
March 31	
Inventory balances	
Raw materials	$ 60,000
Work in process	145,000
Finished goods	80,000
During March	
Costs of raw materials purchased	$120,000
Costs of direct labor	100,000
Costs of manufacturing overhead	63,000
Sales revenues	380,000

Required

a. Prepare a schedule of cost of goods manufactured and sold.

b. Calculate the amount of gross margin on the income statement.

Exercise 10-14 *Upstream and downstream costs*   LO 10-2

During 2014, Welch Manufacturing Company incurred $67,000,000 of research and development (R&D) costs to create a long-life battery to use in computers. In accordance with FASB standards, the entire R&D cost was recognized as an expense in 2014. Manufacturing costs (direct materials, direct labor, and overhead) are expected to be $250 per unit. Packaging, shipping, and sales commissions are expected to be $50 per unit. Welch expects to sell 2,000,000 batteries before new research renders the battery design technologically obsolete. During 2014, Welch made 440,000 batteries and sold 400,000 of them.

Required

a. Identify the upstream and downstream costs.

b. Determine the 2014 amount of cost of goods sold and the ending inventory balance.

c. Determine the sales price assuming that Welch desires to earn a profit margin that is equal to 25 percent of the *total cost* of developing, making, and distributing the batteries.

d. Prepare an income statement for 2014. Use the sales price developed in Requirement *c.*

e. Why would Welch price the batteries at a level that would generate a loss for the 2014 accounting period?

Exercise 10-15 *Using JIT to minimize waste and lost opportunity*   LO 10-4

Kate Connor, a teacher at Meadow Middle School, is in charge of ordering the T-shirts to be sold for the school's annual fund-raising project. The T-shirts are printed with a special Meadow School logo. In some years, the supply of T-shirts has been insufficient to satisfy the number of sales orders. In other years, T-shirts have been left over. Excess T-shirts are normally donated to some charitable organization. T-shirts cost the school $7 each and are normally sold for $15 each. Ms. Connor has decided to order 800 shirts.

Required

a. If the school receives actual sales orders for 725 shirts, what amount of profit will the school earn? What is the cost of waste due to excess inventory?

b. If the school receives actual sales orders for 825 shirts, what amount of profit will the school earn? What amount of opportunity cost will the school incur?

c. Explain how a JIT inventory system could maximize profitability by eliminating waste and opportunity cost.

LO 10-4

Exercise 10-16   *Using JIT to minimize holding costs*

Ray Pet Supplies purchases its inventory from a variety of suppliers, some of which require a six-week lead time before delivering the goods. To ensure that she has a sufficient supply of goods on hand, Ms. Jelavich, the owner, must maintain a large supply of inventory. The cost of this inventory averages $46,000. She usually finances the purchase of inventory and pays an 8 percent annual finance charge. Ms. Jelavich's accountant has suggested that she establish a relationship with a single large distributor who can satisfy all of her orders within a two-week time period. Given this quick turnaround time, she will be able to reduce her average inventory balance to $4,000. Ms. Jelavich also believes that she could save $5,600 per year by reducing phone bills, insurance, and warehouse rental space costs associated with ordering and maintaining the larger level of inventory.

Required

a. Is the new inventory system available to Ms. Jelavich a pure or approximate just-in-time system?

b. Based on the information provided, how much of Ms. Jelavich's inventory holding cost could be eliminated by taking the accountant's advice?

LO 10-5

Exercise 10-17   *Professional conduct and code of ethics*

In February 2006, former senator Warren Rudman of New Hampshire completed a 17-month investigation of an $11 billion accounting scandal at Fannie Mae (a major enterprise involved in home mortgage financing). The Rudman investigation concluded that Fannie Mae's CFO and controller used an accounting gimmick to manipulate financial statements in order to meet earnings-per-share (EPS) targets. Meeting the EPS targets triggered bonus payments for the executives. Fannie Mae's problems continued after 2006, and on September 8, 2008, it went into conservatorship under the control of the Federal Housing Financing Agency. The primary executives at the time of the Rudman investigation were replaced, and the enterprise reported a $59.8 billion loss in 2008. By June 2012, the federal government had spent $170 million to assist Fannie Mae as a result of mismanagement.

Required

Review the statement of ethical professional practice shown in Exhibit 10.17. Identify and comment on which of the ethical principles the CFO and controller violated.

LO 10-6

Exercise 10-18   *Value chain analysis (Appendix)*

Audiomax Company manufactures and sells high-quality audio speakers. The speakers are encased in solid walnut cabinets supplied by Serle Cabinet, Inc. Serle packages the speakers in durable moisture-proof boxes and ships them by truck to Audiomax's manufacturing facility, which is located 50 miles from the cabinet factory.

Required

Identify the nonvalue-added activities that occur between the companies described in the above scenario. Provide a logical explanation as to how these nonvalue-added activities could be eliminated.

PROBLEMS

≡ connect | **All applicable Problems are available with McGraw-Hill**
ACCOUNTING | ***Connect® Accounting.***

Problem 10-19   *Product versus selling, general, and administrative costs*

LO 10-2

Issa Manufacturing Company was started on January 1, 2014, when it acquired $78,000 cash by issuing common stock. Issa immediately purchased office furniture and manufacturing equipment costing $21,000 and $49,000, respectively. The office furniture had a seven-year useful life and a zero salvage value. The manufacturing equipment had a $4,000 salvage value and an expected useful life of five years. The company paid $12,000 for salaries of administrative personnel and $21,000 for wages to production personnel. Finally, the company paid $26,000 for raw materials that were used to make inventory. All inventory was started and completed during the year. Issa completed production on 8,000 units of product and sold 7,200 units at a price of $15 each in 2014. (Assume that all transactions are cash transactions.)

Required

a. Determine the total product cost and the average cost per unit of the inventory produced in 2014.
b. Determine the amount of cost of goods sold that would appear on the 2014 income statement.
c. Determine the amount of the ending inventory balance that would appear on the December 31, 2014, balance sheet.
d. Determine the amount of net income that would appear on the 2014 income statement.
e. Determine the amount of retained earnings that would appear on the December 31, 2014, balance sheet.
f. Determine the amount of total assets that would appear on the December 31, 2014, balance sheet.
g. Determine the amount of net cash flow from operating activities that would appear on the December 31, 2014 statement of cash flows.
h. Determine the amount of net cash flow from investing activities that would appear on the December 31, 2014 statement of cash flows.

Problem 10-20   *Effect of product versus period costs on financial statements*

LO 10-2

Gunn Manufacturing Company experienced the following accounting events during its first year of operation. With the exception of the adjusting entries for depreciation, assume that all transactions are cash transactions.

1. Acquired $80,000 cash by issuing common stock.
2. Paid $9,200 for the materials used to make its products, all of which were started and completed during the year.
3. Paid salaries of $3,800 to selling and administrative employees.
4. Paid wages of $12,000 to production workers.
5. Paid $9,600 for furniture used in selling and administrative offices. The furniture was acquired on January 1. It had a $1,600 estimated salvage value and a four-year useful life.
6. Paid $16,000 for manufacturing equipment. The equipment was acquired on January 1. It had a $1,000 estimated salvage value and a five-year useful life.
7. Sold inventory to customers for $38,000 that had cost $18,000 to make.

Required

Explain how these events would affect the balance sheet, income statement, and statement of cash flows by recording them in a horizontal financial statements model as indicated here. Also, in the Cash Flow column, indicate whether the cash flow is for operating activities

(OA), investing activities (IA), or financing activities (FA). The first event is recorded as an example.

	Financial Statements Model												
	Assets					Equity							
Event No.	Cash	+	Inventory	+	Manuf. Equip.*	+	Office Furn.*	=	Com. Stk.	+	Ret. Ear.	Rev.	−	Exp.	=	Net Inc.	Cash Flow
1.	80,000								80,000							80,000 FA

*Record accumulated depreciation as negative amounts in these columns.

LO 10-2

Problem 10-21   *Product versus selling, general, and administrative costs*

The following transactions pertain to 2015, the first-year operations of Bailey Company. All inventory was started and completed during 2015. Assume that all transactions are cash transactions.

1. Acquired $7,000 cash by issuing common stock.
2. Paid $2,800 for materials used to produce inventory.
3. Paid $1,900 to production workers.
4. Paid $1,300 rental fee for production equipment.
5. Paid $350 to administrative employees.
6. Paid $400 rental fee for administrative office equipment.
7. Produced 500 units of inventory of which 450 units were sold at a price of $17.50 each.

Required

Prepare an income statement, a balance sheet, and statement of cash flows.

LO 10-2

Problem 10-22   *Service versus manufacturing companies*

Lang Company began operations on January 1, 2014, by issuing common stock for $64,000 cash. During 2014, Lang received $95,000 cash from revenue and incurred costs that required $75,000 of cash payments.

Required

Prepare an income statement, a balance sheet, and a statement of cash flows for Lang Company for 2014, under each of the following independent scenarios.

a. Lang is a promoter of rock concerts. The $75,000 was paid to provide a rock concert that produced the revenue.

b. Lang is in the car rental business. The $75,000 was paid to purchase automobiles. The automobiles were purchased on January 1, 2014, and have five-year useful lives, with no expected salvage value. Lang uses straight-line depreciation. The revenue was generated by leasing the automobiles.

c. Lang is a manufacturing company. The $75,000 was paid to purchase the following items:

   (1) Paid $12,000 cash to purchase materials that were used to make products during the year.

   (2) Paid $22,000 cash for wages of factory workers who made products during the year.

   (3) Paid $5,000 cash for salaries of sales and administrative employees.

   (4) Paid $36,000 cash to purchase manufacturing equipment. The equipment was used solely to make products. It had a three-year life and a $6,000 salvage value. The company uses straightline depreciation.

   (5) During 2014, Lang started and completed 2,000 units of product. The revenue was earned when Lang sold 1,500 units of product to its customers.

d. Refer to Requirement *c*. Could Lang determine the actual cost of making the 500th unit of product? How likely is it that the actual cost of the 500th unit of product was exactly the same as the cost of producing the 501st unit of product? Explain why management may be more interested in average cost than in actual cost.

Problem 10-23   *Importance of cost classification*

Naoki Manufacturing Company (NMC) was started when it acquired $50,000 by issuing common stock. During the first year of operations, the company incurred specifically identifiable product costs (materials, labor, and overhead) amounting to $30,000. NMC also incurred $24,000 of engineering design and planning costs. There was a debate regarding how the design and planning costs should be classified. Advocates of Option 1 believe that the costs should be classified as general, selling, and administrative costs. Advocates of Option 2 believe it is more appropriate to classify the design and planning costs as product costs. During the year, NMC made 4,000 units of product and sold 3,000 units at a price of $30 each. All transactions were cash transactions.

Required

a. Prepare an income statement, a balance sheet, and a statement of cash flows under each of the two options.

b. Identify the option that results in financial statements that are more likely to leave a favorable impression on investors and creditors.

c. Assume that NMC provides an incentive bonus to the company president equal to 25 percent of net income. Compute the amount of the bonus under each of the two options. Identify the option that provides the president with the higher bonus.

d. Assume a 35 percent income tax rate. Determine the amount of income tax expense under each of the two options. Identify the option that minimizes the amount of the company's income tax expense.

e. Comment on the conflict of interest between the company president as determined in Requirement *c* and the owners of the company as indicated in Requirement *d*. Describe an incentive compensation plan that would avoid a conflict of interest between the president and the owners.

Problem 10-24   *Schedule of cost of goods manufactured and sold*

Antioch Company makes eBook readers. The company had the following amounts at the beginning of 2014: Cash, $660,000; Raw Materials Inventory, $51,000; Work in Process Inventory, $18,000; Finished Goods Inventory, $43,000; Common Stock, $583,000; and Retained Earnings, $189,000. Antioch experienced the following accounting events during 2014. Other than the adjusting entries for depreciation, assume that all transactions are cash transactions.

1. Paid $23,000 of research and development costs.
2. Paid $47,000 for raw materials that will be used to make eBook readers.
3. Placed $83,000 of the raw materials cost into the process of manufacturing eBook readers.
4. Paid $60,000 for salaries of selling and administrative employees.
5. Paid $91,000 for wages of production workers.
6. Paid $90,000 to purchase equipment used in selling and administrative offices.
7. Recognized depreciation on the office equipment. The equipment was acquired on January, 1, 2014. It has a $10,000 salvage value and a five-year life. The amount of depreciation is computed as [(Cost − salvage) ÷ useful life]. Specifically, ($90,000 − $10,000) ÷ 5 = $16,000.
8. Paid $165,000 to purchase manufacturing equipment.
9. Recognized depreciation on the manufacturing equipment. The equipment was acquired on January 1, 2014. It has a $25,000 salvage value and a seven-year life. The amount of depreciation is computed as [(Cost − salvage) ÷ useful life]. Specifically, ($165,000 − $25,000) ÷ 7 = $20,000.
10. Paid $45,000 for rent and utility costs on the manufacturing facility.

11. Paid $70,000 for inventory holding expenses for completed eBook readers (rental of warehouse space, salaries of warehouse personnel, and other general storage cost).

12. Completed and transferred eBook readers that had total cost of $240,000 from work in process inventory to finished goods.

13. Sold 1,000 eBook readers for $420,000.

14. It cost Antioch $220,000 to make the eBook readers sold in Event 13.

Required

a. Show how these events affect the balance sheet, income statement, and statement of cash flows by recording them in a horizontal financial statements model.

b. Explain why Antioch's recognition of cost of goods sold had no impact on cash flow.

c. Prepare a schedule of cost of goods manufactured and sold, a formal income statement, and a balance sheet for the year.

d. Distinguish between the product costs and the upstream costs that Antioch incurred.

e. The company president believes that Antioch could save money by buying the inventory that it currently makes. The warehouse manager said that would not be a good idea because the purchase price of $230 per unit was above the $220 average cost per unit of making the product. Assuming the purchased inventory would be available on demand, explain how the company could be correct and why the production manager could be biased in his assessment of the option to buy the inventory.

LO 10-4

Problem 10-25   *Using JIT to reduce inventory holding costs*

Torre Manufacturing Company obtains its raw materials from a variety of suppliers. Torre's strategy is to obtain the best price by letting the suppliers know that it buys from the lowest bidder. Approximately four years ago, unexpected increases in demand resulted in materials shortages. Torre was unable to find the materials it needed even though it was willing to pay premium prices. Because of the lack of raw materials, Torre was forced to close its manufacturing facility for two weeks. Its president vowed that her company would never again be at the mercy of its suppliers. She immediately ordered her purchasing agent to perpetually maintain a one-month supply of raw materials. Compliance with the president's orders resulted in a raw materials inventory amounting to approximately $2,000,000. Warehouse rental and personnel costs to maintain the inventory amounted to $9,000 per month. Torre has a line of credit with a local bank that calls for a 10 percent annual rate of interest. Assume that Torre finances the raw materials inventory with the line of credit.

CHECK FIGURE
a. $308,000

Required

a. Based on the information provided, determine the annual holding cost of the raw materials inventory.

b. Explain how a JIT system could reduce Torre's inventory holding cost.

c. Explain how most-favored customer status could enable Torre to establish a JIT inventory system without risking the raw materials shortages experienced in the past.

LO 10-4

Problem 10-26   *Using JIT to minimize waste and lost opportunity*

CHECK FIGURES
a. $1,200
b. $7,100

CMA Review, Inc., provides review courses twice each year for students studying to take the CMA exam. The cost of textbooks is included in the registration fee. Text material requires constant updating and is useful for only one course. To minimize printing costs and ensure availability of books on the first day of class, CMA Review has books printed and delivered to its offices two weeks in advance of the first class. To ensure that enough books are available, CMA Review normally orders 10 percent more than expected enrollment. Usually there is an oversupply and books are thrown away. However, demand occasionally exceeds expectations by more than 10 percent and there are too few books available for student use. CMA Review has been forced to turn away students because of a lack of textbooks. CMA Review expects to enroll approximately 110 students per course. The tuition fee is $1,500 per student. The cost of teachers is $36,000 per course, textbooks cost $80 each, and other operating expenses are estimated to be $40,000 per course.

Required

a. Prepare an income statement, assuming that 95 students enroll in a course. Determine the cost of waste associated with unused books.

b. Prepare an income statement, assuming that 115 students attempt to enroll in the course. Note that five students are turned away because of too few textbooks. Determine the amount of lost profit resulting from the inability to serve the five additional students.

c. Suppose that textbooks can be produced through a high-speed copying process that permits delivery *just in time* for class to start. The cost of books made using this process, however, is $90 each. Assume that all books must be made using the same production process. In other words, CMA Review cannot order some of the books using the regular copy process and the rest using the high-speed process. Prepare an income statement under the JIT system assuming that 95 students enroll in a course. Compare the income statement under JIT with the income statement prepared in Requirement *a*. Comment on how the JIT system would affect profitability.

d. Assume the same facts as in Requirement *c* with respect to a JIT system that enables immediate delivery of books at a cost of $90 each. Prepare an income statement under the JIT system, assuming that 115 students enroll in a course. Compare the income statement under JIT with the income statement prepared in Requirement *b*. Comment on how the JIT system would affect profitability.

e. Discuss the possible effect of the JIT system on the level of customer satisfaction.

Problem 10-27   *Value chain analysis (Appendix)*   LO 10-6

Vernon Company invented a new process for manufacturing ice cream. The ingredients are mixed in high-tech machinery that forms the product into small round beads. Like a bag of balls, the ice cream beads are surrounded by air pockets in packages. This design has numerous advantages. First, each bite of ice cream melts rapidly when placed in a person's mouth, creating a more flavorful sensation when compared to ordinary ice cream. Also, the air pockets mean that a typical serving includes a smaller amount of ice cream. This not only reduces materials cost but also provides the consumer with a low-calorie snack. A cup appears full of ice cream, but it is really half full of air. The consumer eats only half the ingredients that are contained in a typical cup of blended ice cream. Finally, the texture of the ice cream makes scooping it out of a large container a very easy task. The frustration of trying to get a spoon into a rock-solid package of blended ice cream has been eliminated. Vernon Company named the new product Sonic Cream.

Like many other ice cream producers, Vernon Company purchases its raw materials from a food wholesaler. The ingredients are mixed in Vernon's manufacturing plant. The packages of finished product are distributed to privately owned franchise ice cream shops that sell Sonic Cream directly to the public.

Vernon provides national advertising and is responsible for all research and development costs associated with making new flavors of Sonic Cream.

Required

a. Based on the information provided, draw a comprehensive value chain for Vernon Company that includes its suppliers and customers.

b. Identify the place in the chain where Vernon Company is exercising its opportunity to create added value beyond that currently being provided by its competitors.

ANALYZE, THINK, COMMUNICATE

ATC 10-1   Business Applications Case   *Financial versus managerial accounting*

The following information was taken from Starbucks Corporation's 2011 and 2012 Form 10-Ks.

	Fiscal Year Ended	
	September 30, 2012	October 2, 2011
Number of global employees	160,000	149,000
Number of employees in the U.S.	120,000	112,000
Revenues (in millions)	$13,300	$11,700
Properties used for roasting warehouse and distribution	2,171,000 square feet	2,396,000 square feet
Total assets (in millions)	$8,219	$7,360
Company-owned stores	9,045	9,007
Net earnings (in millions)	$1,384	$1,246

Required

a. Explain whether each line of information in the table above would best be described as being primarily financial accounting or managerial accounting in nature.

b. Provide some additional examples of managerial and financial accounting information that could apply to Starbucks.

c. If you analyze only the data you identified as financial in nature, does it appear that Starbucks' 2012 fiscal year was better or worse than its 2011 fiscal year? Explain.

d. If you analyze only the data you identified as managerial in nature, does it appear that Starbucks' 2012 fiscal year was better or worse than its 2011 fiscal year? Explain.

e. Did Starbucks appear to be using its roasting and distribution facilities more efficiently or less efficiently in 2012 than in 2011?

ATC 10-2   Group Assignment   *Product versus upstream and downstream costs*

Victor Holt, the accounting manager of Sexton, Inc., gathered the following information for 2014. Some of it can be used to construct an income statement for 2014. Ignore items that do not appear on an income statement. Some computation may be required. For example, the cost of manufacturing equipment would not appear on the income statement. However, the cost of manufacturing equipment is needed to compute the amount of depreciation. All units of product were started and completed in 2014.

1. Issued $864,000 of common stock.
2. Paid engineers in the product design department $10,000 for salaries that were accrued at the end of the previous year.
3. Incurred advertising expenses of $70,000.
4. Paid $720,000 for materials used to manufacture the company's product.
5. Incurred utility costs of $160,000. These costs were allocated to different departments on the basis of square footage of floor space. Mr. Holt identified three departments and determined the square footage of floor space for each department to be as shown in the table below.

Department	Square Footage
Research and development	10,000
Manufacturing	60,000
Selling and administrative	30,000
Total	100,000

6. Paid $880,000 for wages of production workers.
7. Paid cash of $658,000 for salaries of administrative personnel. There was $16,000 of accrued salaries owed to administrative personnel at the end of 2014. There was no beginning balance in the Salaries Payable account for administrative personnel.
8. Purchased manufacturing equipment two years ago at a cost of $10,000,000. The equipment had an eight-year useful life and a $2,000,000 salvage value.

9. Paid $390,000 cash to engineers in the product design department.

10. Paid a $258,000 cash dividend to owners.

11. Paid $80,000 to set up manufacturing equipment for production.

12. Paid a one-time $186,000 restructuring cost to redesign the production process to implement a just-in-time inventory system.

13. Prepaid the premium on a new insurance policy covering nonmanufacturing employees. The policy cost $72,000 and had a one-year term with an effective starting date of May 1. Four employees work in the research and development department and eight employees work in the selling and administrative department. Assume a December 31 closing date.

14. Made 69,400 units of product and sold 60,000 units at a price of $70 each.

Required

a. Divide the class into groups of four or five students per group, and then organize the groups into three sections. Assign Task 1 to the first section of groups, Task 2 to the second section of groups, and Task 3 to the third section of groups.

Group Tasks

(1) Identify the items that are classified as product costs and determine the amount of cost of goods sold reported on the 2014 income statement.

(2) Identify the items that are classified as upstream costs and determine the amount of upstream cost expensed on the 2014 income statement.

(3) Identify the items that are classified as downstream costs and determine the amount of downstream cost expensed on the 2014 income statement.

b. Have the class construct an income statement in the following manner. Select a member of one of the groups assigned Group Task (1), identifying the product costs. Have that person go to the board and list the costs included in the determination of cost of goods sold. Anyone in the other groups who disagrees with one of the classifications provided by the person at the board should voice an objection and explain why the item should be classified differently. The instructor should lead the class to a consensus on the disputed items. After the amount of cost of goods sold is determined, the student at the board constructs the part of the income statement showing the determination of gross margin. The exercise continues in a similar fashion with representatives from the other sections explaining the composition of the upstream and downstream costs. These items are added to the income statement started by the first group representative. The final result is a completed income statement.

ATC 10-3 Research Assignment *Identifying product costs at Snap-on Inc.*

Use the 2011 Form 10-K for Snap-on Inc. to complete the requirements below. To obtain the Form 10-K, you can use the EDGAR system following the instructions in Appendix A, at the back of this text, or it can be found under "Corporate Information" on the company's corporate website at www.snapon.com. Read carefully the following portions of the document:

■ "Products and Services" on page 5.

"Consolidated Statement of Earnings" on page 64.

The following parts of Note 1 on page 71:
- "Shipping and handling"
- "Advertising and promotion"

■ "Note 4: Inventories" on page 79.

■ "Note 5: Property and equipment" on page 79.

Required

a. Does the level of detail that Snap-on provides regarding costs incurred to manufacture its products suggest the company's financial statements are designed primarily to meet the needs of external or internal users?

b. Does Snap-on treat shipping and handling costs as product or period costs?

c. Does Snap-on treat advertising and promotion costs as product or period costs?

d. Earlier in this course you learned about a class of inventory called merchandise inventory. What categories of inventory does Snap-on report in its annual report?

e. What is the cost of the land owned by Snap-on? What is the cost of its machinery and equipment?

ATC 10-4   Writing Assignment   *Emerging practices in managerial accounting*

On April 14, 2012, Best Buy Company, Inc., issued a press release from which the following excerpt was taken:

> *April 14, 2012—Best Buy announced plans March 29, 2012, to close 50 U.S. stores as part of a number of key initiatives for this year. . . . This was not an easy decision to make. We chose these stores carefully, and are working to ensure the impact to our employees will be as minimal as possible, while serving all customers in a convenient and satisfying way. But we also recognize the impact this news has on the people who deserve respect for the contributions they have made to our business. . . . More broadly, our previously announced retail store actions are intended to increase points of presence, while decreasing overall square footage, for increased flexibility—including key store remodels with a new Connected Store format, while continuing to build out the successful Best Buy Mobile small format stores throughout the U.S. . . . We are committed to making it easier for customers to shop with us, whenever and wherever they want.*

The restructuring cost Best Buy $40 million and disrupted the lives of many of the company's employees.

Required

Assume that you are Best Buy's vice president of human relations. Write a letter to the employees who are affected by the restructuring. The letter should explain why it was necessary for the company to undertake the restructuring. Your explanation should refer to the ideas discussed in the section "Emerging Trends in Managerial Accounting" of this chapter (see Appendix).

ATC 10-5   Ethical Dilemma   *Product cost versus selling and administrative expense*

Emma Emerson is a proud woman with a problem. Her daughter has been accepted into a prestigious law school. While Ms. Emerson beams with pride, she is worried sick about how to pay for the school; she is a single parent who has worked hard to support herself and her three children. She had to go heavily into debt to finance her own education. Even though she now has a good job, family needs have continued to outpace her income and her debt burden is staggering. She knows she will be unable to borrow the money needed for her daughter's law school.

Ms. Emerson is the chief financial officer (CFO) of a small manufacturing company. She has just accepted a new job offer. Indeed, she has not yet told her employer that she will be leaving in a month. She is concerned that her year-end incentive bonus may be affected if her boss learns of her plans to leave. She plans to inform the company immediately after receiving the bonus. She knows her behavior is less than honorable, but she believes that she has been underpaid for a long time. Her boss, a relative of the company's owner, makes twice what she makes and does half the work. Why should she care about leaving with a little extra cash? Indeed, she is considering an opportunity to boost the bonus.

Ms. Emerson's bonus is based on a percentage of net income. Her company recently introduced a new product line that required substantial production start-up costs. Ms. Emerson is fully aware that GAAP requires these costs to be expensed in the current accounting period, but no one else in the company has the technical expertise to know exactly how the costs should be treated. She is considering misclassifying the start-up costs as product costs. If the costs are misclassified, net income will be significantly higher, resulting in a nice boost in her incentive bonus. By the time the auditors discover the misclassification, Ms. Emerson will have moved on to her new job. If the matter is brought to the attention of her new employer, she will simply plead ignorance. Considering her daughter's needs, Ms. Emerson decides to classify the start-up costs as product costs.

Required

a. Based on this information, indicate whether Ms. Emerson believes the number of units of product sold will be equal to, less than, or greater than the number of units made. Write a brief paragraph explaining the logic that supports your answer.

b. Explain how the misclassification could mislead an investor or creditor regarding the company's financial condition.

c. Explain how the misclassification could affect income taxes.

d. Review the Statement of Ethical Professional Practice shown in Exhibit 10.17 and identify at least two ethical principles that Ms. Emerson's misclassification of the start-up costs violated.

CHAPTER 11

Cost Behavior, Operating Leverage, and Profitability Analysis

LEARNING OBJECTIVES

After you have mastered the material in this chapter, you will be able to:

LO 11-1   Identify and describe fixed, variable, and mixed cost behavior.

LO 11-2   Demonstrate the effects of operating leverage on profitability.

LO 11-3   Prepare an income statement using the contribution margin approach.

LO 11-4   Calculate the magnitude of operating leverage.

LO 11-5   Determine the sales volume necessary to break even or to earn a desired profit.

LO 11-6   Calculate and interpret the margin of safety measure.

 Video lectures and accompanying self-assessment quizzes are available for all learning objectives through McGraw-Hill Connect® Accounting.

CHAPTER OPENING

Three college students are planning a vacation. One of them suggests inviting a fourth person along, remarking that four can travel for the same cost as three. Certainly, some costs will be the same whether three or four people go on the trip. For example, the hotel room costs $800 per week, regardless of whether three or four people stay in the room. In accounting terms, the cost of the hotel room is a **fixed cost.** The total amount of a fixed cost does not change when volume changes. The total hotel room cost is $800 whether 1, 2, 3, or 4 people use the room. In contrast, some costs vary in direct proportion with changes in volume. When volume increases, total variable cost increases; when volume decreases, total variable cost decreases. For example, the cost of tickets to a theme park is a **variable cost.** The total cost of tickets increases proportionately with each vacationer who goes to the theme park. Cost behavior (fixed versus variable) can significantly impact profitability. This chapter explains cost behavior and ways it can be used to increase profitability.

The Curious Accountant

News flash! On April 16, 2012, Charles Schwab Company announced that its first quarter's revenues decreased 1.5 percent compared to the same quarter in 2011, yet its earnings had decreased by 19.8 percent. On April 19, 2012, Union Pacific Corporation announced that an increase in revenue of 14 percent for the just-ended quarter would cause its earnings to increase 35 percent compared to the same quarter in 2011. On April 18, 2012, Qualcomm, Inc., reported that its revenue for the quarter had increased by 28 percent compared to the previous year, but its earnings increased by 123 percent.

Can you explain why such relatively small changes in these companies' revenues resulted in such relatively large changes in their earnings or losses? In other words, if a company's sales increase 10 percent, why do its earnings not also increase 10 percent? (Answer on page 407.)

FIXED COST BEHAVIOR

LO 11-1

Identify and describe fixed, variable, and mixed cost behavior.

How much more will it cost to send one additional employee to a sales meeting? If more people buy our products, can we charge less? If sales increase by 10 percent, how will profits be affected? Managers seeking answers to such questions must consider **cost behavior.** Knowing how costs behave relative to the level of business activity enables managers to more effectively plan and control costs. To illustrate, consider the entertainment company Star Productions, Inc. (SPI).

SPI specializes in promoting rock concerts. It is considering paying a band $48,000 to play a concert. Obviously, SPI must sell enough tickets to cover this cost. In this example, the relevant activity base is the number of tickets sold. The cost of the band is a fixed cost because it does not change regardless of the number of tickets sold. Exhibit 11.1 illustrates the fixed cost behavior pattern, showing the *total cost* and the *cost per unit* at three different levels of activity.

Total versus *per-unit* fixed costs behave differently. The total cost for the band remains constant (fixed) at $48,000. In contrast, fixed cost per unit decreases as volume (number of tickets sold) increases. The term *fixed cost* is consistent with the behavior of *total cost.* Total fixed cost remains constant (fixed) when activity changes. However, there is a contradiction between the term *fixed cost per unit* and the *per-unit behavior pattern of a fixed cost.* Fixed cost per unit is *not* fixed. It changes with the number of tickets sold. This contradiction in terminology can cause untold confusion. Study carefully the fixed cost behavior patterns in Exhibit 11.2.

EXHIBIT 11.1

Fixed Cost Behavior

Number of tickets sold (a)	2,700	3,000	3,300
Total cost of band (b)	$48,000	$48,000	$48,000
Cost per ticket sold (b ÷ a)	$17.78	$16.00	$14.55

EXHIBIT 11.2

Fixed Cost Behavior

	When Activity Increases	When Activity Decreases
Total fixed cost	Remains constant	Remains constant
Fixed cost **per unit**	Decreases	Increases

The fixed cost data in Exhibit 11.1 help SPI's management decide whether to sponsor the concert. For example, the information influences potential pricing choices. The per-unit costs represent the minimum ticket prices required to cover the fixed cost at various levels of activity. SPI could compare these per-unit costs to the prices of competing entertainment events (such as the prices of movies, sporting events, or theater tickets). If the price is not competitive, tickets will not sell and the concert will lose money. Management must also consider the number of tickets to be sold. The volume data in Exhibit 11.1 can be compared to the band's track record of ticket sales at previous concerts. A proper analysis of these data can reduce the risk of undertaking an unprofitable venture.

OPERATING LEVERAGE

LO 11-2

Demonstrate the effects of operating leverage on profitability.

Heavy objects can be moved with little effort using *physical* leverage. Business managers apply **operating leverage** to magnify small changes in revenue into dramatic changes in profitability. The *lever* managers use to achieve disproportionate changes between revenue and profitability is fixed costs. The leverage relationships between revenue, fixed costs, and profitability are displayed in Exhibit 11.3.

When all costs are fixed, every sales dollar contributes one dollar toward the potential profitability of a project. Once sales dollars cover fixed costs, each

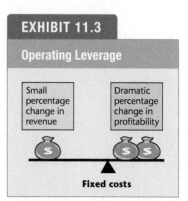

EXHIBIT 11.3

Operating Leverage

Small percentage change in revenue

Dramatic percentage change in profitability

Fixed costs

FOCUS ON INTERNATIONAL ISSUES

THE EFFECTS OF A TSUNAMI AND FIXED COSTS ON TOYOTA'S PERFORMANCE

On March 11, 2011, a major earthquake and tsunami hit a coastal area of Japan where automobile production facilities were located. Both Toyota and Honda were affected by these events, and both of these companies end their fiscal years on March 31. Presented below are data for Toyota Motor Corporation for the quarter ending on June 30, 2011, the first full quarter after the tsunami, and for the same quarter of 2010.

| | Quarter Ended | | |
	June 30, 2011	June 30, 2010	Percentage Change
Sales in units	1,221,374	1,819,995	(32.9)
Sales in billions of yen	¥3,441.1	¥4,871.8	(29.4)
Operating income in billions of yen	(¥108.0)	¥211.7	(151.0)

As the data above reveal, Toyota's earnings declined much more than the decline in its sales. This is due to the fact that its fixed costs did not decrease when its sales declined. Fortunately for Toyota, a year later things had greatly improved. During the quarter ended June 30, 2012, Toyota sold 2,268,563 vehicles and its operating earnings were ¥353.1 billion.

One might think the impact of the tsunami would have been limited mostly to Toyota's operations in Japan. After all, Toyota manufactures about 72 percent of its vehicles in countries outside of Japan. However, like many modern international companies, Toyota's operations are integrated. Cars assembled in the United States rely on some parts that are produced in Japan, so effects of the Japanese tsunami were felt throughout the world.

---

additional sales dollar represents pure profit. As a result, a small change in sales volume can significantly affect profitability. To illustrate, assume SPI estimates it will sell 3,000 tickets for $18 each. A 10 percent difference in actual sales volume will produce a 90 percent difference in profitability. Examine the data in Exhibit 11.4 to verify this result.[1]

EXHIBIT 11.4

Effect of Operating Leverage on Profitability

Number of tickets sold	2,700	⇐ −10% ⇐	3,000	⇒ +10% ⇒	3,300
Sales revenue ($18 per ticket)	$ 48,600		$ 54,000		$ 59,400
Cost of band (fixed cost)	(48,000)		(48,000)		(48,000)
Gross margin	$ 600	⇐ −90% ⇐	$ 6,000	⇒ +90% ⇒	$ 11,400

Calculating Percentage Change

The percentages in Exhibit 11.4 are computed as follows:

$$(\text{Alternative measure} - \text{Base measure}) \div \text{Base measure} = \% \text{ change}$$

The base measure is the starting point. To illustrate, compute the percentage change in gross margin when moving from 3,000 units (base measure) to 3,300 units (the alternative measure).

$$(\text{Alternative measure} - \text{Base measure}) \div \text{Base measure} = \% \text{ change}$$

$$(\$11,400 - \$6,000) \div \$6,000 = 90\%$$

---

[1]Do not confuse operating leverage with financial leverage. Companies employ *financial leverage* when they use debt to profit from investing money at a higher rate of return than the rate they pay on borrowed money. Companies employ *operating leverage* when they use proportionately more fixed costs than variable costs to magnify the effect on earnings of changes in revenues.

The percentage *decline* in profitability is similarly computed:

$$\text{(Alternative measure} - \text{Base measure)} \div \text{Base measure} = \% \text{ change}$$

$$(\$600 - \$6,000) \div \$6,000 = (90\%)$$

Risk and Reward Assessment

Risk refers to the possibility that sacrifices may exceed benefits. A fixed cost represents a commitment to an economic sacrifice. It represents the ultimate risk of undertaking a particular business project. If SPI pays the band but nobody buys a ticket, the company will lose $48,000. SPI can avoid this risk by substituting *variable costs* for the *fixed cost.*

VARIABLE COST BEHAVIOR

To illustrate variable cost behavior, assume SPI arranges to pay the band $16 per ticket sold instead of a fixed $48,000. Exhibit 11.5 shows the total cost of the band and the cost per ticket sold at three different levels of activity.

EXHIBIT 11.5

Variable Cost Behavior

Number of tickets sold (a)	2,700	3,000	3,300
Total cost of band (b)	$43,200	$48,000	$52,800
Cost per ticket sold (b ÷ a)	$16	$16	$16

Since SPI will pay the band $16 for each ticket sold, the *total* variable cost increases in direct proportion to the number of tickets sold. If SPI sells one ticket, total band cost will be $16 (1 × $16); if SPI sells two tickets, total band cost will be $32 (2 × $16); and so on. The total cost of the band increases proportionately as ticket sales move from 2,700 to 3,000 to 3,300. The variable cost *per ticket* remains $16, however, regardless of whether the number of tickets sold is 1, 2, 3, or 3,000. The behavior of variable cost *per unit* is contradictory to the word *variable.* Variable cost per unit remains *constant* regardless of how many tickets are sold. Study carefully the variable cost behavior patterns in Exhibit 11.6.

EXHIBIT 11.6

Variable Cost Behavior

	When Activity Increases	When Activity Decreases
Total variable cost	Increases proportionately	Decreases proportionately
Variable cost **per unit**	Remains constant	Remains constant

Risk and Reward Assessment

Shifting the cost structure from fixed to variable enables SPI to avoid the fixed cost risk. Recall that under the fixed cost structure, SPI was locked into a $48,000 cost for the band regardless of how many tickets are sold. If no tickets are sold, SPI will have to report a $48,000 loss on its income statement. The risk of incurring this loss is eliminated by the variable cost structure that requires SPI to only pay the band $16 per ticket sold. If SPI sells zero tickets, then the cost of the band is zero. For each ticket sold, SPI earns a $2 profit ($18 ticket sales price − $16 fee paid to band).

Shifting the cost structure from fixed to variable reduces not only the level of risk but also the potential for profits. Managers cannot avoid the risk of fixed costs without also

EXHIBIT 11.7						
Variable Cost Eliminates Operating Leverage						
Number of tickets sold	2,700	⇐−10%⇐	3,000	⇒+10%⇒	3,300	
Sales revenue ($18 per ticket)	$48,600		$54,000		$59,400	
Cost of band ($16 variable cost)	(43,200)		(48,000)		(52,800)	
Gross margin	$ 5,400	⇐−10%⇐	$ 6,000	⇒+10%⇒	$ 6,600	

sacrificing the benefits. Variable costs do not offer operating leverage. Exhibit 11.7 shows that a variable cost structure produces a proportional relationship between sales and profitability. A 10 percent increase or decrease in sales results in a corresponding 10 percent increase or decrease in profitability.

☑ CHECK YOURSELF 11.1

Suppose that you are sponsoring a political rally at which Ralph Nader will speak. You estimate that approximately 2,000 people will buy tickets to hear Mr. Nader's speech. The tickets are expected to be priced at $12 each. Would you prefer a contract that agrees to pay Mr. Nader $10,000 or one that agrees to pay him $5 per ticket purchased?

Answer   Your answer would depend on how certain you are that 2,000 people will purchase tickets. If it were likely that many more than 2,000 tickets would be sold, you would be better off with a fixed cost structure, agreeing to pay Mr. Nader a flat fee of $10,000. If attendance numbers are highly uncertain, you would be better off with a variable cost structure, thereby guaranteeing a lower cost if fewer people buy tickets.

Answers to The Curious Accountant

The explanation for how a company's earnings can rise faster, as a percentage, than its revenue is operating leverage, and operating leverage is due entirely to fixed costs. As the chapter explains, when a company's output goes up, its fixed cost per unit goes down. As long as it can keep prices about the same, this lower unit cost will result in higher profit per unit sold. In real-world companies, the relationship between changing sales levels and changing earnings levels can be very complex, but the existence of fixed costs helps to explain why a 14 percent rise in revenue can cause a 35 percent rise in net earnings.

☑ CHECK YOURSELF 11.2

If both Kroger Food Stores and Delta Airlines were to experience a 5 percent increase in revenues, which company would be more likely to experience a higher percentage increase in net income?

Answer   Delta would be more likely to experience a higher percentage increase in net income because a large portion of its cost (e.g., employee salaries and depreciation) is fixed, while a large portion of Kroger's cost is variable (e.g., cost of goods sold).

AN INCOME STATEMENT UNDER THE CONTRIBUTION MARGIN APPROACH

LO 11-3

Prepare an income statement using the contribution margin approach.

The impact of cost structure on profitability is so significant that managerial accountants frequently construct income statements that classify costs according to their behavior patterns. Such income statements first subtract variable costs from revenue; the resulting subtotal is called the **contribution margin.** The contribution margin represents the amount available to cover fixed expenses and thereafter to provide company profits. Net income is computed by subtracting the fixed costs from the contribution margin. A contribution margin style income statement cannot be used for public reporting (GAAP prohibits its use in external financial reports), but it is widely used for internal reporting purposes. Exhibit 11.8 illustrates income statements prepared using the contribution margin approach.

EXHIBIT 11.8		
Income Statements		
	Company Name	
	Bragg	**Biltmore**
Variable cost per unit (a)	$ 6	$ 12
Sales revenue (10 units × $20)	$ 200	$ 200
Variable cost (10 units × a)	(60)	(120)
Contribution margin	140	80
Fixed cost	(120)	(60)
Net income	$ 20	$ 20

MEASURING OPERATING LEVERAGE USING CONTRIBUTION MARGIN

LO 11-4

Calculate the magnitude of operating leverage.

A contribution margin income statement allows managers to easily measure operating leverage. The magnitude of operating leverage can be determined as follows:

$$\text{Magnitude of operating leverage} = \frac{\text{Contribution margin}}{\text{Net income}}$$

Applying this formula to the income statement data reported for Bragg Company and Biltmore Company in Exhibit 11.8 produces the following measures.

Bragg Company:

$$\text{Magnitude of operating leverage} = \frac{\$140}{\$20} = 7$$

Biltmore Company:

$$\text{Magnitude of operating leverage} = \frac{\$80}{\$20} = 4$$

The computations show that Bragg is more highly leveraged than Biltmore. Bragg's change in profitability will be seven times greater than a given percentage change in revenue. In contrast, Biltmore's profits change by only four times the percentage change in revenue. For example, a 10 percent increase in revenue produces a 70 percent increase (10 percent × 7) in profitability for Bragg Company and a 40 percent increase (10 percent × 4) in profitability for Biltmore Company. The income statements in Exhibits 11.9 and 11.10 confirm these expectations.

EXHIBIT 11.9			
Comparative Income Statements for Bragg Company			

EXHIBIT 11.9

Comparative Income Statements for Bragg Company

Units (a)	10		11
Sales revenue ($20 × a)	$ 200	⇒ +10% ⇒	$ 220
Variable cost ($6 × a)	(60)		(66)
Contribution margin	140		154
Fixed cost	(120)		(120)
Net income	$ 20	⇒ +70% ⇒	$ 34

EXHIBIT 11.10

Comparative Income Statements for Biltmore Company

Units (a)	10		11
Sales revenue ($20 × a)	$ 200	⇒ +10% ⇒	$ 220
Variable cost ($12 × a)	(120)		(132)
Contribution margin	80		88
Fixed cost	(60)		(60)
Net income	$ 20	⇒ +40% ⇒	$ 28

Operating leverage itself is neither good nor bad; it represents a strategy that can work to a company's advantage or disadvantage, depending on how it is used. The next section explains how managers can use operating leverage to create a competitive business advantage.

✓ CHECK YOURSELF 11.3

Boeing Company's 2012 10-K annual report filed with the Securities and Exchange Commission refers to "operating margins in our Commercial Airplanes business." Is Boeing referring to gross margins or contribution margins?

Answer   Since the data come from the company's external annual report, the reference must be to gross margins (revenue − cost of goods sold), a product cost measure. The contribution margin (revenue − variable cost) is a measure used in internal reporting.

COST BEHAVIOR SUMMARIZED

The term *fixed* refers to the behavior of *total* fixed cost. The cost *per unit* of a fixed cost *varies inversely* with changes in the level of activity. As activity increases, fixed cost per unit decreases. As activity decreases, fixed cost per unit increases. These relationships are graphed in Exhibit 11.11.

The term *variable* refers to the behavior of *total* variable cost. Total variable cost increases or decreases proportionately with changes in the volume of activity. In contrast, variable cost *per unit* remains *fixed* at all levels of activity. These relationships are graphed in Exhibit 11.12.

The relationships between fixed and variable costs are summarized in the chart in Exhibit 11.13. Study these relationships thoroughly.

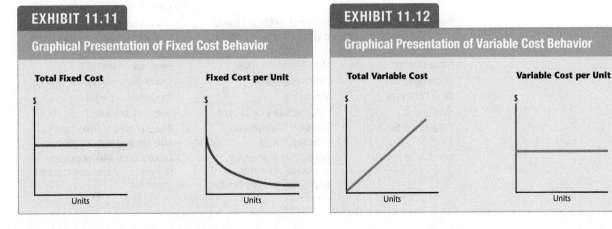

EXHIBIT 11.11

Graphical Presentation of Fixed Cost Behavior

Total Fixed Cost / Fixed Cost per Unit (Units)

EXHIBIT 11.12

Graphical Presentation of Variable Cost Behavior

Total Variable Cost / Variable Cost per Unit (Units)

EXHIBIT 11.13

Fixed and Variable Cost Behavior

When Activity Level Changes	Total Cost	Cost per Unit
Fixed costs	Remains constant	Changes *inversely*
Variable costs	Changes in direct proportion	Remains constant

Mixed Costs (Semivariable Costs)

Mixed costs (semivariable costs) include both fixed and variable components. For example, suppose Star Productions, Inc., has to pay for janitorial services. The charge for these services includes a base fee of $1,000 plus $20 per hour required to do a cleanup. The $1,000 base fee is fixed. It is the same no matter how many hours it takes to accomplish the cleanup. In contrast, the $20 hourly cost is a variable cost because the total cost increases with each additional hour it takes to complete the cleanup. Since the total janitorial cost is composed of fixed and variable components, it is frequently called a mixed cost. It may also be called a semivariable cost.

Given the $1,000 base plus $20 per hour cost components, the total janitorial cost for any cleanup can be easily computed as shown below:

$$\text{Total cost} = \text{Fixed cost} + (\text{Variable cost per hour} \times \text{Number of hours})$$

If 60 hours are required to accomplish a cleanup, the total mixed cost is:

$$\text{Total cost} = \$1,000 + (\$20 \times 60) = \$2,200$$

If 90 hours are required to accomplish a cleanup, the total mixed cost is:

$$\text{Total cost} = \$1,000 + (\$20 \times 90) = \$2,800$$

Exhibit 11.14 illustrates a variety of mixed costs businesses commonly encounter.

EXHIBIT 11.14

Examples of Mixed Costs

Type of Cost	Fixed Cost Component(s)	Variable Cost Component(s)
Cost of sales staff	Monthly salary	Bonus based on sales volume
Truck rental	Monthly rental fee	Cost of gas, tires, and maintenance
Legal fees	Monthly retainer	Reimbursements to attorney for out-of-pocket costs (copying, postage, travel, filing fees)
Outpatient service cost	Salaries of doctors and nurses, depreciation of facility, utilities	Medical supplies such as bandages, sterilization solution, and paper products
Phone services	Monthly connection fee	Per-minute usage fee
LP gas utility cost	Container rental fee	Cost of gas consumed
Cable TV services	Monthly fee	Pay-per-view charges
Training cost	Instructor salary, facility cost	Textbooks, supplies
Shipping and handling	Salaries of employees who process packages	Boxes, packing supplies, tape, and other shipping supplies, postage
Inventory holding cost	Depreciation on inventory warehouse, salaries of employees managing inventory	Delivery costs, interest on funds borrowed to finance inventory, cost of supplies

The Relevant Range

Suppose SPI, the rock concert promoter mentioned earlier, must pay $5,000 to rent a concert hall with a seating capacity of 4,000 people. Is the cost of the concert hall fixed or variable? Since total cost remains unchanged regardless of whether one ticket, 4,000 tickets, or any number in between is sold, the cost is fixed relative to ticket sales. However, what if demand for tickets is significantly more than 4,000? In that case, SPI might rent a larger concert hall at a higher cost. In other words, *the cost is fixed only for a designated range of activity (1 to 4,000).*

A similar circumstance affects many variable costs. For example, a supplier may offer a volume discount to buyers who purchase more than a specified number of products. The point is that descriptions of cost behavior pertain to a specified range of activity. The range of activity over which the definitions of fixed and variable costs are valid is commonly called the **relevant range.**

Context-Sensitive Definitions of Fixed and Variable

The behavior pattern of a particular cost may be either fixed or variable, depending on the context. For example, the cost of the band was fixed at $48,000 when SPI was considering hiring it to play a single concert. Regardless of how many tickets SPI sold, the total band cost was $48,000. However, the band cost becomes variable if SPI decides to hire it to perform at a series of concerts. The total cost and the cost per concert for one, two, three, four, or five concerts are shown in Exhibit 11.15.

EXHIBIT 11.15

Cost Behavior Relative to Number of Concerts

Number of concerts (a)	1	2	3	4	5
Cost per concert (b)	$48,000	$48,000	$ 48,000	$ 48,000	$ 48,000
Total cost (a × b)	$48,000	$96,000	$144,000	$192,000	$240,000

In this context, the total cost of hiring the band increases proportionately with the number of concerts while cost per concert remains constant. The band cost is therefore variable. The same cost can behave as either a fixed cost or a variable cost, depending on the **activity base.** When identifying a cost as fixed or variable, first ask, fixed or variable *relative to what activity base?* The cost of the band is fixed relative to *the number of tickets sold for a specific concert;* it is variable relative to *the number of concerts produced.*

☑ CHECK YOURSELF 11.4

Is the compensation cost for managers of Pizza Hut Restaurants a fixed cost or a variable cost?

Answer   The answer depends on the context. For example, since a store manager's salary remains unchanged regardless of how many customers enter a particular restaurant, it can be classified as a fixed cost relative to the number of customers at a particular restaurant. However, the more restaurants that Pizza Hut operates, the higher the total managers' compensation cost will be. Accordingly, managers' salary cost would be classified as a variable cost relative to the number of restaurants opened.

DETERMINING THE BREAK-EVEN POINT

LO 11-5

Determine the sales volume necessary to break even or to earn a desired profit.

Bright Day Distributors sells nonprescription health food supplements including vitamins, herbs, and natural hormones in the northwestern United States. Bright Day recently obtained the rights to distribute the new herb mixture Delatine. Recent scientific research found that Delatine delayed aging in laboratory animals. The researchers hypothesized that the substance would have a similar effect on humans. Their theory could not be confirmed because of the relatively long human life span. The news media reported the research findings; as stories turned up on television and radio news, talk shows, and in magazines, demand for Delatine increased.

Bright Day plans to sell the Delatine product at a price of $36 per bottle. Delatine costs $24 per bottle. Bright Day's management team suspects that enthusiasm for Delatine will abate quickly as the news media shift to other subjects. To attract customers immediately, the product managers consider television advertising. The marketing manager suggests running a campaign of several hundred cable channel ads at an estimated cost of $60,000.

Bright Day's first concern is whether it can sell enough units to cover its costs. The president made this position clear when he said, "We don't want to lose money on this product. We have to sell at least enough units to break even." In accounting terms, the **break-even point** is where profit (income) equals zero. So how many bottles of Delatine must be sold to produce a profit of zero? The break-even point is commonly computed using either the *equation method,* the *contribution margin per unit method,* or the *contribution margin ratio method.* All three of these approaches produce the same result. They are merely different ways to arrive at the same conclusion.

Equation Method

The **equation method** begins by expressing the income statement as follows:

$$\text{Sales} - \text{Variable costs} - \text{Fixed costs} = \text{Profit (Net income)}$$

As previously stated, profit at the break-even point is zero. Therefore, the break-even point for Delatine is computed as follows:

$$\text{Sales} - \text{Variable costs} - \text{Fixed costs} = \text{Profit}$$
$$\$36N - \$24N - \$60,000 = \$0$$
$$\$12N = \$60,000$$
$$N = \$60,000 \div \$12$$
$$N = 5,000 \text{ Units}$$

Where:

N = Number of units

$36 = Sales price per unit

$24 = Variable cost per unit

$60,000 = Fixed costs

✓ CHECK YOURSELF 11.5

B-Shoc is an independent musician who is considering whether to independently produce and sell a CD. B-Shoc estimates fixed costs of $5,400 and variable costs of $2.00 per unit. The expected selling price is $8.00 per CD. Use the equation method to determine B-Shoc's break-even point.

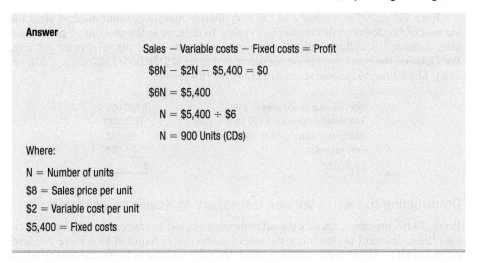

Answer

$$Sales - Variable\ costs - Fixed\ costs = Profit$$

$$\$8N - \$2N - \$5,400 = \$0$$

$$\$6N = \$5,400$$

$$N = \$5,400 \div \$6$$

$$N = 900\ Units\ (CDs)$$

Where:

N = Number of units
$8 = Sales price per unit
$2 = Variable cost per unit
$5,400 = Fixed costs

Contribution Margin per Unit Method

Recall that the *total contribution margin* is the amount of sales minus total variable cost. The **contribution margin per unit** is the sales price per unit minus the variable cost per unit. Therefore, the contribution margin per unit for Delatine is:

Sales price per unit	$ 36
Less: Variable cost per unit	(24)
Contribution margin per unit	$ 12

For every bottle of Delatine it sells, Bright Day earns a $12 contribution margin. In other words, every time Bright Day sells a bottle of Delatine, it receives enough money ($24) to cover the variable cost of the bottle of Delatine and still has $12 left to go toward paying the fixed cost. Bright Day will reach the break-even point when it sells enough bottles of Delatine to cover its fixed costs. Therefore the break-even point can be determined as follows:

$$\text{Break-even point in units} = \frac{\text{Fixed costs}}{\text{Contribution margin per unit}}$$

$$\text{Break-even point in units} = \frac{\$60,000}{\$12}$$

$$\text{Break-even point in units} = 5,000\ \text{Units}$$

This result is the same as that determined under the equation method. Indeed, the contribution margin per unit method formula is an abbreviated version of the income statement formula used in the equation method. In other words, both methods are simply different derivations of the same formula. The proof is provided in the footnote below.[2]

---

[2]The formula for the *contribution margin per unit method* is (where N is the number of units at the break-even point):

N = Fixed costs ÷ Contribution margin per unit

The income statement formula for the *equation method* produces the same result as shown below (where N is the number of units at the break-even point):

Sales − Variable costs − Fixed costs = Profit
Sales price per unit (N) − Variable cost per unit (N) − Fixed costs = Profit
Contribution margin per unit (N) − Fixed costs = Profit
Contribution margin per unit (N) − Fixed costs = 0
Contribution margin per unit (N) = Fixed costs
N = Fixed costs ÷ Contribution margin per unit

Both the *equation method* and the *contribution margin per unit method* yield the amount of break-even sales measured *in units.* To determine the amount of break-even sales measured *in dollars,* multiply the number of units times the sales price per unit. For Delatine, the break-even point measured in dollars is $180,000 (5,000 units × $36 per unit). The following income statement confirms this result:

Sales revenue (5,000 units × $36)	$ 180,000
Total variable expenses (5,000 units × $24)	(120,000)
Total contribution margin (5,000 units × $12)	60,000
Fixed expenses	(60,000)
Net income	$ 0

Determining the Sales Volume Necessary to Reach a Desired Profit

Bright Day's president decides the ad campaign should produce a $40,000 profit. He asks the accountant to determine the sales volume that is required to achieve this level of profitability. Using the *equation method,* the sales volume in units required to attain the desired profit is computed as follows:

$$\text{Sales} - \text{Variable costs} - \text{Fixed costs} = \text{Profit}$$

$$\$36N - \$24N - \$60,000 = \$40,000$$

$$\$12N = \$60,000 + \$40,000$$

$$N = \$100,000 \div \$12$$

$$N = 8,333 \text{ Units}$$

Where:

N = Number of units

$36 = Sales price per unit

$24 = Variable cost per unit

$60,000 = Fixed costs

$40,000 = Desired profit

The accountant used the *contribution margin per unit method* to confirm these computations as follows:

$$\text{Sales volume in units} = \frac{\text{Fixed costs} + \text{Desired profit}}{\text{Contribution margin per unit}}$$

$$= \frac{\$60,000 + \$40,000}{\$12} = 8,333.33 \text{ Units}$$

The required volume in sales dollars is this number of units multiplied by the sales price per unit (8,333.33 units × $36 = $300,000). The following income statement confirms this result; all amounts are rounded to the nearest whole dollar.

Sales revenue (8,333.33 units × $36)	$ 300,000
Total variable expenses (8,333.33 units × $24)	(200,000)
Total contribution margin (8,333.33 units × $12)	100,000
Fixed expenses	(60,000)
Net income	$ 40,000

In practice, the company will not sell partial bottles of Delatine, so the accountant rounds 8,333.33 bottles to 8,334 whole units. For planning and decision making, managers frequently make decisions using approximate data. Accuracy is desirable, but it is not as important as relevance. Do not be concerned when computations do not produce whole numbers. Rounding and approximation are common characteristics of managerial accounting data.

REALITY BYTES

The relationship among the costs to produce goods, the volume of goods produced, the price charged for those goods, and the profit earned is relevant to all industries, but perhaps no industry demonstrates the effects of these relationships more dramatically than automobile manufacturing. The automobile industry is characterized by having a lot of fixed production costs for things such as buildings, equipment, and research and development, as well as financing costs associated with borrowed funds, such as interest expense on bonds.

In the 1980s, foreign automobile manufacturers began increasing their market share, thus decreasing the market share of domestic companies such as General Motors (GM). As GM's relative level of production fell, its fixed cost per unit increased. In response, GM and others tried to regain market share by lowering prices, largely through rebates. Unfortunately this did not work, so the lower prices,

combined with the higher relative fixed costs, seriously eroded profits. These problems reached a crisis in 2008 and 2009, when GM sought financial help from the government and entered expedited bankruptcy proceedings.

What did GM hope to achieve by entering bankruptcy? Primarily it needed to lower its costs—especially its fixed costs. As a result of bankruptcy proceedings it was able to greatly reduce interest and principal payments on outstanding bonds (fixed costs), reduce the number of brands (fixed costs), shut down some plants (fixed costs), reduce health care costs to retirees (fixed costs), and reduce the number of dealers. While reducing the number of dealers did reduce some cost to the companies, it also reduced price competition among the dealers, which had the potential of allowing GM to charge more for its cars. All of these changes, it was hoped, would allow GM to return to profitability.

However, before a company can be profitable, it must break even. At one time, GM's break-even point was estimated to be around 16 million vehicles per year. GM's CEO until 2000, Rick Wagoner, had implemented changes that reduced the company's break-even point to 12 million units. On March 29, 2009, as a condition of receiving government financial support, the administration of President Barack Obama asked Mr. Wagoner to resign as GM's CEO. A fact perhaps overlooked by many amid the news coverage of Mr. Wagoner's resignation were reports that officials at the U.S. Treasury Department also asked the new leadership at GM to take steps to reduce the company's break-even point to 10 million units.

It would be a major achievement if GM were able to reduce its break-even point from 16 million units to 10 million units in the span of a few years. In 2008, GM sold only 8.8 million units, and its sales in the first quarter of 2009 were even lower than the same quarter of 2008, so even selling 10 million units was not a sure thing. Furthermore, it should be remembered that the objective of businesses is not simply to break even, but to make a profit.

Did the strategy work? As of December 31, 2011, the answer seems to be yes. The table below shows GM's results for the two years preceding and the two years following its bankruptcy. As the data show, the break-even level is now less than 10 million units.

	"New" GM		"Old" GM	
	2011	2010	2008	2007
Sales in units (thousands)	9,286	8,144	8,714	9,267
Sales in dollars (millions)	$150,276	$135,592	$148,979	$179,984
Operating income (millions)	$5,656	$5,108	($4,863)	($16,095)

☑ CHECK YOURSELF 11.6

VolTech Company manufactures small engines that it sells for $130 each. Variable costs are $70 per unit. Fixed costs are expected to be $100,000. The management team has established a target profit of $188,000. Use the contribution margin per unit method to determine how many engines VolTech must sell to attain the target profit.

Answer

Contribution margin per unit approach:

$$\text{Sales volume in units} = \frac{\text{Fixed costs} + \text{Desired profit}}{\text{Contribution margin per unit}} = \frac{\$100,000 + \$188,000}{\$130 - \$70} = 4,800 \text{ Units}$$

CALCULATING THE MARGIN OF SAFETY

The final meeting of Bright Day's management team focused on the reliability of the data used to construct the CVP chart. The accountant called attention to the sales volume figures in the area of profitability. Recall that Bright Day must sell 4,375 bottles of Delatine to earn the desired profit. In dollars, budgeted sales are $122,500 (4,375 bottles × $28 per bottle). The accountant highlighted the large gap between these budgeted sales and break-even sales. The amount of this gap, called the *margin of safety,* can be measured in units or in sales dollars as shown here.

	In Units	In Dollars
Budgeted sales	4,375	$122,500
Break-even sales	(1,875)	(52,500)
Margin of safety	2,500	$ 70,000

The **margin of safety** measures the cushion between budgeted sales and the break-even point. It quantifies the amount by which actual sales can fall short of expectations before the company will begin to incur losses.

To help compare diverse products or companies of different sizes, the margin of safety can be expressed as a percentage. Divide the margin of safety by the budgeted sales volume[3] as shown here.

$$\text{Margin of safety} = \frac{\text{Budgeted sales} - \text{Break-even sales}}{\text{Budgeted sales}}$$

$$\text{Margin of safety} = \frac{\$122,500 - \$52,500}{\$122,500} = 57.14\%$$

This analysis suggests actual sales would have to fall short of expected sales by more than 57 percent before Bright Day would experience a loss on Delatine. The large margin of safety suggests the proposed radio advertising program to market bottles of 30 mg Delatine capsules has minimal risk. As a result, the project team recommends that Delatine be added to the company's line of products.

☑ CHECK YOURSELF 11.7

Suppose that Bright Day is considering the possibility of selling a protein supplement that will cost Bright Day $5 per bottle. Bright Day believes that it can sell 4,000 bottles of the supplement for $25 per bottle. Fixed costs associated with selling the supplement are expected to be $42,000. Does the supplement have a wider margin of safety than Delatine?

Answer   Calculate the break-even point for the protein supplement.

$$\text{Break-even volume in units} = \frac{\text{Fixed costs}}{\text{Contribution margin per unit}} = \frac{\$42,000}{\$25 - \$5} = 2,100 \text{ Units}$$

Calculate the margin of safety. Note that the margin of safety expressed as a percentage can be calculated using the number of units or sales dollars. Using either units or dollars yields the same percentage.

$$\text{Margin of safety} = \frac{\text{Budgeted sales} - \text{Break-even sales}}{\text{Budgeted sales}} = \frac{4,000 - 2,100}{4,000} = 47.5\%$$

The margin of safety for Delatine (57.14 percent) exceeds that for the protein supplement (47.5 percent). This suggests that Bright Day is less likely to incur losses selling Delatine than selling the supplement.

---

[3]The margin of safety percentage can be based on actual as well as budgeted sales. For example, an analyst could compare the margins of safety of two companies under current operating conditions by substituting actual sales for budgeted sales in the computation, as follows: [(Actual sales − Break-even sales) ÷ Actual sales].

A Look Back

To plan and control business operations effectively, managers need to understand how different costs behave in relation to changes in the volume of activity. Total *fixed cost* remains constant when activity changes. Fixed cost per unit decreases with increases in activity and increases with decreases in activity. In contrast, total *variable cost* increases proportionately with increases in activity and decreases proportionately with decreases in activity. Variable cost per unit remains constant regardless of activity levels. The definitions of fixed and variable costs have meaning only within the context of a specified range of activity (the relevant range) for a defined period of time. In addition, cost behavior depends on the relevant volume measure (a store manager's salary is fixed relative to the number of customers visiting a particular store but is variable relative to the number of stores operated). A mixed cost has both fixed and variable cost components.

Fixed costs allow companies to take advantage of *operating leverage.* With operating leverage, each additional sale decreases the cost per unit. This principle allows a small percentage change in volume of revenue to cause a significantly larger percentage change in profits. The *magnitude of operating leverage* can be determined by dividing the contribution margin by net income. When all costs are fixed and revenues have covered fixed costs, each additional dollar of revenue represents pure profit. Having a fixed cost structure (employing operating leverage) offers a company both risks and rewards. If sales volume increases, fixed costs do not increase, allowing profits to soar. Alternatively, if sales volume decreases, fixed costs do not decrease and profits decline significantly more than revenues. Companies with high variable costs in relation to fixed costs do not experience as great a level of operating leverage. Their costs increase or decrease in proportion to changes in revenue. These companies face less risk but fail to reap disproportionately higher profits when volume soars.

Under the contribution margin approach, variable costs are subtracted from revenue to determine the *contribution margin.* Fixed costs are then subtracted from the contribution margin to determine net income. The contribution margin represents the amount available to pay fixed costs and provide a profit. Although not permitted by GAAP for external reporting, many companies use the contribution margin format for internal reporting purposes.

The *break-even point* (the point where total revenue equals total cost) in units can be determined by dividing fixed costs by the contribution margin per unit. The break-even point in sales dollars can be determined by multiplying the number of break-even units by the sales price per unit. To determine sales in units to obtain a designated profit, the sum of fixed costs and desired profit is divided by the contribution margin per unit.

The *margin of safety* is the number of units or the amount of sales dollars by which actual sales can fall below expected sales before a loss is incurred. The margin of safety can also be expressed as a percentage to permit comparing different size companies. The margin of safety can be computed as a percentage by dividing the difference between budgeted sales and break-even sales by the amount of budgeted sales.

A Look Forward >>

The next chapter begins investigating cost measurement. Accountants seek to determine the cost of certain objects. A cost object may be a product, a service, a department, a customer, or any other thing for which the cost is being determined. Some costs can be directly traced to a cost object, while others are difficult to trace. Costs that are difficult to trace to cost objects are called *indirect costs,* or *overhead.* Indirect costs are assigned to cost objects through *cost allocation.* The next chapter introduces the basic concepts and procedures of cost allocation.

Video lectures and accompanying self-assessment quizzes are available for all learning objectives through McGraw-Hill *Connect® Accounting*.

SELF-STUDY REVIEW PROBLEM 1

Mensa Mountaineering Company (MMC) provides guided mountain climbing expeditions in the Rocky Mountains. Its only major expense is guide salaries; it pays each guide $4,800 per climbing expedition. MMC charges its customers $1,500 per expedition and expects to take five climbers on each expedition.

Part 1

Base your answers on the preceding information.

Required

a. Determine the total cost of guide salaries and the cost of guide salaries per climber assuming that four, five, or six climbers are included in a trip. Relative to the number of climbers in a single expedition, is the cost of guides a fixed or a variable cost?

b. Relative to the number of expeditions, is the cost of guides a fixed or a variable cost?

c. Determine the profit of an expedition assuming that five climbers are included in the trip.

d. Determine the profit assuming a 20 percent increase (six climbers total) in expedition revenue. What is the percentage change in profitability?

e. Determine the profit assuming a 20 percent decrease (four climbers total) in expedition revenue. What is the percentage change in profitability?

f. Explain why a 20 percent shift in revenue produces more than a 20 percent shift in profitability. What term describes this phenomenon?

Part 2

Assume that the guides offer to make the climbs for a percentage of expedition fees. Specifically, MMC will pay guides $960 per climber on the expedition. Assume also that the expedition fee charged to climbers remains at $1,500 per climber.

Required

g. Determine the total cost of guide salaries and the cost of guide salaries per climber assuming that four, five, or six climbers are included in a trip. Relative to the number of climbers in a single expedition, is the cost of guides a fixed or a variable cost?

h. Relative to the number of expeditions, is the cost of guides a fixed or a variable cost?

i. Determine the profit of an expedition assuming that five climbers are included in the trip.

j. Determine the profit assuming a 20 percent increase (six climbers total) in expedition revenue. What is the percentage change in profitability?

k. Determine the profit assuming a 20 percent decrease (four climbers total) in expedition revenue. What is the percentage change in profitability?

l. Explain why a 20 percent shift in revenue does not produce more than a 20 percent shift in profitability.

Solution to Part 1, Requirement *a*

Number of climbers (a)	4	5	6
Total cost of guide salaries (b)	$4,800	$4,800	$4,800
Cost per climber (b ÷ a)	1,200	960	800

Because the total cost remains constant (fixed) regardless of the number of climbers on a particular expedition, the cost is classified as fixed. Note that the cost per climber decreases as the number of climbers increases. This is the *per unit* behavior pattern of a fixed cost.

Solution to Part 1, Requirement *b*

Because the total cost of guide salaries changes proportionately each time the number of expeditions increases or decreases, the cost of salaries is variable relative to the number of expeditions.

Solution to Part 1, Requirements *c*, *d*, and *e*

Number of Climbers	4	Percentage Change	5	Percentage Change	6
Revenue ($1,500 per climber)	$6,000	⇐ (20%) ⇐	$7,500	⇒ +20% ⇒	$9,000
Cost of guide salaries (fixed)	4,800		4,800		4,800
Profit	$1,200	⇐ (55.6%) ⇐	$2,700	⇒ +55.6% ⇒	$4,200

Percentage change in revenue: ±$1,500 ÷ $7,500 = ±20%
Percentage change in profit: ±$1,500 ÷ $2,700 = ±55.6%

Solution to Part 1, Requirement *f*

Because the cost of guide salaries remains fixed while volume (number of climbers) changes, the change in profit, measured in absolute dollars, exactly matches the change in revenue. More specifically, each time MMC increases the number of climbers by one, revenue and profit increase by $1,500. Because the base figure for profit ($2,700) is lower than the base figure for revenue ($7,500), the percentage change in profit ($1,500 ÷ $2,700 = 55.6%) is higher than percentage change in revenue ($1,500 ÷ $7,500). This phenomenon is called *operating leverage*.

Solution for Part 2, Requirement *g*

Number of climbers (a)	4	5	6
Per climber cost of guide salaries (b)	$ 960	$ 960	$ 960
Cost per climber (b × a)	3,840	4,800	5,760

Because the total cost changes in proportion to changes in the number of climbers, the cost is classified as variable. Note that the cost per climber remains constant (stays the same) as the number of climbers increases or decreases. This is the *per unit* behavior pattern of a variable cost.

Solution for Part 2, Requirement *h*

Because the total cost of guide salaries changes proportionately with changes in the number of expeditions, the cost of salaries is also variable relative to the number of expeditions.

Solution for Part 2, Requirements *i*, *j*, and *k*

Number of Climbers	4	Percentage Change	5	Percentage Change	6
Revenue ($1,500 per climber)	$6,000	⇐ (20%) ⇐	$7,500	⇒ +20% ⇒	$9,000
Cost of guide salaries (variable)	3,840		4,800		5,760
Profit	$2,160	⇐ (20%) ⇐	$2,700	⇒ +20% ⇒	$3,240

Percentage change in revenue: ±$1,500 ÷ $7,500 = ±20%
Percentage change in profit: ±$540 ÷ $2,700 = ±20%

Solution for Part 2, Requirement *l*

Because the cost of guide salaries changes when volume (number of climbers) changes, the change in net income is proportionate to the change in revenue. More specifically, each time the number of climbers increases by one, revenue increases by $1,500 and net income increases by $540 ($1,500 − $960). Accordingly, the percentage change in net income will always equal the percentage change in revenue. This means that there is no operating leverage when all costs are variable.

Video lectures and accompanying self-assessment quizzes are available for all learning objectives through McGraw-Hill *Connect® Accounting*.

SELF-STUDY REVIEW PROBLEM 2

Sharp Company makes and sells pencil sharpeners. The variable cost of each sharpener is $20. The sharpeners are sold for $30 each. Fixed operating expenses amount to $40,000.

Required

a. Determine the break-even point in units and sales dollars.

b. Determine the sales volume in units and dollars that is required to attain a profit of $12,000. Verify your answer by preparing an income statement using the contribution margin format.

c. Determine the margin of safety between sales required to attain a profit of $12,000 and break-even sales.

Solution to Requirement *a*

Formula for Computing Break-even Point in Units

Sales − Variable costs − Fixed costs = Profit
Sales price per unit (N) − Variable cost per unit (N) − Fixed costs = Profit
Contribution margin per unit (N) − Fixed costs = Profit
N = (Fixed costs + Profit) ÷ Contribution margin per unit
N = ($40,000 + 0) ÷ ($30 − $20) = 4,000 Units

Break-even Point in Sales Dollars

Sales price	$ 30
× Number of units	4,000
Sales volume in dollars	$120,000

Solution to Requirement *b*

**Formula for Computing Unit Sales
Required to Attain Desired Profit**

Sales − Variable costs − Fixed costs = Profit
Sales price per unit (N) − Variable cost per unit (N) − Fixed costs = Profit
Contribution margin per unit (N) − Fixed costs = Profit
N = (Fixed costs + Profit) ÷ Contribution margin per unit
N = ($40,000 + 12,000) ÷ ($30 − $20) = 5,200 Units

**Sales Dollars Required
to Attain Desired Profit**

Sales price	$ 30
× Number of units	5,200
Sales volume in dollars	$156,000

Income Statement	
Sales volume in units (a)	5,200
Sales revenue (a × $30)	$156,000
Variable costs (a × $20)	(104,000)
Contribution margin	52,000
Fixed costs	(40,000)
Net income	$ 12,000

Solution to Requirement *c*

Margin of Safety Computations	Units	Dollars
Budgeted sales	5,200	$156,000
Break-even sales	(4,000)	(120,000)
Margin of safety	1,200	$ 36,000

Percentage Computation

$$\frac{\text{Margin of safety in \$}}{\text{Budgeted sales}} = \frac{\$36,000}{\$156,000} = 23.08\%$$

KEY TERMS

Activity base 411
Break-even point 412
Contribution
   margin 408

Contribution margin
   per unit 413
Cost behavior 404
Equation method 412

Fixed cost 402
Margin of safety 416
Mixed costs (semivariable
   costs) 410

Operating leverage 404
Relevant range 411
Variable cost 402

QUESTIONS

1. Define *fixed cost* and *variable cost* and give an example of each.

2. How can knowing cost behavior relative to volume fluctuations affect decision making?

3. Define the term *operating leverage* and explain how it affects profits.

4. How is operating leverage calculated?

5. Explain the limitations of using operating leverage to predict profitability.

6. If volume is increasing, would a company benefit more from a pure variable or a pure fixed cost structure? Which cost structure would be advantageous if volume is decreasing?

7. Explain the risk and rewards to a company that result from having fixed costs.

8. Are companies with predominately fixed cost structures likely to be most profitable?

9. How is the relevant range of activity related to fixed and variable cost? Give an example of how the definitions of these costs become invalid when volume is outside the relevant range.

10. Which cost structure has the greater risk? Explain.

11. The president of Bright Corporation tells you that he sees a dim future for his company. He feels that his hands are tied because fixed costs are too high. He says that fixed costs do not change and therefore the situation is hopeless. Do you agree? Explain.

12. All costs are variable because if a business ceases operations, its costs fall to zero. Do you

agree with the statement? Explain.

13. Verna Salsbury tells you that she thinks the terms fixed cost and variable cost are confusing. She notes that fixed cost per unit changes when the number of units changes. Furthermore, variable cost per unit remains fixed regardless of how many units are produced. She concludes that the terminology seems to be backward. Explain why the terminology appears to be contradictory.

14. What does the term *break-even point* mean? Name the two ways it can be measured.

15. How does a contribution margin income statement differ from the income statement used in financial reporting?

16. If Company A has a projected margin of safety of

22 percent while Company B has a margin of safety of 52 percent, which company is at greater risk when actual sales are less than budgeted?

17. Mary Hartwell and Jane Jamail, college roommates, are considering the joint purchase of a computer that they can share to prepare class assignments. Ms. Hartwell wants a particular model that costs $2,000; Ms. Jamail prefers a more economical model that costs $1,500. In fact, Ms. Jamail is adamant about her position, refusing to contribute more than $750 toward the purchase. If Ms. Hartwell is also adamant about her position, should she accept Ms. Jamail's $750 offer and apply that amount toward the purchase of the more expensive computer?

MULTIPLE-CHOICE QUESTIONS

Multiple-choice questions are provided on the text website at www.mhhe.com/edmondssurvey4e.

EXERCISES

≣ connect | **All applicable Exercises are available with McGraw-Hill**
ACCOUNTING | **Connect® Accounting.**

LO 11-1

Exercise 11-1 *Identifying cost behavior*

Molly's Restaurant, a fast-food restaurant company, operates a chain of restaurants across the nation. Each restaurant employs eight people; one is a manager paid a salary plus a bonus equal to 3 percent of sales. Other employees, two cooks, one dishwasher, and four waitresses, are paid salaries. Each manager is budgeted $3,000 per month for advertising costs.

Required

Classify each of the following costs incurred by Molly's Restaurant as fixed, variable, or mixed:

a. Manager's compensation relative to the number of customers.
b. Waitresses' salaries relative to the number of restaurants.
c. Advertising costs relative to the number of customers for a particular restaurant.
d. Rental costs relative to the number of restaurants.
e. Cooks' salaries at a particular location relative to the number of customers.
f. Cost of supplies (cups, plates, spoons, etc.) relative to the number of customers.

LO 11-1

Exercise 11-2 *Identifying cost behavior*

At the various activity levels shown, Yates Company incurred the following costs:

	Units Sold	20	40	60	80	100
a.	Total cost of shopping bags	$ 2.00	$ 4.00	$ 6.00	$ 8.00	$ 10.00
b.	Cost per unit of merchandise sold	90.00	90.00	90.00	90.00	90.00
c.	Rental cost per unit of merchandise sold	36.00	18.00	12.00	9.00	7.20
d.	Total phone expense	80.00	100.00	120.00	140.00	160.00
e.	Cost per unit of supplies	1.00	1.00	1.00	1.00	1.00
f.	Total insurance cost	480.00	480.00	480.00	480.00	480.00
g.	Total salary cost	1,200.00	1,600.00	2,000.00	2,400.00	2,800.00
h.	Total cost of goods sold	1,800.00	3,600.00	5,400.00	7,200.00	9,000.00
i.	Depreciation cost per unit	240.00	120.00	80.00	60.00	48.00
j.	Total rent cost	3,200.00	3,200.00	3,200.00	3,200.00	3,200.00

Required

Identify each of these costs as fixed, variable, or mixed.

LO 11-1

Exercise 11-3 *Determining fixed cost per unit*

Munoz Corporation incurs the following annual fixed costs:

Item	Cost
Depreciation	$ 75,000
Officers' salaries	160,000
Long-term lease	38,000
Property taxes	12,000

Required

Determine the total fixed cost per unit of production, assuming that Munoz produces 4,000, 4,500, or 5,000 units.

Exercise 11-4   *Determining total variable cost*

LO 11-1

The following variable production costs apply to goods made by Raeburn Manufacturing Corporation:

Item	Cost per Unit
Materials	$ 8.00
Labor	3.50
Variable overhead	2.50
Total	$14.00

Required

Determine the total variable production cost, assuming that Raeburn makes 5,000, 15,000, or 25,000 units.

Exercise 11-5   *Fixed versus variable cost behavior*

LO 11-1

Nasenko Company's cost and production data for two recent months included the following:

	March	April
Production (units)	200	400
Rent	$1,800	$1,800
Utilities	$ 600	$1,200

Required

a. Separately calculate the rental cost per unit and the utilities cost per unit for both March and April.

b. Identify which cost is variable and which is fixed. Explain your answer.

Exercise 11-6   *Fixed versus variable cost behavior*

LO 11-1

Varina Trophies makes and sells trophies it distributes to little league ballplayers. The company normally produces and sells between 6,000 and 12,000 trophies per year. The following cost data apply to various activity levels:

Number of Trophies	6,000	8,000	10,000	12,000
Total costs incurred				
Fixed	$48,000			
Variable	48,000			
Total costs	$96,000			
Cost per unit				
Fixed	$ 8.00			
Variable	8.00			
Total cost per trophy	$ 16.00			

Required

a. Complete the preceding table by filling in the missing amounts for the levels of activity shown in the first row of the table. Round all cost-per-unit figures to the nearest whole penny.

b. Explain why the total cost per trophy decreases as the number of trophies increases.

LO 11-1

Exercise 11-7 *Graphing fixed cost behavior*

The following graph setups depict the dollar amount of fixed cost on the vertical axes and the level of activity on the horizontal axes:

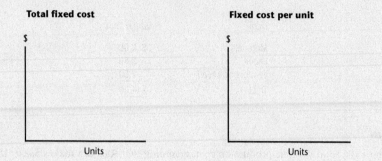

Total fixed cost   **Fixed cost per unit**

Required

a. Draw a line that depicts the relationship between total fixed cost and the level of activity.
b. Draw a line that depicts the relationship between fixed cost per unit and the level of activity.

LO 11-1

Exercise 11-8 *Graphing variable cost behavior*

The following graph setups depict the dollar amount of variable cost on the vertical axes and the level of activity on the horizontal axes:

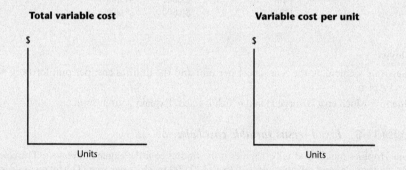

Total variable cost   **Variable cost per unit**

Required

a. Draw a line that depicts the relationship between total variable cost and the level of activity.
b. Draw a line that depicts the relationship between variable cost per unit and the level of activity.

LO 11-1

Exercise 11-9 *Mixed cost at different levels of activity*

Veasy Corporation paid one of its sales representatives $7,500 during the month of March. The rep is paid a base salary plus $25 per unit of product sold. During March, the rep sold 200 units.

Required

Calculate the total monthly cost of the sales representative's salary for each of the following months:

Month	April	May	June	July
Number of units sold	240	150	250	160
Total variable cost				
Total fixed cost				
Total salary cost				

Exercise 11-10   *Fixed versus variable cost behavior*

LO 11-1, 11-2

Moore Entertainment sponsors rock concerts. The company is considering a contract to hire a band at a cost of $105,000 per concert.

Required

a. What are the total band cost and the cost per person if concert attendance is 2,000, 2,500, 3,000, 3,500, or 4,000?

b. Is the cost of hiring the band a fixed or a variable cost?

c. Draw a graph and plot total cost and cost per unit if attendance is 2,000, 2,500, 3,000, 3,500, or 4,000.

d. Identify Moore's major business risks and explain how they can be minimized.

Exercise 11-11   *Fixed versus variable cost behavior*

LO 11-1, 11-2

Moore Entertainment sells souvenir T-shirts at each rock concert that it sponsors. The shirts cost $9 each. Any excess shirts can be returned to the manufacturer for a full refund of the purchase price. The sales price is $15 per shirt.

Required

a. What are the total cost of shirts and cost per shirt if sales amount to 2,000, 2,500, 3,000, 3,500, or 4,000?

b. Is the cost of T-shirts a fixed or a variable cost?

c. Draw a graph and plot total cost and cost per shirt if sales amount to 2,000, 2,500, 3,000, 3,500, or 4,000.

d. Comment on Moore's likelihood of incurring a loss due to its operating activities.

Exercise 11-12   *Using fixed cost as a competitive business strategy*

LO 11-2

The following income statements illustrate different cost structures for two competing companies:

Income Statements		
	Company Name	
	Kent	Trent
Number of customers (a)	100	100
Sales revenue (a × $250)	$ 25,000	$ 25,000
Variable cost (a × $175)	N/A	(17,500)
Variable cost (a × $0)	0	N/A
Contribution margin	25,000	7,500
Fixed cost	(17,500)	0
Net income	$ 7,500	$ 7,500

Required

a. Reconstruct Kent's income statement, assuming that it serves 200 customers when it lures 100 customers away from Trent by lowering the sales price to $150 per customer.

b. Reconstruct Trent's income statement, assuming that it serves 200 customers when it lures 100 customers away from Kent by lowering the sales price to $150 per customer.

c. Explain why the price-cutting strategy increased Kent Company's profits but caused a net loss for Trent Company.

Exercise 11-13   *Prepare an income statement using the contribution margin approach*

LO 11-3

AJ Manufacturing Company incurred $50,000 of fixed product cost and $40,000 of variable product cost during its first year of operation. Also during its first year, AJ incurred $16,000 of fixed selling and administrative costs and $13,000 of variable selling and administrative costs. The company sold all of the units it produced for $160,000.

Required

a. Prepare an income statement using the format required by generally accepted accounting Principles (GAAP).

b. Prepare an income statement using the contribution margin approach.

c. Explain why both statements have the same amount of net income.

LO 11-3

Exercise 11-14   *Determining contribution margin from incomplete cost data*

Estrada Corporation produced 300,000 watches that it sold for $35 each. The company determined that fixed manufacturing cost per unit was $14 per watch. The company reported a $2,700,000 gross margin on its income statement.

Required

Determine the variable cost per unit, the total variable cost, and the total contribution margin.

LO 11-3, 11-4

Exercise 11-15   *Using contribution margin format income statement to measure the magnitude of operating leverage*

The following income statement was drawn from the records of Butler Company, a merchandising firm:

BUTLER COMPANY	
Income Statement	
For the Year Ended December 31, 2014	
Sales revenue (2,000 units × $275)	$ 550,000
Cost of goods sold (2,000 units × $146)	(292,000)
Gross margin	258,000
Sales commissions (10% of sales)	(55,000)
Administrative salaries expense	(80,000)
Advertising expense	(38,000)
Depreciation expense	(50,000)
Shipping and handling expenses (2,000 units × $1.50)	(3,000)
Net income	$ 32,000

Required

a. Reconstruct the income statement using the contribution margin format.

b. Calculate the magnitude of operating leverage.

c. Use the measure of operating leverage to determine the amount of net income Butler will earn if sales increase by 10 percent.

LO 11-4

Exercise 11-16   *Assessing the magnitude of operating leverage*

The following income statement applies to Nagano Company for the current year:

Income Statement	
Sales revenue (250 units × $60)	$15,000
Variable cost (250 units × $36)	(9,000)
Contribution margin	6,000
Fixed costs	(2,000)
Net income	$ 4,000

Required

a. Use the contribution margin approach to calculate the magnitude of operating leverage.

b. Use the operating leverage measure computed in Requirement *a* to determine the amount of net income that Nagano Company will earn if it experiences a 10 percent increase in revenue. The sales price per unit is not affected.

c. Verify your answer to Requirement *b* by constructing an income statement based on a 10 percent increase in sales revenue. The sales price is not affected. Calculate the percentage change in net income for the two income statements.

Exercise 11-17　*Break-even point*　LO 11-5

Agassi Corporation sells products for $90 each that have variable costs of $60 per unit. Agassi's annual fixed cost is $450,000.

Required

Determine the break-even point in units and dollars.

Exercise 11-18　*Desired profit*　LO 11-5

Lindo Company incurs annual fixed costs of $80,000. Variable costs for Lindo's product are $40 per unit, and the sales price is $64 per unit. Lindo desires to earn an annual profit of $40,000.

Required

Determine the sales volume in dollars and units required to earn the desired profit.

Exercise 11-19　*Margin of safety*　LO 11-6

Information concerning a product produced by Ender Company appears here:

Sales price per unit	$200
Variable cost per unit	$80
Total annual fixed manufacturing and operating costs	$600,000

Required

Determine the following:

a. Contribution margin per unit.
b. Number of units that Ender must sell to break even.
c. Sales level in units that Ender must reach to earn a profit of $240,000.
d. Determine the margin of safety in units, sales dollars, and as a percentage. Round the percentage to one decimal place.

Exercise 11-20　*Margin of safety*　LO 11-6

Otto Company makes a product that sells for $5 per unit. The company pays $3 per unit for the variable costs of the product and incurs fixed costs of $50,000. Otto expects to sell 30,000 units of product.

Required

Determine Otto's margin of safety in units, sales dollars, and as a percentage. Round the percentage to one decimal place.

PROBLEMS

■ connect | ACCOUNTING | **All applicable Problems are available with McGraw-Hill *Connect® Accounting*.**

Problem 11-21　*Identifying cost behavior*　LO 11-1

Required

Identify the following costs as fixed or variable:

Costs related to plane trips between New York, New York, and Los Angeles, California, follow. Pilots are paid on a per-trip basis.

a. Pilots' salaries relative to the number of trips flown.
b. Depreciation relative to the number of planes in service.

c. Cost of refreshments relative to the number of passengers.

d. Pilots' salaries relative to the number of passengers on a particular trip.

e. Cost of a maintenance check relative to the number of passengers on a particular trip.

f. Fuel costs relative to the number of trips.

Guaranty National Bank operates several branch offices in grocery stores. Each branch employs a supervisor and two tellers. Costs related to Guaranty's branch operations follow.

g. Tellers' salaries relative to the number of tellers in a particular district, which is composed of branches.

h. Supplies cost relative to the number of transactions processed in a particular branch.

i. Tellers' salaries relative to the number of customers served at a particular branch.

j. Supervisors' salaries relative to the number of branches operated.

k. Supervisors' salaries relative to the number of customers served in a particular branch.

l. Facility rental costs relative to the size of customer deposits.

Costs related to operating a fast-food restaurant follow.

m. Depreciation of equipment relative to the number of restaurants.

n. Building rental cost relative to the number of customers served in a particular restaurant.

o. Manager's salary of a particular store relative to the number of employees.

p. Food cost relative to the number of customers.

q. Utility cost relative to the number of restaurants in operation.

r. Company president's salary relative to the number of restaurants in operation.

s. Land costs relative to the number of hamburgers sold at a particular restaurant.

t. Depreciation of equipment relative to the number of customers served at a particular restaurant.

LO 11-1

CHECK FIGURES

c. Total supplies cost for cleaning 30 houses: $150

d. Total cost for 20 houses: $2,200

Problem 11-22   *Cost behavior and averaging*

Kara Buchanan has decided to start Kara Cleaning, a residential housecleaning service company. She is able to rent cleaning equipment at a cost of $900 per month. Labor costs are expected to be $60 per house cleaned and supplies are expected to cost $5 per house.

Required

a. Determine the total expected cost of equipment rental and the average expected cost of equipment rental per house cleaned, assuming that Kara Cleaning cleans 10, 20, or 30 houses during one month. Is the cost of equipment a fixed or a variable cost?

b. Determine the total expected cost of labor and the average expected cost of labor per house cleaned, assuming that Kara Cleaning cleans 10, 20, or 30 houses during one month. Is the cost of labor a fixed or a variable cost?

c. Determine the total expected cost of supplies and the average expected cost of supplies per house cleaned, assuming that Kara Cleaning cleans 10, 20, or 30 houses during one month. Is the cost of supplies a fixed or a variable cost?

d. Determine the total expected cost of cleaning houses, assuming that Kara Cleaning cleans 10, 20, or 30 houses during one month.

e. Determine the average expected cost per house, assuming that Kara Cleaning cleans 10, 20, or 30 houses during one month. Why does the cost per unit decrease as the number of houses increases?

f. If Ms. Buchanan tells you that she prices her services at 25 percent above cost, would you assume that she means average or actual cost? Why?

LO 11-1

CHECK FIGURE

b. Average teller cost for 60,000 transactions: $1.60

Problem 11-23   *Context-sensitive nature of cost behavior classifications*

Atlantic Bank's start-up division establishes new branch banks. Each branch opens with three tellers. Total teller cost per branch is $96,000 per year. The three tellers combined can process up to 90,000 customer transactions per year. If a branch does not attain a volume of at least 60,000 transactions during its first year of operations, it is closed. If the demand for services exceeds 90,000 transactions, an additional teller is hired and the branch is transferred from the start-up division to regular operations.

Required

a. What is the relevant range of activity for new branch banks?

b. Determine the amount of teller cost in total and the average teller cost per transaction for a branch that processes 60,000, 70,000, 80,000, or 90,000 transactions. In this case (the activity base is the number of transactions for a specific branch), is the teller cost a fixed or a variable cost? Round year figures to 2 decimal points.

c. Determine the amount of teller cost in total and the average teller cost per branch for Atlantic Bank, assuming that the start-up division operates 10, 15, or 25 branches. In this case (the activity base is the number of branches), is the teller cost a fixed or a variable cost?

Problem 11-24 *Context-sensitive nature of cost behavior classifications*

LO 11-1

Lisa Dunkley operates a sales booth in computer software trade shows, selling an accounting software package, *Abacus*. She purchases the package from a software company for $150 each. Booth space at the convention hall costs $8,000 per show.

CHECK FIGURES
a. Average cost at
   400 units: $170
b. Average price at
   250 units: $227

Required

a. Sales at past trade shows have ranged between 200 and 400 software packages per show. Determine the average cost of sales per unit if Ms. Dunkley sells 200, 250, 300, 350, or 400 units of *Abacus* at a trade show. Use the following chart to organize your answer. Is the cost of booth space fixed or variable? Round your computation to 2 decimal points.

	Sales Volume in Units (a)				
	200	250	300	350	400
Total cost of software (a × $150)	$30,000				
Total cost of booth rental	8,000				
Total cost of sales (b)	$38,000				
Average cost per unit (b ÷ a)	$190.00				

b. If Ms. Dunkley wants to earn a $45 profit on each package of software she sells at a trade show, what price must she charge at sales volumes of 200, 250, 300, 350, or 400 units?

c. Record the total cost of booth space if Ms. Dunkley attends one, two, three, four, or five trade shows. Record your answers in the following chart. Is the cost of booth space fixed or variable relative to the number of shows attended?

	Number of Trade Shows Attended				
	1	2	3	4	5
Total cost of booth rental	$8,000				

d. Ms. Dunkley provides decorative shopping bags to customers who purchase software packages. Some customers take the bags; others do not. Some customers stuff more than one software package into a single bag. The number of bags varies in relation to the number of units sold, but the relationship is not proportional. Assume that Ms. Dunkley uses $30 of bags for every 50 software packages sold. What is the additional cost per unit sold? Is the cost fixed or variable?

Problem 11-25 *Effects of operating leverage on profitability*

LO 11-2

Rohr Training Services (RTS) provides instruction on the use of computer software for the employees of its corporate clients. It offers courses in the clients' offices on the clients' equipment. The only major expense RTS incurs is instructor salaries; it pays instructors $4,000 per course taught. RTS recently agreed to offer a course of instruction to the employees of Basemera Incorporated at a price of $600 per student. Basemera estimated that 20 students would attend the course.

Base your answers on the preceding information.

430   Chapter 11

Part 1:

Required

a. Relative to the number of students in a single course, is the cost of instruction a fixed or a variable cost?

b. Determine the profit, assuming that 20 students attend the course.

c. Determine the profit, assuming a 10 percent increase in enrollment (i.e., enrollment increases to 22 students). What is the percentage change in profitability?

d. Determine the profit, assuming a 10 percent decrease in enrollment (i.e., enrollment decreases to 18 students). What is the percentage change in profitability?

e. Explain why a 10 percent shift in enrollment produces more than a 10 percent shift in profitability. Use the term that identifies this phenomenon.

Part 2:

The instructor has offered to teach the course for a percentage of tuition fees. Specifically, she wants $360 per person attending the class. Assume that the tuition fee remains at $600 per student.

Required

f. Is the cost of instruction a fixed or a variable cost?

g. Determine the profit, assuming that 20 students take the course.

h. Determine the profit, assuming a 10 percent increase in enrollment (i.e., enrollment increases to 22 students). What is the percentage change in profitability?

i. Determine the profit, assuming a 10 percent decrease in enrollment (i.e., enrollment decreases to 18 students). What is the percentage change in profitability?

j. Explain why a 10 percent change in enrollment produces a proportional 10 percent change in profitability.

Part 3:

RTS sells a workbook with printed material unique to each course to each student who attends the course. Any workbooks that are not sold must be destroyed. Prior to the first class, RTS printed 20 copies of the books based on the client's estimate of the number of people who would attend the course. Each workbook costs $30 and is sold to course participants for $50. This cost includes a royalty fee paid to the author and the cost of duplication.

Required

k. Calculate the workbook cost in total and per student, assuming that 18, 20, or 22 students attempt to attend the course. Round your computation to 2 decimal points.

l. Classify the cost of workbooks as fixed or variable relative to the number of students attending the course.

m. Discuss the risk of holding inventory as it applies to the workbooks.

n. Explain how a just-in-time inventory system can reduce the cost and risk of holding inventory.

LO 11-2

Problem 11-26   *Effects of fixed and variable cost behavior on the risk and rewards of business opportunities*

Orlando and Diego Universities offer executive training courses to corporate clients. Orlando pays its instructors $4,600 per course taught. Diego pays its instructors $230 per student enrolled in the class. Both universities charge executives a $400 tuition fee per course attended.

Required

a. Prepare income statements for Orlando and Diego, assuming that 20 students attend a course.

b. Orlando University embarks on a strategy to entice students from Diego University by lowering its tuition to $220 per course. Prepare an income statement for Orlando assuming that the university is successful and enrolls 40 students in its course.

c. Diego University embarks on a strategy to entice students from Orlando University by lowering its tuition to $220 per course. Prepare an income statement for Diego, assuming that the university is successful and enrolls 40 students in its course.

Cost Behavior, Operating Leverage, and Profitability Analysis   431

d. Explain why the strategy described in Requirement *b* produced a profit but the same strategy described in Requirement *c* produced a loss.

e. Prepare income statements for Orlando and Diego Universities, assuming that 10 students attend a course, and assuming that both universities charge executives a $400 tuition fee per course attended.

f. It is always better to have fixed rather than variable cost. Explain why this statement is false.

g. It is always better to have variable rather than fixed cost. Explain why this statement is false.

Problem 11-27 *Analyzing operating leverage*   LO 11-4

Palvo Sorokin is a venture capitalist facing two alternative investment opportunities. He intends to invest $1 million in a start-up firm. He is nervous, however, about future economic volatility. He asks you to analyze the following financial data for the past year's operations of the two firms he is considering and give him some business advice.

	Company Name	
	Wood	Lake
Variable cost per unit (a)	$ 16.00	$ 8.00
Sales revenue (8,000 units × $25)	$200,000	$200,000
Variable cost (8,000 units × a)	(128,000)	(64,000)
Contribution margin	$ 72,000	$136,000
Fixed cost	(24,000)	(88,000)
Net income	$ 48,000	$ 48,000

Required

Round your figures to 2 decimal points in all required computation.

a. Use the contribution margin approach to compute the operating leverage for each firm.

b. If the economy expands in coming years, Wood and Lake will both enjoy a 10 percent per year increase in sales, assuming that the selling price remains unchanged. Compute the change in net income for each firm in *dollar amount* and in *percentage*. (*Note:* Since the number of units increases, both revenue and variable cost will increase.)

c. If the economy contracts in coming years, Wood and Lake will both suffer a 10 percent decrease in sales volume, assuming that the selling price remains unchanged. Compute the change in net income for each firm in *dollar amount* and in *percentage*. (*Note:* Since the number of units decreases, both total revenue and total variable cost will decrease.)

d. Write a memo to Palvo Sorokin with your analyses and advice.

CHECK FIGURES
b. % of change for Lake: 28.33
c. % of change for Wood: (15.00)

Problem 11-28 *Determining the break-even point and preparing a contribution margin income statement*   LO 11-3, 11-5

Lucent Manufacturing Company makes a product that it sells for $75 per unit. The company incurs variable manufacturing costs of $30 per unit. Variable selling expenses are $9 per unit, annual fixed manufacturing costs are $240,000, and fixed selling and administrative costs are $165,000 per year.

Required

Determine the break-even point in units and dollars using each of the following approaches:

a. Equation method.

b. Contribution margin per unit.

c. Confirm your results by preparing a contribution margin income statement for the break-even sales volume.

CHECK FIGURE
a. 11,250 units

Problem 11-29 *Margin of safety and operating leverage*   LO 11-4, 11-6

Carmon Company is considering the addition of a new product to its cosmetics line. The company has three distinctly different options: a skin cream, a bath oil, or a hair coloring gel.

Relevant information and budgeted annual income statements for each of the products follow.

Relevant Information			
	Skin Cream	Bath Oil	Color Gel
Budgeted sales in units (a)	100,000	180,000	60,000
Expected sales price (b)	$7.00	$4.00	$10.00
Variable costs per unit (c)	$2.00	$1.00	$6.00
Income statements			
Sales revenue (a × b)	$ 700,000	$ 720,000	$ 600,000
Variable costs (a × c)	(200,000)	(180,000)	(360,000)
Contribution margin	500,000	540,000	240,000
Fixed costs	(420,000)	(480,000)	(100,000)
Net income	$ 80,000	$ 60,000	$ 140,000

Required

a. Determine the margin of safety as a percentage for each product. Round your figures to 2 decimal points.

b. Prepare revised income statements for each product, assuming a 20 percent increase in the budgeted sales volume.

c. For each product, determine the percentage change in net income that results from the 20 percent increase in sales. Which product has the highest operating leverage? Round your figures to 2 decimal points.

d. Assuming that management is pessimistic and risk averse, which product should the company add to its cosmetics line? Explain your answer.

e. Assuming that management is optimistic and risk aggressive, which product should the company add to its cosmetics line? Explain your answer.

ANALYZE, THINK, COMMUNICATE

ATC 11-1   Business Applications   *Operating leverage*

Description of Business for Merck & Co., Inc.

Merck & Co., Inc., is a global health care company that delivers innovative health solutions through its prescription medicines, vaccines, biologic therapies, animal health, and consumer care products, which it markets directly and through its joint ventures. The company's operations are principally managed on a products basis and are comprised of four operating segments, which are the Pharmaceutical, Animal Health, Consumer Care, and Alliances segments, and one reportable segment, which is the Pharmaceutical segment.

Merck & Company	2011	2010
Revenue	$48,047	$45,987
Operating earnings	7,334	1,653

Description of Business for Costco Wholesale Corporation

We at Costco Wholesale Corporation operate membership warehouses based on the concept that offering our members low prices on a limited selection of nationally branded and private-label products in a wide range of merchandise categories will produce high sales volumes and rapid inventory turnover. . . .

Because of our high sales volume and rapid inventory turnover, we generally sell inventory before we are required to pay many of our merchandise vendors, even though we take advantage of early payment discounts when available. To the extent that sales increase and inventory turnover becomes more rapid, a greater percentage of inventory is financed through payment terms provided by suppliers rather than by our working capital.

Costco Corporation	2011	2010
Revenue	$88,915	$77,946
Operating earnings	2,439	2,077

Required

a. Determine which company appears to have the higher operating leverage.

b. Write a paragraph or two explaining why the company you identified in Requirement *a* might be expected to have the higher operating leverage.

c. If revenues for both companies declined, which company do you think would likely experience the greater decline in operating earnings? Explain your answer.

ATC 11-2   Group Assignment   *Operating leverage*

The Parent Teacher Association (PTA) of Meadow High School is planning a fund-raising campaign. The PTA is considering the possibility of hiring Eric Logan, a world-renowned investment counselor, to address the public. Tickets would sell for $28 each. The school has agreed to let the PTA use Harville Auditorium at no cost. Mr. Logan is willing to accept one of two compensation arrangements. He will sign an agreement to receive a fixed fee of $10,000 regardless of the number of tickets sold. Alternatively, he will accept payment of $20 per ticket sold. In communities similar to that in which Meadow is located, Mr. Logan has drawn an audience of approximately 500 people.

Required

a. In front of the class, present a statement showing the expected net income assuming 500 people buy tickets.

b. The instructor will divide the class into groups and then organize the groups into four sections. The instructor will assign one of the following tasks to each section of groups.

Group Tasks

    (1) Assume the PTA pays Mr. Logan a fixed fee of $10,000. Determine the amount of net income that the PTA will earn if ticket sales are 10 percent higher than expected. Calculate the percentage change in net income.

    (2) Assume that the PTA pays Mr. Logan a fixed fee of $10,000. Determine the amount of net income that the PTA will earn if ticket sales are 10 percent lower than expected. Calculate the percentage change in net income.

    (3) Assume that the PTA pays Mr. Logan $20 per ticket sold. Determine the amount of net income that the PTA will earn if ticket sales are 10 percent higher than expected. Calculate the percentage change in net income.

    (4) Assume that the PTA pays Mr. Logan $20 per ticket sold. Determine the amount of net income that the PTA will earn if ticket sales are 10 percent lower than expected. Calculate the percentage change in net income.

c. Have each group select a spokesperson. Have one of the spokespersons in each section of groups go to the board and present the results of the analysis conducted in Requirement *b*. Resolve any discrepancies between the computations presented at the board and those developed by the other groups.

d. Draw conclusions regarding the risks and rewards associated with operating leverage. At a minimum, answer the following questions:

    (1) Which type of cost structure (fixed or variable) produces the higher growth potential in profitability for a company?

    (2) Which type of cost structure (fixed or variable) faces the higher risk of declining profitability for a company?

    (3) Under what circumstances should a company seek to establish a fixed cost structure?

    (4) Under what circumstances should a company seek to establish a variable cost structure?

ATC 11-3 Research Assignment *Fixed versus variable cost*

Use the 2011 Form 10-K for Black & Decker Corp. (B&D) (not Stanley Black & Decker) to complete the requirements below. To obtain the Form 10-K, you can use the EDGAR system (see Appendix A at the back of this text for instructions), or it can be found under "Investor Relations" on the company's corporate website at www.bdk.com. Be sure to read carefully the following portions of the document:

■ "General Development of the Business" on pages 3–4.
■ "Consolidated Statement of Operations" on page 65.

Required

a. Calculate the percentage increase in B&D's sales and its "earnings from continuing operations" from 2010 to 2011.

b. Would fixed costs or variable costs be more likely to explain why B&D's operating earnings increased by a bigger percentage than its sales?

c. On page 105, B&D reported that it incurred research and development costs of $147.2 million in 2011. If this cost is thought of in the context of the number of units of products sold, should it be considered as primarily fixed or variable in nature?

d. If the research and development costs are thought of in the context of the number of new products developed, should they be considered as primarily fixed or variable in nature?

ATC 11-4 Writing Assignment *Operating leverage, margin of safety, and cost behavior*

Early versions of cellular phones could do one thing—make and receive voice phone calls. Later versions were developed that could send and receive text messages, but due to their typing interface, performing this task was cumbersome. Then a company named Research in Motion (RIM) brought its BlackBerry phone to the market with an integrated keyboard that made typing text much easier. The BlackBerry became the phone of choice for users who wanted to send and receive e-mail messages via their cell phone, and its success soared.

Unfortunately for RIM, Apple Inc. began selling the iPhone to the world in June of 2007. The iPhone was not only capable of dealing with e-mail messages efficiently, but it also allowed users to search the Internet using a popular touchscreen interface. The popularity of RIM's BlackBerry began to decline. RIM's sales declined 14 percent in its 2012 fiscal year compared to its sales in 2011, but its operating earnings declined 32 percent.

Required

Write a memorandum that explains how a 14 percent decline in sales could cause a 32 percent decline in profits. Your memo should address the following:

a. An identification of the accounting concept involved.

b. A discussion of how various major types of costs incurred by RIM were likely affected by the decline in its sales.

c. The effect of the decline in sales on RIM's margin of safety.

ATC 11-5 Ethical Dilemma *Profitability versus social conscience (effects of cost behavior)*

Advances in biological technology have enabled two research companies, Bio Labs, Inc., and Scientific Associates, to develop an insect-resistant corn seed. Neither company is financially strong enough to develop the distribution channels necessary to bring the product to world markets. World Agra Distributors, Inc., has negotiated contracts with both companies for the exclusive right to market their seed. Bio Labs signed an agreement to receive an annual royalty of $1,000,000. In contrast, Scientific Associates chose an agreement that provides for a royalty of $0.50 per pound of seed sold. Both agreements have a 10-year term. During 2014, World Agra sold approximately 1,600,000 pounds of the Bio Labs, Inc., seed and 2,400,000 pounds of the Scientific Associates seed. Both types of seed were sold for $1.25 per pound. By the end of 2014, it was apparent that the seed developed by Scientific Associates was superior. Although insect infestation was virtually nonexistent for both types of seed, the seed developed by Scientific Associates produced corn that was sweeter and had consistently higher yields.

World Agra Distributors' chief financial officer, Roger Weatherstone, recently retired. To the astonishment of the annual planning committee, Mr. Weatherstone's replacement, Ray Borrough, adamantly recommended that the marketing department develop a major advertising campaign to promote the seed developed by Bio Labs, Inc. The planning committee reluctantly approved the recommendation. A $100,000 ad campaign was launched; the ads emphasized the ability of the Bio Labs seed to avoid insect infestation. The campaign was silent with respect to taste or crop yield. It did not mention the seed developed by Scientific Associates. World Agra's sales staff was instructed to push the Bio Labs seed and to sell the Scientific Associates seed only on customer demand. Although total sales remained relatively constant during 2015, sales of the Scientific Associates seed fell to approximately 1,300,000 pounds while sales of the Bio Labs, Inc., seed rose to 2,700,000 pounds.

Required

a. Determine the amount of increase or decrease in profitability experienced by World Agra in 2015 as a result of promoting the Bio Labs seed. Support your answer with appropriate commentary.

b. Did World Agra's customers in particular and society in general benefit or suffer from the decision to promote the Bio Labs seed?

c. Review the statement of ethical professional practice in Exhibit 10.17 of Chapter 10 and comment on whether Mr. Borrough's recommendation violated any of the standards in the code of ethical conduct.

d. Comment on your belief regarding the adequacy of the statement of ethical professional practice in terms of directing the conduct of management accountants.

GLOSSARY

absolute amounts   Dollar totals reported in accounts on financial reports that can be misleading because they make no reference to the relative size of the company being analyzed. *p. 327*

accelerated depreciation methods   Depreciation methods that recognize depreciation expense more rapidly in the early stages of an asset's life than in the later stages of its life. *p. 214*

account balance   Difference between total debits and total credits in an account. *p. 602*

account receivable   Expected future cash receipt arising from permitting a customer to *buy now and pay later;* typically a relatively small balance due within a short time period. *pp. 51, 162*

accounting   Service-based profession that provides reliable and relevant financial information useful in making decisions. *p. 3*

accounting equation   Expression of the relationship between the assets and the claims on those assets. *p. 12*

accounting event   Economic occurrence that causes changes in an enterprise's assets, liabilities, or equity. *p. 13*

accounting period   Span of time covered by the financial statements, normally one year, but may be a quarter, a month or some other time span. *p. 23*

accounts   Records used for classifying and summarizing transaction data; subclassifications of financial statement elements. *p. 11*

accounts receivable turnover   Financial ratio that measures how fast accounts receivable are turned into cash; computed by dividing sales by accounts receivable. *p. 333*

accrual   Recognition of events before exchanging cash. *p. 49*

accrual accounting   Accounting system that recognizes expenses or revenues when they occur regardless of when cash is exchanged. *p. 49*

accrued expenses   Expenses that are recognized before cash is paid. An example is accrued salaries expense. *p. 52*

accrued interest   Interest revenue or expense that is recognized before cash has been exchanged. *p. 173*

accumulated conversion factors   Factors used to convert a series of future cash inflows into their present value equivalent and that are applicable to cash inflows of equal amounts spread over equal interval time periods and that can be determined by computing the sum of the individual single factors used for each period. *p. 573*

accumulated depreciation   Contra asset account that indicates the sum of all depreciation expense recognized for an asset since the date of acquisition. *p. 212*

acid-test ratio   (quick ratio) Measure of immediate debt-paying ability; calculated by dividing very liquid assets (cash, receivables, and marketable securities) by current liabilities. *p. 332*

activities   The actions taken by an organization to accomplish its mission. *p. 381*

activity base   Factor that causes changes in variable cost; is usually some measure of volume when used to define cost behavior. *p. 411*

activity-based management (ABM)   Management of the activities of an organization to add the greatest value by developing products that satisfy the needs of that organization's customers. *p. 381*

adjusting entry   Entry that updates account balances prior to preparing financial statements. *pp. 52, 174*

adverse opinion   Opinion issued by a certified public accountant that means one or more departures from GAAP in a company's financial statements are so very material the auditors believe the financial statements do not fairly represent the company's status; contrast with *unqualified opinion. p. 147*

aging of accounts receivable   Classifying each account receivable by the number of days it has been outstanding. The aging schedule is used to develop an estimate of the amount of the allowance for doubtful accounts. *p. 171*

AICPA (American Institute of Certified Public Accountants)   National association that serves the educational and professional interests of members of the public accounting profession; membership is voluntary. *p. 143*

allocation   Process of dividing a total cost into parts and apportioning the parts among the relevant cost objects. *p. 440*

allocation base   Cost driver used as the basis for the allocation process. *p. 441*

allocation rate   Factor used to allocate or assign costs to a cost object; determined by taking the total cost to be allocated and dividing it by the appropriate cost driver. *p. 441*

allowance for doubtful accounts   Contra asset account that contains an amount equal to the accounts receivable that are expected to be uncollectible. *p. 164*

allowance method of accounting for uncollectible accounts   Method of accounting for bad debts in which bad debts are estimated and expensed in the same period in which the corresponding sales are recognized. The receivables are reported in the financial statements at net realizable value (the amount expected to be collected in cash). *p. 164*

amortization   Method of systematically allocating the costs of intangible assets to expense over their useful lives; also term for converting the discount on a note or a bond to interest expense over a designated period. *pp. 208, 254*

amortizing   See *amortization.*

annual report   Document in which an organization provides information to stockholders, usually on an annual basis. *p. 28*

annuity   Series of equal payments made over a specified number of periods. *p. 573*

appropriated retained earnings   Retained earnings restricted by the board of directors for a specific purpose (e.g., to repay debt or for future expansion); although a part of total retained earnings, not available for distribution as dividends. *p. 307*

articles of incorporation   Items on an application filed with a state agency for the formation of a corporation; contains such information as the corporation's name, its purpose, its location, its expected life, provisions for its capital stock, and a list of the members of its board of directors. *p. 294*

articulation   Characteristic of financial statements that means they are interrelated. For example, the amount of net income reported on the income statement is added to beginning retained earnings as a component in calculating the ending retained earnings balance reported on the statement of changes in stockholders' equity. *p. 21*

asset exchange transaction   A transaction that decreases one asset while increasing another asset so that total assets do not change; for example, the purchase of land with cash. *pp. 14, 51*

asset source transaction   Transaction that increases an asset and a claim on assets; three types of asset source transactions are acquisitions from owners (equity), borrowings from creditors (liabilities), or earnings from operations (revenues). *pp. 13, 50*

asset turnover ratio   The amount of net income divided by average total assets. *p. 328*

asset use transaction   Transaction that decreases an asset and a claim on assets; the three types are distributions (transfers to owners), liability payments (to creditors), or expenses (used to operate the business). *pp. 15, 51*

assets   Economic resources used by a business to produce revenue. *p. 11*

audits   Detailed examination of some aspect of a company's accounting records or operating procedures in order to report the results to interested parties. *p. 145*

authority manual   A document that outlines the chain of command for authority and responsibility. The authority manual provides guidelines for specific positions such as personnel officer as well as general authority such as all vice presidents are authorized to spend up to a designated limit. *p. 133*

authorized stock   Number of shares that the corporation is approved by the state to issue. *p. 299*

average cost   The total cost of making products divided by the total number of products made. *p. 366*

average number of days to collect receivables   Length of the average collection period for accounts receivable; computed by dividing 365 by the accounts receivable turnover ratio. *p. 334*

average number of days to sell inventory   Financial ratio that measures the average number of days that inventory stays in stock before being sold. *p. 334*

avoidable costs   Future costs that can be avoided by taking a specified course of action. To be avoidable in a decision-making context, costs must differ among the alternatives. For example, if the cost of material used to make two different products is the same for both products, that cost could not be avoided by choosing to produce one product over the other. Therefore, the material's cost would not be an avoidable cost. *p. 472*

balanced score card   A management evaluation tool that includes financial and nonfinancial measures. *p. 551*

balance sheet   Statement that lists the assets of a business and the corresponding claims (liabilities and equity) on those assets. *p. 23*

bank reconciliation   Schedule that identifies and explains differences between the cash balance reported by the bank and the cash balance in the firm's accounting records. *p. 137*

bank statement   Statement issued by a bank (usually monthly) that denotes all activity in the bank account for that period. *p. 137*

bank statement credit memo   Memorandum that describes an increase in the account balance. *p. 137*

bank statement debit memo   Memorandum that describes a decrease in the account balance. *p. 137*

basket purchase   Acquisition of several assets in a single transaction with no specific cost attributed to each asset. *p. 209*

batch-level costs   The costs associated with producing a batch of products. For example, the cost of setting up machinery to produce 1,000 products is a batch-level cost. The classification of batch-level costs is context sensitive. Postage for one product would be classified as a unit-level cost. In contrast, postage for a large number of products delivered in a single shipment would be classified as a batch-level cost. *p. 473*

benchmarking   Identifying the best practices used by world-class competitors. *p. 381*

best practices   Practices used by world-class companies. *p. 381*

board of directors   Group of individuals elected by the stockholders of a corporation to oversee its operations. *p. 296*

bond certificates   Debt securities used to obtain long-term financing in which a company borrows funds from a number of lenders, called *bondholders;* usually issued in denominations of $1,000. *p. 257*

bond discount   Difference between the selling price and the face amount of a bond sold for less than the face amount. *p. 262*

bond premium   Difference between the selling price and the face amount of a bond that is sold for more than the face amount. *p. 266*

bondholder   The party buying a bond (the lender or creditor). *p. 257*

book of original entry   A journal in which transactions are first recorded. *p. 603*

book value   Historical (original) cost of an asset minus the accumulated depreciation; alternatively, undepreciated amount to date. *p. 212*

book value per share   Value of stock determined by dividing the total stockholders' equity by the number of shares of stock. *pp. 299, 340*

break-even point   Point where total revenue equals total cost; can be expressed in units or sales dollars. *p. 412*

budgeting   Form of planning that formalizes a company's goals and objectives in financial terms. *p. 504*

capital budgeting   Financial planning activities that cover the intermediate range of time such as whether to buy or lease equipment, whether to purchase a particular investment, or whether to increase operating expenses to stimulate sales. *p. 506*

capital expenditures   (on an existing asset) Substantial amounts of funds spent to improve an asset's quality or to extend its life. *p. 220*

capital investments   Expenditures for the purchase of operational assets that involve a long-term commitment of funds that can be critically important to the company's ultimate success; normally recovered through the use of the assets. *p. 570*

carrying value   Face amount of a bond liability less any unamortized bond discount or plus any unamortized bond premium. *p. 263*

cash   Coins, currency, checks, balances in checking and certain savings accounts, money orders, bank drafts, certificates of deposit, and other items that are payable on demand. *p. 135*

cash budget   A budget that focuses on cash receipts and payments that are expected to occur in the future. *p. 515*

cash discount   Discount offered on merchandise sold to encourage prompt payment; offered by sellers of merchandise and represent sales discounts to the seller when they are used and purchase discounts to the purchaser of the merchandise. *p. 100*

certified check   Check guaranteed by a bank to be drawn on an account having funds sufficient to pay the check. *p. 139*

certified public accountant (CPA)   Accountant who, by meeting certain educational and experiential requirements, is licensed by the state government to provide audit services to the public. *p. 145*

certified suppliers   Suppliers who have gained the confidence of the buyer by providing quality goods and services at desirable prices and usually in accordance with strict delivery specifications; frequently provide the buyer with preferred customer status in exchange for guaranteed purchase quantities and prompt payment schedules. *p. 478*

chart of accounts   List of all ledger accounts and their corresponding account numbers. *p. 603*

checks   Prenumbered forms, sometimes multicopy, with the name of the business issuing them preprinted on the face, indicating to whom they are paid, the amount of the payment, and the transaction date. *p. 137*

claims   Owners' and creditors' interests in a business's assets. *p. 12*

claims exchange transaction   Transaction that decreases one claim and increases another so that total claims do not change. For example, the accrual of interest expense is a claims exchange transaction; liabilities increase, and the recognition of the expense causes retained earnings to decrease. *p. 53*

classified balance sheet   Balance sheet that distinguishes between current and noncurrent items. *p. 268*

closely held corporation Corporation whose stock is exchanged between a limited number of individuals. *p. 294*

closing See *closing the books.*

closing the books Process of transferring balances from temporary accounts (Revenue, Expense, and Dividends) to the permanent account (Retained Earnings). *p. 25*

Code of Professional Conduct A set of guidelines established by the American Institute of Certified Public Accountants (AICPA) to promote high ethical conduct among its membership. *p. 143*

collateral Assets pledged as security for a loan. *pp. 173, 267*

common costs Costs that are incurred to support more than one cost object but cannot be traced to any specific object. *p. 440*

common size financial statements Financial statements in which amounts are converted to percentages to allow a better comparison of period-to-period and company-to-company financial data since all information is placed on a common basis. *p. 109*

common stock Basic class of corporate stock that carries no preferences as to claims on assets or dividends; certificates that evidence ownership in a company. *pp. 12, 300*

confidentiality Code of ethics requirement that prohibits CPAs from voluntarily disclosing information they acquire as a result of accountant-client relationships. *p. 147*

conservatism A principle that guides accountants in uncertain circumstances to select the alternative that produces the lowest amount of net income. *p. 58*

consistency The generally accepted accounting principle that a company should, in most circumstances, continually use the same accounting method(s) so that its financial statements are comparable across time. *p. 183*

contingent liability A potential obligation, the amount of which depends on the outcome of future events. *p. 250*

continuity Concept that describes the fact that a corporation's life may extend well beyond the time at which any particular shareholder decides to retire or to sell his or her stock. *p. 296*

continuous improvement Total quality management (TQM) feature that refers to an ongoing process through which employees learn to eliminate waste, reduce response time, minimize defects, and simplify the design and delivery of products and services to customers. *p. 381*

contra asset account Account subtracted from another account with which it is associated; has the effect of reducing the asset account with which it is associated. *pp. 166, 212*

contribution margin Difference between a company's sales revenue and total variable cost; represents the amount available to cover fixed cost and thereafter to provide a profit. *p. 408*

contribution margin per unit The contribution margin per unit is equal to the sales price per unit minus the variable cost per unit. *p. 413*

controllability concept Evaluating managerial performance based only on revenue and costs under the manager's direct control. *p. 538*

controllable costs Costs that can be influenced by a particular manager's decisions and actions. *p. 440*

copyright Legal protection of writings, musical compositions, and other intellectual property for the exclusive use of the creator or persons assigned the right by the creator. *p. 223*

corporation Legal entity separate from its owners; formed when a group of individuals with a common purpose join together in an organization according to state laws. *p. 294*

cost Measure of resources used to acquire an asset or to produce revenue. *p. 59*

cost accumulation Process of determining the cost of a particular object by accumulating many individual costs into a single total cost. *p. 438*

cost allocation Process of dividing a total cost into parts and assigning the parts to relevant objects. *pp. 372, 439*

cost behavior How a cost reacts (goes up, down, or remains the same) relative to changes in some measure of activity (e.g., the behavior pattern of the cost of raw materials is to increase as the number of units of product made increases). *p. 404*

cost center Type of responsibility center which incurs costs but does not generate revenue. *p. 538*

cost driver Any factor, usually some measure of activity, that causes cost to be incurred, sometimes referred to as *activity base* or *allocation base*. Examples are labor hours, machine hours, or some other measure of activity whose change causes corresponding changes in the cost object. *p. 438*

cost method of accounting for treasury stock Method of accounting for treasury stock in which the purchase of treasury stock is recorded at its cost to the firm but does not consider the original issue price or par value. *p. 304*

cost objects Objects for which managers need to know the cost; can be products, processes, departments, services, activities, and so on. *p. 436*

cost of capital Return paid to investors and creditors for the use of their assets (capital); usually represents a company's minimum rate of return. *p. 571*

cost of goods available for sale Total costs paid to obtain goods and to make them ready for sale, including the cost of beginning inventory plus purchases and transportation-in costs, less purchase returns and allowances and purchase discounts. *p. 95*

cost of goods sold Total cost incurred for the goods sold during a specific accounting period. *p. 95*

cost-plus pricing Pricing strategy that sets the price at cost plus a markup equal to a percentage of the cost. *p. 365*

cost pool A collection of costs organized around a common cost driver. The cost pool as opposed to individual costs is allocated to cost objects using the common cost driver thereby promoting efficiency in the allocation process. *p. 442*

cost tracing Relating specific costs to the objects that cause their incurrence. *p. 439*

credit Entry that increases liability and equity accounts or decreases asset accounts. *p. 602*

creditors Individuals or institutions that have loaned goods or services to a business. *p. 4*

cumulative dividends Preferred dividends that accumulate from year to year until paid. *p. 301*

current (short-term) assets Assets that will be converted to cash or consumed within one year or an operating cycle, whichever is longer. *pp. 206, 267*

current (short-term) liability Obligation due within one year or an operating cycle, whichever is longer. *p. 267*

current ratio Measure of liquidity (short-term debt-paying ability); calculated by dividing current assets by current liabilities. *p. 332*

date of record Date that establishes who will receive the dividend payment: shareholders who actually own the stock on the record date will be paid the dividend even if the stock is sold before the dividend is paid. *p. 305*

debit Entry that increases asset accounts or decreases liability and equity accounts. *p. 602*

debt to assets ratio Financial ratio that measures a company's level of risk. *p. 335*

debt to equity ratio Financial ratio that compares creditor financing to owner financing, expressed as the dollar amount of liabilities for each dollar of stockholder's equity. *p. 335*

decentralization Practice of delegating authority and responsibility for the operation of business segments. *p. 538*

declaration date Date on which the board of directors actually declares a dividend. *p. 305*

deferral Recognition of revenue or expense in a period after the cash is exchanged. *p. 49*

depletion Method of systematically allocating the costs of natural resources to expense as the resources are removed from the land. *p. 208*

deposits in transit Deposits recorded in a depositor's books but not received and recorded by the bank. *p. 138*

deposit ticket Bank form that accompanies checks and cash deposited into a bank account; normally specifies the account number, name of the account, and a record of the checks and cash being deposited. *p. 137*

depreciable cost Original cost minus salvage value (of a long-term depreciable asset). *p. 210*

depreciation Decline in value of long-term tangible assets such as buildings, furniture, or equipment. It is systematically recognized by accountants as depreciation expense over the useful lives of the affected assets. *p. 208*

depreciation expense Portion of the original cost of a long-term tangible asset systematically allocated to an expense account in a given period. *p. 210*

differential revenues Future-oriented revenues that differ among the alternatives under consideration. *p. 472*

direct cost Cost that is easily traceable to a cost object and for which the sacrifice to trace is small in relation to the information benefits attained. *p. 439*

direct labor Wages paid to production workers whose efforts can be easily and conveniently traced to products. *p. 369*

direct raw materials Costs of raw materials used to make products that can be easily and conveniently traced to those products. *p. 369*

disclaimer of opinion Report on financial statements issued when the auditor is unable to obtain enough information to determine if the statements conform to GAAP; is neither positive nor negative. *p. 147*

discount on bonds payable Contra liability account used to record the amount of discount on a bond issue. *p. 262*

dividend Transfer of wealth from a business to its owners. *p. 16*

dividends in arrears Cumulative dividends on preferred stock that have not been paid; must be paid prior to paying dividends to common stockholders. *p. 301*

dividend yield Ratio for comparing stock dividends paid in relation to the market price; calculated as dividends per share divided by market price per share. *p. 341*

double-declining-balance depreciation Depreciation method that recognizes larger amounts of depreciation in the early stages of an asset's life and progressively smaller amounts as the asset ages. *p. 214*

double-entry accounting (bookkeeping) Method of keeping records that provides a system of checks and balances by recording transactions in a dual format. *pp. 13, 602*

double taxation Policy to tax corporate profits distributed to owners twice, once when the income is reported on the corporation's income tax return and again when the dividends are reported on the individual's return. *p. 295*

downstream costs Costs, such as delivery costs and sales commissions, incurred after the manufacturing process is complete. *p. 375*

earnings The difference between revenues and expenses. Same as net income or profit. *p. 4*

earnings per share Measure of the value of a share of common stock in terms of company earnings; calculated as net income available to common stockholders divided by the average number of outstanding common shares. *p. 340*

effective interest rate Yield rate of bonds, equal to the market rate of interest on the day the bonds are sold. *p. 262*

effective interest rate method Method of amortizing bond discounts and premiums that bases interest computations on the carrying value of liability. As the liability increases or decreases, the amount of interest expense also increases or decreases. *p. 270*

elements Primary components of financial statements including assets, liabilities, equity, contributions, revenue, expenses, distributions, and net income. *p. 10*

entity See *reporting entities*.

entrenched management Management that may have become ineffective but because of political implications may be difficult to remove. *p. 297*

equation method Cost-volume-profit analysis technique that uses the algebraic relationship among sales, variable costs, fixed costs, and desired net income before taxes to solve for required sales volume. *p. 412*

equipment replacement decisions Decisions regarding whether existing equipment should be replaced with newer equipment based on identification and comparison of the avoidable costs of the old and new equipment to determine which equipment is more profitable to operate. *p. 482*

equity Portion of assets remaining after the creditors' claims have been satisfied (i.e., Assets Liabilities Equity); also called *residual interest* or *net assets*. *p. 10*

estimated useful life Time for which an asset is expected to be used by a business. *p. 210*

ex-dividend Stock traded after the date of record but before the payment date; does not receive the benefit of the upcoming dividend. *p. 306*

expenses Economic sacrifices (decreases in assets or increase in liabilities) that are incurred in the process of generating revenue. *pp. 15, 54*

face value Amount of the bond to be paid back (to the bondholders) at maturity. *p. 257*

facility-level costs Costs incurred on behalf of the whole company or a segment of the company; not related to any specific product, batch, or unit of production or service and unavoidable unless the entire company or segment is eliminated. *p. 473*

favorable variance Variance that occurs when actual costs are less than standard costs or when actual sales are higher than standard sales. *p. 542*

fidelity bond Insurance policy that a company buys to insure itself against loss due to employee dishonesty. *p. 133*

financial accounting Field of accounting designed to meet the information needs of external users of business information (creditors, investors, governmental agencies, financial analysts, etc.); its objective is to classify and record business events and transactions to facilitate the production of external financial reports (income statement, balance sheet, statement of cash flows, and statement of changes in equity). *pp. 6, 362*

Financial Accounting Standards Board (FASB) Privately funded organization with the primary authority for the establishment of accounting standards in the United States. *pp. 8, 365*

financial resources Money or credit supplied to a business by investors (owners) and creditors. *p. 4*

financial statement audit Detailed examination of a company's accounting records and the documents that support the information reported in the financial statements; includes testing the reliability of the underlying accounting system used to produce the financial reports. *p. 146*

financial statements Primary means of communicating the financial information of an organization to the external users. The four general-purpose financial statements are the income statement, statement of changes in equity, balance sheet, and statement of cash flows. *p. 10*

financing activities Cash inflows and outflows from transactions with investors and creditors (except interest). These cash flows include cash receipts from the issue of stock, borrowing activities, and cash disbursements associated with dividends. *p. 24*

finished goods inventory   Asset account used to accumulate the product costs (direct materials, direct labor, and overhead) associated with completed products that have not yet been sold. *pp. 178, 374*

first-in, first-out (FIFO) cost flow method   Inventory cost flow method that treats the first items purchased as the first items sold for the purpose of computing cost of goods sold. *p. 178*

fixed cost   Cost that in total remains constant when activity volume changes; varies per unit inversely with changes in the volume of activity. *p. 402*

fixed cost volume variance   The difference between the budgeted fixed cost and the applied fixed cost. *p. 542*

fixed interest rate   Interest rate (charge for the use of money) that does not change over the life of the loan. *p. 253*

flexible budgets   Budgets that show expected revenues and costs at a variety of different activity levels. *p. 539*

flexible budget variances   Differences between budgets based on standard amounts at the actual level of activity and actual results; caused by differences in standard and actual unit cost since the volume of activity is the same. *p. 543*

FOB (free on board) destination   Term that designates the seller as the responsible party for freight costs (transportation-in costs). *p. 101*

FOB (free on board) shipping point   Term that designates the buyer as the responsible party for freight costs (transportation-in costs). *p. 101*

franchise   Exclusive right to sell products or perform services in certain geographic areas. *p. 223*

full disclosure   The accounting principle that financial statements should include all information relevant to an entity's operations and financial condition. Full disclosure frequently requires adding footnotes to the financial statements. *p. 183*

gains   Increases in assets or decreases in liabilities that result from peripheral or incidental transactions. *p. 105*

general authority   Policies and procedures that apply across different levels of a company's management, such as everyone flies coach class. *p. 133*

general journal   Journal in which all types of accounting transactions can be entered but which is commonly used to record adjusting and closing entries and unusual types of transactions. *p. 603*

general ledger   Complete set of accounts used in accounting systems. *pp. 16, 603*

generally accepted accounting principles (GAAP)   Rules and regulations that accountants agree to follow when preparing financial reports for public distribution. *pp. 8, 365*

general uncertainties   Uncertainties inherent in operating a business, such as competition and damage from storms. Unlike contingent liabilities, these uncertainties arise from future rather than past events. *p. 250*

going concern assumption   Accounting presumption that a company will continue to operate indefinitely, benefiting from its assets and paying its obligations in full; justifies reporting assets and liabilities in the financial statements. *p. 19*

goodwill   Added value of a successful business that is attributable to factors—reputation, location, and superior products—that enable the business to earn above-average profits; stated differently, the excess paid for an existing business over the appraised value of the net assets. *p. 224*

gross margin (gross profit)   Difference between sales revenue and cost of goods sold; the amount a company makes from selling goods before subtracting operating expenses. *p. 96*

gross profit   See *gross margin.*

historical cost concept   Actual price paid for an asset when it was purchased. *pp. 16, 209*

horizontal analysis   Analysis technique that compares amounts of the same item over several time periods. *p. 327*

horizontal statements model   Arrangement of a set of financial statements horizontally across a sheet of paper. *p. 26*

income   Added value created in transforming resources into more desirable states. *p. 4*

income statement   Statement that measures the difference between the asset increases and the asset decreases associated with running a business. This definition is expanded in subsequent chapters as additional relationships among the elements of the financial statements are introduced. *p. 21*

incremental revenue   Additional cash inflows from operations generated by using an additional capital asset. *p. 577*

independent auditor   Licensed certified public accountant engaged to audit a company's financial statements; not an employee of the audited company. *p. 146*

indirect cost   Cost that cannot be easily traced to a cost object and for which the economic sacrifice to trace is not worth the informational benefits. *pp. 371, 439*

information overload   Situation in which presentation of too much information confuses the user of the information. *p. 326*

installment notes   Obligations that require regular payments of principal and interest over the life of the loan. *p. 254*

intangible assets   Assets that may be represented by pieces of paper or contracts that appear tangible; however, the true value of an intangible asset lies in the rights and privileges extended to its owners. *p. 208*

interest   Fee paid for the use of borrowed funds; also refers to revenue from debt securities. *pp. 4, 173*

internal controls   A company's policies and procedures designed to reduce the opportunity for fraud and to provide reasonable assurance that its objectives will be accomplished. *p. 132*

internal rate of return   Rate that will produce a present value of an investment's future cash inflows that equals cash outflows required to acquire the investment; alternatively, the rate that produces in a net present value of zero. *p. 576*

International Accounting Standards Board (IASB)   Private, independent body that establishes International Financial Reporting Standards (IFRS). The IASB's authority is established by various governmental institutions that require or permit companies in their jurisdiction to use IFRS. To date, more than 100 countries require or permit companies to prepare their financial statements using IFRS. One notable exception is the United States of America. *p. 9*

International Financial Reporting Standards (IFRS)   Pronouncement established by the International Accounting Standards Board (IASB) that provides guidance for the preparation of financial statements. *p. 9*

inventory cost flow methods   Methods used to allocate the cost of goods available for sale between cost of goods sold and inventory. *p. 180*

inventory holding costs   Costs associated with acquiring and retaining inventory including cost of storage space; lost, stolen, or damaged merchandise; insurance; personnel and management costs; and interest. *p. 376*

inventory turnover   Ratio of cost of goods sold to inventory that indicates how many times a year the average inventory is sold (turned over). *p. 334*

investing activities   One of the three categories of cash inflows and outflows shown on the statement of cash flows; includes cash received and spent by the business on operating assets and investments in the debt and equity of other companies. *p. 24*

investment center   Type of responsibility center for which revenue, expense and capital investments can be measured. *p. 538*

investors   Company or individual who gives assets or services in exchange for security certificates representing ownership interests. *p. 4*

issued stock   Stock sold to the public. *p. 299*

issuer   Individual or business that issues a note payable, bonds payable, or stock (the party receiving cash). See also *maker. pp. 248, 257*

journals   Books of original entry in which accounting data are entered chronologically before posting to the ledger accounts. *p. 603*

just in time (JIT)   Inventory flow system that minimizes the amount of inventory on hand by making inventory available for customer consumption on demand, therefore eliminating the need to store inventory. The system reduces explicit holding costs including financing, warehouse storage, supervision, theft, damage, and obsolescence. It also eliminates hidden opportunity costs such as lost revenue due to the lack of availability of inventory. *p. 376*

labor resources   Both intellectual and physical efforts of individuals used in the process of providing goods and services to customers. *p. 5*

last-in, first-out (LIFO) cost flow method   Inventory cost flow method that treats the last items purchased as the first items sold for the purpose of computing cost of goods sold. *p. 178*

legal capital   Amount of assets that should be maintained as protection for creditors; the number of shares multiplied by the par value. *p. 299*

liabilities   Obligations of a business to relinquish assets, provide services, or accept other obligations. *p. 12*

limited liability   Concept that investors in a corporation may not be held personally liable for the actions of the corporation (the creditors cannot lay claim to the owners' personal assets as payment for the corporation's debts). *p. 296*

limited liability companies (LLC)   Organizations offering many of the best features of corporations and partnerships and with many legal benefits of corporations (e.g., limited liability and centralized management) but permitted by the Internal Revenue Service to be taxed as a partnership, thereby avoiding double taxation of profits. *p. 295*

line of credit   Preapproved credit arrangement with a lending institution in which a business can borrow money by simply writing a check up to the approved limit. *p. 257*

liquidation   Process of dividing up the assets and returning them to the resource providers. Creditors normally receive first priority in business liquidations; in other words, assets are distributed to creditors first. After creditor claims have been satisfied, the remaining assets are distributed to the investors (owners) of the business. *p. 19*

liquidity   Ability to convert assets to cash quickly and meet short-term obligations. *pp. 23, 175*

liquidity ratios   Measures of short-term debt-paying ability. *p. 331*

long-term liabilities   Liabilities with maturity dates beyond one year or the company's operating cycle, whichever is longer; noncurrent liabilities. *p. 253*

long-term operational assets   Assets used by a business to generate revenue; condition of being used distinguishes them from assets that are sold (inventory) and assets that are held (investments). *p. 206*

losses   Decreases in assets or increases in liabilities that result from peripheral or incidental transactions. *p. 105*

low-ball pricing   Pricing a product below competitors' price to lure customers away and then raising the price once customers depend on the supplier for the product. *p. 478*

maker   The party issuing a note (the borrower). *p. 173*

making the numbers   Expression that indicates marketing managers attained the planned master budget sales volume. *p. 541*

management by exception   The philosophy of focusing management attention and resources only on those operations where performance deviates significantly from expectations. *p. 545*

managerial accounting   Branch of accounting that provides information useful to internal decision makers and managers in operating an organization. *pp. 6, 362*

manufacturing business   Companies that make the goods they sell to customers. *p. 27*

manufacturing overhead   Production costs that cannot be traced directly to products. *p. 371*

margin   Component in the determination of the return on investment. Computed by dividing operating income by sales. *p. 547*

margin of safety   Difference between break-even sales and budgeted sales expressed in units, dollars, or as a percentage; the amount by which actual sales can fall below budgeted sales before a loss is incurred. *p. 416*

market   Group of people or entities organized to buy and sell resources. *p. 4*

market rate of interest   Interest rate currently available on a wide range of alternative investments with similar levels of risk. *p. 266*

market value   The price at which securities sell in the secondary market; also called fair value. *p. 299*

master budget   Composition of the numerous separate but interdependent departmental budgets that cover a wide range of operating and financial factors such as sales, production, manufacturing expenses, and administrative expenses. *p. 508*

matching concept   Process of matching expenses with the revenues they produce; three ways to match expenses with revenues include matching expenses directly to revenues, matching expenses to the period in which they are incurred, and matching expenses systematically with revenues. *pp. 21, 57, 174*

material   The point at which knowledge of information would influence a user's decision; can be measured in absolute, percentage, quantitative, or qualitative terms. The concept allows nonmaterial matters to be handled in any convenient way, such as charging a pencil sharpener to expense rather than recording periodic depreciation over its useful life. *p. 146*

materiality   Concept that recognizes practical limits in financial reporting by allowing flexible handling of matters not considered material; information is considered material if the decisions of a reasonable person would be influenced by its omission or misstatement; can be measured in absolute, percentage, quantitative, or qualitative terms. *p. 327*

maturity date   The date a liability is due to be settled (the date the borrower is expected to repay a debt). *p. 173*

merchandise inventory   Supply of finished goods held for resale to customers. *p. 92*

merchandising businesses   Companies that buy and resell merchandise inventory. *pp. 27, 92*

minimum rate of return   Minimum amount of profitability required to persuade a company to accept an investment opportunity; also known as *desired rate of return, required rate of return, hurdle rate, cutoff rate,* and *discount rate. p. 571*

mixed costs (semivariable costs)   Costs composed of a mixture of fixed and variable components. *p. 410*

multistep income statement   Income statement format that matches particular revenue items with related expense items and distinguishes between recurring operating activities and nonoperating items such as gains and losses. *p. 106*

natural resources   Mineral deposits, oil and gas reserves, and reserves of timber, mines, and quarries are examples; sometimes called *wasting assets* because their value wastes away as the resources are removed. *p. 208*

net income   Increase in net assets resulting from operating the business. *p. 21*

net loss   Decrease in net assets resulting from operating the business. *p. 21*

net margin   Profitability measurement that indicates the percentage of each sales dollar resulting in profit; calculated as net income divided by net sales. *p. 337*

net present value   Evaluation technique that uses a desired rate of return to discount future cash flows back to their present value equivalents and then subtracts the cost of the investment from the present value equivalents to determine the net present value. A zero or positive net present value (present value of cash inflows equals or exceeds the present value of cash outflows) implies that the investment opportunity provides an acceptable rate of return. *p. 575*

net realizable value   Face amount of receivables less an allowance for accounts whose collection is doubtful (amount actually expected to be collected). *p. 164*

net sales   Sales less returns from customers and allowances or cash discounts given to customers. *p. 109*

non-sufficient-funds (NSF) check   Customer's check deposited but returned by the bank on which it was drawn because the customer did not have enough funds in its account to pay the check. *p. 139*

nonvalue-added activities   Tasks undertaken that do not contribute to a product's ability to satisfy customer needs. *p. 381*

note payable   A liability that results from executing a legal document called a *promissory note* which describes the interest rate, maturity date, collateral, and so on. *p. 248*

notes receivable   Notes that evidence rights to receive cash in the future from the maker of a *promissory note;* usually specify the maturity date, interest rate, and other credit terms. *p. 163*

not-for-profit entities   Organizations (also called *nonprofit* or *nonbusiness entities*) established primarily for motives other than making a profit, such as providing goods and services for the social good. Examples include state-supported universities and colleges, hospitals, public libraries, and public charities. *p. 6*

operating activities   Cash inflows and outflows associated with operating the business. These cash flows normally result from revenue and expense transactions including interest. *p. 24*

operating budgets   Budgets prepared by different departments within a company that will become a part of the company's master budget; typically include a sales budget, an inventory purchases budget, a selling and administrative budget, and a cash budget. *p. 508*

operating cycle   Time required to turn cash into inventory, inventory into receivables, and receivables back to cash. *p. 267*

operating income (or loss)   Income statement subtotal representing the difference between operating revenues and operating expenses, but before recognizing gains and losses from peripheral activities which are added to or subtracted from operating income to determine net income or loss. *p. 106*

operating leverage   Operating condition in which a percentage change in revenue produces a proportionately larger percentage change in net income; measured by dividing the contribution margin by net income. The higher the proportion of fixed cost to total costs, the greater the operating leverage. *p. 404*

operations budgeting   Short-range planning activities such as the development and implementation of the master budget. *p. 506*

opportunity   An element of the fraud triangle that recognizes weaknesses in internal controls that enable the occurrence of fraudulent or unethical behavior. *p. 144*

opportunity cost   Cost of lost opportunities such as the failure to make sales due to an insufficient supply of inventory or the wage a working student forgoes to attend class. *pp. 366, 470*

ordinary annuity   Annuity whose cash inflows occur at the end of each accounting period. *p. 574*

outsourcing   The practice of buying goods and services from another company rather than producing them internally. *p. 477*

outstanding checks   Checks deducted from the depositor's cash account balance but not yet presented to the bank for payment. *p. 139*

outstanding stock   Stock owned by outside parties; normally the amount of stock issued less the amount of treasury stock. *p. 299*

overhead   Costs associated with producing products that cannot be cost effectively traced to products including indirect costs such as indirect materials, indirect labor, utilities, rent, and depreciation. *p. 336*

overhead costs   Indirect costs of doing business that cannot be directly traced to a product, department, or process, such as depreciation. *p. 439*

paid-in capital in excess of par (or stated) value   Any amount received above the par or stated value of stock when stock is issued. *p. 302*

participative budgeting   Budget technique that allows subordinates to participate with upper-level managers in setting budget objectives, thereby encouraging cooperation and support in the attainment of the company's goals. *p. 508*

partnership agreement   Legal document that defines the responsibilities of each partner and describes the division of income and losses. *p. 294*

partnerships   Business entities owned by at least two people who share talents, capital, and the risks of the business. *p. 294*

par value   Arbitrary value assigned to stock by the board of directors. *p. 299*

patent   Legal right granted by the U.S. Patent Office ensuring a company or an individual the exclusive right to a product or process. *p. 222*

payback method   Technique that evaluates investment opportunities by determining the length of time necessary to recover the initial net investment through incremental revenue or cost savings; the shorter the period, the better the investment opportunity. *p. 584*

payee   The party collecting cash. *p. 173*

payment date   Date on which a dividend is actually paid. *p. 306*

percentage analysis   Analysis of relationships between two different items to draw conclusions or make decisions. *p. 328*

percent of receivables method   Estimating the amount of the allowance for doubtful accounts as a percentage of the outstanding receivables balance. The percentage is typically based on a combination of factors such as historical experience, economic conditions, and the company's credit policies. *p. 170*

percent of revenue method   Estimating the amount of uncollectible accounts expense as a percentage of the revenue earned on account during the accounting period. The percentage is typically based on a combination of factors such as historical experience, economic conditions, and the company's credit policies. *p. 169*

period costs   General, selling, and administrative costs that are expensed in the period in which the economic sacrifice is made. *pp. 57, 95, 371*

periodic inventory system   Method of accounting for changes in the Inventory account only at the end of the accounting period. *p. 112*

permanent accounts   Accounts that contain information transferred from one accounting period to the next. *p. 25*

perpetual (continuous) budgeting   Continuous budgeting activity normally covering a 12-month time span by replacing the current month's budget at the end of each month with a new budget; keeps management constantly involved in the budget process so that changing conditions are incorporated on a timely bases. *p. 506*

perpetual inventory system   Method of accounting for inventories that increases the Inventory account each time merchandise is purchased and decreases it each time merchandise is sold. *p. 96*

physical flow of goods   Physical movement of goods through the business; normally a FIFO flow so that the first goods purchased are the first goods delivered to customers, thereby reducing the likelihood of obsolete inventory. *p. 178*

physical resources   Natural resources that businesses transform to create more valuable resources. *p. 5*

plant assets to long-term liabilities   Financial ratio that suggests how well a company manages its long-term debt. *p. 337*

postaudit   Repeat calculation using the techniques originally employed to analyze an investment project; accomplished with the use of actual data available at the completion of the investment project so that the actual results can be compared with expected results based on estimated data at the beginning of the project. Its purpose is to provide feedback as to whether the expected results were actually accomplished in improving the accuracy of future analysis. *p. 587*

posting   Process of copying information from journals to ledgers. *p. 603*

predetermined overhead rate   Allocation rate calculated before actual costs or activity are known; determined by dividing the estimated overhead costs for the coming period by some measure of estimated total production activity for the period, such as the number of labor-hours or machine-hours. The base should relate rationally to overhead use. The rate is used throughout the accounting period to allocate overhead costs to work in process inventory based on actual production activity. *p. 451*

preferred stock   Stock that receives some form of preferential treatment (usually as to dividends) over common stock; normally has no voting rights. *p. 300*

premium on bonds payable   Difference between the selling price and the face amount of a bond that is sold for more than the face amount. *p. 266*

prepaid items   Deferred expenses. An example is prepaid insurance. *p. 59*

present value index   Present value of cash inflows divided by the present value of cash outflows. Higher index numbers indicate higher rates of return. *p. 580*

present value table   Table that consists of a list of factors to use in converting future values into their present value equivalents; composed of columns that represent different return rates and rows that depict different periods of time. *p. 572*

pressure   An element of the fraud triangle that recognizes conditions that motivate fraudulent or unethical behavior. *p. 145*

price-earnings (P/E) ratio   Measurement used to compare the values of different stocks in terms of earnings; calculated as market price per share divided by earnings per share. *p. 340*

principal   Amount of cash actually borrowed. *p. 173*

procedures manual   Manual that sets forth the accounting procedures to be followed. *p. 133*

product costing   Classification and accumulation of individual inputs (materials, labor, and overhead) for determining the cost of making a good or providing a service. *p. 365*

product costs   All costs related to obtaining or manufacturing a product intended for sale to customers; are accumulated in inventory accounts and expensed as cost of goods sold at the point of sale. For a manufacturing company, product costs include direct materials, direct labor, and manufacturing overhead. *pp. 95, 365*

product-level costs   Costs incurred to support different kinds of products or services; can be avoided by the elimination of a product line or a type of service. *p. 473*

profit   Value added by transforming resources into products or services desired by customers. *p. 4*

profit center   Type of responsibility center for which both revenues and costs can be indentified. *p. 538*

profitability ratios   Measurements of a firm's ability to generate earnings. *p. 337*

pro forma financial statements   Budgeted financial statements prepared from the information in the master budget. *p. 508*

promissory note   A legal document representing a credit agreement between a lender and a borrower. The note specifies technical details such as the maker, payee, interest rate, maturity date, payment terms, and any collateral. *p. 172*

property, plant, and equipment   Category of assets, sometimes called *plant assets,* used to produce products or to carry on the administrative and selling functions of a business; includes machinery and equipment, buildings, and land. *p. 208*

purchase discount   Reduction in the gross price of merchandise extended under the condition that the purchaser pay cash for the merchandise within a stated time (usually within 10 days of the date of the sale). *p. 100*

purchase returns and allowances   A reduction in the cost of purchases resulting from dissatisfaction with merchandise purchased. *p. 99*

qualified opinion   Opinion issued by a certified public accountant that means the company's financial statements are, for the most part, in compliance with GAAP, but there is some circumstance (explained in the auditor's report) about which the auditor has reservations; contrast with *unqualified opinion. p. 147*

qualitative characteristics   Nonquantifiable features such as company reputation, welfare of employees, and customer satisfaction that can be affected by certain decisions. *p. 472*

quantitative characteristics   Numbers in decision making subject to mathematical manipulation, such as the dollar amounts of revenues and expenses. *p. 472*

quick ratio   See *acid-test ratio. p. 332*

ratio analysis   See *percentage analysis. p. 330*

rationalization   An element of the fraud triangle that recognizes a human tendency to justify fraudulent or unethical behavior. *p. 145*

raw materials   Physical commodities (e.g., wood, metal, paint) used in the manufacturing process. *p. 369*

raw materials inventory   Asset account used to accumulate the costs of materials (such as lumber, metals, paints, chemicals) that will be used to make a company's products. *p. 374*

realization   A term that usually refers to actually collecting cash. *p. 49*

recognition   Reporting an accounting event in the financial statements. *p. 49*

recovery of investment   Recovery of the funds used to acquire the original investment. *p. 586*

reengineering   Business practices designed by companies to make production and delivery systems more competitive in world markets by eliminating or minimizing waste, errors, and costs. *p. 381*

reinstate   Recording an account receivable previously written off back into the accounting records, generally when cash is collected long after the original due date. *p. 168*

relative fair market value method   Method of assigning value to individual assets acquired in a basket purchase in which each asset is assigned a percentage of the total price paid for all assets. The percentage assigned equals the market value of a particular asset divided by the total of the market values of all assets acquired in the basket purchase. *p. 209*

relevant costs   Future-oriented costs that differ between business alternatives; also known as *avoidable costs. p. 471*

relevant information   Decision-making information about costs, costs savings, or revenues that have these features: (1) future-oriented information and (2) the information differs between the alternatives; decision-specific (information that is relevant in one decision may not be relevant in another decision). *p. 470*

relevant range   Range of activity over which the definitions of fixed and variable costs are valid. *p. 411*

reporting entities   Particular businesses or other organizations for which financial statements are prepared. *p. 9*

residual income   Approach that evaluates managers on their ability to maximize the dollar value of earnings above some targeted level of earnings. *p. 548*

responsibility accounting   Performance measure that evaluates managers based on how well they maximize the dollar value of earning above some target level of earnings. *p. 536*

responsibility center   Point in an organization where the control over revenue or expense items is located. *p. 538*

restrictive covenants   Special provisions specified in the loan contract that are designed to prohibit management from taking certain actions that place creditors at risk. *p. 267*

retail companies   Companies that sell goods to consumers. *p. 92*

retained earnings   Portion of stockholders' equity that includes all earnings retained in the business since inception (revenues minus expenses and distributions for all accounting periods). *p. 12*

return on assets   Profitability measure based on earnings a company generates relative to its asset base; calculated as net income divided by average total assets. *p. 338*

return on equity   Measure of the profitability of a firm based on earnings generated in relation to stockholders' equity; calculated as net income divided by stockholders' equity. *p. 339*

return on investment   Measure of profitability based on the asset base of the firm. It is calculated as net income divided by average total assets. ROI is a product of net margin and asset turnover. *pp. 338, 546*

return on sales   Percent of net income generated by each $1 of sales; computed by dividing net income by net sales. *p. 337*

revenue   The economic benefit (increase in assets or decrease in liabilities) gained by providing goods or services to customers. *p. 64*

revenue expenditures   Costs incurred for repair or maintenance of long-term operational assets; recorded as expenses and subtracted from revenue in the accounting period in which incurred. *p. 219*

salaries payable   Amounts of future cash payments owed to employees for services that have already been performed. *p. 52*

sales discount   Cash discount extended by the seller of goods to encourage prompt payment. When the buyer of the goods takes advantage of the discount to pay less than the original selling price, the difference between the selling price and the cash collected is the sales discount. *p. 107*

sales price variance   Difference between actual sales and expected sales based on the standard sales price per unit times the actual level of activity. *p. 543*

sales return and allowances   A reduction in sales revenue resulting from dissatisfaction with merchandise sold. *p. 109*

sales volume variance   Difference between sales based on a static budget (standard sales price times standard level of activity) and sales based on a flexible budget (standard sales price times actual level of activity). *p. 541*

salvage value   Expected selling price of an asset at the end of its useful life. *p. 210*

schedule of cost of goods manufactured and sold   Internal accounting report that summarizes the manufacturing product costs for the period; its result, cost of goods sold, is reported as a single line item on the company's income statement. *p. 374*

schedule of cost of goods sold   Schedule that reflects the computation of the amount of the cost of goods sold under the periodic inventory system; an internal report not shown in the formal financial statements. *p. 112*

Securities Act of 1933 and Securities Exchange Act of 1934   Acts passed after the stock market crash of 1929 designed to regulate the issuance of stock and govern the stock exchanges; created the Securities and Exchange Commission (SEC), which has the authority to establish accounting policies for companies registered on the stock exchanges. *p. 295*

Securities and Exchange Commission (SEC)   Government agency responsible for overseeing the accounting rules to be followed by companies required to be registered with it. *p. 365*

segment   Component part of an organization that is designated as a reporting entity. *p. 479*

selling and administrative costs   Costs that cannot be directly traced to products that are recognized as expenses in the period in which they are incurred. Examples include advertising expense and rent expense. *p. 95*

selling, general, and administrative costs (SG&A)   All costs not associated with obtaining or manufacturing a product; sometimes called *period costs* because they are normally expensed in the period in which the economic sacrifice is incurred. *p. 371*

separation of duties   Internal control feature of, whenever possible, assigning the functions of authorization, recording, and custody to different individuals. *p. 132*

service business   Organizations such as accounting and legal firms, dry cleaners, and insurance companies that provide services to consumers. *p. 27*

service charges   Fees charged by a bank for services performed or a penalty for the depositor's failing to maintain a specified minimum cash balance throughout the period. *p. 139*

shrinkage   A term that reflects decreases in inventory for reasons other than sales to customers. *p. 104*

signature card   Bank form that records the bank account number and the signatures of the people authorized to write checks on an account. *p. 136*

single-payment (lump-sum)   A one-time receipt of cash which can be converted to its present value using a conversion factor. *p. 572*

single-step income statement   Single comparison between total revenues and total expenses. *p. 106*

sole proprietorships   Businesses (usually small) owned by one person. *p. 294*

solvency   Ability of a business to pay liabilities in the long run. *p. 335*

solvency ratios   Measures of a firm's long-term debt-paying ability. *p. 335*

source documents   Documents such as a cash register tape, invoice, time card, or check stub that provide accounting information to be recorded in the accounting journals and ledgers. *p. 602*

special journals   Journals designed to improve the efficiency of recording specific types of repetitive transactions. *p. 603*

special order decisions   Decisions of whether to accept orders from nonregular customers who want to buy goods or services significantly below the normal selling price. If the order's relevant revenues exceed its avoidable costs, the order should be accepted. Qualitative features such as the order's effect on the existing customer base if accepted must also be considered. *p. 474*

specific authorizations   Policies and procedures that apply to designated levels of management, such as the policy that the right to approve overtime pay may apply only to the plant manager. *p. 133*

specific identification   Inventory method that allocates costs between cost of goods sold and ending inventory using the cost of the specific goods sold or retained in the business. *p. 178*

spending variance   The difference between the actual fixed overhead costs and the budgeted fixed overhead costs. *p. 542*

stakeholders   Parties interested in the operations of a business, including owners, lenders, employees, suppliers, customers, and government agencies. *p. 5*

stated interest rate   Rate of interest specified in the bond contract that will be paid at specified intervals over the life of the bond. *p. 258*

stated value   Arbitrary value assigned to stock by the board of directors. *p. 299*

statement of cash flows Statement that explains how a business obtained and used cash during an accounting period. *p. 24*

statement of changes in stockholders' equity Statement that summarizes the transactions occurring during the accounting period that affected the owners' equity. *p. 23*

static budgets Budgets such as the master budget based solely on the level of planned activity; remain constant even when volume of activity changes. *p. 539*

stewardship A duty to protect and use the assets of a business for the benefit of the owners. *p. 18*

stock certificate Evidence of ownership interest issued when an investor contributes assets to a corporation; describes the rights and privileges that accompany ownership. *p. 294*

stock dividend Proportionate distribution of additional shares of the declaring corporation's stock. *p. 306*

stockholders Owners of a corporation. *pp. 12, 296*

stockholders' equity Stockholders' equity represents the portion of the assets that is owned by the stockholders. *p. 12*

stock split Proportionate increase in the number of outstanding shares; designed to reduce the market value of the stock and its par value. *p. 307*

straight-line amortization Method of amortization in which equal amounts of the account being reduced (e.g., Bond Discount, Bond Premium, Patent) are transferred to the appropriate expense account over the relevant time period. *p. 263*

straight-line depreciation Method of computing depreciation that allocates the cost of an asset to expense in equal amounts over its life. The formula for calculating straight line depreciation is [(Cost − Salvage)/Useful Life]. *p. 211*

strategic planning Planning activities associated with long-range decisions such as defining the scope of the business, determining which products to develop, deciding whether to discontinue a business segment, and determining which market niche would be most profitable. *p. 506*

suboptimization Situation in which managers act in their own self-interests even though the organization as a whole suffers. *p. 548*

sunk costs Costs that have been incurred in past transactions and therefore are not relevant for decision making. *p. 470*

T-account Simplified account form, named for its shape, with the account title placed at the top of a horizontal bar, debit entries listed on the left side of the vertical bar, and credit entries shown on the right side. *p. 602*

tangible assets Assets that can be touched, such as equipment, machinery, natural resources, and land. *p. 208*

temporary accounts Accounts used to collect information for a single accounting period (usually revenue, expense, and distribution accounts). *p. 25*

times interest earned ratio Ratio that computes how many times a company would be able to pay its interest by using the amount of earnings available to make interest payments; amount of earnings is net income before interest and income taxes. *pp. 335–336*

time value of money Recognition that the present value of a promise to receive a dollar some time in the future is worth less than a dollar because of interest, risk, and inflation factors. For example, a person may be willing to pay $0.90 today for the right to receive $1.00 one year from today. *p. 570*

total quality management (TQM) Management philosophy that includes: (1) a continuous systematic problem-solving philosophy that engages personnel at all levels of the organization to eliminate waste, defects, and nonvalue-added activities; and (2) the effort to manage quality costs in a manner that leads to the highest level of customer satisfaction. *p. 381*

trademark Name or symbol that identifies a company or an individual product. *p. 222*

transaction Particular event that involves the transfer of something of value between two entities. *p. 13*

transferability Concept referring to the practice of dividing the ownership of corporations into small units that are represented by shares of stock, which permits the easy exchange of ownership interests. *p. 296*

transportation-in (freight-in) Cost of freight on goods purchased under terms FOB shipping point that is usually added to the cost of inventory and is a product cost. *p. 101*

transportation-out (freight-out) Freight cost for goods delivered to customers under terms FOB destination; a period cost expensed when it is incurred. *p. 101*

treasury stock Stock first issued to the public and then bought back by the corporation. *p. 299*

trend analysis Study of the performance of a business over a period of time. *p. 327*

trial balance List of ledger accounts and their balances that provides a check on the mathematical accuracy of the recording process. *p. 605*

true cash balance Actual balance of cash owned by a company at the close of business on the date of the bank statement. *p. 137*

turnover Component in the determination of the return on investment. Computed by dividing sales by operating assets. *p. 547*

2/10, n/30 Expression meaning the seller will allow the purchaser a 2 percent discount off the gross invoice price if the purchaser pays cash for the merchandise within 10 days from the date of purchase. *p. 100*

unadjusted bank balance Ending cash balance reported by the bank as of the date of the bank statement. *p. 137*

unadjusted book balance Balance of the Cash account as of the date of the reconciliation before making any adjustments. *p. 137*

unadjusted rate of return Measure of profitability computed by dividing the average incremental increase in annual net income by the average cost of the original investment (original cost ÷ 2). *p. 585*

uncollectible accounts expense Expense associated with uncollectible accounts receivable; the amount recognized may be estimated using the percent of revenue or the percent of receivables method, or actual losses may be recorded using the direct write-off method. *p. 165*

unearned revenue Revenue for which cash has been collected but the service has not yet been performed. *p. 60*

unfavorable variance Variance that occurs when actual costs exceed standard costs or when actual sales are less than standard sales. *p. 542*

unit-level costs Costs incurred each time a company makes a single product or performs a single service and that can be avoided by eliminating a unit of product or service. Likewise, unit-level costs increase with each additional product produced or service provided. *p. 472*

units-of-production depreciation Depreciation method based on a measure of production rather than a measure of time; for example, an automobile may be depreciated based on the expected miles to be driven rather than on a specific number of years. *p. 217*

unqualified opinion Opinion issued by a certified public accountant that means the company's financial statements are, in all material respects, in compliance with GAAP; the auditor has no reservations. Contrast with qualified opinion. *p. 147*

upstream costs Costs incurred before the manufacturing process begins, for example, research and development costs. *p. 375*

users Individuals or organizations that use financial information for decision making. Also called *stakeholders*. *p. 5*

value-added activity Any unit of work that contributes to a product's ability to satisfy customer needs. *p. 381*

value-added principle The benefits attained (value added) from the process should exceed the cost of the process. *p. 365*

620   Glossary

value chain   Linked sequence of activities that create value for the customer. *p. 381*

variable cost   Cost that in total changes in direct proportion to changes in volume of activity; remains constant per unit when volume of activity changes. *p. 402*

variable cost volume variance   The difference between a variable cost calculated at the planned volume of activity and the same variable cost calculated at the actual volume of activity. *p. 541*

variable interest rate   Interest rate that fluctuates (may change) from period to period over the life of the loan. *p. 253*

variances   Differences between standard and actual amounts. *p. 540*

vertical analysis   Analysis technique that compares items on financial statements to significant totals. *p. 329*

vertical integration   Attainment of control over the entire spectrum of business activity from production to sales; as an example a grocery store that owns farms. *p. 478*

vertical statements model   Arrangement of a full set of financial statements on a single page with account titles arranged from the top to the bottom of the page. *p. 66*

warranties   Promises to correct deficiencies or dissatisfactions in quality, quantity, or performance of products or services sold. *p. 251*

weighted-average cost flow method   Inventory cost flow method in which the cost allocated between inventory and cost of goods sold is based on the average cost per unit, which is determined by dividing total costs of goods available for sale during the accounting period by total units available for sale during the period. If the average is recomputed each time a purchase is made, the result is called a *moving average*. *p. 178*

wholesale companies   Companies that sell goods to other businesses. *p. 92*

withdrawals   Distributions to the owners of proprietorships and partnerships. *p. 297*

work in process inventory   Asset account used to accumulate the product costs (direct materials, direct labor, and overhead) associated with incomplete products that have been started but are not yet completed. *p. 374*

working capital   Current assets minus current liabilities. *pp. 331, 577*

working capital ratio   Another term for the current ratio; calculated by dividing current assets by current liabilities. *p. 332*